ALWD Guide to Legal Citation

Aspen Coursebook Series

ALWD Guide to Legal Citation

Seventh Edition

Association of Legal Writing Directors

and

Carolyn V. Williams
Associate Professor of Legal Writing and
Assistant Clinical Professor of Law
University of Arizona
James E. Rogers College of Law

Dedicated to Tamara S. Herrera for introducing me to the *ALWD Guide* as a law student and Gary D. Williams

Published by Wolters Kluwer in New York.

Wolters Kluwer Legal & Regulatory U.S. serves customers worldwide with CCH, Aspen Publishers, and Kluwer Law International products. (www.WKLegaledu.com)

Cover image: J. Barmack/The Froebe Group.

To contact Customer Service, e-mail customer.service@wolterskluwer.com, call 1-800-234-1660, fax 1-800-901-9075, or mail correspondence to:

Wolters Kluwer
Attn: Order Department
PO Box 990
Frederick, MD 21705

Printed in the United States of America.

1 2 3 4 5 6 7 8 9 0

ISBN 978-1-5438-0777-6

Library of Congress Cataloging-in-Publication Data

Names: Williams, Carolyn V., author. | Association of Legal Writing Directors.
Title: ALWD guide to legal citation / Association of Legal Writing Directors and Carolyn V. Williams, Associate Professor of Legal Writing and Assistant Clinical Professor of Law, University of Arizona, James E. Rogers College of Law.
Other titles: ALWD citation manual. | Association of Legal Writing Directors guide to legal citation
Description: Seventh edition. | New York : Wolters Kluwer, 2021. | Series: Aspen coursebook series | Includes bibliographical references and index. | Summary: "This book is a comprehensive guide to legal citation style"—Provided by publisher.
Identifiers: LCCN 2021012019 (print) | LCCN 2021012020 (ebook) | ISBN 9781543807776 (paperback) | ISBN 9781543831221 (ebook)
Subjects: LCSH: Citation of legal authorities—United States. | Annotations and citations (Law—United States.
Classification: LCC KF245 .A45 2021 (print) | LCC KF245 (ebook) | DDC 808.02/7—dc23
LC record available at https://lccn.loc.gov/2021012019
LC ebook record available at https://lccn.loc.gov/2021012020

The SFI label applies to the text stock

About Wolters Kluwer Legal & Regulatory U.S.

Wolters Kluwer Legal & Regulatory U.S. delivers expert content and solutions in the areas of law, corporate compliance, health compliance, reimbursement, and legal education. Its practical solutions help customers successfully navigate the demands of a changing environment to drive their daily activities, enhance decision quality and inspire confident outcomes.

Serving customers worldwide, its legal and regulatory portfolio includes products under the Aspen Publishers, CCH Incorporated, Kluwer Law International, ftwilliam.com and MediRegs names. They are regarded as exceptional and trusted resources for general legal and practice-specific knowledge, compliance and risk management, dynamic workflow solutions, and expert commentary.

Summary of Contents

Table of Contents

About the Authors

The Association of Legal Writing Directors is a learned society for professors who coordinate legal writing instruction in legal education. ALWD members teach at nearly all American law schools. ALWD is headquartered at the University of Michigan Law School, 625 South State Street, Ann Arbor, MI, 48109-1215.

Carolyn V. Williams is an Associate Professor of Legal Writing at the University of Arizona James E. Rogers College of Law where she teaches legal writing, research, and advocacy courses. In law school, she was Editor-in-Chief of the *Arizona State Law Journal*. As a professor, she became the faculty advisor for the *Journal* and mentored subsequent EICs. She is now an Article Editor of the *Journal of Appellate Practice and Process*, a faculty-edited law review that has used *ALWD Guide* citation format since 2000. Carolyn is also a sought-after consultant who frequently teaches continuing legal education courses for those in the larger legal community, including lawyers in the Air Force, court staff, and law review editors. Carolyn holds positions in each of the national legal writing organizations, including ALWD, the Legal Writing Institute, and the Legal Writing, Reasoning, and Research Section of AALS.

Before joining academia, Carolyn spent eight years in big firm practice where she litigated a range of complex commercial and land use matters, including cases involving condemnation, data breach class actions, complex judgment collections, and shareholder disputes at the state and federal levels. Super Lawyers named her a Rising Star in 2016, an honor bestowed on no more than 2.5 percent of the lawyers in Arizona.

Preface

Legal citations serve multiple purposes. Naturally, they record the sources selected by writers to support their statements concerning the law. They provide readers with the information they'll need to access those sources. They give credit to the original authors of text and ideas. But they also underscore the weight, the relevance, and the influence that a particular source possesses. And they even tell us something about the legal writers who drafted them — including how current, how extensive, and how careful their research was — and consequently, the degree to which the writers' work will be perceived as trustworthy, complete, accurate, and ethical.

The *ALWD Guide to Legal Citation* exists to assist legal writers in building citations to serve those purposes. From its inaugural publication in 2000 (under the title *The ALWD Citation Manual*), this book has prioritized the forms of citations used by the overwhelming majority of today's legal writers. In the twenty-one ensuing years, the *ALWD Guide* has found ways to improve its content and structure, while continuing to serve its users and their legal writing needs.

The *ALWD Guide to Legal Citation* has the following goals:

- To help beginners learn the conventions of legal citation, both for constructing their own citations and for understanding citations written by others;
- To explain the functions of the specific components for citations to various types of legal sources;
- To give its users a text that makes sense and that provides a step-by-step guide to constructing accurate citations;
- To offer legal writing and research professors a text that is easy to use, well organized, and self-contained;
- To arrange its contents so that legal professionals can easily find what they need to construct the citations used in practice-based documents; and
- To identify and make easy to find the small changes needed to modify citations for the constraints of scholarly writing in academic journals.

The *ALWD Guide* places its greatest focus on the primary and secondary sources most often cited in practice-based and academic writing. Each primary or secondary source rule begins with a **Fast Formats** page that previews and refreshes understanding of essential components for both full and short citations. Rules for case law, statutes, and restatements feature **Snapshots** of actual pages, illustrating where to find essential components. The *ALWD Guide* features abundant **Charts** with abbreviations and other essentials, *within* the rules they relate to. **Sidebars** help students understand the "why" of legal citations and steer them away from common errors or misconceptions. Templates at the beginning of each source's rule diagram the order and relationship of essential components. Each primary and secondary source rule features component-by-component explanations and illustrations, including the use of red triangles ▲ to illustrate required spacing of components within the citation.

As was the case in the sixth edition, the seventh edition takes pains to ensure that writers do not confuse the citation formats of academic writing with those used by lawyers in practice. Each academic formatting rule number ends with the suffix FN. The academic rule and its examples are further marked with unmistakable visual cues; they are set off by a vertical red line and accompanied by a warning icon.

ACADEMIC FORMATTING

The *ALWD Guide* also aims to demystify certain features of legal citation. For example, it addresses curious features, such as star pagination; confounding features, such as whether, when, and why to provide a parallel citation or a public domain citation; confusing features, such as the geographic coverage of a regional reporter; challenging features, such as determining whether to append subsequent history to a case citation, and if so, in what manner; and missing features, such as how to cite to documents in a shared drive, which is not addressed by any other legal citation manual.

In response to suggestions and inquiries by our users, we have made some changes that facilitate the *ALWD Guide*'s use for all law reviews. First, **Parts 1–5** and **Appendix 6** have callouts that cross-reference the information in the text of the *ALWD Guide* to the corresponding rule in the twenty-first edition of *The Bluebook: A Uniform System of Citation Bluebook*. Consequently, law review students can confidently use the *ALWD Guide* no matter the law review's stated preference. This new development also helps students understand that they are learning legal citation and how to use reference tools, not memorizing a book. Second, **Appendix 5** that lists full abbreviations for periodical titles is available online for free. One of the more difficult tasks of law review staff is to understand and apply the myriad of rules surrounding how to craft lengthy periodical abbreviations. That makes **Appendix 5** a time saver for stressed law students. And allowing all interested individuals access to it for free is our way of giving back. See **Appendix 5** in the back of the *ALWD Guide* for directions to access it online.

Next, we reevaluated the nature of the sources relied upon by today's legal writers. We found that traditional legal citation does not adequately address—or fails to address—many technological sources of information. Accordingly, we extensively revised a number of rules by visualizing the multitude of ways that people access information now, crafting several new examples and illustrations to account for those, and adding detailed explanations of how to construct legal citations for each new source. For example, we revised **Rule 26** (speeches, addresses, and other oral presentations) to answer questions such as what to do if you are citing to a presentation on an online conference platform; **Rule 27** (interviews, letters, and memoranda) to demonstrate how to cite to a virtual video interview or to an unpublished letter posted online; **Rule 28** (video and visual programs) to explain how to cite private videos people take on their personal devices that they do not post online; and **Rule 33** (email, listservs, shared drives, and other short electronic messages) to show examples of citations to chats in shared workspaces, to texts, and to documents in shared drives. This reimagining also led to expanded coverage of commercial databases and online sources for all primary and secondary source rules.

We then talked to attorneys around the country about the way law is practiced after the global pandemic that forced the legal profession to adapt in significant ways. This indicated the need to overhaul **Rule 25** (citing court documents in your own case) and **Rule 12.15** (citing court documents in published or pending cases) to better reflect how practitioners identify practice documents now. We asked practitioners, judges, and professors from each of the fifty states to weigh in on the local rules of practice for their state that are contained in **Appendix 2**. The response was awe-inspiring and thoughtful. We made significant updates to those local rules as a result. And in gratitude for the outpouring of support for this effort, we decided to make **Appendix 2** available online for free to all as well. As part of our civic duty, we wanted the collective knowledge of local practices to benefit everyone. It also helps us to update this rapidly changing information in a timely fashion.

Finally, we revised many of the examples and illustrations to better reflect the diverse viewpoints and cultures that comprise our world. ALWD adopted a Diversity Strategic Action Plan in 2017 that prioritizes cultural competency among its members and creating an inclusive organization with a welcoming atmosphere for all. In line with this mission, we turned a critical eye on what and who was represented in the *ALWD Guide*. Sometimes the improvements were making sure that every state was represented in an example or illustration in **Rule 15** (legislative materials). At other times, we made sure that the subjects of the sources themselves — movies, speeches, podcasts, etc. — that we used as examples represented gender, sexual orientation, racial, political, and cultural diversity. And we made a concerted effort to include authors or other people represented in citations (such as editors, presenters, or interviewees) with diverse backgrounds. Although we will continually strive for inclusion, we hope that this small effort brings a smile to any user who sees themself represented in the *ALWD Guide*. Strength lies in differences.

We are confident that the *ALWD Guide to Legal Citation* will meet your needs for a legal citation reference work. Should you find any errors or omissions, or if you have suggestions for our next edition, please send them to the Association of Legal Writing Directors, alwd@alwd.org, or to Carolyn Williams, cvwilliams@email.arizona.edu.

CVW and ALWD

Acknowledgments to the Seventh Edition

In law school, I learned legal citation using the *ALWD Citation Manual* (what is now the *ALWD Guide to Legal Citation*). I remember it as the easiest textbook to understand during my first year. As a student, I was grateful. As a professor, I have witnessed this same relief in my students who used prior editions of the *Guide*. Again, I was grateful to the authors — Darby Dickerson for taking on the monumental task of creating a simple, clear citation manual and to Coleen Barger for carrying that concept forward. Over the past year, my respect and admiration for these remarkable women grew as I revised the *Guide*. I am grateful beyond words for their work, and I hope I made them proud.

It is humbling to read the voluminous number of names in the first six editions' acknowledgments. I won't repeat the many individuals and organizations that have contributed to the production and success of the *ALWD Guide* over the past twenty years, but I am indebted to them all and echo the thanks expressed by the last two authors. Even in the midst of a global pandemic, when the world was on lockdown for most of the year and the work of professors, judges, and attorneys tripled and mutated in unexpected ways, the following people stepped up to assist me with the seventh edition, for which I am eternally grateful:

Fantastic peer reviewers who pushed me to think outside the box and gave me outstanding suggestions and guidance: Deborah L. Borman, Brooke J. Bowman, Jason L. Cassidy, Alexa Z. Chew, Tessa L. Dysart, John D. Edwards, Jessica R. Gunder, Steven K. Homer, Heather T. Horrocks, Jeffery D. Jackson, Sylvia J. Lett, Shakira D. Pleasant, Joseph Regalia, and Diana Simon.

Brooke Bowman who selflessly labored over almost all the past editions of the *Guide* and accompanying teaching materials for providing me her institutional knowledge, keen eye, and honest feedback. Her grace is extraordinary, and something I will not forget.

Andrea Gass for her tireless editing of my writing, unbelievable attention to detail, inspired suggestions, and kind emotional support. I am so thankful for her skills and friendship.

My student research assistants Christina Billhartz and Christina Poletti for accomplishing the impossible in a short amount of time. Their precision and cheerfulness made our work manageable.

Edward D. Garcia for answering my incessant questions about technology and for saving my work when my computer crashed.

The officers, directors, and membership of the Association of Legal Writing Directors (ALWD) for entrusting me to carry out their vision of the *Guide*. In particular, I wish to thank the four ALWD presidents I've worked with: Megan McAlpin, Jodi Wilson, Anne Mullins, and Katrina Lee. I am also grateful for the support of the *ALWD Guide* Task Force for their work in spreading the word about the *Guide*.

The administration and faculty of the University of Arizona James E. Rogers College of Law for providing generous support and ongoing encouragement for the project. Special thanks to my legal writing colleagues Susie Salmon, Tessa Dysart, Diana Simon, Sylvia Lett, and Joy Herr-Cardillo for sharing course materials, shielding me from extra projects while I wrote, and making me laugh when I was overwhelmed. Thanks to Debbie Martin for excellent clerical services.

The judges, attorneys, and professors from all fifty states who reviewed local rules.

The many users who took the time to write with questions, ideas, and suggestions.

The publisher Wolters Kluwer, and in particular to Justin Billing, Stacie Goosman, and Natalie Danner. I am especially grateful for the outstanding editorial work of The Froebe Group and the efforts of Jessica Barmack, Renee Cote, and Paul Sobel.

Finally, a special thanks to my sweet son Thor for entertaining himself during lockdown and teaching himself third grade online while I wrote. And to the love of my life, Gary Williams: thank you for indulging my eccentricities, cooking me food, cleaning around me at my desk, decorating for holidays I forgot, and all the other things you did to support me. I could not accomplish half that I do without you.

As Darby said, all errors are mine. If you see any, please let me know.

Carolyn V. Williams
cvwilliams@email.arizona.edu
University of Arizona James E. Rogers College of Law
Tucson, Arizona
April 2021

I am also grateful to the following copyright holders for permission to reprint material in the Seventh Edition:

- Screenshots of caption page and textual excerpt from *Gideon v. Wainwright*. Westlaw Edge. Reprinted with permission from Thomson Reuters/West. Copyright © 2020 Thomson Reuters/West.
- Screenshots of caption page and textual excerpt from *Foster v. Winston-Salem Joint Venture*. Lexis+. LexisNexis. Copyright © 2020.
- Pages 812 and 813 of *United States v. Roviaro. Federal Reporter, Second Series*. Reprinted with permission from Thomson Reuters/West. Copyright © 2020 Thomson Reuters/West.
- Title page and page 78. Restatement (Third) of the Law of Foreign Relations of the United States. American Law Institute. Copyright © 1987.

Acknowledgments to the First Edition

I would like to thank and recognize the following people and organizations without whom the *ALWD Citation Manual* would not have become a reality:

The Association of Legal Writing Directors (ALWD), whose officers and directors conceived the idea of a new citation system and provided guidance and support throughout the process.

Members of the ALWD Citation Manual Advisory Committee who reviewed draft manuscripts and provided valuable input, support, and suggestions: Coleen Barger, Mary Beth Beazley, Maria Ciampi, Eric B. Easton, Ruth Ann McKinney, Craig T. Smith, Kathleen Elliott Vinson, Marilyn R. Walter, and Ursula H. Weigold.

Special thanks to the co-chairs of the ALWD Citation Manual Advisory Committee, Steven D. Jamar and Amy E. Sloan, to Richard K. Neumann, Jr., who served as a liaison between ALWD and the publisher and provided invaluable assistance and advice from the beginning of the project through the end, and to Jan Levine, who conceived the idea of the *Manual* and supported and contributed to it throughout the process.

The four presidents of ALWD who served during the pendency of this project and who helped facilitate its completion: Jan Levine, Katie McManus, Maureen Straub Kordesh, and Sue Liemer.

The other ALWD officers, including Molly Warner Lien, who supported and nurtured the project.

Henry T. Wihnyk for participating in the initial stages of the project.

Joe Kimble and Christy B. Nisbett for providing insightful and detailed comments on a prior draft of the *Manual.*

The anonymous reviewers who provided helpful critiques of earlier drafts of the *Manual.*

The administration and faculty of Stetson University College of Law for providing generous financial support and ongoing encouragement for the project.

Professor Peter L. Fitzgerald for sharing his knowledge about international treaties and Internet sources.

The Stetson University College of Law Reference Librarians — Pamela Burdett, Dorothy Clark, Michael Dahn, Earlene Kuester, Madison Mosley, and Sally Waters — for locating difficult-to-find material, processing many interlibrary loan requests, and serving as excellent sources of bibliographic information.

The Stetson University College of Law Faculty Support Services Department, headed by Connie P. Evans, for superb clerical services and moral support.

The following Stetson University College of Law students who provided top-notch research assistance: Robert Taylor Bowling, Christopher H. Burrows, Victoria L. Cecil, David F. Chalela, Julianne J. Flynn, Darren D. McClain, Ashkan Najafi, Nicole D. Quinn, Tyra Nicole Read, Jeffrey P. Rosato, and Debra A. Tuomey.

Students Victoria J. Avalon, Danielle M. Bonett, Pamela H. Cazares, and Kevin M. Iurato deserve special recognition for their painstaking and detail-oriented work on several appendices and other portions of the *Manual.*

Aspen Law & Business for recognizing the value of this project and enhancing the quality of the manuscript. Within Aspen, I would like to specifically recognize Dan Mangan, Melody Davies, Ellen Greenblatt, Carol McGeehan, and Linda Richmond for their creativity, persistence, and hard work.

Finally, a special thanks to my husband, Michael P. Capozzi, for understanding why I have not been around much during the last year.

Darby Dickerson
Stetson University College of Law
April 2000

Acknowledgments to the Second Edition

As with many projects, there are so many people to thank and such little space in which to express that thanks. Over the years, many individuals and organizations have contributed to the production and success of the *ALWD Citation Manual*. In addition to those recognized in the *Manual*'s first edition, I would like to thank the following for their assistance with the second edition:

The Association of Legal Writing Directors (ALWD) and its officers, directors, and members, who have supported this project from the beginning.

Specifically, I would like to thank the following ALWD presidents who have served since the first edition was published and while the second edition was being prepared: Sue Liemer, Pamela Lysaght, Nancy Schultz, and Amy Sloan.

The members of the *ALWD Citation Manual* Advisory Committee for the Second Edition, who provided invaluable input and guidance: Tracy L. Bach, Coleen Barger, Jan Levine, Tracy McGaugh, Judith Rosenbaum, Arnold I. Siegel, and Grace Tonner.

Richard K. Neumann, Jr. and Jan Levine, who conceived the idea of the *Manual* and have provided input, suggestions, and support since that time.

Members of the *ALWD Citation Manual* Adoption Committee for their work in spreading the word about the *Manual*. Special thanks go to co-chairs Coleen Barger, Wayne Schiess, and Hether Macfarlane.

My former student and now colleague Brooke J. Bowman for her assistance with so many of the painstaking details.

The following current and former Stetson University College of Law students who provided excellent research assistance: Irene Bosco, Tracy Carpenter, Catherine Shannon Christie, Tanya Dentamaro, Dale Goerne (tax appendix), Moein Marashi, Susan St. John, Bridget Remington, and Natsha Wolfe.

Stetson University College of Law, for continued support and resources.

The anonymous reviewers of the new tax appendix.

The many law librarians and state reporters of decisions who took time to complete surveys regarding the *Manual*.

The many users who took the time to write with comments and changes. A special thanks goes to C. Edward Good for his comments.

The many research and writing professionals who took the time to write reviews of the first edition.

Aspen Publishers, for helping in so many ways to make the *Manual* a success. I would like to extend special thanks to Dan Mangan, Melody Davies, Carol McGeehan, Michael Gregory, Barbara Lasoff, and Paul Sobel for their hard work on this project.

Despite all of the help, all errors remain my own.

Darby Dickerson
November 2002

Acknowledgments to the Third Edition

To be a success, a project the magnitude of the *ALWD Citation Manual* requires the expertise and assistance of many people. As with the first two editions, I have many people to thank for helping to bring the third edition to fruition, including the following:

The Association of Legal Writing Directors (ALWD) and its officers, directors, and members for continuing to support this project.

The ALWD presidents who have served and supported the *Manual* since the second edition was printed: Jo Anne Durako, Brad Clary, and Kristin Gerdy.

The members of the *ALWD Citation Manual* Advisory Committee, who provided outstanding advice and guidance: Pam Armstrong, Brooke J. Bowman, Pamela Lysaght, Tracy McGaugh, Amy E. Sloan, Tracy Weissman, and Melissa H. Weresh.

The members of the *ALWD Citation Manual* Adoptions Committee, who have generated many creative ideas over the years. A special thanks goes to Hether Macfarlane, who has chaired that committee for many years.

Molly Lien, for providing material on foreign and international citations for Rule 21.

My Stetson colleague Brooke J. Bowman, who helped to update several rules and appendices, and was a source of constant support and encouragement during this project.

My assistants Roxane Latoza and Vicky Baumann, for managing the office while I was locked away preparing this edition.

Stetson law students Paula Bentley, Sarah Lahlou-Amine, and Josephine Thomas for their assistance in updating rules and examples.

The Stetson reference librarians, and particularly Sally G. Waters, who helped to locate sources and materials for this edition.

Members and editors of the *Stetson Law Review* for passing along suggestions to help improve the *Manual.*

Stetson University and Stetson University College of Law for continued support and resources.

The many users who took the time to write with questions, ideas, and suggestions.

The research and writing professionals who took the time to write reviews of the first and second editions, and who showed confidence in the *Manual* by adopting it in their classes.

Aspen Publishers, for its continued efforts to make the *Manual* a success. I would like to extend special thanks to Carol McGeehan, Melody Davies, Barbara Lasoff, Laurel Ibey, Michael Gregory, and George Serafin for their help over the years and for their hard work on the third edition.

And, as usual, despite all of the help, all errors remain my own.

Darby Dickerson
November 2005

Acknowledgments to the Fourth Edition

As we celebrate the *ALWD Citation Manual*'s tenth anniversary, I thank all of the faculty members, attorneys, judges, students, and other individuals who have used the *Manual*. Your support has been critical to the book's continued success and improvement. I send a heartfelt thanks to the professors who adopted the *Manual*, sometimes at risk to their own careers, because they believe it is the best teaching tool for legal citation.

I reserve special thanks for two individuals who made the fourth edition a better product because of their effort: Professor Coleen Barger and Professor Brooke J. Bowman, co-authors of *The ALWD Companion: A Citation Practice Book*, which will be published soon after this fourth edition. Professor Bowman is my former student and current Stetson Law colleague. She is passionate (yes . . . that's correct) about legal citation and has contributed outstanding suggestions, eagle eyes, and valuable time to this edition. Professor Barger is a nationally recognized expert on legal writing and citation who has served as a reviewer for every edition. I'm thrilled that she was able to join us as a Visiting Professor at Stetson in Fall 2009. As I've come to expect, Professor Barger offered fabulous ideas, was willing to ask the tough questions, and combed through the *Manual* multiple times to help think about what should be updated, added, or revised.

Once again, I could not have updated the appendices without tremendous help from the Stetson Law Librarians. Professor and Law Library Director Rebecca Trammell assisted with Appendices 5 and 7, among others. Pamela Burdett, Whitney Curtis, Alyssa Folse, Earlene Kuester, Wanita Scroggs, Jules Stevens, and Sally ("Queen of Reference") Waters helped check and re-check sources for accuracy and track down difficult-to-locate sources. Thank you for all that you do!

The Association of Legal Writing Directors (ALWD) has been an outstanding partner for this project, and I again thank its officers, directors, and members for their continuing support. The ALWD presidents who have served and supported the *Manual* since the third edition was printed are Craig Smith, Terrill Pollman, Judy Stinson, and Mary Beth Beazley.

My student assistant Stephanie Sawchuk performed assignments admirably and completed less-than-glamorous tasks professionally and cheerfully. Thanks also go to Stetson Law student Kaleena Barnes for helping with various projects. Among other things, she gamely tested draft rules for some of the "new media" sources.

My assistants Roxane Latoza and Charmaine Rushing were, as always, amazing throughout the updating process.

I am grateful to Stetson University and Stetson University College of Law for providing support and resources for me to complete this and earlier editions.

Finally, thanks go to the talented staff at Wolters Kluwer/Aspen Publishers for their patience, hard work, and determination to make the fourth edition as perfect as possible. They truly have added great value to this project. Carol

McGeehan, Melody Davies, Michael Gregory, and George Serafin have been with the project since inception. They have all become friends and treasured colleagues who always have great ideas and sage advice. And it has been a great pleasure to work with Barbara Roth, Darren Kelly, and Lisa Wehrle to prepare this edition for publication. I know that working with a sitting law dean who travels constantly was not the easiest assignment. You deserve great credit for bringing the project to successful conclusion.

As always, all errors are mine. If you see any, please let me know!

Darby Dickerson
March 2010

Acknowledgments to the Fifth Edition

The fifth edition of the *ALWD Guide to Legal Citation* was inspired by and owes its development to many people, without whom it could not have come into being. I thank the officers, directors, and membership of the Association of Legal Writing Directors, who recognized the direction in which the *Guide* needed to go and who have been so supportive. In particular, I wish to thank the three ALWD presidents under whose watch I've worked on this project: J. Lyn Entrikin, Anthony Niedwiecki, and Kathleen Elliott Vinson.

I am so fortunate for the guidance and suggestions of the members of the ALWD Citation Advisory Committee: Professors Cindy Archer, Mary Beth Beazley, Luellen Curry, Jan Levine, Deborah Panek Paruch, Mary Rose Strubbe, and Dean Maria Perez Crist. The project has also enjoyed the support of ALWD Publication Committee chairs J. Lyn Entrikin and Ted Becker. And for those times when the project seemed daunting, I appreciate the encouragement of Professors Richard Neumann and Grace Tonner.

Three people provided extraordinary levels of help and feedback during the editing process: Professors Jessica Clark, Jan Levine, and Samantha Moppett. Thank you, guys. I would also like to thank Professor Brooke Bowman and the *ALWD Companion* scholars, updating its exercises to guide law students in mastering legal citation: Professors Jessica Clark (again!), Cassandra Hill, Erin Karsman, and Samantha Moppett.

At UALR, I owe so many thanks to my student research assistants: Luke Burton, Kayleigh Collins Dulaney, Katie Beck, and Kristen Garner. My faculty assistant, Colleen Godley, was a great help in updating several sources' Snapshots. Thank you to UALR law librarians Jessie Burchfield and Melissa Serfass for your wise advice. And of course, I couldn't have done this without the generous research support and personal encouragement of UALR deans John DiPippa, Paula Casey, and Michael Hunter Schwartz.

At Aspen, special thanks go to Carol McGeehan, Christine Hannan, Aaron Reid, Dana Wilson, and Susan Junkin. Additional thanks go to talented book designer Claire Seng-Niemoeller.

I owe a mountainous debt of gratitude to Dean Darby Dickerson, who created the original *ALWD Citation Manual* and whose clear explanations, sensible organization, remarkable consistency, and generous examples in the four earlier editions continue to inspire this book.

Finally, thanks go to my husband, Gary Barger, for his patience, wisdom, and unwavering support, and for listening to hours of citation minutiae during our walks!

Please let me know your suggestions, and without question, let me know if you find problems. My email address is below.

Coleen M. Barger
University of Arkansas Little Rock
February 2014

Acknowledgments to the Sixth Edition

In my experience, writing the new edition to an established text is not an easy job. It isn't just a matter of adding (or subtracting) some abbreviations or correcting errors and omissions (although these tasks were certainly necessary). I've listened to and learned from complaints about the inherent nature of books about citation — from my students, from my legal writing comrades across the country, and from those directed to another publication. The complaints (let's relabel them as "concerns") range from "It's too long/bulky/detailed/heavy" to "It doesn't adequately explain X" and "I wish it covered Y." Reconciling these competing concerns has been an adventure. I've been making notes for months, and I've collected and implemented a host of helpful suggestions.

I am most appreciative for the generous help of Professors Brooke Bowman, John Edwards, Lyn Entrikin, Lindsey Gustafson, Jan Levine, and Judy Rosenbaum, who shared their wise observations and gave me so many good ideas.

I could not have done without the able assistance of my three research assistants, Andrew Trevino, Samantha Lambert, and the amazing Lauren Kuhlmann. Lauren's help extends as far back as her first-year legal writing class, where she found errors, asked questions, and evolved into a true citation geek (a badge of honor, in my estimation).

The Association of Legal Writing Directors has now entrusted me with two editions of this essential text, and I am forever in its debt for that trust and support. In particular, I want to give heartfelt thanks to the officers, President Wanda Temm, President-Elect Megan McAlpin, Secretary Tamara Herrera, and Treasurer Catherine Wasson, and to the members of the 2016-17 Board of Directors (Mary Adkins, David Cleveland, Lucy Jewel, Tonya Kowalski, Katrina Lee, Ellie Margolis, Suzanne Rabe, Amy Vorenberg, and Jodi Wilson).

Thanks go as well to our publisher, Wolters Kluwer, and in particular to Nicole Pinard, Donna Gridley, Maureen Kenealy, and Sherri Meek. I am especially grateful for the outstanding editorial work of The Froebe Group and the efforts of Paul Sobel, Kathy Langone, and Renee Cote.

At the University of Arkansas Little Rock, many thanks are due to Dean Michael Hunter Schwartz, Associate Dean Michael Flannery, and my former assistant Colleen Godley (the Career Services office lucked out when you joined them). A special note of appreciation goes to Professor Jeff Woodmansee, law librarian extraordinaire, who helped to unravel the mysteries of Internal Revenue Service publications.

Finally, thank you to my husband, Gary Barger, for once again giving his support, showing his wisdom, and putting up with me while I worked.

I welcome your suggestions, and I encourage you to contact me if you have any questions, spot any problems, or just want to connect with another citation geek.

Coleen M. Barger
April 2017

Introductory Material

A Purposes and Uses of Citations

Legal citations are shorthand references to sources a writer wants to bring to a reader's attention. The sources used in legal writing are *primary* or *secondary* authorities. A primary authority is *the law itself* as determined by one of the three branches of federal or state government (judicial, legislative, and executive/administrative). Within the jurisdiction of the governmental body that issued it, a primary authority is mandatory until it is changed by subsequent governmental action (e.g., repeal of a statute, overruling of a case). A secondary authority is a source that *talks about* the law (or a legal topic); unlike a primary authority, it has no force of law.

Depending on the nature of the source, the components of a legal citation typically indicate the source's author or origin, its title, the location of pertinent data within the source (such as a volume, page, or paragraph number), and its date of issuance or publication.

Legal citations serve many purposes. First, by indicating *the nature* of a source, a legal citation tells law-trained readers *where to find the source*, such as within a set of statutes or a volume of a law review. A citation's format also indicates to law-trained readers whether the source is in print or online. Because readers often want to retrieve a source themselves, whether to verify what it says or to learn additional details, its citation should provide everything necessary to locate both the source and any internal reference.

Second, law-trained readers learn much about a source's *weight and persuasiveness* from its citation. For example, a case citation can inform the reader that the case was later reversed. A legal citation may reveal other relevant facts about a source's influence, such as its author's identity, its age, its hierarchical position among other relevant authorities, and its current validity.

Third, a citation conveys the *type and degree of support* provided for a particular proposition. For example, the signal preceding a case citation can show whether the case provides strong, direct support for the writer's assertion or support that is more inferential. A citation can indicate that an authority contradicts or challenges an opponent's assertion. Law-trained readers can discern the type and degree of support from the citation itself or from the signal used to introduce it.

Fourth, attorneys use citations *to demonstrate that their positions are well researched and well supported.* Law-trained readers expect to see evidence that writers have thoroughly researched the authorities for and against particular propositions. Careful writers document their research with citations to the sources they have consulted.

Finally, legal writers use citations to *give credit* to those who originated the ideas incorporated in their writing. The principles of effective and ethical legal writing demand that legal writers give proper attribution to those whose words and ideas have informed them.

B How to Use the *ALWD Guide*

The seventh edition of the *ALWD Guide to Legal Citation* assists writers in developing citations to sources used in their legal writing. The *ALWD Guide* codifies the rules of legal citation most commonly followed. While no citation system can anticipate every source a writer might need or choose to cite, the *ALWD Guide* gives rules and examples for frequently cited materials and guidelines for citing new or less familiar materials.

The *ALWD Guide* focuses on United States law, both federal and state. It does not address international or foreign sources, except for treaties binding on the United States. To cite a legal source from another country or an international law source, consult the *Guide to Foreign and International Legal Citations* (2d ed. 2009), prepared by the editors of New York University School of Law's *Journal of International Law and Politics*, or Part IV of the Oxford University Standard for Citation of Legal Authorities (OSCOLA), http://www.law.ox.ac.uk/sites/files/oxlaw/oscola_2006_citing_international_law.pdf.

The *ALWD Guide*'s citation system applies to all forms of legal writing, both practice-based and scholarly. Where scholarly writing requires modifications to citation format, the *ALWD Guide* identifies those modifications and provides examples.

1 Overall Organization

The *ALWD Guide* is organized into six parts:

- **Part 1**, "Citation Basics," addresses key concepts applicable to a variety of citations, including typeface, abbreviations, numbers, pinpoint references, and full or short citations.
- **Part 2**, "Citing Specific Sources," diagrams and explains citations to the primary and secondary authorities most often used in legal writing, whether in print or online.
- **Part 3**, "Online Sources," addresses sources *not covered* in **Part 2**, including those available on the internet, on commercial databases, and other electronic media such as blogs, email, listserv postings, and social media.
- **Part 4**, "Incorporating Citations into Documents," illustrates the placement of citations in text, including citation sentences, citation clauses, embedded citations, and citations in academic footnotes. It provides guidance for choosing which authorities to cite and for organizing citations to multiple authorities. It also addresses the functions of signals and parentheticals.
- **Part 5**, "Quotations," covers the essentials for incorporating quotations into legal documents, including correct punctuation and formatting. It

also demonstrates how to make alterations to or indicate omissions from a quoted text.

- **Part 6**, "Appendices," collects essential information for constructing legal citations, including general and specialized abbreviations for official and unofficial reporters, statutes, and administrative publications, as well as complete abbreviations for legal periodicals. Where federal or state courts have adopted local rules affecting citation of primary sources, the *ALWD Guide* gathers references to both online and print sources of those local rules.

2 Organization Within Each Part of the *ALWD Guide*

Parts 1 through **5** condense legal citation into forty rules, divided into subsections. Each rule gives detailed explanations for citing a particular source or applying a particular concept. Examples illustrate key points and exceptions to the general rules.

Rules for citing a particular source begin with a diagram of required components and an example that represents the components used in a full citation. The diagrams are highlighted in gray for easy identification. They use a vertical line (|) to separate components of a full citation; the line does not, however, indicate the placement of spaces in a citation. Instead, the *ALWD Guide* uses red triangles (▲) in the component examples below the diagrams to designate required spaces. Using ordinary type, *italics*, or LARGE AND SMALL CAPITALS, the diagrams show components that must be rendered in those typefaces. The diagrams show the placement of necessary punctuation such as commas or parentheses. All punctuation and any words that will always appear exactly as they appear in the diagram are in black font. The text in red font indicates that the component is variable—the words it represents change with each source's citation. For example, in the diagram below, "*Case name*" would be replaced with the actual, italicized name of a case. Brackets indicate components that may not always be a part of the citation, depending on the circumstances. Think of brackets as indicating inclusion of this component (and any of its punctuation) only if it is available, exists, or is applicable. For example, in the component diagram below, the brackets around "[, *Subsequent history designation*,]" indicate that you may include the applicable designation, set off by commas, only if a case has subsequent history, and if so, the designation would be italicized. Do not include the brackets, red triangles, or red text in the final citation.

This component diagram and accompanying example is from **Rule 12 (Cases)**:

Case name, | Reporter volume | Reporter abbreviation | Initial page, | Pinpoint reference | (Court abbreviation | Date) | [, *Subsequent history designation*,] | [Subsequent history citation].

Example

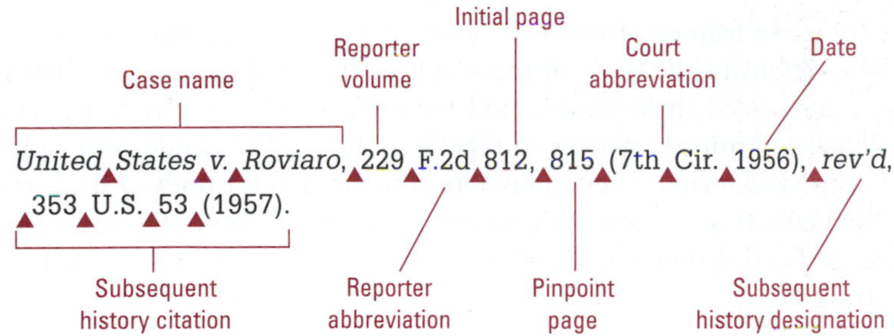

Following the diagram, the rule explains each component of the full citation and provides additional examples.

Rules 12 through **29** and **Rules 31** through **33** offer special features to help you construct accurate citations. These rules are preceded by "Fast Formats," tables containing representative citations to commonly cited materials. Consult a rule's Fast Formats to quickly preview basic citation components or refresh your memory. "Snapshots" of sources show you where to look to find necessary components for a full citation. Several rules are augmented by "Charts" collecting abbreviations or other components that frequently appear in citations addressed by those rules. Finally, throughout the *ALWD Guide*, "Sidebars" present useful background information about particular publications, caveats about common mistakes, and tips for citing particular sources.

Callouts in **Parts 1–5** and **Appendix 6** after some sentences in the rules are a new feature of the seventh edition that is generally most useful for those working on law reviews. The corresponding callouts can be found in **Appendix 8**, under the part and rule number. There, the callouts indicate cross-references for select information in the text of the *ALWD Guide* to the corresponding rule in *The Bluebook: A Uniform System of Citation* (Columbia Law Review Ass'n et al. eds., 21st ed. 2020). For example, *ALWD Guide* **Rule 1.3(d)** has "7" as a callout after the first sentence. In **Appendix 8**, after the headings **Part 1** and **Rule 1**, the seventh entry is "7 2.1(a)." That means that the information in the first sentence in **Rule 1.3(d)** of the *ALWD Guide* correlates to the information found in *Bluebook* **Rule 2.1(a)**. Occasionally, there are law reviews or local rules that require citations conform to the *Bluebook*, and this new feature simply assures the user that citations crafted using the *Guide* do just that. Lack of a callout does not indicate nonconformance. On the contrary, it generally indicates that the twenty-first edition of the *Bluebook* does not contain that information — it is silent on how to treat a particular source, does not explicitly explain a rule, or does not include clarifying background information. In those instances, the *ALWD Guide* fills the gaps that would likely frustrate or confuse legal writers.

3 Citations in Text or in Footnotes

A distinctive feature of everyday legal writing is its preference for placement of citations in the body of the text itself. In scholarly writing, however, citations are placed in footnotes, and for some sources, footnote placement requires certain minor changes in typeface. The *ALWD Guide* addresses the construction and format of citations appearing both in the body of the text and in academic footnotes. Academic formatting rules for footnotes end with the superscript [FN], and they are set off with a vertical red line and an "Academic Formatting" icon.

4 Automatic Formatting in Your Word-Processing Software

Preexisting settings in your word-processing software can adversely affect your citations. Unless modified or disabled, default settings or auto-correct features can make changes you did not intend and, consequently, create errors. For example, your software may automatically insert spaces after a period, even though you are trying to type a citation component that uses no spaces after periods (e.g., U.S.C.). It may recognize your attempt to type an ellipsis, yet convert your correctly spaced ellipsis points to three unspaced periods (e.g., from . . . to...). It may erroneously convert ordinal contractions to superscript (e.g., 4th to 4th) while leaving others alone (e.g., 2d and 3d). It may automatically convert subsection references to other symbols, such as converting (c) to ©. And if you type an internet address, the software may automatically convert the URL (Uniform Resource Locator) to an active hyperlink.

Test your software to see whether it makes these unwanted changes. If it does, consult the developer's website for help in modifying, turning off, or disabling these features.

5 Finding What You Need (and Quickly)

To understand the *ALWD Guide*'s overall organization or to quickly locate rules on the major sources of law, check the Table of Contents. To find a specific source or concept, see the Fast Formats Locator on the inside front cover or look for the topic in the Index.

6 Citing Sources Not Covered in the *ALWD Guide*

If your writing requires citation to a source not covered by the *ALWD Guide*, follow the rule for the source most analogous to the source you have found. By analogizing to the most similar source, you stand the best chance of providing readers with the information they need to find the source.

7 Nonconforming Citations

Citation rules and practices evolve, and writers always seek guidance in constructing citations to new types of sources. In your research, you may encounter citations inconsistent with those you see in the *ALWD Guide*. They may differ because they reflect older or superseded rules and practices. Legal publishers are known to employ their proprietary citation formats in specific contexts (e.g., the running header of a case reporter). Many courts have *local rules* governing citations that attorneys must follow when submitting documents to those courts (see **Appendix 2**). Unless you are following a court's local rules in a document to be submitted to that court, when you encounter nonconforming citations, do not copy them as shown in the publication. Instead, look up the relevant rules in the *ALWD Guide* and revise the citations to conform to current citation standards.

8 Sources for Additional Guidance

For more guidance on matters of capitalization, punctuation, style, and special citation formats not addressed in the *ALWD Guide*, consult the most recent editions of these works:

- *U.S. Government Publishing Office Style Manual* (2016), a free download from https://www.govinfo.gov/content/pkg/GPO-STYLEMANUAL-2016/pdf/GPO-STYLEMANUAL-2016.pdf.
- *The Solicitor General's Style Guide* (Jack Metzler ed., 3d ed. 2018).
- *Bryan A. Garner, The Redbook: A Manual on Legal Style* (4th ed. 2018).
- *The Chicago Manual of Style* (17th ed. 2017), available in print or online at http://www.chicagomanualofstyle.org/home.html.

9 Citing the *ALWD Guide*

Cite this book as Carolyn V. Williams, ALWD, *ALWD Guide to Legal Citation* (7th ed. 2021).

ALWD Guide to Legal Citation

Part 1
Citation Basics

1 Typeface for Citations

1.1 Typeface Choices

Legal citations use four typefaces: ordinary type, *italics* (or its equivalent, underlining), and LARGE AND SMALL CAPITAL LETTERS.[1]

1.2 When to Use Ordinary Type

Most citation components use ordinary type, i.e., uppercase and lowercase letters with no enhancements. Use ordinary type for everything not listed in **Rule 1.3** or **1.4**.[2]

1.3 When to Use *Italics* or Underlining

1.3(a) Components to *italicize* or underline

Where the *ALWD Guide* directs the use of italics, you may substitute underlining.[3] The modern trend, however, is to use underlining only if a local court rule or a professor's course requirements demand it. In those situations, any rule in the *ALWD Guide* specifying the use of italics will be satisfied with underlining. Never use underlining in academic footnotes.[4] **Chart 1.1** identifies citation components to italicize or underline.

1.3(b) Italicized or underlined punctuation

Italicize or underline punctuation marks such as apostrophes, commas, periods, question marks, and quotation marks only when they are located within other components of the citation using the same formatting (e.g., within case names, signals, titles of books or law review articles, or as part of an abbreviation).[5] Do not italicize or underline punctuation that follows such components.[6]

Examples (*italicized* or underlined punctuation in red)

Tomlinson v. Goldman, Sachs & Co., 682 F. Supp. 2d 845, 848 (N.D. Ill. 2009), *aff'd sub nom. Premium Plus Partners, L.P. v. Goldman, Sachs & Co.*, 648 F.3d 533 (7th Cir. 2011).

Tomlinson v. Goldman, Sachs & Co., 682 F. Supp. 2d 845, 848 (N.D. Ill. 2009), aff'd sub nom. Premium Plus Partners, L.P. v. Goldman, Sachs & Co., 648 F.3d 533 (7th Cir. 2011).

Esther M. Schonfeld, *"To Be or Not to Be a Parent?" The Search for a Solution to Custody Disputes over Frozen Embryos*, 15 Touro L. Rev. 305, 311–12 (1998).

CHART 1.1	Components to *Italicize* or Underline
Internal cross-references *supra* and *infra*	10.2FN
Short citations *id.* and *supra*	11.3, 11.4
Case names in full citations (except in academic footnotes)	12.2(a), 18.5(a), 24.1
Phrases indicating subsequent or prior history of a case (such as *aff'd, cert. denied*)	12.8, 12.9
Case names in short citations	12.16
Titles of congressional hearings, debates, and name of committee	15.5(a)–(b), 15.10(a)(1), 15.16(a), 15.18(b)
Titles of jury instructions	16.3(a)
Titles of books, treatises, dictionaries, other nonperiodic materials, and forthcoming works (except in academic footnotes)	15.7(a), 15.9(a), 15.17(a), 20.1(c), 20.3(b), 20.5(a)–(d), 22.1, 24.2, 29.1
Titles of works in periodicals	21.2(c), 21.3(b)
Defined terms, topics, or titles in annotations, dictionaries, and legal encyclopedias	22.1, 22.3(c), 22.5(b)
Titles of visual or audio media	28.1(a), 28.1(b), 28.2, 28.3(b), 28.4, 28.5, 28.7, 28.8
Titles of websites and CD-ROMs	31.1(b), 33.6
Titles of individual postings in blogs, social media platforms, and wikis	31.2
Signals (such as *see, cf.*)	35

Esther M. Schonfeld, "To Be or Not to Be a Parent?" The Search for a Solution to Custody Disputes over Frozen Embryos, 15 Touro L. Rev. 305, 311–12 (1998).

See id. at 325.

See id. at 325.

1.3(c) Possessive endings

Do not italicize or underline possessive endings ('s or ') added to case names, publication names, or similar components.

Examples (possessive endings in red)

Counsel for the petitioner argued that *Tinker*'s protection of student free speech did not apply to teachers while they were in the classroom.

The court adopted Black's Law Dictionary's definition of "affiliate."

1.3(d) Italicized or underlined words within similarly formatted component

When words ordinarily italicized under a rule in the *ALWD Guide* appear within an italicized component (e.g., a case name in the title of a law review article), write those words in ordinary type.[7] The same principle applies to underlined components.[8]

Examples

Zachary M. Vaughn, Note, *The Reach of the Writ*: Boumediene v. Bush *and the Political Question Doctrine*, 99 Geo. L.J. 869, 872 (2011).

Rob Atkinson, *Liberating Lawyers: Divergent Parallels in* Intruder in the Dust *and* To Kill a Mockingbird, 49 Duke L.J. 601, 647 (1999).

Nina W. Tarr, <u>A Different Ethical Issue in</u> Anatomy of a Murder<u>: Friendly Fire from the Cowboy-Lawyer</u>, 32 J. Legal Prof. 137, 157–58 (2008).

1.3(e) Adding emphasis

Emphasize words by italicizing or underlining them, but use this technique sparingly. When you emphasize words in quotations in the text, append a parenthetical note to the quoted source's citation to indicate the added emphasis.[9] Read **Rule 39.4(b)** for more guidance. It is unnecessary to parenthetically note emphasis appearing in a source's original language.[10]

Example

"A written provision in any maritime transaction or a contract evidencing a transaction involving commerce to settle by arbitration a controversy . . . shall be valid, irrevocable, and enforceable, *save upon such grounds as exist at law or in equity for the revocation of any contract.*" 9 U.S.C. § 2 (emphasis added).

1.3(f) Foreign words and abbreviations

You may italicize or underline foreign words not commonly seen in English.[11] Latin terms that are common to the law do not need italics or underlining. **Chart 1.2** shows examples of Latin words and abbreviations that are not italicized or underlined unless used within a component that itself requires the formatting, such as a case name or the title of a law review article. To determine whether to italicize or underline other foreign words or abbreviations, consult the most current edition of *Black's Law Dictionary*.

CHART 1.2 Latin Words and Abbreviations Ordinarily Not Italicized or Underlined

ab initio	e.g.	mens rea
ad hoc	en banc	modus operandi
amicus curiae	et al.	obiter dictum
certiorari	et seq.	prima facie
corpus juris	etc.	quid pro quo
de facto	habeas corpus	res gestae
de jure	i.e.	res ipsa loquitur
de novo	in personam	res judicata
dicta, dictum	in rem	viz.,

1.4FN When to Use LARGE AND SMALL CAPITAL LETTERS

ACADEMIC FORMATTING

Use large and small capital letters only in academic footnote citations, such as those found in books, treatises, and law review articles.[12] See **Sidebar 1.1** for instructions on how to format text in large and small capital letters. For footnotes in any other context, such as a memorandum of authorities or an appellate brief, use ordinary type and italics or underlining for components.[13]

Do not use large and small capital letters for any citation in the body of the text[14] or for any citation used as a part of speech[15] (see **Rule 34.1(b)FN**). **Chart 1.3** identifies citation components that in academic footnotes require use of large and small capital letters.

Examples

---

11 U.S. CONST. art. IV.

12 OR. REV. STAT. § 215.080 (2011).

13 S. REP. NO. 112-202, at 8 (Aug. 2, 2012).

14 8TH CIR. R. 28A(i).

15 LOUDON CNTY., VA., CODIFIED ORDINANCES § 684.03 (2009).

16 STEPHEN BREYER, MAKING OUR DEMOCRACY WORK: A JUDGE'S VIEW 42–44 (2010).

17 Andrew Jay McClurg, *Fight Club: Doctors vs. Lawyers — A Peace Plan Grounded in Self-Interest*, 83 TEMP. L. REV. 309, 345 (2011).

18 *Parody*, DICTIONARY.COM, http://www.dictionary.com/browse/parody (last visited Nov. 13, 2016).

19 RESTATEMENT (SECOND) OF PROP.: LANDLORD AND TENANT §§ 1.4–1.8 (1977).

SIDEBAR 1.1 Using Your Word Processor to Format Large and Small Capital Letters

In Microsoft Word, you can create large and small caps in two ways. First, type your word in ordinary type, highlight it, and then press Control+Shift+K. Alternatively, type the word in ordinary type, highlight it, pull down the font menu at the top of the screen, and check "Small caps." It is not possible to use large and small caps in Google Docs unless you install a specific plug-in.

CHART 1.3 Components Using Large and Small Capital Letters in Academic Footnotes

Abbreviated titles of constitutions	13.2(e)[FN]
Abbreviated titles of statutory codes	14.2(i)[FN], 14.4(d)[FN], 14.5(b)[FN]
Names of authors, titles, and abbreviated titles of numbered congressional reports, documents, and prints	15.7(h)[FN], 15.8(b)[FN], 15.9(b)[FN], 15.9(c)(2)[FN], 15.10(a)(7)[FN], 15.10(b)(2)[FN], 15.10(c)(2)[FN], 15.10(d)(2)[FN], 15.11(b)[FN], 15.11(c)(2)[FN], 15.12(b)[FN], 15.17(h)[FN], 15.17(j)[FN], 15.18(g)[FN], 15.19(b)[FN], 15.20(b)[FN], 15.20(d)[FN]
Abbreviated titles of court rules, jury instructions	16.1(f)[FN], 16.3(b)[FN], 16.3(d)[FN], 16.3(f)[FN]
Titles of codified ordinances	17.3[FN], 17.4(b)[FN]
Senate treaty or executive documents	19.3[FN]
Names of authors and titles of books, treatises, and other nonperiodic materials	20.1(f)[FN], 20.3(e)[FN], 20.4(d)[FN], 20.6(d)[FN]
Abbreviated names of periodicals	21.6[FN], 21.7(b)[FN]
Titles of dictionaries, encyclopedias, and American Law Reports series	22.1(d)[FN], 22.2(b)[FN], 22.3(g)[FN], 22.4(b)[FN], 22.4(d)[FN], 22.5(g)[FN], 22.6(b)[FN]
Titles of restatements, principles of law, model codes and acts, uniform laws, and sentencing guidelines	23.1(f)[FN], 23.3(c)[FN], 23.5(c)[FN], 23.6(d)[FN]
Homepage name in an online source	31.1(h)[FN]

2 Abbreviations

2.1 Using Abbreviations

2.1(a) Standard and non-standard abbreviations

Legal writers use abbreviations to shorten words in citation components such as case names, court names, statutes, and periodical names. The **Appendices** in **Part 7** contain tables of standard abbreviations. While most abbreviations of words end in periods, others are contractions formed with apostrophes; such abbreviations do not end with a period.[1] Abbreviations for ordinal numbers use neither periods nor apostrophes (see **Rule 4.3(b)**).[2]

Through your research, you may encounter non-standard or obsolete abbreviations. Look for their current counterparts in the appendices, and substitute the abbreviations shown there for the non-standard or obsolete ones. If a word does not appear in the applicable appendix, or if the appendix prohibits creation of abbreviations for longer words, spell out the word. Do not substitute another abbreviation unless a local court rule requires its use in documents submitted to that court.

2.1(b) Abbreviations used for multiple words

A few abbreviations stand for multiple words or multiple forms of a word. For example, "J." is an abbreviation for "Joint," "Journal," "Judge," or "Justice," depending on the source or context, and "Elec." stands for "Electric," "Electrical," "Electricity," or "Electronic." Consult the appropriate appendix for the type of source your citation represents.

2.2 Spacing

2.2(a) Spaces between abbreviations when at least one abbreviation has multiple letters

When a citation uses two or more adjacent abbreviations, insert a space between the abbreviations, unless two adjacent words' abbreviations consist of single letters.[3] See **Rule 2.2(b)** if two or more single letters in an abbreviation are adjacent. (*Note:* Many of the examples in the *ALWD Guide* and all of the abbreviations in Appendices 1, 3, 4, 5, and 7 illustrate required spaces with a red triangle (▲).)

Examples (spaces denoted by ▲)

Ent.▲&▲Sports▲L.

Fordham▲Env't▲L.▲Rev.

Hamline▲J.▲Pub.▲L.▲&▲Pol'y

Brook.▲L.▲Rev.

2.2(b) Single-letter abbreviations

When an abbreviation uses consecutive single letters, omit spaces between the letters, except when abbreviating names of certain periodicals, as explained in **Rule 21.2(e)** and illustrated in **Appendix 5(A)**.[4] Retain the spaces between abbreviations with multiple letters and those with single letters.[5]

Examples (spaces denoted by ▲)

N.C.	H.R.	Ariz.▲St.▲L.J.	Or.▲T.C.
U.S.C.	S.D.N.Y.	Colum.▲J.L.▲&▲Arts	B.C.▲J.L.▲&▲Soc.▲Just.

2.2(c) Ordinal contractions treated as single-letter abbreviations

Treat an ordinal contraction, such as 2d or 5th, as a single letter.[6] For more information about ordinal contractions, see **Rule 4.3(b)**.

Examples (spaces denoted by ▲)

1st	3d
5th	13th
20▲P.3d▲100	L.▲Ed.▲2d

2.2(d) Symbols

Do not treat an ampersand (&), a single section symbol (§), or a single paragraph symbol (¶) as a single letter; instead, always insert a space before and after the symbol.[7] While you should also insert a space before and after double section (§§) or paragraph (¶¶) symbols, *do not* insert a space between the double symbols.[8]

Examples (spaces denoted by ▲)

N.D.▲Cent.▲Code▲§▲14-18-05▲(2009).

3▲Jack▲B.▲Weinstein▲&▲Margaret▲A.▲Berger,▲*Weinstein's*▲*Federal*▲*Evidence*▲¶¶▲502–04▲(2005).

2.2(e) Spacing in court documents

You may choose to close spaces in reporter name abbreviations to conserve space in documents filed with the court, even if the abbreviations for words in reporter names would normally be separated by a space.[9] Courts often impose word count limits on briefs and other filings; this rule helps conserve words for the substance of your arguments.

Examples

Academic footnote abbreviation	Court document abbreviation
So. ▲2d	So.2d
F. ▲Supp. ▲3d	F.Supp.3d
Fed. ▲Cl.	Fed.Cl.

2.3 Referring to Cases and Constitutions in Textual Sentences

In general, do not abbreviate words in a case name used as a part of speech in a textual sentence (e.g., a case name used as the object of a preposition), including a case name in an embedded citation.[10] For more information about embedded citations, see **Rule 34.1(c)**.

It is nonetheless permissible to use well-known acronyms (e.g., FBI, NAACP) in case names in textual sentences.[11] For guidance on using acronyms in case names, see **Rule 12.2(e)(3)**. In addition, if a word listed in **Chart 2.1** appears in a case name in a textual sentence *or* in an embedded citation, you may abbreviate it as shown there or in **Appendix 3(E)**. But do not abbreviate the words in **Chart 2.1** if they begin a party's name in a textual sentence.[12]

Examples

Correct: In *Performance Coal Co. v. Federal Mine & Health Review Commission*, the court disagreed with the government's interpretation of the statute.

Incorrect: In *Performance Coal Co. v. Fed. Mine & Health Rev. Comm'n*, the court disagreed with the government's interpretation of the statute.

CHART 2.1 Words to Abbreviate in Textual Sentences and Embedded Citations

Word	Abbreviation	Word	Abbreviation
and	&	Corporation	Corp.
Association	Ass'n	Incorporated	Inc.
Brothers	Bros.	Limited	Ltd.
Company	Co.	Number	No.

When referring to a constitutional provision in a textual sentence, do not use its citation format; instead, spell out the reference to the provision.[13] Capitalize textual references to subdivisions of the United States Constitution, even though they are not capitalized in a citation. Do not capitalize a textual reference to a state constitution's subdivision unless it is the first word of a sentence.

Do not confuse references to these authorities within textual sentences with their references in citation clauses. Citation clauses are set off from the text by commas; they are not grammatical elements of those sentences. See **Rule 34.1(b)** for more information on citation clauses, **Rule 34.1(c)** for more information about using citations in sentences, and **Rule 34.1(d)** for information on textual references.

3 Spelling and Capitalization

3.1 Spelling in Titles and Text

Do not alter the original spelling of words in a title or subtitle. When quoting a source with spelling errors in the text, however, you may choose whether to reproduce the errors or to correct them.[1] See **Rule 39.6** for guidance on indicating errors in the original or making corrections.

3.2 Capitalization in Titles and Subtitles

The modern trend is to use lowercase letters unless a specific rule requires the use of a capital letter.

3.2(a) General rule for capitalizing titles and subtitles

Capitalize the first letter of the following:

- The first word in a citation or in a title;
- The first word after a colon or a dash, no matter its part of speech; and
- Any other word in the citation *except* an article ("a," "an," "the"); a coordinating conjunction ("and," "but," "for," "or," "nor," "yet," "so"); a preposition of four or fewer letters (e.g., "in," "of," "with"); and "to" when used in an infinitive (e.g., "to decide," "to reconsider").[2]

Examples (titles and subtitles in practice-based documents and in academic footnotes)

Tomiko Brown-Nagin, *Courage to Dissent: Atlanta and the Long History of the Civil Rights Movement* 338 (2011).

Kim D. Chanbonpin, *Between Black and White: The Coloring of Asian Americans*, 14 Wash. U. Glob. Stud. L. Rev. 637, 653 (2015).

ACADEMIC FORMATTING

[17] Tomiko Brown-Nagin, Courage to Dissent: Atlanta and the Long History of the Civil Rights Movement 338 (2011).

[25] Kim D. Chanbonpin, *Between Black and White: The Coloring of Asian Americans*, 14 Wash. U. Glob. Stud. L. Rev. 637, 653 (2015).

3.2(b) Capitalizing hyphenated words in titles or subtitles

When words in a title or subtitle are joined by a hyphen, capitalize the first letter of the first word in the hyphenated phrase. Capitalize the first letter of a word following a hyphen unless it is an article, preposition, coordinating conjunction, or a modifier for a musical term (e.g., "flat," "sharp"). If a title uses spelled-out numbers or fractions, capitalize words on either side of the hyphen (e.g., "Twenty-Second," "Three-Fourths").

SIDEBAR 3.1 Common Prepositions

This list of common prepositions is not exhaustive. If you are uncertain whether a word is a preposition, consult a dictionary or style manual. In titles and subtitles, capitalize the first letter of a preposition when it has five or more letters (whether or not in this list).

aboard	beyond	onto
about	but	out
above	by	outside
according to	considering	over
across	down	prior to
after	during	since
against	except	than
ahead of	for	through
along	from	throughout
around	in	to
as	inside	toward
at	into	until
before	like	under
behind	near	up
below	next	upon
beneath	next to	versus
beside	of	with
besides	off	within
between	on	without

Examples

Shyamkrishna Balganesh, *Quasi-Property: Like, but Not Quite Property*, 160 U. Pa. L. Rev. 1889, 1909 (2012).

Lynn Foster, *Fifty-One Flowers: Post-Perpetuities War Law and Arkansas's Adoption of USRAP*, 29 U. Ark. Little Rock L. Rev. 411, 426 (2007).

ACADEMIC FORMATTING

65 Christopher J. Peters, *Under-the-Table Overruling*, 54 Wayne L. Rev. 1067, 1090 (2008).

84 Scott W. McKinley, Comment, *The Need for Legislative or Judicial Clarity on the Four-Fifths Rule and How Employers in the Sixth Circuit Can Survive the Ambiguity*, 37 Cap. U. L. Rev. 171, 176–77 (2008).

3.3 Capitalization in Text

3.3(a) Capitalizing proper nouns

Capitalize proper nouns, including names of people, entities, organizations, and places. Capitalize the shortened form of a proper noun.[3]

Examples

Samuel Langhorne Clemens	the National Archives
Helen Keller International	the Grand Canyon
the Chicago Bulls	the Bulls

3.3(b) Capitalizing proper adjectives

Capitalize adjectives derived from words that exist solely as proper nouns (e.g., American, Lincolnesque). However, when a word does not exist exclusively as a proper noun, do not capitalize the adjective derived from it (e.g., congressional, presidential).[4] Unless an ordinal number is part of a proper noun phrase, do not capitalize the number when used as an adjective.

Examples

European   constitutional   twenty-first century

3.3(c) Capitalizing defined terms

When a term is defined to thereafter represent a person or an entity, it becomes a proper noun that should subsequently be capitalized.

Example

Jackson Elementary School ("Buyer") agrees to purchase five hundred half-pint cartons of milk each week from Smart Dairy, Inc. ("Seller"). Buyer will pay Seller within thirty days of receiving an invoice from Seller.

3.3(d) Capitalizing professional or honorific titles of persons

Capitalize a person's professional title or a title of honor or respect that immediately precedes or follows the person's name or that substitutes for the name. Capitalize titles in the second person (e.g., Your Honor) or third person (e.g., Her Majesty).

Examples

Jeane Kirkpatrick, United States Ambassador to the United Nations

Justice Oliver Wendell Holmes

the Justice

3.4 Capitalizing Specific Words

Capitalize words shown in **Chart 3.1** when they are used in the contexts described.[5] For words not listed here or covered by **Rules 3.2** and **3.3**, consult the most recent edition of the *United States Government Publishing Office Style Manual*, *The Redbook: A Manual on Legal Style*, or *The Chicago Manual of Style*.

CHART 3.1 Capitalizing Specific Words

Word	Capitalization rule	Examples
Act	Capitalize when referring to a specific legislative act or when referring to a previously named act.	The Americans with Disabilities Act requires . . . Interpreting that provision of the Act, the trial court . . .
Appellant, Appellee	Capitalize within a court document (such as a brief) only when referring to a party in the pending case.	As for whether the condition was met, Appellant incorrectly argues . . . But: Court rules require an appellant's opening brief to contain . . .
Board, Commission, Department	Capitalize when used in a proper name or when referring to a governmental entity.	Members of the Board of Visitors of George Mason University are appointed by . . . But: The chair of the department called a meeting for . . .
Circuit	Capitalize when used with a judicial circuit number.	Eleventh Circuit But: The circuit court held . . .
Code	Capitalize when referring to a named code.	*United States Code*, *Code of Federal Regulations*, *Indiana Code* But: Many states have codes that address . . .
Committee, Subcommittee	Capitalize when used in a proper name or when referring to a governmental committee.	Committee for Education Funding, Senate Committee on Armed Services, Subcommittee on Personnel But: The committee ordinarily meets on Wednesdays.

(*Continued*)

CHART 3.1	Capitalizing Specific Words (*Continued*)	
Word	**Capitalization rule**	**Examples**
Commonwealth, People, State	Capitalize when part of the full name of a state or federation of states or when referring to a state or federation of states as a governmental actor or party to litigation.	State of Tennessee, Commonwealth of Virginia The People argued that the conviction was . . . But: As a commonwealth develops politically, it often develops economically.
Constitution, Article, Amendment	Capitalize when referring to the United States Constitution or when naming any constitution in full. Capitalize names of parts of the United States Constitution when referring to them in textual sentences.	Texas Constitution, First Amendment, Equal Protection Clause The defendant violated Article IV, Section 2, Clause 1 of the Constitution. But: The attorney general argued that the state's constitution did not authorize . . . U.S. Const. art. IV, § 2, cl. 1.
Court	Capitalize when referring to the United States Supreme Court, when using the full name of any court, or within a court document (such as a complaint, a motion, or a brief) when referring to the court in which the document was filed, no matter what the court's level.	Ohio Supreme Court, West Virginia Court of Claims Defendant asks this Court to certify . . . But: An executor usually files a petition with the probate court.
Defendant, Plaintiff	Capitalize within a court document (such as a complaint, a motion, or a brief) when referring to a party in the pending case.	Plaintiff requests that the Court grant his motion to . . . But: In *State v. Hudson*, the defendant argued that . . .
Federal	Capitalize when the word or phrase it modifies is capitalized.	Federal Aviation Administration, Federal Rules of Evidence But: The federal government

(*Continued*)

CHART 3.1 Capitalizing Specific Words (*Continued*)

Word	Capitalization rule	Examples
Judge, Justice	Capitalize when used as a title or when referring to a Justice of the United States Supreme Court.	Judge Brita Dahlberg, Chief Justice Rehnquist But: The circuit judge recused herself due to a conflict of interest.
Nation, National	Capitalize "Nation" when used as part of a proper name or as a synonym for the United States of America. Capitalize "National" when the word it modifies is capitalized.	United Nations, Cherokee Nation, National Guard But: The ambassadors of several nations gathered at . . .
President, Vice President	Capitalize when used as a title or when referring to the chief executives of a government.	President Truman, Vice President The Vice President campaigned in Florida last night. But: Mr. Jones serves as vice president of the club.
Secretary	Capitalize when used as a title or when referring to a cabinet-level official of a government.	Secretary of Defense Leon Panetta The Secretary traveled to Beijing in order to . . . But: The secretary contacted the judge's clerk to ask . . .
Term	Capitalize when indicating United States Supreme Court Terms.	Because of the pandemic, the United States Supreme Court held oral arguments remotely this Term. But: Governors of fourteen states have no term limits.

4 Numbers in General

4.1 Numbers in Citations

Present numbers as numerals in citations, unless the number appears in a title or subtitle. In titles and subtitles, reproduce the number as it appears in the source, whether spelled out or shown as a numeral.

In citations and text using numbers of four digits or more (1,000 and above), use commas to place the numbers into three-digit groups (e.g., 12,843,675).[1] Do not, however, create three-digit groups for numbers in statutory sections, database identifier numbers, docket numbers, URLs, or any other source that does not use commas itself to split numbers into three-digit groups.[2] Additionally, if a page or section number in a case, periodical, or book has four digits and the source does not use a comma to separate them into three-digit groups, do not use a comma for those four-digit numbers either.[3]

Examples

11 U.S.C. § 1202(a).

Fed. R. Civ. P. 45.

Ruthann Robson, *Thirteen False Blackbirds*, 37 N.Y.U. Rev. L. & Soc. Change 3115, 3118 (2013).

Max Stul Oppenheimer, *Patents 101: Patentable Subject Matter and Separation of Powers*, 15 Vand. J. Ent. & Tech. L. 1, 30–31 (2012).

Certain Lined Paper Products from the People's Republic of China, 78 Fed. Reg. 34,640, 34,640–41 (June 10, 2013).

Butler v. Smith, No. 3:10CV00172-JMM-BD, 2010 WL 4680293 (E.D. Ark. Nov. 10, 2010).

Carla Hayden, *Race in America: Jason Reynolds & Jacqueline Woodson*, Library of Congress (June 19, 2020), https://www.loc.gov/item/webcast-9222/.

Paul M. Trueger, Accounting Guide for Defense Contracts 1039–41 (6th ed. 1971).

4.2 Numbers in Textual Sentences

4.2(a) Representing numbers as words or numerals

When referring to numbers in textual or footnote sentences, spell out zero through ninety-nine and round numbers (e.g., one thousand, two million), and use numerals (e.g., 476) for everything else.[4] Always use Arabic numerals if any number has a decimal point.[5] When you have numbers in a series, and at least one of those numbers is 100 or greater, you may use numerals for the entire list.[6] In some contexts, numbers are nonetheless treated in a particular manner, as explained later in this rule. If you are dissatisfied with the way a number should be handled, consider revising the sentence structure to accommodate your preference.

Examples

The court listed five reasons for denying the motion.

The jury awarded the plaintiff compensatory damages of more than one million dollars.

Even though the firm logged 735 billable hours in preparing for trial, the court ruled that its fees were too high.

4.2(b) Numbers that begin a sentence

Always spell out a number that begins a sentence.[7] Preface statutory numbers with an appropriate noun indicating the statute's position within the code (e.g., chapter, section, title).[8]

Examples

One hundred thirty-five prisoner petitions are pending before the court.

Section 26-10C-1 describes the state's putative father registry.

According to title 18 U.S.C. § 922, certain individuals are prohibited from possessing firearms, ammunition, or explosives.

4.2(c) Arabic and Roman numerals

In general, use Arabic numerals (1, 4, 25) in preference to Roman numerals (I, IV, XXV).[9] Use capitalized Roman numerals in the names of monarchs, popes, and similar persons; in personal names; in names of certain events; in outlines; in constitutions; and in names of vehicles or vessels. Use lowercase Roman numerals for page numbers in the front matter of books or appellate briefs. See **Rule 20.1(a)** for the way to indicate the volume number of a book within a multivolume work.

Examples

Chapter 13 bankruptcy	Appendix 3	Interstate 40
Queen Elizabeth II	World War I	Thomas Michael Adams IV
U.S. Const. amend. XVIII, § 1.	III. Conclusion	The preface begins on page ii.

4.2(d) Additional information for numbers in text

For more guidance on using numbers in text, see the most recent edition of the *United States Government Publishing Office Style Manual*, *The Redbook: A Manual on Legal Style*, or *The Chicago Manual of Style*.

4.3 Ordinal Numbers

4.3(a) Ordinal numbers in general

An ordinal number designates a position in a series, whether spelled out (e.g., first, fiftieth) or within an ordinal contraction using numbers and letters (e.g., 3d, 21st, 75th). Represent ordinal numbers as words or numbers according to the principles set out in **Rule 4.2(a)** when they are in textual or footnote sentences. Ordinal numbers in citations are represented as numerals.[10]

Examples

The court agreed with the appellant's fifth argument.

Robert Wolfe, *The OECD Contribution to the Evolution of Twenty-First Century Trade Law*, 43 Geo. Wash. Int'l L. Rev. 277, 284–85 (2011).

Michael A. Olivas, *Commemorating the 50th Anniversary of* Hernandez v. Texas, 25 Chicano-Latino L. Rev. 1, 4 (2005).

4.3(b) Ordinal contractions

Ordinal contractions appear in a variety of references, such as abbreviations for publications issued in series (e.g., Am. Jur. 2d, F.3d) and court name abbreviations (e.g., 2d Cir., 9th Cir.). When representing ordinal contractions in legal citations, use just the letter "d" to represent the "nd" and "rd" endings of contractions for "second" and "third" (e.g., 3d, 22d). When representing ordinal numbers in textual sentences, however, represent ordinal number two as "2nd" and ordinal number three as "3rd."[11]

Do not end ordinal contractions with a period (e.g., write 3d rather than 3d.). Do not use superscript to represent letters in ordinal contractions (e.g., write 21st rather than 21st)[12]; if necessary, disable the automatic superscript feature of your word-processing software.

Examples (in citations)

First:	1st	**Fourth:**	4th
Second:	2d	**Fifty-first:**	51st

Examples (in text)

22nd Justice of the Supreme Court   203rd representative

4.3(c) Ordinal numbers and dates

Do not use ordinal numbers when writing dates in a full date format (e.g., write June 17, 2020, rather than June 17th, 2020). If the day comes before the month in the sentence, without referencing a year, you can choose to write it as an ordinal or spell out the day (e.g., write either 17th of June or the seventeenth of June). If the date includes only the day in a textual sentence, you can choose to either write it as an ordinal or spell it out.

Examples

The commissioner signed the order on July 11, 2019.

The commissioner signed the order on the 11th of July.

The commissioner signed the order on the eleventh of July.

The commissioner signed the order on July 11.

The commissioner signed the order on the eleventh.

The commissioner signed the order on the 11th.

5 Page Numbers

5.1 Initial Pages

5.1(a) Definition of "initial page"

The "initial page" is the page on which a paginated source begins. For example, a case's initial page is the page on which the case caption appears; a law review article's initial page is its title page.

5.1(b) When to refer to initial page

To assist readers in locating a paginated source that is one of several published within a larger work (e.g., a case within a regional reporter, an article within an issue of a periodical), the full citation to that source must always provide the initial page.[1] When you cite a paginated source that stands on its own (e.g., a book, a treatise, a pamphlet), there is no need to refer to the initial page of that source.[2]

Examples (initial page, where required, in red)

Teen Ranch v. Udow, 389 F. Supp. 2d 827, 831 (W.D. Mich. 2005).

Steven K. Green, *Federalism and the Establishment Clause: A Reassessment*, 38 Creighton L. Rev. 761, 764–65 (2005).

Akhil Reed Amar, *The Bill of Rights: Creation and Reconstruction* 277 (1998).

5.1(c) Abbreviations "p." and "pp."

Do not use the abbreviations "p." or "pp." before page numbers in a citation. Use these abbreviations only in a document's internal cross-references to its own pages (see **Rule 10.2(a)^FN^**).[3]

5.2 Pinpoint Pages

5.2(a) Definition of "pinpoint page"

The term "pinpoint page" refers to the specific page(s) of a cited source on which a quotation or relevant passage appears. The terms "pincite," "pin," "pinpoint reference," "jump citation," "jump cite," and "jump page" are synonyms.

SIDEBAR 5.1 **Importance of Using Pinpoint References**

Pinpoint references are essential. Readers are frustrated when citations do not indicate the specific pages or other subdivisions where the referenced material appears. When a judge or judicial law clerk cannot find support in the cited authority for your assertion, you may lose credibility, or the court may discount your position. Make a point to always insert a pinpoint reference.

5.2(b) When to refer to pinpoint pages

Pinpoint pages indicate the exact location of cited material within a paginated source. Whether you quote from or refer to specific information within a source, add a pinpoint page reference to that location. For example, when you refer to the holding of a case, indicate the page(s) on which the holding appears.

In a full citation, when the pinpoint page is also the initial page, add a comma and repeat the number of the first page.[4] Doing so tells your readers that the cited material not only begins on the cited page but is also found on that page.

Examples (pinpoint pages in red)

Teen Ranch v. Udow, 389 F. Supp. 2d 827, 832 (W.D. Mich. 2005).

Steven K. Green, *Federalism and the Establishment Clause: A Reassessment*, 38 Creighton L. Rev. 761, 764–65 (2005).

Akhil Reed Amar, *The Bill of Rights: Creation and Reconstruction* 277 (1998).

P.D.T. v. State, 996 So. 2d 919, 919 (Fla. Dist. Ct. App. 2008).

5.2(c) Preventing confusion in references to numbers in titles

When a source's title ends with a number, when the cited work uses Roman numerals to indicate its pagination, or any other time the pinpoint page could be mistaken for another part of the citation, insert a comma and the preposition "at" before the citation's pinpoint page reference.[5]

Examples

John C. Maxwell, *Attitude 101*, at 56–57 (2003).

Robert M. Utley, *Frontier Regulars: The United States Army and the Indian, 1866–1891*, at 302 (1973).

Constance Backhouse, *Carnal Crimes: Sexual Assault Law in Canada, 1900–1975*, at 276 (2008).

N.Y. Exec. Order No. 134, at 3 (Jan. 5, 2005).

Robert T. Anderson et al., *American Indian Law: Cases and Commentary*, at ii (2d ed. 2010).

5.3 Consecutive Pinpoint Pages

To provide a pinpoint reference to material on consecutive pages (a "page span"), set out the beginning and ending page numbers of the span, joined by a hyphen (-), an en dash (–), or the word "to."[6] Hyphens and en dashes are used interchangeably, as described in **Sidebar 5.2**. Only substitute the word "to" for a hyphen or an en dash, however, when it will avoid ambiguity or confusion.[7] For example, some publications use hyphenated numbers to indicate pages or sections (e.g., 53-01). Using a hyphen or en dash to denote a span in that instance could confuse readers (53-01–53-04); avoid this confusion by using the word "to" in the span (53-01 to 53-04).

SIDEBAR 5.2 **The Difference Between Hyphens and En Dashes**

In everyday documents, such as memoranda or briefs, writers typically use hyphens (-) to denote such spans of pages. In published materials, such as law review articles and books, page spans are normally denoted with an en dash (–). What's the difference? The length: An en dash is the width of the letter N; a hyphen is shorter. (The "em dash" is the width of the letter M (—). Don't use it in a span.)

If pages in the span are numbered 100 or higher, drop repetitious digits from the concluding number, retaining only the last two digits.[8] If the source uses star pagination (see **Rule 5.5**), drop the star preceding the concluding digit(s).[9]

Examples (consecutive page spans in red)

State v. Spikes, 961 A.2d 426, 434–35 (Conn. App. Ct. 2008).

Cynthia S. Duncan, Note, *The Need for Change: An Economic Analysis of Marijuana Policy*, 41 Conn. L. Rev. 1701, 1736–38 (2009).

State v. Biskner, No. E2000-01440-CCA-R3-CD, 2001 Tenn. Crim. App. LEXIS 887, at *23–25 (July 25, 2001).

Ariz. Rev. Stat. Ann. §§ 5-101 to -03 (2018).

5.4 Nonconsecutive Pinpoint Pages

When providing a pinpoint reference to pages that are not consecutive, separate the page numbers with a comma and one space. Do not use an ampersand (&) or the word "and" before the final page number in the group.[10] If the nonconsecutive pages use star pagination (see **Rule 5.5**), retain the star in front of the nonconsecutive page numbers.[11]

Examples

Correct:	5, 14, 26
	*88, *91, *95–97
Incorrect:	5, 14 & 26
	5, 14, and 26
	*88, 91, 95–97

5.5 Star Pagination

5.5(a) Definition of "star pagination"

The terms "star pagination" and "star page" refer to supplemental page numbering that indicates a source's pagination in two or more publications or media. There are four types of star pagination: (1) star pages in sources in online databases indicating where a new page number in the print version of the source occurs (see **Rule 5.5(b)**); (2) star pages in cases printed in unofficial reporters indicating where a page in the official reporter begins (see **Rule 5.5(c)**); (3) star pages indicating pages in online sources that have no print counterparts (see **Rule 5.5(d)**); and (4) star pages in a reprint of a classic work indicating pages in the original classic work (see **Rule 5.5(e)**). Each of these is addressed in depth below. There is no space between the star and the page number.[12]

5.5(b) Star pages in online databases that reflect pages in print sources

Star pagination helps researchers correlate a screen display to the actual page numbers used in print versions of the same source. For example, some publishers preface a page number with a single asterisk to one print source, with two asterisks to indicate a page in another print source, and so on. Other publishers place brackets around star pages (e.g., [*34]). Despite the method of star pagination displayed online, when you insert the pinpoint page reference in the citation, omit the asterisks or brackets.

Examples

Caption from case in Westlaw Edge:

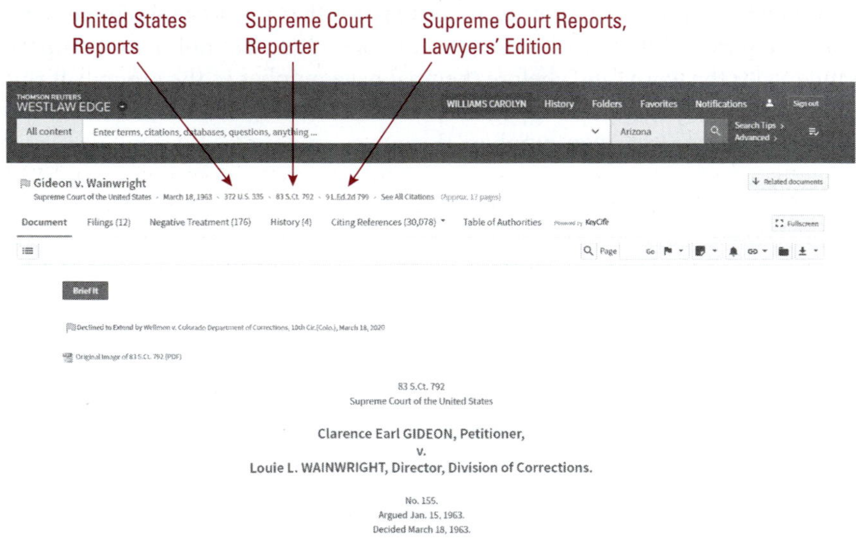

Reprinted from Westlaw Edge with the permission of Thomson Reuters.

Textual excerpt displaying asterisked star pages (in red squares):

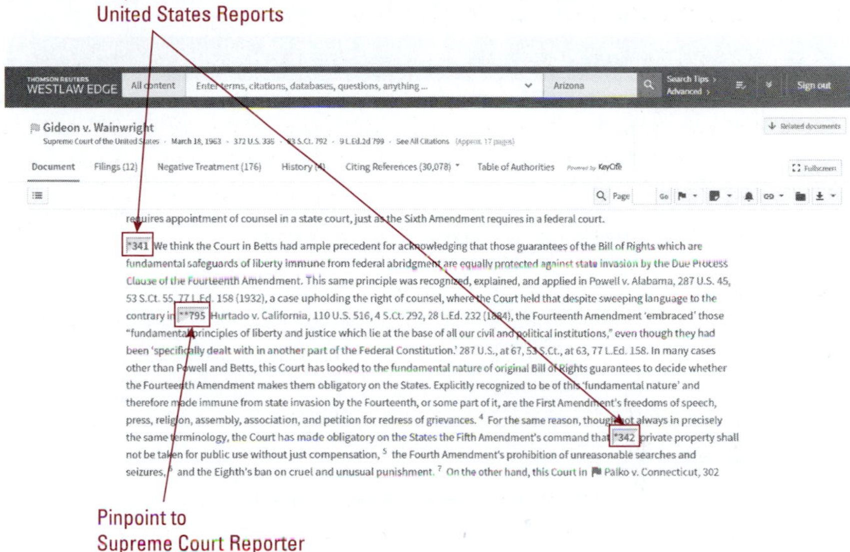

Gideon v. Wainwright
Supreme Court of the United States · March 18, 1963 · 372 U.S. 335 · 83 S.Ct. 792 · 9 L.Ed.2d 799 · See All Citations

Document | Filings (12) | Negative Treatment (176) | History (4) | Citing References (30,078) | Table of Authorities

requires appointment of counsel in a state court, just as the Sixth Amendment requires in a federal court.

*341 We think the Court in Betts had ample precedent for acknowledging that those guarantees of the Bill of Rights which are fundamental safeguards of liberty immune from federal abridgment are equally protected against state invasion by the Due Process Clause of the Fourteenth Amendment. This same principle was recognized, explained, and applied in Powell v. Alabama, 287 U.S. 45, 53 S.Ct. 55, 77 L.Ed. 158 (1932), a case upholding the right of counsel, where the Court held that despite sweeping language to the contrary in **795 Hurtado v. California, 110 U.S. 516, 4 S.Ct. 292, 28 L.Ed. 232 (1884), the Fourteenth Amendment 'embraced' those "fundamental principles of liberty and justice which lie at the base of all our civil and political institutions," even though they had been 'specifically dealt with in another part of the Federal Constitution.' 287 U.S., at 67, 53 S.Ct., at 63, 77 L.Ed. 158. In many cases other than Powell and Betts, this Court has looked to the fundamental nature of original Bill of Rights guarantees to decide whether the Fourteenth Amendment makes them obligatory on the States. Explicitly recognized to be of this 'fundamental nature' and therefore made immune from state invasion by the Fourteenth, or some part of it, are the First Amendment's freedoms of speech, press, religion, assembly, association, and petition for redress of grievances.[4] For the same reason, though not always in precisely the same terminology, the Court has made obligatory on the States the Fifth Amendment's command that *342 private property shall not be taken for public use without just compensation,[5] the Fourth Amendment's prohibition of unreasonable searches and seizures,[6] and the Eighth's ban on cruel and unusual punishment.[7] On the other hand, this Court in Palko v. Connecticut, 302

Reprinted from Westlaw Edge with the permission of Thomson Reuters.

Explanation: The top of the caption from Westlaw Edge indicates that *Gideon v. Wainwright* was published in three different reporters—volume 372 of the *United States Reports* beginning at page 335 (372 U.S. 335), in volume 83 of the *Supreme Court Reporter* beginning on page 792 (83 S. Ct. 792), and in volume 9 of *Supreme Court Reports, Lawyers Edition, Second Series* beginning on page 799 (9 L. Ed. 2d 799). Westlaw Edge places one or more asterisks in front of star pages to indicate which pages correspond to each of the three sources in which the case appears. For example, star pages *341 and *342 reflect the beginning of pages 341 and 342, respectively, in volume 372 of the official *United States Reports*. Star page **795 indicates the beginning of page 795 in volume 83 of the unofficial *Supreme Court Reporter*. Because **Rule 12.4(b)(3)** requires citation to the Supreme Court's official reporter where available, the citation needs the pinpoint page number from *United States Reports* (*341), not the pinpoint page number from the *Supreme Court Reporter*.

Correct citation: *Gideon v. Wainwright*, 372 U.S. 335, 341 (1963).

Caption from case in Lexis+:

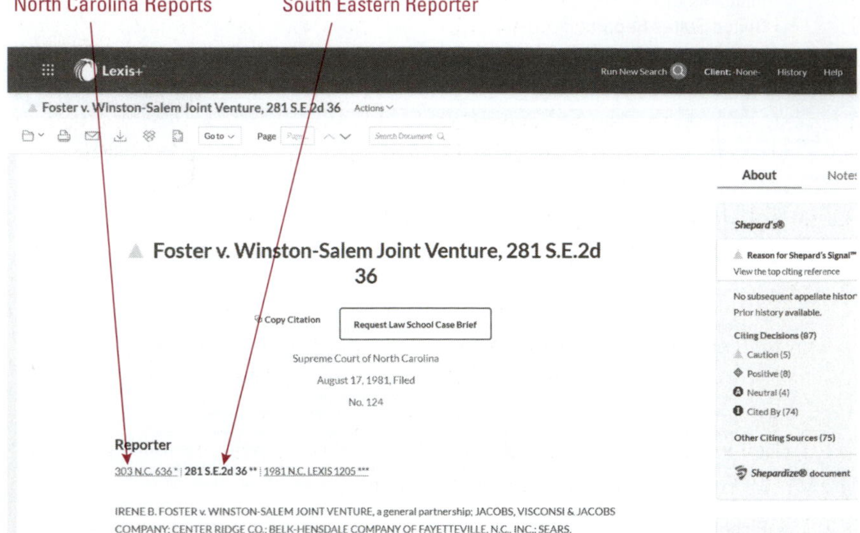

Textual excerpt displaying bracketed star pages (in red squares):

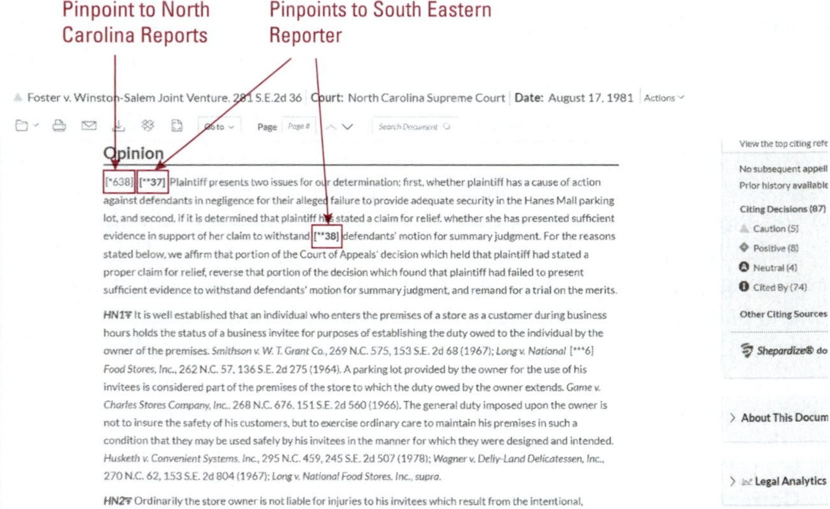

Explanation: The top of the caption from Lexis+ indicates that *Foster v. Winston-Salem Joint Venture* was published in two different reporters—volume 303 of the *North Carolina Reports* beginning at page 636 (303 N.C. 636), and in volume 281 of the *South Eastern Reporter, Second Series* beginning at page 36 (281 S.E.2d 36). Lexis+ encloses star pages in square brackets with one or more asterisks. Star page [**37] reflects the beginning of page 37 in volume 281 of the unofficial *South Eastern Reporter, Second Series*; it could not indicate the *North Carolina Reports*' page because in that reporter, the case does not begin until page 636. Instead, [*638] indicates that this excerpt begins on page 638 of volume 303 of the *North Carolina Reports*. By clicking on the different reporters in the caption on Lexis+, the star pages associated with that reporter are bolded. In the excerpt above, because [**37] and [**38] are in bold, you know you are viewing the *South Eastern Reporter, Second Series* version. Because **Rule 12.4(b)(5)** requires citation to the regional reporter in West's National Reporter System, the citation needs the pinpoint page number from the *South Eastern Reporter, Second Series* (37–38), not the pinpoint page number from the *North Carolina Reports* [*638].

Correct citation: *Foster v. Winston-Salem Joint Venture*, 281 S.E.2d 36, 37–38 (N.C. 1981).

5.5(c) Star pages in unofficial print reporters that reflect pages in official print reporters

Legal publisher Thomson Reuters West uses star pagination in hard copies of unofficial print reporters to indicate the beginning of pages in its official reporter counterparts. While you may rely on star pagination to locate a page in an official print reporter, when you provide the pinpoint reference in the citation, omit the asterisk(s).

5.5(d) Star pages in online sources with no print counterparts

Some online providers use asterisked star pagination in an electronic source that has no print counterpart. For example, star pagination may reflect the top of a page in an unpublished case (see **Rule 12.14**).[13] To refer to these star pages as pinpoint references, insert a comma, a space, and the word "at" after the database identifier, followed by a space, one asterisk, and the page number(s). Because this kind of star pagination does not correlate to a print source, retain the asterisk preceding the first page of a consecutive span of pages and each page of scattered references.[14]

Examples

Jones v. Scotti, No. 11-2213, 2012 WL 4373655, at *4–5 (1st Cir. Sept. 26, 2012).

Goodman v. Genesee County, 2008 Mich. App. LEXIS 161, at *14, *19 (Mich. Ct. App. Jan. 24, 2008).

5.5(e) Star pages in star editions

Many classic sources, such as William Blackstone's *Commentaries* (published 1765–1769, original edition not easily accessed), have been republished in "star editions" whose page numbering reflects that of the original work.[15] When working with a star edition, follow **Rule 20.2** to format its page numbers.

5.6 *Passim*

When pinpoint references would be so numerous as to be unwieldy, you may use the italicized word *passim* to indicate as much.[16] Similarly, you may use *passim* in a brief's table of authorities to indicate the location of a source repeatedly cited. Because *passim* does not tell the reader exactly where to find the references, use it only where warranted.

Examples

In pinpoint reference:

For a defense of Judge Arnold's conclusions, see Polly J. Price, *Precedent and Judicial Power After the Founding*, 42 B.C. L. Rev. 81 *passim* (2001).

In table of authorities:

Sutton v. United Airlines, Inc., 527 U.S. 471 (1999) . . . . *passim*

6 Sections and Paragraphs

6.1 Sources Divided Solely by Sections or Paragraphs

When a source is divided solely by sections (§) or by paragraphs (¶), whether they are numbered or lettered, use the symbol § or ¶, then a space, and then the referenced section or paragraph.[1] Citations to two or more sections or paragraphs should use the symbols §§ or ¶¶.[2]

6.1(a) Pinpoint references to subdivisions

Citations to sources divided by sections or paragraphs should indicate, to the extent possible, the exact location of the cited material. Provide pinpoint references to subdivisions, including subsections or subparagraphs, if any.[3]

In general, use the punctuation or formatting of the original source to differentiate subdivisions from the main sections or paragraphs to which they belong. Omit reference to subsections or subparagraphs when the cited material refers to a level that encompasses all such subdivisions. If you are citing to an example within a section or paragraph or citing to the text of a section or paragraph that has flush language, append a parenthetical immediately following the citation indicating that.[4]

Examples

¶ 4(a)(1)

§ 55.12.104

¶ 21 [pinpoint reference includes all subparagraphs, e.g., (a), (b), and (c)]

Treas. Reg. § 1.704-2(f)(7) (example 2).

6.1(b) Spacing and punctuation of section and paragraph symbols

Insert a space between the section or paragraph symbol and the numbers or letters that follow.[5] Do not insert a space between a main section and its own subdivision(s).[6] Do not insert a space between two section or paragraph symbols.[7]

Section designations (particularly those in statutes, regulations, and rules) may be comprised of both numbers and letters (e.g., "§ 2000e-2"). Because these letters do not refer to subsections of the source, do not separate them from the numbers.[8]

Examples (spaces denoted by ▲)

Correct:	§▲1710(b)(3)	¶¶▲A–C	§§▲22.05(a),▲22.07
Incorrect:	§1710(b)(3)	¶¶A–C	§▲§▲22.05(a),22.07

When the source displays no specific punctuation (e.g., periods, hyphens) to differentiate numbered or lettered subdivisions of sections or paragraphs, place the subdivision designations in parentheses.[9]

Example

Textual excerpt of United States Code with the provisions to be cited in red:

Title 42 § 2000e-4

. . .

(d) Seal; judicial notice

The Commission shall have an official seal which shall be judicially noticed.

. . .

(h) Cooperation with other departments and agencies in performance of educational or promotional activities; outreach activities

(1) The Commission shall, in any of its educational or promotional activities, cooperate with other departments and agencies in the performance of such educational and promotional activities.

(2) In exercising its powers under this subchapter, the Commission shall carry out educational and outreach activities (including dissemination of information in languages other than English) targeted to—

(A) individuals who historically have been victims of employment discrimination and have not been equitably served by the Commission; and

(B) individuals on whose behalf the Commission has authority to enforce any other law prohibiting employment discrimination, concerning rights and obligations under this subchapter or such law, as the case may be.

Explanation: There are no parentheses around the "e" or "4" after "§ 2000" because the full number of this subsection of this statute includes them as the statute number. Even though there are two subsections cited, because they are in the same statute section, there is only one section symbol in the citation. And the subsections, sub-subsections, and sub-sub-subsections are designated by placing a set of parentheses around each.

Correct citation (spaces denoted by ▲):

42▲U.S.C.▲§▲2000e-4(d),▲(h)(2)(A).

6.1(c) Section and paragraph symbols in short citations

Do not use the preposition "at" before a section or paragraph symbol, especially in short citations.[10]

Examples

Correct: *Id.* § 35.

Incorrect: *Id.* at § 35.

6.2 Consecutive Sections or Paragraphs

6.2(a) Indicating span of specific sections or paragraphs

To provide a pinpoint reference to a span of consecutive sections or paragraphs, set out the beginning and ending subdivisions of the span, separated with a hyphen (-), an en dash (–), or the word "to."[11] See **Rule 5.3** for when to choose each. Use only two section (§§) or paragraph (¶¶) symbols, even if the span contains three or more sections or paragraphs.[12] While you should ordinarily retain all digits or letters on either side of the span, you may omit identical digits or letters that precede a period if doing so is unlikely to confuse a reader.[13]

Examples (spaces denoted by ▲)

§§▲1–55 §§▲1961–1965

§§▲1997e(d)▲to▲1997e(g) ¶¶▲14.30–.50

6.2(b) Et seq.

Avoid using the abbreviation "et seq." to denote a span of sections.[14] "Et seq." simply means "and the following." Set out the actual span.

Example

Correct: 15 U.S.C. §§ 2301–2310.

Incorrect: 15 U.S.C. §§ 2301 et seq.

6.2(c) Indicating consecutive subdivisions within a single section or paragraph

To provide a pinpoint reference to consecutive subsections or subparagraphs contained within a single section or paragraph, follow **Rule 6.2(a)**, but use a single section (§) or paragraph (¶) symbol.[15]

Examples (spaces denoted by ▲)

§▲22(a)–(c) §▲14(a)(1)–(4)

¶▲3601(a)–(c) ¶▲3601(a)▲to▲(c)

6.3 Scattered Sections or Paragraphs

6.3(a) Indicating scattered sections or paragraphs

To provide a pinpoint reference to nonconsecutive sections or paragraphs, use two section (§§) or paragraph (¶¶) symbols followed by a space and the section or paragraph numbers, separated by commas and spaces.[16] Do not use an ampersand (&) or the word "and" before the final number.

Examples (spaces denoted by ▲)

§§▲1961,▲1963,▲1965

¶¶▲47(c),▲58(m),▲107(a)

¶¶▲33(b)(7),▲33(c)(5)

6.3(b) Indicating scattered subdivisions within a single section or paragraph

To provide a pinpoint reference to multiple, nonconsecutive subdivisions within a single section or paragraph, follow **Rule 6.3(a)**, but use a single section (§) or paragraph (¶) symbol.[17]

Examples (spaces denoted by ▲)

§▲1961(a),▲(c),▲(e)

¶▲47(c),▲(m)

6.4 Unnumbered Paragraphs

For sources containing indented, but unnumbered, paragraphs, use the abbreviation "para." (plural, "paras.") rather than the paragraph symbol.[18] If a source is normally cited by page number, however, do not cite to an indented, unnumbered paragraph.[19]

Example

18 U.S.C. § 1546(a) para. 3.

6.5 Sources Divided Both by Pages and by Sections or Paragraphs

When a source is divided both by pages and by sections or paragraphs, you may refer to both the page and the section or paragraph to narrow down the cited subject matter, unless the citation refers to an entire section or paragraph.[20] See **Sidebar 6.1** regarding the limit of this rule. Set out the section or paragraph number first, followed by a comma and space, followed by the page number on which the cited material appears.

When it may be unclear, however, whether a citation refers to a paragraph or section number or to a page number, you may insert ", at" before a pinpoint *page* number.[21] For example, a reader may think a citation refers to scattered section numbers when in fact it refers to certain sections on a page.

Examples (spaces denoted by ▲)

Julian▲Conrad▲Juergensmeyer▲&▲Thomas▲E.▲Roberts,▲*Land▲Use▲Planning▲and▲Control▲Law*▲§▲10.4,▲425▲(2d▲ed.▲2007).

Bernard▲J.▲Hibbitts,▲*The▲Technology▲of▲Law*,▲102▲Law▲Libr.▲J.▲¶¶▲25–28,▲at▲105–06▲(2010).

SIDEBAR 6.1 When Not to Cite to Both Pages and Sections or Paragraphs

Rule 6.5 typically applies only when a section of a book, treatise, or legal encyclopedia takes up multiple pages. Unless a local rule says differently, it does not apply to court documents. Typically, court documents that have both numbered paragraphs and page numbers—such as complaints, answers, or separate statements of facts that accompany a motion for summary judgment—use only the paragraph number as the pinpoint. Court documents that have unnumbered paragraphs—such as motions or briefs—normally use the page number as the pinpoint. See **Rule 25.2(b)** for more about citing to court documents. **Rule 6.5** also does not apply to any enacted law. Use section or rule numbers for pincites in enacted law and not a page number. For more on pinpoints in statutes, regulations, or rules, see **Rule 14.6(e)**.

6.6 Referring to Sections or Paragraphs in Text

To refer to a specific section or paragraph within a textual sentence, you should generally spell out the word.[22] But if you are referring to a section of the United States Code or a federal regulation in a textual sentence, use the section symbol.[23] Never begin a sentence with a symbol; always use a noun to identify the section or paragraph.[24]

Examples

Parents can secure temporary parenting time under section 25-404.

The police officers sought immunity under § 1983.

Section 1983 might provide a defense for police officers charged with conducting an illegal search.

7 Footnotes and Endnotes

7.1 Citing Footnotes or Endnotes Within a Source

7.1(a) Single footnote or endnote

For footnotes, set out the page of the source on which the note begins (even if it spans two or more pages), followed by the abbreviation "n." and the note reference number, with no space between n. and the reference number.[1] For endnotes, cite the same way except cite the actual page on which the note appears, not the page containing its note reference number.[2]

To cite only a specific page of a single footnote or endnote that spans multiple pages, set out the specific page, followed by the note reference number.[3]

To cite both textual material and a footnote appearing on the same page, first indicate the page number and then add an ampersand (&) followed by the abbreviation "n." and the note reference number.[4] If you are citing to a span of pages and also to a single footnote on only one of those pages, cite the page span, then the footnote as described above, separating the span and the note citation with a comma.[5]

Examples (spaces denoted by ▲)

Citation to a single footnote:	Sarah▲Howard▲Jenkins,▲*Application▲of▲the▲U.C.C.▲to▲Nonpayment▲Virtual▲Assets▲or▲Digital▲Art*,▲11▲Duq.▲Bus.▲L.J.▲245,▲248▲n.8▲(2009).
	Sanders▲v.▲Mountain▲Am.▲Fed.▲Credit▲Union,▲689▲F.3d▲1138,▲1142▲n.2▲(10th▲Cir.▲2012).
Citation to a single endnote:	Gerald▲Lebovits,▲*The▲Bottom▲Line▲on▲Footnotes▲and▲Endnotes*,▲75▲N.Y.▲St.▲Bar▲Ass'n▲J.▲61,▲64▲n.2▲(2003).
Citation to the whole note spanning multiple pages:	Howard▲J.▲Bashman,▲*Recusal▲on▲Appeal:▲An▲Appellate▲Advocate's▲Perspective*,▲7▲J.▲App.▲Prac.▲&▲Process▲59,▲64▲n.9▲(2005).
Citation to single page of a note spanning multiple pages:	Howard▲J.▲Bashman,▲*Recusal▲on▲Appeal:▲An▲Appellate▲Advocate's▲Perspective*,▲7▲J.▲App.▲Prac.▲&▲Process▲59,▲65▲n.9▲(2005).
Citation to page in text and note on same page:	Roy▲Stuckey▲et▲al.,▲*Best▲Practices▲for▲Legal▲Education:▲A▲Vision▲and▲a▲Road▲Map*▲110▲&▲n.323▲(2007).
Citation to span of pages and note on only one of those pages:	Roy▲Stuckey▲et▲al.,▲*Best▲Practices▲for▲Legal▲Education:▲A▲Vision▲and▲a▲Road▲Map*▲110–13,▲110▲n.323▲(2007).

7.1(b) Consecutive notes

To cite consecutive notes on a single page, indicate the page number on which the notes appear, immediately followed by the abbreviation "nn." and the note reference numbers, joined with a hyphen (-) or an en dash (–).[6] Do not insert a comma between the page number and the note reference. To cite consecutive notes on a span of pages, indicate the page span before adding "nn." and the note reference numbers.[7]

Examples (spaces denoted by ▲)

Citation to consecutive notes on a single page: John▲J.▲Brunetti,▲*Searching*▲*for*▲*Methods*▲*of*▲*Trial*▲*Court*▲*Fact-Finding*▲*and*▲*Decision-Making*,▲49▲Hastings▲L.J.▲1491,▲1494▲nn.15–17▲(1998).

Citation to consecutive notes on span of pages: *Daimler*▲*AG*▲*v.*▲*Bauman*,▲134▲S.▲Ct.▲746,▲754–55▲nn.4–6▲(2014).

7.1(c) Nonconsecutive notes

To cite nonconsecutive notes on a single page, join the final two note numbers with an ampersand (&).[8] To cite scattered notes on nonconsecutive pages, set out the page on which the first note begins, followed by the note reference number and a comma; then do the same for each of the other notes.[9] To cite both a page in the source and a note on that page, set out the page number, followed by an ampersand (&), the abbreviation "n." (or "nn."), and the note reference number(s).[10]

Examples (spaces denoted by ▲)

Citation to scattered notes on a single page: Susanna▲L.▲Blumenthal,▲*Law*▲*and*▲*the*▲*Creative*▲*Mind*,▲74▲Chi.-Kent▲L.▲Rev.▲151,▲158▲nn.15,▲19▲&▲23▲(1998).

Citation to scattered notes on nonconsecutive pages: John▲H.▲Langbein,▲*Chancellor*▲*Kent*▲*and*▲*the*▲*History*▲*of*▲*Legal*▲*Literature*,▲93▲Colum.▲L.▲Rev.▲547,▲567▲n.100,▲569▲n.108▲(1993).

7.1(d) Footnotes or endnotes in online sources

Determine whether the online source uses footnotes or endnotes. Online documents are ordinarily not paginated, and their note reference numbers function as hyperlinks, either to something resembling an endnote or as a link to an external source. To cite a hyperlinked note, insert the abbreviation "n." followed by the note reference number.

Online documents displaying footnotes may be copies of a print source in PDF format. Alternatively, they may employ star pagination (**Rule 5.5**). Only an online document that has permanent page numbers, such as a PDF, should use page numbers for pinpoint references; indicate the page number followed by the abbreviation "n." and the note reference number. If the document does not display page numbers, insert just the note reference number, preceded by "n."

Example

Digital Object Identifier, Wikipedia n.4, https://en.wikipedia.org/wiki/Digital_object_identifier#cite_ref-4 (last modified Aug. 5, 2020, 9:35 UTC).

7.1(e) Preventing confusion in a single citation's references to notes and pages

Note references are always preceded by the abbreviations "n." or "nn." However, in order to avoid confusing readers over which numbers in a citation refer to pages and which refer to notes, you may wish to provide two citations, the first to the referenced notes and the next to the later page.

Examples

Potentially confusing:	D.H. Kaye, *Choice and Boundary Problems in* Logerquist, Hummert, *and* Kumho Tire, 33 Ariz. St. L.J. 41, 51 nn.52–54, 52 (2001).
Less confusing:	D.H. Kaye, *Choice and Boundary Problems in* Logerquist, Hummert, *and* Kumho Tire, 33 Ariz. St. L.J. 41, 51 nn.52–54 (2001); *id.* at 52.

7.2 Footnotes or Endnotes in Short Citations

You have two alternatives for providing pinpoint references to footnotes or endnotes when *id.* is the short citation. (*Note:* Although the examples below are from academic footnotes, the short citations are formatted the same way in practice-based documents.)

First alternative:

ACADEMIC FORMATTING

[5] Harold J. Berman, *The Historical Foundations of Law*, 54 Emory L.J. 13, 16 nn.2–5 (2005).

[6] *Id.* at 16 n.4.

[7] *Id.* at 18 n.7.

Second alternative:

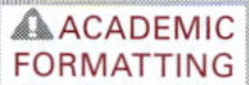

[5] Harold J. Berman, *The Historical Foundations of Law*, 54 EMORY L.J. 13, 16 nn.2–5 (2005).

[6] *Id.* at n.4.

[7] *Id.* at 18 n.7.

In the first alternative, footnote 6 repeats the pinpoint page from the previous footnote, while in the second alternative, footnote 6 does not repeat the page. The second alternative is technically more accurate under **Rule 11.3**, but many writers prefer the first alternative. Once you select an alternative to follow, use it consistently.

Short citations are discussed generally in **Rule 11.2** and are discussed specifically within relevant rules in **Parts 3** and **4**.

8 Supplements

Many legal texts are regularly updated by pocket parts or supplemental pamphlets. The material to be cited may be located solely in the supplement, solely in the main volume of a supplemented work, or in both the main volume and the supplement. Use this rule to indicate the location of the material by modifying the citation's date parenthetical.

8.1 Sources Found Only in Supplements

To indicate a source that appears solely in a supplement, insert the abbreviation "Supp." after the opening parenthesis of the citation's date parenthetical. If the supplement is numbered or its name is otherwise modified, include that information. Set out the year of the supplement's publication, and close the parentheses.[1]

If the supplement updates a later edition of the main work, insert the abbreviation "Supp." and its publication date after the abbreviation for the edition.

Examples

18 U.S.C. § 1965 (Supp. 2010).

42 U.S.C. § 3796hh (Supp. I 2001).

Or. Rev. Stat. Ann. § 540.520 (West Supp. 2009).

John Wesley Hall, Jr., *Professional Responsibility in Criminal Defense Practice* § 9:3.50 (3d ed. Supp. 2012).

8.2 Sources Found Only in Main Volume of a Supplemented Work

To indicate a source that appears solely in the main volume of a work with supplements, use only the publication date of the main volume in the date parenthetical. Omit reference to the supplement. Consult the rule for the specific source being cited (e.g., **Rule 14.2(f)** for statutes).

Examples

18 U.S.C. § 1965.

John Wesley Hall, Jr., *Professional Responsibility in Criminal Defense Practice* § 14:2 (3d ed. 2005).

8.3 Sources Found in Both Main Volume and Supplement

To indicate source material that appears in both a main volume and its supplement, use both dates in the date parenthetical. Set out the date of the main volume first, followed by an ampersand (&) and a reference to the supplement and its date.[2]

Examples

18 U.S.C. § 1965 (2000 & Supp. IV 2004).

John Wesley Hall, Jr., *Professional Responsibility in Criminal Defense Practice* § 28:19 (3d ed. 2005 & Supp. 2012).

8.4 Sources Found in Multiple Supplements

If a cited source appears in multiple supplements, cite the supplements in chronological order.

Examples

Multiple supplements, different years:	(Supps. IV 1999 & V 2000).
Multiple supplements, same year:	(Supps. IV & V 1994).
Main volume and supplements in different years:	(1988 & Supps. I 1989, II 1990, III 1991, IV 1992, V 1993).
Supplements to later edition:	(2d ed. Supps. 1994 & 1996).

9 Graphical Material, Appendices, and Other Subdivisions

9.1 Graphical Material

To cite graphical material such as tables, charts, graphs, or figures, set out the pinpoint page number on which the material begins, followed by the abbreviation from **Appendix 3(C)** (if any) for the particular type of material cited and, without any space in between, the number, letter, or other designation for the material (if any).[1] For information on citing photographs or illustrations, see **Rule 28.8**.

To cite multiple graphics, analogize to citing multiple sections or paragraphs (see **Rule 6**). Do not use a hyphen or en dash for spans of graphical material; use commas and ampersands.[2]

Examples (spaces denoted by ▲)

Bryan▲A.▲Garner,▲*The*▲*Winning*▲*Brief*▲413▲chart▲(2d▲ed.▲2004).

Endale▲Alemu▲Hora,▲*Factors*▲*that*▲*Affect*▲*Women*▲*Participation*▲*in*▲*Leadership*▲*and*▲*Decision*▲*Making*▲*Position*,▲1▲Asian▲J.▲Human.▲Art▲&▲Literature▲97,▲104▲figs.1,▲2▲&▲3▲(2014).

ACADEMIC FORMATTING

[87] Gary▲L.▲Blasi,▲*What*▲*Lawyers*▲*Know:*▲*Lawyering*▲*Expertise,*▲*Cognitive*▲*Science,*▲*and*▲*the*▲*Functions*▲*of*▲*Theory,*▲45▲J.▲LEGAL▲EDUC.▲313,▲370▲fig.4▲(1995).

9.2 Preventing Confusion in References to Graphical Material

To prevent reader confusion about which numbers refer to pages, sections, or paragraphs and which refer to graphical material, you may deviate from the general rule. In such instances, analogize to the solutions in **Rules 6.5** and **7.1(e)**.

9.3 Appendices

9.3(a) Entire appendix

To cite an entire appendix, determine whether it belongs to the entire source (e.g., an appendix to a law review article) or to a specific portion of the source (e.g., an appendix to a book chapter). Place the abbreviation "app." immediately following the appropriate component of the citation.[3] For example, if an appendix is attached to a law review article, provide the initial page of the law review article and then designate the appendix. If the appendix is attached to a particular chapter of a book, provide the book's chapter number, and then refer to the appendix.

When the appendix is designated by a number or letter, insert one space between "app." and the designation. The abbreviation for multiple appendices is "apps." To cite multiple appendices, analogize to citing multiple sections and paragraphs (**Rules 6.2–6.5**).

Examples (spaces denoted by ▲)

Federal▲Advisory▲Committee▲Act,▲5▲U.S.C.▲app.▲(2012).

M.H.▲Sam▲Jacobson,▲*Providing*▲*Academic*▲*Support*▲*Without*▲*an*▲*Academic*▲*Support*▲*Environment*,▲3▲Legal▲Writing▲241▲app.▲B▲(1997).

Thompson▲*v.*▲*Oklahoma*,▲487▲U.S.▲815▲apps.▲A–F▲(1988).

9.3(b) Material within an appendix

To refer to specific material within an appendix, insert the pinpoint reference directly after the abbreviation "app." Insert "at" before a pinpoint page reference.[4]

Examples (spaces denoted by ▲)

Federal▲Advisory▲Committee▲Act,▲5▲U.S.C.▲app.▲§▲4▲(2012).

M.H.▲Sam▲Jacobson,▲*Providing*▲*Academic*▲*Support*▲*Without*▲*an*▲*Academic*▲*Support*▲*Environment*,▲3▲Legal▲Writing▲241▲app.▲B▲at▲261–63▲(1997).

9.4 Other Subdivisions

To cite a subdivision or appended material not specifically described in **Rules 5** through **9.3**, use the most similar subdivision as an analogy.[5] Consult **Appendix 3(C)** for abbreviations.

Examples

Chapter:	Philip C. Kissam, *The Discipline of Law Schools: The Making of Modern Lawyers* ch. 3 (2003).
Comment:	Model Rules of Pro. Conduct r. 7.3 cmt. 5 (Am. Bar Ass'n 2013).
Historical notes:	Mass. Gen. Laws Ann. ch. 211, § 2A hist. nn. (West 2005 & Supp. 2013).

10 Internal Cross-References

10.1 Definition of "Internal Cross-Reference"

An "internal cross-reference" refers readers to material in another part of the document, such as text, appendices, footnotes, photographs, or pages. Internal cross-references are most commonly used in academic footnotes or endnotes, but you may encounter them in other kinds of sources, such as judicial opinions. Do not use an internal cross-reference to cite a source outside the document, such as a case or a statute; instead use an appropriate short citation to that source. Short citations are addressed in **Rules 11.2** through **11.4**.

10.2FN Constructing an Internal Cross-Reference

ACADEMIC FORMATTING

10.2(a)FN Indicating location of cross-references with *supra* and *infra*

Provide the most specific reference possible, and if warranted, introduce the cross-reference with a signal (**Rule 35**). To cross-reference material that appears earlier in the document, use the appropriate signal before the italicized term *supra* (Latin for "above"), followed by a reference to the specific location of the material. For material appearing later in the document, use the appropriate signal and the italicized term *infra* (Latin for "below").[1] (For information about using *supra* in a short citation, rather than as a cross-reference, see **Rule 11.4**.)

Unless cross-referencing specific pages within a document, do not abbreviate any cross-references to its footnotes, tables, figures, appendices, or other internal subdivisions. To cross-reference the document's own pages, use the abbreviations "p." or "pp." before the page number(s).[2] If pages in the span are numbered 100 or higher, the repetitious digits should be dropped from the concluding number, retaining only the last two digits.[3]

Examples

Cross-referencing an earlier discussion:	125 *See supra* text accompanying note 75.
Cross-referencing a later portion of document:	133 *See infra* Part IV.
Cross-referencing an internal subdivision:	233 *See generally* Figure 4.
Cross-referencing specific pages:	88 *But see infra* pp. 225–26.

10.2(b)FN Adding explanatory parentheticals to cross-references

ACADEMIC FORMATTING

If the accompanying text or citation does not adequately identify the subject of the cross-reference, add an explanatory parenthetical. For more information about using explanatory parentheticals, see **Rule 37**.

Examples

[34] *See supra* notes 20–31 (examining history of Supreme Court's decisions on attorney advertising).

[47] *See infra* Part C(1) (explaining proper deposition objections).

11 Full and Short Citation Formats

11.1 Full Citation Format

11.1(a) Definition of "full citation"

A "full citation" contains every component needed for the first reference to a source. It gives readers necessary and sufficient information to locate that source in print or in an online version.

11.1(b) Components of a full citation

Rules 12 through **29** and **Rules 31** through **33** begin with a list and illustrations of full citations to the sources they cover. A full citation typically includes the author's name (if any); the title or name of the source; a specific reference to the volume, page, section, or other subdivision within which the referenced material is located; and a publication date.

11.1(c) Frequency of full citations

Provide a source's full citation the first time you cite it. If desired, or when required by local court rule (see **Appendix 2**), you may cite in full more frequently, such as the first time you cite the source in a new section of the document you are writing. For more guidance on how often to cite, see **Rule 34.2**.

11.1(d)FN Frequency of full citations in academic footnotes

ACADEMIC FORMATTING

Repeat the full citation to a *primary authority* if the authority has not been cited in full or in short citation (including *id.*) in one of the previous five footnotes.[1] It is unnecessary to repeat full citations to *secondary* materials; instead, use the *supra* short citation to send readers to the original footnote containing the secondary source's full citation (see **Rule 11.4**).[2]

11.2 Short Citations

Once you have cited a source in full, use a "short citation" in later references to it. A short citation omits some components of a source's full citation while still providing enough information to identify the source and to match it to the earlier full citation. Short citations save space and are less disruptive to the flow of text than are full citations.

Use short citations when the reader will neither be confused about the source being referenced nor have trouble quickly locating the source's full citation. The type of short citation varies, depending on the nature of the source, the location of the short citation in relation to the full citation, and whether the citation appears in a practice-based document, such as an office memorandum or a brief, or in an academic footnote, such as those used in law review articles and treatises.

Each rule in **Part 3** of the *ALWD Guide* contains in-depth information about and examples of full and short citations to the source covered by that rule. The remainder of **Rule 11** deals with general short citation formats to use for almost any source.

11.3 *Id.* as a Short Citation

11.3(a) Definition of "*id.*"

"*Id.*" abbreviates the Latin word "*idem*," meaning "the same." *Id.* refers to everything that is *id*entical to the previous citation, including the page number or other pinpoint reference, if it has not changed. *Id.* tells readers you are citing the same source just cited.[3] (*Note: Id.* is used in legal citations the same way *ibid.* is used in non-legal citation systems.) Where it is appropriate (see **Rule 11.3(c)**), *id.* is the preferred short citation.[4]

11.3(b) Typeface and capitalization of *id.*

Italicize *id.* and its period.[5] If you use underlining, underline the period (id.). When the word *id.* begins a short citation, capitalize the letter "I." When *id.* is not the first word in a short citation, use a lowercase letter "i."[6]

Examples

Italicized citations (text): Any object may suffice as a simulated deadly weapon, provided the victim reasonably perceives it to be an actual weapon. *State v. Felix*, 737 P.2d 393, 394 (Ariz. Ct. App. 1986). When the defendant in *Felix* pressed a nasal inhaler against his victim's back, declaring that he had a gun, the victim was convinced that the object he felt was a gun. *Id.* at 396.

Underlined citations (text): Any object may suffice as a simulated deadly weapon, provided the victim reasonably perceives it to be an actual weapon. State v. Felix, 737 P.2d 393, 394 (Ariz. Ct. App. 1986). When the defendant in Felix pressed a nasal inhaler against his victim's back, declaring that he had a gun, the victim was convinced that the object he felt was a gun. Id. at 396.

Italicized citations (academic footnotes): ⚠ ACADEMIC FORMATTING

[18] State v. Felix, 737 P.2d 393, 394 (Ariz. Ct. App. 1986).

[19] *Id.* at 396.

11.3(c) Appropriate uses of *id.*

Use *id.* to cite the same source cited in the immediately preceding citation.[7] Because *id.* refers to the identical source, do not use *id.* if the previous citation refers to a different source, and do not use *id.* if the previous citation is part of a string citation (see **Rule 36.1**).[8] In a parallel case citation, *id.* replaces the first cited source, but not the second. For more information about parallel citations, see **Rules 12.4(c)** and **12.16(d)**.

Use *id.* for any source except an appellate record (**Rule 25.7**), unless using it will save significant space, or an internal cross-reference (**Rule 10**).[9] And only use *id.* as a short form for court documents that are in the case you are litigating if doing so will save significant space (**Rule 25.5**).

Examples

	Different policy considerations animate courts' rulings on surrogacy agreements. In California, for example, surrogacy contracts do not violate the policies governing the termination of parental
Full citation for first reference to *Johnson*	rights. *Johnson v. Calvert*, 851 P.2d 776, 784 (Cal. 1993). The court reached this conclusion because the contract was based on services, not on the
Id. refers to same case and page	termination of parental rights. *Id.* Other states, however, have refused to enforce surrogacy agreements. In Massachusetts, for example, a contract in which the birth mother receives payment for her services is not enforceable if the payment is used to influence her decision to relinquish
Full citation for first reference to *R.R.*	custody. *R.R. v. M.H.*, 689 N.E.2d 790, 796 (Mass. 1998). In *R.R.*, the surrogate was artificially inseminated with the
Id. refers to *R.R.* but to page 791	intended father's sperm. *Id.* at 791. Because the contract indicated that the surrogate would receive $10,000 for delivering the child, the court refused to enforce the contract, reasoning that the payment vitiated the surrogate's intent.
Id. refers to page 796 of *R.R.*	*Id.* at 796. While the Michigan court was focused on the payment, the California court described compelling public policy reasons for enforcing surrogacy contracts.
Reference to *Johnson* does not use *id.* because *R.R.* was last source cited	*Johnson*, 851 P.2d at 784.

Subsequent references to *Freeman* and *Stanton* do not use *id.* because their first references are in a string citation

The problems of sexual assault at colleges and universities—usually fueled by alcohol—have continued to vex courts. Two important decisions have occurred since 1999 that are potentially reconcilable with our theory: *Freeman v. Busch*, 349 F.3d 582 (8th Cir. 2003); *Stanton v. Univ. Me. Sys.*, 773 A.2d 1045 (Me. 2001). Both cases involved female students being sexually assaulted in residence halls. *See Freeman*, 349 F.3d at 585; *Stanton*, 773 A.2d at 1047–48.

11.3(d) *Id.* followed by pinpoint reference

When citing a source whose pinpoint reference *has not* changed from the immediately preceding citation, use *id.* by itself to refer both to the source and to the pinpoint reference.[10] If the source is the same but the pinpoint reference (e.g., a section, a subsection, a paragraph) *has* changed, use *id.* followed by the new pinpoint reference.[11] When citing a source that uses page numbers, insert the preposition "at" between *id.* and the new page number. Do not use "at" before other types of pinpoint references.[12]

Examples

Page number:	*Id.* at 321.
Section number:	*Id.* § 14.3.
Subsection number:	*Id.* § 200(a)(3).
Paragraph number:	*Id.* ¶ 6.
Other reference:	*Id.* app. 1.
	Id. R. 56(c)(1)(A).

11.3(e) *Id.* referring to shorter work within a collection

When citing a shorter work in a collection, use *id.* to refer to the shorter work, not to the overall collection.[13] For examples, see **Rule 20.6(b)**.

11.3(f) Intervening sources

Sources referenced in an explanatory parenthetical (**Rule 37**), in subsequent history (**Rule 12.8**), or in prior history (**Rule 12.9**) are not considered intervening sources for determining whether to use *id.*[14]

Examples

Practice-based document:

Full citation for first reference to *Ruston*

Id. refers to *Ruston* and has intervening source in a parenthetical

Id. still refers to *Ruston*

An abuse of discretion standard applies to the district court's failure to conduct a mental competency hearing. *United States v. Ruston*, 565 F.3d 892, 901 (5th Cir. 2009) ("Whether the district court erred in not *sua sponte* holding a competency hearing is reviewed for abuse of discretion."). It is clear, however, that "the court must consider three factors: (1) the existence of a history of irrational behavior, (2) the defendant's demeanor at trial, and (3) prior medical opinion on competency." *Id.* at 902 (citing *United States v. Messervey*, 317 F.3d 457, 463 (5th Cir. 2002)). Although all three factors are relevant to determining whether further inquiry is warranted, under certain circumstances, "even one of these factors standing alone" may be sufficient. *Id.*

Academic footnotes:

ACADEMIC FORMATTING

Id. still refers to *Hawaii Housing Authority* even though the prior cite has a parenthetical

Id. still refers to *Gazza* even though the prior cite has subsequent history

100 Haw. Hous. Auth. v. Midkiff, 467 U.S. 229, 241 (1984) (quoting United States v. Gettysburg Elec. Ry., 160 U.S. 668, 680 (1896)).

101 *Id.* at 242.

102 Gazza v. N.Y. State Dep't Env't Conservation, 634 N.Y.S.2d 740 (App. Div. 1995), *aff'd*, 679 N.E.2d 1035 (N.Y. 1997).

103 *Id.* at 741.

11.4 *Supra* in a Short Citation

11.4(a) Definition of "*supra*"

The term "*supra*" (Latin for "above") indicates that a full citation to the cited source can be found earlier in the document.[15] This use of *supra* differs from the internal cross-reference use of *supra* described in **Rule 10.2(a)**[FN].

11.4(b) Appropriate uses of *supra*

Supra cannot be used for every type of source or cross-reference. Do not use *supra* to refer to an earlier citation to primary sources of law such as cases, enacted law (statutes, administrative regulations, constitutions, etc.), or legislative materials. Do not use *supra* to refer back to restatements or model codes either. For these, use the short citation formats shown in the authority's rule in **Part 3**. You may, however, use *supra* to refer to earlier full citations of secondary sources such as books, treatises, periodicals, court filings, legislative hearings (but not other types of legislative materials), or unpublished materials.[16]

Use *supra* only after the source has been cited once in full. Do not use *supra* when *id.* is appropriate.[17]

11.4(c) Short citations using *supra*

Use this format for the *supra* short citation:

Author's last name or if no author, the title of the work, | *supra*, | [at] | Pinpoint reference.

If the pinpoint reference is a page of the cited work, insert the preposition "at" before the new page number. Do not insert "at" before paragraph or section symbols.[18]

Example

Since the days of the Salem witch trials, the accuracy of children's testimony has been suspect. Michelle L. Morris, *Li'l People, Little Justice: The Effects of the Witness Competency Standard in California on Children in Sexual Abuse Cases*, 22 J. Juv. L. 113, 114 (2001–2002). The reason, however, is not the child's age. Even the United States Supreme Court has upheld the competency of children as witnesses, stating that there is no minimum age. *See Wheeler v. United States*, 159 U.S. 523, 526 (1895). Refusing to declare a five-year-old absolutely incompetent to testify in a murder trial, the Court explained, "While no one would think of calling an infant of only two or three years old, there is no precise age which determines the question of competency." *Id.* However, a judge still must assess the child's qualifications for testifying. "This [is] a conditional competency standard, not a per se rule declaring children competent to testify." Morris, *supra*, at 114.

11.4(d)FN Appropriate uses of *supra* in academic footnotes

ACADEMIC FORMATTING

In academic writing, *supra* is appropriate only in referring to the source's full citation in an earlier footnote. Do not use *supra* for short citation references to the following primary sources of law: cases, statutes, session laws, ordinances, legislative materials (other than hearings), constitutions, or administrative regulations. Use *supra* for short citation references to other administrative, legislative, or executive materials and for references to secondary sources such as books, law review articles, and websites.[19]

11.4(e)FN Short citations using *supra* in academic footnotes

ACADEMIC FORMATTING

Use this format for the *supra* short citation in an academic footnote:

Author's last name or if no author, the title of the work, | *supra* | note | Number of footnote containing full citation to source, | [at] | Pinpoint reference.

Do not abbreviate the word "note." Do not insert "at" before paragraph or section symbols. When the pinpoint reference is to a page of the cited work, insert the preposition "at" before the new page number.[20]

Examples

[45] Kristen David Adams, *Do We Need a Right to Housing?*, 9 NEV. L.J. 275, 303 (2009).

. . .

[57] Adams, *supra* note 45, at 318.

. . .

[84] JOSHUA DRESSLER, UNDERSTANDING CRIMINAL LAW § 10.04[A][1] (3d ed. 2001).

. . .

[95] DRESSLER, *supra* note 84, § 10.03.

11.5 Designating a Shortened Reference with [Hereinafter]

11.5(a) Function of [hereinafter] reference

The "[hereinafter]" reference appended to a full citation alerts readers to a shortened name of that source in subsequent citations. It can provide a shorter *supra* citation or truncate a long title.[21] Its primary use is in academic footnotes, as shown in the examples in **Rule 11.5(c)FN**.

11.5(b) Format of [hereinafter] reference

Immediately following the first full citation to the source, insert one space and an opening square bracket, followed by the term "hereinafter" (in ordinary type), one space, the shortened reference, and a closing square bracket. Depending on the nature of the source, the shortened reference may be an author's surname and a shortened version of the title, or if no author, just a shortened title. Present citation components following [hereinafter] in the same typeface as they appear in the full citation. Place the [hereinafter] reference before any explanatory parenthetical.[22]

Example

As a general matter, "courts have had a fair amount of trouble developing standards for distinguishing frivolous cases from ordinary losers." Charles M. Yablon, *The Good, the Bad, and the Frivolous Case: An Essay on Probability and Rule 11*, 44 UCLA L. Rev. 65, 66 (1996) [hereinafter Yablon, *Essay on Probability*]. A study of Rule 11 reversals by the federal courts of appeals revealed that in 19 percent of those cases, the appellate courts concluded that the cases had merit, even though the district courts had not viewed them as such. Fed. Jud. Ctr., *Rule 11: Final Report to the Advisory Committee on Civil Rules of the Judicial Conference of the United States* 21 (1991). Certainly this statistic shows that courts can disagree about what makes a case frivolous. Yablon, *Essay on Probability*, 44 UCLA L. Rev. at 94.

11.5(c)FN Appropriate uses of [hereinafter] in academic footnotes

ACADEMIC FORMATTING

Use [hereinafter] in these circumstances:

- When no author is attributed to the cited source and the title is long.

Examples

65 *Terrorism: Victims' Access to Terrorist Assets: Hearing Before the Senate Committee on the Judiciary*, 106th Cong. 17 (1999) [hereinafter *Terrorism Hearing*].

. . .

74 *Terrorism Hearing*, *supra* note 65, at 19.

- When full citations to two or more works from the *same* author appear in the same academic footnote (to prevent confusion in subsequent short citations over which author's work is being cited).[23]

Examples

5 Lani Guinier, *Lessons and Challenges of Becoming Gentlemen*, 24 N.Y.U. Rev. L. & Soc. Change 1, 11 (1998) [hereinafter Guinier, *Lessons*]; Lani Guinier, *Reframing the Affirmative Action Debate*, 86 Ky. L.J. 505, 517–18 (1997–1998) [hereinafter Guinier, *Reframing Debate*].

. . .

[18] Guinier, *Lessons*, *supra* note 5, at 12–15.

[19] *Id.* at 13, 17.

[20] Guinier, *Reframing Debate*, *supra* note 5, at 520.

- When the regular shortened form might confuse the reader, or when the [hereinafter] designation would help readers more easily recognize the source.[24]

Example

[14] Winston Churchill, Speech to the House of Commons (June 18, 1940) [hereinafter Their Finest Hour] (transcript available at http://www.winstonchurchill.org/resources/speeches/1940-the-finest-hour/122-their-finest-hour).

. . .

[20] Their Finest Hour, *supra* note 14.

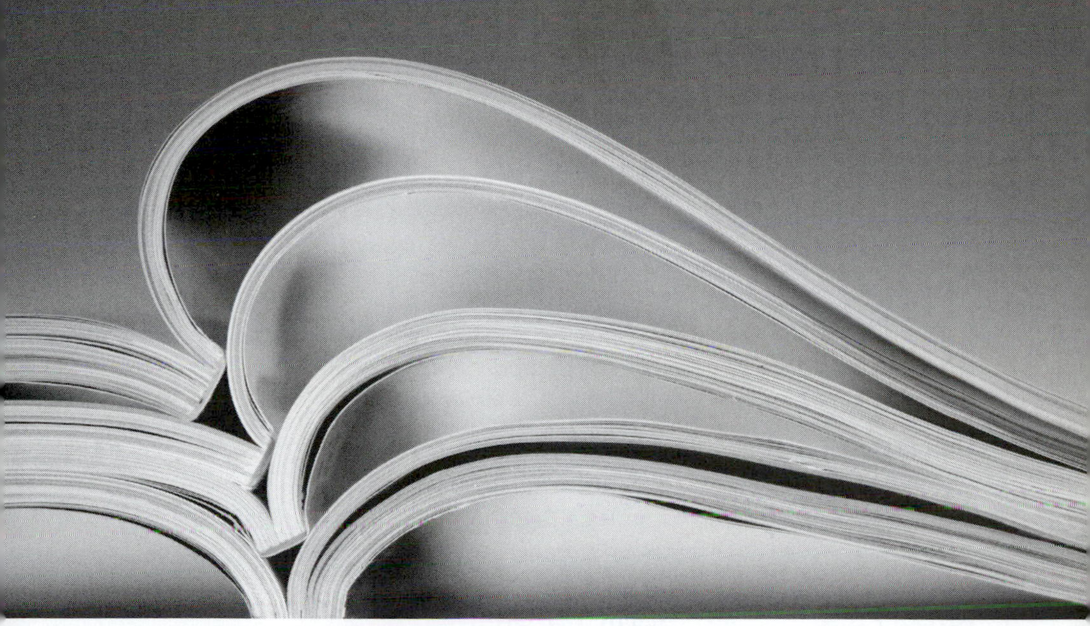

Part 2
Citing Specific Sources

Fast Formats

Cases	
United States Supreme Court	*Citizens United v. Fed. Election Comm'n*, 558 U.S. 310, 365–66 (2010).
United States Court of Appeals	*United States v. Mahin*, 668 F.3d 119, 123 (4th Cir. 2012). *Bradley v. Looten*, 450 F. App'x 558, 559 (8th Cir. 2012).
United States District Court	*Woollard v. Sheridan*, 863 F. Supp. 2d 462, 469 (D. Md. 2012).
State supreme court	*Firstland Vill. Assocs. v. Law.'s Title Ins. Co.*, 284 S.E.2d 582, 584 (S.C. 1981).
State intermediate appellate court	*Oberlander v. Handy*, 913 N.E.2d 734, 738 (Ind. Ct. App. 2009).
Subsequent history	*Cutshall v. Sundquist*, 980 F. Supp. 928, *aff'd in part, rev'd in part*, 193 F.3d 466 (6th Cir. 1999).
Minority opinion	*Polsky v. Virnich*, 804 N.W.2d 80, 81 (Wis. 2011) (Abrahamson, C.J., dissenting).
Unpublished opinion in commercial database	*In re Weisinger*, No. 14-12-00558-CV, 2012 WL 3861960 (Tex. App. Sept. 6, 2012).
Parallel citation	*Walder v. Lobel*, 339 Pa. Super. 203, 211–12, 488 A.2d 622, 626 (1985).
Citation in academic footnote	[153] *See* Quan v. Gonzales, 428 F.3d 883, 888–89 (9th Cir. 2005). ACADEMIC FORMATTING
Short citations	913 N.E.2d at 737. *Oberlander*, 913 N.E.2d at 736. *Id.* at 213, 488 A.2d at 627. [155] *Quan*, 428 F.3d at 889.

Snapshot
CASES

reporter volume

initial page number

812 | 229 FEDERAL REPORTER, 2d SERIES

Before we can order the release of a state prisoner for failure to obtain a "speedy trial," we must be convinced that the failure resulted in the taking of the prisoner's liberty or property without due process of law.

[11, 12] The right to a speedy trial is relative and must always be judged by the surrounding circumstances. Beavers v. Haubert, 198 U.S. 77, 25 S.Ct. 573, 49 L.Ed. 950; United States ex rel. Hanson v. Ragen, 7 Cir., 166 F.2d 608. Under the circumstances shown by the record in this case the delay in bringing Sawyer to trial was not so unreasonable as to contravene his Constitutional rights.

The record shows that Sawyer was indicted on April 25, 1950, and the following day was released on bail. He has been at liberty on bail ever since, so that the delay in bringing him to trial has not resulted in any additional imprisonment.

Sawyer was arraigned on May 5, 1951, more than a year after he was indicted. This is not an unreasonable amount of time considering the fact that Sawyer filed an affidavit of prejudice against the Municipal Judge necessitating the appointment of a special judge, and the fact that Sawyer twice moved to dismiss the indictment listing sixteen grounds.

The state elected to try Krause first on charges that did not involve Sawyer. Krause was convicted and appealed to the Supreme Court of Wisconsin. His principal argument on appeal was that the grand jury, which had indicted both him and Sawyer, had been unlawfully constituted. If the court had upset Krause's indictment, it would have upset Sawyer's as well. It was only reasonable for the state to wait until the validity of the grand jury's action had been determined by the Supreme Court of Wisconsin before going to trial with the Sawyer case.

The only request for extra time made by the state was made on June 5, 1951, when it decided to try Krause first and Sawyer later. This delay was reasonable since the prosecutor could not try them both at the same time, and Krause had been indicted first.

[13] Not only has Sawyer failed to show that the delay in bringing him to trial was unreasonable, but also he failed to ask the court before which his case was pending for an immediate trial. Acquiescence in the delay, by failing to ask the court for immediate trial, waives the right to speedy trial. Miller v. Overholser, 92 U.S.App.D.C. 110, 206 F.2d 415; Fowler v. Hunter, 10 Cir., 164 F.2d 668; Shepherd v. United States, 8 Cir., 163 F.2d 974; United States v. Albrecht, 7 Cir., 25 F.2d 93. Also see Annotation 129 A.L.R. 572.

Since it involves no prejudicial error, the judgment of the District Court is

Affirmed.

The UNITED STATES of America, Plaintiff-Appellee,

v.

Albert ROVIARO, Defendant-Appellant.

No. 11616.

United States Court of Appeals Seventh Circuit.

Feb. 7, 1956.

Rehearing Denied March 7, 1956.

Defendant was convicted of illegal sale of narcotics and of illegal carriage and possession of same. The United States District Court for the Northern District of Illinois, Eastern Division, Win G. Knock, J., rendered judgment, and defendant appealed. The Court of Appeals, Lindley, Circuit Judge, held, inter alia, that where there was evidence, without disclosure of identity of informer, to sustain conviction on second count and guilt under second count was suffi-

First party's name: Use Rule 12.2(h) for United States.

Second party's name: Use Rule 12.2(d) for an individual.

Court: Use Appendix 4 to determine abbreviation.

Date of decision: Use Rule 12.7. Ignore the date the rehearing was denied.

First Page of a Case in a Reporter

Snapshot
CASES

UNITED STATES v. ROVIARO 813
Cite as 229 F.2d 812

cient to support sentence imposed, disclosure of identity of informer was not necessary, although he was named as purchaser in the first count.

Judgment affirmed.

1. Indictment and Information ⚷121(1)
Witnesses ⚷268(1)

If a person is named in an indictment as an informer and nothing more, defendant is not entitled to have his identity disclosed by bill of particulars or cross-examination.

2. Poisons ⚷9

In prosecution for illegal possession and carriage of narcotics, proof of possession and carriage alone furnished prima facie evidence of guilt, and left defendant with burden to prove that he possessed the narcotics lawfully. Narcotic Drugs Import and Export Act, § 2 (c) as amended 21 U.S.C.A. § 174.

3. Poisons ⚷9

In respect to prosecution for illegal possession and carriage of narcotics, wherein there was testimony by government agent that they saw defendant pick up and carry package of narcotics, proof of identity of person to whom defendant sold narcotics was not involved, and disclosure of this person's identity was not required. Narcotic Drugs Import and Export Act, § 2(c) as amended 21 U.S.C.A. § 174.

4. Criminal Law ⚷1177

Where a sentence does not exceed that which may lawfully be imposed under any single count, judgment must be affirmed if evidence is sufficient to sustain any one of the counts.

5. Criminal Law ⚷1177

In prosecution for illegal sale of narcotics and illegal possession and carriage thereof, wherein there was evidence, without disclosure of identity of informer, to sustain conviction on second count and guilt under second count was sufficient to support sentence imposed, disclosure of identity of informer was not necessary, although he was named as purchaser in the first count. 26 U.S.C.A. (I.R.C.1939) § 2554(a); Narcotic Drugs Import and Export Act, § 2(c) as amended 21 U.S.C.A. § 174.

6. Criminal Law ⚷627½

In narcotics prosecution, wherein there was testimony that several arresting officers participated in the discovery of narcotics in an automobile and wherein one officer testified that he found a package, envelope in which package was preserved and which bore label stating that narcotics had been found by a different participating officer was not required to be produced.

7. Criminal Law ⚷627½

Where a witness does not use his notes or memoranda in court, a party has no absolute right to have them produced and to inspect them, and trial judge has a large discretion in this respect.

Maurice J. Walsh, Chicago, Ill., for appellant.

Robert Tieken, U. S. Atty., John Peter Lulinski, Asst. U. S. Atty., Chicago, Ill., Chester E. Emanuelson Asst. U. S. Atty., Chicago, Ill., of counsel, for appellee.

Before FINNEGAN, LINDLEY and SCHNACKENBERG, Circuit Judges.

LINDLEY, Circuit Judge.

In a trial before the court without a jury, defendant was found guilty upon the two counts of an indictment charging that he (1) on August 12, 1954, sold to one John Doe heroin in violation of 26 U.S.C. § 2554(a), and (2) on the same date, in the city of Chicago, knowingly received, concealed and facilitated the transportation, after importation, of heroin in violation of 21 U.S.C.A. § 174. The court entered a general sentence, ordering defendant imprisoned for two years and fined.

Upon appeal, defendant aserts error in that the court (1) denied his petition for a bill of particulars disclosing the home address and occupation of John Doe; (2) unduly limited the cross-examination concerning the identity of the said Doe;

Second Page of a Case in a Reporter

12.1 Full Citations to Cases

A full case citation contains as many as nine components, depending on the publication source(s) and the case's history[1]:

Case name, | Reporter volume | Reporter abbreviation | Initial page, | Pinpoint reference | (Court abbreviation | Date) | [, *Subsequent history designation*,] | [Subsequent history citation].

Example

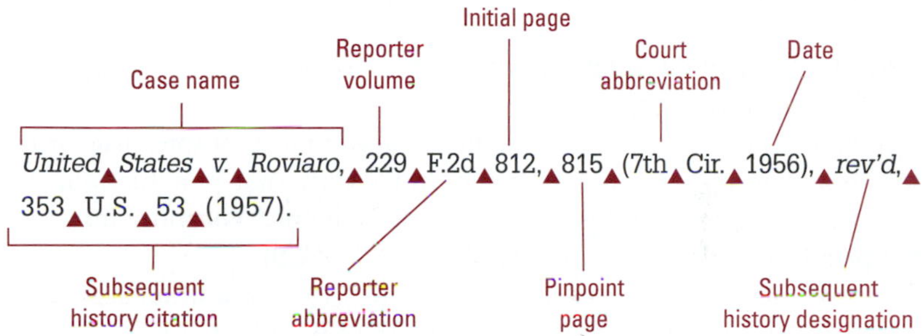

12.2 Case Names

To construct the case name component, examine the caption preceding the opinion itself (see the example in the **Snapshot** on page 55).[2] The caption displays the names and procedural roles of the parties, the case's identification number (also known as a "docket" or "case management" number; see **Sidebar 12.7** for more information about docket numbers), the name of the presiding court, and the date of the opinion. Your job is to represent the names of the parties shown in the caption, but in abbreviated form and in compliance with the subsections of **Rules 12.2(b)** through **12.2(s)**. Do not rely on a publisher's shortened version of a case name or the abbreviations the publisher uses; they may not comply with these rules.

12.2(a) Typeface for case name

12.2(a)(1) Typeface alternatives

Present the case name, the "v." abbreviation, and any internal punctuation *within* the case name in *italics* (or underlining, if you have been directed by a court rule or other instruction to use that formatting; see **Rule 1.3(a)**).[3] Use this typeface regardless whether the citation appears in a full citation or a short citation (**Rule 12.16**), whether it appears in a citation sentence, a citation clause, or an embedded citation (**Rule 34.1**), and whether it appears as simply a case name in a main text sentence or a footnote sentence.[4] Use ordinary type for the comma that separates the case name from the remainder of the citation.[5]

Examples

Singh v. Ashcroft, 393 F.3d 903, 905 (9th Cir. 2004).

Singh, 393 F.3d at 904.

Although it recognized that the First Amendment generally prohibits discrimination against religion, *Church of the Lukumi Babalu Aye, Inc. v. City of Hialeah*, 508 U.S. 520, 533 (1993), the Supreme Court has subsequently refused to extend *Lukumi*'s holding to other factual settings, *see Locke v. Davey*, 540 U.S. 712, 720 (2004).

12.2(a)(2)^FN Typeface for case names in academic footnotes

ACADEMIC FORMATTING

When presenting a *full citation* in an academic footnote, use ordinary type—not italics—for the case name and its internal punctuation, if any, but italicize any procedural phrases used in the name.[6] For more information about procedural phrases, see **Rules 12.2(o)** and **12.2(p)**.

However, when an academic footnote refers to a case in a short citation, italicize the case name reference (see **Rule 12.16(g)^FN**).[7] Use ordinary type for the comma that separates the case name from the remainder of the citation.[8]

Examples

[5] Singh v. Ashcroft, 393 F.3d 903, 905 (9th Cir. 2004).

[6] Locke v. Davey, 540 U.S. 712, 720 (2004).

[7] *Singh*, 393 F.3d at 904.

12.2(b) Consolidated case or case with two names

If two or more cases have been consolidated for a single opinion, cite only the first case listed in the caption.[9] If a single case has two names, use the name shown first, unless it is a bankruptcy case.[10] Bankruptcy cases with two names are governed by **Rule 12.2(p)(2)**.

SIDEBAR 12.1 Distinguishing Case Names from Party Names

In a textual sentence, in both academic writing and other documents, use *italics* (or <u>underlining</u>) to refer to a case name,[11] but use ordinary type to refer to the person after whom the case is named. See **Rule 2.3** and **Chart 2.1** for guidance on abbreviating words in case names within textual sentences.

Case name: In *Smith*, the court imposed a ten-year sentence on the defendant.

Person: Smith was sentenced to ten years.

Example

Caption (consolidated cases):	Case name:
VIKING PUMP, INC., Plaintiff, v. CENTURY INDEMNITY COMPANY, et al., Defendants. Warren Pumps LLC, Third-Party Plaintiff, v. Century Indemnity Company, et al., Third-Party Defendants. Viking Pump, Inc., Third-Party Plaintiff, v. John Crane, Inc., Houdaille Industries, Inc., Third-Party Defendants	*Viking Pump, Inc. v. Century Indem. Co.*,

12.2(c) First-named party

Using the caption for reference, select the first-named *adversarial* party on each side of the case.[12] No matter whether the caption uses "*v.*," "*vs.*," or "*versus*" to separate them, insert a lowercase "*v.*" between the names of the adversarial parties.[13] If the case consolidates more than one action (see **Rule 12.2(b)**), use only the first-named party in the first action.[14] If the party named first on either side is a relator (see **Rule 12.2(o)** for definition of relator), begin with the relator's name (but see **Rule 12.2(o)** when the relator is not the first-named party).[15] If a party's name is lengthy, you may drop words not essential to its representation.[16]

Print reporters and commercial databases frequently use all capital letters to display the surname of each side's first-named party; despite that presentation, capitalize only the first letter of each word used in the party's name (see **Rule 3.2(a)**). Omit phrases such as "*et al.*" ("and others"), "*et ux.*" ("and spouse"), or other terms that designate additional or unnamed parties.[17] Omit a caption's references to parties' designations or roles, such as plaintiff, defendant, appellant, appellee, petitioner, respondent, intervenor, administrator, executor, guardian, licensee, or trustee.[18]

Examples

Caption:	Case name:
Robert J. Tarbox et al. v. Stephen W. Blaisdell et al.	*Tarbox v. Blaisdell*,
Kathy SMITH, as Executrix for the Estate of Kenneth Smith, Deceased, and Kathy Smith, Individually, Appellant, v. Linda ROHRBAUGH, Appellee	*Smith v. Rohrbaugh*,

Caption:	Case name:
William RICCARD, Plaintiff-Appellant, Robert W. Rasch, Interested Party-Appellant, v. PRUDENTIAL INSURANCE COMPANY, Defendant-Appellee. William Riccard, Plaintiff-Appellant, v. Prudential Insurance Company of America, a New Jersey corporation, Defendant-Appellee. William Riccard, Plaintiff-Appellant, v. Prudential Insurance Company of America, a foreign corporation, Defendant-Appellee, Mary Ann Caso, Claims Administrator for the Prudential Insurance Company of America, Inc., Mark Martin, General Manager for the Prudential Insurance Company of America, Inc., Defendants.	*Riccard v. Prudential Ins. Co.*,

12.2(d) Individual as party

12.2(d)(1) Surname

When a case name refers to an individual, use only that person's surname as it is spelled in the caption.[19] Retain all words in a surname, even if it is hyphenated or contains two or more words.[20] Omit surname suffixes such as "Jr." and "III."[21] Omit alternative names for the party introduced by phrases such as "a/k/a" or "aka" ("also known as").[22] If you are unsure whether a word is part of an individual's surname, consult the index to the reporter in which the case appears; cases are indexed by surnames.[23] Do not abbreviate anything in an individual's surname.[24] If the caption uses a phrase such as "Estate of [Surname]" or "Will of [Surname]," keep the phrase before the surname.[25] For public officials individually named as parties, see **Rule 12.2(m)**.

Examples

Caption:	Case name:
Juma Mussa v. Nikki Palmer-Mussa	*Mussa v. Palmer-Mussa*,
William S. Bailey v. Vernon L. Lanou, Jr.	*Bailey v. Lanou*,
Estate of Joe S. DOYLE et al., Floyd Street Investments Co. et al., and Charles Weisberg, movants, v. City of Louisville, Kentucky	*Estate of Doyle v. City of Louisville*,

12.2(d)(2) Family surname

If a caption displays a family surname preceding a party's given name (e.g., parties of Asian heritage such as Chinese, Korean, or Vietnamese), set out the family and given names as shown in the caption.[26] If the caption displays a party name consisting of two family surnames, one representing each parent (e.g., parties of Portuguese or Spanish heritage), set out both family surnames as shown in the caption (whether hyphenated or joined by the conjunction "y").[27] Do not capitalize "y" in a family surname.[28] (Hint: If unsure, look at the way the name is represented in the index to the reporter.)

Examples

Caption:	**Case name:**
TUAN AHN DU, Plaintiff-Appellant, v. Michael J. ASTRUE, Commissioner of Social Security, Defendant-Appellee	*Tuan Ahn Du v. Astrue,*
The PEOPLE of the State of New York, Respondent, v. Pedro Luis RODRIGUEZ Y PAZ, Appellant	*People v. Rodriguez y Paz,*

12.2(d)(3) Initials of individual

Although you should normally omit given names and initials of an individual,[29] there are a couple exceptions. Case captions may use initials to refer to a party whose identity is being shielded (e.g., a juvenile). If a party is designated solely by initials, use all of them as the party name, omitting spaces between consecutive capital letters (see **Rule 2.2(b)**). If a party is represented with a given name and an initial for the surname, retain both the given name and the initial.

Examples (spaces denoted by ▲)

Caption:	**Case name:**
D.P.G., Plaintiff-Appellant, v. L.G., Defendant-Respondent	*D.P.G.▲v.▲L.G.,*
Ruben M., Appellant, v. Arizona Department of Economic Security, Latina M., Isaiah M., Reynaldo M., Estella T., Appellees	*Ruben▲M.▲v.▲Ariz.▲Dep't▲of▲Econ.▲Sec.,*

12.2(e) Organization as party

12.2(e)(1) Name of organization

Organizations include legally recognized business entities as well as nonprofit or charitable institutions. Set out the full name of the organization as represented by the caption, abbreviating words as described in **Rule 12.2(e)(2)**.[30] If the organization is named after a person, keep the person's full name as shown in the caption, and do not abbreviate it.[31]

The name of an organization often ends with a business designation (e.g., Ass'n, Co.). If an organization's name contains two business designations, you may omit the second but only if it is clear from the shortened name that the party is a business; if the shortened name could imply the party was anything else, such as the name of a natural person or a city, do not omit the second business designation.[32] See **Chart 12.1** for a list of common business designations; for other organizational or business abbreviations, see **Appendix 3(E)**.

Omit "the" as the first word of an organization's name (see also **Rule 12.2(r)**).[33] Omit phrases that come after the organization's name such as "d/b/a" or "dba" ("doing business as"), "f/k/a" ("formerly known as"), and the words following such phrases.[34] For letters in the organization's name, use the same case (lower case or upper case) as the organization itself does, despite the capitalization instructions in **Rule 3**.

Examples

Caption:	**Case name:**
Margaret HOWARD and Robert Howard, Co-Executors of the Estate of John C. Ravert, Deceased v. A.W. CHESTERTON CO., Ace Hardware Corp., Monsey Products Co., Pecora Corp. and Union Carbide Corp.	*Howard v. A.W. Chesterton Co.*,
Goodwyn, Mills & Cawood Company, Inc., a corporation, Plaintiff, v. Black Swamp, Inc. d/b/a Black Swamp Mitigation Bank, a corporation, and Murphree Evans, an individual, Defendants	*Goodwyn, Mills & Cawood Co. v. Black Swamp, Inc.*,
Florida Bar, Petitioner, v. Went For It, Inc., and John T. Blakely, Respondents.	*Fla. Bar v. Went For It, Inc.*, 515 U.S. 618 (1995).

12.2(e)(2) Abbreviated words in organization name

Abbreviate all words in an organization's name (apart from a person's name) that appear in **Appendix 3(E)**.[35] For abbreviations of geographic terms in organization names, see **Rule 12.2(f)** and **Appendix 3(B)**. If the caption uses an abbreviation that differs from the abbreviation for the same word shown in **Appendices 3(B)**, **3(E)**, or **Chart 12.1**, use the ALWD abbreviation.

CHART 12.1 Common Organization and Business Designations[41]

Where the chart indicates options between abbreviations *with* or *without* periods, use the option shown in the caption, if any. For other entity designations, see **Appendix 3(E)**.

Association	Ass'n	Limited Partnership	LP *or* L.P.
Board	Bd.	National Association	N.A.
Company	Co.	National Trust and Savings Association	NT & SA *or* N.T. & S.A.
Cooperative	Coop.	Organization	Org.
Corporation	Corp.	Partnership	P'ship
Federal Savings Bank	F.S.B.	Professional Association	PA *or* P.A.
Incorporated	Inc.	Professional Corporation	PC *or* P.C.
Institute	Inst.	Professional Limited Liability Company	PLLC *or* P.L.L.C.
Limited	Ltd.	Registered Limited Liability Partnership	RLLP *or* R.L.L.P.
Limited Liability Company	LLC *or* L.L.C.	Railroad	R.R.
Limited Liability Limited Partnership	LLLP *or* L.L.L.P.	Railway	Ry.
Limited Liability Partnership	LLP *or* L.L.P.	Society	Soc'y

Unless otherwise indicated in **Appendix 3(E)**, form an abbreviation's plural by adding "s" to the end.[36] You may abbreviate other words of eight or more letters if the abbreviation will save substantial space and will be easily understood by readers.[37]

Examples

Caption:

Ronald M. Bendalin, Appellant,
v.
Youngblood & Associates, a Texas General Partnership, Eldon L. Youngblood, Hilary Youngblood, and David Pederson, Appellees

Case name:

Bendalin v. Youngblood & Assocs.,

MEDIA GENERAL CABLE OF FAIRFAX, INC., Plaintiff-Appellant, v. SEQUOYAH CONDOMINIUM COUNCIL OF CO-OWNERS; AMSAT Communication, Incorporated, Defendants-Appellees	*Media Gen. Cable of Fairfax, Inc. v. Sequoyah Condo. Council of Co-Owners,*

12.2(e)(3) Commonly known initials in organization name

"Commonly known initials" or acronyms are a form of abbreviation that people tend to use—in ordinary speech—in place of an organization's full name (e.g., ACLU, EEOC, NBC, NAACP, SEC).[38] Organizations include government agencies (**Rule 12.2(k)**). When there is no danger of confusion, you may substitute commonly known initials for an organizational party's complete name.[39] Do not insert periods or spaces between commonly known initials.[40] If you are uncertain whether the initials are commonly known, use the appropriate abbreviations for words in the organization's complete name (e.g., Nat'l Broad. Co.).

Example

Caption:	**Case name:**
Alliance for Community Media, et al., Petitioners, v. Federal Communications Commission, et al., Respondents	*All. for Cmty. Media v. FCC,*

12.2(f) Geographic reference in organizational party name

Many organizational party names contain geographic references. Abbreviate any word that appears in **Appendix 3(B)**.[42] If the words "United States" are part of an *organization's* name, abbreviate them as "U.S."[43] This rule does not apply to a governmental entity. Follow **Rule 12.2(h)** when the United States of America is itself a party; **Rule 12.2(i)** when a state or commonwealth is a party; and **Rule 12.2(j)** when a city or municipality is a party. Except in union names (see **Rule 12.2(g)**), if an organization has a national or larger geographic reference (e.g., "of America," "of Russia," "of Asia"), do not omit it.[44]

The guiding principle pertaining to geographic terms in an organization's name is that if it is part of the full name of a business or organization, do not omit it.[45] In any other instance, follow the remaining rules for organizations. If there are two geographic references in an organization name (such as a town name, a comma, and the state), omit the one after the comma.[46] If the geographic term does not follow the term "City" and is a prepositional phrase with a location, omit it unless it would only leave one word in a party name.[47] Retain all geographic terms that are not part of a prepositional phrase.[48]

Examples

Caption:	Case name:
Kathleen GASPER, appellant, v. RUFFIN HOTEL CORPORATION OF MARYLAND, INC., appellee.	*Gasper v. Ruffin Hotel Corp. of Md., Inc.*,
Leo O. LaBRANCHE, Jr., petitioner, v. UNITED STATES OLYMPIC COMMITTEE, respondent.	*LaBranche v. U.S. Olympic Comm.*,
PLANNED PARENTHOOD OF COLORADO, plaintiff, v. The City of DENVER, COLORADO, defendant.	*Planned Parenthood of Colo. v. City of Denver*,
VERMONT ASSOCIATION OF TRUSTEES, petitioner, v. SONY CORPORATION OF AMERICA, respondent.	*Vt. Ass'n of Trs. v. Sony Corp. of Am.*,

12.2(g) Union as party

Indicate the name of a union as it is shown in the caption.[49] If the party is a local unit of the union, omit the caption's subsequent references to larger affiliations (e.g., AFL-CIO),[50] and omit all prepositional phrases indicating location (e.g., "of America," or "of New York").[51] Retain only the first craft or industry designation and omit the others.[52] Otherwise, follow **Rule 12.2(e)** for organization names.

Examples

Caption:	Case name:
Road Sprinkler Fitters Local Union No. 669, U.A., AFL-CIO, Plaintiff-Appellant, v. Dorn Sprinkler Company; Dorn Fire Protection, LLC; Christopher Dorn; David Dorn, Defendants-Appellees	*Road Sprinkler Fitters Local Union No. 669 v. Dorn Sprinkler Co.*,
Jesse James, Plaintiff, v. Enterprise Association of Steamfitters Local 638 of the United Association of Steam, Hot Water, Hydraulic and General Pipe Fitters of New York and Vicinity, Defendant	*James v. Enter. Ass'n of Steamfitters Local 638*,

12.2(h) United States as party

When the government of the United States of America is a party, refer to it as "United States"; do not abbreviate it as "US" or "U.S.," regardless of how it may appear in the caption.[53] If the words "of America" are displayed in the caption, omit them.[54] However, when the caption displays the words "United States" as part of the name of a federal department or agency (**Rule 12.2(k)**) or as part of an organization's name (**Rule 12.2(e)**), abbreviate them as "U.S."[55]

Examples

Caption:	**Case name:**
United States of America, Plaintiff-Appellee, v. Johnny E. Hatcher, Defendant-Appellant	*United States v. Hatcher,*
UNITED STATES DEPARTMENT OF COMMERCE, et al., Appellants v. MONTANA, et al., Appellees	*U.S. Dep't of Com. v. Montana,*
Toth v. United States Steel Corp.	*Toth v. U.S. Steel Corp.,*

12.2(i) State, commonwealth, or territory as party

When an American state or territory is a party, examine the caption to determine whether the case was decided by a *court of the same jurisdiction* (e.g., the State of Texas in a case decided by the Texas Supreme Court; the People of Colorado in a case decided by the Colorado Court of Appeals). In this situation, retain only the word "State," "Commonwealth," or "People," depending on which noun appears in the caption, omitting the prepositional phrase containing the state's or territory's name.[56]

The case may, however, have been decided by a *court in a different jurisdiction* (e.g., the State of Texas in a case decided by the United States Court of Appeals for the Fifth Circuit; the People of Colorado in a case decided by the United States Supreme Court). Here, omit the phrase "State of," "Commonwealth of," or "People of," and do not abbreviate the state's or territory's name.[57]

Examples

Caption:	**Case name:**
Richard Daniel Peters, Jr. v. Commonwealth of Virginia. Court of Appeals of Virginia.	*Peters v. Commonwealth,*

Caption:	Case name:
Lois Sharer; Steven Humber, Plaintiffs-Appellants, v. State of Oregon; Peter Ozanne; Peter Gartlan, Defendants-Appellees. United States Court of Appeals, Ninth Circuit.	*Sharer v. Oregon*,

12.2(j) City, municipality, or other local government as party

When a city, municipality, or other form of local government is a party, set out its full name, without abbreviating any of the words, omit "the" if that article is the first word of the party's name (**Rule 12.2(r)**),[58] and omit the name(s) of any larger geographic units that are set off from the city or municipality name by a comma (e.g., a county name or a state name).[59] Omit "City of," "County of," "Village of," "Township of," and similar phrases unless that phrase begins a party name.[60]

Examples

Caption:	Case name:
HISTORIC CHARLESTON FOUNDATION and Preservation Society of Charleston, Respondents, v. The CITY OF CHARLESTON, The City of Charleston City Council and Library Associates, LLC, Appellants	*Historic Charleston Found. v. City of Charleston*,
Mary Peters SCHRAMEL, et al., Appellants, v. Collegeville Township, Minnesota, Respondent	*Schramel v. Collegeville Township*,
Harry B. TREMENT, et al., Petitioner, v. BOARD OF ADJUSTMENT OF THE VILLAGE OF SPRINGFIELD, Respondent.	*Trement v. Bd. of Adjustment of Springfield*,

12.2(k) Other governmental entity as party

When a governmental agency, department, or other entity is the first-named party on either side of a case, follow **Rule 12.2(e)**, citing the name of that entity as you would that of an organization.[61] Represent the party's name as it appears in the caption, but abbreviate any words appearing in **Appendices 3(B)** or **3(E)**.[62] See **Rule 12.2(h)** for dealing with "United States" in the entity's name. Omit "City of," "County of," "Village of," "Township of," and similar phrases unless that phrase begins a party name.[63]

When there is no danger of confusion, you may substitute commonly known initials (e.g., FAA, NLRB, OSHA, SEC) for the entity's name, as explained in **Rule 12.2(e)(3)**.[64]

Examples

Caption:	**Case name:**
Sylvester Grandberry, Petitioner, v. Department of Homeland Security, Respondent	*Grandberry v. Dep't of Homeland Sec.*,
UNITED STATES DEPARTMENT OF JUSTICE, et al., Petitioners, v. REPORTERS COMMITTEE FOR FREEDOM OF THE PRESS, et al., Respondents	*U.S. Dep't of Just. v. Reps. Comm. for Freedom of the Press*,

12.2(l) Commissioner of Internal Revenue as party

Typically abbreviate "Commissioner" as "Comm'r"; omit the prepositional phrase "of Internal Revenue."[65] It is not uncommon, however, for tax specialists and tax publications to use the unabbreviated term "Commissioner." (For more information about tax cases, see **Appendix 6**.)

Example

Caption:	**Case name:**
Lawrence VIVENZIO and Gloria E. Vivenzio, Petitioners, v. COMMISSIONER OF INTERNAL REVENUE, Respondent	*Vivenzio v. Comm'r*,

12.2(m) Public official as party

When an individual who is a public official is the first-named party on either side of a case, follow **Rule 12.2(d)** to refer to him or her by surname, and omit reference to the person's governmental title. See **Sidebar 12.2** for guidance in citing cases in which a public official is replaced by a successor.

SIDEBAR 12.2 **Public Official Named as Party**

When a federal public official is a party to an action in his or her official capacity and the official leaves office during the pendency of the case, the case name changes to that of the successor. Fed. R. Civ. P. 25(d). Many state rules of civil procedure contain similar provisions about substituting public officials.

For example, although Mickey Kantor was Secretary of Commerce when Abraham Friedman brought suit in the Court of International Trade in 1996, by the time the case was appealed to the Federal Circuit, William Daley was the Secretary of Commerce. Thus the case *Friedman v. Kantor*, 977 F. Supp. 1242 (Ct. Int'l Trade 1997) was affirmed on appeal *sub nom. Friedman v. Daley*, 156 F.3d 1358 (Fed. Cir. 1998). (See **Rule 12.8(e)** for more about "*sub nom.*," a Latin abbreviation meaning "under the name of.")

Example

Caption:	**Case name:**
Ralph E. Price, Plaintiff-Appellant, v. Leon E. Panetta, Secretary of Defense, Department of Defense, and United States, Defendants-Appellees	*Price v. Panetta*,

12.2(n) Real or personal property as party

When a caption lists real or personal property as a party, cite only the first-listed item of such property.[66] If the caption displays an address for real property, use only the street address.[67] Omit words following the first comma in the party's name, such as larger geographic designations or vehicle identification numbers.[68] Abbreviate any words found in **Appendix 3(E)**.[69]

Examples

Caption:	**Case name:**
UNITED STATES of America, Plaintiff, v. REAL PROPERTY LOCATED AT 6415 NORTH HARRISON AVE., FRESNO COUNTY, et al., Defendants	*United States v. 6415 N. Harrison Ave.*,
United States of America, Plaintiff, v. One 1987 Chevrolet Corvette, VIN 1G1YY3189H5125250, Defendant	*United States v. One 1987 Chevrolet Corvette*,

12.2(o) Relator as party; procedural phrase *ex rel.*

A "relator" is a person or entity who sues or defends on behalf of another interested party or entity who cannot act in its own capacity, such as a parent on behalf of a minor child, a guardian on behalf of a ward, or an agency on behalf of a claimant. The procedural phrase "*ex rel.*" indicates that a relator stands in for the affected party. These relationships are also indicated by relationship phrases in the caption such as "by and through," "for the use of," "on behalf of," and "on the relation of," to name a few.

Begin with the relator's name, followed by the italicized procedural phrase *ex rel.* (in place of any other relationship phrase used in the caption) and then the name of the interested party or entity.[70]

When a caption shows multiple relators or interested parties, cite only the first-named relator or interested party per side.[71] When a caption lists the interested party first, *change the order* so as to begin the case name with that of the relator. (It is impossible for the *interested party* to act on the *relator*'s behalf.) When a caption identifies a party as participating both individually and as a relator, use the status indicated first (i.e., only use the relator status if that one is indicated first); if a person is first identified as acting individually, omit reference to the person as a relator.

Examples

Caption:	Case name:
Wayne MYLES, Appellant, v. FLORIDA DEPARTMENT OF REVENUE on behalf of Natricia A. BATCHELOR, Appellee	*Myles v. Fla. Dep't of Revenue ex rel. Batchelor,*
Nydreeka Williams, by and through her Mother and next friend, Theresa Raymond, and Theresa Raymond, as Administrator of the Estate of Robert Earl Williams, Deceased v. Wal-Mart Stores East, L.P., and Martha Parker	*Raymond ex rel. Williams v. Wal-Mart Stores E., L.P.,*
Keisha Hunt, Individually and on Behalf of her Minor Child, M.H. v. McNeil Consumer Healthcare, et al.	*Hunt v. McNeil Consumer Healthcare,*

12.2(p) Procedural phrases *in re* and *ex parte*

12.2(p)(1) General rules for using *in re* and *ex parte*

Use the italicized procedural phrases "*in re*" and "*ex parte*" when they or their synonyms appear in case names. If a caption displays more than one procedural phrase, use only the first.

The phrase "*in re*" ("concerning" or "with regard to") labels an in rem proceeding, one that involves a thing or a status, such as a foreclosure or a proposed public project. "*In re*" replaces synonyms such as "in the matter of," "matter of," "petition of," and "application of."[72]

"*Ex parte*" means "from or on behalf of only one side to a lawsuit." It labels an action made by, for, or on behalf of one party, often without notice to or contest by the other side. For example, an *ex parte* divorce hearing is one in which only one spouse participates and the other does not appear. Habeas corpus proceedings for wrongful convictions often display "*ex parte*" case names on behalf of the prisoner.

When a caption places one of these procedural phrases before an adversarial party name (look for the "*v.*"), drop the procedural phrase.[73] If a caption displays more than one procedural phrase, use only the first.[74] For procedural phrases in bankruptcy cases, see **Rule 12.2(p)(2)**.

Examples

Caption:	**Case name:**
In the Matter of the Adoption of F.I.T.	*In re Adoption of F.I.T.*,
In the Matter of the Administrative Order with Penalty Issued to Architektur, Inc., Philip Carlson and Virginia Carlson, a/k/a Gina Carlson	*In re Admin. Order with Penalty Issued to Architektur, Inc.*,
Ex parte Sherman D. GEORGE	*Ex parte George*,
Ex parte TYSON FOODS, INC., et al. (In re Reba Kirkley, as administratrix of the estate of Allen Hayes, deceased v. Tyson Foods, Inc., et al.)	*Ex parte Tyson Foods, Inc.*,
In re L. Dennis KOZLOWSKI, Petitioner-Respondent, v. NEW YORK STATE BOARD OF PAROLE, Respondent-Appellant	*Kozlowski v. N.Y. State Bd. of Parole*,

12.2(p)(2) Procedural phrase in bankruptcy case name

Captions for bankruptcy cases often display two names, one adversarial (*Party v. Party*) and one non-adversarial (typically using "*in re*").[75] If the caption for a bankruptcy case displays two names, use the adversarial name, even if it is not listed first.[76] If desired, you may supply the non-adversarial name in parentheses following the adversarial case name.[77]

Example

Caption: In re Frank Lamont Swain and Esther Marie Swain, Debtors
Frank Lamont Swain and Esther Marie Swain, Plaintiffs-Appellants v. Dredging, Inc., d/b/a Scott's Concrete and Jane Ellen Martin, Defendants-Appellees

Case name: *Swain v. Dredging, Inc.,*

Alternative: *Swain v. Dredging, Inc. (In re Swain),*

12.2(q) Case known by popular name

A case occasionally becomes well known by a popular name, as opposed to the formal name that appears in its caption.[78] If the case is always referred to in the literature by its popular name, you may replace the formal name that appears in the reporter with the popular name, or you may add the popular name parenthetically after the case's formal name.[79] However, if the case is often referred to by its formal name as well as its popular name, use the formal name for the citation; you may then parenthetically indicate the popular name, if desired.[80] If used in a parenthetical, the popular name should be italicized, but the parentheses should not.[81] Do not omit "The" in a popular name's citation, but do omit it in a textual sentence.[82]

Example

Caption: UNITED STATES v. STANLEY.; UNITED STATES v. RYAN.; UNITED STATES v. NICHOLS.; UNITED STATES v. SINGLETON.; ROBINSON & Wife v. MEMPHIS AND CHARLESTON RAILROAD COMPANY.

Case name: *The Civil Rights Cases,*
or
United States v. Stanley (The Civil Rights Cases),

12.2(r) "The" as first word of party's name

Omit "the" when it is the first word in a party's name, unless it is part of the name of an object in an in rem action (see **Rule 12.2(p)**), it refers to an established popular name (see **Rule 12.2(q)**), or it refers to "The King" or "The Queen" as a party.[83]

Examples

Caption:	**Case name:**
The New Yorker Magazine, Inc., Appellant, v. Lawrence E. Gerosa, Comptroller of the City of New York, and George M. Bragalini, Treasurer of the City of New York	*New Yorker Magazine, Inc. v. Gerosa*,
In re The EXXON VALDEZ	*In re The Exxon Valdez*,
Barry Victor Randall, Appellant, v. The Queen, Respondent	*Randall v. The Queen*,

12.2(s) Case with multiple decisions

When multiple decisions have been issued in a single case, it may help readers to enumerate each decision parenthetically with a short case name followed by a Roman numeral.[84] The enumeration may either be embedded within non-italicized parentheses following the formal case name or set out in a [hereinafter] construction following the court/date parenthetical (**Rule 11.5**).[85] The enumeration may also be used in textual sentences.[86]

Examples

In 1999, the Tenth Circuit Court of Appeals vacated its 1998 decision in the same case. In writing about both decisions, an author may differentiate the cases with enumerations.

Case reference options:	*United States v. Singleton*, 144 F.3d 1343 (10th Cir. 1998) (*Singleton I*).
	United States v. Singleton, 165 F.3d 1297 (10th Cir. 1999) [hereinafter *Singleton II*].
Textual reference:	In *Singleton II*, the court held . . .

12.3 Reporter Volume

Reporters are hard-copy books that print case opinions in chronological order. Some reporters print cases from only one particular state (state reporters) and some collect cases from multiple states and print them together (regional reporters). Sometimes cases are "unreported," meaning that they are not published in bound publications at all, and you should consult **Rule 12.14** for how to cite to those. A case is customarily cited to its publication in a print reporter, even when the researcher has located the case through a commercial database or some other source. Following the italicized case name and its concluding comma in ordinary type, insert the volume number of the cited reporter, in ordinary type and set off with a space on either side.[87] (For citations to cases reported in other media, see **Rules 12.11–12.14**; for cases not published in a reporter, see **Rule 12.14.**)

Example (reporter volume in red)

Jenkins v. Hestand's Grocery, Inc., 898 S.W.2d 30 (Ark. 1995).

12.4 Reporter Name

12.4(a) Abbreviation and series

Following the reporter volume number, insert the reporter's abbreviation (**Rule 12.4(b)**), in ordinary type and followed by one space.[88] **Chart 12.2** shows abbreviations for the most commonly used reporters, with red triangles (▲) indicating required spaces. For names and abbreviations of other reporters (e.g., those utilized by specialized federal courts or official reporters containing a specific state's cases), consult the jurisdiction's entry in **Appendix 1(A)** or **1(B)**.[89] If you are drafting a document you will file in court, consult **Rule 2.2(a)** for information on closing spaces in reporter abbreviations.

Once a reporter reaches a set number of volumes (typically 999, but sometimes fewer), its publisher issues a new series and begins numbering the volumes again. For series subsequent to the first, add the series number to the reporter abbreviation, using an ordinal contraction (**Rule 4.3(b)**).[90] If the ordinal contraction follows a single-letter abbreviation, omit space between the abbreviation and the contraction, as shown in **Chart 12.2**.[91]

12.4(b) Reporter selection

Unless the case is published in a single reporter, select the most appropriate reporter for your situation, considering the type of document you are drafting, the availability of the desired version, the identity of the court issuing the opinion, and the expectations or requirements of the courts or other readers. A case may be published in its jurisdiction's "official reporter" (by government authorization publishing solely the decisions of that jurisdiction) or in a "regional reporter" (an unofficial reporter containing decisions of several jurisdictions). See **Chart 12.2**. The remainder of **Rule 12.4(b)** provides instruction for selecting the appropriate reporter for published opinions. For cases in the public domain, slip opinions, cases in forthcoming publications, or unpublished cases, see **Rules 12.11–12.14**.

12.4(b)(1) Selecting reporter for citation in court document

In court documents such as motions and briefs, cite the reporter(s) required by the court's local rule, if any.[92] For links and citations to local rule sources, see **Appendices 2(A)** and **2(B)**. In the absence of a local rule, select the

CHART 12.2 **Abbreviations for Commonly Used Reporters[93] (spaces denoted by ▲)**

United States Reports	U.S.
Supreme Court Reporter	S.▲Ct.
United States Supreme Court Reports, Lawyers' Edition	L.▲Ed. L.▲Ed.▲2d
United States Law Week	U.S.L.W.
Federal Reporter (federal circuit courts of appeal)	F. F.2d F.3d
Federal Appendix (federal cases not designated for publication in *Federal Reporter)*	F.▲App'x
Federal Supplement (federal district courts, United States Customs Court, United States Court of Federal Claims, United States Court of International Trade, Judicial Panel on Multidistrict Litigation)	F.▲Supp. F.▲Supp.▲2d F.▲Supp.▲3d
Federal Rules Decision (federal district courts)	F.R.D.
Bankruptcy Reporter	B.R.
Atlantic Reporter (Connecticut, Delaware, District of Columbia, Maine, New Hampshire, New Jersey, Pennsylvania, Rhode Island, Vermont)	A. A.2d A.3d
California Reporter	Cal.▲Rptr. Cal.▲Rptr.▲2d Cal.▲Rptr.▲3d
New York Supplement	N.Y.S. N.Y.S.2d N.Y.S.3d
North Eastern Reporter (Illinois, Indiana, Massachusetts, New York, Ohio)	N.E. N.E.2d N.E.3d
North Western Reporter (Iowa, Michigan, Minnesota, Nebraska, North Dakota, South Dakota, Wisconsin)	N.W. N.W.2d
Pacific Reporter (Alaska, Arizona, California, Colorado, Hawai'i, Idaho, Kansas, Montana, Nevada, New Mexico, Oklahoma, Oregon, Utah, Washington, Wyoming)	P. P.2d P.3d

(*Continued*)

CHART 12.2 **Abbreviations for Commonly Used Reporters[93] (spaces denoted by ▲ (*Continued*)**

South Eastern Reporter (Georgia, North Carolina, South Carolina, Virginia, West Virginia)	S.E. S.E.2d
South Western Reporter (Arkansas, Kentucky, Missouri, Tennessee, Texas)	S.W. S.W.2d S.W.3d
Southern Reporter (Alabama, Florida, Louisiana, Mississippi)	So. So.▲2d So.▲3d

reporter following the order of preference set out for non-court documents in **Rule 12.4(b)(2)**. An official reporter is not necessarily the preferred reporter. **Appendices 1(A)** and **1(B)** list reporters in order of citation preference.[94]

Local rules of court may require citation to an official reporter (including an official public domain version, addressed in **Rule 12.11**).[95] In some states, you may be required to cite both the official reporter or public domain version and a regional reporter (a practice known as "parallel citation," covered in **Rule 12.4(c)**).[96] Consult the jurisdiction's entry in **Appendix 1(B)** to determine the official reporter for the state's appellate courts. Official reporters are marked with a red star [★]. It is common for a state to have two official reporters, one for cases decided by its highest appellate court and another for cases from its intermediate appellate court.

12.4(b)(2) Selecting reporter for citation in non-court document

In non-court documents such as office memoranda, seminar papers, and law review articles, cite a published case to a single reporter, as addressed more fully below.[97] Local court rules do not apply to these kinds of documents, and if you are citing a case that is awaiting publication in a reporter (**Rule 12.13**), you do not need parallel citations to two or more reporters (**Rule 12.4(c)**).

12.4(b)(3) Selecting reporter for published federal case

When selecting a reporter for a published federal case, distinguish between cases from the United States Supreme Court and cases from lower federal courts. All cases from the United States Supreme Court are published.

Cite a *United States Supreme Court* case decided *later than 1874* to a single reporter, in the order of preference set out below.[98]

- *United States Reports*;
- *Supreme Court Reporter*;

- *Rapp's In Chambers Opinions*;
- *United States Supreme Court Reports, Lawyers' Edition;*
- *United States Law Week*.

Cite a published case from a *lower federal court* (circuit court of appeals, district court, or specialty federal court) to a West federal reporter, whether a general or specialty reporter (e.g., *Federal Reports*, *Federal Supplement*, *Bankruptcy Reporter*, *Veterans Appeals Reporter*).[99] For *unpublished cases*, see **Rule 12.14** and **Sidebar 12.8**.

12.4(b)(4) Supreme Court case in nominative reporter

The first ninety volumes of *United States Reports* (containing cases decided *in or before 1874*) were named for the editors who compiled the cases for publication (hence the term "nominative reporter").[100] Citations to cases in *United States Reports* from that period should include a parenthetical reference to the corresponding volume and abbreviation of the nominative reporter.[101] Place the parenthetical immediately after "U.S.," the abbreviation for *United States Reports*.[102] See **Sidebar 12.3** for the nominative reporter abbreviations, their corresponding volumes of *United States Reports*, and the years each nominative reporter published Supreme Court cases. If the page numbering in the nominative reporter differs from that in *United States Reports*, present the two reporters as parallel citations, following **Rule 12.4(c)**.[103]

SIDEBAR 12.3 United States Supreme Court Nominative Reporters[104]

Nominative Reporter (Abbreviation):	Corresponding U.S. Volumes:	Years of Publication:
Dallas (Dall.)	1–4	1789–1800
Cranch (Cranch)	5–13	1801–1815
Wheaton (Wheat.)	14–25	1816–1827
Peters (Pet.)	26–41	1828–1842
Howard (How.)	42–65	1843–1860
Black (Black)	66–67	1861–1862
Wallace (Wall.)	68–90	1863–1874

The dates of the Court's decisions are not shown in the captions of the first 107 volumes of *United States Reports* (from 1789 through the 1882 term). Because a case citation requires a date (**Rule 12.7**), consult a reliable source, such as *Dates of Supreme Court Decisions and Arguments: United States Reports Volumes 2–107, 1791–1882*, https://www.supremecourt.gov/opinions/datesofdecisions.pdf.

Examples

United States v. Hudson, 11 U.S. (7 Cranch) 32, 34 (1812).

Trs. of Dartmouth Coll. v. Woodward, 17 U.S. (14 Wheat.) 518, 644 (1819).

12.4(b)(5) Selecting publication source for state case

In non-court documents, unless the case has been reported under an *official* public domain citation (**Rule 12.11**) or unless a parallel citation is needed (**Rule 12.4(c)**), cite a published case from a state supreme or intermediate appellate court to a single publication source, in the following order of preference[105]:

- the regional reporter in West's National Reporter System (see **Chart 12.2**);
- for a case from California or New York, West's *California Reporter* or *New York Supplement*;
- an official state reporter (e.g., *New Jersey Superior Court Reports*, *Oregon Reports*, *Pennsylvania State Reports*);
- a preferred unofficial reporter;
- a commercial database such as Westlaw Edge, Lexis+, or Bloomberg Law;
- a looseleaf reporter or service (**Rule 24**);
- a slip opinion (**Rule 12.12**);
- an internet source; or
- a newspaper.

When citing a case that appears in both the *Pacific Reporter* and West's *California Reporter*, or in both the *North Eastern Reporter* and West's *New York Supplement*, cite the *Pacific Reporter* or *North Eastern Reporter* version. Do not cite a state-specific unofficial reporter unless you are submitting a court document to a court in a jurisdiction that requires or prefers citation to West's state-specific reporters.[106]

ACADEMIC FORMATTING

For academic writing, if a case is available as an official public domain citation, you must use that citation first, and include a parallel citation to a regional reporter in West's National Reporter System.[107]

12.4(c) Indicating reporters in parallel citations

A parallel citation displays two or more publication sources for the same case, typically one in an official reporter and another in an unofficial reporter.[108] Provide a parallel citation in only the following situations:

- when a local rule of court requires parallel citation (see jurisdiction's entry in **Appendix 2(B)**);[109]
- when the case is published in a print reporter, but it has also been assigned an official public domain citation (**Rule 12.11**);[110] or
- when the case's publication in a print reporter is forthcoming (**Rule 12.13**).

When parallel citation is required, set out the official reporter or public domain citation first, followed by citation to the unofficial print reporter.[111] Consult **Appendix 1** to determine which reporters are official (marked with a red star [★]) and which are unofficial. For pinpoint references in parallel citations, see **Rule 12.5(c)**.

Examples

O'Connell v. Kirchner, 513 U.S. 1303, 1304, 115 S. Ct. 891, 892, 130 L. Ed. 2d 873, 875 (1995).

In re Estate of Netherton, 62 Ill. App. 3d 55, 57–58, 378 N.E.2d 800, 802 (1978).

For forthcoming publications, the parallel citation indicates the intended print reporter, followed by a citation to its version in a commercial database, as described and illustrated in **Rule 12.13**.

SIDEBAR 12.4 Locating Parallel Citations

When a case is published in only a single reporter, it will not have a parallel citation. When you must provide a parallel citation, you may find references to parallel reporters by consulting:

- the first page of the West reporter version;
- the first page of the official reporter version;
- the running head or caption of the Bloomberg Law, Lexis, or Westlaw version; or
- the case's entry in a citator such as BCite, KeyCite, or Shepard's.

12.5 Page Numbers

A case's full citation requires the initial page number in the publication, followed by a pinpoint page reference to the specific material cited.[112] A commercial database version will indicate the pagination used by the print reporter(s). See **Rule 5.5(b)** for help distinguishing page numbers on Westlaw Edge or Lexis+.

12.5(a) Initial page number

Following the reporter abbreviation, insert a space and the case's initial page number, i.e., the page on which the caption appears, signaling the beginning of the published case.[113] In parallel citations, provide the initial page for the case in each reporter, immediately after the reporter abbreviation (see examples in **Rule 12.5(c)**).[114]

12.5(b) Pinpoint references in general

When you refer to specific material in a case, add a comma after the initial page, a space, and a pinpoint reference.[115] Most published cases use page numbers as pinpoint references (see **Rule 5.2**). If the pinpoint reference spans more than one page, indicate the entire span, dropping all repetitious digits but the final two.[116] Remember that **Rule 4.1** does not apply to case reporters that do not themselves insert a comma to create groups of three numerals when a number is four or more numerals long.[117]

Many states now number paragraphs in their opinions. Use **Appendix 2(B)** to identify states that require public domain citations that indicate pinpoint references by paragraph numbers.[118] See **Rule 12.5(e)** to indicate pinpoint references to paragraph numbers in states that do not use public domain citation. In both instances, refer to **Rule 6** for more rules about citing to paragraphs. For specific information about handling pinpoint references for cases that do not fit the norm for print reporters, see **Rule 12.5(e)** (cases), **Rule 12.11** (public domain), **Rule 12.12** (slip opinions), **Rule 12.13** (forthcoming publication), and **Rule 12.14** (*Federal Appendix*, commercial databases, looseleaf services, and internet).

Examples

Chambers v. Bowersox, 157 F.3d 560, 566 (8th Cir. 1998).

In re Estate of Hewitt, 721 A.2d 1082, 1085–86 (Pa. 1998).

12.5(c) Pinpoint references in parallel citations

In a parallel citation to an official print reporter and an unofficial reporter (**Rule 12.4(c)**), provide pinpoint references to pages in both the official and the unofficial reporter.[119] If the official public domain version uses subdivisions other than pages for pinpoint references, such as paragraphs, use those subdivisions as the pinpoint reference.[120]

It may not be necessary to consult both versions of the case to determine internal pagination; some print reporters—and all commercial databases—have devised methods to embed pagination for parallel reporters within the text of the case, a practice known as "star pagination" (see **Rule 5.5**). These devices include a variety of formats to indicate parallel page numbers in another reporter, such as numbers in superscript or bracketed subscript, or numbers preceded by one or more asterisks. For example, opinions in the unofficial *United States Supreme Court Reports, Lawyers' Edition* contain bracketed references to pagination used in those opinions in their official reporter, *United States Reports*. Where a public domain version uses paragraph numbers, these will be retained in the print reporter or commercial database.

Examples

Commonwealth v. Sell, 504 Pa. 46, 65, 470 A.2d 457, 467 (1983).

Tinker v. Des Moines Indep. Cmty. Sch. Dist., 393 U.S. 503, 506, 89 S. Ct. 733, 736, 21 L. Ed. 2d 731, 737 (1969).

Galle v. Isle of Capri Casino, Inc., 2013-CT-00024-SCT, ¶¶ 13–14, 180 So. 3d 619, 622 (Miss. 2015).

12.5(d) Pinpoint references in dissenting or concurring opinions

Following reference to the initial page of the case (**Rule 12.5(a)**), insert a pinpoint reference to the location of a dissenting or concurring opinion containing the cited material. See **Rule 12.10(b)** for additional requirements in citing dissenting or concurring opinions.

Example

Purkett v. Elam, 514 U.S. 765, 775 (Stevens & Brennan, JJ., dissenting).

12.5(e) Paragraph numbers as pinpoint references in published cases

Some jurisdictions number the paragraphs in opinions published in their official reporters, in addition to having page numbers, and require by local rule that attorneys use either the paragraph number alone or the paragraph number in addition to the page number as the pinpoint reference. If you are in such a jurisdiction, immediately following the comma after the pinpoint page number, insert a space, a paragraph symbol, a space, and the paragraph number. If the local rule does not require you to include the pinpoint page number in addition to the pinpoint paragraph number, omit the pinpoint page number, and in its place insert a paragraph symbol, a space, and the paragraph number. Follow the other rules about paragraphs in **Rule 6**. Do not follow **Rule 12.5(e)** for academic citations or if the opinion does not number the paragraphs in cases (i.e., do not count the paragraphs yourself). Follow the public domain citation format in **Appendix 2(B)** when citing to paragraphs in cases from states that require their own public domain citation format.

Examples

Scenic Ariz. v. Phx. Bd. of Adjustment, 228 Ariz. 419, ¶ 5 (2011).

or

Scenic Ariz. v. Phx. Bd. of Adjustment, 228 Ariz. 419, 422, ¶ 5 (2011).

12.6 Court Abbreviations

12.6(a) General rule for identifying court of decision

Each case citation must identify, in some form, the court that decided the matter, typically in a court/date parenthetical immediately following the initial page and pinpoint page references.[121] To create the parenthetical, insert an opening parenthesis, followed by the abbreviation for the court's name, as shown in **Appendices 1(A)**, **1(B)**, **4(A)**, or **4(B)**.[122] (Close the parentheses after inserting the date of decision (**Rule 12.7**).)[123]

Examples

Howard v. Wal-Mart Stores, Inc., 160 F.3d 358, 360 (7th Cir. 1998).

Webb v. Dixie-Ohio Express Co., 165 S.W.2d 539, 541 (Ky. 1942).

When the identity of the court can be discerned by other information in the citation (e.g., by an official reporter name), it is unnecessary to put the court's abbreviation (or its entire abbreviation) into the court/date parenthetical.[124] See **Rule 12.6(b)** for United States Supreme Court cases, **Rule 12.4(c)** for parallel citations, **Rule 12.11** for public domain citations, and **Rule 12.13** for cases not yet available in a print reporter.

Examples

Schutz v. La Costita III, Inc., 364 Or. 536, 541 (2019).

Miller v. Elisea, 302 Or. App. 188, 194 (2020).

But: *N.C. Farm Bureau Mutual Ins. Co. v. Lunsford*, 843 S.E.2d 677, 680 (N.C. Ct. App. 2020).

12.6(b) Identifying United States Supreme Court

When you cite a case to a reporter that publishes only cases from the United States Supreme Court, there is no question which court decided the case.[125] Therefore, omit the court abbreviation from the court/date parenthetical. Identify the court, however, when citing the case in *United States Law Week* ("U.S.L.W."),[126] a looseleaf service that published decisions of several different courts until it ceased publication in August 2018.

Examples

Correct:	*Penry v. Lynaugh*, 492 U.S. 302 (1989).
Incorrect:	*Penry v. Lynaugh*, 492 U.S. 302 (U.S. 1989).
Correct:	*Kloeckner v. Solis*, 81 U.S.L.W. 4018 (U.S. Dec. 10, 2012).
Incorrect:	*Kloeckner v. Solis*, 81 U.S.L.W. 4018 (Dec. 10, 2012).

12.6(c) Additional jurisdictional information in court name

12.6(c)(1) Federal court abbreviations

Citations to federal cases omit reference to divisions or units of federal district courts or circuit courts of appeals except as noted below in **Rules 12.6(c)(2)** and **12.6(c)(3)**.[127] When identifying a court of the United States Courts of Appeals, omit reference to the state in which the case originated.[128] Represent the ordinal numbers of a circuit court according to **Rule 4.3(b)**. Consult **Appendix 4(A)** for federal court abbreviations.

Examples

Correct: *Lipford v. Carnival Corp.*, 346 F. Supp. 2d 1276, 1278 (S.D. Fla. 2004).

Incorrect: *Lipford v. Carnival Corp.*, 346 F. Supp. 2d 1276, 1278 (S.D. Fla. Miami Div. 2004).

Correct: *Ezell v. City of Chicago*, 651 F.3d 684, 704 (7th Cir. 2011).

Incorrect: *Ezell v. City of Chicago*, 651 F.3d 684, 704 (7th Cir. (Ill.) 2011).

If a U.S. Supreme Court Justice took part in a decision in his or her capacity as a Circuit Justice in a lower court, immediately before the court abbreviation in the parenthetical, include the Justice's last name, a comma and a space, then "Circuit Justice,".[129]

Example

United States v. Spilotora, 800 F.2d 959, 967 (Kennedy, Circuit Justice, 9th Cir. 1986).

12.6(c)(2) Fifth Circuit split

On October 1, 1981, the United States Court of Appeals for the Fifth Circuit was divided to create two circuits, the Fifth and the Eleventh.[130] When the caption for a Fifth Circuit case preceding that date labels the court as "Unit A" or "Unit B," indicate that unit after the "5th Cir." abbreviation, and add the abbreviated month of decision.[131] If the caption contains a "Former Fifth Circuit" reference and the case was decided after September 30, 1981, use "Former 5th Cir." as the court abbreviation; omit the month of decision.[132]

Examples

Gullatte v. Potts, 654 F.2d 1007, 1012 (5th Cir. Unit B Aug. 1981).

Summer v. Land & Leisure, Inc., 664 F.2d 965, 969 (Former 5th Cir. 1981).

12.6(c)(3) Historic federal courts

In the original districts of Maine and Kentucky, and in many states admitted to the Union during the nineteenth century, the United States district court also exercised appellate jurisdiction until a district was incorporated into a specific judicial circuit. Only in 1889 did Congress provide for a circuit court of appeals to cover every judicial district, ending the expanded jurisdiction of certain district courts. When citing a case from an early federal district court exercising appellate jurisdiction, add the abbreviation "C.C." before the district court abbreviation,[133] and if shown in the caption, add the case's docket number in a separate parenthetical following the court/date parenthetical. See **Sidebar 12.7** for more information on docket numbers.

Similarly, when citing cases from the old federal circuits, which were abolished on June 1, 1912, follow the format for current United States Court of Appeals cases, but use the abbreviation "C.C." instead of "Cir." in the court/date parenthetical,[134] and add the case's docket number in a separate parenthetical.

For any other early court whose name differs from that of the modern court serving the jurisdiction, abbreviate the court name as it appears in the caption, analogizing to court abbreviations in **Appendices 1(A)** or **1(B)**.

Examples

Pierson v. Philips, 36 F. 837 (C.C.E.D. Tex. 1888).

United States v. Burr, 25 F. Cas. 55, 156–57 (C.C.D. Va. 1807) (No. 14,693).

United States ex rel. Stokes v. Kendall, 26 F. Cas. 702, 713 (C.C.D.C. 1837) (No. 15,517), *aff'd*, 37 U.S. (12 Pet.) 524 (1838).

12.6(c)(4) State court abbreviations

When you indicate a state court, use the court abbreviation shown in that state's entry in **Appendix 1(B)** or **Appendix 4(B)**.[135] If the decision is one from the highest court in the state, and you are citing to a regional reporter, use only the abbreviation for the state in a parenthetical, not the full name of the highest court.[136] Omit reference to departments, districts, counties, or other subdivisions unless the information is relevant.[137] If so, present the information in the order and numerical style used by that court, abbreviating any words found in **Appendix 3(G)**.[138]

Examples

Court abbreviation:	*Griffin v. Paul*, 901 So. 2d 1034, 1034 (Fla. Dist. Ct. App. 2005).
Relevant district:	*Griffin v. Paul*, 901 So. 2d 1034, 1034 (Fla. 2d Dist. Ct. App. 2005).
Decision from highest court in state reporter:	*Keodalah v. Allstate Ins. Co.*, 194 Wash. 2d 339, ¶ 6 (2019).
Decision from highest court in regional reporter:	*Keodalah v. Allstate Ins. Co.*, 449 P.3d 1040, ¶ 6 (Wash. 2019).

12.6(c)(5) Omission of court abbreviation in parallel and other citations

In a parallel citation or in any citation in which the name of the reporter unambiguously represents the court's identity, omit all or part of the court abbreviation in the court/date parenthetical if the name of one of the reporters clearly indicates the court of decision (e.g., *Iowa Reports*, *North Carolina Court of Appeals Reports*, Miss. App. LEXIS).[139]

Examples

Miller v. Commonwealth, 5 Va. App. 22, 25, 359 S.E.2d 841, 842 (1987).

State v. Davis, 283 Conn. 280, 299, 929 A.2d 278, 313 (2007).

People v. Albanese, 38 A.D. 1015, 1017, 831 N.Y.S.2d 280, 283 (2007).

Vancamp v. Decision HR 30, Inc., 2015 Fla. App. LEXIS 12452, at *1 (Aug. 19, 2015) (per curiam).

Fox v. Mize, 2018 OK 75, ¶ 5, 428 P.3d 314, 319.

12.7 Date of Decision

Set out the date on which the case was decided in the same parenthetical as the court abbreviation (if any).[140] For cases cited to print reporters, including the *Federal Appendix* and other reporters that print cases marked "unpublished," provide only the year of the decision.[141] For cases that are not published in reporters, provide the exact date (Month Day, Year) of the decision, abbreviating the month.[142] Local court rules addressing public domain citations have their own methods to indicate the date of decision; consult the jurisdiction's entry in **Appendix 2(B)**.

Examples

Guinan v. Tenet Healthsystems of Hilton Head, Inc., 677 S.E.2d 32, 36 (S.C. Ct. App. 2009).

Allen v. Adams, 2004 U.S. Dist. LEXIS 6313, at *4 (W.D. Tex. Mar. 30, 2004).

12.8 Subsequent History

An essential step in legal research is determining whether anything significant has happened to affect the precedential or persuasive value of a case since it was decided. Use citator tools like *Shepard's*, *BCite*, or *KeyCite* to check a case's subsequent history. Add subsequent history to the full citation of a case if the form of history—or an analogous form of history having similar effect—is addressed in **Rule 12.8(a)**. Some forms of subsequent history may be ignored, as explained in **Rule 12.8(b)**. For information on citing a case's *prior* history, see **Rule 12.9**.

12.8(a) Subsequent history to include

Chart 12.3 lists phrases and abbreviations for the most common forms of subsequent history; it is not an exhaustive list. Add the forms of subsequent history in the chart marked with an asterisk (*) *only if the cited case*—not the disposition or ruling indicated in the history—was decided within the last two years *or* if that case's history is particularly important to the discussion.[143] See **Sidebar 12.5** for a discussion of the certiorari petition, one form of history that can be "particularly important." Forms of subsequent history marked in the chart with a dagger (†) should be ignored after a *higher* court later makes some disposition of the cited case.

Many subsequent history phrases are abbreviated, as **Chart 12.3** illustrates. For other abbreviations that may be useful in constructing a subsequent history phrase, see **Appendix 3(G)**, but do not substitute an abbreviation from that appendix for the abbreviation shown in the chart. Pay attention to the presence or absence of a comma following the phrase; do not insert a comma following phrases ending in the prepositions "by," "from," or "to."[144] In other words, if the direct object of an abbreviation or phrase in **Chart 12.3** is a case citation (e.g., "*rev'g* [case citation]" or "*denying cert. to*" [case citation]), there is no comma after the abbreviation.[145] But if the abbreviation describes what happened to the case (e.g., "*aff'd*," or "*appeal denied*,"), you should include a non-italicized comma after the abbreviation.[146]

If relevant, the subsequent history phrase may use an expanded explanation for the disposition, such as *cert. dismissed as improvidently granted*, *vacated as moot*, *rev'd without opinion*, or *aff'd by an equally divided court*.[147]

12.8(b) Subsequent history to ignore

Ignore history concerning remands, rehearings, rehearings en banc, and similar matters unless the history is particularly relevant to the purpose for which the case is cited.[148] Similarly, unless it is relevant to the proposition for which a case is cited, ignore a denial of certiorari or a denial of a permissive appeal when *more than two years* have passed since the case's date of decision.[149] (For more information about certiorari petitions, see **Sidebar 12.5**.) Ignore history when the deciding court withdraws a disposition (e.g., when a court affirms a decision but then decides differently on a rehearing).[150]

12.8(c) Placement, format, and components of subsequent history phrases

Indicate subsequent history when citing a case in full.[151] *Do not* attach subsequent history to a short citation.[152]

Insert the subsequent history designation after the court/date parenthetical.[153] Italicize the history phrase but not the commas (if any) that precede or follow it.[154] Following the history phrase, set out the volume number, reporter

CHART 12.3	Subsequent History Phrases		
Abrogated by	*abrogated by*	Dismissing appeal from	*dismissing appeal from*
Affirmed	*aff'd,*	Enforced	*enforced,*
Affirmed on rehearing	*aff'd*	Invalidated by	*invalidated by*
Affirmed in part and reversed in part	*aff'd in part, rev'd in part,*	Mandamus denied	*mandamus denied,*
Affirmed on other grounds	*aff'd on other grounds,*	Modified	*modified,*
Affirmed on rehearing	*aff'd on reh'g,*	Overruled by	*overruled by*
Amended by	*amended by*	*Permissive appeal denied	*perm. app. denied,*
*Appeal denied	*appeal denied,*	†Permissive appeal granted	*perm. app. granted,*
*Appeal dismissed	*appeal dismissed,*	†Petition for certiorari filed	*petition for cert. filed,*
†Appeal docketed	*appeal docketed,*	Probable jurisdiction noted	*prob. juris. noted,*
†Appeal filed	*appeal filed,*	Rehearing granted	*reh'g granted,*
Argued	*argued,*	Rehearing denied	*reh'g denied,*
Certifying question to	*certifying question to*	Reversed	*rev'd,*
*Certiorari denied	*cert. denied,*	Reversed in part and affirmed in part	*rev'd in part, aff'd in part,*
*Certiorari dismissed	*cert. dismissed,*	Superseded by	*superseded by*
†Certiorari granted	*cert. granted,*	Vacated	*vacated,*
Depublished by	*depublished by*	Withdrawn	*withdrawn,*

abbreviation, initial page, and court/date parenthetical of the history case.[155] When the subsequent history is something other than a denial of certiorari and the case name has changed on appeal, however, follow **Rule 12.8(e)**.[156]

When a case's history is not separately reported but is denoted in the case's caption, set out the appropriate history phrase followed by a parenthetical with the court abbreviation and exact date (Month Day, Year) of the disposition; there is no additional reporter to cite.

If the history itself has history, set it out using another history designation.[157] Connect multiple decisions by a *single* court with the italicized word "*and*."[158]

Examples

Saregama India Ltd. v. Mosley, 687 F. Supp. 2d 1325 (S.D. Fla. 2009), *aff'd*, 635 F.3d 1284 (11th Cir. 2011).

EEOC v. Ilona of Hung. Inc., 108 F.3d 1569, 1574–75 (7th Cir. 1996, *modified on reh'g en banc*, Mar. 6, 1997).

Shell Oil Co. v. Meyer, 684 N.E.2d 504 (Ind. Ct. App. 1997), *vacated*, 698 N.E.2d 1183 (Ind.), *and aff'd in part, vacated in part*, 705 N.E.2d 962 (Ind. 1998).

SIDEBAR 12.5 Petition for Writ of Certiorari

A writ of certiorari is a device used by courts of last resort, such as the United States Supreme Court, that have discretion to select the cases they hear. If the party who lost in the court below seeks such discretionary review, that party files a "Petition for Writ of Certiorari." If the court grants the petition, it will hear the appeal. If the court denies the petition, it will not hear the appeal. A state's process for pursuing a "permissive appeal" operates similarly.

"*Cert. pending*" and "*Cert. granted*"

The process of appeal puts the correctness of the *lower court's* ruling in question; therefore, during the pendency of the appellate proceedings, a citation to the lower court's opinion must indicate that a higher court has agreed to review that ruling.[159]

When a citator flags a case to show that the losing party is seeking appellate review, indicate that status with a "*cert. pending*" subsequent history phrase. Once the higher court opts to hear the appeal, we can replace the "*cert. pending*" phrase with "*cert. granted*." When the higher court decides the appeal, whether affirming or reversing, the lower court case's *cert. granted* history becomes irrelevant.

"*Cert. denied*"

Denials of certiorari carry no precedential value; they do not indicate that the higher court agreed with the lower court's decision. Accordingly, denials of certiorari typically are not treated as subsequent history.[160] However, because these denials inform readers that the *lower court's* decision has become final, provide the history when the cited decision is two years old or less at the time of your document's preparation.[161] Two years reflects the time within which most cases are resolved on appeal. Look at the date in the caption of the lower court's opinion to determine whether two years have passed since it was issued.

Once the two-year period has passed, do not indicate a denial of certiorari unless that denial is particularly important to your topic or argument.[162] A denial of certiorari is important when the case is the focus of the discussion. It also is important when the higher court issues an opinion explaining why a petition for certiorari was denied, or when a judge issues a dissenting opinion concerning the denial of certiorari.

When one of these subsequent history phrases is required or important, append it to the citation of the lower court's case; the phrase tells readers its status during the time the case's fate is in question. Do not copy "*cert. pending*," "*cert. granted*," or "*cert. denied*" information from other sources, as they may not reflect the current status of a case.

12.8(d) Subsequent history in same year as original decision

When a case develops subsequent history in the same year that it was originally reported, the full citation omits the year from the court/date parenthetical component.[163] It instead sets out the year solely in the court/date parenthetical for the history case.[164]

Example

Nat. Res. Def. Council, Inc. v. Winter, 518 F.3d 658 (9th Cir.), *rev'd*, 555 U.S. 7 (2008).

12.8(e) Case name changed on appeal

When the subsequent history of a case indicates that its name changed in later proceedings, even when the difference is minor, indicate the new case name in the subsequent history phrase by using the italicized abbreviation "*sub nom.*" (meaning "under the name of").[165] Insert "*sub nom.*" and the new case name immediately after the history designation, followed by the rest of the subsequent history case components.[166] Do not put a comma after "*sub nom.*"[167]

Do not provide the case name after the subsequent history phrase when one of the following situations is present:

- The only change is a reversal of the parties' names;[168]
- The designation of a state shifts between "Commonwealth," "People," or "State," and the state's proper name (e.g., when a federal court hears an appeal from a case previously decided by a state court);[169] or
- The subsequent history is solely a denial of certiorari or rehearing.[170]

Examples

Macias v. Mine Safety Appliances Co., 244 P.3d 978 (Wash. Ct. App. 2010), *rev'd sub nom. Macias v. Saberhagen Holdings, Inc.*, 282 P.3d 1069 (Wash. 2012).

In re Iraq & Afg. Detainees Litig., 479 F. Supp. 2d 85, 105 (D.D.C. 2007), *aff'd sub nom. Ali v. Rumsfeld*, 649 F.3d 762 (D.C. Cir. 2011).

McHenry v. Fla. Bar, 808 F. Supp. 1543 (M.D. Fla. 1992), *aff'd*, 21 F.3d 1038 (11th Cir. 1994), *rev'd sub nom. Fla. Bar v. Went For It, Inc.*, 515 U.S. 618 (1995).

12.8(f) Abrogated, overruled, or superseded cases

The precedential effect of a case may be directly or indirectly altered by the subsequent actions of courts or legislatures. For example, a court may explicitly overrule one of its earlier cases, or it may abrogate one of its earlier decisions by deciding an outcome inconsistent with it. A statute may be enacted or a constitutional amendment may be approved in order to supersede the common law in a specific judicial decision. These actions must be treated as subsequent history appended to the full citation.[171]

When the same court that decided the case or a court with appellate jurisdiction over the original deciding court explicitly states in an opinion that it is overruling the cite you are citing, designate that case as "*overruled by*."[172] But if the same court or a court with appellate jurisdiction over the original deciding court only implicitly overrules the decision to which you are citing, indicate that with the phrase "*abrogated by*."[173] Do not use the phrase "*sub nom.*" before the name of a history case that overrules or abrogates the case you are citing; two different cases are involved, and the second case is not an appeal from the first.

When the legislature enacted a law with the intent to change the law stated in a case you are citing, you *must* indicate that the case was superseded by the law.[174] When citing to the law, use the session law citation, if available.[175] If a case decided after the law changed explicitly recognizes that the law was meant to overturn the case you are citing, you can choose to indicate that using "*as recognized in*."[176]

Examples

Baldasar v. Illinois, 446 U.S. 222 (1980), *overruled by Nichols v. United States*, 511 U.S. 738 (1994).

United States v. Barrett, 198 F. Supp. 2d 1046 (S.D. Iowa 2002), *abrogated by United States v. Griner*, 358 F.3d 979 (8th Cir. 2004).

Sutton v. United Air Lines, Inc., 527 U.S. 471 (1999), *superseded by statute*, ADA Amendments Act of 2008, Pub. L. No. 110-325, 122 Stat. 3553 (2008), *as recognized in Allen v. SouthCrest Hosp.*, 455 F. App'x 827 (10th Cir. 2011).

12.8(g) Parenthetical information regarding history

When a cited case is not extensively discussed in the text, it may be useful to provide an explanatory parenthetical, appended to the citation, summarizing the holding of the cited case, explaining its relevance, or providing a pertinent quotation.[177]

Follow **Rule 37** regarding placement of parentheticals, commentary, and treatment. If the parenthetical concerns the cited case, it should follow that case's full citation.[178] If the parenthetical concerns the history case, it should follow the history case's citation.[179]

For parentheticals relating to minority opinions or to the weight of authority, see **Rule 12.10**.

Examples

Parenthetical relates to cited case:	*Mapp v. Ohio*, 166 N.E.2d 387 (Ohio 1960) (holding that contraband obtained by an unlawful search is admissible evidence), *rev'd*, 347 U.S. 643 (1961).
Parenthetical relates to history case:	*Mapp v. Ohio*, 166 N.E.2d 387 (Ohio 1960), *rev'd*, 347 U.S. 643 (1961) (holding that evidence obtained by an unconstitutional search is inadmissible).

CHART 12.4	Prior History Phrases		
Acquiescing	*acq.*	Modifying	*modifying*
Acquiescing in result	*acq. in result*	Reversing	*rev'g*
Affirming	*aff'g*	Vacating	*vacating*
Enforcing	*enforcing*	Vacating as moot	*vacating as moot*

12.9 Prior History

"Prior history" concerns rulings and dispositions that took place before the cited opinion was reported. Add prior history to a citation only when it is significant to a point addressed in the document.[180] For example, a law review article discusses what happened in a case when it was still in the lower courts; in that instance, the writer might add its prior history to the citation. (On the other hand, when a case's early history is important, you may wish to cite those earlier rulings directly.)

Insert the prior history immediately following the case's full citation, in the same manner as subsequent history is appended (**Rule 12.8(c)**).[181] Do not attach prior history to a short citation. For prior history phrases, refer to the examples in **Chart 12.4** or modify abbreviations shown in **Chart 12.3**.

If citing both prior and subsequent histories, provide the prior history first.[182] Insert a comma followed by the italicized historical phrase before the subsequent history.[183]

Examples

Prior history in citation: *Edwards v. Nat'l Audubon Soc'y, Inc.*, 556 F.2d 113 (2d Cir. 1977), rev'g 423 F. Supp. 516 (S.D.N.Y. 1976).

Prior history and subsequent history in same citation: *McHenry v. Fla. Bar*, 21 F.3d 1038 (11th Cir. 1994), *aff'g* 808 F. Supp. 1543 (M.D. Fla. 1992), *rev'd sub nom. Fla. Bar v. Went For It, Inc.*, 515 U.S. 618 (1995).

12.10 Parenthetical Information

12.10(a) Parenthetical reference to weight of authority

You may parenthetically provide information about the precedential weight of a case.[184] For example, the parenthetical can identify an en banc decision or a per curiam opinion; identify the split among the judges who decided the case;

label the cited proposition as dictum as opposed to holding; and state whether a case was decided without an opinion, a disposition known as a "memorandum opinion" (abbreviated "mem.").[185] See **Rule 37.2** and **Sidebar 37.1** for additional information about placing and ordering parentheticals.

Examples

Ellis v. Anderson Tully Co., 727 So. 2d 716, 719–20 (Miss. 1998) (en banc).

Aguilar v. Felton, 473 U.S. 402, 414 (1985) (affirming 5–4).

Beer v. United States, 564 U.S. 1050, 1050 (2011) (mem.).

12.10(b) En banc, per curiam, plurality, dissenting, concurring, or in-chambers opinions

An "en banc" decision is one made by all of the judges of a particular court; it usually determines the outcome of a contested ruling made by a three-judge panel of that court. You may identify such a decision with a parenthetical that follows the case's *full citation*.[186]

A "plurality" decision is one in which no single judge or justice's opinion in a case (or on a discrete issue therein) received the support of a majority of the court, although it garnered more support than any other opinion. Indicate a plurality opinion with a parenthetical following the case's full citation, and omit reference to the names of the judges or justices who supported that opinion.[187]

A "per curiam" decision is an unsigned opinion attributed to the entire court, not to any particular judge.[188] You may indicate a per curiam opinion with a parenthetical appended to the case's *full citation*.[189]

Always identify a minority opinion (e.g., a dissent or a concurrence) in a parenthetical that follows the citation, no matter if it is a *full citation* or a *short citation* (including *id.*).[190] Set out the surname(s), a comma, and the title abbreviation(s) of all justices or judges who joined the opinion, in the order they are listed there.[191] See **Chart 12.5** for judicial title abbreviations. Only if a court has two justices or judges with the same surname should you include their first name in the citation.[192] Following the title abbreviation, add a comma, and indicate the type of minority opinion (e.g., "concurring," "concurring in part," "dissenting," "dissenting from Parts II and III of the opinion").[193]

An "in-chambers opinion" is one in which a single Supreme Court Justice rules on an application for a stay, bail, or injunction on behalf of the Court as a whole.[194] In-chambers decisions after 1969—and even a few before then—are published in the *United States Reports*.[195] Cite to the *United States Reports* for all in-chambers opinions, whether pre- or post-1969, if printed therein.[196] If citing to a pre-1969 case that was not published in the *United States Reports*, cite to it as part of *In Chamber Opinions by Justices of the Supreme Court of the United States* by Cynthia Rapp; state the case name, followed by a comma and a space, the volume number and a space, "Rapp," a space, the initial page

CHART 12.5 Abbreviations for Titles of Judges and Other Judicial Officials

Administrative Law Judge	A.L.J.	Judge, Justice	J.
Arbitrator	Arb.	Judges, Justices	JJ.
Assembly[man, member, woman]	Assemb.	Magistrate, Magistrate Judge	Mag.
Attorney General	Att'y Gen.	Master of the Rolls	M.R.
Baron	B.	Mediator	Med.
Chancellor	C.	Referee	Ref.
Chief Judge, Chief Justice	C.J.	Representative	Rep.
Commissioner	Comm'r	Senator	Sen.
Delegate	Del.	Vice Chancellor	V.C.
Honorable	Hon.		

number and a space, and the year in a parenthetical.[197] For all in-chambers opinions, indicate so with a parenthetical appended to the case's *full citation*.[198]

Do not italicize the terms used to indicate any of these opinions.[199]

Examples

United States v. Andis, 333 F.3d 886, 889–90 (8th Cir. 2003) (en banc).

Lease v. Tipton, 722 S.W.2d 379, 379 (Tenn. 1986) (per curiam).

Missouri v. Seibert, 542 U.S. 600, 606 (2004) (plurality).

United States v. Anderson, 895 F.2d 641, 647 (9th Cir. 1990) (Kozinski, J., dissenting).

Nat'l Fed'n of Indep. Bus. v. Sebelius, 567 U.S. 519, 590 (2012) (Ginsburg, J., with Breyer, Sotomayor and Kagan, JJ., concurring in part, concurring in the judgment in part, and dissenting in part).

Whalen v. Roe, 423 U.S. 1313, 1316–17 (1975) (Marshall, J., in chambers).

Orloff v. Willoughby, 1 Rapp 76 (1952) (Douglas, J., in chambers).

When citing different opinions within the same case, provide a designating parenthetical each time you switch opinions.[200] As illustrated by footnotes 60 and 64 in the examples below, when you use *id.* to refer successively to the same minority opinion, you need not repeat the parenthetical.[201] When citing the majority opinion or a *different* minority opinion immediately after having cited a minority opinion, prevent reader confusion by indicating the majority parenthetically.[202] The examples below are from a document with academic footnotes, but the rule also applies to citations in practice-based documents.

Examples

ACADEMIC FORMATTING

[59] *Id.* at 381 (Alito, J., concurring).

[60] *Id.*

[61] *Id.* at 387 (Scalia, J., dissenting).

[62] *Id.* at 382 (Alito, J., concurring).

[63] *Id.* at 369 (majority opinion).

[64] *Id.* at 371.

12.11 Cases in the Public Domain

A public domain citation does not refer to a particular publisher's source (such as a West regional reporter) or to a particular type of source (such as a print reporter or a commercial database). Synonymous terms for "public domain" citations are "medium-neutral," "vendor-neutral," and "universal" citations.

In submitting a document to a court, use public domain citations when required by local court rule.[203] Consult **Appendices 1(B)** and **2(B)** to determine whether a state court uses or requires public domain citations (see **Sidebar 12.6**). Even in non-court documents, however, if the case you wish to cite has an officially assigned public domain citation, include it as a parallel citation to the print reporter citation.[204]

If the court does not dictate the format, or if the public domain citation is in a document not being submitted to a court, use these components:[205]

Case name, | Year of decision | State's two-letter postal code abbreviation | [Court abbreviation] | Opinion number[U], | Pinpoint reference.

Only include a court abbreviation if the deciding court was one other than the state's highest court.[206] When a public domain opinion is explicitly designated as "unpublished," append the letter "U" to the opinion number.[207]

Include a pinpoint reference whenever possible.[208] Most public domain citations use a paragraph number for a pinpoint reference instead of a page number.[209] If the opinion displays page numbers, insert the preposition "at" before the pinpoint page reference. If the opinion displays paragraph numbers, do not use the preposition "at"; instead, insert paragraph symbol(s) ¶ or ¶¶ directly before the cited paragraph number(s).[210]

Examples (spaces denoted by ▲)

Johnson▲*v.*▲*Traynor*,▲1998▲ND▲115,▲¶¶▲8–9.

Anderson▲*v.*▲*State*,▲2009▲AR▲App.▲230U,▲at▲6–7.

Gen.▲*Steel*▲*Domestic*▲*Sales*,▲*LLC*▲*v.*▲*Bacheller*,▲2012▲CO▲68,▲¶▲3.

Meleski▲*v.*▲*Schbohm*▲*LLC*,▲2012▲WI▲App.▲63,▲¶▲6,▲341▲Wis.▲2d▲716,▲720,▲817▲N.W.2d▲887,▲889.

SIDEBAR 12.6 **Jurisdictions Using Public Domain Citations**

As of late 2020, sixteen states and three U.S. territories use public domain citations: Arkansas, Colorado, Illinois, Louisiana, Maine, Mississippi, Montana, New Mexico, North Dakota, Ohio, Oklahoma, South Dakota, Utah, Vermont, Wisconsin, Wyoming, Guam, Northern Mariana Islands, and Puerto Rico. For more information about public domain citation rules, see the jurisdiction's entry in **Appendix 2(B)**.

12.12 Slip Opinions

A "slip opinion" is the first public issuance of a court's decision, typically printed in pamphlet form prior to its publication in a reporter.

Case name, | No. | Docket number, | slip op. | [at] | [Initial page number,] | Pinpoint reference | (Court abbreviation | Month Day, Year).

When citing a case that is available solely in a slip opinion, how the pinpoint reference looks depends on whether the case in the slip opinion is separately paginated.[211] If it is, omit the initial page number and comma after it.[212] Omit "at" if the opinion uses other subdivisions.[213] If the case is issued in a publication with other cases and is thus not separately paginated, omit "at" and use the case's initial page and comma following it before the pinpoint reference.[214] If the case was renumbered, include the old docket number, a comma and space, and the year of the term that number was used, then "; renumbered" and the new docket number, a comma and space, and the year of the term that number was used.[215] See **Sidebar 12.7** for more on representing docket numbers.

In the court/date parenthetical, set out the court's abbreviation (see **Appendices 1(A)**, **1(B)**, **4(A)**, or **4(B)**) and the exact date (Month Day, Year) of the disposition, abbreviating the month as shown in **Appendix 3(A)**.[216] If the docket number unambiguously indicates the identity of the court issuing the opinion, you may omit the court abbreviation from this parenthetical. If the date reference is not the date of disposition, indicate its significance by inserting an appropriate description between the court abbreviation and the date in the court/date parenthetical.[217]

To assist readers in locating a slip opinion online when it is not in an electronic database, you may append its URL after the court/date parenthetical, set off by a comma and one space.[218]

SIDEBAR 12.7 Docket Numbers

Courts assign every litigated case a unique identification number (typically called a "docket" number) at the time the complaint for the case is filed that links all documents connected to that case. Follow local court rules (consult **Appendix 2**) for specific instructions regarding the representation of a docket number. In the absence of a local rule, use the docket number assigned by the clerk of court at the time the case was initiated. Depending on the practice of the court, docket numbers may be entirely numeric, or they may use a combination of letters and numbers. No matter the form of the docket number, represent it exactly as it was assigned.

Examples

In re Hostess Brands, Inc., No. 12-22052 (RDD), slip op. at 11–13 (Bankr. S.D.N.Y. Jan. 7, 2013).

Woods v. Wyeth Labs. Inc., No. 94-1493, slip op. at 1 (W.D. Pa. filed Sept. 1, 1994).

In re M.W., No. 2016-Ohio-5452, slip op. ¶ 1 (Aug. 23, 2016), http://www.supremecourt.ohio.gov/rod/docs/pdf/0/2016/2016-Ohio-5452.pdf.

Greffin v. Lorent, No. 90-756, slip op. 2358, 2365 (1st Cir. Mar. 2, 1991).

United States v. Johnson, 425 F.2d 630 (9th Cir. 1970), *cert. granted*, 403 U.S. 956 (1971) (No. 577, 1970 Term; renumbered No. 70-8, 1971 Term).

12.13 Forthcoming Case Publications

When a case is marked for publication in a print reporter, the number of the bound volume number may not yet be available. Page numbers cannot be assigned until the bound volume is prepared. A citation will therefore indicate its to-be-published status, and it will include a parallel citation to a commercial database containing the case.

Immediately after the case name, insert a comma, the abbreviation "No." and the docket number, followed by another comma and a space. If the docket number has a digit before a colon or the judge's initials at the end of the docket number, those can be omitted, but retain all other parts of the docket number. The docket number provides a unique means of identification that will retrieve the case no matter which commercial database you use. See **Sidebar 12.7** for more about docket numbers.

Replace both the volume number of reporter and the initial page number with three underlined spaces, followed by a comma, a space, and a parallel citation to its version in the commercial database. In the court/date parenthetical, provide the court abbreviation (if not apparent from the database identifier) and the exact date (Month Day, Year). Abbreviate the month.

Examples (fictitious)

In re Sofia B., No. 18-16-0520, ___ N.E.2d ___, 2018 Ill. App. LEXIS 52006 (May 20, 2018).

Jett v. McAlister, No. 19-cv-1951, ___ F. Supp. 3d ___, 2019 WL 71909 (W.D. Ark. Dec. 26, 2019).

12.14 "Unpublished" (Nonprecedential) Cases

A significant number of appellate court decisions (and almost all trial court decisions) are never published in print because they are not binding precedent or because, in the court's estimation, they add nothing of value to the existing body of authority in the jurisdiction. Despite their "unpublished" status, such cases are often available in online media, whether on a court's website or in a commercial database. In addition, Thomson Reuters (West) collects many cases not designated for publication by federal appellate courts and prints them in its unofficial *Federal Appendix* reporter.

Although the general rule is that unpublished cases are not binding precedent and therefore should not be cited, with the adoption of Federal Rule of Appellate Procedure 32.1 (applicable to cases decided after January 1, 2007), federal courts no longer prohibit their citation; similarly, many state courts permit their citation. For more information about citing unpublished cases, see **Sidebar 12.8**.

12.14(a) Unpublished case in the *Federal Appendix* reporter

Since 2001, the West *Federal Appendix* reporter has collected decisions of the federal circuit courts of appeal that are not designated for publication. Cite the *Federal Appendix* in preference to another source in which the case is available. Follow the format for citing cases from the United States Courts of Appeals, using the abbreviation "F. App'x" for the reporter name.[219]

Example

Scarborough v. Morgan, 21 F. App'x 279, 280 (6th Cir. 2001).

12.14(b) Unpublished case in commercial database

When a case is not published in a reporter but is available online in a commercial database such as Bloomberg Law, Westlaw Edge, or Lexis+, cite directly to the database.[220] Do not cite to an online database when citing a case if it is available in a print reporter.

Case name, | No. | Docket number, | Database identifier, | at | *Pinpoint reference | (Court abbreviation | Month Day, Year).

SIDEBAR 12.8 **Court Rules Prohibiting or Limiting Citation of Unreported Cases**

Courts have differing rules on whether litigants may cite unpublished cases in briefs or other documents presented to them. While some courts permit these cases to be cited, others prohibit such citation or limit the precedential value they carry.

Before citing an opinion designated as "unpublished," check controlling court rules. Federal Rule of Appellate Procedure 32.1, applying to cases issued on or after January 1, 2007, provides that a federal court of appeals "may not prohibit or restrict the citation" of federal judicial decisions that have been "designated as 'unpublished,' 'not for publication,' 'nonprecedential,' 'not precedent,' or the like." As for pre-2007 federal appellate unpublished decisions, court rules differ from circuit to circuit. While many local rules permit their citation, e.g., 9th Cir. Fed. R. App. Proc. 32.1, others explicitly label the practice as "disfavored," e.g., 4th Cir. R. 32.1. Some expressly declare that unpublished cases are "not precedent," e.g., 8th Cir. R. 32.1A and 3d Cir. I.O.P. 5.7. Similarly, local rules for state courts vary regarding their treatment of unpublished cases (see, e.g., Ariz. Sup. Ct. R. 111).

If you are considering citing an unpublished case in a brief or other court document, always consult the presiding court's local rules to determine its requirements, practices, and restrictions. See **Appendices 2(A)** and **2(B)** for citations to local court rules and links to rules on court websites.

If the docket number has a digit before a colon or the judge's initials at the end of the docket number, those can be omitted, but retain all other parts of the docket number.[221] See **Sidebar 12.7** for more information on docket numbers.

The database identifier in Bloomberg Law uses the year, the abbreviation BL, and a document number. Similarly, the database identifier in Westlaw uses the year, the abbreviation WL, and a document number. The database identifier in Lexis+ uses the year, an abbreviation for the court (or type of court), the abbreviation LEXIS, and a document number. In less well known electronic databases, the name of the database may be unclear from the database identifier; in that case, include the name of the database parenthetically at the end.[222]

If the database identifier sufficiently indicates the identity of the court deciding the case (as is often the case with Lexis+), all or part of the court abbreviation in the court/date parenthetical may be omitted.

Omit reference to an initial page number.[223] Refer to star pages, if available, as the pinpoint reference, following the directions in **Rule 5.5(d)**. If the online source indicates pagination to several sources, determine which page numbers belong to the online database itself, using **Rule 5.5** as guidance. If the online database assigns paragraph numbers instead of star pages, use a paragraph symbol, a space, and the paragraph number as the pinpoint reference.[224]

Examples

Va. Dep't of Transp. v. EPA, No. 12-CV-775, 2013 WL 53741, at *3–4 (E.D. Va. Jan. 3, 2013).

Cent. Delivery Serv. of Wash., Inc. v. Va. Emp't Comm'n, No. 2046-00-2, 2001 Va. App. LEXIS 617, at *5 (Nov. 6, 2001).

Jalesko v. Gartes, No. 85892-1, 2002 OR 0023008, ¶ 14 (Or. Feb. 5, 2002) (VersusLaw).

12.14(c) Unpublished case in looseleaf service or website

Do not cite a case to its publication in a looseleaf service if it has subsequently become available in a reporter or in a commercial database. To cite a case in a looseleaf service, follow **Rule 24.1**.

Example

Collins v. Vill. of Woodridge, 84 Fair Empl. Prac. Cas. (BNA) 787, 788 (N.D. Ill. Oct. 19, 1999).

Do not cite a case published on the internet if it is available in a print reporter, a commercial database, or a looseleaf service.[225] The internet may be useful, however, for locating recent slip opinions, opinions of lower courts whose decisions are not published, or cases from other countries. Choose a reliable site, such as governmental websites hosting unofficial versions or public-access sites such as the Legal Information Institute.

To cite a case published on the internet, provide the case name, the docket number (if apparent), and a parenthetical with the court abbreviation and exact date (Month Day, Year). Following the court/date parenthetical, add a comma, a space, and the website's URL.[226] It is not necessary to preface the URL with the phrase "available at" or to indicate the date you visited the website.

Example

Menna v. Walmart, No. 08-2610 (N.Y. Sup. Ct. Suffolk Cty. July 10, 2013), http://www.nycourts.gov/reporter/3dseries/2013/2013_51255.htm.

It may not be possible to provide pinpoint references for court decisions published on the internet. Some courts, however, provide page or paragraph numbering in the opinion. If the opinion has page numbers, use the preposition "at" before the pinpoint page reference. If the opinion has paragraph numbers, use the paragraph symbol ¶ or ¶¶ before the cited paragraph(s); do not use "at."[227]

For more information about citing sources on the internet, see **Rule 31.1**.

Examples

Page number:	*In re Russell*, No. SC-11-1, slip op. at 3–4 (N.C. Cherokee Ct. Aug. 15, 2011), http://turtletalk.files.wordpress.com/2011/08/in-re-russell.pdf.
Paragraph number:	*El-Masri v. Former Yugoslav Republic of Maced.*, 66 Eur. Ct. H.R. ¶¶ 79–90 (2012), http://hudoc.echr.coe.int/sites/eng/pages/search.aspx?i=001-115621.

12.15 Court Documents in Published or Pending Cases

12.15(a) Scope of rule

Two rules govern the citation of court documents, this one and **Rule 25**. Follow this rule to cite court documents or other materials filed in connection with a case *other than* the same one for which you are currently writing a document (e.g., when writing a paper about pending certiorari petitions and amicus briefs filed with the Supreme Court). To cite documents or other materials filed earlier in the *same case* for which you are writing (e.g., writing an appellate brief, referring to the trial court's order on appeal, or referring to a complaint when drafting a motion for the same case), follow **Rule 25**.

12.15(b) Full citations to court documents in published or pending cases

To cite the document, begin with its title as indicated on its cover or first page, set in ordinary type, followed by one space, "at" if the pinpoint reference is a page number, another space, and then a pinpoint reference, if needed, to specific pages or subdivisions within the document.[228] Do not abbreviate words in the document's title unless they are listed in **Chart 2.1**.[229] If the document being cited is an amicus brief, and there are more than two signatories on the brief, use "et al." after the first signatory's name in the document title and omit the others.[230] Follow the instructions in **Rule 25.2(b)** for pinpoint references. The remaining components depend on whether the case the documents were filed in is published or not. To cite to a document in a case that is published, use the following components:

Document name | at | Pinpoint reference, | [Full citation to case in which the court document was filed] | (Docket number), | [ECF No. | Electronic Case Filing number], | [Parallel citation to electronic database or website].

Example (spaces denoted by ▲)

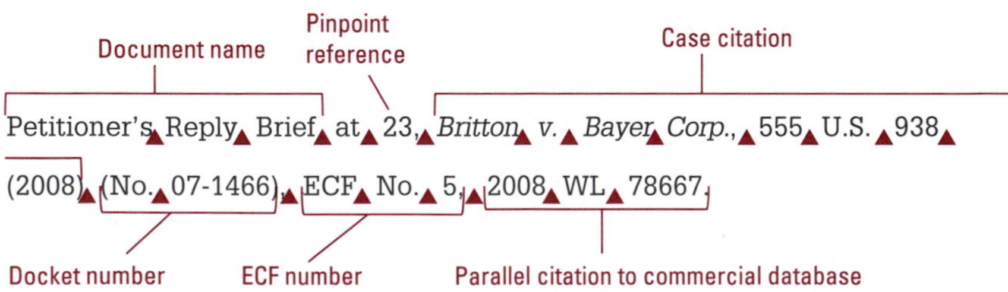

To cite to a document in a case that is not published or has no reported citation, use the following components:

Document name | at | Pinpoint reference, | *Case name*, | Docket number, | (Court abbreviation | Document's filing date), | [ECF No. | Electronic Case Filing number], | [Parallel citation to electronic database or website].

Example (spaces denoted by ▲)

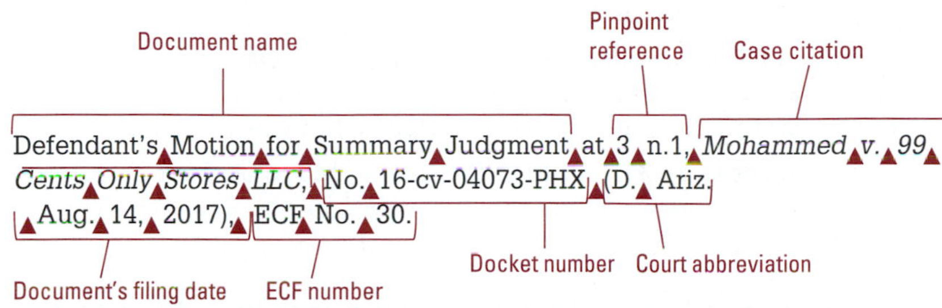

If the case in which the document was filed has been published in a reporter, a commercial database, or on a website, append a full citation to that case, and add a second parenthetical containing the case's docket number immediately after the court/date parenthetical.[231] If the case is still pending, the date in the parenthetical should reflect the date of the document's filing, and the case's docket number should be used in place of a reporter volume number, reporter name, and reporter page number.[232] In either event, the case name should be italicized and abbreviated as described in **Rule 12.2**.

If the docket number has a digit or digits before a colon (usually representing the year the complaint in the case was filed) or the judge's initials at the end of the docket number, those can be omitted, but retain all other parts of the docket number.[233] See **Sidebar 12.7** for more information on docket numbers. If the Electronic Case Filing (ECF) number is available, you may include that as well, but it is not required unless the ECF number is necessary to locate the document.[234] See **Sidebar 25.1** for more information about ECF numbers.

If you think a parallel citation to an electronic database or website would be helpful, you may provide it by putting a comma after the last component in the citation and then the commercial database number or URL.[235] If you include an electronic database identifier, and the document cited has a pinpoint citation immediately after the document name, you must also provide a pinpoint citation to the electronic database after the database identifier.[236]

If you need to cite to an audio or visual recording of an oral argument, deposition, or hearing rather than the transcript, the same general rules apply.[237] You may use a descriptive title and designate pinpoint citations using time markers.[238]

Examples

Complaint ¶¶ 84–88, *United States v. Huseby*, 862 F. Supp. 2d 951 (D. Minn. 2012) (No. 009CV03737).

Petitioner's Reply Brief at 23, *Britton v. Bayer Corp.*, 555 U.S. 938 (2008) (No. 07-1466).

Government's Proposed Jury Instructions at 9, *United States v. Stile*, 11-CR-00185 (D. Me. Oct. 28, 2014), ECF No. 532, 2014 WL 6992361, at *9.

Brief for Fetal Monitors, Inc. et al. as Amici Curiae Supporting Respondents at 24, *Fultz v. Denver Health, Inc.*, 450 U.S. 630 (1995) (No. 94-998) [hereinafter Brief for Fetal Monitors].

Transcript of Oral Argument at 6:16–23, *McGirt v. Oklahoma*, 140 S. Ct. 2452 (2020) (No. 18-9526), https://www.supremecourt.gv/oral_arguments/argument_transcripts/audio/2019/18-9526_n758.pdf.

Oral Argument at 13:20, *McGirt v. Oklahoma*, 140 S. Ct. 2452 (2020) (No. 18-9526), https://www.supremecourt.gov/oral_arguments/audio/2019/18-9526.

12.15(c) Short citations to court documents in published or pending cases

After citing a court document in full that uses the full citation to a case, you can shorten the case citation as you would according to **Rule 12.16**. You must always include the docket number of the case in any short form of court documents. If the document name is too unwieldy, you can use hereinafter to designate a shorter name.[239] In addition, you can always use *id.* as a short form for court documents in published or pending cases.[240]

Examples

Full citation: Appellant's Opening Brief at 27, *Chalker v. Chalker*, No. 2 CA-CV 20-0013 (Ariz. Ct. App. Mar. 30, 2020).

Short citation: Appellant's Opening Brief at 29, *Chalker*, No. 2 CA-CV 20-0013.

Full citation: Brief for Fetal Monitors, Inc. et al. as Amici Curiae Supporting Respondents at 24, *Fultz v. Denver Health, Inc.*, 450 U.S. 630 (1995) (No. 94-998) [hereinafter Brief for Fetal Monitors].

Short citation: Brief for Fetal Monitors at 21, *Fultz*, 450 U.S. 630 (No. 94-998).

ACADEMIC FORMATTING

Although *supra* should not be used for cases, it can be used for a short citation to a court document. However, the *supra* short form for a court document does not count as part of one of the five preceding footnotes for purposes of **Rule 12.16(g)^FN^**. You should use the document name as the *supra* reference.[241]

[23] Oral Argument Transcript at 6:16–23, *McGirt v. Oklahoma*, 140 S. Ct. 2452 (2020) (No. 18-9526), https://www.supremecourt.gov/oral_arguments/argument_transcripts/2019/18-9526_n758.pdf.

. . .

[25] Oral Argument Transcript, *supra* note 23, at 15:30.

12.16 Short Citations to Cases

12.16(a) *Id.* as the preferred short citation

Use *id.* only to refer to the case cited in the immediately preceding citation; do not use *id.* when the preceding citation contains a string citation (see **Rule 34.3**).[242] When *id.* is appropriate, use it as the short citation (see **Rule 11.3**).[243] When deciding whether *id.* is appropriate, ignore citations to sources in explanatory parentheticals, explanatory phrases, prior history parentheticals, and subsequent history parentheticals.[244] Refer to **Rule 12.10(b)** when using *id.* to refer to citations to the same case, but to a different opinion in that case (e.g., a dissenting opinion or concurring opinion).

When *id.* is not appropriate, use a citation format from those described below in **Rules 12.16(b)–(f)**.

12.16(b) Short citations when textual sentence has no reference to case name

When the textual sentence supported by the citation does not contain a reference to all or part of the cited case's name, use the following components:[245]

Single party's name including procedural phrase, if any, | Reporter volume | Reporter abbreviation | at | Pinpoint reference.

Example (short citation in red)

A trial court generally has discretion whether to grant a motion for a continuance. *Seel v. Van Der Veur*, 971 P.2d 924, 926 (Utah 1998). "[T]o constitute reversible error, the error complained of must be sufficiently prejudicial that there is a reasonable likelihood of a more favorable result for the defendant in its absence." *State v. Featherson*, 781 P.2d 424, 431 (Utah 1989). Where the record supports a conclusion that the trial's outcome would be no different had the continuance been granted, a defendant has not been denied due process of law. *Seel*, 971 P.2d at 927.

Incorrect: *Seel*, at 927.

Use the first party's name unless that name would cause confusion; if so, use the second party's name.[246] For example, if you wrote about two cases in which the first party's name was *Smith*, your readers might be unsure which *Smith* case you were discussing; similarly, if you wrote about a series of cases involving a federal criminal appeal, you might have several cases in which *United States* is the first party. Do not use the name of a common litigant such as a government entity, government official, or a geographic unit as the short form of the case name.[247] In these instances, using the second party's name distinguishes these short citations from one another.

If a party's name is long, include enough of it for recognition.[248]

Examples

Full citation:	*United States v. Chairse*, 18 F. Supp. 2d 1021, 1023 (D. Minn. 1998).
Short citation:	*Chairse*, 18 F. Supp. 2d at 1024.
Full citation:	*Metro E. Ctr. for Conditioning & Health v. Qwest Commc'ns Int'l, Inc.*, 294 F.3d 924, 929 (7th Cir. 2002).
Short citation:	*Metro E. Ctr.*, 294 F.3d at 928.

12.16(c) Short citations when textual sentence uses all or part of case name

When you use all or part of the case name in the textual sentence supported by the citation, don't repeat the case name in the short citation.[249] Use only these components:

Volume number | Reporter abbreviation | at | Pinpoint reference.

Example (short citation in red)

The decision in *International Shoe* specifically addressed minimum contacts relating to *in personam* jurisdiction. 326 U.S. at 316.

When you use the short form for the case name in main or footnote text when referring to your own analysis, you do not have to give a citation at the end as long as it has been cited in full in the same general discussion.[250]

Example

The reasoning in *Friesia* is just as applicable today.

12.16(d) Short citations in parallel citations

Id. alone is inadequate as a short form for a parallel citation.[251] *Id.* refers to a single publication source, while a parallel citation refers to two or more publication sources.[252] However, unless a local court rule prohibits your doing so, use *id.* to refer to the *first* source in the parallel citation, and for each succeeding publication source, provide its volume number, reporter abbreviation, and pinpoint reference.[253]

Examples

Full citation:	*Dow Chem. Co. v. Mahlum*, 114 Nev. 1468, 970 P.2d 98 (1998).
Short citation:	*Id.* at 1469, 970 P.2d at 99.
Full citation:	*Meleski v. Schbohm LLC*, 2012 WI App. 63, ¶ 6, 341 Wis. 2d 716, 720, 817 N.W.2d 887, 889.
Short citation:	*Id.*, 341 Wis. 2d at 720, 817 N.W.2d at 889.

Where you cannot use *id.*, consult **Rule 12.16(b)**, **(c)** to determine whether the short citation needs a party name. If it does, select a single party name, set out the volume number and reporter abbreviation for the first-cited reporter, and preface a pinpoint page reference with the preposition "at." Then add a comma, a space, and for the second-cited reporter, its volume number, reporter abbreviation, "at" and a pinpoint page reference. Do not use "at" before a different subdivision. Where the number of the bound volume is not yet available or where a pinpoint page reference is not available, use three underlined blank spaces to represent the missing number(s).

Examples

Full citation: *Abel v. Fox*, 247 Ill. App. 3d 811, 813, 221 Ill. Dec. 129, 131, 654 N.E.2d 591, 593 (4th Dist. 1995).

Short citation: *Abel*, 247 Ill. App. 3d at 813, 221 Ill. Dec. at 131, 654 N.E.2d at 593.

Full citation: *Minneci v. Pollard*, ___ U.S. ___, 132 S. Ct. 617, 181 L. Ed. 2d 606 (2012).

Short citation: *Minneci*, ___ U.S. at ___, 132 S. Ct. at 626, 181 L. Ed. 2d at 616–17.

12.16(e) Short citations to cases in commercial databases

Select a single party name (following the guidance in **Rule 12.16(b)**).[254] Omit the docket number, but retain the full database identifier. For a pinpoint reference, use the preposition "at," one space, and a single asterisk, with no space, before the pinpoint page number(s). If you added a parenthetical reference to the database source because it is not apparent in the database identifier (see **Rule 12.14(b)**), retain that parenthetical in the short citation.[255]

Example

Full citation: *State ex rel. Knotts v. Facemire*, 2009 W. Va. LEXIS 50 (June 5, 2009).

Short citation: *Facemire*, 2009 W. Va. LEXIS at *19–20.

Full citation: *Staats v. Brown*, No. 65681-9, 2000 WA 0042007, ¶ 25 (Wash. Jan. 6, 2000) (VersusLaw).

Short citation: *Staats*, 2000 WA 0042007, ¶ 25 (VersusLaw).

12.16(f) Short citations to slip opinions

Select a single party name.[256] In place of a reporter reference, use the phrase "slip op. at" before the pinpoint page number(s).[257] Do not use "at" before a different subdivision. If you are citing to two different slip opinions from the same case, you can choose to either assign a unique identifier to each slip opinion in its full citation or use the jurisdiction/date parenthetical in the short form.[258]

Example

Full citation:	*St. Joseph Abbey v. Castille*, No. 11-30756, slip op. at 10 (5th Cir. Oct. 23, 2012).
Short citation:	*St. Joseph Abbey*, slip op. at 9.
Full citation:	*In re Hostess Brands, Inc. (Hostess III)*, No. 12-22052 (RDD), slip op. at 11–13 (Bankr. S.D.N.Y. Jan. 7, 2013).
Short citation:	*Hostess III*, slip op. at 11–13. **or** *In re Hostess Brands, Inc.*, slip op. at 11–13 (Bankr. S.D.N.Y. Jan. 7, 2013).

12.16(g)FN Short citations to cases in academic footnotes

ACADEMIC FORMATTING

Use *id.* to refer to a single case previously cited within the *same* footnote or cited in the immediately preceding footnote **(Rule 11.3(c))**.[259] Where you cannot use *id.*, consult **Rule 12.16(b)**, **(c)** to determine whether the short citation needs a party name. If it does, select a single party name, and present it in *italics*.[260] (Reminder: Full case names in academic footnotes are presented in ordinary type (**Rule 12.2(a)(2)FN**).[261]) Present the remainder of the short citation in accordance with **Rule 12.16(b)**, **(c)**, **(d)**, **(e)**, or **(f)**, as applicable.

If the case has not previously been cited in the same footnote or in any of the five immediately preceding footnotes, however, do not use a short citation.[262] Repeat the full citation.[263] Never use *supra* as a short citation to a case.[264] See **Rules 11.1(d)FN** and **11.4.**

Examples

The wave of post-*Chevron* deference arguably crested in 1997 with *Auer v. Robbins*,[256] a unanimous decision authored by Justice Scalia.[257] . . . The dispute in *Auer* involved a claim by St. Louis police officers that the City had erroneously designated them "exempt" from the wage and hour provisions of the Fair Labor Standards Act (FLSA).[263] The Secretary of Labor, carrying out specific rulemaking authority conferred by the FLSA,[264] had issued regulations defining the scope of the exemption,[265] which in part turned on the outcome of the "salary basis test,"[266] defined in the agency's regulations.[267] As one condition for exempt status, an employee's salary could not be subject to reduction for variations in "work performance."[268] The officers argued that the mere possibility that their salaries might be reduced was sufficient to defeat exempt status. The City argued that to be nonexempt, the officers had to be realistically vulnerable to an actual pay reduction; a theoretical possibility was not enough.[269]

256 519 U.S. 452 (1997).

257 *Id.* at 454.

. . .

263 Auer v. Robbins, 519 U.S. 452, 455 (1997).

264 29 U.S.C. § 213(a)(1).

265 *Auer*, 519 U.S. at 456.

266 *Id.* at 456–57.

267 *See* 29 C.F.R. §§ 541.1(f), 541.2(e), 541.3(e) (1996).

268 *Auer*, 519 U.S. at 456 (citing 29 C.F.R. § 541.118(a) (1996)) (defining "salary basis" test).

269 *Id.* at 459.

13 Constitutions

Fast Formats

United States Constitution (provision currently in force)	U.S. Const. art. IV, § 5(b).
United States Constitution (provision not currently in force)	U.S. Const. amend. XVIII (repealed 1933). **or** U.S. Const. amend. XVIII, *repealed by* U.S. Const. amend. XXI.
State constitution (provisions currently in force)	Conn. Const. art. XIII, § 1.
State constitution (provision not currently in force)	Cal. Const. art. XVII (repealed 1976). **or** Cal. Const. art. XVII, *repealed by* Cal. Const. art. XXI.
Citation in academic footnote	[42] U.S. CONST. art. II, § 4. ACADEMIC FORMATTING
Short citation	*Id.* amend. V.

13.1 Which Source to Cite

You will ordinarily cite the constitution currently in force, using a print source. For citations to constitutions in commercial databases or official websites, see **Rule 13.2(d)**. For citations to historic constitutions or to specific constitutional provisions no longer in force, see **Rule 13.3**.

13.2 Full Citations to Constitutions Currently in Force

A full citation to a print source of a constitution currently in force has three components: the jurisdiction's abbreviated name, "Const.," and a pinpoint reference.[1]

Abbreviated jurisdiction name | Const. | Pinpoint reference.

Example (spaces denoted by ▲)

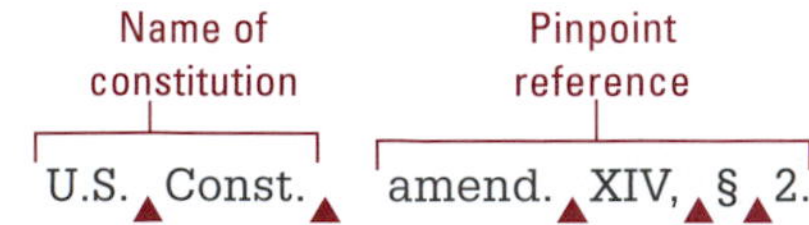

13.2(a) Name of constitution

A constitution's name uses the abbreviation of its jurisdiction (U.S. or a state's abbreviation, as shown in **Appendix 3(B)**), a space, and the abbreviation "Const."[2] Use ordinary type.[3] For constitution names used as a part of speech in a textual sentence, including reference to a constitution in an embedded citation, see **Rule 2.3**.

Examples (spaces denoted by ▲)

U.S.▲Const.▲amend.▲XXVI.

N.J.▲Const.▲art.▲XI,▲§▲7.

13.2(b) Pinpoint references

Following the abbreviated name of the constitution, set out the pinpoint reference. To abbreviate a subdivision, see **Appendix 3(C)**.[4] When citing the United States Constitution, use Roman numerals for articles and amendments; use Arabic numbers for smaller subsections, such as sections and clauses.[5] For a state constitution, use the numbering system it displays. Use commas to separate multiple subdivisions within the same article, section, or amendment.[6] For additional guidance, see **Rule 4** (numbers) and **Rule 6** (subdivisions).

If you are referring to multiple amendments, sections in the same article, or clauses in the same section, you can cite to them as if they were multiple pinpoint references in one source.[7] Otherwise, you will need to cite the subdivisions separately using *id.*[8]

Examples (spaces denoted by ▲)

U.S.▲Const.▲art.▲I,▲§▲9,▲cl.▲2.

U.S.▲Const.▲pmbl.

Fla.▲Const.▲art.▲X,▲§§▲4,▲6.

Kan.▲Const.▲Bill▲of▲Rights▲§▲15.

U.S.▲Const.▲amends.▲I,▲V.

Utah▲Const.▲art.▲IV,▲§▲1;▲*id.*▲art.▲IX,▲§▲1.

13.2(c) Date

Citations to constitutional provisions currently in force ordinarily omit dates.[9] However, if information about a date relates to the point for which the provision is being cited (e.g., date of an amendment's adoption), you may include it parenthetically or put a comma and a space after the full citation and then cite the repealing provision in full.[10]

Examples (spaces denoted by ▲)

U.S.▲Const.▲amend.▲XIV,▲§▲2.

Iowa▲Const.▲art.▲I,▲§▲1▲(amended▲1998).

13.2(d) Publication in commercial database or official website

To cite a constitutional provision published in a commercial database such as Bloomberg Law, Lexis, or Westlaw, add a parenthetical identifying the database and its currency, as indicated by the database itself.[11]

Example (spaces denoted by ▲)

When a constitution is available online in an *official* version that is published, edited, or compiled by or under the supervision of governmental officials, no parenthetical is needed; cite the constitution the same as its print version.[12]

13.2(e)FN Full citations to constitutions in academic footnotes

ACADEMIC FORMATTING

Follow **Rule 13.2(a)–(d)**, but use large and small capital letters for the name of the constitution and ordinary type for subdivisions such as articles, amendments, and clauses.[13]

Examples

23 U.S. CONST. amend. XXVI.

39 WASH. CONST. art. I, § 24.

64 N.J. CONST. art. XI, § 7.

13.3 Full Citations to Historic Constitutions or Constitutional Provisions No Longer in Force

13.3(a) Historic constitution

When citing a historic constitution that is completely superseded or otherwise no longer in force, set out the abbreviated name of the constitution followed by the preposition "of" and the date of that constitution's adoption.[14] You may add a pinpoint reference to a particular provision.[15] Put the year the particular provision was adopted in a parenthetical if it was different from the year the entire constitution was adopted.[16]

Examples

Ind. Const. of 1816.

Ga. Const. of 1777, art. IX, § 1.

Ark. Const. of 1868, art. III, § 2 (1873).

13.3(b) Constitutional provision no longer in force

You have two options for indicating when a specific provision of a current constitution is no longer in force (e.g., one that is amended, repealed, or superseded).[17] Always begin with the citation format for the current constitution and the pinpoint reference. Your first option is to add a parenthetical, in ordinary type, stating the reason the specific provision is no longer in force and the year the provision lost effect.[18] If the provision was repealed, refer to the year of repeal. If the provision was amended, refer to the year of amendment.[19] The second option is to append a clause with an italicized reference to the action affecting the provision, followed by a full citation to the repealing or amending provision.[20]

Examples

U.S. Const. amend. XVIII (repealed 1933).

Cal. Const. art. XXV (repealed 1949).

U.S. Const. amend. XVIII, *repealed by* U.S. Const. amend. XXI.

La. Const. art. I, § 6 (1921), *superseded by* La. Const. art. I, § 22.

13.4 Short Citations to Constitutions

When appropriate (**Rule 11.3(c)**), use *id.* as the short citation.[21] Insert a pinpoint reference immediately following *id.*[22] When *id.* is not appropriate, repeat the full citation.[23]

Example

Full citation: U.S. Const. art. I, § 10, cl. 3.

Short citation: *Id.* art. VI, cl. 2.

14 Statutory Codes and Session Laws

Fast Formats

United States Code	19 U.S.C. § 2411.
***United States Code Annotated* (supplement)**	5 U.S.C.A. § 552 (West Supp. 2016).
***United States Code Service* (main volume and supplement)**	17 U.S.C.S. § 115 (LexisNexis 2011 & Supp. 2016).
State statute (see Appendix 1(B) for each state's format)	Wyo. Stat. Ann. § 4-10-902 (2011). N.Y. Exec. Law § 63-b (McKinney 2010). Conn. Gen. Stat. Ann. § 9-325 (West 2013).
Statute in commercial database	Ariz. Rev. Stat. Ann. § 12-2604(A) (Westlaw Edge through 2d Reg. Sess. of 54th Leg.). Mass. Ann. Laws ch. 56, § 59 (Lexis+ through ch. 176 of the 2020 2d Ann. Legis. Sess.).
Federal session law	Pub. L. No. 109-2, 119 Stat. 12 (2005). Economic Espionage Act of 1996, Pub. L. No. 104-294, § 201, 110 Stat. 3488, 3491.
State session law (see Appendix 1(B) for each state's format)	1985 N.J. Laws 308.
Citations in academic footnotes	⚠ ACADEMIC FORMATTING [33] 18 U.S.C. § 2314. [119] MO. REV. STAT. § 287.835 (2011).
Short citations to federal and state statutes	*Id.* § 2412. 19 U.S.C. § 2412. Or. Rev. Stat. Ann. § 258.036.
Short citations to session laws	119 Stat. at 13. Economic Espionage Act § 201. § 201, 110 Stat. at 3492. 1996 Alaska Sess. Laws at 53.

Snapshot

UNITED STATES CODE

United
States
Code

2012 Edition

TITLE
7
§§ 901–END

3

UNITED STATES CODE

2012 EDITION

CONTAINING THE GENERAL AND PERMANENT LAWS
OF THE UNITED STATES ENACTED THROUGH THE
112TH CONGRESS

(ending January 2, 2013, the last law of which was signed on January 15, 2013)

Prepared and published under authority of Title 2, U.S. Code, Section 285b,
by the Office of the Law Revision Counsel of the House of Representatives

VOLUME THREE

TITLE 7—AGRICULTURE
§§ 901–END

UNITED STATES
GOVERNMENT PRINTING OFFICE
WASHINGTON : 2013

78-402 D Sig-1

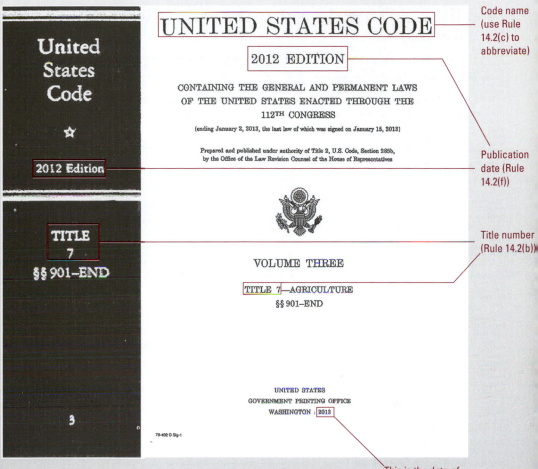

Code name (use Rule 14.2(c) to abbreviate)

Publication date (Rule 14.2(f))

Title number (Rule 14.2(b))

This is the date of printing. Do not use this date (Rule 14.2(f)).

Spine and Title Page

Snapshot

UNITED STATES CODE

Section number (Rule 14.2(d)). Use only the section number, not the subtitle that follows it.

ducted under subchapters I, III, and III-A of this chapter, and that such evaluations cover no fewer than five countries sampled from the developing regions (Asia, Africa, Latin America, and Caribbean), and assess the nutritional and other impacts, achievements, problems, and future prospects for programs thereunder, for provisions that, not later than November 1 of each calendar year the President submit to the House Committee on Agriculture, the House Committee on International Relations, the Senate Committee on Agriculture and Forestry, and the Senate Committee on Foreign Relations a revised global assessment of food production and needs, and revised planned programming of food assistance for the current fiscal year, to reflect, to the maximum extent feasible, the actual availability of commodities for food assistance.

Subsecs. (d), (e). Pub. L. 95-113 added subsecs. (d) and (e).

1975—Pub. L. 94-161 designated existing provisions as subsec. (a), substituted "fiscal" for "calendar" in first sentence, and added subsecs. (b) and (c).

EFFECTIVE DATE OF 2008 AMENDMENT

Amendment by Pub. L. 110-246 effective May 22, 2008, see section 4(b) of Pub. L. 110-246, set out as an Effective Date note under section 8701 of this title.

EFFECTIVE DATE OF 1990 AMENDMENT

Amendment by Pub. L. 101-624 effective Jan. 1, 1991, see section 1513 of Pub. L. 101-624, set out as a note under section 1691 of this title.

EFFECTIVE DATE OF 1985 AMENDMENT

Amendment by Pub. L. 99-83 effective Oct. 1, 1985, see section 1301 of Pub. L. 99-83, set out as a note under section 2151-1 of Title 22, Foreign Relations and Intercourse.

EFFECTIVE DATE OF 1981 AMENDMENT

Amendment by Pub. L. 97-98 effective Dec. 22, 1981, see section 1801 of Pub. L. 97-98, set out as an Effective Date note under section 4301 of this title.

EFFECTIVE DATE OF 1977 AMENDMENTS

Amendment by Pub. L. 95-113 effective Oct. 1, 1977, see section 1901 of Pub. L. 95-113, set out as a note under section 1307 of this title.

Amendment by Pub. L. 95-88 effective Oct. 1, 1977, see section 215 of Pub. L. 95-88, set out as a note under section 1702 of this title.

EFFECTIVE DATE

Section effective Jan. 1, 1967, see section 5 of Pub. L. 89-808, set out as an Effective Date of 1966 Amendment note under section 1691 of this title.

§§1736c, 1736d. Repealed. Pub. L. 104-127, title II, §§218, 219, Apr. 4, 1996, 110 Stat. 957

Section 1736c, act July 10, 1954, ch. 469, title IV, §409, as added Nov. 11, 1966, Pub. L. 89-808, §2(E), 80 Stat. 1537; amended July 29, 1968, Pub. L. 90-436, §1, 82 Stat. 450; Nov. 30, 1970, Pub. L. 91-524, title VII, §701, 84 Stat. 1379; Aug. 10, 1973, Pub. L. 93-86, §1(25), 87 Stat. 237; Sept. 29, 1977, Pub. L. 95-113, title XII, §1208, 91 Stat. 957; Dec. 22, 1981, Pub. L. 97-98, title XII, §1216, 95 Stat. 1282; Dec. 23, 1985, Pub. L. 99-198, title XI, §1105, 99 Stat. 1466; Nov. 28, 1990, Pub. L. 101-624, title XV, §1512, 104 Stat. 3653; Dec. 13, 1991, Pub. L. 102-237, title III, §322, 105 Stat. 1857, required promulgation of regulations to implement chapter not later than 180 days after Nov. 28, 1990.

Section 1736d, act July 10, 1954, ch. 469, title IV, §410, as added Nov. 11, 1966, Pub. L. 89-808, §2(E), 80 Stat. 1538; amended Nov. 28, 1990, Pub. L. 101-624, title XV, §1512, 104 Stat. 3653; Dec. 13, 1991, Pub. L. 102-237, title III, §322, 105 Stat. 1857, provided for independent evaluation of programs under subchapters II, III, and III-A of this chapter and report to Congress.

§1736e. Debt forgiveness

(a) Authority

The President, taking into account the financial resources of a country, may waive payments of principal and interest that such country would otherwise be required to make to the Commodity Credit Corporation under dollar sales agreements under subchapter II of this chapter if—

(1) that country is a least developed country; and

(2) either—

(A) an International Monetary Fund standby agreement is in effect with respect to that country;

(B) a structural adjustment program of the International Bank for Reconstruction and Development or of the International Development Association is in effect with respect to that country;

(C) a structural adjustment facility, enhanced structural adjustment facility, or similar supervised arrangement with the International Monetary Fund is in effect with respect to that country; or

(D) even though such an agreement, program, facility, or arrangement is not in effect, the country is pursuing national economic policy reforms that would promote democratic, market-oriented, and long term economic development.

(b) Request for debt relief by President

The President may provide debt relief under subsection (a) of this section only if a notification is submitted to Congress at least 10 days prior to providing the debt relief. Such a notification shall—

(1) specify the amount of official debt the President proposes to liquidate; and

(2) identify the countries for which debt relief is proposed and the basis for their eligibility for such relief.

(c) Appropriations action required

Subsection (Rule 14.2(d))

The aggregate amount of principal and interest waived under this section may not exceed the amount approved for such purpose in an Act appropriating funds to carry out this chapter.

(d) Limitation on new credit assistance

If the authority of this section is used to waive payments otherwise required to be made by a country pursuant to this chapter, the President may not provide any new credit assistance for that country under this chapter during the 2-year period beginning on the date such waiver authority is exercised, unless the President provides to the Congress, before the assistance is provided, a written justification for the provision of such new credit assistance.

(e) Applicability

The authority of this section applies with respect to credit sales agreements entered into before November 28, 1990.

(July 10, 1954, ch. 469, title IV, §411, as added Pub. L. 91-524, title VII, §704, Nov. 30, 1970, as added Pub. L. 93-86, §1(26), Aug. 10, 1973, 87 Stat. 237; amended Pub. L. 101-624, title XV, §1512, Nov. 28, 1990, 104 Stat. 3654; Pub. L. 102-237, title

76-402 D Sig-16

Inside page

14.1 Sources of Statutory Law

You are not required to cite to an official code, especially if it is not readily available, but it is preferred.[1] Federal statutes are cited either to the official print version of the *United States Code* (preferred, although it is rarely up to date (see **Sidebar 14.1**)) or to the authenticated online version of the code in the Government Publishing Office's govinfo.gov website ("govinfo"). It can be found here: https://www.govinfo.gov/app/collection/uscode/. Authenticated online content is identified with a seal of authenticity, a graphic of an eagle beside the phrase "Authenticated U.S. Government Information." Cite an authenticated federal statute in govinfo the same way you cite it in print (**Rule 14.2**).[2]

Similarly, citing official versions of state statutes is preferrable, if available, but not required.[3] Official compilations are indicated with a red star (★) in **Appendix 1(B)**. Some states publish authenticated versions of their statutes online, and online compilations are increasingly common. However, do not assume that any online compilation is official, even when on a governmental website; look for specific language indicating its status as official or authenticated.

When the official or authenticated code and its supplement are not readily available or do not yet contain the cited statute, cite another version of the federal or state statute, in this order of preference[4]:

- unofficial code or its supplement (including those designated as "certified");
- official session laws (**Rules 14.6** and **14.8**);
- unofficial session laws;
- Westlaw or Lexis commercial database;
- other commercial database (e.g., Bloomberg Law, Fastcase);
- looseleaf service;
- unofficial website; or
- newspaper.

SIDEBAR 14.1 **Publication Dates of Official and Unofficial Versions of the *United States Code***

A new print edition of the official *United States Code* is published every six years. Some titles in the most recent edition were published in 2018, although as of late 2020, some titles still had not been printed. The next edition is scheduled for publication in 2024. If possible, use the most recent print version of the official code (or its supplements) unless you are doing historical research and need to cite a statute no longer in the official code.

(*Continued*)

SIDEBAR 14.1 **Publication Dates of Official and Unofficial Versions of the *United States Code* (*Continued*)**

The Government Publishing Office provides authenticated versions of the *United States Code* at govinfo.gov. Even so, it advises, "While every effort has been made to ensure that the U.S. Code on govinfo is accurate, those using it for legal research should verify their results against the printed version of the U.S. Code available through the Government Publishing Office."

Individual volumes of the unofficial *United States Code Annotated* and *United States Code Service* are republished as needed (e.g., when a pocket part becomes too large to fit within the volume's back cover); different volumes of these unofficial codes are likely to have different publication dates.

Similarly, commercial databases update statutory collections on their own schedules, and they do so more frequently than their print counterparts. Do not assume that the date through which an online statute is current will be the same as its print counterpart or as its counterpart in a different database.

14.2 Full Citations to Federal Statutes Currently in Force

A full citation to a federal statute currently in force has four to eight components, depending on whether it has an official name, whether the source is official or unofficial, whether the source is in print or online, and whether a publication date is required.

[Official name,] | Title number | Code abbreviation | §[§] | Section number[s] [pinpoint subdivision] | ([Publisher, if citing unofficial code] | [Publication date] [or Database | through | Currency information]), [URL].

Examples (spaces denoted by ▲)

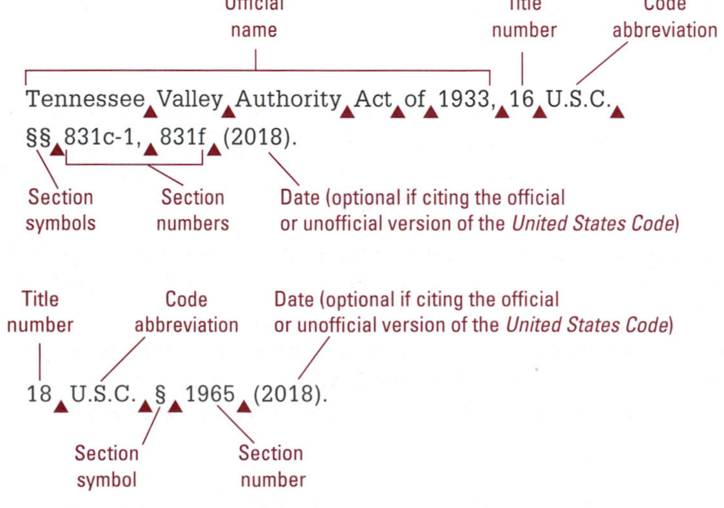

14.2(a) Official or popular name of statute

When the official name of a cited statute will assist your readers in identifying it, or when a statute is referenced by its popular name, you may begin with the official name, popular name, or both, set out in ordinary type.[5] (You can find official and popular name tables at the end of the general indexes to the *United States Code* and its two unofficial codifications.)

Omit "The" when it prefaces a statute's name.[6] Capitalize words in the name according to the guidelines in **Rule 3.2**, **Rule 3.3**, and **Chart 3.1**. When a statute's official name includes reference to a year, keep it.[7] If the statute is typically cited using its original section number, add that reference to the title.[8]

Examples

Americans with Disabilities Act of 1990, 42 U.S.C. §§ 12101–12117.

Securities Exchange Act of 1934 § 10(b), 15 U.S.C. § 78j(b).

14.2(b) Title number

Federal statutes are grouped within numbered titles. The current edition of the *United States Code* has fifty-three titles, each addressing specific topics (Title 53 is presently reserved). When a citation begins with the statute's name, add a comma and a space, followed by the title number and a space.[9] Otherwise, begin the citation with the title number, followed by a space.[10]

Title 26 is the Internal Revenue Code; in citations to that title, you may substitute the abbreviation "I.R.C." for "26 U.S.C."[11] See **Appendix 6** for more information on citing to the Internal Revenue Code.

14.2(c) Abbreviated name of code

Following the title number, insert the abbreviated name of the code, in ordinary type, followed by a space.[12] The official code for federal statutes is the *United States Code* ("U.S.C."), whether in print or in the authenticated online version on the Government Publishing Office's website, govinfo.gov (see **Rule 14.1**).[13]

The two preferred unofficial codes are the *United States Code Annotated* ("U.S.C.A.") and the *United States Code Service* ("U.S.C.S."), available in print and in their publishers' commercial databases (**Rule 14.2(f)**).[14]

14.2(d) Sections and subsections

Following the code abbreviation, insert one or two section symbols (§ or §§), depending on whether you are citing one or multiple sections of the code.[15] Omit references to subtitles, parts, chapters, or subchapters.[16]

Insert a space after the symbol(s);[17] avoid putting a space *between* two section symbols.[18] Set out the section number(s) and subsection(s), if any, making as specific a reference as possible.[19] Some sections of the *United States Code* are designated by numbers plus one or more letters (uppercase or lowercase, and sometimes attached to the numbers with hyphens); do not treat these letters as subsections, and do not insert a space before them.[20] See **Rule 6** for more information on citing sections and subsections, particularly for consecutive or scattered subsections. If a statute appears in so many scattered sections or titles that it is difficult or confusing to cite to that many parts of the code, cite to the session laws (see **Rule 14.6**) and indicate in a parenthetical the general location of those sections in the code.[21]

Examples (spaces denoted by ▲):

Single section:	28▲U.S.C.▲§▲2671▲(2012).
	or
	28▲U.S.C.▲§▲2671.
Section designated by number and letters:	18▲U.S.C.▲§▲3600A.
Consecutive sections:	21▲U.S.C.▲§§▲2001–2003.
Consecutive subsections:	28▲U.S.C.▲§▲2631(a)–(c).
Scattered sections:	15▲U.S.C.▲§§ 80a-7,▲80a-10.
Scattered subsections:	18▲U.S.C.▲§▲1962(a),▲(d).

14.2(e) Statutory appendices and other subdivisions

To cite material in a statutory appendix when the statute is numbered and otherwise looks like it were part of the code, insert a space and the abbreviation "app." immediately after the title number and code abbreviation, a space, and a pinpoint reference to section(s) and subsection(s), if any.[22]

To cite notes or other types of information accompanying a statute, insert the word "note" or an abbreviation for the specific subdivision immediately after the section number (use **Appendix 3(C)**).[23] You may use a parenthetical to identify one of multiple named notes beneath a section, as illustrated in the fourth example below.[24]

Examples

46 U.S.C. app. §§ 1300–1315.

5 U.S.C. § 801 note.

49 U.S.C. § 40105 hist. nn.

15 U.S.C. § 78s note (Construction of 1993 Amendment).

14.2(f) Publication parenthetical

A statute's publication parenthetical immediately follows the statute's section number(s) and pinpoint reference(s), and includes the year that the source was published (i.e., its publication date).[25] When citing to statutes currently in effect in either an official or unofficial *United States Code*, you may, but are not required to, provide a publication date.[26] Thus, because an authenticated or official code, such as the *United States Code*, makes no reference to the publisher, there is no publication parenthetical when citing to those unless you choose to include the year of publication.[27] The publication parenthetical for an *unofficial* print or online version of the *United States Code* begins with the name of the publisher, and if you choose to include the date of publication, follow the publisher's name with one space and the year of publication.[28]

The publication date indicates the currency of the source you selected to cite. Do not confuse the date of publication with the statute's date of legislative enactment. For example, a statute enacted in 1930 may be in effect today; its citation should indicate the current code in which the statute is published. Do not presume that the publication date of an unofficial version of the code is the same as the date of an official version (or vice versa).

Locate the publication date of a statute's print version on the spine of the volume, the title page, or the copyright page, in that order.[29] Where a statute appears both in the main volume and in a supplement (abbreviated "Supp." whether separately bound or a pocket part), indicate the date of each, as shown in **Rule 8.3**.[30] See **Rule 8.1** to cite solely to a code's supplement. Use the year of a supplement as it appears on the title page of the supplement or the latest copyright year of the supplement, in that order of preference.[31] If the supplement spans more than one year, give all years in the publication parenthetical.[32]

Citations to commercial database versions demonstrate the means through which the statute is current in the database. Use the database name (in addition to the publisher, if required by this rule) and the date information provided by the database itself, which may be a year, an exact date, a particular legislative enactment, a legislative session, a date within a legislative session, or some combination thereof.[33] Use abbreviations found in **Appendix 3(F)** if they appear in the commercial database's currency information.

Examples

Main volume:	18 U.S.C. § 1965 (2012).
	or
	18 U.S.C. § 1965.
Supplement:	12 U.S.C. §§ 5381–5394 (Supp. V 2011).
Both main volume and supplement:	38 U.S.C. § 312(c) (2012 & Cum. Supp. 2015).
Commercial database:	42 U.S.C.A. § 1751 (West, Westlaw Edge through Pub. L. No. 114-219).
	Wis. Stat. Ann. § 19.43 (West, Westlaw Edge through 2019 Act 186).

14.2(g) Parentheticals in statutory citations

To any statute's citation, you may append a parenthetical with explanations of, commentary about, or treatment of the statute.[34] The explanatory parenthetical immediately follows the publication parenthetical.[35] For more information about explanatory parentheticals, see **Rule 37**.

Examples

35 U.S.C. § 1 (enacted under Patent Act of 1952, 66 Stat. 792 (1952)).

17 U.S.C. § 109(a) (providing that "the owner of a particular copy . . . lawfully made under this title, or any person authorized by such owner, is entitled, without the authority of the copyright owner, to sell or otherwise dispose of the possession of that copy").

14.2(h) Citations to online sources

When you cite to an authentic, official statutory source online, you may cite it exactly as you would in print; both have the same weight.[36] If you are citing to an unofficial source in a commercial database online, the only difference between citing to the online source and the print source is that you must include the publisher's information as explained in **Rule 14.2(f)**. If neither of those apply, and you are citing an unofficial version of a statute available online that is not in a commercial database, you must add the URL after the publication parenthetical;[37] if the code is not published, edited, or compiled by, or under the supervision of, government officials, you must also include the publisher's information as explained in **Rule 14.2(f)**.[38] See **Rule 30.2** for more information on URLs.

Example

6 U.S.C. § 765(a)(3) (Legal Information Institute), https://www.law.cornell.edu/uscode/text/6/765.

14.2(i)FN Full citations to federal statutes in academic footnotes

ACADEMIC FORMATTING

Follow **Rule 14.2(a)–(h)**, but use large and small capital letters for the abbreviated name of the code.[39]

Examples

155 11 U.S.C. § 721.

156 Securities Exchange Act of 1934 § 10(b), 15 U.S.C. § 78j(b).

157 I.R.C. § 170(b).

14.3 Full Citations to Federal Statutes No Longer in Force

For a statute no longer in force, cite to the current official or unofficial code if it still appears therein, the last edition of the official or unofficial code in which the statute does appear, the session law, or a secondary source, in that order of preference.[40] The exception to this rule is if you are citing to the historical fact of a statute's enactment, amendment, or repeal, in which case see **Rule 14.7**.

14.3(a) Federal statutes repealed or amended

When citing a federal statute that has been repealed or amended, follow the basic format in **Rule 14.2**, adding a parenthetical indicating both the fact of and the year of the repeal or amendment.[41] Alternatively, forgo the parenthetical and instead append a clause with an italicized reference to the repeal or amendment, followed by a full citation to the repealing or amending statute or session law.[42] For amended statutes, you may also cite to the current amended version parenthetically.[43] In any event, if citing to an earlier version of a statute that was amended, you must indicate it somehow, even if the specific subsection you are citing was not amended.[44]

Examples

26 U.S.C. § 1071(a) (repealed 1995).

26 U.S.C. § 1071(a), *repealed by* Act of Apr. 11, 1995, Pub. L. No. 104-7, § 2(a), 109 Stat. 93.

15 U.S.C. § 18 (amended 1996).

15 U.S.C. § 18, *amended by* Act of Feb. 8, 1996, Pub. L. No. 104-104, Title VI, § 601(b)(3), 110 Stat. 143.

Clayton Act, ch. 323, § 7, 38 Stat. 730, 731–32 (1914) (current version at 15 U.S.C. § 18).

14.3(b) Federal statutes invalidated or declared unconstitutional

When citing a federal statute that has been invalidated or held unconstitutional by a court, follow the basic format in **Rule 14.2**, and append a clause with an italicized reference to the court's action, followed by a full citation to the case addressing the statute.[45]

Example

Flag Protection Act of 1989, 18 U.S.C. § 700, Pub. L. No. 101-131, 103 Stat. 777, *held unconstitutional by United States v. Eichman*, 496 U.S. 310 (1990).

14.4 Full Citations to State Statutes

14.4(a) Full citation to state statute

Each state has at least one code containing its statutes. The components and arrangement of state statutory citations vary widely. Consult the jurisdiction's entry in **Appendix 1(B)** for its components, format, order, and abbreviations. Analogize to the federal rules for specific components;[46] see **Chart 14.1** for cross-references to those rules. See **Rule 6.1** for guidance in citing section or paragraph numbers.

To the extent consistent with the state's entry in **Appendix 1(B)**, analogize to similar components in the rules for federal statutes:

Examples

Del. Code Ann. tit. 13, § 711A (2012).

Fla. Stat. Ann. § 608.4225(1)(b) (West 2007).

65 Ill. Comp. Stat. 5/11-61-2 (2006).

Ariz. Rev. Stat. Ann. § 8-303 (Westlaw through 2d Reg. Sess. of 52d Leg.).

Haw. Rev. Stat. Ann. § 201B-1 (Lexis+ through 2019 2d Spec. Sess.).

SIDEBAR 14.2 Local Practices When Citing Statutes

Rule 14.4 and **Appendix 1(B)** reflect a uniform system of citation for statutes across all jurisdictions. Legal writers should use them to craft citations for a national legal audience, such as when drafting a book or law review article. This is so legal readers can understand the citation no matter what jurisdiction they are in. In contrast, **Appendix 2(B)** reflects local citation practices. Citations for state statutes that are crafted using local practices may look different than the standardized citations found in **Rule 14.4** and **Appendix 1(B)**. For example, an Illinois statute's citation according to **Rule 14.4(a)** may look like this: 65 Ill. Comp. Stat. 5/11-61-2 (2006). But if you were practicing in Illinois and drafting a document to file in court there, the same citation would look like this: 65 ILCS 5/11-61-2 (2006). An Illinois court would know what "ILCS" means because it is the local custom to abbreviate the code that way. But if you used that abbreviation in a document meant for readers outside Illinois who are unfamiliar with the term "ILCS," they will not know to which state's statute that acronym refers. Illinois, perhaps, but maybe it refers to Idaho, Indiana, or Iowa. Whether you use **Appendix 2(B)** or **Rule 14.4** to cite to a state's statutory code depends on your audience.

CHART 14.1 **Analogous Rules for Statutory Components**

To the extent they are consistent with the state's entry in **Appendix 1(B)**, analogize the components of a state statute to similar components in the rules for federal statutes.

Component:	Rule(s):
Official or popular name of statute	14.2(a)
Section symbols and section numbers	6.1, 14.2(d)
Appendices and other subdivisions	14.2(e)
Publisher or commercial database	14.2(f)
Publication date or current-through information	14.2(f)
Explanatory parentheticals	14.2(g)
Statute no longer in force	14.3

14.4(b) State code with subject-matter designations

A few states (California, Louisiana, Maryland, New York, Texas) use subject-matter designations for their code volumes. In general, use the subject-matter designations in the statute's citation;[47] consult the state's entry in **Appendix 1(B)** for those codes' abbreviations.

Examples

Cal. Prob. Code § 4264(c) (West 2009).

N.Y. Gen. Oblig. Law § 5-1501 (McKinney 2011 & Supp. 2013).

14.4(c) Publication date rules specific to state statutes

Some state codes have more than one year on the spine or title page. If so, include all the years covered.[48] Use the year of a replacement volume, not the year of the original, if a state code volume replaces an earlier edition.[49]

14.4(d) Citing to online sources for state statutes

When a state publishes its official code online, you may cite to it as you would in print, but you must append the URL.[50] You must also add the URL after the publication parenthetical when you are citing an unofficial version of a state statute available online.[51]

Examples

W. Va. Code § 1-5-3 (2020), http://www.wvlegislatCure.gov/WVCODE/code.cfm?chap=1&art=5#01.

Haw. Rev. Stat. § 431C-3 (2019), https://law.justia.com/codes/hawaii/2019/title-24/chapter-431c/section-431c-3/.

14.4(e)FN Full citations to state statutes in academic footnotes

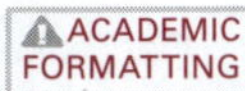

Follow **Rule 14.4(a)–(d)**, but use large and small capital letters for the abbreviated name of the state code, including its subject-matter designations, if any.[52]

Examples

[11] Tenn. Code Ann. § 55-50-405(a)(1)(C) (2012).

[42] Mo. Ann. Stat. § 404.710.6(3) (West 2011 & Supp. 2013).

14.5 Short Citations to Federal and State Statutes

14.5(a) Using *id.* or other short citations to statutes

When a citation refers to a statute *within the same title, chapter, or part* as a statute cited in the immediately preceding citation, use *id.*, changing the section or paragraph number as needed (see **Rules 6.1** and **11.3(c)**).[53]

Examples

Id. § 12102. *Id.* ¶¶ 73–107.

When *id.* is not appropriate, use one of the short citation options illustrated below.[54] If the citation is to a source from an electronic database, you must include the name of the database in the short form.[55] And for any source in which the full citation requires a URL (see **Rules 14.2(h)** and **14.4(d)**), omit the URL in any short form.[56] In selecting an option, choose one with enough information for the reader to easily recognize the source.

Examples

Full citation (federal with optional date):	42 U.S.C. § 12101 (2012).
Short citation options:	42 U.S.C. § 12101.
	§ 12101.
Full citation (named statute with optional date):	Administrative Procedure Act § 5(d), 5 U.S.C. § 554(e) (2012).
Short citation options:	Administrative Procedure Act § 5(d).
	§ 5(d).
	5 U.S.C. § 554(e).
	§ 554(e).
Full citation (state with numbered codes):	Okla. Stat. tit. 22, § 258 (2003 & Supp. 2012).

Short citation options:	Okla. Stat. tit. 22, § 258.
	Tit. 22, § 258.
	§ 258.
Full citation (state with named codes):	Cal. Fin. Code § 4995 (West 2018).
Short citation option:	Fin. § 4995.
Full citation with publisher:	Del. Code Ann. tit. 4, § 512D (West, Westlaw Edge through ch. 281 of the 150th Gen. Assemb.).
Short citation option:	Tit. 4 § 512D (Westlaw Edge).
	§ 512D (Westlaw Edge).
Full citation with URL:	Utah Code § 10-3c-202 (2017), https://le.utah.gov/xcode/Title10/Chapter3C/10-3c-S202.html?v=C10-3c-S202_2017031420170314.
Short citation option:	§ 10-3c-202.

When referring to the *United States Code* in main or footnote text, you may either spell out "section" or use a section symbol (§).[57] When referring to any other statutory code, always spell out the word "section" in main or footnote text, but use a section symbol (§) in both full and short citations.[58]

14.5(b)FN Short citations to statutes in academic footnotes

ACADEMIC FORMATTING

When appropriate (**Rule 11.3(c)**), use *id.* as the short citation.[59] When *id.* is not appropriate, either use all components of the full citation except the date, or use a format illustrated in **Rule 14.5(a)**.[60] Repeat the full citation when the statute has not been cited, in full or in short form (including *id.*) in the same footnote or one of the previous five footnotes. Do not use *supra* (**Rule 11.4**).[61]

Examples

in Federal:	in State:
[121] 18 U.S.C. § 1965.	[73] MICH. COMP. LAWS § 445.84 (2008).
[122] *Id.* § 1961.	[74] *Id.* § 445.86.
. . .	. . .
[124] § 1965.	[87] MICH. COMP. LAWS § 445.86 (2008).
. . .	. . .
[138] 18 U.S.C. § 1965.	[90] § 445.86.

14.6 Full Citations to Federal Session Laws Currently in Force

Once a legislative enactment has been signed into law, but before it is codified, it is cited as a session law (also referred to in the singular as a "slip law"). A full citation to a federal session law currently in force contains the following components[62]:

[Title of act,] | Law abbreviation | No. | Law number, | Pinpoint reference, | Volume number | Stat. | Initial page, | Pinpoint reference | [(Date)].

Example (spaces denoted by ▲)

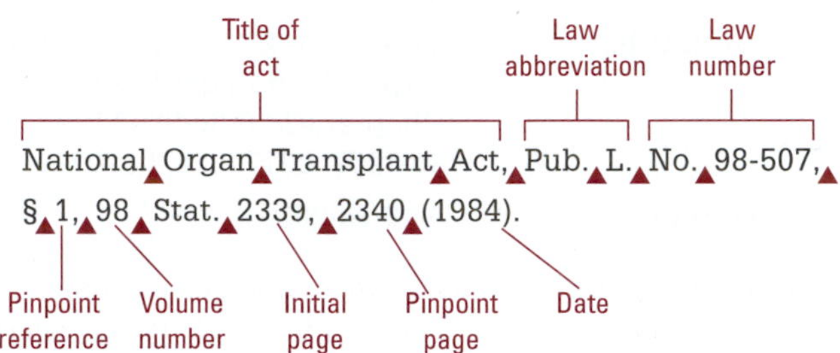

14.6(a) Title of act

Begin the citation with the title or popular name of the act, or both, in ordinary type.[63] Omit "the" if it is the first word.[64] Insert a comma and one space after the title. When an act is untitled, identify it with its date of enactment ("Act of . . .") or date of effectiveness ("Act effective . . .") (Month Day, Year).[65] You may add additional identifying information in a parenthetical.[66] Follow **Rule 3.2**, **Rule 3.3**, and **Chart 3.1** for capitalization and **Appendix 3(A)** for calendar abbreviations. Do not abbreviate the words in the title.[67]

Examples

Jumpstart Our Business Startups Act, Pub. L. No. 112-106, 126 Stat. 306, 307–08 (2012).

Act of Nov. 7, 2011, Pub. L. No. 112-45, 125 Stat. 535, 536–37.

14.6(b) Session law abbreviations for public and private laws

Federal session laws are enacted either as public laws ("Pub. L."), applying generally to all persons, or as private laws ("Priv. L."), applying only to specific individuals or groups. Private laws are not always published in the *United States Code*. If a private law you are citing is not, cite to the session law or a secondary source, in that order of preference.[68] For laws published in the *United*

States Code, use the appropriate abbreviation for the session law, in ordinary type, followed by one space.[69]

14.6(c) Public or private law number

Federal session law numbers are hyphenated (e.g., 107-49). The number preceding the hyphen identifies the Congress that enacted the law (e.g., the 107th Congress). The number following the hyphen indicates the sequential order of the enactment (e.g., the 49th law enacted by the 107th Congress). After the session law abbreviation, set out the abbreviation "No." followed by a space and the number of the public or private law.[70] Insert a comma and one space after the session law number.[71]

Example

Priv. L. No. 112-1

14.6(d) *Statutes at Large*

At the end of each session of Congress, session laws are compiled and collectively published in *United States Statutes at Large* (abbreviated "Stat."). Following the session law number, set out the volume number of *Statutes at Large* in which the cited session law is published.[72] Insert one space after the volume number, followed by the abbreviation "Stat." in ordinary type, and one space.[73]

Example

Credit Card Accountability Responsibility and Disclosure Act of 2009, Pub. L. No. 111-24, § 148(b)(1), 123 Stat. 1734, 1738.

When a session law is not yet available in print in *Statutes at Large*, cite its authenticated online version in govinfo.gov exactly as you would cite the print source. You may also cite an unofficial source for these session laws, such as the advance sheets of West's *United States Code Congressional and Administrative News* (abbreviated "U.S.C.C.A.N.")[74] or commercial databases such as Lexis+, Westlaw Edge, or Bloomberg Law.

14.6(e) Initial page and pinpoint references

After "Stat.," insert the initial page number for the cited law.[75] When citing specific sections of a session law, indicate them with section numbers immediately following the public law number, and provide corresponding page numbers from *Statutes at Large* immediately following the initial page number from that source.[76] See **Rule 5.2** for more information on pinpoint page references.

Example

Economic Espionage Act of 1996, Pub. L. No. 104-294, § 201, 110 Stat. 3488, 3491.

14.6(f) Enactment or effective date

Following the page reference(s), set out in parentheses the year of the session law's enactment, or if no enactment date is available, the law's effective date.[77] Omit this date reference when the year is part of the session law's title.[78]

Examples

Air Carriage of International Mail Act, Pub. L. No. 110-405, § 2(a), 122 Stat. 4287, 4287–90 (2008).

Act of Aug. 16, 2012, Pub. L. No. 112-170, 126 Stat. 1303, 1304.

14.6(g) Information regarding codification of session law

Once a session law is codified, cite the law in its codified version rather than the session law version. If the session law itself is the focus of your writing, however, indicate parenthetically the statutory code in which the session law has been ("codified as") or will be codified ("to be codified at").[79]

Examples

Cruise Vessel Security and Safety Act of 2010, Pub. L. No. 111-207, § 3, 124 Stat. 2243, 2244–51 (codified as 46 U.S.C. §§ 3507–3508 (2012)).

Every Student Succeeds Act, Pub. L. No. 114-95, 129 Stat. 1802 (2015) (to be codified at 20 U.S.C. § 6301).

14.6(h)FN Full citations to federal session laws in academic footnotes

ACADEMIC FORMATTING

There are no differences between citations to federal session laws in academic footnotes and those in practice-based documents.

14.7 Full Citations to Historical Facts and Federal Session Laws No Longer in Force

To cite support for the historical fact of a statute's enactment, amendment, or repeal, cite to the session law.[80] You may choose to add a parenthetical describing the historical fact.[81]

Example

Pub. L. No. 87-301, § 5, 75 Stat. 650, 651–53 (1961) (repealed 1996).

When citing a session law for a federal statute that is no longer in force, follow **Rule 14.6**, but add a parenthetical notation regarding the date that the statute was repealed, invalidated, amended, or superseded.[82] Alternatively, forgo the parenthetical and instead append a clause with an italicized reference to the repeal or amendment, followed by a full citation to the repealing or amending statute or session law.[83]

Example

Supplemental Appropriation Act of 1955, Pub. L. No. 663, 68 Stat. 800 (1954) (amended 1959).

Religious Freedom of Restoration Act (RFRA) of 1993, Pub. L. No. 103-141, 107 Stat. 1488, *invalidated by City of Boerne v. Flores*, 521 U.S. 507 (1997).

Act of Sept. 9, 1959, Pub. L. No. 115-334, 132 Stat. 4685 (repealed Dec. 20, 2018).

Farm Credit Act of 1971, Pub. L. No. 92-181, 105 Stat. 1874, *amended by* Farm Credit System Reform Act of 1996, Pub. L. No. 104-105, 110 Stat. 168.

14.8 Full Citations to State Session Laws

To cite state session laws, follow the formats and use the abbreviations shown in the state's entry in **Appendix 1(B)**, setting out all components in ordinary type.[84] To the extent the state session law's components are comparable to federal session law components, analogize to **Rule 14.6**.[85] When a state session law is no longer in force, analogize to **Rule 14.7**. Whether you are citing a state session law from a print source or from an authenticated or official online source, the format is the same.

Examples

2009 S.D. Sess. Laws ch. 9 § 3.

2015 Tenn. Pub. Acts ch. 166 (to be codified at Tenn. Code Ann. § 29-34-209).

14.9 Short Citations to Federal and State Session Laws

14.9(a) Using *id.* or other short citations to session laws

When a citation refers to the same session law as in the immediately preceding citation, use *id.*, changing the section number, paragraph number, or pinpoint pages as needed.[86] When *id.* is not appropriate (**Rule 11.3(c)**), use one of the options shown in the examples.[87] Select an option that will not confuse the reader.

Examples

Full citation (with title of act):	Economic Espionage Act of 1996, Pub. L. No. 104-294, § 201, 110 Stat. 3488, 3491.
Short citation options:	§ 201.
	Economic Espionage Act § 201.
	§ 201, 110 Stat. at 3491.

14.9(b)FN Short citations to session laws in academic footnotes

ACADEMIC FORMATTING

When appropriate (**Rule 11.3(c)**), use *id.* as the short citation.[88] When *id.* is not appropriate, either use all components of the full citation except the date, or use a format illustrated in **Rule 14.9(a)**.[89] Repeat the full citation when the session law has not been cited, in full or in short form (including *id.*), in the same footnote or one of the previous five footnotes.[90] Do not use *supra* (**Rule 11.4**).[91]

Examples

[45] Rosa's Law, Pub. L. No. 111-256, § 4, 124 Stat. 2643, 2645 (2010).

[46] *Id.* § 3, 124 Stat. at 2645.

. . .

[49] § 2, 124 Stat. at 2643–44.

[50] *Id.*

. . .

[61] Rosa's Law, Pub. L. No. 111-256, § 4, 124 Stat. 2643, 2645 (2010).

15 Legislation and Other Legislative Materials

Fast Formats

House bill	H.R. 6, 109th Cong. § 142 (2005).
Senate simple resolution	S. Res. 262, 103d Cong. (1994).
House concurrent resolution	H.R. Con. Res. 133, 112th Cong. (2012).
House joint resolution	H.R.J. Res. 2, 113th Cong. (2013).
Congressional hearing	*Department of Defense Mustard Gas Testing: Hearing Before the Subcomm. on Comp., Pension & Ins. of the H. Comm. on Veterans' Affs.*, 102d Cong. 12–16 (1993) (statement of Constance M. Pechura) [hereinafter *Mustard Gas Testing*].
Congressional report	S. Rep. No. 113-9, at 6–7 (2013).
Congressional debate, bound edition	147 Cong. Rec. 13,463 (2001).
Congressional debate, daily edition	158 Cong. Rec. H1923 (daily ed. Apr. 18, 2012).
Congressional journal	S. Journal, 115th Cong. 131–34 (2017).
State house bill	H.R. 4660, 97th Leg., 1st Sess. § 31 (Mich. 2013).
State senate resolution	S. Res. 76, 130th Gen. Assemb., Reg. Sess. (Ohio 2013).
State legislative hearing	*Hearing to Evaluate Governor's Program Bill 44 Before the S. Standing Comm. on Banks*, 2008 Leg., 232d Sess. 11, 17 (N.Y. 2008) (prepared testimony of Paul J. Richman, vice president of state gov't affs., Mortg. Bankers Ass'n).
State legislative report or document	S. Rules Comm. Off. of S. Floor Analyses, *Report on Senate Bill No. 1471*, 1995–1996 Reg. Sess., at 2–3 (Cal. 1996).

State legislative debate	S., *55th Legislative Day, Senate Transcripts*, 101st Gen. Assemb., Reg. Sess. 40–45 (Ill. 2019).
Citations in academic footnotes	[24] Social Security Solvency and Sustainability Act, S. 804, 112th Cong. § 3 (2011). ⚠ ACADEMIC FORMATTING [109] S. REP. NO. 113-9, at 6–7 (2013). [168] 147 CONG. REC. 13,463 (2001). [249] FINAL LEGIS. REP., 57th Leg., at 198 (Wash. 2001).
Short citations	H.R. 6, 109th Cong. § 141. H.R.J. Res. 2. *Mustard Gas Testing*, *supra* note 199, at 12–16. 147 Cong. Rec. at 13,464. Mich. H.R. 4660, 97th Leg., 1st Sess. § 31. Ohio S. Res. 76, 130th Gen. Assemb., Reg. Sess.

15.1 Full Citations to Federal Unenacted Measures

A full citation to an unenacted measure of the United States Senate or House of Representatives contains up to seven components.[1] Congress uses four types of measures: the bill, the simple resolution, the concurrent resolution, and the joint resolution. The first three, when *unenacted*, are treated here in **Rule 15.1**. For enacted federal bills and joint resolutions, see **Rule 15.3**. For enacted simple and concurrent resolutions, see **Rule 15.4**.

Title of measure, | Designation of measure | Measure number, | Congress number | Pinpoint reference | ([Session number if an older measure] | Year).

Example (House bill)

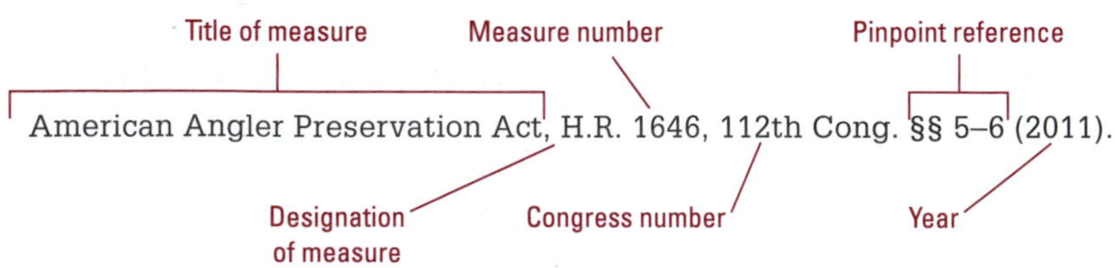

Other examples (spaces denoted by ▲)

House simple resolution:	H.R.▲Res.▲438,▲109th▲Cong.▲(2005).
Senate bill (with title):	Border▲Security,▲Economic▲Opportunity,▲and▲Immigration▲Modernization▲Act,▲S.▲744,▲113th▲Cong.▲§▲2101▲(2013).
Senate bill (with session reference):	S.▲109,▲25th▲Cong.▲(3d▲Sess.▲1839).

15.1(a) Title of measure

Each measure bears a "long title," beginning with words identifying it as a bill or a form of resolution and serving as its official name. Citations to legislative measures rarely refer to their long titles. However, many measures are given a "short title" intended as an easier and more memorable reference to the measure. You may begin the citation to a measure with its short title, if any, followed by a comma and one space.[2] Set out the title in ordinary type.[3] Capitalize words according to **Rule 3.2**, **Rule 3.3**, and **Chart 3.1**.

Examples

Long title:	A Bill to Amend the Animal Welfare Act to Provide Further Protection for Puppies
Citation with short title, as designated in the act itself:	Puppy Uniform Protection and Safety Act, S. 395, 113th Cong. (2013).

15.1(b) Designation of measure

Each measure begins with an abbreviation indicating the chamber in which it was introduced ("H.R." or "S."), followed by an abbreviation for the form of the measure.[4] Present the designation in ordinary type, followed by one space.[5] The abbreviations below denote those spaces with red triangles (▲). For more information on forms of legislative measures, see **Sidebar 15.1**.

Examples (spaces denoted by ▲)

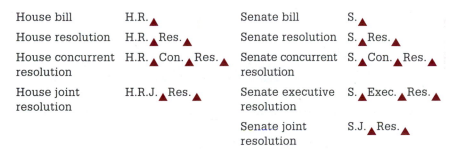

House bill	H.R.▲	Senate bill	S.▲
House resolution	H.R.▲Res.▲	Senate resolution	S.▲Res.▲
House concurrent resolution	H.R.▲Con.▲Res.▲	Senate concurrent resolution	S.▲Con.▲Res.▲
House joint resolution	H.R.J.▲Res.▲	Senate executive resolution	S.▲Exec.▲Res.▲
		Senate joint resolution	S.J.▲Res.▲

15.1(c) Number of measure

Following the abbreviation for the measure's designation, insert its number, a comma, and one space.[6]

15.1(d) Congress number

Following the measure's number, designate the Congress in which the measure was introduced, in ordinary type, using an ordinal contraction (**Rule 4.3(b)**).[7] Insert a space and the abbreviation "Cong." (e.g., 103d Cong., 111th Cong.), followed by another space.[8]

15.1(e) Pinpoint references

When referring to only a portion of a measure, provide its pinpoint reference immediately following the Congress number.[9] Bills and resolutions are typically divided into sections. Insert one space after the pinpoint reference.[10] For more information on citing sections and other subdivisions, see **Rule 6.1**.

Examples (spaces denoted by ▲)

S.▲3978,▲109th▲Cong.▲§§▲2–3▲(2005).

H.R.▲Res.▲97,▲110th▲Cong.▲§▲1(B)▲(2007).

SIDEBAR 15.1 Forms of Legislative Measures

Legislative measures are presented in one of four forms: the bill, the joint resolution, the concurrent resolution, and the simple resolution. The most common is the bill. Once a bill has been approved by the chamber in which it was introduced, it goes to the other chamber for consideration. When it has been approved in identical form by both chambers, it goes to the President for signature, and if signed, becomes law. Alternatively, it may become law if the President fails to veto it within ten days after receiving it, or if vetoed, by a two-thirds override vote of each of the two chambers. Similarly, a joint resolution must be approved by both chambers and the President to become law. Joint resolutions typically deal with limited matters such as proposed amendments to the Constitution or specific appropriations.

Concurrent and simple resolutions deal with rules and procedures concerning Congress itself. A concurrent resolution requires the agreement of both chambers, but it is not signed by the President. A simple resolution applies only to the chamber that proposed and passed it.

For descriptions of the versions of bills and resolutions as they move through the legislative process, visit the U.S. Government Publishing Office, *About Congressional Bills*, https://www.govinfo.gov/help/bills (last visited Nov. 3, 2020).

15.1(f) Year of publication, version of measure, and session number

Following the Congress number and the pinpoint reference, if any, add a parenthetical indicating the year of publication.[11] Depending on the age of the measure, the parenthetical may also need to indicate the session of Congress in which the measure was introduced.[12]

Congress formerly met in three sessions. When citing a House or Senate bill or resolution published before the 60th Congress (1907), indicate in the date parenthetical the session in which the measure was introduced.[13] Use an ordinal contraction for the session ("1st," "2d," or "3d"), followed by a space, the abbreviation "Sess.," and the year.[14] Today's Congress meets in two sessions: the first session occurs in odd-numbered years, and second session occurs in even-numbered years. Because the session number can be inferred from the year, omit the session number from the date parenthetical.[15] Occasionally, Congress will meet in a third session; if you are citing materials from a third session, you must indicate that parenthetically.[16]

Examples

H.R. Res. 88, 39th Cong. (1st Sess. 1866).

Nonprofit Energy Efficiency Act, S. 717, 113th Cong. (2013).

Legislative measures can go through multiple versions as they move through the political process. To cite a particular version of a measure, replace the year of publication with the measure's status on a specific date (e.g., "as introduced, [Month Day, Year]," "as passed by Senate [on Month Day, Year]," "as reported by H.R. Comm. on Ways & Means [on Month Day, Year]").[17] In referring to names of congressional committees and subcommittees, you may abbreviate words appearing in **Appendix 3(F)**.[18] Abbreviate months in accordance with **Appendix 3(B)**.

Examples

H.R. 203, 107th Cong. § 6 (as introduced, Jan. 3, 2001).

H.R. 203, 107th Cong. § 6 (as reported by H.R Comm. on Small Business, Sept. 21, 2001).

H.R. 203, 107th Cong. § 6 (as passed by House, Oct. 2, 2001).

15.1(g) Commercial databases, other online sources, and other parallel citations

Where possible, cite an official version of a legislative measure, whether it is in print or online.[19] Obtain official online versions of congressional measures from Congress.gov or the Government Publishing Office's website govinfo.gov. Cite an official online version in the same manner as its print counterpart.[20] While it is not a necessary component,[21] you may append a parallel citation containing the URL.[22]

Example

Birthright Citizenship Act of 2011, H.R. 140, 112th Cong. (2011–2012), https://www/congress.gov/bill/112th-congress/house-bill/140/text.

To assist readers in locating the measure, you may also provide a parallel citation to a published committee hearing (**Rule 15.5**), a committee report (**Rule 15.7**), or a congressional debate (**Rule 15.10**).[23]

When your source for the measure is a commercial database, add a parallel citation indicating the unique database identifier, if any, followed by a parenthetical with the name of the database provider, if it is not otherwise clear from the database identifier itself.[24] If you are citing to an unofficial online source other than a commercial database, append a URL.[25]

Examples

Parallel citation to committee report:

Sleeping Bear Dunes National Lakeshore Conservation and Recreation Act, S. 140, 112th Cong. (2011), S. Rep. No. 112-104 (2012).

Parallel citation to commercial database:

Sleeping Bear Dunes National Lakeshore Conservation and Recreation Act, S. 140, 112th Cong. (2011), S. Rep. No. 112-104 (2012), 2012 WL 112045.

Every Student Succeeds Act, S. 1177, 113th Cong. (2015), 2015 S. 1177, 114 S. 1177 (Lexis+).

Parallel citation to unofficial online version:

Pursuing Equity in Mental Health Act, H.R. 5469, 116th Cong. (as introduced Dec. 17, 2019), https://docs.house.gov/billsthisweek/20200928/BILLS-116hr5469-SUS.pdf.

15.1(h)[FN] Full citations to unenacted measures in academic footnotes

ACADEMIC FORMATTING

Follow **Rule 15.1(a)–(g)**. There is no difference in the full citation format used in academic footnotes.[26]

15.2 Short Citations to Federal Unenacted Measures

15.2(a) Using *id.* or other short citations to unenacted measures

Use the short citation *id.* to cite the same unenacted measure cited in the immediately preceding citation, even if the pinpoint reference has changed.[27]

Do not use *id.* if the previous citation was in a string citation with one or more other sources (**Rule 11.3(c)**).[28]

For materials divided by sections or other subdivisions, see **Rules 6** and **9**.

When *id.* is not appropriate (**Rule 11.3(c)**), use the designation of the measure and its number.[29] Change the pinpoint reference if necessary. If you are citing to a source in a commercial electronic database, the short form must include the unique database identifier, if any, and include the parenthetical with the name of the database provider.[30] You do not need to include the URL in a short citation if you included it in a source's full citation.[31]

Examples

Full citations: H.R. 988, 109th Cong. § 702 (2005).

H.R. 561, 116th Cong. § 2 (2020), 2019 CONG US HR 561 (Westlaw Edge).

Sleeping Bear Dunes National Lakeshore Conservation and Recreation Act, S. 140, 112th Cong. (2011), 2012 WL 112045.

Short citations: H.R. 988 §§ 701–703.

H.R. 561 § 1, 2019 CONG US HR 561 (Westlaw Edge).

S. 140, 2012 WL 112045.

15.2(b)FN Short citations to unenacted measures in academic footnotes

ACADEMIC FORMATTING

Repeat the full citation if the unenacted measure has not been cited, in full or in short form (including *id.*) in the same footnote or in one of the previous five footnotes.[32] Otherwise, use the applicable short citation described in **Rule 15.2(a)**.[33] Do not use *supra* (**Rule 11.4**).[34]

Examples

59 Graduation for All Act, H.R. 547, 109th Cong. §§ 201–203 (2005).

60 *Id.*

. . .

63 H.R. 547 § 202.

. . .

77 Graduation for All Act, H.R. 547, 109th Cong. §§ 201–203 (2005).

15.3 Citations to Federal Enacted Bills or Joint Resolutions

15.3(a) Full citation to federal enacted bill or joint resolution

Cite an enacted federal bill or joint resolution as a statute, using **Rule 14.1**, unless you are using the bill or joint resolution to document legislative history.[35] In such instances, cite the bill or resolution following **Rule 15.1**.[36]

Examples

House joint resolution:	H.R.J. Res. 75, 107th Cong. (2001).
	H.R.J. Res. 76, 116th Cong. (2020), https://www.congress.gov/bill/116th-congress/house-joint-resolution/76/text.
Senate joint resolution:	S.J. Res. 23, 110th Cong. (2007).
	S.J. Res. 323, 101st Cong. (1990), PL 101–469 (SJRes 323), 104 Stat 1090 (Westlaw Edge).

15.3(b) Short citations to federal enacted bills or joint resolutions

15.3(b)(1) Using *id.* or other short citations to enacted bills or joint resolutions

Follow **Rule 15.2(a)** for short citations to unenacted bills or joint resolutions.[37]

Examples

Full citations:	S.J. Res. 5, 106th Cong. §§ 1–4 (2000).
	H.R.J. Res. 80, 116th Cong. (2020), 2020 WL 755010.
	H.R. Res. 116, 115th Cong. (2017), 2017 H. Res. 116 (Lexis+).
Short citations:	S.J. Res. 5 § 1.
	H.R.J. Res. 80, 2020 WL 755010.
	H.R. Res. 116, 2017 H. Res. 116 (Lexis+).

15.3(b)(2)FN Full and short citations to enacted bills or joint resolutions in academic footnotes

ACADEMIC FORMATTING

For full citations, follow **Rule 15.3(a)**. There is no difference in the full citation format used in academic footnotes.[38]

For short citations, repeat the full citation if the enacted bill or joint resolution has not been cited, in full or in short form (including *id.*) in the same footnote or in one of the previous five footnotes.[39] Otherwise, use the short citation described in **Rule 15.3(b)(1)**.[40] Do not use *supra* **Rule 11.4**.[41]

Examples

[20] H.R.J. Res. 110, 112th Cong. § 1 (2012).

[21] *Id.* § 3.

. . .

[24] H.R.J. Res. 110 § 3.

. . .

[38] H.R.J. Res. 110, 112th Cong. §§ 1, 3 (2012).

15.4 Citations to Federal Enacted Simple or Concurrent Resolutions

15.4(a) Full citation to federal enacted simple or concurrent resolution

Cite an enacted simple or concurrent resolution of either chamber like an unenacted bill or resolution under **Rule 15.1** (including **Rule 15.1(g)** for online versions and those in commercial databases) but add a parenthetical containing the term "enacted."[42]

Examples

H.R. Res. 723, 108th Cong. (2004) (enacted).

S. Con. Res. 115, 108th Cong. (2005) (enacted), https://www.congress.gov/bill/108th-congress/senate-concurrent-resolution/115/text.

H.R. Con. Res. 75, 116th Cong. (2019), 2019 WL 6221668 (enacted).

Provide parallel citations if it would help the reader locate the enacted statute.[43] For simple resolutions, cite the *Congressional Record*; follow **Rule 15.10(a)(4)** in constructing the date parenthetical and place it after the pinpoint reference of the *Congressional Record* abbreviation.[44] Place the "enacted" parenthetical after the date parenthetical at the end of the parallel citation.[45] For concurrent resolutions, cite the *Statutes at Large*, omit the "(enacted)" parenthetical, but provide a parenthetical with the year of publication.[46]

Examples

Simple resolution, parallel citation to *Congressional Record* (daily edition):

H.R. Res. 188, 109th Cong., 151 Cong. Rec. H1802 (daily ed. Apr. 6, 2005) (enacted).

Concurrent resolution, parallel citation to *Statutes at Large*:

H.R. Con. Res. 464, 107th Cong., 116 Stat. 3150 (2002).

15.4(b) Short citations to federal enacted simple or concurrent resolutions

15.4(b)(1) Using *id.* or other short citations to enacted simple or concurrent resolutions

Follow **Rule 15.2(a)** for short citations to unenacted simple or concurrent resolutions.[47]

Example (enacted simple or concurrent resolution)

Full citation: S. Con. Res. 8, 109th Cong. § 1, 151 Cong. Rec. S825 (daily ed. Feb. 1, 2005) (enacted).

Short citation: S. Con. Res. 8 § 1.

15.4(b)(2)[FN] Full and short citations to enacted simple or concurrent resolutions in academic footnotes

ACADEMIC FORMATTING

For full citations, follow **Rule 15.4(a)**. There is no difference in the full citation format used in academic footnotes.[48]

For short citations, repeat the full citation if the resolution has not been cited, in full or in short form (including *id.*) in the same footnote or one of the previous five footnotes.[49] Otherwise, use the short citation described in **Rule 15.4(b)(1)**.[50] Do not use *supra* (**Rule 11.4**).[51]

Example

36 S. Con. Res. 115, 108th Cong. (2005) (enacted).

37 *Id.*

. . .

39 S. Con. Res. 115.

. . .

56 S. Con. Res. 115, 108th Cong. (2005) (enacted).

15.5 Full Citations to Congressional Committee Hearings

A full citation to a congressional committee hearing contains four to seven components.[52]

Full title: | *Hearing* [on *Designation of Measure and Measure number*] | *Before the* | *Name of Subcommittee and/or Committee*, | Congress number | Pinpoint reference | ([Session number] | Year of publication).

Example (spaces denoted by ▲)

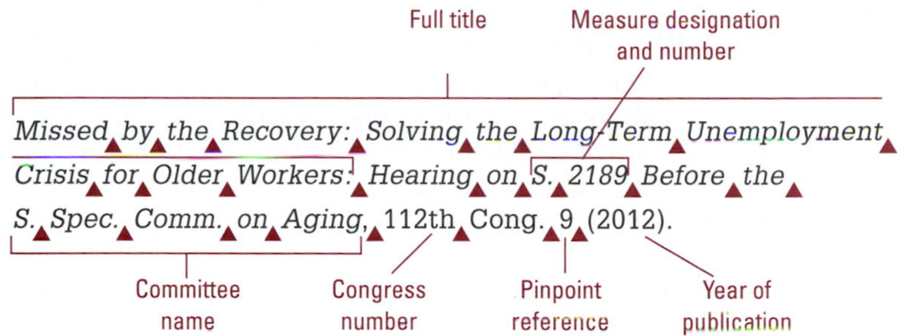

15.5(a) Title of hearing

In italics, present the full title of the hearing, as set out at the top of its cover page, followed by a colon and one space.[53] When a hearing concerns a measure, its title should include the designation of the measure and its number.[54]

15.5(b) Name of committee or subcommittee

Provide the abbreviated name of the committee before which the hearing was held in italics.[55] If the hearing was before a subcommittee, also indicate the name of the committee to which the subcommittee is subordinate.[56] You may abbreviate any words in the committee or subcommittee name that are listed in **Appendices 3(B)**, **3(E)**, and **3(F)**.[57] Insert a comma and one space after the name.[58]

15.5(c) Congress number

Follow **Rule 15.1(d)**.[59]

15.5(d) Pinpoint references

If the citation refers to a specific portion of the hearing, insert a pinpoint reference following the Congress number.[60]

15.5(e) Year of publication; session number

Follow **Rule 15.1(f)**.[61]

15.5(f) Parenthetical information about congressional hearings

You may add a parenthetical after the citation to explain the reference or otherwise assist readers, such as identifying the person testifying before the committee.[62] Abbreviate titles of governmental officials as shown in **Appendices 3(B)** and **3(F)** and **Chart 12.5**.[63]

Examples

S. 2205, S. 2421, S. 2564, and S. 2717: Hearing Before the S. Comm. on Indian Affs., 114th Cong. 9–10 (2016) (statement of Sen. Jeff Flake).

Proposed Federal Water Grabs and Their Potential Impacts on States, Water and Power Users, and Landowners: Oversight Hearing Before the H. Subcomm. on Water, Power & Oceans of the H. Comm. on Nat. Res., 114th Cong. 7–8 (2015) (statement of James Ogsbury, Exec. Dir., W. Governors' Ass'n, Denver, Colo.).

15.5(g) Commercial databases and other online sources

Follow the directions in **Rule 15.1(g)** regarding citations to official and unofficial online sources and commercial databases.[64]

15.5(h)FN Full citations to congressional committee hearings in academic footnotes

ACADEMIC FORMATTING

Follow **Rule 15.5(a)–(g)**. There is no difference in the full citation format used in academic footnotes.[65]

15.6 Short Citations to Congressional Hearings

15.6(a) Using *id.* or other short citations to congressional hearings

Use the short citation *id.* to cite the same congressional hearing cited in the immediately preceding citation, even if the pinpoint reference has changed.[66] Do not use *id.* if the previous citation was in a string citation with one or more other sources (**Rule 11.3(c)**).[67]

When *id.* is not appropriate (**Rule 11.3(c)**), use the hearing title (or a shortened title as indicated by a [hereinafter] reference in the full citation), the Congress number, and the preposition "at" before the pinpoint reference. See **Rule 11.5** for more information about using [hereinafter]. If you are citing to a source in a commercial electronic database, the short form must include the unique database identifier, if any, and include the parenthetical with the name of the database provider.[68] You do not need to include the URL in a short citation if you included it in a source's full citation.[69]

Example

Full citation:	*Roundtable Discussions on Comprehensive Health Care Reform: Hearings Before the S. Comm. on Fin.*, 111th Cong. 120 (2009) [hereinafter *Roundtable Discussions*].
Short citation:	*Roundtable Discussions*, 111th Cong. at 137 (testimony of Edward Kleinbard, Chief of Staff, Joint Comm. on Taxation).

15.6(b)FN Short citations to congressional hearings in academic footnotes

ACADEMIC FORMATTING

When *id.* is not appropriate (**Rule 11.3(c)**), use *supra* to refer the reader to the footnote containing the full citation.[70] Indicate the new pinpoint reference, preceded by ", at."[71] See **Rule 11.4** for more information on using *supra*.

Hearing title, | *supra* | note | Note number, | at | Pinpoint reference.

Example

[19] *Health Care Reform: Recommendations to Improve Coordination of Federal and State Initiatives: Hearing Before the Subcomm. on Health, Emp't, Labor & Pensions of the H. Comm. on Educ. & Labor*, 110th Cong. 46 (2007) [hereinafter *Health Care Reform*].

[20] *Id.*

. . .

[29] *Health Care Reform*, *supra* note 19, at 44.

15.7 Full Citations to Numbered Congressional Reports and Documents

Congressional reports address proposed legislation and issues under a committee's investigation. Senate executive reports relate to nominations of individuals or to treaties between the United States and other countries. House and Senate documents address a variety of materials that Congress has ordered to be printed. Senate treaty documents contain treaty text as submitted to the Senate for presidential ratification.

Because numbered congressional reports and documents are most easily accessed by their numbers, a full citation contains between five and nine components.[72]

[Author, *Title*,] | Abbreviation for type of document | No. | Report or document number, | at | Pinpoint reference | ([Session] | Year of publication).

Example (spaces denoted by ▲)

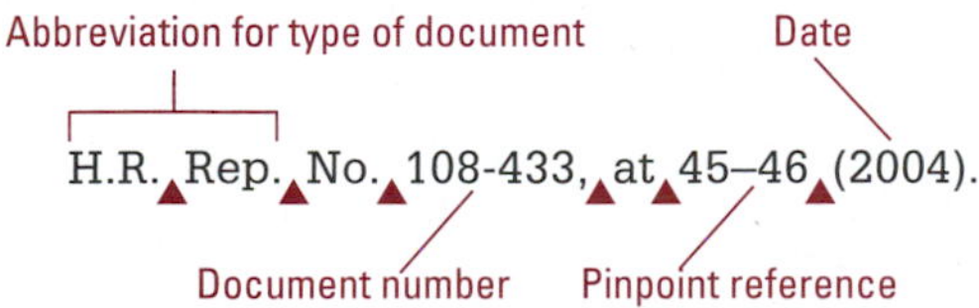

15.7(a) Author and title option

If desired, begin the citation with the author and title of the report or document.[73] Do not indicate a title without also giving the name of the author.[74] For an institutional author, follow **Rule 20.1(b)(3)**, abbreviating words in **Appendices 3(E)** and **3(F)**.[75] Use ordinary type for the author name and italics for the title.[76]

Example

Permanent Subcomm. on Investigations of the S. Comm. on Governmental Affs., *Phony Identification and Credentials Via the Internet*, S. Rep. No. 107-133, at 25–29 (2002).

15.7(b) Abbreviation for numbered report or document

Following the author and title, or as the first component of the citation, abbreviate the type of numbered report or document, beginning with an abbreviation for the chamber in which it originated, followed by one space.[77] Indicate conference reports by adding a parenthetical with the abbreviation "Conf. Rep." after the date parenthetical.[78]

Example

H.R. Rep. No. 108-724, pt. 3 (2004) (Conf. Rep.).

Type of document:	Abbreviation (spaces denoted by ▲):
House Report	H.R.▲Rep.▲
House Document	H.R.▲Doc.▲
House Miscellaneous Document	H.R.▲Misc.▲Doc.▲
Senate Report	S.▲Rep.▲
Senate Executive Report	S.▲Exec.▲Rep.▲
Senate Executive Document	S.▲Exec.▲Doc.▲
Senate Document	S.▲Doc.▲
Senate Treaty Document	S.▲Treaty▲Doc.▲

15.7(c) Report or document number

To create the report or document number, insert the abbreviation "No.," followed by a space and the Congress number, a hyphen, and the number shown on the report or document, followed by another space.[79] If the document or report does not have a number, follow **Rule 15.9**.

Example

No. 103-42 — Report or document number

Congress number

15.7(d) Pinpoint references

When referring to only part of the report or document, indicate the subdivision.[80] Use ", at" only when referring to *pages*, not to other types of subdivisions.[81] For more information on pinpoint subdivisions, see **Rule 5.2**. Insert one space after the pinpoint reference.[82]

Examples

H.R. Doc. No. 111-113, at 7–9 (2010).

S. Treaty Doc. No. 111-5, pt. 4, at 63 (2010).

15.7(e) Year of publication; session designation for older Congresses

Indicate the year in which the report, document, or print was ordered to be printed, enclosed in parentheses.[83]

When citing a House Report published earlier than the 47th Congress (1881) or a Senate Report published earlier than the 40th Congress (1867), indicate whether the measure was introduced during that Congress's first, second, or third session.[84] Place the session designation before the year of publication. Use an ordinal contraction for the session ("1st," "2d," or "3d"), followed by a space and the abbreviation "Sess."[85] For later Congresses, the session can be inferred from the year and thus should not be stated.[86]

15.7(f) Parallel citation to U.S.C.C.A.N., commercial databases, or other online sources

Provide a parallel citation to the report or document, if possible, in the annual bound edition of *United States Code Congressional and Administrative News* ("U.S.C.C.A.N."), introduced by the italicized phrase "*reprinted in*" (for complete reprint of a document) or "*as reprinted in*" (for a partial reprint) and continuing with the year (which serves as the volume number), the abbreviation "U.S.C.C.A.N." and a pinpoint page reference.[87]

Example

H.R. Rep. No. 94-1487, at 7 (1976), *reprinted in* 1976 U.S.C.C.A.N. 6604, 6605–06.

Beginning with the 104th Congress, federal committee reports are also available on Congress.gov and govinfo.gov. Cite them the same way you cite their print versions.[88] If the source you are citing is not available on any of those, but is in a commercial database, add a parallel citation indicating the unique database identifier, if any, followed by a parenthetical with the name of the database provider, if it is not otherwise clear from the database identifier itself.[89] If you are citing to another online source, check **Rules 30.2** and **30.3** to see if you need to append a URL.[90]

Example

> H. Agric. Comm, *Agriculture and Nutrition Act of 2018 Report of the Committee on Agriculture Together with Dissenting Views to Accompany H.R. 2*, H.R. Rep. No. 115-661, 115th Cong. (2018), 2017 Legis. Bill Hist. US H.B. 2 (Lexis+).

15.7(g) Parallel citations to separately bound legislative histories

Some significant acts' legislative histories are published in separately bound books; examples of significant acts include the Administrative Procedures Act, Titles VII and IX of the Civil Rights Act of 1964, the Clean Air Act Amendments of 1970, the Equal Employment Opportunity Act, the Internal Revenue Acts, the National Labor Relations Act, the Occupational Safety and Health Act of 1970, and the Securities Exchange Act of 1934.[91] To determine if an act's compiled legislative history exists, consult the sources on The Library of Congress's website, located at https://www.loc.gov/law/help/leghist.php. If an act's legislative history has been compiled and separately bound and citation to it would help the reader locate the legislative materials more easily, you can give a parallel citation to the bound book. After the citation of the enacting bill, add a ", *reprinted in*" and the citation to the separately bound legislative history. Cite these publications as you would a book, according to **Rule 20**.[92]

Example

> H.R. Rep. No. 1370, at 1 (1962), *reprinted in* U.S. Equal Emp. Opportunity Comm'n, *Legislative History of Titles VII and XI of Civil Rights Act of 1964*, at 2155 (1965).

15.7(h)FN Full citations to numbered congressional reports or documents in academic footnotes

ACADEMIC FORMATTING

Follow **Rule 15.7(a)–(g)**, but use large and small capital letters for both the abbreviation of the report or document and the abbreviation "No."[93] If the citation includes an author name and title, also present them in large and small capital letters.[94] If you are citing to a separately bound legislative history according to **Rule 15.7(g)**, use large and small caps for the author and title of the separately bound publication.[95]

Examples

> 68 H.R. REP. NO. 108-724, pt. 3 (2004) (Conf. Rep.).

> 113 GEORGE W. BUSH, STATE OF THE UNION MESSAGE, H.R. DOC. NO. 109-3 (2005).

> 121 H.R. REP. NO. 1370, at 1 (1962), *reprinted in* U.S. EQUAL EMP. OPPORTUNITY COMM'N, LEGISLATIVE HISTORY OF TITLES VII AND XI OF CIVIL RIGHTS ACT OF 1964, at 2155 (1965).

15.8 Short Citations to Numbered Congressional Reports and Documents

15.8(a) Using *id.* or other short citations to numbered congressional reports or documents

Use the short citation *id.* to cite the same report or document cited in the immediately preceding citation, even if the pinpoint reference has changed.[96] Do not use *id.* if the previous citation was in a string citation with one or more other sources (**Rule 11.3(c)**).[97] For materials divided by sections, see **Rule 6** for guidance on pinpoint references.

When *id.* is not appropriate (**Rule 11.3(c)**), omit the date parenthetical (and conference parenthetical, if any), and if you included the committee name, author, and title in the full citation, you may omit those as well.[98] Keep all other elements of the full citation.[99] If you are citing to a source in a commercial electronic database, the short form must include the unique database identifier, if any, and include the parenthetical with the name of the database provider.[100] You do not need to include the URL in a short citation if you included it in a source's full citation.[101]

Example

Full citation:	H.R. Rep. No. 109-123, §§ 2–4 (2005) (Conf. Rep.).
	H.R. Doc. No. 109-751, r. XI, cl. 2 (2007), https://www.congress.gov/congressional-report/109th-congress/house-report/751/1.
	H.R. Rep. No. 111-156 (2009), 2009 WL 1664631.
Short citation:	H.R. Rep. No. 109-123, § 3.
	H.R. Doc. No. 109-751, r. XI, cl. 2.
	H.R. Rep. No. 111-156, 2009 WL 1664631.

15.8(b)FN Short citations to numbered congressional reports or documents in academic footnotes

Repeat the full citation if the numbered report or document has not been cited, in full or in short form (including *id.*) in the same footnote or one of the previous five footnotes.[102] Otherwise, use the short citation described in **Rule 15.8(a)**.[103] Do not use *supra* (**Rule 11.4**).[104] If you are citing to a separately bound legislative history according to **Rule 15.7(g)**, repeat all components of that publication except the date parenthetical.

Example

33 S. Rep. No. 94-755, at 81 (1976).

34 *Id.*

35 H.R. Rep. No. 1370, at 1 (1962), *reprinted in* U.S. Equal Emp. Opportunity Comm'n, Legislative History of Titles VII and XI of Civil Rights Act of 1964, at 2155 (1965).

. . .

39 S. Rep. No. 94-755, at 80.

40 H.R. Rep. No. 1370, at 1, *reprinted in* U.S. Equal Emp. Opportunity Comm'n, Legislative History of Titles VII and XI of Civil Rights Act of 1964, at 2155.

15.9 Citations to Unnumbered Reports, Documents, and Committee Prints

15.9(a) Full citation to unnumbered report, document, or committee print

Begin with the name of the congressional entity who wrote the unnumbered report, document, or committee print.[105] Treat the entity as an institutional author under **Rule 20.1(b)(3)**, abbreviating any words found in **Appendices 3(E)** and **3(F)**.[106] Treat the Congress number as part of the author's name.[107] Use ordinary type for the author name and italics for the title.[108] For pinpoint references, follow **Rule 15.7(e)**. Using **Appendix 3(F)**, abbreviate the type of document and insert it at the beginning of the date parenthetical.[109] When your source is a commercial database, add a parallel citation indicating the unique database identifier, if any, followed by a parenthetical with the name of the database provider, if it is not otherwise clear from the database identifier itself.[110] If you are citing to an online source other than a commercial database, check **Rules 30.2** and **30.3** to see if you need to append a URL.[111]

Example

Staff of S. Comm. on Banking, Hous. & Urban Affs., 94th Cong., *Report of the Securities and Exchange Commission on Questionable and Illegal Corporate Payments and Practices* 2–3 (Comm. Print 1976).

Staff of H. Comm. on Sci., Space & Tech, 116th Cong., *Compilation of Space Law U.S. & International Space Law, Documents and Agreements* 19–23 (Comm. Print 2019), https://www.govinfo.gov/content/pkg/CPRT-116HPRT38136/pdf/CPRT-116HPRT38136.pdf.

15.9(b)FN Full citations to unnumbered reports, documents, or committee prints in academic footnotes

Follow **Rule 15.9(a)**, but use large and small capital letters for the name of the author and the title.[112]

Example

> 23 Staff of S. Comm. on Banking, Hous. & Urban Affs., 94th Cong., Report of the Securities and Exchange Commission on Questionable and Illegal Corporate Payments and Practices 2–3 (Comm. Print 1976).

15.9(c) Short citations to unnumbered reports, documents, or committee prints

15.9(c)(1) Using *id.* or other short citations to unnumbered reports, documents, or prints

Use the short citation *id.* to cite the same unnumbered report, document, or committee print cited in the immediately preceding citation, even if the pinpoint reference has changed.[113] Do not use *id.* if the previous citation was in a string citation with one or more other sources (**Rule 11.3(c)**).[114]

When *id.* is not appropriate (**Rule 11.3(c)**), omit the date parenthetical, but keep all other elements of the full citation.[115] If you are citing to a source in a commercial electronic database, the short form must include the unique database identifier, if any, and include the parenthetical with the name of the database provider.[116] You do not need to include the URL in a short citation if you included it in a source's full citation.[117]

15.9(c)(2)FN Short citations to unnumbered reports, documents, or prints in academic footnotes

ACADEMIC FORMATTING

Repeat the full citation if the report, document, or print has not been cited, in full or in short form (including *id.*) in the same footnote or one of the previous five footnotes.[118] Otherwise, use the short citation described in **Rule 15.9(c)(1)**.[119] Do not use *supra* (**Rule 11.4**).[120]

Example

> 23 Staff of S. Comm. on Banking, Hous. & Urban Affs., 94th Cong., Report of the Securities and Exchange Commission on Questionable and Illegal Corporate Payments and Practices 2–3 (Comm. Print 1976).
>
> 24 *Id.*
>
> . . .
>
> 27 Staff of S. Comm. on Banking, Hous. & Urban Affs., 94th Cong., Report of the Securities and Exchange Commission on Questionable and Illegal Corporate Payments and Practices 7.

15.10 Citations to Congressional Debates

15.10(a) Full citations to post-1873 congressional debates

Cite congressional debates occurring *after* 1873 to the *Congressional Record*.[121] (For earlier debates, see **Rule 15.10(c)**.) The *Congressional Record* is published daily while either house is in session. At the end of the session, a bound volume of the *Congressional Record* (the "bound edition") is published; it is the preferred citation source.[122] Cite the daily edition only for material not yet available in the bound edition.[123]

A full citation to a post-1873 congressional debate contains four to six components, depending on whether it uses the debate's title and whether it refers to the daily edition or the bound edition of the *Congressional Record*.[124]

Examples (spaces denoted by ▲)

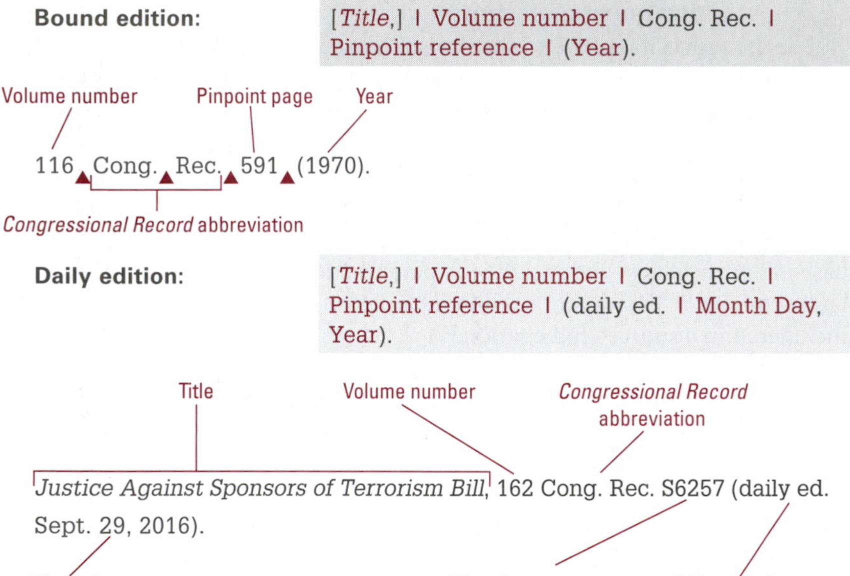

15.10(a)(1) Title of debate

If desired, begin the citation with the title of the debate, in italics. Capitalize words according to **Rule 3.2**, **Rule 3.3**, and **Chart 3.1**.

Example

Suicide Prevention, 155 Cong. Rec. S7445, S7447 (daily ed. July 14, 2009).

Nomination of Amy Coney Barrett, 166 Cong. Rec. S6009, S6010 (daily ed. Oct. 1, 2020) (speech by Sen. McConnell).

15.10(a)(2) Volume number and abbreviation for *Congressional Record*

Following the title (if any), indicate the volume number of the *Congressional Record* in which the debate appears, followed by one space, and the abbreviation "Cong. Rec." in ordinary type.[125]

15.10(a)(3) Pinpoint pages

After the *Congressional Record* abbreviation, insert one space, followed by the page number(s) on which the debate appears.[126] In the daily edition, page numbers are preceded by single letter prefixes corresponding to one of the four sections published in each issue: H for proceedings of the House of Representatives, S for proceedings of the Senate, E for Extensions of Remarks, and D for the Daily Digest (e.g., H____, S____, E___, D___). Each section is separately paginated. The bound edition uses continuous pagination and drops the prefixes.[127] For guidance on citing consecutive or scattered pages, see **Rule 5.3** and **Rule 5.4**.

Examples

Bound edition: 124 Cong. Rec. 25,267 (1978).

Daily edition: 149 Cong. Rec. H9748–50 (daily ed. Oct. 21, 2003).

15.10(a)(4) Edition and date

When citing the bound edition, set out the year of publication in a date parenthetical, even if the debate occurred in a different year.[128] When citing the daily edition, begin the date parenthetical with the phrase "daily ed." followed by one space and the issue's exact date (Month Day, Year).[129] Abbreviate the month according to **Appendix 3(A)**. See examples in **Rule 15.10(a)(3)**.

15.10(a)(5) Parenthetical information

You may include parenthetically any other information that might assist readers, such as the name of the cited speaker,[130] and you may abbreviate words appearing in **Appendix 3(F)**.[131]

Example

51 Cong. Rec. S546–47 (daily ed. Jan. 26, 2005) (statement of Sen. Jeff Bingaman).

15.10(a)(6) Commercial databases and other online sources

Cite an official electronic version of a congressional debate in the same manner as its print counterpart.[132] When your source is a commercial database, add a parallel citation indicating the unique database identifier, if any, followed by a parenthetical with the name of the database provider, if it is not otherwise clear from the database identifier itself.[133] If you are citing to an unofficial online source, append a URL.[134]

Examples

135 Cong. Rec. 329 (1989) (statement of Rep. Philip M. Crane), 135 Cong Rec 329 (Lexis+).

43 Cong. Rec. 11 (1875) (statement of Rep. Williams A. Wheeler), https://memory.loc.gov/cgi-bin/ampage?collId=llcr&fileName=004/llcr004.db&recNum=12.

15.10(a)(7)[FN] Full citations to post-1873 congressional debates in academic footnotes

ACADEMIC FORMATTING

Follow **Rule 15.10(a)(1)–(6)**, but abbreviate *Congressional Record* using large and small capital letters ("Cong. Rec.").[135]

Examples

[145] *Suicide Prevention*, 155 Cong. Rec. S7445, S7447 (daily ed. July 14, 2009).

[152] *Partial-Birth Abortion Ban Act of 2000*, 146 Cong. Rec. 4491, 4501 (2000) (speech by Rep. DeLay).

15.10(b) Short citations to post-1873 congressional debates

15.10(b)(1) Using *id.* or other short citations to post-1873 congressional debates

Use the short citation *id.* to cite the same debate cited in the immediately preceding citation, even if the pinpoint reference has changed.[136] Do not use *id.* if the previous citation was in a string citation with one or more other sources (**Rule 11.3(c)**).[137]

When *id.* is not appropriate (**Rule 11.3(c)**), use all components except the date parenthetical; insert "at" before the pinpoint page(s).[138] If you are citing to a source in a commercial electronic database, the short form must include the unique database identifier, if any, and include the parenthetical with the name of the database provider.[139] You do not need to include the URL in a short citation if you included it in a source's full citation.[140]

Examples

Full citations:	124 Cong. Rec. 32,408 (1978).
	138 Cong. Rec. 1121 (1992) (statement of Rep. Andrews), 138 Cong Rec 1121 (Lexis+).
Short citations:	124 Cong. Rec. at 32,409.
	138 Cong. Rec. at 1121, 138 Cong Rec 1121 (Lexis+).

15.10(b)(2)FN Short citations to post-1873 congressional debates in academic footnotes

Abbreviate *Congressional Record* using large and small capital letters ("CONG. REC.").[141] Repeat the full citation if the congressional debate has not been cited, in full or in short form (including *id.*), in the same footnote or one of the previous five footnotes.[142] Otherwise, follow the short citation described in **Rule 15.10(b)(1)**.[143] Do not use *supra* (**Rule 11.4**).[144]

Example

> 29 150 CONG. REC. S11,653 (daily ed. Nov. 19, 2004).
>
> 30 *Id.*
>
> . . .
>
> 33 150 CONG. REC. at S11,653.

15.10(c) Full citations to pre-1873 congressional debates

15.10(c)(1) Publication sources and formats

For congressional debates taking place *up to and through* 1873, there are three publication sources, covering different periods and different Congresses: the *Annals of Congress*, the *Register of Debates*, and the *Congressional Globe*, with a few years' overlap in coverage by the latter two.[145] Represent the publication's components in ordinary type.[146] If you are citing to an online source, append a URL.[147]

Cite the *Annals of Congress* (1st Cong. to 18th Cong., 1st Sess., 1789–1824) as:

Volume number | Annals of Cong. | Pinpoint reference | (Year).

If you are citing the first volume of the *Annals of Congress*, the year in the parenthetical will be the year of the debate.[148] Then include a space after the year parenthetical and include a second parenthetical with the name(s) of the editor(s), the abbreviation "ed.," another space and the year of its publication.[149]

Cite the *Register of Debates* (18th Cong., 2d Sess. to 25th Cong., 1st Sess., 1824–1833) as:

Volume number | Reg. Deb. | Pinpoint reference | (Year).

Cite the *Congressional Globe* (25th Cong., 2d Sess. to 42d Cong., 2d Sess., 1833–1873) as:

Cong. Globe, | Congress ordinal number | Cong., | Session ordinal number | Sess. | Pinpoint reference | (Year).

Examples

1 Annals of Cong. 516 (1792) (Joseph Gales and Williams Seaton eds., 1849).

18 Annals of Cong. 1766 (1819).

11 Reg. Deb. 130 (1835).

Cong. Globe, 41st Cong., 1st Sess. 500–01 (1869).

15.10(c)(2)^FN Full citations to pre-1873 congressional debates in academic footnotes

ACADEMIC FORMATTING

Follow **Rule 15.10(c)(1)**, but use large and small capital letters for the abbreviated name of the publication source.[150]

Examples

56 37 ANNALS OF CONG. 47 (1820).

64 12 REG. DEB. 2331 (1836).

198 *See* CONG. GLOBE, 26th Cong., 1st Sess. 150–51 (1840).

15.10(d) Short citations to pre-1873 congressional debates

15.10(d)(1) Using *id.* or other short citations to pre-1873 congressional debates

Use the short citation *id.* to cite the same debate cited in the immediately preceding citation, even if the pinpoint reference has changed.[151] Do not use *id.* if the previous citation was in a string citation with one or more other sources (**Rule 11.3(c)**).[152]

When *id.* is not appropriate (**Rule 11.3(c)**), keep all components except the date parenthetical, and insert "at" before the pinpoint page(s).[153] You do not need to include the URL in a short citation if you included it in a source's full citation.[154]

Example

Full citation: 18 Annals of Cong. 1766 (1819).

Cong. Globe, 37th Cong., 1st Sess. 310 (1861), https://memory.loc.gov/cgi-bin/ampage?collId=llcg&fileName=057/llcg057.db&recNum=327.

Short citation: 18 Annals of Cong. at 1766.

Cong. Globe, 37th Cong., 1st Sess. at 311.

15.10(d)(2)FN Short citations to pre-1873 congressional debates in academic footnotes

Use large and small capital letters for the abbreviated name of the publication source.[155] Repeat the full citation if the congressional debate has not been cited, in full or in short form (including *id.*) in the same footnote or one of the previous five footnotes.[156] Otherwise, follow the short citation described in **Rule 15.10(d)(1)**.[157] Do not use *supra* (**Rule 11.4**).[158]

Example

> 59 CONG. GLOBE, 41st Cong., 1st Sess. 500–01 (1869), http://lcweb2.loc.gov/cgi-bin/ampage.
>
> 60 *Id.*
>
> . . .
>
> 63 CONG. GLOBE, 41st Cong., 1st Sess. at 500.

15.11 Citations to Congressional Journals

15.11(a) Full citations to congressional journals

The House of Representatives and the Senate publish official proceedings in journals at the end of each session. The journals record motions, actions taken, and roll-call votes but not the text of debates or other proceedings.

A full citation to a congressional journal contains six components, all rendered in ordinary type. Although the word "Journal" is abbreviated in other citation contexts, to avoid possible confusion with joint resolutions, do not abbreviate it here.[159]

Chamber abbreviation | Journal, | Congress number | Cong. | [, Session number | Sess.] | Pinpoint reference | (Year of publication).

Example (spaces denoted by ▲)

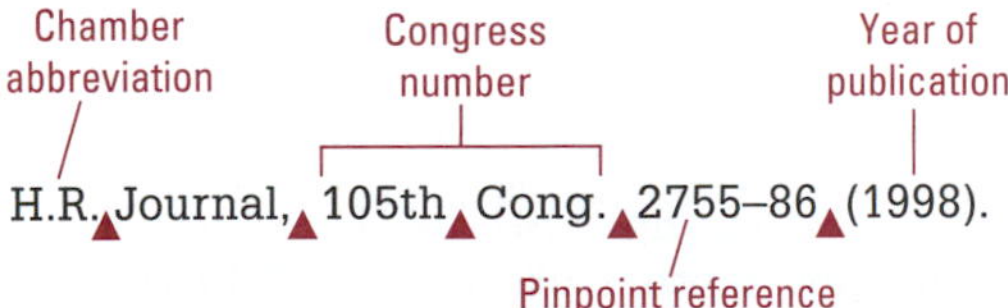

Both the Congress number and session numbers should be written as ordinals (see **Rules 4.3(b)** and **15.1(d)**, **(f)**). In accordance with **Rule 15.1(f)**, only include the session number for journals published before the 60th Congress (1907) or if you are citing materials from a third session.[160]

When your source for the journal is a commercial database, add a parallel citation indicating the unique database identifier, if any, followed by a parenthetical with the name of the database provider, if it is not otherwise clear from the database identifier itself.[161] If you are citing to an online source other than a commercial database, check **Rules 30.2** and **30.3** to see if you need to append a URL.

Examples

S. Journal, 109th Cong. 2–7 (2006), https://www.govinfo.gov/content/pkg/GPO-CPUB-109pub30/pdf/GPO-CPUB-109pub30.pdf.

H.R. Journal, 115th Cong. 1821–2608 (2017), 2017 Part 2 J. H.R. U.S. (HeinOnline).

15.11(b)[FN] Full citations to congressional journals in academic footnotes

ACADEMIC FORMATTING

Follow **Rule 15.11(a)**, but use large and small capital letters for the chamber abbreviation and Journal.[162]

Example

[79] S. JOURNAL, 34th Cong., 3d Sess. 132 (1857) (petition for relief of shipwrecked mariners).

15.11(c) Short citations to congressional journals

15.11(c)(1) Using *id.* or other short citations to congressional journals

Use the short citation *id.* to cite the same journal cited in the immediately preceding citation, even if the pinpoint reference has changed.[163] Do not use *id.* if the previous citation was in a string citation with one or more other sources (**Rule 11.3(c)**).[164]

When *id.* is not appropriate (**Rule 11.3(c)**), keep all components except the date parenthetical, and insert "at" before the pinpoint page(s).[165] If you are citing to a source in a commercial electronic database, the short form must include the unique database identifier, if any, and include the parenthetical with the name of the database provider.[166] You do not need to include the URL in a short citation if you included it in a source's full citation.[167]

Examples

Full citations:	S. Journal, 38th Cong., 1st Sess. 51–55 (1863).
	H.R. Journal, 114th Cong. 2101–07 (2015), https://www.govinfo.gov/content/pkg/GPO-HJOURNAL-2015/pdf/GPO-HJOURNAL-2015-2-2.pdf.
Short citations:	S. Journal, 38th Cong., 1st Sess. at 54.
	H.R. Journal, 114th Cong. at 2103.

15.11(c)(2)FN Short citations to congressional journals in academic footnotes

ACADEMIC FORMATTING

Use large and small capital letters for the abbreviated name of the journal.[168] Repeat the full citation if the congressional journal has not been cited, in full or in short form (including *id.*) in the same footnote or one of the previous five footnotes.[169] Otherwise, follow the short citation described in **Rule 15.11(c)(1)**.[170] Do not use *supra* (**Rule 11.4**).[171]

Example

96 S. Journal, 1st Cong., 1st Sess. 117 (1789).

97 *Id.*

. . .

99 S. Journal, 1st Cong., 1st Sess. at 118.

15.12 *The Declaration of Independence*

15.12(a) Citations to *The Declaration of Independence*

A full citation to *The Declaration of Independence* includes its italicized title, a pinpoint reference, and a parenthetical with its date (1776).[172] If it might be unclear whether the citation refers to the *Declaration* of the United States or that of another country, add the abbreviation "U.S." to the date parenthetical, before the year. Because the *Declaration* uses indented but unnumbered paragraphs, use the abbreviation "para." instead of a paragraph symbol (**Rule 6.3**).[173] For short citations, where *id.* is not appropriate (**Rule 11.3(c)**), omit the date parenthetical, and change the pinpoint reference if necessary.

Example

The Declaration of Independence para. 1 (U.S. 1776).

15.12(b)FN Citations to *The Declaration of Independence* in academic footnotes

ACADEMIC FORMATTING

Follow **Rule 15.12(a)**, but use large and small capital letters for the title.[174]

Example

80 The Declaration of Independence para. 2 (U.S. 1776).

15.13 Full Citations to State Unenacted Measures

A full citation to an unenacted measure from a state legislative body is similar to its federal counterpart (**Rule 15.1**), but it may contain additional components.[175] You may encounter measure names that differ from those used by the

United States Congress (e.g., a "file" instead of a "bill"). Similarly, you may find that the names of legislative bodies differ (e.g., Assembly, House of Delegates). To the extent the information is available or applicable, a full citation uses the following components.[176]

[Title of measure,] | Designation of measure | Measure number, | Legislature number, | [Session designation | Sess.] | [Pinpoint reference] | (State abbreviation | Year).

Example (Alaska House Bill) (spaces denoted by ▲)

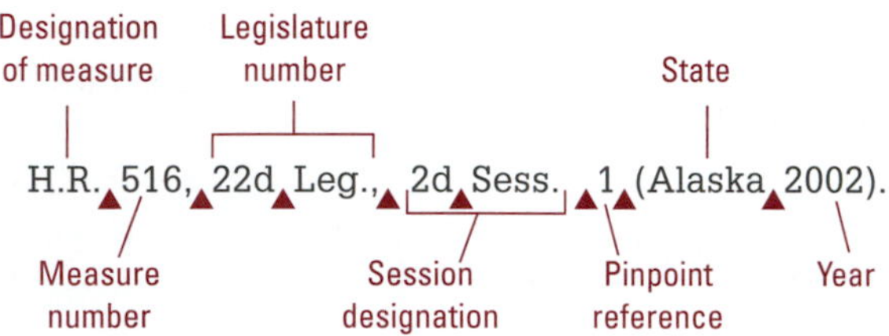

Other examples (spaces denoted by ▲)

Arizona Senate Bill:	S.▲6114,▲46th▲Leg.,▲2d▲Reg.▲Sess.▲(Ariz.▲2004).
Nebraska Legislative Resolution:	Legis.▲Res.▲100,▲101st▲Leg.,▲1st▲Reg.▲Sess.▲(Neb.▲2009).
Wisconsin Assembly Bill:	Assemb.▲15,▲2013–2014▲Leg.,▲2013▲Reg.▲Sess.▲§▲11▲(Wis.▲2013).
Maryland House of Delegates Bill:	H.D.▲367,▲2017▲Leg.,▲437th▲Sess.▲(Md.▲2017).
Georgia Senate Bill:	C.J's▲Law,▲S.▲1,▲155th▲Gen.▲Assemb.,▲Reg.▲Sess.▲(Ga.▲1999).
Utah House of Representatives Joint Resolution:	H.R.J.▲Res.▲33,▲55th▲Leg.,▲Gen.▲Sess.▲(Utah▲1989).
Louisiana Senate Resolution:	S.▲Res.▲1,▲2020▲Leg.,▲2d▲Extraordinary▲Sess.▲(La.▲2020).
Oregon House of Representatives Concurrent Resolution:	H.R.▲Con.▲Res.▲212▲80th▲Leg.▲Spec.▲Sess.▲(Or.▲2020).

15.13(a) Title of state measure

If desired, begin the citation with the state measure's "short title," if any, followed by a comma and one space. Use ordinary type. For more information about measure titles, see **Rule 15.1(a)**. Capitalize words in the title according to **Rule 3.2**, **Rule 3.3**, and **Chart 3.1**.

Example

Same Sex Marriage — Business Not Required to Participate, H.R. 296, 131st Gen. Assemb., Reg. Sess. (Ohio 2015).

15.13(b) Designation and number of state measure

Designate the measure by abbreviating the chamber in which it was introduced and indicating the measure's form.[177] Use ordinary type.[178] If a word in the designation is not listed below or in **Appendix 3(F)**, spell it out.[179] Required spaces in the abbreviations below are indicated with red triangles (▲). Do not abbreviate the word "bill." After the designation, insert the measure's number, followed by a comma and one space.[180]

Note: Some states use the word "Assembly" to refer to the lower chamber of the legislature (e.g., California State Assembly, Wisconsin State Assembly), while in others, it refers to the entire legislature (e.g., Indiana General Assembly, Maryland General Assembly).

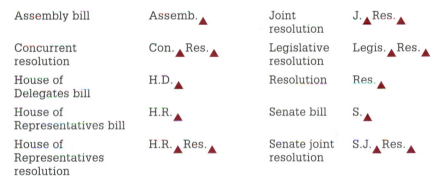

Assembly bill	Assemb.▲	Joint resolution	J.▲Res.▲
Concurrent resolution	Con.▲Res.▲	Legislative resolution	Legis.▲Res.▲
House of Delegates bill	H.D.▲	Resolution	Res.▲
House of Representatives bill	H.R.▲	Senate bill	S.▲
House of Representatives resolution	H.R.▲Res.▲	Senate joint resolution	S.J.▲Res.▲

Examples (spaces denoted by ▲)

Delaware House concurrent resolution:

H.R.▲Con.▲Res.▲29,▲146th▲Gen.▲Assemb.▲(Del.▲2012).

Wisconsin Senate bill:

S.▲73,▲2011–2012▲Leg.,▲100th▲Reg.▲Sess.▲§▲2▲(Wis.▲2011).

Vermont House concurrent resolution:

H.R.▲Con.▲Res.▲1,▲Gen.▲Assemb.▲(Vt.▲2019).

15.13(c) State legislature and session designation

Following the number of the measure, identify the legislature in which the measure was introduced.[181] If the state numbers its legislature or assembly (e.g., 107th General Assembly), begin with an ordinal contraction for the number (**Rule 4.3(b)**).[182] If the state does not number its legislature or assembly, use any other description used by the state (e.g., 2010–2011 Legislature).[183]

When available, identify the legislative session.[184] Designate a numbered session with an ordinal contraction or designate it with the description used by the state.[185] Insert one space after the session designation.[186] For both the legislature and the session, abbreviate words found in **Appendix 3(F)**.[187]

Examples

H.R. 2192, 79th Gen. Assemb., 2d Sess. (Iowa 2002).

S. 10, 47th Leg., 1st Spec. Sess. (Okla. 1999).

15.13(d) Pinpoint references

When referring to only a portion of a measure, provide a pinpoint reference to the particular subdivision, such as a section number or a page, followed by one space. For more information on citing pages, sections, and other subdivisions, see **Rules 5** through **9**.

Examples

H.R. 471, Gen. Assemb., 2019 Sess. § 1 (N.C. 2019).

S. 8, 100th Gen. Assemb., 1st Extraordinary Sess. ¶ 4 (Mo. 2020), https://www.senate.mo.gov/20info/pdf-bill/E1/intro/SB8.pdf.

15.13(e) State and date parenthetical

In a parenthetical, set out the abbreviation of the state, as shown in **Appendix 3(B)**, followed by one space and the year in which the measure was enacted, or if unenacted, the year it was published.[188]

Example

H.R. 95, Reg. Sess. 12–14 (Miss. 2020).

15.13(f) Commercial databases and other online sources

Cite an official electronic version of a state legislative measure in the same manner as its print counterpart.[189] When your source for the measure is a commercial database, add a parallel citation indicating the unique database identifier, followed by a parenthetical with the name of the database provider, if it is not otherwise clear from the database identifier itself.[190] If you are citing to an unofficial online source other than a commercial database, append a URL.[191]

Examples

S. 1105, 89th Gen. Assemb., Reg. Sess. (Ark. 2013), 2013 Bill Text AR S.B. 1105 (Lexis+).

S. Res. 1, 165th Gen. Ct., Reg. Sess. ¶ 3 (N.H. 2017), 2017 Bill Text NH S.R. 1 (Lexis+).

S. 2273, 219th Leg., Reg. Sess. 5–6 (N.J. 2020), https://www.njleg.state.nj.us/2020/Bills/S2500/2273_R1.PDF.

H.R. 8, Gen. Assemb., Reg. Sess. ¶ 9 (Ky. 2020), 2020 KY H.B. 8 (NS) (Westlaw Edge).

15.13(g)FN Full citations to state unenacted measures in academic footnotes

ACADEMIC FORMATTING

Follow **Rule 15.13(a)–(f)**.[192] There is no difference in the full citation format used in academic footnotes.

15.14 Short Citations to State Unenacted Measures

15.14(a) Using *id.* or other short citations to state unenacted measures

Use the short citation *id.* to cite the same unenacted measure cited in the immediately preceding citation, even if the pinpoint reference has changed.[193] Do not use *id.* if the previous citation was in a string citation with one or more other sources (**Rule 11.3(c)**).[194] For materials divided by sections or other subdivisions, see **Rules 6** and **9**.

When *id.* is not appropriate (**Rule 11.3(c)**), place the state abbreviation before the abbreviated name of the measure, using **Appendix 3(B)** and **Appendix 3(F)**.[195] Omit reference to numbers of the legislative body or the legislative session, and omit the date parenthetical.[196] Change the pinpoint reference as needed; insert "at" before a pinpoint *page* reference.[197] If you are citing to a source in a commercial electronic database, the short form must include the unique database identifier, if any, and include the parenthetical with the name of the database provider.[198] You do not need to include the URL in a short citation if you included it in a source's full citation.[199]

Examples

Full citations:	S. 1359, 1999 Reg. Sess. 2 (Conn. 1999).
	H.R. 3327, 119th Gen. Assemb., 1st Sess. (S.C. 2011), 2011 Bill Text SC H.B. 3327 (Lexis+).
Short citations:	Conn. S. 1359, at 2.
	S.C. H.R. 3327, 2011 Bill Text SC H.B. 3327 (Lexis+).

15.14(b)FN Short citations to state unenacted measures in academic footnotes

ACADEMIC FORMATTING

Repeat the full citation if the measure has not been cited, in full or in short form (including *id.*) in the same footnote or one of the previous five footnotes.[200] Otherwise, use the short citations described in **Rules 15.14(a)**.[201] Do not use *supra* (**Rule 11.4**).[202]

Example

12 S. 7, 2021 Reg. Sess. (Ala. 2021), 2021 AL S.B. 7 (NS) (Westlaw).

13 *Id.*

. . .

16 Ala. S. 7, 2021 AL S.B. 7 (NS) (Westlaw).

. . .

33 S. 7, 2021 Reg. Sess. (Ala. 2021), 2021 AL S.B. 7 (NS) (Westlaw).

15.15 Citations to State Enacted Measures and Joint Resolutions

15.15(a) Full citations to state enacted measures and joint resolutions

Cite state enacted measures and joint resolutions as statutes under **Rule 14.4**, unless using the measure to document legislative history.[203] In that case, analogize to **Rule 15.3**, with the additional requirement of including the legislative session after the state legislature as explained in **Rule 15.13(c)**.[204]

Examples

S.J. Res. 07-037, 66th Gen. Assemb., 1st Reg. Sess. (Colo. 2007).

H.R.J. Res. 5, 65th Leg., 2d Reg. Sess. (Idaho 2020), https://legislature .idaho.gov/wp-content/uploads/sessioninfo/2020/legislation/HJR005.pdf.

S. 78, 58th Leg. (Wyo. 2005), 2005 Bill Text WY S.B. 78 (Lexis+).

15.15(b) Short citations to state enacted measures and joint resolutions

Follow **Rule 15.14(a)**.[205]

Example

Full citation: S.J. Res. 07-037, 66th Gen. Assemb., 1st Reg. Sess. 1 (Colo. 2007).

Short citation: Colo. S.J. Res. 07-037, at 1.

15.15(c)FN Full and short citations to state enacted measures and joint resolutions in academic footnotes

For full citations, follow **Rule 15.15(a)**.[206] There is no difference in the full citation format used in academic footnotes.

For short citations, follow **Rule 15.14(b)FN**.[207]

Examples

91 S.J. Res. 7, 120th Gen. Assemb., 1st Reg. Sess. (Ind. 2017), 2017 Ind. Legis. Serv. P.L. 271-2017 (S.J.R. 7) (Westlaw Edge).

92 *Id.*

. . .

94 Ind. S.J. Res. 7, 2017 Ind. Legis. Serv. P.L. 271-2017 (S.J.R. 7) (Westlaw Edge).

. . .

111 S.J. Res. 7, 120th Gen. Assemb., 1st Reg. Sess. (Ind. 2017), 2017 Ind. Legis. Serv. P.L. 271-2017 (S.J.R. 7) (Westlaw Edge).

15.16 Citations to State Legislative Hearings

15.16(a) Full citations to state legislative hearings

A full citation to a state legislative hearing follows the format for federal committee hearings (**Rule 15.5**), but substitutes the legislature's number for the number of Congress and identifies the legislative session.[208] It also inserts the state abbreviation (**Appendix 3(B)**) into the date parenthetical.[209]

Example

Creation of Commission to Study Sexual Assault, Misconduct, and Harassment by Staff Against Inmates in State Correctional Facilities: Hearing on S.J. Res. 79 Before the S.L. & Pub. Safety Comm., 219th Leg. 6–15 (N.J. 2020) (statement of Brenda V. Smith, Dean & Professor at Am. Univ. Coll. of L.), https://www.njleg.state.nj.us/legislativepub/pubhear/slp05122020.pdf.

15.16(b) Short citations to state legislative hearings

Analogize to **Rule 15.6(a)**, but place the state abbreviation before the abbreviated number and session.[210]

Example

Full citation: *Section 71.051 Forum Non Conveniens: Hearing on S. 2 Before the S. Econ. Dev. Comm.*, 73d Leg., Reg. Sess. 73 (Tex. 1993) [hereinafter *Forum Non Conveniens*].

Short citation: *Forum Non Conveniens*, Tex. 73d Leg., Reg. Sess., at 74.

15.16(c)FN Full and short citations to state legislative hearings in academic footnotes

ACADEMIC FORMATTING

For full citations, follow **Rule 15.16(a)**.[211] There is no difference in the full citation format used in academic footnotes.

For short citations, analogize to **Rule 15.6(b)FN**.

Examples

[67] *Section 71.051 Forum Non Conveniens: Hearing on S. 2 Before the S. Econ. Dev. Comm.*, 73d Leg., Reg. Sess. 73 (Tex. 1993) [hereinafter *Forum Non Conveniens*].

[68] *Id.*

. . .

[109] *Forum Non Conveniens*, *supra* note 67, at 77.

15.17 Full Citations to State Legislative Reports and Documents

A full citation to a state legislative report or document has six to nine components.[212]

[Committee or author name, | *Title*,] | Abbreviation for type of document | [No.] | [Legislature-document number,] | [Session designation] | Pinpoint reference | (State abbreviation | Year of publication).

Example (spaces denoted by ▲)

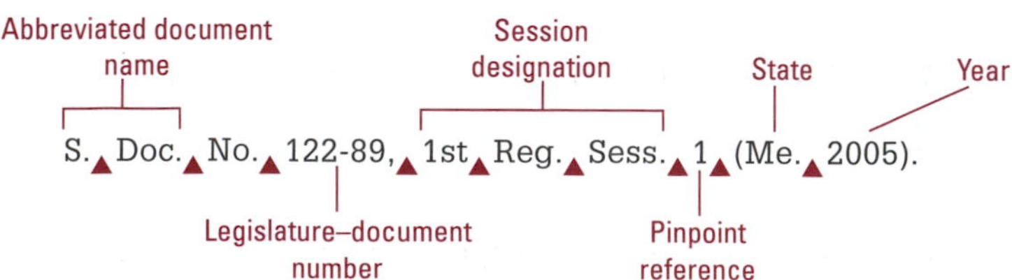

15.17(a) Committee name, author, and title option

If desired, begin the citation with the committee name or author's name and the title.[213] If you use one, you must include the other.[214] For an institutional author, follow **Rule 20.1(b)(3)**, abbreviating words found in **Appendices 3(B)**, **3(E)**, and **3(F)**.[215] Use ordinary type for the committee or author name and italics for the title.[216]

Examples

S. Comm. on Child., Families & Elder Affs., *Review of the Baker Act*, Interim S. Rep. No. 2009-15, at 2 (Fla. 2008).

J. Comm. on State Bldg. Constr., *Report on the Joint Committee on State Building Construction*, J. Rep., 2019 Sess. 2-1 to 2-5 (Kan. 2019), http://www.kslegresearch.org/KLRD-web/Publications/CommitteeReports/2019CommitteeReports/jt_SBC-session-cr.pdf.

15.17(b) Abbreviation for type of report or document

Abbreviate the type of report or document (using **Appendix 3(F)**), including an abbreviation for the chamber in which it originated, followed by one space.[217] Required spaces in the abbreviations below are indicated with red triangles (▲).

House of Representatives report	H.R.▲Rep.▲
House of Delegates report	H.D.▲Rep.▲
Joint report	J.▲Rep.▲
Assembly document	Assemb.▲Doc.▲

15.17(c) Legislature-document number

If the report or document is numbered, create a legislature-document number beginning with the abbreviation "No." and a space.[218] Then, using a hyphen, combine the number of the legislature with the number of the report or document.[219] For more information about legislature numbers, see **Rule 15.13(c)**.

Example

J. Comm. on Health Care, *The Dispensing of Drugs and Devices Pursuant to Pharmacy Collaborative Practice Agreements, Standing Orders, and Statewide Protocols*, H.R. Doc. No. 2019-2, 2019-2020 Sess. 2 (Va. 2020).

15.17(d) State session designation

Follow **Rule 15.13(c)**.[220]

Example

1997 Final Legislative Report, J. Rep. 55th Leg., 1997 Reg. Sess. 400 (Wash. 1997), http://leg.wa.gov/LIC/Documents/Historical/Final%20Legislative%20Reports/1997FinalLegRpt.pdf.

15.17(e) Pinpoint references

When referring to only part of the report or document, cite the particular subdivision.[221] For more information on subdivisions, see **Rules 5**, **6**, and **9**. Insert one space after the subdivision information.[222]

Example

H.R. State Affs. Comm., *Feb. 21, 2020 Minutes*, H.R. Doc. 95th Leg., Reg. Sess. 2 (S.D. 2020).

15.17(f) State and date parenthetical

Unless the name of the state appears in the author or title component, begin the date parenthetical with the state's abbreviation (see **Appendix 3(B)**), followed by one space.[223] In the same parenthetical, indicate the year of the report's or document's publication.[224]

Example

Spec. Legis. Comm'n to Study Pesticide Control Reguls., *Findings and Recommendations*, S. Rep. 145th Legis., Reg. Sess. 100 (R.I. 2018), http://www.rilegislature.gov/Reports/PESTICIDE%20COMN%20Rept%20FINAL.pdf.

15.17(g) Commercial databases and other online sources

Follow **Rule 15.13(f)** when you are citing to an online source for a state legislative report or document.

Examples

Legis. Comm. for the Rev. & Oversight of the Tahoe Reg'l Plan. Agency & the Marlette Lake Water Sys., *Work Session Document*, Comm. Rep. 80th Leg., 2019 Sess. 2 (Nev. 2020), https://www.leg.state.nv.us/App/InterimCommittee/REL/Document/16005.

H.R. B. Summary, *House Bill 192*, 110th Gen. Assemb., Reg. Sess. (Tenn. 2018), TN B. Summ., 2018 Reg. Sess. H.B. 192 (Westlaw Edge).

15.17(h)FN Full citations to state legislative reports or documents in academic footnotes

ACADEMIC FORMATTING

Use large and small capital letters for the following components, if present: the name of the committee, the author, the title, the abbreviation of the report or document, and the abbreviation "No."[225]

Example

56 S. Comm. on Children, Families & Elder Affs., Review of the Baker Act, Interim S. Rep. No. 2009-15, Reg. Sess. 2 (Fla. 2008).

15.17(i) Using *id.* or other short citations to state legislative reports or documents

Follow **Rule 15.8(a)** for the short citations to state legislative reports or documents.

Example

Full citation: H.R.J. Mem'l No. 50-183603.1, 1st Sess. (N.M. 2011).

Short citation: H.R.J. Mem'l No. 50-183603.1.

15.17(j)[FN] Short citations to state legislative reports or documents in academic footnotes

ACADEMIC FORMATTING

Repeat the full citation if the report or document has not been cited, in full or in short form (including *id.*) in the same footnote or one of the previous five footnotes.[226] Otherwise, use the short citation described in **Rule 15.17(i)**, but use large and small capital letters for the following components, if present: the name of the committee, the author, the title, the abbreviation of the report or document, and the abbreviation "No."[227] Do not use *supra* (**Rule 11.4**).[228]

15.18 Full Citations to State Legislative Debates

A full citation to a state legislative debate contains the following components, depending on whether the debate is published and on the type of legislature and session designations used in the state.

Chamber abbreviation, | *Title or description of debate,* | [Publication source,] | [Legislature designation,] | [Session designation] | [Pinpoint reference] | (State abbreviation | Month Day, Year) | [(Location of transcript or recording)].

Examples (spaces denoted by ▲)

Published debate:

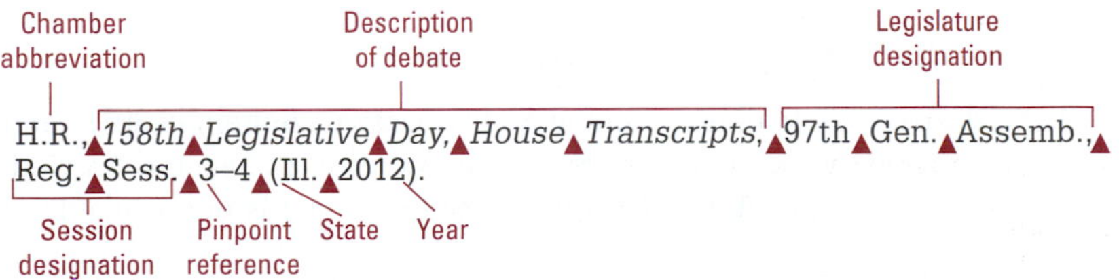

Unpublished debate:

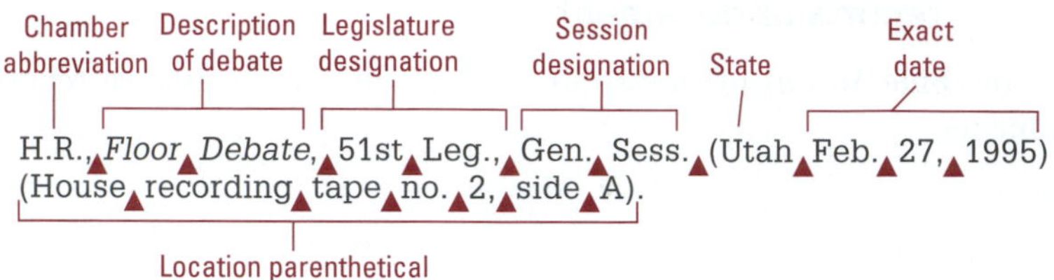

15.18(a) Chamber abbreviation

Begin the citation with an abbreviation for the legislative chamber in which the debate took place (**Appendix 3(F)**), followed by a comma and one space.

15.18(b) Title or description of debate; publication source

If the debate is published, provide its title, in italics, and the name of the publication, also in italics, followed by a comma and one space. If the debate is not published, provide a concise description of the debate, in italics (e.g., *Floor Debate*, *Debate on H.R. 1731*). If providing both a description and the publication, put the description first. See **Rule 15.18(f)** for citing an unpublished debate.

Example

Assem., *Debate on Assembly No. A08226-B, Rules Report No. 63, 6-9-20 Session Proceedings*, 2020 Leg., Spec. Sess. 8–10 (N.Y. June 9, 2020).

15.18(c) State legislature and session designations

Follow **Rule 15.13(c)**.

15.18(d) Pinpoint references

Follow **Rule 15.13(d)**.

Example

H.R., *House Session Transcript for 07/23/2020*, 2020 Conn. Gen. Assemb., Spec. Sess. 366–73 (Conn. July 23, 2020).

15.18(e) State and date parenthetical

Begin the parenthetical with the state's abbreviation (**Appendix 3(B)**), and if available, provide the exact date of the debate (Month Day, Year), abbreviating the month according to **Appendix 3(A)**. If the exact date is not available, use the year.

15.18(f) Location of transcript or recording of unpublished debate

If the debate is not published, following the state and date parenthetical, add a second parenthetical indicating the location of a transcript or audio recording of the debate, if it is in a physical location. If the source is online, append a URL instead of using a parenthetical or parallel citation indicating the location.[229]

Examples

S., *Debate on S. 31*, 74th Leg., Reg. Sess. 1 (Tex. Feb. 1, 1995) (transcript available from Senate Staff Services Office).

Assem., *Debate on Assembly Res. No. 854, 3-30-2020 Session Proceedings*, 2020 Leg., Reg. Sess. 4–5 (N.Y. Mar. 30, 2020), https://nyassembly.gov/av/session/.

15.18(g)[FN] Full citations to state legislative debates in academic footnotes

ACADEMIC FORMATTING

Use large and small capital letters for the chamber abbreviation and the title.[230]

Example

[115] S., DEBATE ON S. 31, 74th Leg., Reg. Sess. 1 (Tex. Feb. 1, 1995) (transcript available from Senate Staff Services Office).

15.19 Short Citations to State Legislative Debates

15.19(a) Using *id.* or other short citations to state legislative debates

Whether the debate is published or unpublished, use the short citation *id.* to cite the same debate cited in the immediately preceding citation, even if the pinpoint reference has changed.[231] Do not use *id.* if the previous citation was in a string citation referring to the debate and one or more other sources (**Rule 11.3(c)**).[232]

When *id.* is not appropriate (**Rule 11.3(c)**), keep all components except the state/date parenthetical, physical location parenthetical, or URL.[233] Move the state's abbreviation to precede the name of the chamber, and use the preposition "at" before a pinpoint page reference.[234]

Example

Full citation:	S., *Debate on S. 31*, 74th Leg., Reg. Sess. 1 (Tex. Feb. 1, 1995) (transcript available from Senate Staff Services Office).
Short citation:	Tex. S., *Debate on S. 31*, 74th Leg., Reg. Sess., at 2.

15.19(b)FN Short citations to state legislative debates in academic footnotes

ACADEMIC FORMATTING

Repeat the full citation if the debate has not been cited, in full or in short form (including *id.*) in the same footnote or one of the previous five footnotes.[235] Otherwise, omit the state/date parenthetical, and if any, the physical location parenthetical and URL. But put the state abbreviation before the abbreviated name of the chamber, and render both of those and the words "Debate on" in large and small capital letters.[236] Use the preposition "at" before a pinpoint page reference.[237] Do not use *supra* (**Rule 11.4**).[238]

Examples

115 S., Debate on S. 31, 74th Leg., Reg. Sess., at 1 (Tex. Feb. 1, 1995) (transcript available from Senate Staff Services Office).

116 *Id.* at 3.

. . .

120 Tex. S., Debate on S. 31, 74th Leg., Reg. Sess., at 2.

15.20 Citations to State Legislative Journals

15.20(a) Full citations to state legislative journal

Cite a state legislative journal as follows[239]:

Chamber abbreviation | Journal, | [Legislature designation,] | [Session designation] | Pinpoint reference | (State abbreviation | Date).

Examples (spaces denoted by ▲)

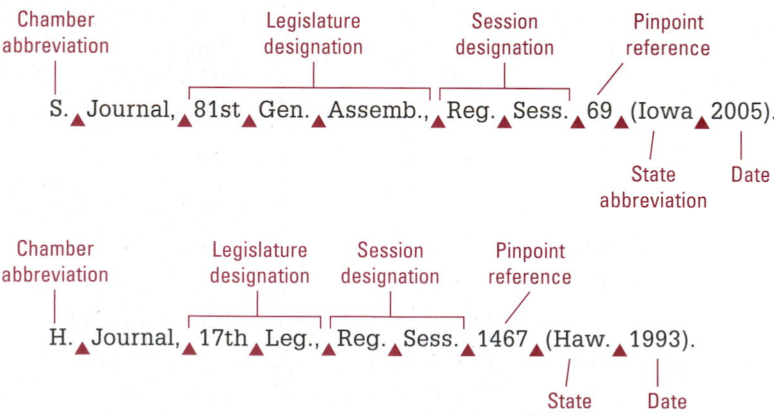

When your source for the journal is a commercial database, add a parallel citation indicating the unique database identifier, if any, followed by a parenthetical with the name of the database provider, if it is not otherwise clear from the database identifier itself.[240] If you are citing to an online source other than a commercial database, append a URL.[241]

Examples

H. Journal, 83d Leg., Reg. Sess. 20 (W. Va. 2018), https://www.wvlegislature.gov/legisdocs/publications/journal/house/HJournal_2018_Vol1.pdf.

H. Journal, 2017 Leg., Reg. Sess. 27 (Mass. 2017), MA H.R. Jour. 1/15/2017 (Westlaw Edge).

S. Journal, 91st Leg., 4th Spec. Sess. 12–14 (Minn. 2020), https://www.senate.mn/journals/2019-2020/2020091101_ss4.pdf.

H. Journal, 66th Leg., 8th Legis. Day 4 (Mont. 2019).

15.20(b)[FN] Full citations to state legislative journals in academic footnotes

ACADEMIC FORMATTING

Follow **Rule 15.20(a)**, but use large and small capital letters for the chamber abbreviation and the name of the journal.[242]

Examples

[87] S. JOURNAL, 99th Leg., Reg. Sess. 404 (Mich. 2017).

[88] H. JOURNAL, 66th Leg., Reg. Sess. 820 (N.D. 2019), https://www.legis.nd.gov/assembly/66-2019/journals/hr-dailyjnl-30.pdf#Page820/.

15.20(c) Using *id.* or other short citations to state legislative journals

Use the short citation *id.* to cite the same journal cited in the immediately preceding citation, even if the pinpoint reference has changed.[243] Do not use *id.* if the previous citation was in a string citation referring to the journal and one or more other sources (**Rule 11.3(c)**).[244]

When *id.* is not appropriate (**Rule 11.3(c)**), use the full citation format, but put the state's abbreviation (**Appendix 3(B)**) in front of the journal reference and omit the date parenthetical. Use the preposition "at" before a pinpoint page reference.[245] If you are citing to a source in a commercial electronic database, the short form must include the unique database identifier, if any, and include the parenthetical with the name of the database provider.[246] You do not need to include the URL in a short citation if you included it in a source's full citation.[247]

Examples

Iowa S. Journal, 81st Gen. Assemb., Reg. Sess., at 70.

Haw. H. Journal, 17th Leg., Reg. Sess., at 1469.

15.20(d)FN Short citations to state legislative journals in academic footnotes

Use large and small capital letters for the chamber abbreviation and the name of the journal.[248] Repeat the full citation if the journal has not been cited, in full or in short form (including *id.*) in the same footnote or one of the previous five footnotes.[249] Otherwise, use the short citation described in **Rule 15.20(c)**, but use large and small capital letters for the state abbreviation, too.[250] Do not use *supra* (**Rule 11.4**).[251]

Examples

92 S. Daily Journal, 2009–2010 Leg., Reg. Sess., at 2332–33 (Cal. 2009).

93 *Id.* at 2333.

94 H. Journal, 161st Gen. Assemb., Reg. Sess., vol. 5, at 3663–64 (Pa. 1978).

. . .

98 Cal. S. Daily Journal, 2009–2010 Leg., Reg. Sess., at 2334.

99 Pa. H. Journal, 161st Gen. Assemb., Reg. Sess., vol. 5, at 3664.

16 Court Rules, Judicial Administrative Orders, Ethics Opinions, and Jury Instructions

Fast Formats

Federal Rule of Civil Procedure	Fed. R. Civ. P. 56.
Federal Rule of Criminal Procedure	Fed. R. Crim. P. 21(a).
Federal Rule of Evidence	Fed. R. Evid. 801.
State rule of procedure	Mo. R. Civ. P. 56.01(b)(3).
Judicial administrative order	*In re: Motions for Johnson Sentencing Reductions Pursuant to 28 U.S.C. § 2255*, Admin. Or. No. 2016-05 (E.D.N.Y. June 9, 2016).
Ethics opinion	ABA Standing Comm. on Ethics & Pro. Resp., Formal Op. 07-446 (2007).
Pattern jury instruction	*Ill. Pattern Jury Instr. Crim.* 1.01 (4th ed. 2000).
Citations in academic footnotes	ACADEMIC FORMATTING 21 FED. R. CRIM. P. 21(a). 22 ABA Standing Comm. on Ethics & Pro. Resp., Formal Op. 07-446 (2007). 23 11TH CIR. PATTERN JURY INSTR. § 6 (2000).
Short citations	Fed. R. Civ. P. 56. ABA Standing Comm. on Ethics & Pro. Resp., Formal Op. 07-446, at 3–4.

16.1 Court Rules and Judicial Administrative Orders

Court rules and judicial administrative orders govern the operation of courts and an array of judicial processes. Court rules operate within a given jurisdiction (e.g., the rules of evidence applicable to federal court proceedings, a state's rules of civil or criminal procedure), but they may have more limited application to particular courts (e.g., bankruptcy appellate panels) or to a single court.

An administrative order concerns the operation of the courts in the jurisdiction. Typically issued by the chief judge of the court, administrative orders can affect a variety of lower courts, such as courts within a subdivision of a larger division or courts dealing with specialized matters; they may deal with such diverse topics as the imposition of fees, the use of standardized forms, the appointment of civil process servers, or the prohibition of smartphones in a courtroom.

When you cite a court rule or an administrative order in a document to be submitted to a court, follow that court's local rules governing citation, if any (see the jurisdiction's entry in **Appendix 2(A)** or **2(B)**).

16.1(a) Full citations to court rules currently in force

Unless a local rule otherwise specifies the form of citation, a full citation to a court rule currently in force contains two components.[1]

Code or Rule compilation abbreviation | Rule number.

Example (spaces denoted by ▲)

Rule compilation abbreviation — Rule number (with subdivision)

Fed.▲R.▲Civ.▲P.▲11(a).

16.1(b) Code or rule compilation abbreviation

Unless you are citing a rule of the United States Supreme Court, begin with a geographic reference to the jurisdiction, followed by the abbreviation for the code or rule compilation that contains the cited rule.[2] If the jurisdiction is identified in **Appendix 3(B)** (states, territories, major cities), use the abbreviation shown there; otherwise, spell out the jurisdiction's name.

Use **Appendices 3(C)**, **3(E)**, and **3(G)** for abbreviations to other words in the name of the code or compilation (e.g., abbreviating "Supreme" as "Sup.").[3] See **Rule 2.2** for guidance on spacing abbreviations. Omit prepositions (e.g., "of," "on") and articles ("a," "an, "the").[4] Use ordinary type for all components.[5] Insert one space between the abbreviation and the rule number.[6]

Examples (spaces denoted by ▲)

Fed.▲R.▲Crim.▲P.▲21(a).
Fla.▲R.▲Crim.▲Evid.▲3.380.
8th▲Cir.▲R.▲30A.
Fed.▲R.▲Civ.▲P.▲26(a)(1)(A)(iii).
Tex.▲R.▲App.▲P.▲38.
Nev.▲Sup.▲Ct.▲R.▲42.
Sup.▲Ct.▲R.▲37.2(b).
Fed.▲R.▲App.▲P.▲5(c)(1).

16.1(c) Rule number and subdivisions

Following the code or compilation abbreviation, insert the rule number, as shown in the source, and a pinpoint reference to its relevant subdivision(s), if any.[7] When applicable, add reference to an internal operating procedure ("I.O.P.") or similar information immediately after the rule number.

Examples (spaces denoted by ▲)

Mo.▲R.▲Civ.▲P.▲56.01(b)(3).

Haw.▲R.▲Pro.▲Conduct▲1.18(d)(2)(i)▲cmt.▲7.

11th▲Cir.▲R.▲34-4▲I.O.P.▲2(b).

16.1(d) Court rule no longer in force

To cite a court rule that is no longer in force, follow **Rule 16.1(a)–(c)**, but add a parenthetical with the date of the most recent official source in which the rule appears, and add a second parenthetical indicating the date of the repeal.[8]

Examples

Fed. R. Civ. P. 34 (1948) (repealed 1970).

Ohio Code Pro. Resp. DR 7-103 (1970) (repealed 2007).

16.1(e) Full citations to judicial administrative orders

Set out the full title of the judicial administrative order.[9] Follow the capitalization guidelines in **Rule 3.2**, **Rule 3.3**, and **Chart 3.1**. After the title, insert a comma and one space, followed by the abbreviation "Admin. Or. No." and the order's assigned number, both in ordinary type. If it is an amended order, insert the word "Amended" before that abbreviation. If the order is untitled, provide its abbreviation and number, if any, or any other identifying label given to it.

Following the title or other designation, insert a pinpoint reference, if applicable. Following the title or pinpoint reference, insert one space and a parenthetical indicating the abbreviated name of the court and the exact date (Month Day, Year) of the order's issuance, analogous to the court/date parenthetical used for case citations (**Rules 12.6–12.7**). For court name abbreviations, see **Appendices 1** and **4**.

If the order is published in a reporter, set out the order's full title followed by the volume number, reporter abbreviation, initial page, pinpoint page(s), and in parentheses, the year of publication.[10] If the identity of the court cannot be determined by the reporter name, insert the abbreviation for the issuing court before the year of issuance.

Examples

Authorization of Pilot Project to Study Feasibility and Effectiveness of Mediation in the Court of Appeals, Admin. Or. No. 2015-8 (Mich. Sept. 16, 2015).

Appellate Court Technology Committee, Admin Or. No. AOSC20-57 (Fla. June 25, 2020).

Amendments to the Federal Rules of Bankruptcy Procedure, 572 U.S. 1169, 1175 (2013).

16.1(f)FN Full citations to court rules or judicial administrative orders in academic footnotes

For a court rule, use large and small capital letters for the name of the code or rule compilation; the remainder of the citation is in ordinary type.[11]

To cite a judicial administrative order follow **Rule 16.1(e)**.

Examples

[2] FED. R. EVID. 1006.

[13] FLA. R. CRIM. EVID. 3.380.

[21] WIS. STAT. R. 809.19(2)(b).

[30] In re: Motions for *Johnson* Sentencing Reductions Pursuant to 28 U.S.C. § 2255, Admin. Or. No. 2016-05 (E.D.N.Y. June 9, 2016).

16.1(g) Short citations to court rules or judicial administrative orders

When appropriate (**Rule 11.3(c)**), use *id.* as the short citation to a court rule or judicial administrative order, whether current or no longer in force.[12] When *id.* is not appropriate, use all the components of the full citation to a court rule. In a short citation to an administrative order that is not published in a reporter, omit the court/date parenthetical. You may add a pinpoint reference to the rule or order. In a short citation to an administrative order that is published in a reporter, omit the date parenthetical and initial page number and in its place, insert "at" and the pinpoint reference.

Examples

Full citations:

Alternative Dispute Resolution Educational and Certification Requirements, Admin. Or. No. AOSC20-24 (Fla. Apr. 7, 2020).

Amendments to the Federal Rules of Appellate Procedure, 572 U.S. 1161, 1166 (2013).

Short citations: Alternative Dispute Resolution Educational and Certification Requirements, Admin. Or. No. AOSC20-24 at pt. IV.

Amendments to the Federal Rules of Appellate Procedure, 572 U.S. at 1166.

ACADEMIC FORMATTING

Short citations in academic footnotes should use the typefaces described in **Rule 16.1(f)FN**.[13]

16.2 Ethics Opinions

16.2(a) Full citation to ethics opinion

A full citation to an ethics opinion contains four or five components, depending on whether a pinpoint reference is available.[14]

Abbreviated name of issuing entity, | [Type of opinion] | Opinion number | [, at] | [Pinpoint reference] | (Date).

Refer to **Appendices 3(B)**, **3(E)**, and **3(G)** for abbreviating the name of the entity issuing the opinion and the type of opinion. For purposes of this rule, "American Bar Association" may be abbreviated as "ABA."[15] Do not omit prepositions or articles from the entity's name.[16] Present the opinion number as it is displayed in the source.[17] Use ordinary type for all components of the citation.[18]

Example (spaces denoted by ▲)

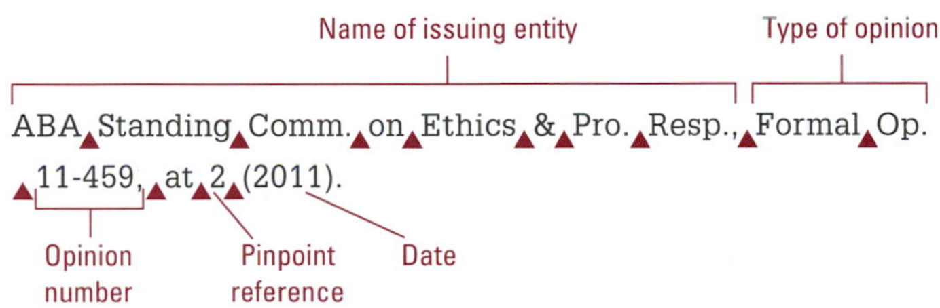

Where possible, provide a pinpoint reference after the opinion number. Use the preposition "at" before a pinpoint *page* number.[19] See **Rules 5, 6, 7,** and **9** for more information about pinpoint references.

To cite an opinion that has been superseded or withdrawn, analogize to **Rule 16.1(d)**. When an opinion has been revised, note that information parenthetically. You can also use a parenthetical to convey the subject of the opinion.[20] For the ABA model code or rules of professional responsibility, see **Rule 23.5**.

Examples

Ohio Bd. of Comm'rs on Grievances & Discipline, Op. 2001-6, at 3–4 (2001).

ABA Comm. on Ethics & Pro. Resp., Informal Op. 1414 (1978) (repealed 2007).

16.2(b) Short citations to ethics opinions

When appropriate (**Rule 11.3(c)**), use *id.* as the short citation to ethics opinions.[21] When *id.* is not appropriate, use all the components of the full citation except the date parenthetical. There are no differences in the short citations used in academic footnotes.

Example

Full citation: Or. Bar Ass'n, Formal Op. 2005-164, at 452 (2005).

Short citation: Or. Bar Ass'n, Formal Op. 2005-164, at 453–54.

16.3 Jury Instructions

16.3(a) Full citation to pattern, standard, or approved instruction

A full citation to a jury instruction in a pattern, standard, or approved set may contain up to five components, depending on whether the instruction is published in a single volume or a multivolume set and whether it is published in an edition subsequent to the first.

Example (spaces denoted by ▲)

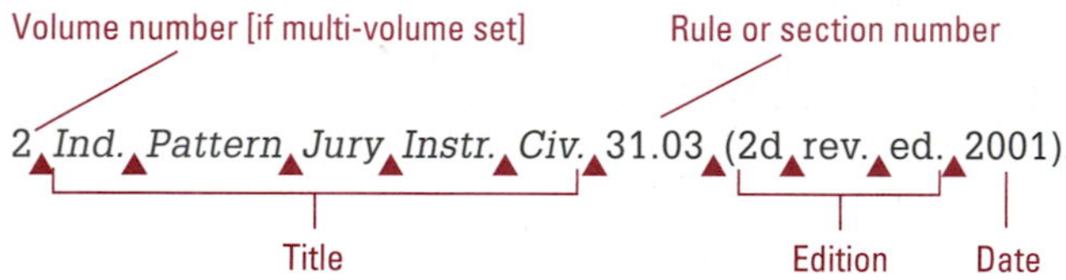

Italicize and abbreviate words in the title of the instruction, using **Appendices 3(B)** and **3(G)**. Set out the rule or section number as shown in the source. Add a parenthetical with the edition number, if any, and the year of publication. When the instruction comes from a multivolume set, put the volume number before the name of the set of instructions, analogizing to **Rule 20.1(a)**.

Examples

Ill. Pattern Jury Instr. Crim. 1.01 (4th ed. 2000).

11th Cir. Pattern Jury Instr. § 6 (2000).

16.3(b)FN Full citations to pattern, standard, or approved instructions in academic footnotes

ACADEMIC FORMATTING

Use the components described in **Rule 16.3(a)**, but instead of italics, use large and small capital letters for the title.

Examples

[14] ILL. PATTERN JURY INSTR. CRIM. 1.01 (4th ed. 2000).

[23] 11TH CIR. PATTERN JURY INSTR. § 6 (2000).

16.3(c) Full citation to unofficial jury instruction

Cite an unofficial jury instruction, including a model instruction, in the same manner as a book, including the volume, if any, author, title, and publication data (see **Rule 20.1**). Do not abbreviate words in the author name or the title. Use ordinary type for the author name and italics for the title. Include pinpoint references where possible.

Example

2 Kevin F. O'Malley et al., *Fed. Jury Prac. & Instr.* § 23.05 (6th ed. 2006).

16.3(d)FN Full citations to unofficial jury instructions in academic footnotes

ACADEMIC FORMATTING

Follow **Rule 16.3(c)**, but use large and small capital letters for both the author name and the title.

Example

[37] 2 KEVIN F. O'MALLEY ET AL., FED. JURY PRAC. & INSTR. § 23.05 (6th ed. 2006).

16.3(e) Short citations to jury instructions

For any jury instruction, use *id.* as a short citation when appropriate (**Rule 11.3(c)**).[22] For a standard, pattern, or approved jury instruction, use the components shown in **Rule 16.3(a)**, but omit the publication parenthetical. For an unofficial jury instruction, analogize to **Rule 20.6(a)**.

Examples

Pattern instruction: *11th Cir. Pattern Jury Instr.* § 6.

Unofficial instruction: O'Malley, *supra*, § 23.03.

16.3(f)FN Short citations to jury instructions in academic footnotes

ACADEMIC FORMATTING

Use *id.* when appropriate (**Rule 11.3(c)**). When *id.* is not appropriate, set out the volume number (if applicable) and the author's surname, followed by a *supra* cross-reference to the earlier footnote containing the full citation (**Rule 11.4**) and a pinpoint reference.[23]

Examples

[37] 2 KEVIN F. O'MALLEY ET AL., FED. JURY PRAC. & INSTR. § 23.05 (6th ed. 2006).

[38] *Id.* § 23.04.

. . .

[45] O'MALLEY, *supra* note 37, § 23.03.

17 Ordinances

Fast Formats

Codified ordinance	Village of Richfield, Ohio, Codified Ordinances § 1513.05(f) (2011).
Uncodified ordinance	Moreno Valley, Cal., Ordinance 556 (Dec. 14, 1999).
Citations in academic footnotes	ACADEMIC FORMATTING 56 VILLAGE OF RICHFIELD, OHIO, CODIFIED ORDINANCES § 1513.05(f) (2011). 71 MORENO VALLEY, CAL., ORDINANCE 556 (Dec. 14, 1999).
Short citations	Village of Richfield, Ohio, Codified Ordinances § 1513.05(f). *Id.* § 1513.05(e).

17.1 Full Citations to Codified Ordinances

A full citation to a codified ordinance contains five components.[1]

Name of political subdivision, | State abbreviation, | Name of code | Pinpoint reference | (Publication date).

Example (spaces denoted by ▲)

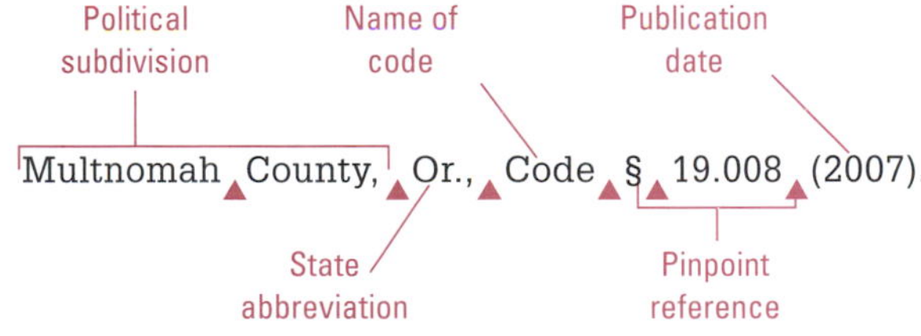

17.1(a) Name of political subdivision and code

Begin the citation with the name of the municipality, county, or other political subdivision enacting the ordinance, followed by a comma, one space, and the abbreviated name of the state.[2] Use abbreviations in **Appendix 3(B)** for certain city names and for states; do not otherwise abbreviate the name of the political subdivision.[3] Following the state abbreviation, insert a comma, one space, and the name of the code containing the cited ordinance, abbreviating any words found in **Appendix 3(E)**.[4] Omit articles ("a," "an," "the") and prepositions (e.g., "of," "for").[5] Use ordinary type for the name of the political subdivision and code.[6]

Example (spaces denoted by ▲)

Allentown,▲Pa.,▲Codified▲Ordinances▲§▲710.02▲(2013).

17.1(b) Pinpoint references

Provide a pinpoint reference to the specific subdivision(s) of the code containing the cited ordinance, followed by a space.[7] Codified ordinances may be designated by sections, articles, chapters, or other subdivisions. See **Rules 5**, **6**, and **9** for guidance on citing specific types of subdivisions.

17.1(c) Publication parenthetical; official or unofficial online source

In parentheses, indicate the publication date of the source to which you are citing the ordinance, analogizing to **Rule 14.2(f)**.[8] If possible, use an authenticated or official source, whether in print or online.[9] When citing an ordinance from an online source, whether official or unofficial, immediately following the publication parenthetical, insert a comma and one space, followed by the source's URL.[10] For more information about citing sources online, see **Rules 30** and **31**.

Examples

Loudon County, Va., Codified Ordinances § 684.03 (2009).

Owasso, Okla. Zoning Code § 9.1.2 (2019), https://cityofowasso.com/DocumentCenter/View/2378/Owasso-Zoning-Code-PDF?bidId=.

Orange Beach, Ala., Code of Ordinances § 78-24 (2016), https://www.municode.com/library/al/orange_beach/codes/ (from menu bar, select "Chapter 78 Waterways," then scroll to § 78-24).

17.2 Full Citations to Uncodified Ordinances

A full citation to an uncodified ordinance contains four components.[11]

Name of political subdivision, | State abbreviation, | Ordinance [Number or name or other pinpoint reference] | (Month Day, Year).

Example (spaces denoted by ▲)

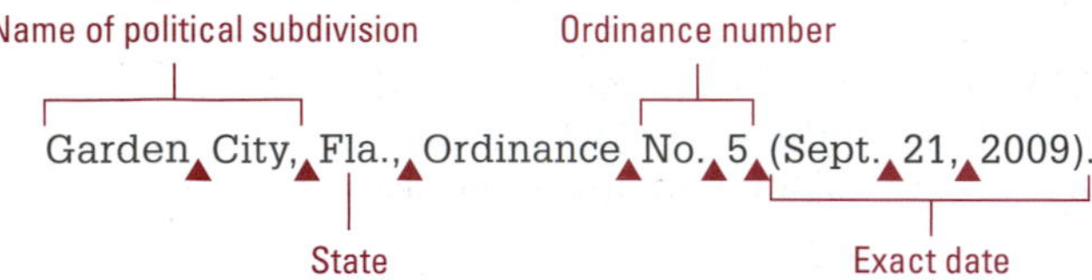

17.2(a) Name of political subdivision and state

Begin with the name of the political subdivision and state, in ordinary type.[12] Follow **Rule 17.1(a)** for spacing and abbreviations.[13]

17.2(b) Number or name

Following the state abbreviation, insert the phrase "Ordinance" followed by one space and the ordinance number, or if the ordinance is not numbered, the name of the ordinance, in ordinary type.[14] Capitalize words in the name of an ordinance according to **Rule 3.2**, **Rule 3.3**, and **Chart 3.1**.

Examples

Moreno Valley, Cal., Ordinance 556 (Dec. 14, 1999).

Campbell County, Va., Airport Development Area Special Service District § 4 (Apr. 3, 2006).

17.2(c) Date of enactment

In parentheses, set out the exact date (Month Day, Year) on which the uncodified ordinance was enacted.[15] Abbreviate the month according to **Appendix 3(A)**.[16] For ordinances published in online sources, follow **Rule 17.1(c)**.

17.3FN Full Citations to Codified or Uncodified Ordinances in Academic Footnotes

ACADEMIC FORMATTING

Follow **Rule 17.1** or **Rule 17.2**, but in a citation to a codified ordinance, use large and small capital letters for the name of the political subdivision and the name of the code.[17] If the ordinance is uncodified, use ordinary type for all components.[18]

Examples

26 ALLENTOWN, PA., CODIFIED ORDINANCES § 710.02 (2013).

85 Campbell County, Va., Airport Development Area Special Service District § 4 (Apr. 3, 2006).

17.4 Short Citations to Codified or Uncodified Ordinances

17.4(a) Using *id.* or other short citations to ordinances

When a citation refers to a codified ordinance within the same title, chapter, or part as an ordinance cited in the immediately previous citation, use *id.* as the short citation, changing the section number as needed (see **Rule 11.3(d)**).[19]

When a citation refers to an uncodified ordinance, use *id.* only to refer to the same ordinance cited in the immediately previous citation.[20]

When *id.* is not appropriate (**Rule 11.3(c)**), use one of the short citation options illustrated below, selecting one with enough information for the reader to easily recognize the source.

Examples

Full citation (codified ordinance):	Loudon County, Va., Codified Ordinances § 684.03 (2009).
Short citation options:	Loudon County, Va., Codified Ordinances § 684.03.
	§ 684.03.
Full citation (uncodified ordinance):	Moreno Valley, Cal., Ordinance 556 (Dec. 14, 1999).
Short citation options:	Moreno Valley, Cal., Ordinance 556.
	Ordinance 556.

17.4(b)FN Short citations to ordinances in academic footnotes

ACADEMIC FORMATTING

When *id.* is not appropriate (**Rule 11.3(c)**), you may use all required components of the full citation, omitting the date, or you may use any format illustrated in **Rule 17.4(a)**. Repeat the full citation when the ordinance has not been cited, in full or in short form (including *id.*) in the same footnote or one of the previous five footnotes.[21] Do not use *supra* (**Rule 11.4**).[22]

Examples

33 LOUDON COUNTY, VA., CODIFIED ORDINANCES § 684.03 (2009).

34 *Id.* § 684.02.

. . .

37 LOUDON COUNTY, VA., CODIFIED ORDINANCES § 684.02.

. . .

51 LOUDON COUNTY, VA., CODIFIED ORDINANCES § 684.03 (2009).

18 Administrative and Executive Materials

Fast Formats

Code of Federal Regulations	31 C.F.R. § 515.329 (2014).
Federal Register	Importation of Wood Packaging Material, 69 Fed. Reg. 55,719, 55,720–21 (Sept. 16, 2004).
Federal agency decision	*Bath Iron Works Corp.*, 345 N.L.R.B. 499, 506 (2005). *Limitation of Access to Through-Highways Crossing Public Lands*, 62 Interior Dec. 158, 161 (1955).
Federal advisory opinion	Lawfulness of Recess Appointments During a Recess of the Senate Notwithstanding Periodic Pro Forma Sessions, 36 Op. O.L.C. 9 n.13 (2012).
Federal executive order	Exec. Order No. 13,588, 3 C.F.R. 281 (2012).
State administrative code	312 Ind. Admin. Code 5-2-7 (2013). Utah Admin. Code r. 105-1-10 (2013).
State administrative register	Notice of Hearing on Proposed Administrative Regulations of State Corporation Commission, 32 Kan. Reg. 456 (May 2, 2013).
State advisory opinion	Colo. Att'y Gen. Op. 09-03 (June 9, 2009), 2009 Colo. AG LEXIS 3.
State executive order	Cal. Exec. Order No. B-29-15 (Apr. 1, 2015).
Citations in academic footnotes	ACADEMIC FORMATTING [22] 31 C.F.R. § 515.329 (2014). [27] Importation of Wood Packaging Material, 69 Fed. Reg. 55,719, 55,720–21 (Sept. 16, 2004). [28] Bath Iron Works Corp., 345 N.L.R.B. 499, 506 (2005). [35] Exec. Order No. 13,588, 3 C.F.R. 281 (2012).
Short citations	31 C.F.R. § 515.329. Fisheries of the Caribbean, Gulf of Mexico, and South Atlantic, 78 Fed. Reg. at 25,049–50. *Bath Iron Works Corp.*, 345 N.L.R.B. at 505. 37 Op. Att'y Gen. at 60.

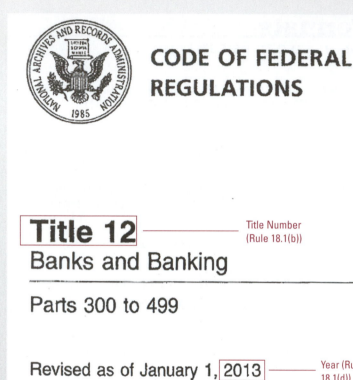

CODE OF FEDERAL REGULATIONS

Title 12

Title Number (Rule 18.1(b))

Banks and Banking

Parts 300 to 499

Revised as of January 1, 2013

Year (Rule 18.1(d))

Containing a codification of documents
of general applicability and future effect

As of January 1, 2013

Published by the Office of the Federal Register
National Archives and Records Administration
as Special Edition of the Federal Register

Cover

Pinpoint reference
(Rule 18.1(c))

or provided services), an assessment may be imposed against any such person or jointly and severally against any combination of such persons.

§ 308.503 Investigations.

(a) If an investigating official concludes that a subpoena pursuant to the authority conferred by 31 U.S.C. 3804(a) is warranted:

(1) The subpoena will identify the person to whom it is addressed and the authority under which the subpoena is issued and will identify the records or documents sought;

(2) The investigating official may designate a person to act on his or her behalf to receive the documents sought; and

(3) The person receiving such subpoena will be required to provide the investigating official or the person designated to receive the documents a certification that the documents sought have been produced, or that such documents are not available, and the reasons therefor, or that such documents, suitably identified, have been withheld based upon the assertion of an identified privilege.

(b) If the investigating official concludes that an action under the PFCRA may be warranted, the investigating official will submit a report containing the findings and conclusions of such investigation to the reviewing official.

(c) Nothing in this section will preclude or limit an investigating official's discretion to refer allegations directly to the United States Department of Justice (DOJ) for suit under the False Claims Act (31 U.S.C. 3729 *et seq.*) or other civil relief, or to preclude or limit the investigating official's discretion to defer or postpone a report or referral to the reviewing official to avoid interference with a criminal investigation or prosecution.

(d) Nothing in this section modifies any responsibility of an investigating official to report violations of criminal law to the Attorney General.

§ 308.504 Review by the reviewing official.

(a) If, based on the report of the investigating official under § 308.503(b) of this subpart, the reviewing official determines that there is adequate evidence to believe that a person is liable under § 308.502 of this subpart, the reviewing official will transmit to the Attorney General a written notice of the reviewing official's intention to issue a complaint under § 308.506 of this subpart.

(b) Such notice will include:

(1) A statement of the reviewing official's reasons for issuing a complaint;

(2) A statement specifying the evidence that supports the allegations of liability;

(3) A description of the claims or statements upon which the allegations of liability are based;

(4) An estimate of the amount of money or the value of property, services, or other benefits requested or demanded in violation of § 308.502 of this subpart;

(5) A statement of any exculpatory or mitigating circumstances that may relate to the claims or statements known by the reviewing official or the investigating official; and

(6) A statement that there is a reasonable prospect of collecting an appropriate amount of penalties and assessments. Such a statement may be based upon information then known, or upon an absence of any information indicating that the person may be unable to pay such amount.

§ 308.505 Prerequisites for issuing a complaint.

(a) The reviewing official may issue a complaint under § 308.506 of this subpart only if:

(1) The DOJ approves the issuance of a complaint in a written statement described in 31 U.S.C. 3803(b)(1); and

(2) In the case of allegations of liability under § 308.502(a) of this subpart with respect to a claim (or a group of related claims submitted at the same time as defined in paragraph (b) of this section) the reviewing official determines that the amount of money or the value of property or services demanded or requested does not exceed $150,000.

(b) For the purposes of this section, a group of related claims submitted at the same time will include only those claims arising from the same transaction (e.g., grant, loan, application, or

Inside Page

Rule 18 contains instructions for citing only the most popular administrative and executive materials. There are a multitude of administrative agencies and other executive bodies that develop their own citation formats and conventions that change intermittently. If you are writing a document to submit to an administrative agency or other executive body, you should research and comply with that agency's or body's citation conventions, if they differ.

18.1 Full Citations to *Code of Federal Regulations*

You must cite federal rules and regulations to the *Code of Federal Regulations* ("C.F.R.") whenever possible.[1] The C.F.R. is an annual codification of general and permanent rules and regulations of the departments and agencies of the federal government. The rules and regulations are published in a paperbound print version, but they are also available as an official PDF through the Government Publishing Office's website govinfo.gov. Each is updated annually. A full citation to the C.F.R. has four or five components.[2]

[Name of the rule or regulation,] | Title number | C.F.R. | § | Pinpoint reference | (Year).

Example (spaces denoted by ▲)

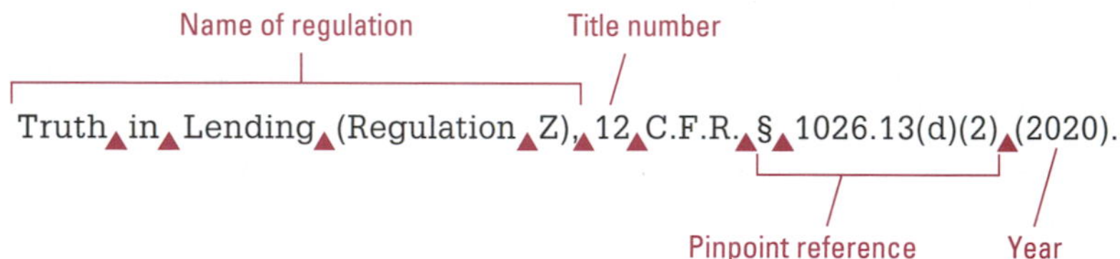

18.1(a) Name of rule or regulation

When a rule or regulation is commonly referenced by its name, or when the name of a rule or regulation will assist your readers in its identification, you may set out that name before the title number, followed by a comma and one space.[3] Use ordinary type, and refer to **Rules 3.2**, **Rule 3.3**, and **Chart 3.1** for capitalization.[4] You may also start with the issuing agency's name, abbreviated according to common conventions (e.g., Federal Communications Commission becomes "FCC" and Federal Trade Commission becomes "FTC").[5] You may shorten a long name for easier reference.[6]

Examples

FTC Credit Practices Rule, 16 C.F.R. § 444.3(a)(1) (2020).

or

Credit Practices Rule, 16 C.F.R. § 444.3(a)(1) (2020).

18.1(b) Title number

If you do not use the name of the rule or regulation, begin with the number of the C.F.R. volume containing the cited rule or regulation, followed by one space, the abbreviation "C.F.R." in ordinary type, and another space.[7] For *Treasury Regulations* (in Title 26) and *Federal Acquisition Regulations* (in Title 48), see **Rule 18.1(f)**. For presidential orders and other executive documents (in Title 3), see **Rule 18.9**.

18.1(c) Pinpoint references

Although each C.F.R. title is divided into chapters and further subdivided into parts covering specific regulatory areas, most titles are organized by sections. Cite the most specific section or other subdivision containing the referenced rule or regulation. Insert one space after the pinpoint reference.[8] For more information on subdivisions, see **Rules 5**, **6**, and **9**.

Examples (spaces denoted by ▲)

11▲C.F.R.▲§§▲4.4(a)(4), 4.5(d) (2020).

36▲C.F.R.▲§▲703.4(a) (2020),▲85▲FR▲70948▲(Westlaw).

6▲C.F.R.▲ch.▲I▲(2020).

14▲C.F.R.▲pt.▲25,▲app.▲C▲(2020).

18.1(d) Date parenthetical

Unless you intend to cite a provision from an earlier edition of the C.F.R., cite the current edition, setting out the volume's year of publication in parentheses.[9] When citing a provision in a historic edition, use the year of that edition.

Examples

Current annual edition (print or official PDF):	38 C.F.R. § 3.343(c)(2) (2020).
Historic version:	20 C.F.R. § 404.140 (1998).

18.1(e) Commercial databases and other online sources

If you cite a provision from the online, official C.F.R. on govinfo.gov, it is unnecessary to indicate its publication by the Government Publishing Office or to add the URL.[10] In other words, cite to it as you would the print publication. Likewise, if you cite to any online authenticated or exact copy of the C.F.R., cite to it as the original and do not append a URL.[11] The e-CFR, in contrast, while reflecting the most current version of a federal regulation, is not official (see **Sidebar 18.1**); consequently, in the full citation, indicate the exact

SIDEBAR 18.1 **Currency of C.F.R. Volumes**

The *Code of Federal Regulations* is presently divided into 50 subject-matter titles representing broad areas under federal regulation, contained in over 200 volumes. Although each volume is annually updated, the set is also revised quarterly, as follows:

Title numbers	Revision date
1–16	January 1
17–27	April 1
28–41	July 1
42–50	October 1

The current official annual edition of the C.F.R. is available in print and online in PDF format from the Government Publishing Office's website govinfo, available at https://www.govinfo.gov/app/collection/CFR.

Govinfo also publishes the unofficial *Electronic Code of Federal Regulations* ("e-CFR") at https://www.ecfr.gov/cgi-bin/ECFR?page=browse. The e-CFR is updated daily, compiling C.F.R. provisions and *Federal Register* amendments. Other unofficial electronic versions of the C.F.R. are available from commercial publishers such as Bloomberg Law, Lexis, and Westlaw. Because unofficial versions of the C.F.R. may contain material not present in the current annual print or official online edition, if you cite the C.F.R. from one of these unofficial sources, convey that information as described in **Rule 18.1(e)**.

date (Month Day, Year) through which the provision is current, and append its URL after the publication parenthetical.[12]

If you cite to a C.F.R. provision in a commercial database, after the date parenthetical, include any unique database identifiers; if the database name is not clear from the unique identifier, add the name of the database to a second parenthetical with the database name at the end of the citation.[13]

Examples

e-CFR daily update version:	8 C.F.R. § 60.2 (Nov. 3, 2020), https://www.ecfr.gov/cgi-bin/text-idx?SID=d411ca853de28595b7727eec96a5dbb6&mc=true&node=se10.2.60_12&rgn=div8.
Commercial database version:	27 C.F.R. § 72.21(b) (2020), WL 27 CFR § 72.21.

18.1(f) *Treasury Regulations; Federal Acquisition Regulations*

The *Treasury Regulations* in Title 26 and the *Federal Acquisition Regulations* in Title 48 are not typically cited to their C.F.R. title numbers.[14] Replace the title number and C.F.R. abbreviation with the abbreviations shown below, in ordinary type.[15]

Treasury Regulations:	Treas. Reg.	Treas. Reg. § 1.921-2 (2016).
Federal Acquisition Regulations:	FAR	FAR 9.403 (2016).

18.2 Short Citations to *Code of Federal Regulations*

18.2(a) Using *id.* or other short citations to C.F.R.

When appropriate, use *id.* as the short citation.[16] When *id.* is not appropriate (**Rule 11.3(c)**), use one of the short citations illustrated below, omitting the publication date parenthetical.[17] If the reader could easily recognize the citation from the context of the discussion, you may omit the title number and C.F.R. abbreviation.[18]

Example

Full citation options:	Cuban Assets Control Regulations, 31 C.F.R. § 515.329 (2016).
	31 C.F.R. § 515.329 (2016).
Short citation options:	31 C.F.R. § 515.329.
	§ 515.329.

18.2(b)[FN] Short citations to C.F.R. in academic footnotes

ACADEMIC FORMATTING

When *id.* is not appropriate (**Rule 11.3(c)**), use one of the formats illustrated in **Rule 18.2(a)**.[19] Repeat the full citation when the C.F.R. provision has not been cited, in full or in short form (including *id.*) in the same footnote or one of the previous five footnotes.[20] Do not use *supra* (**Rule 11.4**).[21]

18.3 Full Citations to *Federal Register*

Cite the *Federal Register* for proposed rules and regulations, notices that are not transferred to the C.F.R., and final regulations not yet printed in the C.F.R. The *Federal Register* (abbreviated "Fed. Reg.") is published daily in print, official online sources, and unofficial online sources. A full citation to the *Federal Register* contains the following components[22]:

[Title of rule or regulation] | Volume number | Fed. Reg. | Initial page, | Pinpoint reference | ([proposed] Month Day, Year) | [(to be codified at | C.F.R. citation)] | [(amending | C.F.R. citation)].

Example (spaces denoted by ▲)

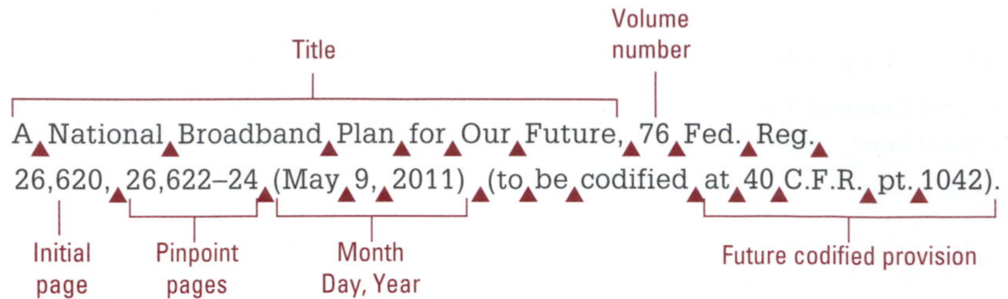

18.3(a) Title of rule or regulation

If the rule or regulation has a commonly used name, begin with the title of the notice, rule, or regulation, in ordinary type, followed by a comma and one space.[23] Use **Rule 3.2**, **Rule 3.3**, and **Chart 3.1** for capitalization. You may shorten lengthy titles so long as they remain descriptive.[24] Administrative notices can begin with a commonly used name or begin with a description.[25]

Examples

September 11th Victim Compensation Fund of 2001, 67 Fed. Reg. 11,233 (Mar. 13, 2002).

Notice, 74 Fed. Reg. 28,877 (June 18, 2009).

18.3(b) Volume number

Following the title or description, if any, set out the number of the *Federal Register* volume containing the cited material, one space, the abbreviation "Fed. Reg." in ordinary type, and another space.[26] Omit reference to the register volume's specific issue number.[27]

Example

Consolidated Federal Oil and Gas and Indian Coal Valuation Reform, 85 Fed. Reg. 62,016 (Oct. 1, 2020), 85 FR 62016 (Lexis+).

18.3(c) Initial page and pinpoint references

Provide the initial page of the notice, rule, or regulation, and if citing only a portion, add the pinpoint page(s) of more specific material.[28] Separate the initial page from the pinpoint page with a comma and one space.[29] With page numbers of five digits or more, use a comma to separate the thousands from the hundreds.[30] See **Rule 5.2** for more information about numbers and pinpoint pages.

Examples

Notice, 74 Fed. Reg. 14,790, 14,792 (Apr. 1, 2009), 2009 WL 834096.

Certain Lined Paper Products from the People's Republic of China, 78 Fed. Reg. 34,640, 34,640–41 (June 10, 2013).

18.3(d) Exact date; status of proposed rule or regulation

Because the *Federal Register* is published daily, the date parenthetical should refer to the exact date (Month Day, Year) of publication.[31] Abbreviate the month according to **Appendix 3(A)**. When citing a proposed rule or regulation, indicate that status in the date parenthetical, preceding the date.[32]

Example

Approval and Promulgation of Air Quality Implementation Plans, 74 Fed. Reg. 25,205 (proposed May 27, 2009).

18.3(e) Cross-references to C.F.R.

When the *Federal Register* indicates that a rule or regulation will be codified or will amend an existing provision in the *Code of Federal Regulations*, provide that information in a parenthetical following the date parenthetical, as illustrated below.[33]

Examples

Candidate Solicitation at State, District, and Local Party Fundraising Events, 70 Fed. Reg. 9013 (proposed Feb. 24, 2005) (to be codified at 11 C.F.R. § 300.64(a)).

86 Fed. Reg. 7503 (Jan. 29, 2021) (amending 16 C.F.R. pt. 1015).

18.3(f) Commercial databases and other online sources

If you cite to the *Federal Register* on a government website such as https://www.federalregister.gov or govinfo.gov (i.e., an official online source), follow **Rules 18.3(a)–(e)**.[34] When citing a commercial database for the *Federal Register*, give the unique database codes or identifiers in a parallel citation after the full citation.[35] Include the database name in a separate parenthetical after that if the database is not clear from the unique identifier.[36] If you are citing to an online source other than one of these, check **Rules 30.2** and **30.3** to see if you need to append a URL or cite the source as an internet page.

Examples

DHS Ratification of Department Actions, 85 Fed. Reg. 59,651, 59,654 (Sept. 23, 2020), 85 FR 59651 (Lexis+).

Notice, 74 Fed. Reg. 14,786, 14,788 (Apr. 1, 2009), 2009 WL 834094.

18.4 Short Citations to *Federal Register*

18.4(a) Using *id.* or other short citations to *Federal Register*

When appropriate, use *id.* as the short citation.[37] When *id.* is not appropriate (see **Rule 11.3(c)**), omit the date parenthetical and any cross-references to the C.F.R.[38] Insert "at" before a pinpoint reference.[39]

Example

Full citation: Fisheries of the Caribbean, Gulf of Mexico, and South Atlantic, 78 Fed. Reg. 25,047, 25,047–48 (proposed Apr. 29, 2013) (amending 50 C.F.R. pt. 622).

Short citation: Fisheries of the Caribbean, Gulf of Mexico, and South Atlantic, 78 Fed. Reg. at 25,049–50.

18.4(b)FN Short citations to *Federal Register* in academic footnotes

ACADEMIC FORMATTING

When *id.* is not appropriate (**Rule 11.3(c)**), use the format illustrated in **Rule 18.4(a)**.[40] Repeat the full citation when the rule or regulation in the *Federal Register* has not been cited, in full or in short form (including *id.*) in the same footnote or one of the previous five footnotes.[41] Do not use *supra* (**Rule 11.4**).[42]

18.5 Full Citations to Federal Agency Decisions

A full citation to an administrative decision such as an agency adjudication or arbitration should generally follow the format for citing cases in **Rule 12**, with the exceptions noted in this rule.[43] These citations typically contain six components[44]:

[*Case name or Title*,] | Volume number | Reporter abbreviation | Initial page, | Pinpoint reference | (Year).

Example (spaces denoted by ▲)

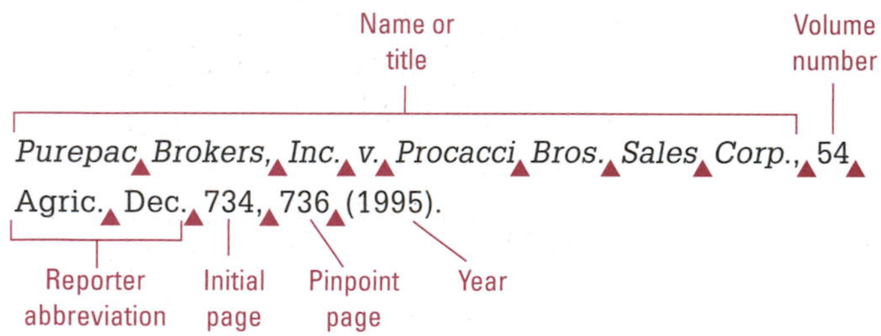

18.5(a) Name or title

If the decision involves adverse parties, the name of the proceeding is analogous to a case name; follow **Rule 12.2**, indicating the first-listed party on each side, but omitting any procedural phrases that may be present.[45] In non-adversarial proceedings, the title of an adjudicative matter may indicate the stage and nature of the proceeding; you may remove that information from the title and indicate it in a parenthetical appended to the full citation.[46] In either situation, abbreviate words found in **Appendix 3(E)**,[47] and present the name or title in italics.[48]

Example

Boltless Steel Shelving Units Prepackaged for Sale from China: Sales at Less Than Fair Value, 80 Fed. Reg. 51,779 (Dep't of Commerce Aug. 26, 2015) (final determination).

18.5(b) Volume number and reporter abbreviation

There is no single publication source for federal agency decisions. When the decision is printed in an agency's official reporter, cite the volume number of that reporter, followed by one space and the abbreviation for the reporter.[49] See **Appendix 7(A)** for abbreviations to many federal agencies' official reporters.[50]

Agency decisions are also unofficially published in topical looseleaf services. When the decision is not available in an official reporter, but is available from a looseleaf service, follow **Rule 24**.[51] Provide the full date in the date parenthetical, any helpful publication number, and any case number.[52] If the source indicates the decision will be in a bound volume, use the volume number, the reporter abbreviation, and the initial page number; if the initial page number is unavailable, use the case number as the initial page number.[53]

If the decision is available only from the agency's website, follow **Rules 30.2**, **30.3**, and **31**.[54] In any instance, you may add a parallel citation to the decision in a commercial database such as Westlaw, Bloomberg Law, or Lexis.[55] When citing an unpublished decision directly to a commercial database, analogize to **Rule 12.14(b)**.[56] If you are citing to an online source other than one of these, check **Rules 30.2** and **30.3** for how to cite it.[57]

Examples

Official reporter:	*Clinton Milk Co.*, 31 Agric. Dec. 1231, 1238–40 (1972).
	Seattle Crescent Container Serv., Inc. v. Port of Seattle, 28 F.M.C. 336, 336 (1986).
Agency website:	*Bio-Chi Inst. of Massage Therapy*, No. 14-37-SP (U.S. Dep't of Educ. Dec. 18, 2014), https://oha.ed.gov/oha/files/2019/03/2014-37-SP-S.pdf.
Official reporter with parallel citation to commercial database:	*Cavazos v. Wanxiang Am. Corp.*, 10 OCAHO 1138 (Apr. 27, 2011), 2011 WL 824675.
Unpublished opinion in a commercial database:	*City of Effingham*, No. 25-WH-244790, 2019 NLRB LEXIS 611, *2 (Nov. 8, 2019).

18.5(c) Subdivision and pinpoint reference

After the reporter abbreviation, insert a reference to the initial subdivision.[58] In bound reports, the initial subdivision will likely be a page number; however, in looseleaf services, the subdivision may be a paragraph or another division (see **Rule 24.1(e)**).[59] Provide a pinpoint reference if possible. See **Rules 5**, **6**, and **9** for more information on pinpoint references.

18.5(d) Date parenthetical

Indicate the date of the decision, following **Rule 12.7**.[60]

18.5(e) Agency abbreviation

If the identity of the agency that issued the decision cannot be determined from the reporter name, add the agency's abbreviation to the date parenthetical, using abbreviations from **Appendix 7(B)**.[61] Insert one space between the agency abbreviation and the date.[62] For a current list of federal agencies, go to USA.gov, *A–Z Index of U.S. Government Departments and Agencies*, https://www.usa.gov/agencies.

18.5(f) Arbitrator

When citing the decision of an arbitrator, add a parenthetical following the date parenthetical and provide the surname of the arbitrator, followed by a comma and the abbreviation "Arb."[63]

Example (looseleaf service)

Am. Fed'n of Gov't Emps., Local 2270 v. Dep't of Veterans Affs., 111 LRP 13172 (2010) (Zeiser, Arb.).

18.5(g)FN Full citations to federal agency decisions in academic footnotes

ACADEMIC FORMATTING

Follow the relevant provisions of **Rule 18.5**, but use ordinary type for the case name, analogizing to **Rule 12.2(a)(2)FN**.[64]

SIDEBAR 18.2 Citing Federal Tax Materials

Citation information for commonly used federal tax materials is contained in **Appendix 6**. For tax materials not contained in **Appendix 6**, consult Joni Larson & Dan Sheaffer, *Federal Tax Research* (2d ed. 2011) (updates available at https://cap-press.com/books/isbn/9781594608575/Federal-Tax-Research-Second-Edition), or Gail Levin Richmond, *Federal Tax Research: Guide to Materials and Techniques* (10th ed. 2018).

18.6 Short Citations to Federal Agency Decisions

Follow the relevant subdivisions of **Rule 12.16**.[65]

18.7 Full Citations to Advisory Opinions

A full citation to an advisory opinion of the Attorney General of the United States or the Justice Department's Office of Legal Counsel contains up to six components.[66]

[Title,] | Volume number | Source abbreviation | Initial page, | Pinpoint reference | (Date).

Examples (spaces denoted by ▲)

Attorney General opinion:

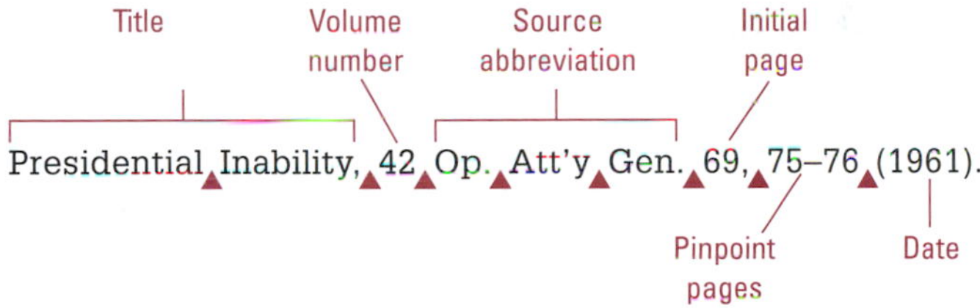

Office of Legal Counsel opinion:

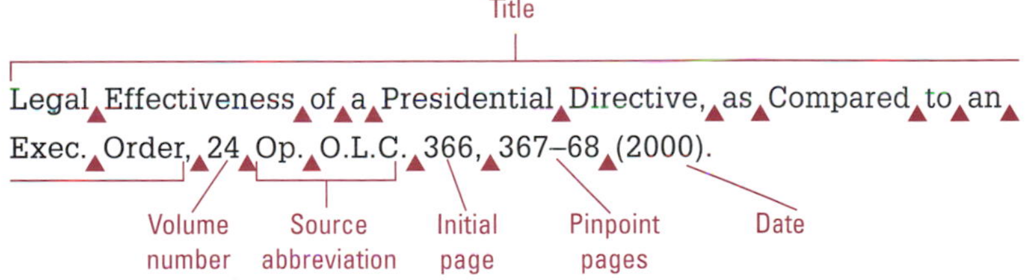

18.7(a) Title

Begin with the title of the advisory opinion, if any, abbreviating words found in **Appendices 3(B)**, **(E)**, **(F)**, or **(G)**.[67] Present the title in ordinary type.[68] Insert a comma and one space after the title.[69]

Example

Whether a Presidential Pardon Expunges Jud. & Exec. Branch Rec. of a Crime, 30 Op. O.L.C. 1 (2006).

18.7(b) Volume number and source abbreviation

Following the title, set out the number of the volume containing the cited opinion, followed by one space, an abbreviation for the publication source, and another space.[70] Abbreviate *Opinions of the Attorneys General of the United States* as "Op. Att'y Gen."[71] Abbreviate *Opinions of the Office of Legal Counsel* as "Op. O.L.C."[72]

Example

Relative Rank of Navy & Army Officers, 34 Op. Att'y Gen. 521, 523 (1925).

18.7(c) Initial page and pinpoint references

Following the source abbreviation, indicate the initial page on which the cited material begins.[73] To cite a particular part of the opinion, add a comma, one space, and a pinpoint page reference (see **Rule 5.2**).[74]

18.7(d) Date parenthetical

In parentheses, indicate the volume's year of publication.[75]

18.7(e) Commercial databases and other online sources

When citing to a commercial database, give the unique database codes or identifiers in a parallel citation after the full citation.[76] Include the database name in a separate parenthetical after that if the database is not clear from the unique identifier.[77] If you are citing to an online source other than a commercial database, check **Rules 30.2** and **30.3** to determine the proper format.[78]

Examples

Promotions of Judge Advocs. Gen., 32 Op. O.L.C. 70, 73 (2008), https://www.justice.gov/olc/file/477051/download.

Applicability of 18 U.S.C. § 281 to Selling Activities of Retired Mil. Officers, 5 Op. O.L.C. 360, *6 (1981), 1981 OLC LEXIS 61.

18.8 Short Citations to Advisory Opinions

18.8(a) Using *id.* or other short citations to advisory opinions

When appropriate, use *id.* as the short citation.[79] When *id.* is not appropriate (**Rule 11.3(c)**), indicate the volume number and the source abbreviation. Insert "at" before a pinpoint page reference. If you are citing to a source in a commercial electronic database, the short form must include the unique database identifier, if any, and include the parenthetical with the name of the database provider.[80] You do not need to include the URL in a short citation if you included it in a source's full citation.[81]

Example

Full citation: Rev. of Final Order in Alien Emp. Sanctions Cases, 13 Op. O.L.C. 370, 371 (1989).

Short citation: 13 Op. O.L.C. at 371.

18.8(b)FN Short citations to advisory opinions in academic footnotes

ACADEMIC FORMATTING

Repeat the full citation when the advisory opinion has not been cited, in full or in short form (including *id.*) in the same footnote or one of the previous five footnotes.[82] Do not use *supra* (**Rule 11.4**).[83]

18.9 Full Citations to Executive Documents

A full citation to a document such as an executive order, a proclamation, a determination, a finding, a memorandum, a notice, or a reorganization plan prepared by the President of the United States contains six or seven components.[84]

[Title,] | Document identification | No. | Document number, | Source abbreviation | Initial subdivision, | Pinpoint reference | (Date).

Example (spaces denoted by ▲)

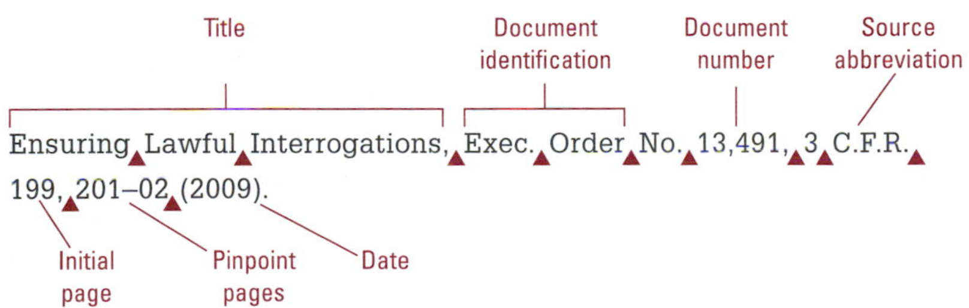

18.9(a) Title, document identification, and document number

Begin with the title of the document, if any, followed by a comma and one space.[85] Do not abbreviate any words in the title, use ordinary type, and capitalize according to **Rule 3.2**, **Rule 3.3**, and **Chart 3.1**.[86] Next, identify the form of the executive document (e.g., executive order, proclamation) and indicate its number, if any, as it appears in the source.[87] Abbreviate "Executive" as "Exec." and "Number" as "No.,"[88] but do not otherwise abbreviate words in the document identification.

Examples

National Defense Resources Preparedness, Exec. Order No. 13,603, 77 Fed. Reg. 16,651 (Mar. 22, 2012).

Proclamation No. 8346, 74 Fed. Reg. 9735 (Feb. 27, 2009).

18.9(b) Source abbreviations

Presidential orders, proclamations, and reorganization plans are usually printed in Title 3 of the *Code of Federal Regulations* ("3 C.F.R."); this is the preferred source to cite.[89] If the document is not in the *Code of Federal Regulations* or has not yet appeared there, cite its publication in the *Federal Register*,[90] following **Rule 18.3**.

Cite executive documents not appearing in the C.F.R. or the *Federal Register* to the sources in which they are published, such as *Public Papers of the Presidents* (abbreviated "Pub. Papers"), the *Weekly Compilation of Presidential Documents* ("Weekly Comp. Pres. Doc."), the *Daily Compilation of Presidential Documents* ("Daily Comp. Pres. Doc."), or the *United States Code Congressional and Administrative News* ("U.S.C.C.A.N.") in that order of preference.[91] Use ordinary type for the source abbreviation.[92]

Examples

Exec. Order No. 12,834, 3 C.F.R. 580 (1993).

Presidential Notice of March 11, 2009, 74 Fed. Reg. 10,999 (Mar. 13, 2009).

Address to the Nation on the Terrorist Attacks, 1 Pub. Papers 1099 (Sept. 11, 2001).

18.9(c) Subdivision and pinpoint references

Indicate the page or other subdivision on which the specific document begins.[93] Unlike other titles of the C.F.R., most documents published in Title 3 use page numbers rather than section numbers, but you may encounter both. To refer to material within the document, insert a comma, one space, and the pinpoint reference.[94] See **Rules 5**, **6**, and **9** for more information on pinpoint pages and other subdivisions.

Examples

Exec. Order No. 12,778, 3 C.F.R. 359, 360 (1992).

Exec. Order No. 12,291, 3 C.F.R. 127, 128 § 2(c) (1981).

18.9(d) Date parenthetical

Because C.F.R. Title 3 prints only current executive orders, when citing an older executive order, use the publication year of the original C.F.R. volume containing the order.[95] When citing an executive order or other executive document to the *Federal Register*, insert the exact date (Month Day, Year) of the cited issue, abbreviating the month using **Appendix 3(A)**.[96] Enclose dates in parentheses.[97]

18.9(e) Parallel citation to document reprint

You may include a parallel citation to another source that reprints the cited document, such as an appendix to the *United States Code*, U.S.C.C.A.N., or *Statutes at Large*.[98] Following the date parenthetical, insert the italicized phrase "*reprinted in*" followed by a full citation to the parallel source.[99]

Examples

Exec. Order No. 11,246, 3 C.F.R. 167 (1965), *reprinted in* 42 U.S.C. § 2000e app. 538–41 (2000).

Exec. Order No. 11,785, 3 C.F.R. 874 (1974), *reprinted in* 1974 U.S.C.C.A.N. 8277.

18.9(f)FN Full citations to executive documents in academic footnotes

ACADEMIC FORMATTING

Follow **Rule 18.9(a)–(e)**, with the following typeface modifications. Use ordinary type for abbreviated references to the *Code of Federal Regulations* or the *Federal Register*, but use large and small capital letters abbreviations to other sources, such as *Public Papers of the Presidents* (**Rule 18.9(b)**).[100]

Example

78 Address to the Nation on the Terrorist Attacks, 1 Pub. Papers 1099 (Sept. 11, 2001).

128 Interagency Working Group on Coordination of Domestic Energy Development and Permitting in Alaska, Exec. Order No. 13,580, 76 Fed. Reg. 4198 (July 15, 2011).

18.10 Short Citations to Executive Documents

18.10(a) Using *id.* or other short citations to executive documents

When appropriate (**Rule 11.3(c)**), use *id.* as the short citation.[101] When *id.* is not appropriate, use the components of the full citation, omitting the initial page number and the date.[102] Insert "at" before a pinpoint page.[103]

Example

Full citation:	Exec. Order No. 12,778, 3 C.F.R. 359, 360 (1992).
Short citation:	Exec. Order No. 12,778, 3 C.F.R. at 360.

18.10(b)FN Short citations to executive documents in academic footnotes

ACADEMIC FORMATTING

When *id.* is not appropriate (**Rule 11.3(c)**), use the format illustrated in **Rule 18.9(f)**.[104] Repeat the full citation when the executive document has not been cited, in full or in short form (including *id.*) in the same footnote or one of the previous five footnotes.[105] Do not use *supra* (**Rule 11.4**).[106]

18.11 Executive Agreements

Follow **Rule 19** for treaties, international conventions, and international agreements.

18.12 Citations to Patents

Begin the citation with the abbreviation "U.S. Patent No." in ordinary type, followed by the patent number and one space.[107] If the date the patent was filed is relevant to the discussion, in parentheses, insert the word "filed" followed by the exact date (Month Day, Year) on which the patent was filed, abbreviating the month (**Appendix 3(A)**).[108] If relevant, you may begin the citation with the name of the patent (in ordinary type) or append a second parenthetical indicating the date on which the patent was issued.[109]

Use the same format for citations to patents in academic footnotes.[110]

ACADEMIC FORMATTING

To cite a specific portion of a patent, insert an appropriate pinpoint reference immediately following the patent number.[111] To cite a specific field code on the patent's title page, you should include that field code in brackets.[112] See **Appendix 3(C)** and **Rule 9** for more information on subdivisions.

In short citations, use the full citation format without the date parenthetical. In textual-sentence references to a patent, you may use an apostrophe followed by the last three digits of the patent number and the word "Patent" (e.g., '854 Patent).[113] Do not use this shortened reference if more than one patent would have the same designation.

Examples

Full citations:	U.S. Patent No. 6,918,136 fig.2 (filed Feb. 1, 2001).
	U.S. Patent No. 4,396,601, at [75] (filed Sept. 3, 1982) (issued Apr. 24, 1984).
	Service Operations on a Computer System, U.S. Patent No. 6,918,055 (filed Mar. 20, 2002).
Short citations:	U.S. Patent No. 6,918,136.
	U.S. Patent No. 6,918,136 fig.3.
Short citation in text:	In challenging the '136 Patent, Jones argued that. . .

18.13 Citations to State Administrative Codes

Each state has its own administrative code, the state's equivalent of the *Code of Federal Regulations*. The citation typically includes a title number, the abbreviated name of the code, a pinpoint subdivision, and the year. The format for each state's code is listed under its entry in **Appendix 1(B)**. If the rule or regulation has a title, you may begin the citation with that title, in ordinary type. Analogize to **Rule 18.1**.[114]

See **Rules 30.2** and **30.3** to determine which rule to use for citations to official government sources published online. For short citations, analogize to **Rule 18.2**.[115]

Examples

Full citations:	Ohio Admin. Code 1501:9-1-08 (2012).
	Rights and Responsibilities of the Public Schools and Public School Students, New Mexico Board of Education, N.M. Admin. Code R. 6.11.2 (Aug. 25, 2020).
	Approved Carbon Monoxide Alarms for Use in Public Schools, Ill. Admin. Code tit. 41, § 112.230 (2016), https://www.ilga.gov/commission/jcar/admincode/041/041001120002300R.html (last visited Nov. 4, 2020).
Short citations:	Ill. Admin. Code tit. 41, § 112.230.
	Tit. 41, § 112.230.
	§ 112.230.

18.14 Citations to State Administrative Registers

Many, but not all, states have administrative registers, similar to the *Federal Register*. Consult **Appendix 1(B)** to determine whether the state has an administrative register and, if so, the citation format to follow. As with the *Federal Register*, refer to the exact date listed on the front cover. See **Rule 18.3** for more guidance.[116] For short citations, analogize to **Rule 18.4**.[117]

Examples

Full citation:	56 D.C. Reg. 5875 (July 31, 2009).
	640 Wis. Admin. Reg. 22 (Apr. 14, 2009).
Short citation:	56 D.C. Reg. at 5875.
	640 Wis. Admin. Reg. at 22.

18.15 Citations to State Agency Decisions

Analogize to **Rule 12** and **Rule 18.5**. If the identity of the agency issuing the decision cannot be determined by the name of the reporter or commercial database, insert the state's abbreviation before the agency abbreviation in the date parenthetical. When citing to a commercial database, give the unique database codes or identifiers in a parallel citation after the full citation.[118] Include the database name in a separate parenthetical after that if the database is not clear from the unique identifier.[119] If you are citing to another source found online, check **Rules 30.2** and **30.3** to see if you need to cite it as an internet source or simply append a URL.[120]

For short citations, analogize to **Rule 12.16**.

Examples

Avista Corp., Order No. 11-080, at 13–14 (Or. Pub. Util. Comm'n Mar. 10, 2011), http://apps.puc.state.or.us/orders/2011ords/11-080.pdf.

L.B. v. Dep't of Children & Family Servs., 2008 Fla. Div. Adm. Hear. LEXIS 232, at *3 (Apr. 30, 2008).

18.16 Citations to State Advisory Opinions

Analogize to **Rule 18.7**, but add the state abbreviation (**Appendix 3(B)**) to the beginning of the opinion's abbreviation. When citing to a commercial database, give the unique database codes or identifiers in a parallel citation after the full citation.[121] Include the database name in a separate parenthetical after that if the database is not clear from the unique identifier.[122] If you are citing to another source found online, check **Rules 30.2** and **30.3** to see if you need to cite it as an internet source or append a URL.[123] If desired, you may include a parallel citation to a state administrative code or register. For short citations, analogize to **Rule 18.8**.

Examples

Full citations:	Tex. Att'y Gen. Op. GA-0734, 34 Tex. Reg. 5621 (Aug. 21, 2009).
	Colo. Att'y Gen. Op. 09-03, 2009 Colo. AG LEXIS 3, at *5 (June 9, 2009).
Short citations:	Tex. Att'y Gen. Op. GA-0734, 34 Tex. Reg. at 5621.
	Colo. Att'y Gen. Op. 09-03, 2009 Colo. AG LEXIS 3, at *5.

18.17 Citations to State Executive Materials

Analogize to **Rule 18.9**, but begin the citation with the state's abbreviation. Because these materials are often most easily located online or in an electronic database, you may add that information using the rules in **Rules 30–32**. If desired, add a parallel citation to a state administrative code or register. For short citations, analogize to **Rule 18.10**.

Examples

Statewide Language Access Policy, N.Y. Exec. Order No. 26 (Oct. 6, 2011), http://www.governor.ny.gov/news/no-26-statewide-language-access-policy (last visited Oct. 5, 2020).

N.J. Exec. Order No. 68 (June 22, 2011), 2010 NJ EO 68 (Westlaw Edge).

18.18 Citations to Other Administrative and Executive Materials

To cite other federal or state administrative and executive materials not specifically addressed above, analogize to the closest rule above or use the following format. If the suggested format does not fit the source, include as much as possible.

Title, | Document abbreviation | No. | Document number | Source abbreviation | Pinpoint reference | (Agency abbreviation | Date).

19 Treaties and International Conventions and Agreements

Fast Formats

Bilateral treaty	Treaty on Measures for the Further Reduction and Limitation of Strategic Offensive Arms, Russ.-U.S., Apr. 8, 2010, S. Treaty Doc. No. 111-5 [hereinafter New START Treaty].
Multilateral treaty	Inter-American Treaty of Reciprocal Assistance, Sept. 2, 1947, 62 Stat. 1681, 21 U.N.T.S. 77.
Convention	Council of Europe, Convention on Cybercrime arts. 16–17, Nov. 23, 2001, C.E.T.S. No. 185, http://conventions.coe.int/Treaty/en/Treaties/Html/185.htm.
Agreement	Agreement for Economic and Technical Cooperation, Iraq-U.S., July 11, 2005, T.I.A.S. No. 13-1218 (entered into force Dec. 18, 2013).
Citation in academic footnote	ACADEMIC FORMATTING 56 Treaty on Measures for the Further Reduction and Limitation of Strategic Offensive Arms, Russ.-U.S., Apr. 8, 2010, S. Treaty Doc. No. 111-5 [hereinafter New START Treaty].
Short citations	New START Treaty. 60 New START Treaty, *supra* note 56.

19.1 Full Citations to Treaties, International Conventions, or International Agreements Currently in Force

A full citation to a treaty, convention, or executive agreement to which a nation or international organization is a party and that is currently in force varies slightly depending on whether it is a bilateral or multilateral agreement.[1] If bilateral, it establishes legal rights and obligations between two nations or a nation and an international organization; when multilateral, it does so among three or more nations or organizations.

A citation to a bilateral treaty, convention, or agreement has up to six components.[2]

Title, | 1st signatory party-2d signatory party, | [Pinpoint reference], | Month Day, Year, | Treaty source.

A citation to a multilateral treaty, convention, or agreement has up to five components.[3]

Title | [Pinpoint reference], | Month Day, Year, | U.S. treaty source, | [International treaty source].

Examples (spaces denoted by ▲)

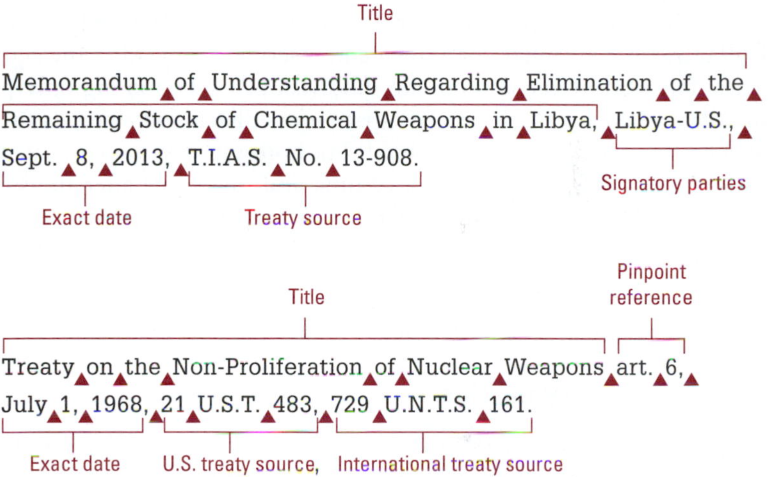

19.1(a) Title of treaty, convention, or agreement

Use the English-language version of the title of a treaty, convention, or agreement if one is available.[4] Indicate the form of agreement (e.g., "Treaty," "Convention," "Protocol," "Agreement") and its subject matter as shown on the document's title page.[5] If the document displays more than one form of agreement, use only the first shown.[6] Present the title in ordinary type, and capitalize words according to **Rule 3.2**, **Rule 3.3**, and **Chart 3.1**. If the citation refers to the entire document (i.e., does not use a pinpoint reference), add a comma and one space.[7]

When the title is lengthy or the document is commonly referenced by a popular name, append a [hereinafter] designation of the alternate name to the end of the full citation.[8] For guidance on using the [hereinafter] designation, see **Rule 11.5**.

Examples

Agreement to Improve International Tax Compliance and to Implement the Foreign Account Tax Compliance Act, Lat.-U.S., June 27, 2014, T.I.A.S. No. 14-1215 (entered into force Dec. 14, 2014).

Treaty on Principles Governing the Activities of States in the Exploration and Use of Outer Space, Including the Moon and Other Celestial Bodies art. III, Jan. 27, 1967, 18 U.S.T. 2410, 610 U.N.T.S. 205 [hereinafter Outer Space Treaty].

19.1(b) Pinpoint references

Pinpoint references to treaties, conventions, and agreements typically indicate a major subdivision, not a page number.[9] When citing only a part of a bilateral treaty, convention, or agreement, insert a comma after the signatory parties, followed by the appropriate subdivision.[10] When citing only part of a multilateral document, insert one space immediately following its title, followed by the appropriate subdivision.[11] For both pinpoints, abbreviate words found in **Appendix 3(C)**.[12] Insert a comma and one space after the subdivision.[13] See **Rules 5**, **6**, and **9** for more information on subdivisions.

Example

Convention for the Protection of Individuals with Regard to Automatic Processing of Personal Data pmbl., Jan. 28, 1981, 20 I.L.M. 317.

19.1(c) Signatory parties

List the signatory parties to a bilateral agreement in alphabetical order, abbreviating their names according to **Appendix 3(B)**, and joining the abbreviations with a hyphen (-).[14] Following the last abbreviation, insert a comma and one space.[15]

In citations to multilateral agreements, the parties' names are typically omitted, and are always omitted in academic footnotes.[16] If you wish to identify them, however, list their abbreviations in alphabetical order, joined by hyphens, before the pinpoint reference.

Examples

Mutual Defense Treaty, Phil.-U.S., Aug. 30, 1951, 3 U.S.T. 3947.

North American Free Trade Agreement, Can.-Mex.-U.S., art. 1120, Dec. 17, 1992, 32 I.L.M. 289 (1993) [hereinafter NAFTA].

19.1(d) Date of signing

When possible, provide the exact date (Month Day, Year) of signing, followed by a comma and one space.[17] Use **Appendix 3(A)** to abbreviate the months.[18]

When citing an agreement or note between only two parties in which the parties signed on different days, list the first date of signing, an en dash (–), and the last date of signing; omit the year of the first date of signing if both dates occurred in the same year (e.g., Mar. 2–May 3, 2020).[19] When citing a treaty that parties signed on different dates, use the date on which the treaty was opened for signature, approved, ratified, or adopted.[20] When doing so, you should italicize the phrase describing the date you used.[21] When the date of signing is not available, use one of the following dates, in this order of preference:

- the effective date;
- the date on which ratifications were exchanged between or among the signatories;
- the date of ratification by the President of the United States;
- the date of ratification by the United States Senate; or
- any other date of significance.

If desired, you may append a parenthetical referencing any additional date of significance.[22]

Examples

One date of signing:	Convention for the Unification of Certain Rules Relating to International Transportation by Air, Oct. 12, 1929, 49 Stat. 3000 [hereinafter Warsaw Convention].
	Convention for the Unification of Certain Rules with Respect to Assistance and Salvage at Sea art. 14, Sept. 23, 1910, 37 Stat. 1658 (entered into force Mar. 1, 1913).
Other dates:	Agreement Relating to the Establishment of a Peace Corps Program in Cameroon, Cameroon-U.S., July 23–Sept. 10, 1962, 13 U.S.T. 2114.
	Agreement Concerning a Joint Project for Planning, Design, Experiment Preparation, Performance and Reporting of Reactor Safety Experiments Concerning Containment Response, *adopted* Jan. 25, 1975, 28 U.S.T. 629, T.I.A.S. No. 8479 [hereinafter Reactor Safety Experiments].

19.1(e) Document sources

Following the date, cite a source in which the treaty, convention, or agreement is published.[23] For bilateral documents between the United States and another party, cite an official source, if available.[24] For multilateral documents to which the United States is a party, cite an official source; if desired, you may add a parallel citation to a source published by an international organization.[25] The *United States Treaties and Other International Agreements* ("U.S.T.") and the *Treaties and Other International Acts Series* ("T.I.A.S.") have not been published in print by the Government Publishing Office since Volume 35, Part 6, 1983–1984. For guidance on locating treaty texts, go to the "Finding Agreements" page on the United States Department of State's website, https://www.state.gov/finding-agreements/.

For agreements to which the United States is *not* a party, cite a source published by an international organization.[26] If the agreement doesn't appear there, cite to the official source of one of the signatories.[27] If it isn't clear from the abbreviation or context which signatory's source it is from, append a parenthetical indicating the jurisdiction, abbreviated according to **Appendix 3(B)**.[28]

When a treaty or agreement is not available in an official source or a source published by an international organization, cite it to International Legal Materials (I.L.M.), if therein; if not, cite to another unofficial source.[29] As a last resort, if you cannot find the treaty, convention, or agreement in any of the sources listed above, you may cite to it in a book, periodical, or online source.[30]

See **Chart 19.1** for a list of document sources, their abbreviations and citation formats, and for official sources, the order of preference for citation.[31] If you are citing to a source found online, check **Rules 30.2** and **30.3** to see if you need to cite it as an internet source or if you need to append a URL.[32]

Examples

Treaty Relating to the Uses of the Waters of the Niagara River, Can.-U.S., art. IV, Feb. 27, 1950, 1 U.S.T. 694.

Inter-American Convention on the Taking of Evidence Abroad art. 4, Jan. 30, 1975, 1438 U.N.T.S. 389, O.A.S.T.S. No. 44, http://www.oas.org/juridico/english/treaties/b-37.html.

19.2 Full Citations to Treaties, Conventions, or Agreements No Longer in Force

When citing an agreement (or part of an agreement) that is no longer in force, use the citation format for current agreements, but append a parenthetical indicating how and when the agreement was terminated or otherwise lost effect.

Example

Mutual Defense Treaty between the United States of America and the Republic of China, China-U.S., art. 10, Dec. 2, 1954, 6 U.S.T. 433 (terminated on Jan. 1, 1980).

CHART 19.1 Document Sources for Treaties, Conventions, and Agreements

Official sources (in order of citation preference)[33]:	**Abbreviation and format (spaces denoted by ▲):**
United States Treaties and Other International Agreements	Volume number▲U.S.T.▲Page number
Statutes at Large	Volume number▲Stat.▲Page number
Treaties and Other International Acts Series	T.I.A.S.▲No.▲Treaty number
Treaty Series	T.S.▲No.▲Treaty number
Executive Agreement Series	E.A.S.▲No.▲Treaty number
United Nations Treaty Series	Volume number▲U.N.T.S.▲Page number
Senate Treaty Documents	S.▲Treaty▲Doc.▲No.▲Treaty number
Senate Executive Documents	S.▲Exec.▲Doc.▲No.▲Document number
Sources from international organizations[34]:	**Abbreviation and format:**
United Nations Treaty Series	Volume number▲U.N.T.S.▲Page number
Council of Europe Treaty Series	C.E.T.S.▲No.▲Treaty number
European Treaty Series	E.T.S.▲No.▲Treaty number
International Legal Materials	Volume number▲I.L.M.▲Page number
League of Nations Treaty Series	Volume number▲L.N.T.S.▲Page number
Organization of American States Treaty Series	O.A.S.T.S.▲No.▲Treaty number
Pan-American Treaty Series	Volume number▲Pan-Am.▲T.S.▲Page number
Unofficial sources (cite I.L.M., if therein; otherwise no citation preference)[35]:	**Abbreviation and format:**
International Legal Materials	Volume number▲I.L.M.▲Page number
Hein's United States Treaties and Other International Agreements	Hein's▲No.▲KAV▲Treaty number
Parry's Consolidated Treaty Series	Volume number▲Consol.▲T.S.▲Page number
Treaties and Other International Agreements of the United States of America (Charles I. Bevans comp.)	Volume number▲Bevans▲Page number

19.3FN Full Citations to Treaties, Conventions, or Agreements in Academic Footnotes

ACADEMIC FORMATTING

Citations to treaties, conventions, or agreements—whether in force or not—use ordinary type for all the components, with one exception. If you are citing to a source in Senate treaty documents or Senate executive documents, the abbreviation for those sources must be in large and small caps.[36]

19.4 Short Citations to Treaties, Conventions, or Agreements

19.4(a) Using *id.* or other short citations to treaties, conventions, or agreements

When appropriate (**Rule 11.3(c)**), use *id.* as the short citation.[37] When *id.* is not appropriate, omit the title but keep the treaty source component, changing the pinpoint reference as needed. Analogize to short citations for statutes (**Rule 14.5**) or session laws (**Rule 14.9**).

Example

Full citation: Treaty on the Protection of Artistic and Scientific Institutions and Historic Monuments, Apr. 13, 1935, 49 Stat. 3267.

Short citation: 49 Stat. at 3268.

19.4(b)FN Short citations to treaties, conventions, or agreements in academic footnotes

ACADEMIC FORMATTING

Do not use *id.* if the treaty, convention, or agreement has not previously been cited in the same footnote or in one of the previous five footnotes.[38] Instead, use the *supra* format illustrated below, cross-referencing the footnote in which the document's full citation is first set out.[39] If the document's full citation uses a [hereinafter] designation, begin with that designation, followed by a comma, one space, and the *supra* cross-reference.[40] See **Rule 11.5** for more information about using [hereinafter].

Example

Full citation: 32 Treaty on the Protection of Artistic and Scientific Institutions and Historic Monuments, Apr. 13, 1935, 49 Stat. 3267 [hereinafter Roerich Pact].

Short citation: 44 Roerich Pact, *supra* note 32, at 3268.

19.5 International and Foreign Legal Sources

For citations to foreign and international legal sources, including the United Nations, consult the most recent edition of *Guide to Foreign and International Legal Citations*, prepared by the editors of New York University School of Law's *Journal of International Law and Politics*. Another useful guide for international law sources is Part IV of the Oxford University Standard for Citation of Legal Authorities (OSCOLA), https://www.law.ox.ac.uk/sites/files/oxlaw/oscola_2006_citing_international_law.pdf.

20 Books, Treatises, and Other Nonperiodic Materials

Fast Formats

Single author	Martha C. Nussbaum, *Sex and Social Justice* 265–66 (1999).
Two authors	Irin Carmon & Shana Knizhnik, *Notorious RBG: The Life and Times of Ruth Bader Ginsburg* 162–63 (2015).
Multivolume treatise, multiple authors	7A Charles Alan Wright, Arthur R. Miller & Mary Kay Kane, *Federal Practice and Procedure* § 1758, 114–15 (3d ed. 2005). 7A Charles Alan Wright et al., *Federal Practice and Procedure* § 1758, 114–15 (3d ed. 2005).
Editor, no listed author	*International Family Law Desk Book* ch. 8 (Ann Laquer Estin ed., 2012).
Author and editor	1 Arthur Linton Corbin, *Corbin on Contracts* § 4.14 (Joseph M. Perillo ed., rev. ed. 1993). Jeremy Bentham, *Of the Limits of the Penal Branch of Jurisprudence* § 4, 42–44 (Philip Schofield ed., Clarendon Press 2010).
Translator	Aldo Schiavone, *The Invention of Law in the West* 170–74 (Jeremy Carden & Antony Shugaar trans., Belknap Press of Harvard Univ. Press 2012).
Collected works of one author	Oliver Wendell Holmes, *Primitive Notions in Modern Law No. II*, *in* 3 *The Collected Works of Justice Holmes* 21, 30–31 (Sheldon M. Novick ed., 1995).
Collected works of multiple authors	Celia Wells, *Medical Manslaughter: Organizational Liability*, *in* 2 *Bioethics, Medicine and the Criminal Law* 192 (Danielle Griffiths & Andrew Sanders eds., 2013).
Commercial database	2 Edward J. Imwinkelreid, *Uncharged Misconduct Evidence* § 9:23 (2020), Westlaw UNMEV § 9:23.
E-book	Karla FC Holloway, *Legal Fictions: Constituting Race, Composing Literature* loc. 10 (2014) (e-book).
Religious work	*Proverbs* 22:6.

Citations in academic footnotes	ACADEMIC FORMATTING [44] OLIVER WENDELL HOLMES, *Primitive Notions in Modern Law No. II*, *in* 3 THE COLLECTED WORKS OF JUSTICE HOLMES 21, 30–31 (Sheldon M. Novick ed., 1995). [74] JEREMY BENTHAM, OF THE LIMITS OF THE PENAL BRANCH OF JURISPRUDENCE § 4, 42–44 (Philip Schofield ed., Clarendon Press 2010). [99] Celia Wells, *Medical Manslaughter: Organizational Liability*, *in* 2 BIOETHICS, MEDICINE AND THE CRIMINAL LAW 192 (Danielle Griffiths & Andrew Sanders eds., 2013).
Short citations	Nussbaum, *supra*, at 267. 7A Wright, § 1757. [86] BENTHAM, *supra* note 74, at 135.

20.1 Full Citations to Books, Treatises, and Other Nonperiodic Materials

A full citation to a treatise, book, or other nonperiodic work in print contains up to ten components.[1]

[Volume number if multivolume work] | Author, | *Title* | [at] | Pinpoint reference | ([Editor name, ed.,] | [Translator name, trans.,] | [Publisher if not the original] | [Edition number if not the 1st ed., ed.] | Year of publication).

Example (spaces denoted by ▲)

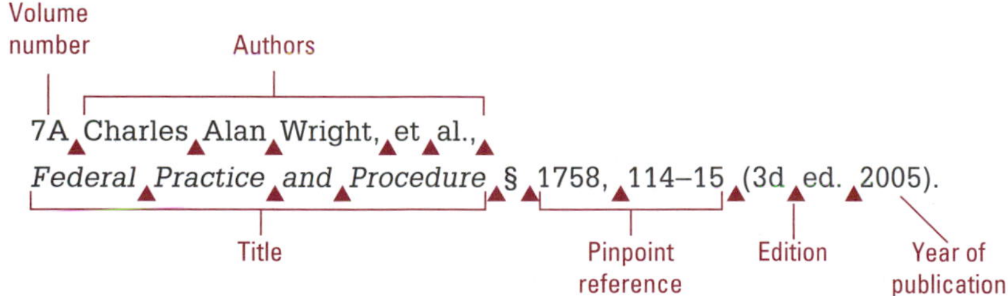

20.1(a) Volume number

If the cited work is from a multivolume set, begin the citation with the volume number, set out as an Arabic numeral in ordinary type, preceding the name of the author(s).[2] When the volume number also includes a letter, capitalize the letter.

Examples

3 *State Constitutions for the Twenty-First Century* 149–54 (G. Alan Tarr & Robert F. Williams eds., 2006).

6A Stuart M. Speiser et al., *The American Law of Torts* § 18:199 (Monique C.M. Leahy ed., 2010 & Cum. Supp. 2012).

33 Robert A. Rubin et al., *New York Construction Law Manual* § 12:13 (2020 ed. 2020).

20.1(b) Authors

20.1(b)(1) Single author

Set out the author's full name, in ordinary type, as represented on the cover or title page of the work, followed by a comma and one space.[3] A full name includes designations such as Jr. and III; only set off those designations with a comma if the author's name is listed that way in the work.[4] A full name does not include academic degrees, such as J.D., Ph.D., or M.D., or titles of respect, such as "Hon.," "Dr.," or "Prof." even if they are included in the work.[5]

Example

Correct:	Diego L. Garcia III,
Incorrect:	Prof. Diego L. Garcia, III, J.D.,

20.1(b)(2) Multiple authors

If the work has *two* authors, set out their full names as represented and in the order in which they appear on the cover or title page of the work and join their names with an ampersand (&).[6]

If the work has *three or more* authors, and the authors' names are not particularly relevant or the citation is a short form, use the first author's name followed by "et al." and omit the other authors' names.[7] There is no period after "et" and no comma *before* "et al."; set the entire phrase in ordinary type.[8] Insert a comma and one space after the phrase "et al."[9]

In a full citation, when the authors' names are particularly relevant, set out the full names of multiple authors, in ordinary type, as represented and in the order in which they appear on the cover or title page of the work.[10] If listing all author names, separate each name from the next with a comma and a space, except for the last two names, which are joined with an ampersand.[11] Insert a comma and one space after the last author's name.[12]

When citing a single volume of a multivolume work, set out only those authors whose names are attributed to that volume.[13]

Examples

Anne Enquist & Laurel Currie Oates,

Ruth Anne Robbins, Steve Johansen & Ken Chestek,

Ruth Anne Robbins et al.,

20.1(b)(3) Institutional author

If an institution or organization is listed as author, use the name appearing on the cover or title page, abbreviating any words (including the first) found in **Appendices 3(B)** or **3(E)**—as long as the author remains clearly identifiable.[14] Abbreviate United States as "U.S."[15] If the name has two business designations (see **Chart 12.1**), omit the second.[16] If the authors of the work are both a person and an institution or organization, give the individual's full name first, a comma and one space, and then the institutional author's name.[17] If no individual author is cited along with an institutional author, use the smallest subdivision of the institution that prepared the work first, if available, then a comma and a space, and then the overall institutional author's name.[18]

Examples

Meghan Spillane, Int'l Bar Ass'n, *International Moot Court: An Introduction* 54 (2008).

Section Tax'n, Am. Bar Ass'n, *The Property Tax Deskbook* (23d ed. 2018).

20.1(b)(4) Prefaces, forewords, introductions, and epilogues written by someone other than the author

If someone other than the author of a work wrote a preface, foreword, introduction, or epilogue to that larger work, follow **Rule 20.3(b)**.[19] If the same material is written by the author of the larger work, do not treat citation to those materials any differently than you would otherwise cite the larger work.[20]

Examples

Introduction written by someone other than the main work's author:	Camille Cauti, *Introduction to* Oscar Wilde, *The Picture of Dorian Gray*, at xiii, xxvii (N.Y., Barnes & Noble Classics 2003) (1891).
Introduction written by the main work's author:	Benjamin Dreyer, *Dreyer's English: An Utterly Correct Guide to Clarity and Style*, at xv (2019).

20.1(b)(5) Unlisted or unknown author

If the work shows no author or the author is unknown or when the work lists only editors, begin the citation with the title.

Example

Sir Gawain and the Green Knight 34 n.3 (Paul Battles ed., 2012).

20.1(c) Title

20.1(c)(1) Words in title; subtitles

Present the title and the subtitle (if any) in italics, but do not italicize information that is italicized in text, such as a case name (see **Rule 1.3** and **Chart 1.1**);

present such information in ordinary type.[21] Spell words in titles and subtitles exactly as shown on the cover or title page, and capitalize them according to **Rule 3.2**, **Rule 3.3**, and **Chart 3.1**.[22] Do not abbreviate any word in a title unless the word is so abbreviated on the work's cover or title page.[23] Do not omit prepositions or other words from a title or subtitle.[24]

Subtitles are optional; include them only if it is relevant.[25] Even if the cover or title page shows no punctuation between the main title and the subtitle, insert a colon and one space between them.[26] If the main title ends with a question mark, exclamation point, or dash, do not change it, and do not insert a colon between it and the subtitle.

If citing to a single volume of a multivolume work, in addition to including the volume number, use the main title of the volume cited, if different from the multivolume work.[27]

Examples

Linda H. Edwards, *Estates in Land & Future Interests: A Step-by-Step Guide* ch. 13 (4th ed. 2013).

James T. Patterson, Brown v. Board of Education*: A Civil Rights Milestone and Its Troubled History* 109–10 (2001).

Eric Foner, *Who Owns History? Rethinking the Past in a Changing World* 144–45 (2002).

6 Charles Fairman, *History of the Supreme Court of the United States: Reconstruction and Reunion 1864-88, Part 1*, at 542–46 (Paul A. Freund ed., 1971).

20.1(c)(2) Title in another language

Represent the title of a work published in a language other than English just as the title of any other book.[28] Capitalize words as they appear on the cover or title page.[29] You may provide an English translation of the title, placed in brackets, immediately following the original title.[30]

Examples

Tratado Teórico, Práctico y Crítico de Derecho Privado Puertorriqueño

Le Droit à la Santé en tant que Droit de l'Homme [The Right to Health as a Human Right]

20.1(d) Pinpoint references

Following the title or subtitle, insert a space and a pinpoint reference directing readers to the portion of the work that relates to the cited proposition or quotation.[31] Most works use Arabic page numbers, although pagination in front matter typically uses lowercase Roman numerals. Treat Roman numerals as you would any other page numbers.[32]

Insert one space after the pinpoint reference.[33] Do not treat a volume number as a pinpoint reference; the volume number is the first component of the citation.[34] See **Rule 20.1(a)** and its examples.

If a reader would be confused about when the title ends and the pinpoint reference begins, such as when the title ends in a numeral or when the pinpoint reference is in Roman numerals, insert ", at" before a pinpoint page, as explained in **Rule 5.2(c)**.[35] For works divided both by pages and by sections or paragraphs, see **Rule 6.5**. For electronic works, including e-books, see **Rule 20.4**. In general, see **Rules 5** through **9** for pinpoint references to pages, sections, chapters, notes, and other subdivisions.[36] Remember that **Rule 4.1** does not apply to books, treatises, or other nonperiodic materials that do not themselves insert a comma to create groups of three numerals when a number is four numerals long, whether the pinpoint reference is by pages or sections.[37]

Examples

Elizabeth Fajans et al., *Writing for Law Practice* 59 n.41 (2d ed. 2010).

Linda A. Pollock, *Forgotten Children: Parent-Child Relations from 1500 to 1900*, at 30 (1983).

4 Charles Alan Wright & Arthur R. Miller, *Federal Practice and Procedure* § 1006 (2d ed. 1987).

Ruth Ann McKinney, *Reading Like a Lawyer*, at xiv (2005).

Paul M. Trueger, *Accounting Guide for Defense Contracts* 1039–41 (6th ed. 1971).

20.1(e) Publication parenthetical

The final component of a citation to a book, treatise, or nonperiodic work is a parenthetical that identifies, at a minimum, the year of publication.[38] Many works have additional features that should be indicated in this parenthetical, such as the names of editors or translators, the names of later publishers, the numbers of later editions or printings, or an indication that the work is part of a larger series.[39]

20.1(e)(1) Editor or translator

When the work lists one editor on the cover or title page, begin the publication parenthetical with the full name of the editor, in ordinary type;[40] if there are two or more editors, analogize to the format in **Rule 20.1(b)(2)** for multiple authors.[41] If the editor is an institution, use the name of that institution, abbreviated according to **Rule 20.1(b)(3)**.[42] Immediately after the name(s), with no intervening punctuation, insert the abbreviation "ed." (plural, "eds."), followed by a comma and a space.[43]

If the work is a translation, add the translator's name, in ordinary type, to the publication parenthetical.[44] Present the translator's full name, followed immediately by the abbreviation "trans.," a comma, and one space.[45] If there are two or more translators, analogize to the format in **Rule 20.1(b)(2)** for multiple authors.[46] If the work has both an editor and a translator, identify the editor first.[47]

Examples

Antitrust Goes Global: What Future for Transatlantic Cooperation? 117–18 (Simon J. Evenett et al. eds., 2000).

Orhan Pamuk, *My Name Is Red* 72 (Erdağ Göknar trans., Vintage Books 2002).

20.1(e)(2) Publisher

Add a publisher to the publication parenthetical only in two instances: (1) when citing a work published by someone *other than* the original publisher[48] or (2) when the work has no named author, editor, or translator.[49] Abbreviate the publisher's name according to **Rule 20.1(b)(3)**.[50]

Example

H.G. Wells, *The Time Machine* 51–52 (Dover Publ'ns, Inc. 1995).

The Chicago Manual of Style § 7.81 (The Univ. Chi. Press 17th ed., 2017).

Dante Alighieri, *Inferno* 281–86 (Giuseppe Mazzotta ed. & Michael Palma trans., W.W. Norton & Co. 2007).

20.1(e)(3) Edition and printing

If possible, cite a current edition unless the prior edition would be especially relevant.[51] For an edition other than the first, indicate its number in the publication parenthetical, using an ordinal contraction (**Rule 4.3(b)**) and the abbreviation "ed." followed by one space.[52] Include all pertinent information about the edition, taking care to use the same terminology the publisher does to describe the edition, abbreviating any words in **Appendix 3(D)** (e.g., "rev. ed." for revised edition).[53]

If a specific printing of a work differs from other printings in a way that affects the substance of the cited material, set out the ordinal contraction of the number of the printing, followed by a space, the abbreviation "prtg.," another space, and the year of the printing.[54]

Examples

Cynthia R. Mabry & Lisa Kelly, *Adoption Law: Theory, Policy, and Practice* 208 (2d ed. 2010).

Karl N. Llewellyn, *The Bramble Bush: On Our Law and Its Study* 70–72 (Oceana Publ'ns 9th prtg. 1991).

20.1(e)(4) Work in a numbered series

When citing a work that is part of a series issued by a specific author, include the series number in the title of the work, using **Appendix 3(C)** to abbreviate any words relating to the series.[55] Insert a comma and one space after the series information.[56]

When someone other than the author issues the series, however, put information about the series into the publication parenthetical, abbreviating any words according to **Rule 20.1(b)(3)**.[57] Insert a comma and one space after the series information.[58]

Examples

U.S. Dep't of Health & Hum. Servs. et al., *Pub. No. 2014-112, Hispanic-Operated Farms, 2008: Youth, Injuries, & Safety* 3–4 (2014).

Arend Lijphart, *Power-Sharing in South Africa* 6 (Inst. of Int'l Studies, Pol'y Papers in Int'l Affs. Ser. No. 24, 1985).

20.1(e)(5) Year of publication

The year of publication is the final component of the publication parenthetical. Set out the year shown on the title page or copyright page of the work, followed by a closing parenthesis.[59] Do this even if the title of the work has the date in it.[60] When citing a single volume of a multivolume work, use the publication year of the cited volume.[61] When citing a work that has supplements, follow **Rule 8**.[62]

Examples

Supplement only:	1 Harvey L. McCormick, *Medicare and Medicaid Claims and Procedures* § 6.7 (4th ed. Supp. 2011).
Main volume and supplement:	Carolyn R. Carter et al., *Repossessions* § 4.1.6 (8th ed. 2012 & Supp. 2015).

For works published before 1900, you may cite a modern edition, the first edition, or another edition, in that order of preference.[63] If citing the original edition, insert the place of publication, a comma, one space, and the abbreviated name of the original publisher before the year of publication.[64] If citing a modern edition of the work, add a second parenthetical with the date of original publication.[65] If citing a well-known work that has been republished, provide the original date of publication in a second parenthetical. When the date of publication is not available, use the abbreviation "n.d." (no date); when the place of publication is unavailable, use the abbreviation "n.p." (no place).[66]

Examples

Hinton Rowan Helper, *The Impending Crisis of the South* 123–25 (N.Y., A.B. Bourdick 1859).

Charles Dickens, *Bleak House* 5 (n.p., Bantam Classics 1983) (1853).

20.1(f)FN Full citations to books, treatises, or other nonperiodic materials in academic footnotes

ACADEMIC FORMATTING

Follow **Rule 20.1(a)–(e)**, but use large and small capital letters for both the author's name and the title and subtitle (if any).[67] When the title contains words that would be italicized in text (e.g., a case name), present them in italicized large and small capital letters.

Examples

[59] JAMES T. PATTERSON, *BROWN V. BOARD OF EDUCATION*: A CIVIL RIGHTS MILESTONE AND ITS TROUBLED HISTORY 109–10, 208 (2001).

[93] 1 ARTHUR LINTON CORBIN, CORBIN ON CONTRACTS § 4.14 (Joseph M. Perillo ed., rev. ed. 1993).

[157] THE CHANGING CONSTITUTION 79–81 (Jeffrey Jowell & Dawn Oliver eds., 7th ed. 2011).

[168] HEINRICH RICKERT, THE LIMITS OF CONCEPT FORMATION IN NATURAL SCIENCE: A LOGICAL INTRODUCTION TO THE HISTORICAL SCIENCES ch. 4, 140–45 (Guy Oakes trans., Cambridge Univ. Press abr. ed. 1986) (1902).

20.2 Star Edition

Many modern reprints of well-known and historic works, such as William Blackstone's *Commentaries* or Greek and Latin classics, indicate the page number of the original work with an asterisk (*) in the margin or in the text, a practice known as "star pagination" (**Rule 5.5(e)**).[68] In citing a star-paginated work, you may ignore the modern edition's pagination, and you may omit the publication parenthetical.[69] Indicate a pinpoint reference by inserting a single asterisk (*) immediately before the page number(s), with no intervening space.[70]

Examples

4 William Blackstone, *Commentaries* *292–93.

[102] ARISTOTLE, NICOMACHEAN ETHICS bk. 5, at *1130b30ff.

ACADEMIC FORMATTING

20.3 Collected Works

20.3(a) Collected works of single author

To cite a single work by one author that is published in a collection of the author's own works, use this format.[71]

Author, | *Title of single work,* | *in* | [Volume number of larger work] | *Title of collected works* | Initial page or subdivision of single work, | Pinpoint reference | ([Editor name ed.,] | [Translator name trans.,] | [Publisher if not the original] | [Edition number if not the 1st ed.] | Year of publication).

Use ordinary type for the author's name and italics for the two titles and the preposition "*in*."[72] Omit components such as editors or translators when they are not applicable to the cited single work.

Example (spaces denoted by ▲)

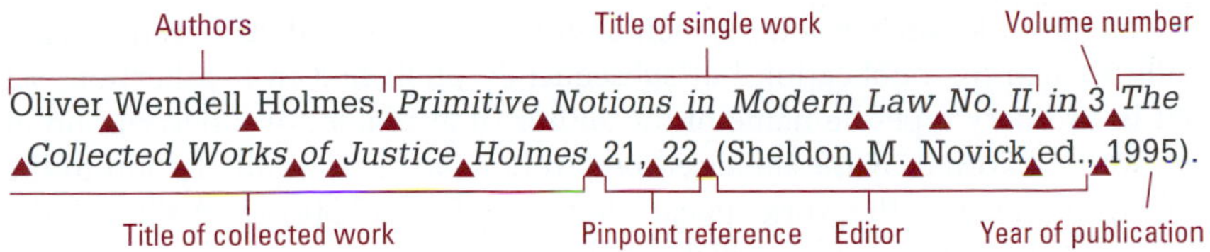

20.3(b) Collected works of multiple authors

To cite a single work within a collection of works by several authors, use this format.[73]

Author of single work, | *Title of single work,* | *in* | [Author(s) of collected works] | *Title of collected works* | Initial page or subdivision of single work, | Pinpoint reference | ([Editor name ed.,] | [Translator name trans.,] | [Publisher if not the original] | [Edition number if not the 1st ed.] | Year of publication).

Follow the rules in **Rule 20.1(b)** for author names; use italics for the two titles and the preposition "*in*."[74] Generally follow the rules in **Rule 20.1** for components after "*in*."[75] Omit components such as editors or translators when they are not applicable to the cited shorter work.[76] Always use the year of publication.[77]

Also use this rule to cite introductions, forewords, prefaces, and similar sections written by persons other than the author or editor of the collected works, using the title or description of the introduction, foreword, or preface as the title of the shorter work and replacing "*in*" with "*to*" (e.g., "*Introduction to*" or "*Preface to*").[78]

Examples

Francis C. Mezzadri, *Perinatal Abuse, in Child Abuse: A Medical Reference* 333, 338–39 (Stephen Ludwig & Allan E. Kornberg eds., 2d ed. 1992).

John Foster Dulles, *Introduction to* Arthur H. Dean, *William Nelson Cromwell 1854–1948: An American Pioneer*, at i, iii (1957).

20.3(c) Reprint collection of previously published work

To cite reprint collections of works previously published elsewhere, begin with the complete citation for the original work followed by a comma, a space, and the italicized phrase "*reprinted in*."[79] Follow that with a full citation to the work containing the reprint.[80]

Example

William Faulkner, *The Bear, in Go Down, Moses and Other Stories* (1942), *reprinted in The Portable Faulkner* 177, 183–84 (Malcolm Cowley ed., rev. & expanded ed. Penguin Books 2003).

20.3(d) Collection of previously unpublished work

To cite works such as letters, memoranda, speeches, and reports not originally written for publication but subsequently published in a collection, set out in ordinary type the name of the author (if available) or a description of the work, followed by the italicized preposition "*in*" and a full citation to the collection in which the work appears, following **Rule 20.3(a)** or **20.3(b)**.[81] If the original date of the work is available, you may append it in a parenthetical following the description of the work.[82]

Example

Letter from Louis Brandeis to Mrs. F.W. Wile (June 19, 1915), *in* 3 *Letters of Louis D. Brandeis* 535, 535–36 (Melvin I. Urofsky & David W. Levy eds., 1973).

20.3(e)FN Full citations to collected works in academic footnotes

ACADEMIC FORMATTING

To cite a single work in the collected works of a single author, use large and small capital letters for the author's name, italics for the title of the single work and the preposition "*in*," and large and small capital letters for the title of the collected works.[83]

To cite a single work within a collection of works by several authors, use ordinary type for the author of the single work and italics for its title and the preposition "*in*"; use large and small capital letters for the author of the collected works and the title of the collected works.[84]

Examples

93 OLIVER WENDELL HOLMES, *Primitive Notions in Modern Law No. II*, *in* 3 THE COLLECTED WORKS OF JUSTICE HOLMES 21, 22 (Sheldon M. Novick ed., 1995).

67 Francis C. Mezzadri, *Perinatal Abuse*, *in* CHILD ABUSE : A MEDICAL REFERENCE 333, 338–39 (Stephen Ludwig & Allan E. Kornberg eds., 2d ed. 1992).

101 John Foster Dulles, *Introduction to* ARTHUR H. DEAN, WILLIAM NELSON CROMWELL 1854–1948: AN AMERICAN PIONEER, at i, iii (1957).

20.4 Books, Treatises, and Other Nonperiodic Materials in Electronic Media

When a work is available in print, cite that version in preference to a version in any electronic medium.[85] There are three ways that nonperiodic material appears in an electronic medium: when a work is in a commercial database, when it is online, and when it is an e-book.

20.4(a) Nonperiodic materials in commercial databases

When your source for the nonperiodic material is a commercial database, after the work's full citation, add a parallel citation indicating name of the database provider and then the unique database identifier, if any.[86]

Example

David H. Kaye et al., *The New Wigmore: Expert Evidence* § 3.2.1 (2016), Westlaw WIGEVEE.

1 David G. Owen & Mary J. Davis, *Owen & Davis on Prod. Liab.* § 1:4 (4th ed. 2020), Westlaw MOPL § 1:4.

20.4(b) Nonperiodic materials online

If the online source exactly reproduces the work in print (e.g., a PDF version of the original that displays and uses the original page numbering), cite the work in the same manner as its print counterpart.[87] You may choose to append a URL if doing so would help the reader locate the source.[88] Books found online and books in print can vary when the online version is not an exact copy (e.g., a PDF version); those two should not be cited interchangeably.[89] If the nonperiodic material is only available online and is not an exact copy, cite to it as you would any other online source (see **Rules 30** through **34**).[90]

Example of exact reproduction online

Int'l L. Comm'n, *Report on the Work of the Seventy-first Session, United Nations* ch. 2, ¶ 20 (2019), https://legal.un.org/ilc/reports/2019/english/chp2.pdf.

20.4(c) Nonperiodic materials in e-books

Only cite e-books if they are the only media through which the book is available.[91]

The citation for books accessed through e-readers such as the Kindle or Kobo depends on the e-book's form of pinpoint reference.[92] The Kindle utilizes location numbers for pinpoint references. The location number is a fixed feature that remains constant even when the font type or size changes; it directs the reader to the same spot no matter what size or style of font is employed. Other e-readers, such as the Kobo, divide the e-book into chapters and enumerate the pages within each chapter (e.g., chapter 7, page 23 of 55).

To designate a location number as a pinpoint reference, use the abbreviation "loc." followed by one space and the location number.[93] Follow the various conventions for page numbers in **Rule 5** — such as citing consecutive or scattered pages — to cite multiple location numbers.

To designate a chapter and page as a pinpoint reference, use the abbreviation "ch." followed by one space and the chapter number, a comma, one space, the preposition "at," and the specific page(s) referenced.

Begin the publication parenthetical with the name of the epublisher, followed by the date of the e-book's publication, which may be different from that of the print edition. Following the publication parenthetical, add a second parenthetical with the word "e-book."[94]

Examples

Ed West, *1215 and All That: A Very, Very Short History of Magna Carta and King John* loc. 51 (Kindle ed. 2015) (e-book).

Chris Davidson, *Winning Techniques for Public Speaking and Presenting: How to Influence People with Social Communication Skills* ch. 3, at 7 (Kobo ed. 2016) (e-book).

20.4(d)^FN Full citations to nonperiodic materials in electronic medium

⚠ ACADEMIC FORMATTING

Follow **Rule 20.1(f)^FN** for citations to nonperiodic materials in commercial databases, in e-books, and in online works that are exact copies; the database provider, the unique database identifier, and the name of the epublisher are not affected.[95] Follow **Rule 31.1(h)^FN** for online nonperiodic materials in academic footnotes that are not exact copies of the print source.[96]

8 ED WEST, 1215 AND ALL THAT : A VERY, VERY SHORT HISTORY OF MAGNA CARTA AND KING JOHN loc. 51 (Kindle ed. 2015) (e-book).

9 DAVID H. KAYE ET AL., THE NEW WIGMORE: EXPERT EVIDENCE § 3.2.1 (2016), Westlaw WIGEVEE.

20.5 Unique Citation Formats for Noteworthy Nonperiodic Materials

20.5(a) Play texts

Cite plays in their written form (as opposed to a particular performance of the play) by referring to the play's act, scene, and line numbers using the following format[97]:

Playwright, | *Play name* | [act | Act number], | [sc. | Scene number,] | [l[l]. | Line number] | [(Year of publication)].

Do not include a date or edition number for Shakespearean plays;[98] for other plays, parenthetically include the year the play was published, if known.

Examples

William Shakespeare, Love's Labour's Lost act 1, sc. 1, ll. 74-81.

Sophie Treadwell, Machinal act 1, sc. 3, l. 15 (1928).

In academic footnotes, the only change in a play's citation is to use large and small caps for the playwright's name and the title of the play.[99]

ACADEMIC FORMATTING

Examples

WILLIAM SHAKESPEARE, LOVE'S LABOUR'S LOST act 1, sc. 1, ll. 74-81.

SOPHIE TREADWELL, MACHINAL act 1, sc. 3, l. 15 (1928).

20.5(b) Religious works: The Bible, the Koran, and the Talmud

To cite a passage from the Bible, begin with the book number, if any, followed by the book's name, italicized.[100] Join the chapter and verse numbers with a colon, omitting spaces.[101] If desired, indicate the translation or version in a publication parenthetical;[102] within the parenthetical, you may abbreviate any word that appears in **Appendices 3(B)**, **3(C)**, and **3(E)**.

Examples

Matthew 5:17.

1 *Corinthians* 10:6 (New Am. Standard).

To cite a passage from the Koran, use the spelling "Koran" or "Qur'an" in ordinary type, followed immediately by chapter and verse numbers, joined with a colon and no spaces. You may indicate a particular translation in the publication parenthetical.

Examples

Koran 2:256.

Qur'an 51:1–10 (Abdullah Yusuf Ali trans.).

The Talmud consists of the Mishnah and Gemara.[103] The Mishnah is divided into six orders, and the Gemara provides a commentary on them. Indicate whether the citation is to the Babylonian Talmud or the Jerusalem Talmud, because they use different Gemara.[104] Begin with the name of the version, in ordinary type, followed by a comma and one space, the book ("tractate") name, one space, and the chapter and section numbers, joined with a colon and no spaces.[105]

Examples

Babylonian Talmud, Eruvin 13b.

Jerusalem Talmud, Terumot 8:4.

In academic footnotes, there is no change when citing the Bible, the Koran, or the Talmud.

ACADEMIC FORMATTING

20.5(c) *The Federalist Papers*

Commonly known simply as "*The Federalist*" until the twentieth century, *The Federalist Papers* are a collection of eighty-five articles and essays authored by James Madison, John Jay, and Alexander Hamilton (under the collective pseudonym "Publius") to encourage the ratification of the United States Constitution. When citing to a particular essay as a whole, begin with the italicized title and abbreviation for number (i.e., "*The Federalist No.*"), a space and the italicized essay number, and then the author's (real) name in a parenthetical.[106] If you are citing more than one essay as a whole, group essays with the same author together as shown in the example below.[107]

If you are citing to a particular part of one essay, rather than the essay as a whole, add a comma after the essay number and a space, the word "at" and the pinpoint page.[108] Then, after the author parenthetical, add a space and a second parenthetical with the editor's full name, "ed.," and the year of the compilation edition you are citing.[109]

Examples

The Federalist No. 9 (Alexander Hamilton).

The Federalist Nos. 9, 33 (Alexander Hamilton), *Nos. 42, 44* (James Madison).

The Federalist No. 80, at 603 (Alexander Hamilton) (Jacob E. Cooke ed., 1982).

ACADEMIC FORMATTING

In academic footnotes, the only change in *The Federalist*'s citation is to use large and small caps for the title and number abbreviation.[110]

Examples

THE FEDERALIST NO. 9 (Alexander Hamilton).

THE FEDERALIST NOS. 9, 33 (Alexander Hamilton), NOS. 42, 44 (James Madison).

THE FEDERALIST NO. 80, at 603 (Alexander Hamilton) (Jacob E. Cooke ed., 1982).

20.5(d) *Manual for Complex Litigation*

The Federal Judicial Center publishes the *Manual for Complex Litigation* for federal judges to use when managing complex cases; it is available for download at https://www.fjc.gov/content/manual-complex-litigation-fourth. When citing the hard copy or the PDF version found at the link on the Federal Judicial Center's website, begin with the italicized title, including the edition printed in a parenthetical as part of the title.[111] Insert a space, a section symbol (§), another space, the pinpoint section, another space, and the year of publication in a parenthetical.[112] Substitute the printing designation and date of a particular reprint only if that printing differs materially with respect to the material you are citing.[113]

Examples

Manual for Complex Litigation (Fourth) § 23.23 (3d prtg. 2020).

Manual for Complex Litigation (Fourth) § 11.422 (2004).

ACADEMIC FORMATTING

In academic footnotes, the only change in the *Manual for Complex Litigation*'s citation is to use large and small caps for the title.[114]

Examples

MANUAL FOR COMPLEX LITIGATION (FOURTH) § 23.23 (3d prtg. 2020).

MANUAL FOR COMPLEX LITIGATION (FOURTH) § 11.422 (2004).

20.6 Short Citations to Books, Treatises, and Other Nonperiodic Materials

This rule applies to all nonperiodic materials, including electronic sources, except online materials that must be cited as an internet source (**Rule 20.4(b)**). In other words, this rule does not apply to online sources that are not an exact copy of a print source or are only available online. If nonperiodic material must be cited as an online source, use **Rule 31.3** for its short form.

The form of the short citation to a book, treatise, or other nonperiodic work varies depending on whether the citation refers to a single work or to a work within a larger collection, whether it refers to a religious text, and whether it is used in an academic footnote.[115]

20.6(a) Using *id.* or other short citations to freestanding works

When appropriate (**Rule 11.3(c)**), use *id.* as the short citation to a freestanding work (i.e., one not published in a larger collection), changing the pinpoint reference if needed.[116] Do not use *id.* if the preceding citation contains references to two or more sources.[117] Do not use *infra.*[118] When *id.* is not appropriate, use one of the following short citation formats.[119]

Author's surname [et al.], | *supra*, | [at] | Pinpoint reference.

or

Title, | *supra*, | [at] | Pinpoint reference.

If the work has one or two named authors, begin the short citation with their surnames, followed by a comma and one space, with the surnames of two authors connected by an ampersand.[120] If the work has three or more authors, use the surname of the first author only, followed by "et al." even if the first citation spelled out all the authors' names.[121] Do not drop any words in an institutional author's name.[122] If the work does not have a named author, begin the short citation with the italicized title, followed by a comma and one space.[123] If the full citation provides a [hereinafter] reference (see **Rule 11.5**), use the shortened name, followed by a comma and one space.[124]

Use the preposition "at" only before a pinpoint *page* reference (see **Rule 5.2(c)**).[125] When the work uses another form of subdivision, directly insert the specific pinpoint reference, consulting **Rules 6** (sections and paragraphs),[126] **7** (footnotes),[127] **8** (supplements),[128] or **9** (graphical material and appendices).[129] Omit the URL if you chose to append one to the full citation of an online source that is an exact copy of the printed source (**Rule 20.4(b)**).[130]

Examples

Full citations:	**Short citations:**
Thomas M. Cooley, *A Treatise on the Constitutional Limitations Which Rest upon the Legislative Power of the States of the American Union* 416–17 (1868).	Cooley, *supra*, at 401.
Peter J. Galie & Christopher Bopst, *The New York State Constitution* 76 (2d ed. 2012).	Galie & Bopst, *supra*, at 74.
Christine Coughlin, Joan Malmud Rocklin & Sandy Patrick, *A Lawyer Writes* 280 (3d ed. 2018).	Coughlin et al., *supra*, at 281.
Chris Davidson, *Winning Techniques for Public Speaking and Presenting: How to Influence People with Social Communication Skills* ch. 3, at 7 (Kobo ed. 2016) (e-book).	Davidson, *supra*, ch. 3 at 6.
1 David G. Owen & Mary J. Davis, *Owen & Davis on Prod. Liab.* § 1:4 (4th ed. 2020) Westlaw MOPL § 1:4.	Owen & Davis, *supra*, § 1.6.

20.6(b) Short citations to collected works

To cite the *same* single work in a collection that was cited in the immediately preceding citation, use *id.*[131] When *id.* is not appropriate (**Rule 11.3(c)**) when citing to the same single work in a collection, set out the surname of the single work's author(s) as described in **Rule 20.6(a)**, followed by a comma and one space, the italicized word "*supra*," another comma and one space, the word "at," and a pinpoint page reference.[132] Omit "at" if the document uses subdivisions other than pages.[133]

If you are citing to the collected works as a whole, rather than only one of the contained works previously cited in full, do not use *id.* Instead, substitute the title of the collected works for the author of the single work, no matter whether the collected works are by one or more authors, and forgo a pinpoint reference.[134]

When you have previously cited one of the single works in a collection but are now citing a different single work within that collection, do not use *id.* to refer to the collection.[135] Use this format[136]:

Full name(s) of new single work's author(s). | *Title of new single work,* | *in* | *Title of collected works,* | *supra,* | [at] | Pinpoint reference.

Examples

Full citation:	Margaret Vandiver, *Capital Punishment and the Families of Victims and Defendants, in The Future of America's Death Penalty: An Agenda for the Next Generation of Capital Punishment Research* 379, 387–89 (Charles S. Lanier et al. eds., 2009) [hereinafter *The Future of America's Death Penalty*].
Short citation referring to Vandiver:	*Id.* at 388. or if *id.* is not appropriate, Vandiver, *supra*, at 388.
Citation to different work in previously cited collection:	Richard C. Dieter, *The Future of Innocence, in The Future of America's Death Penalty*, *supra*, at 225.
Citation to the work as a whole collection:	*The Future of America's Death Penalty*, *supra*.

20.6(c) Short citations to noteworthy nonperiodic materials

To cite one of the noteworthy nonperiodic materials in **Rule 20.5** that was cited in the immediately preceding citation, use *id.*[137] When *id.* is not appropriate (**Rule 11.3(c)**) repeat the full citation to religious works, but follow **Rule 20.6(a)** for play texts and the *Manual for Complex Litigation*. For *The Federalist Papers*, follow **Rule 20.6(b)** using the title, abbreviation "No.," and the essay number in place of the author's name as the first component in the *supra* format.

Examples

Full citations:	**Short citations:**
William Shakespeare, Love's Labour's Lost act 1, sc. 1, l. 74.	*Shakespeare*, *supra*, act 1, sc. 1, l. 74.
Manual for Complex Litigation (Fourth) § 33.22 (2004).	*Manual for Complex Litigation (Fourth)*, *supra*, § 33.22.
The Federalist No. 5, at 17 (John Jay) (Terrance Ball ed., 2003).	*The Federalist No. 5*, *supra*, at 30 (John Jay).

20.6(d)^FN Short citations to books, treatises, or other nonperiodic materials in academic footnotes

Follow **Rule 20.6(a)–(c)** for short citations to books, treatises, and other nonperiodic materials when citing in academic footnotes;[138] when *id.* is not appropriate (**Rule 11.3(c)**), the following exceptions regarding large and small caps and footnote numbers apply.

Use large and small capital letters for the author's name or the title as directed in **Rule 20.1(f)^FN** (nonperiodic material generally),[139] **Rule 20.3(e)^FN** (collected works),[140] **Rule 20.4(d)** (electronic mediums),[141] **Rule 20.5(a)** (plays),[142] **Rule 20.5(c)** (*The Federalist*),[143] **Rule 20.5(d)** (*Manual for Complex Litigation*).[144] Between *supra* and the comma following it, insert one space, the word "note" in plain type, another space, and the footnote number where the full citation can be found.[145]

For freestanding works, the resulting short citations will look like this depending on whether there is an author or not[146]:

AUTHOR'S SURNAME, | *supra* | note | Footnote number, | [at] | Pinpoint reference.

or

TITLE, | *supra* | note | Footnote number, | [at] | Pinpoint reference.

Examples

[19] ANU PESHAWARIA, THE IMMIGRANT'S DREAM 98–99 (2009).

[20] *Id.* at 109.

[21] 3 STATE CONSTITUTIONS FOR THE TWENTY-FIRST CENTURY 149–54 (G. Alan Tarr & Robert F. Williams eds., 2006).

[22] MEGHAN SPILLANE, INT'L BAR ASS'N, INTERNATIONAL MOOT COURT: AN INTRODUCTION 54 (2008).

[23] PESHAWARIA, *supra* note 19, at 102.

[24] ED WEST, 1215 AND ALL THAT: A VERY, VERY SHORT HISTORY OF MAGNA CARTA AND KING JOHN loc. 51 (Kindle ed. 2015) (e-book).

[25] DAVID H. KAYE ET AL., THE NEW WIGMORE: EXPERT EVIDENCE § 3.2.1 (2016), Westlaw WIGEVEE.

[26] *Id.* § 3.2.2.

[27] WEST, *supra* note 24, loc. 55.

[28] 3 STATE CONSTITUTIONS FOR THE TWENTY-FIRST CENTURY, *supra* note 21, at 155.

[29] SPILLANE, INT'L BAR ASS'N, *supra* note 22, at 61.

[30] KAYE ET AL., *supra* note 25, § 3.2.1.

[31] MANUAL FOR COMPLEX LITIGATION (FOURTH) § 33.22 (2004).

[32] THE FEDERALIST NO. 5, at 17 (John Jay) (Terrance Ball ed., 2003).

[33] MANUAL FOR COMPLEX LITIGATION (FOURTH), *supra* note 31, § 33.21.

[34] THE FEDERALIST NO. 81, *supra* note 32, at 393 (Alexander Hamilton).

For a single work that has been cited before in a collection, the resulting short citation would look like this[147]:

Surname of single work's author(s), | *supra* | note | footnote number, | [at] | Pinpoint reference.

For a citation to a *new* single work within a collection when the collection has previously been cited but the particular single work has not, the resulting short citation would use this format[148]:

Full name of single work's author, | *Title of single work,* | *in* | TITLE OF COLLECTED WORKS, | *supra* | note | Number of footnote containing first full citation to collection, | [at] | Initial page of single work, | Pinpoint reference.

Examples

Full citation:

[32] Margaret Vandiver, *Capital Punishment and the Families of Victims and Defendants*, *in* THE FUTURE OF AMERICA'S DEATH PENALTY: AN AGENDA FOR THE NEXT GENERATION OF CAPITAL PUNISHMENT RESEARCH 379, 387–89 (Charles S. Lanier, William J. Bowers & James R. Acker eds., 2009) [hereinafter THE FUTURE OF AMERICA'S DEATH PENALTY].

Short citation referring to Vandiver:	[33] *Id.* at 388.
	or if *id.* is not appropriate,
	[36] Vandiver, *supra* note 32, at 388.
Short citation to different work in previously cited collection:	[38] Richard C. Dieter, *The Future of Innocence*, *in* THE FUTURE OF AMERICA'S DEATH PENALTY, *supra* note 32, at 225, 225–26.

21 Law Reviews and Other Periodicals

Fast Formats

Article in consecutively paginated periodical	Alexa Z. Chew, *Stylish Legal Citation*, 71 Ark. L. Rev. 823, 869 n.270 (2019).
Article in nonconsecutively paginated periodical	Hillary Wandler, *A New Way for Lawyers to Assist Veterans*, Mont. Law., June 2009, at 8, 8.
Student-written article	Lauren E. Franklin, Note, *#MeToo and U.: The Effect of Ineffectual Sexual Assault Remedies at Universities and How #MeToo Could Affect the Pandemic of Underreporting*, 11 Elon L.J. 223, 234 (2019).
Symposium	Symposium, *The Politics of [Evidence] Rulemaking*, 53 Hastings L.J. 733 (2001–2002).
Newspaper	Adam Liptak, *Bucking a Trend, Supreme Court Justices Reject Video Coverage*, N.Y. Times, Feb. 18, 2013, at A15.
Newsletter	Joseph K. Scully, *Taking the Offensive When Defending a Deposition: Questioning Your Own Witness*, 16 Prod. Liab. (ABA Section Litig., Chi., Ill.), Spring 2005, at 13.
Online journal	Denise Amran, *Homosexuality and Child Custody Through the Lenses of Law: Between Tradition and Fundamental Rights*, 15.1 Elec. J. Compar. L., Dec. 2011, at 1, 5–7, http://www.ejcl.org/151/art151-1.pdf.
Citations in academic footnotes	⚠ ACADEMIC FORMATTING [23] Alexa Z. Chew, *Stylish Legal Citation*, 71 ARK. L. REV. 823, 869 n.270 (2019). [50] Hillary Wandler, *A New Way for Lawyers to Assist Veterans*, MONT. LAW., June 2009, at 8, 8.
Short citations	Chew, *supra*, at 870. [28] Chew, *supra* note 23, at 861.

21.1 Consecutive and Nonconsecutive Pagination

Citations to works published in periodicals fall into one of two categories. The first category contains published works where the page numbering continues from issue to issue ("consecutive pagination"). For example, when a law review volume has four issues published throughout the year, and issue 1 of volume 30 begins with page 1 and ends with page 334, and issue 2 of volume 30 begins on page 335 rather than starting back at page 1, that periodical has consecutive pagination. The second category contains published works where the page numbering starts over in each new issue ("nonconsecutive pagination"). For example, a state bar magazine that publishes a new issue every month wherein each issue begins with page 1 uses nonconsecutive pagination. This pagination distinction affects the citation's required components, their order, and their format. Therefore, always make this initial determination before constructing the citation. A red star (★) beside a periodical's entry in **Appendix 5(A)** indicates that the periodical is nonconsecutively paginated. To cite a work in a periodical not listed in **Appendix 5(A)**, examine its preceding and following issues to determine whether the page numbering continues or starts over, and then follow either **Rule 21.2** or **Rule 21.3** based on the pagination.

21.2 Full Citations to Consecutively Paginated Periodicals

A full citation to a work published in a consecutively paginated periodical (e.g., a law review) may contain as many as eight components.[1]

Author, | [Designation of student-written work,] | *Title*, | Volume number | Periodical abbreviation | Initial page, | Pinpoint reference | (Date).

Examples (spaces denoted by ▲)

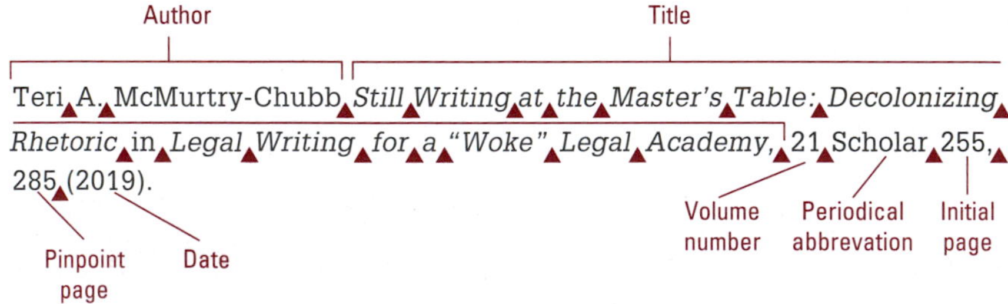

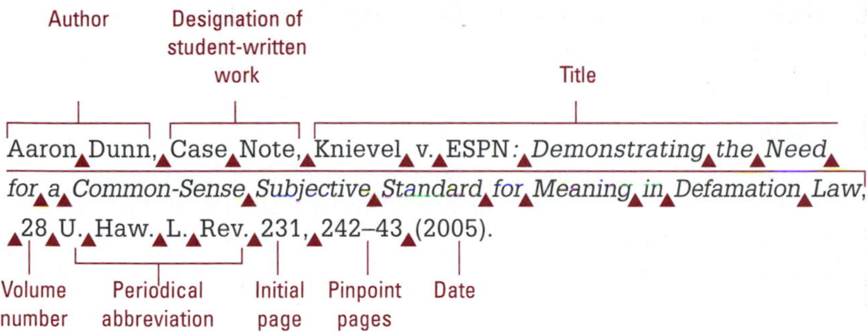

21.2(a) Author

Set out the author's full name as displayed in the work, in ordinary type, followed by a comma and one space.[2] For a single author, follow **Rule 20.1(b)(1)**.[3] For multiple authors, follow **Rule 20.1(b)(2)**.[4] For institutional authors, follow **Rule 20.1(b)(3)**.[5] When a preface, foreword, introduction, or epilogue to a periodical is written by someone other than the periodical piece's author, follow **Rule 20.1(b)(4)**.[6] When the author is not identified, follow **Rule 20.1(b)(5)**.[7] When the author is a student, follow **Rule 21.2(b)** and the rules for a single author or multiple authors.[8]

Example

Olympia Duhart & Hugh Mundy, *Cash Is King: How Market-based Strategies Have Corrupted Classrooms and Criminal Courts in Post-Katrina New Orleans*, 39 Seattle U. L. Rev. 1199, 1211 (2016).

21.2(b) Student author

If the work was written by an identifiable student author (see **Sidebar 21.1**), immediately after the author's name, insert a comma, one space, and the designation of the work given by the periodical (e.g., "Note," "Legislative Note," "Recent Development," "Comment").[9] Present the student author's name and the designation in ordinary type, followed by a comma and one space.[10] If the student author's name is not indicated, begin with the work's designation (e.g., "Note" or "Comment").[11]

Identify any student-written book review, no matter how it is designated in the periodical, as "Book Note."[12] If a book note is unsigned, cite it as any other

SIDEBAR 21.1 Identifying Student Authors

Student-written works are often printed toward the back of the issue. Student-written works are typically designated by terms such as "Note," "Comment," "Case Comment," "Recent Development," "Recent Case," "Recent Statute," or "Recent Decision." In many law reviews, the names of student authors are placed at the end — not the beginning — of the work. Look for a footnote describing the author's background; an author described as a J.D. candidate is a student. If a student only signs a work with initials, that work is considered unsigned.

unsigned student-written work by beginning with the designation.[13] For book notes, parenthetically indicate what work the student is reviewing if it is not clear from the title.[14]

Examples

Nicholas H. Meza, Comment, *A New Approach for Clarity in the Determination of Protected Concerted Activity Online*, 45 Ariz. St. L.J. 329, 339–40 (2013).

Note, *Enabling Television Competition in a Converged Market*, 126 Harv. L. Rev. 2083, 2089–90 (2013).

Catherine Nowak, Book Note, Fair Trade Coffee: The Prospects and Pitfalls of Market-Driven Social Justice, *by Gavin Fridell*, 46 Osgoode Hall L.J. 217, 217 (2008).

Book Note, *Book Notes*, 22 Osgoode Hall L.J. 589, 590 (1984) (reviewing *Judith Areen et al., Law, Science, and Medicine* (1984)).

21.2(c) Title and subtitle

Present the title, including any subtitle, as it appears on the first page of the work.[15] Do not abbreviate or omit any words in a title or subtitle.[16] Italicize the title and the subtitle, if any, but use ordinary type for words italicized in text, such as case names (**Rule 1.3**).[17] Follow **Rule 3.2**, **Rule 3.3**, and **Chart 3.1** for capitalization.[18] For works written in a language other than English, follow **Rule 20.1(c)(2)**.[19]

When a title or subtitle ends with a question mark or exclamation mark, follow it with a comma and one space.[20] When the title or subtitle ends with a quotation, place the comma inside the closing quotation marks.[21]

When the title and subtitle are joined with a dash, retain the subtitle, and do not alter the existing capitalization of the first word following the dash.[22] If no punctuation is shown between a title and subtitle, join them with a colon followed by one space. Capitalize the first word following the colon, no matter what it is.[23]

Examples

Clay Calvert, *Defining Public Concern After* Snyder v. Phelps*: A Pliable Standard Mingles with News Media Complicity*, 19 Vill. Sports & Ent. L.J. 39, 41 (2012).

Assaf Hamdani, *Who's Liable for Cyberwrongs?*, 87 Cornell L. Rev. 901, 940–45 (2002).

Neil Gotanda, *A Critique of "Our Constitution Is Color-Blind,"* 44 Stan. L. Rev. 1, 6 (1991).

John G. Browning, *Keep Your Hands off My Nuts—Airlines, Peanut Allergies, and the Law*, 77 J. Air L. & Com. 3, 8 n.32 (2012).

Marc L. Roark, *"Opening the Barbarians' Gate" or Watching the Barbarians from the Coliseum: A Requiem on the Nomos of the Louisiana Civil Law*, 67 La. L. Rev. 451, 462–63 (2007).

21.2(d) Volume number

Indicate the volume number with an Arabic numeral, followed by one space.[24] If the periodical has no volume number, use its year of publication in place of the volume number, and omit the publication parenthetical described in **Rule 21.2(g)**.[25]

Example

Diana J. Simon, *Cross-cultural Differences in Plagiarism: Fact or Fiction?*, 57 Duq. L. Rev. 73, 85 (2019).

Brandice Canes-Wrone & Tom S. Clark, *Judicial Independence and Nonpartisan Elections*, 2009 Wis. L. Rev. 21, 30–31.

21.2(e) Periodical abbreviation

Always use the title of the periodical as it appears on the title page of the issue you are citing, but use the following rules for abbreviating that title. Following the volume number, set out the **Appendix 5(A)** abbreviation for the periodical, inserting spaces where indicated by the red triangles (▲).[26] If the periodical is not listed in **Appendix 5(A)**, use it and **Appendix 3(E)** to find abbreviations for individual words from the periodical's name.[27] Use abbreviations from **Appendix 3(B)** for geographic terms.[28] If the periodical itself abbreviates a word, use that abbreviation in the title, even if it does not appear in **Appendix 5(A)**, **3(B)**, or **3(E)**.[29] If a word in the periodical name does not appear in one of these appendices, spell it out.[30] Do not use an abbreviation from another appendix, because it may be a word that should not be abbreviated in a periodical name, or it may be abbreviated differently.[31] Set out the periodical abbreviation in ordinary type.[32]

Follow **Rule 2.2** for spacing.[33] If some of the consecutive single letters of an abbreviation indicate an institutional entity, keep them separate from other single letter abbreviations.[34]

Examples

S.C.▲J.▲Int'l▲L.▲&▲Bus. N.Y.U.▲J.L.▲&▲Bus.

N.Y.▲L.J. B.C.▲L.▲Rev.

ABA▲J.

Omit the words "a," "an," "at," "in," "of," and "the," but do not omit the word "on"; if after removing one of those words, the title is only one word long, do not abbreviate the remaining word.[35] Omit commas but retain other punctuation.[36] Unless the periodical's abbreviation in **Appendix 5(A)** indicates otherwise, omit colons and anything following them.[37] Insert one space after the periodical abbreviation.[38]

Examples

Periodical title:	Periodical abbreviation:
Computer/Law Journal	Comput./L.J.
Institute on Planning, Zoning, and Eminent Domain	Inst. on Plan. Zoning & Eminent Domain
The Independent	Independent
Jurist: Studies in Church Law and Ministry	Jurist
Journal of Products Liability	J. Prods. Liab.

21.2(f) Initial page and pinpoint references

Following the periodical abbreviation, set out the initial page number.[39] To refer to specific pages or other subdivisions within the work, add a comma, one space, and the pinpoint reference.[40] Remember that unless a particular periodical inserts commas into its page numbers to create groups of three numerals when a number is four or more numerals long, do not follow **Rule 4.1**;[41] do insert a comma if a number is five digits or more. See **Rules 5** through **9** for more information on pinpoint references.

When a periodical has consecutive, but separate, pagination with a different numbering system, include the special numbering for the initial page and the pinpoint reference.[42]

Examples

Leslie T. Gladstone, *Rule 408: Maintaining the Shield for Negotiation in Federal and Bankruptcy Courts*, 16 Pepp. L. Rev. S237, S243 (1989).

Roseanna Sommers, *Commonsense Consent*, 129 Yale L.J. 2232, 2237 (2020).

21.2(g) Publication parenthetical

Indicate the year of publication in parentheses.[43] Do not use a more specific date or a season, even if displayed in the publication.[44] When a periodical uses the year as the volume number, omit the publication parenthetical.[45] See the example in **Rule 21.2(d)**.

21.2(h) Special issue, symposium, colloquium, or survey

A special issue is one in which all the major articles deal with a single topic or theme. In legal periodicals, this type of special issue may be referred to as a symposium, colloquium, or survey. When citing an *entire* special issue, as opposed to a single article within it, first, in place of author names, set out the capitalized descriptive term used by the periodical, as shown in the first example below, and then for the initial page reference, use the opening page of the special issue.[46]

Cite a single article in a special issue the same as any other work in a consecutively paginated periodical.[47] If it is important to the discussion to let readers know that the single article is part of a special issue, you may note that fact in a second parenthetical following the publication parenthetical.

Some law reviews publish special annual issues that do not follow the periodical's normal consecutive pagination system. Cite these special issues as you normally would, but immediately following the periodical abbreviation, insert a space, the parenthetical "(Special Issue)," and another space before listing the initial page number.[48] For the initial page and pinpoint reference, use the numbering from the special issue.[49]

Examples

Entire issue: Symposium, *An Ocean Apart? Freedom of Expression in Europe and the United States*, 84 Ind. L.J. 803 (2009).

Single articles from special issues: Amy Gajda, *Academic Duty and Academic Freedom*, 91 Ind. L.J. 17, 27 (2016) (part of *Symposium: Academic Freedom for the Next 100 Years*).

Susan Rose-Ackerman, *Comment on Ferejohn and Shipan's "Congressional Influence on Bureaucracy,"* 6 J.L. Econ. & Org. (Special Issue) 21, 25 (1990).

Executive Summary of Proposed Revised Oregon Nonprofit Corporation Act, 1992 Or. L. Rev. (Special Issue) vii, x.

21.2(i) Commentaries, tributes, and in memoriams

When citing an article designated as a "Commentary," "Tribute," "In Memoriam," or other special article designation (as opposed to a full special issue designation), follow **Rule 21.2(a)–(g)**, but after the author's name, insert a comma and a space, the designation in ordinary type, and another comma and space.[50] If the work has no author or the periodical's editors are the author, begin with the designation.[51]

Example

Sandra Day O'Connor, Tribute, *Dean Toni M. Massaro—A Tribute*, 51 Ariz. L. Rev. 254 (2009).

In Memoriam, *Lynn Walker Huntley: A* Columbia Law Review *Alumna and Civil Rights Advocate*, 116 Colum. L. Rev. 1193 (2016).

21.2(j) Multi-part works

To cite a work published in multiple parts in *different volumes* of a consecutively paginated periodical, add a parenthetical following the title that identifies the numbers (or letters) of the parts, followed by the volume number, periodical abbreviation, initial page, and publication parenthetical for each volume.[52]

When all cited parts appear in a *single volume* of the periodical, indicate the part numbers in a parenthetical after the title, and provide the initial page for each part.[53]

To cite a *single part* of a work published in multiple parts, indicate the single part number in parentheses, and cite only the issue in which the part is published.[54]

Examples

All parts in multiple issues:	Vern Countryman, *Executory Contracts in Bankruptcy* (pts. 1 & 2), 57 Minn. L. Rev. 439 (1973), 58 Minn. L. Rev. 479 (1974).
All parts in single issue:	John P. Dawson, *Negotiorum Gestio: The Altruistic Intermeddler* (pts. 1 & 2), 74 Harv. L. Rev. 817, 1073 (1961).
One part in single issue:	Vern Countryman, *Executory Contracts in Bankruptcy* (pt. 2), 58 Minn. L. Rev. 479 (1974).

21.2(k) Non-student-written book reviews

Follow **Rule 21.2(a), (c)–(g)** for book reviews written by authors who are not students.[55] In addition, add a second parenthetical after the date parenthetical.[56] If the work under review isn't clear from the title or discussion of the work and is relevant to the discussion, the second parenthetical should state "reviewing" in ordinary type and then give the full citation to the work.[57] If the work under review is clear from the title or discussion or isn't relevant to the discussion, simply say "book review" in ordinary type in the second parenthetical.[58] If the non-student-written book review is untitled, use the title "Book Review" in ordinary type and forgo the second parenthetical unless it is necessary to the discussion to identify the work.[59]

Examples

Myriam Gilles & Gary Friedman, *Examining the Case for Socialized Law*, 129 Yale L.J. 2078, 2080 (2020) (reviewing Frederick Wilmot-Smith, *Equal Justice: Fair Legal Systems in an Unfair World* (2019)).

Amy Kapczynski, *The Law of Informational Capitalism*, 129 Yale L.J. 1460, 1467 (2020) (book review).

21.3 Full Citations to Nonconsecutively Paginated Periodicals

Nonconsecutively paginated periodicals (see **Rule 21.1**) include publications such as bar association journals, magazines, newspapers, and newsletters. Periodicals that are nonconsecutively paginated are indicated with a red star (★) in **Appendix 5(A)**. The citation to a nonconsecutively paginated journal typically contains the following components.[60]

Author, | *Title*, | Periodical abbreviation, | Publication date, | at | Initial page, | Pinpoint reference.

Example (spaces denoted by ▲)

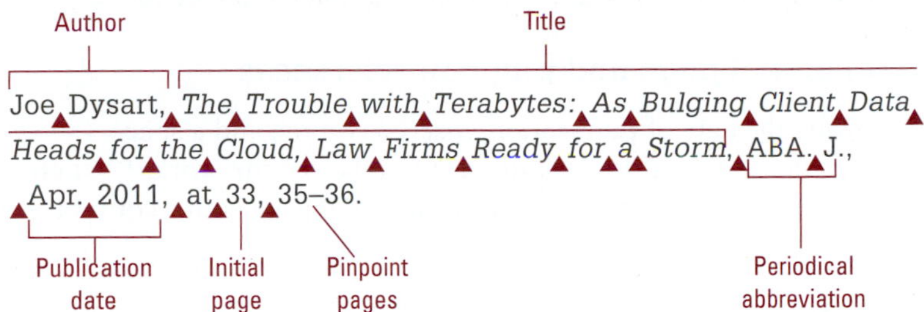

21.3(a) Author

Follow **Rule 21.2(a)** and the rules it cross-references.[61]

21.3(b) Title

Follow **Rule 21.2(c)** and the rules it cross-references.[62]

21.3(c) Periodical abbreviation and volume number

Follow **Rule 21.2(e)** and the rules it cross-references.[63] Abbreviate the name of the periodical as shown in **Appendix 5(A)**; nonconsecutively paginated periodicals are indicated there with a red star (★). Immediately following the periodical abbreviation, insert a comma followed by a space.[64] If the periodical does not include a specific date it was issued but it displays a volume number, set the volume number out *before* the periodical abbreviation.[65]

Examples

Jeffrey R. Young, *Journal Boycott over Online Access Is a Bust*, Chron. Higher Educ., May 31, 2002, at A34.

Andrew E. Taslitz, *The Cold Nose Might Actually Know? Science & Scent Lineups*, 28 Crim. Just., Summer 2013, at 4.

21.3(d) Publication date

Indicate the publication date as shown on the cover or first page of the issue.[66] If the publication date refers to a month, abbreviate it as shown in **Appendix 3(A)**.[67] If the date refers to a season, capitalize the season and insert the year with no comma between them.[68] If the periodical does not indicate a more specific publication date, but shows an issue number instead, in the date position, use the abbreviation "no." followed by the issue number, a comma, one space, and the month and year or season and year of the copyright, if available;[69] indicate the volume number as indicated in **Rule 21.3(c)**.[70]

Examples

Sally H. Scherer, *Our Children—The Legal System's Forgotten Ones*, N.C. St. Bar J., Winter 2011, at 16, 18.

Kevin M. Forde, *What Can a Court Do with Leftover Class Action Funds? Almost Anything!*, 35 Judge's J., no. 3, Summer 1996, at 19.

21.3(e) Initial page and pinpoint references

Following the date of publication, insert a comma and a space, followed by the preposition "at" and the *initial* page number of the work.[71] When a pinpoint page reference is available, follow the initial page with a comma, a space, and the pinpoint page number(s).[72]

21.3(f) Newspaper

Treat a newspaper, whether in print or online, as a nonconsecutively paginated periodical, making the following modifications, as appropriate.[73] If the newspaper is consecutively paginated, follow **Rule 21.2**.[74]

21.3(f)(1) Author and title

Although many newspaper pieces do not indicate an author, if an author name is present, use it as the first component of the citation, following **Rule 21.2(a)**.[75] Treat the headline as a title, following **Rule 21.2(c)**.[76] Present the title in italics, followed by a comma and one space.[77]

To cite an editorial, opinion, or letter to the editor, set out the author's name, if shown, followed by a comma, one space, and the capitalized designation "Editorial," "Opinion," or "Letter to the Editor," in ordinary type.[78] If the piece is titled, present that title in italics, followed by a comma and one space.[79]

Examples

Editorial, *An Endangered Act*, Wash. Post, Dec. 29, 2003, at A16.

Nancy A. Ransom, Letter to the Editor, *Better Eating, Through Home Ec?*, N.Y. Times, Sept. 8, 2003, at A22.

21.3(f)(2) Volume, newspaper abbreviation, and place of publication

No matter the form of the piece, follow it with the volume number of the newspaper, if any, and the newspaper's abbreviation (use **Appendices 3(B)** and **5(A)**) in ordinary type.[80]

If the newspaper's place of publication is not evident from its name, add a parenthetical setting out the place of publication, in ordinary type, after the periodical abbreviation.[81] Use city and state abbreviations from **Appendix 3(B)**.[82] If a city abbreviation is not in that appendix, spell out its name.[83] Insert a comma and one space after the parenthetical information.[84]

Examples

John Noble, *2 Astronauts Float Free in Space, 170 Miles Up*, N.Y. Times, Feb. 7, 1984, at A1.

Bush to Campaign for Bush, Post & Courier (Charleston, S.C.), Jan. 15, 2000, at B4.

21.3(f)(3) Initial page or other reference

When a newspaper in print has multiple sections, preface the initial page reference with the letter of the section in which it appears (e.g., A2, B6).[85] With or without a section letter, indicate the page on which the article appears.[86] Cite only the initial page; omit subsequent pinpoint references.[87]

For an online newspaper, add a comma and one space after the date of the article, followed by the URL.[88] You do not have to include any pagination, but if the date and time of posting is available, include it in parentheses immediately following the newspaper abbreviation, abbreviating months according to **Appendix 3(A)**.[89] For more information about online periodicals, see **Rule 21.5**.

Examples

Atomic Bomb Hits Japan, L.A. Times, Aug. 7, 1945, at A1.

Jamie Williams, Opinion, *Stop the Movement to Exploit America's Federal Lands—Our Lands*, Seattle Times (Oct. 6, 2016, 12:11 PM), http://www.seattletimes.com/opinion/stop-the-movement-to-exploit-americas-federal-lands-our-lands/.

Patricia Cohen, *Pandemic Delivers a Triple Whammy to Working Women*, N.Y. Times (Nov. 17, 2020, 1:28 PM EST), https://www.nytimes.com/2020/11/17/business/economy/women-jobs-economy-recession.html.

21.3(g) Newsletters and other noncommercially distributed periodicals

Follow **Rules 21.2(a)** (author),[90] **21.3(b)** (title),[91] **21.3(c)** (periodical name),[92] and **Appendix 5(A)** (periodical abbreviations) for those components.[93] Following the periodical abbreviation, add a parenthetical with the abbreviated name of the newsletter's issuing organization and its geographic location.[94] Use abbreviations in **Appendices 3(B)** and **3(E)** for the organization name and location, and omit articles and prepositions not needed for clarity.[95]

Example

Gina Bongiovi, *Flying Solo: Marketing*, YLS Newsl. (State Bar Nev. Young Laws. Section, Las Vegas, Nev.), July 2013, at 1.

21.4 Full Citations to Cartoons or Comic Strips

Set out the artist's name, if available (following **Rule 21.2(a)**), the designation "Cartoon" or "Comic Strip" in ordinary type, the italicized title (if any) of the cartoon or comic strip, and information about the periodical in which the cartoon or comic strip appears, including the volume number (if any), the periodical abbreviation (**Appendix 5(A)**), publication date, and pinpoint reference. For cartoons or comic strips published in newspapers, preface the page number with the letter of the section in which it appears (e.g., A2, B6). Treat a caption below a cartoon as a title. For cartoons or comic strips published online, follow **Rules 21.3(f)(3)** or **21.5**, depending on the nature of the periodical.

Examples

Peter Steiner, Cartoon, *On the Internet, Nobody Knows You're a Dog*, 69 New Yorker, July 5, 1993, at 61.

Scott Adams, Comic Strip, *Dilbert*, Bos. Globe, Aug. 15, 2002, at D16.

21.5 Full Citations to Periodicals in Electronic Media

Whenever possible, cite to a print version of a periodical.[96] There are four ways that periodic material appears in an electronic medium: in a commercial database, on an internet website, in an e-reader, or in a phone application.

21.5(a) Periodic materials in commercial databases

When your source for the periodic material is a commercial database, after drafting the work's full citation according to **Rule 21.2** or **Rule 21.3**, add a parallel citation indicating the name of the database provider and then the unique database identifier, if any.[97]

Example

Krysten Crawford, *Too Much in Common: One Troublesome Client,* Am. Law., Nov. 5, 2020, at 88, Lexis+.

Gray Areas Concerning Workers' Compensation Liability, 50 Laws. Brief, Oct. 15, 2020, Westlaw Edge, 50 No. 19 LAWBRIEF-NL 2.

Merritt Schnipper, Note, *Federal Indian Law—Ambiguous Abrogation: The First Circuit Strips the Narragansett Indian Tribe of Its Sovereign Immunity*, 31 W. New Eng. L. Rev. 243 (2009), Westlaw Edge, 31 WNENGLR 243.

21.5(b) Periodic materials online

If a newspaper is in print and online, use the same format as described in **Rule 21.3(f)**; there is no difference in the citations to the print and online newspaper versions.[98]

If a different type of online periodic source exactly reproduces the work in print (e.g., a PDF version of the original that displays and uses the original page numbering), cite the work in the same manner as its print counterpart according to **Rule 21.2** or **Rule 21.3**.[99] You may choose to append a URL if doing so would help the reader locate the source[100] or if the print source is difficult to obtain.[101] If periodic material is *only* available online and is not an exact copy (e.g., a PDF, cite to it as you would any other online source (see **Rules 30** through **34**).[102]

If the online periodical can be accessed only via subscription, you may append a parenthetical with the abbreviation "sub. req." after the publication name.

Examples

Exact copy of periodic material online:

Ann M. Scarlett, *Jury Trial Disparities Between Class Actions and Shareholder Derivative Actions in State Courts*, 72 Okla. L. Rev. 283, 310 (2020), https://digitalcommons.law.ou.edu/cgi/viewcontent.cgi?article=1385&context=olr.

Miriam Marcowitz-Bitton & Emily Michiko Morris, *The Distributive Effects of IP Registration*, 23 Stan. Tech. L. Rev. 306 (2020), https://www.cdn.law.stanford.edu/wp-content/uploads/2020/07/Morris-et-al_Final.pdf.

Denise Amran, *Homosexuality and Child Custody Through the Lenses of Law: Between Tradition and Fundamental Rights*, 15.1 Elec. J. Compar. L., Dec. 2011, at 1, 5–7, http://www.ejcl.org/151/art151-1.pdf.

Periodic material found only online:

Debby Wu & Mark Gurman, *Apple Suspends New Business with Pegatron over Labor Violations*, Bloomberg News (Oct. 9, 2020, 12:15 AM), https://www.bloomberglaw.com/product/blaw/document/QJIJDMT0AFBD?criteria_id=6dd9a03099873fdf5932e32fc942dfbb.

Leslie C. Griffin, *Stigma and the Oral Argument in* Fulton v. City of Philadelphia, Verdict (Nov. 5, 2020), https://verdict.justia.com/2020/11/05/stigma-and-the-oral-argument-in-fulton-v-city-of-philadelphia.

Anne Applebaum, Opinion, *What "Cheese Pizza" Means to the Internet's Conspiracy-Mongers*, Wash. Post (sub. req.) (Dec. 9, 2016) https://www.washingtonpost.com/blogs/post-partisan/wp/2016/12/09/what-cheese-pizza-means-to-the-internets-conspiracy-mongers/?utm_term=.c3ae1823270e.

21.5(c) E-readers and phone applications

More and more e-readers have periodicals such as magazines in their list of offerings. And many magazine and newspapers now have their own applications that you can download to a phone or tablet to access those sources (e.g., the Washington Post Print Edition App). If the periodic material is available in any other format, cite to the material in that other format; citing to an e-reader or app version should be the last resort.

If you must cite to an e-reader or app version, begin by citing the work according to **Rule 21.2** or **Rule 21.3**, depending on whether it is consecutively paginated or not. Include any initial page available in the source, analogizing to **Rule 20.4(c)**, if needed. Begin the publication parenthetical with the name of the epublisher or application, and then a second parenthetical with the word "e-magazine," "e-journal," "e-newsletter," "application," or other similar description.[103]

Examples

Antonia Farzan, *Utah Makes Masks Mandatory Statewide, Issues State of Emergency*, Wash. Post (Washington Post Print Edition App Nov. 8, 2020, 10:58 PM) (application).

Chandra Thomas Whitfield, *Black Judge Magic*, Essence (Kindle Sept./ Oct. 2020) (e-magazine).

21.6FN Full Citations to Periodicals in Academic Footnotes

Follow **Rules 21.2, 21.3, 21.4,** or **21.5**, as needed, but use large and small capital letters for the periodical's abbreviation.[104]

Examples

33 Patricia M. Wald, *Selecting Law Clerks*, 89 MICH. L. REV. 152, 153 (1990).

37 Kathryn J. Ball, Comment, *Horizontal Equity and the Tax Consequences of Attorney-Client Fee Agreements*, 74 TEMP. L. REV. 387, 407–08 (2001).

30 Lewis H. Lazarus & Katherine J. Neikirk, *Litigating in the Court of Chancery*, 31 DEL. LAW., Summer 2013, at 16.

45 Noel Yahanpath & SzeKee Koh, *Strength of Bond Covenants and Bond Assessment Framework*, 6 AUSTRALASIAN ACCT. BUS. & FIN. J., no. 2, 2012, at 71, 81–86.

58 Adam Liptak, *Bucking a Trend, Supreme Court Justices Reject Video Coverage*, N.Y. TIMES, Feb. 18, 2013, at A15.

64 Scott Adams, Comic Strip, *Dilbert*, BOS. GLOBE, Aug. 15, 2002, at D16.

78 Denise Amran, *Homosexuality and Child Custody Through the Lenses of Law: Between Tradition and Fundamental Rights*, 15.1 ELEC. J. COMPAR. L., Dec. 2011, at 1, 5–7, http://www.ejcl.org/151/art151-1.pdf.

21.7 Short Citations to Periodicals

The following rules apply to consecutively and nonconsecutively paginated periodicals, including electronic sources, except online materials that must be cited as an internet source (**Rule 21.5(b)**). In other words, this rule does not apply to online sources that are not an exact copy of a print source or are only available online. If a periodical must be cited as an online source, use **Rule 31.3** for its short form.

21.7(a) Using *id.* or other short citations to periodicals

When appropriate (**Rule 11.3(c)**), use *id.* as the short citation to a work published in any type of periodical, changing the pinpoint reference if needed.[105] *Id.* tells the reader you are the citing the same work just cited in the immediately preceding citation.[106] Do not use *id.* if the preceding citation refers to two or more sources.[107] When *id.* is not appropriate, use one of the following short citation formats[108]:

Author's surname, | *supra*, | [at] | Pinpoint reference.

or

Title or designation or hereinafter reference, | *supra*, | [at] | Pinpoint reference.

Begin the short citation with the surname(s) of the author(s), if any, followed by a comma and one space.[109] If the work does not have a named author, begin the short citation with the italicized title of the work or the designation if there is no title (see **Rules 21.2(i)**, **21.2(k)**, and **21.3(f)(1)**), followed by a comma, one space, and the italicized word *supra*.[110] If there are two authors with the same last name cited in your document, make sure to include a [hereinafter] abbreviated title name for the work so you can differentiate between the two works when using the *supra* citation format.[111] If the full citation provided a [hereinafter] reference for the work (see **Rule 11.5**), begin with its shortened name, followed by a comma, one space, and *supra*.[112]

Use the preposition "at" only before pinpoint *page* references (**Rule 5**).[113] If the work uses another form of subdivision, omit "at" and insert the specific pinpoint reference, consulting **Rules 6** (sections and paragraphs),[114] **7** (footnotes),[115] **8** (supplements),[116] or **9** (graphical material and appendices).[117] For an online periodical without pagination, put a period after *supra*. Do not include the URL if you chose to append one to the full citation of an online source (**Rule 21.5(b)**).[118] Do not include the database identifier (**Rule 21.5(a)**).[119]

Examples

Full citations:

L. Ray Patterson, *Legal Ethics and the Lawyer's Duty of Loyalty*, 29 Emory L.J. 909, 915 (1980).

Sally H. Scherer, *Our Children — The Legal System's Forgotten Ones*, N.C. St. Bar J., Winter 2011, at 16, 18.

Note, *The Death of a Lawyer*, 56 Colum. L. Rev. 606, 608 (1956).

Short citations: Patterson, *supra*, at 919–20.

Scherer, *supra*, at 17.

Note, *supra*, at 608.

21.7(b)FN Short citations to periodicals in academic footnotes

ACADEMIC FORMATTING

Follow **Rule 21.7(a)** for short citations to periodicals, with one addition.[120] When *id.* is not appropriate (**Rule 11.3(c)**), between *supra* and the comma following it, insert one space, the word "note" in plain type, another space, and the footnote number where the full citation can be found.[121] The resulting short citations will look like this depending on whether there is an author or not[122]:

Author's surname, | *supra* | note | Footnote number, | [at] | Pinpoint reference.

or

Title or designation or hereinafter reference, | *supra* | note | Footnote number, | [at] | Pinpoint reference.

Examples

2 L. Ray Patterson, *Legal Ethics and the Lawyer's Duty of Loyalty*, 29 Emory L.J. 909, 915 (1980).

3 *Id.*

. . .

6 Patterson, *supra* note 2, at 919–20.

. . .

52 Sally H. Scherer, *Our Children—The Legal System's Forgotten Ones*, N.C. St. Bar J., Winter 2011, at 16, 18.

53 Editorial, *An Endangered Act*, Wash. Post, Dec. 29, 2003, at A16.

. . .

61 Scherer, *supra* note 52, at 17.

62 Editorial, *supra* note 53.

22 Dictionaries, Encyclopedias, and *American Law Reports*

Fast Formats

Dictionary	*Discharge*, *Merriam-Webster's Collegiate Dictionary* 356 (11th ed. 2012). *Referendum*, *Merriam-Webster*, http://www.merriam-webster .com/dictionary/referendum (last visited Nov. 10, 2020). *Stare Decisis*, *Black's Law Dictionary* (10th ed. 2014).
American Jurisprudence 2d	67 Am. Jur. 2d *Robbery* § 96 (2003).
***Corpus Juris Secundum* online**	3 C.J.S. *Aliens* § 7 (Westlaw through Sept. 2020).
Single-volume encyclopedia with named author	John R. Vile, *Encyclopedia of Constitutional Amendments, Proposed Amendments, and Amending Issues, 1789–2002*, at 133–34 (2d ed. 2003).
Multivolume encyclopedia with named editor	3 *Oxford International Encyclopedia of Legal History* 120–23 (Stanley N. Katz ed., 2009).
American Law Reports	P.H. Vartanian, Annotation, *"Res Ipsa Loquitur" as a Presumption or a Mere Permissible Inference*, 167 A.L.R. 658, 660 (1947). James L. Buchwalter, Annotation, *Construction and Application of Claim Maturity Exception to Compulsory Counterclaim Requirement Under Fed. R. Civ. P. 13(a)(1)*, 6 A.L.R. Fed. 3d Art. 1, § 6 (2015).

Citations in academic footnotes	⚠ACADEMIC FORMATTING 54 *Stare Decisis*, BLACK'S LAW DICTIONARY (10th ed. 2014). 73 67 AM. JUR. 2d *Robbery* § 96 (2003). 90 JOHN R. VILE, ENCYCLOPEDIA OF CONSTITUTIONAL AMENDMENTS, PROPOSED AMENDMENTS, AND AMENDING ISSUES, 1789–2002, at 133–34 (2d ed. 2003). 102 James L. Buchwalter, Annotation, *Construction and Application of Claim Maturity Exception to Compulsory Counterclaim Requirement Under Fed. R. Civ. P. 13(a)(1)*, 6 A.L.R. FED. 3d Art. 1, § 6 (2015).
Short citations	67 Am. Jur. 2d *Robbery*, *supra*, § 97. Buchwalter, *supra*, § 7. 124 VILE, *supra* note 90, at 140.

22.1 Full Citations to Dictionaries

The full citation to a dictionary varies depending on whether the source is a dictionary in print, an online dictionary, or a well-known legal dictionary such as *Black's Law Dictionary*.

22.1(a) Full citations to dictionaries in print

Depending on the nature of the book, a citation to a print dictionary may have as many as eight components.

[*Defined term*], | [Author,] | *Title* | Pinpoint reference | ([Editor name ed.,] | [Edition number if not the 1st ed. | ed.] | Year of publication).

Cite a print dictionary as you would cite a book under **Rule 20.1**.[1] For multi-volume dictionaries, follow **Rule 20.3**.[2] You may begin the citation with the defined term, in italics.[3]

Examples (spaces denoted by ▲)

Eric▲Partridge,▲*A*▲*Dictionary*▲*of*▲*Slang*▲*and*▲*Unconventional*▲*English*▲111▲(8th▲ed.▲1984).

Intemperate,▲*New*▲*World*▲*Dictionary*▲*of*▲*the*▲*American*▲*Language*▲732▲ (David▲B.▲Guralnik▲ed.,▲2d▲college▲ed.▲1980).

22.1(b) Full citations to online dictionaries

A citation to an online dictionary has the following four components[4]:

[*Defined term*], | *Title*, | URL | (Date of access or update).

Begin with the defined term, in italics, followed by a comma and one space.[5] Indicate the title of the primary site for the dictionary, in italics, followed by a comma and one space.[6] Because the defined term is the relevant reference, the citation does not use a pinpoint reference. Use the URL from the page displaying the defined term.[7] Examine the page for the date of its most recent update; if that information is not shown, indicate the date that you last visited the site, in parentheses (Month Day, Year), abbreviating the month according to **Appendix 3(A)**.[8]

Examples (spaces denoted by ▲)

Discipline,▲*Oxford*▲*English*▲*Dictionary*,▲http://www.oed.com/view/Entry/53744▲(last▲visited▲Nov.▲10,▲2020).

Undue,▲*Wiktionary*,▲https://en.wiktionary.org/wiki/undue▲(last▲updated▲Nov.▲9,▲2020).

22.1(c) *Black's Law Dictionary* or *Ballentine's Law Dictionary*

A citation to *Black's Law Dictionary* or *Ballentine's Law Dictionary* has the following components.[9] They are the same whether the source is a print version or a digital version of the dictionary:

Defined Term, | [*Black's Law Dictionary* or *Ballentine's Law Dictionary*] | ([Edition number if not the 1st | ed.] | Year of publication).

Black's capitalizes the first letter of each word in the defined term. If desired, you may capitalize only the first. Following the defined term, insert a comma and one space, followed by the italicized title *Black's Law Dictionary* or *Ballentine's Law Dictionary* and one space.[10] Because the defined term is the relevant reference, the citation does not use a pinpoint reference. In parentheses, set out the edition number and its year of publication.[11] Even if the edition indicates an editor, omit this information from the citation.[12]

Examples

Property, *Black's Law Dictionary* (10th ed. 2014).

Amicitia, *Ballentine's Law Dictionary* (3d ed. 1969).

22.1(d)[FN] Full citations to dictionaries in academic footnotes

ACADEMIC FORMATTING

Follow **Rule 22.1(a)–(c)** for the citation components, but use large and small capital letters for the author's name (if any) and the title of the dictionary or dictionary webpage.[13]

Examples

15 *Discharge*, WEBSTER'S THIRD INTERNATIONAL DICTIONARY 644 (3d ed. 2002).

23 *Ninja*, OXFORD ENGLISH DICTIONARY, http://www.oed.com/view/Entry/240489 (last visited Nov. 10, 2020).

42 *Testator*, BLACK'S LAW DICTIONARY (10th ed. 2014).

22.2 Short Citations to Dictionaries

22.2(a) Using *id.* or other short citations to dictionaries

When citing a dictionary in print, use *id.* and the preposition "at" before the pinpoint page reference (**Rule 11.3(d)**).[14] When *id.* is not appropriate (**Rule 11.3(c)**), use the italicized title of the dictionary, the italicized word *supra*, and the preposition "at" preceding the pinpoint page number.[15] See **Rule 11.4** for more information on using *supra* in a short citation.

To cite an online dictionary or *Black's Law Dictionary*, use its italicized title, followed by a comma, one space, and the italicized word *supra*. Omit pinpoint references. If you cite two or more defined terms from the same dictionary, repeat the defined term at the beginning of the *supra* format in order to avoid reader confusion.

Examples

Full citation:	*Merriam-Webster's Collegiate Dictionary* 1547 (11th ed. 2003).
Short citation:	*Merriam-Webster's Collegiate Dictionary*, *supra*, at 348.
Full citation:	*Qualified privilege*, *Duhaime's Law Dictionary*, http://www.duhaime.org/LegalDictionary/Q/QualifiedPrivilege.aspx (last visited Nov. 9, 2020).
Short citation:	*Qualified privilege*, *Duhaime's Law Dictionary*, *supra*.

22.2(b)FN Short citations to dictionaries in academic footnotes

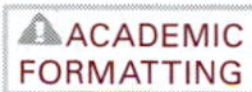

When citing a dictionary in print, use *id.* as the short citation, changing the pinpoint reference when needed.[16] Do not use *id.* when the preceding footnote refers to two or more sources.[17] When *id.* is not appropriate (**Rule 11.3(c)**), use one of the *supra* formats that follow, cross-referencing the footnote in which the work's full citation is set out.[18]

AUTHOR'S SURNAME, | *supra* | note | Footnote number, | [at] | Pinpoint reference.

or

Title, | *supra* | note | Footnote number, | [at] | Pinpoint reference.

Begin with the author's surname(s) in large and small capital letters, followed by a comma and one space.[19] When no author is shown, begin with the title of the work in large and small capital letters, followed by a comma and one space.[20] Add a *supra* reference to the earlier footnote containing the work's full citation (**Rule 11.4**), followed by a comma, a space, and a pinpoint reference.[21]

If citing an online dictionary or *Black's Law Dictionary*, keep *supra* but omit the pinpoint reference. Use large and small capital letters for the title of the dictionary or dictionary webpage.[22]

Examples

45 ALAN GILPIN, DICTIONARY OF ENVIRONMENTAL LAW 42 (2001).

46 *Id.* at 68.

. . .

93 GILPIN, *supra* note 45, at 60.

. . .

123 *Injury*, BLACK'S LAW DICTIONARY (10th ed. 2014).

124 *Duplicitous*, DICTIONARY.COM, https://www/dictionary.com/browse/duplicitous?s=t (last visited Nov. 9, 2020).

. . .

134 BLACK'S LAW DICTIONARY, *supra* note 123.

135 DICTIONARY.COM, *supra* note 124.

22.3 Full Citations to Multivolume Encyclopedias

Use this rule to cite a multivolume legal encyclopedia such as *American Jurisprudence 2d* ("Am. Jur. 2d"), *Corpus Juris Secundum* ("C.J.S."), and similar multivolume encyclopedias. When the encyclopedia has a named author or editor, or if it is a single-volume encyclopedia, follow **Rule 22.4**. A full citation to an entry in a multivolume legal encyclopedia has these components.[23]

Volume number | Encyclopedia abbreviation | *Title or topic* | § | Pinpoint reference | (Year of publication).

Example (spaces denoted by ▲)

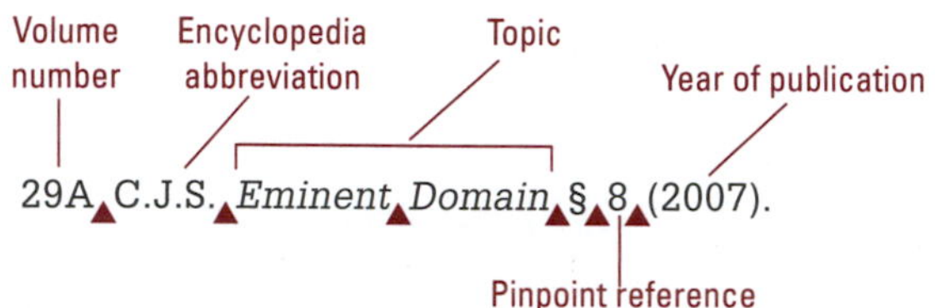

22.3(a) Volume number

Begin with the volume number, set out as an Arabic numeral in ordinary type, followed by a space.[24] When the volume number also includes a letter, capitalize the letter.

Example (spaces denoted by ▲)

60A▲Am.▲Jur.▲2d▲*Pensions*▲§▲1098▲(2003▲&▲Supp.▲2012).

22.3(b) Encyclopedia abbreviation

Following the volume number, set out the abbreviation for the name of the encyclopedia, in ordinary type, followed by one space.[25] **Chart 22.1** has abbreviations for the most widely used legal encyclopedias. To cite an entry in a multivolume encyclopedia not shown in the chart, abbreviate any words in

CHART 22.1 Representative Encyclopedia Abbreviations

Encyclopedia name:	Abbreviation (spaces denoted by ▲):
American Jurisprudence	Am.▲Jur.
American Jurisprudence, Second Series	Am.▲Jur.▲2d
Corpus Juris	C.J.
Corpus Juris Secundum	C.J.S.
California Jurisprudence, Third Series	Cal.▲Jur.▲3d
New York Jurisprudence, Second Series	N.Y.▲Jur.▲2d

its name that appear in **Appendix 3(B)**; analogize to the abbreviations shown in **Chart 22.1** (e.g., N.Y. Jur. 2d). Otherwise, give the full name of the encyclopedia. For an encyclopedia series after the first, use the appropriate ordinal contraction (**Rule 4.3(b)**).[26]

22.3(c) Title or topic name

Following the encyclopedia abbreviation, set out the full main title or topic name of the cited entry, in italics.[27] Capitalize words in the title or topic name according to **Rule 3.2**, **Rule 3.3**, and **Chart 3.1**.[28] Do not omit or abbreviate any words from the title or topic name.[29] However, omit names of subsections or other subdivisions of the entry.[30]

Example

Main title:	*Robbery*
Name of subsection:	§ 91 Unlawful Entry
Correct (main title):	67 Am. Jur. 2d *Robbery* § 91 (2003).
Incorrect (subsection):	67 Am. Jur. 2d *Unlawful Entry* § 91 (2003).

22.3(d) Pinpoint references

Following the title or topic name, insert one or more section symbols, followed by one space and the number(s) of the cited section(s).[31] See **Rule 6** for guidance on citing sections and their subdivisions.

22.3(e) Publication parenthetical

Following the section number(s), add a parenthetical to indicate the year(s) of publication of the cited volume and its supplement, if any.[32] See **Rule 8** for guidance in citing a main volume, a supplement, or both. When citing an encyclopedia entry in a commercial database, add the name of the database provider, and provide the date through which the database is current.[33]

Examples

Main volume:	79A C.J.S. *Securities Regulation* § 4 (2009).
Supplement:	79A C.J.S. *Securities Regulation* § 37 (Supp. 2012).
Both main volume and supplement:	76 Am. Jur. 2d *Trusts* § 1 (2005 & Supp. 2012).
Commercial database:	5 Am. Jur. 2d *Arrest* § 104, Westlaw (database updated Nov. 2020).

22.3(f) Encyclopedias in commercial databases

When your source for the encyclopedia is a commercial database, after the work's full citation, add a parallel citation indicating the name of the database provider and then the unique database identifier, if any.[34] For the publication parenthetical, use the information provided by the database itself, which may be a year, a month, or an exact date.[35]

Example

2 Am. Jur. 2d *Adoption* § 16, Westlaw (database updated Nov. 2020).

22.3(g)FN Full citations to multivolume encyclopedias in academic footnotes

ACADEMIC FORMATTING

Follow **Rule 22.3(a)–(e)**, but present the name of the encyclopedia in large and small capital letters.[36]

Example

62 76 AM. JUR. 2D *Trusts* § 1 (2005 & Supp. 2012).

22.3(h) Short citations to multivolume encyclopedias

When appropriate (**Rule 11.3(c)**), use *id.* as the short citation to an entry in a multivolume encyclopedia.[37] When *id.* is not appropriate, use the full citation of the multivolume encyclopedia without the publication parenthetical. Indicate a pinpoint reference.[38] Use the preposition "at" only before pinpoint *page* references (**Rule 11.3(d)**).[39] When the work uses another form of subdivision, omit "at" and use the specific pinpoint reference,[40] consulting **Rules 6** through **9**.

Example

Full citation:	45C Am. Jur. 2d *Job Discrimination* § 2219 (2012).
Short citation:	45C Am. Jur. 2d *Job Discrimination* § 2219.

22.3(i)FN Short citations to multivolume encyclopedias in academic footnotes

ACADEMIC FORMATTING

When *id.* is not appropriate (**Rule 11.3(c)**), in addition to using large and small capital letters for the name of the encyclopedia, omit the publication parenthetical from the full citation of the multivolume encyclopedia. Then, between the title and the pinpoint reference, insert a *supra* reference to the earlier footnote containing the full citation.[41]

Example

6 45C AM. JUR. 2D *Job Discrimination* § 2219 (2012).

7 *Id.* § 2220.

. . .

13 45C AM. JUR. 2D *Job Discrimination*, *supra* note 6, § 2223.

22.4 Full Citations to Encyclopedias with Named Authors or Editors

22.4(a) Full citation to encyclopedia with named author or editor

Analogize to **Rule 20.1**.[42] To cite a specific author's article within an encyclopedia, refer to **Rule 20.3(b)**.[43]

Examples

J.O. Urmson & Jonathan Rée, *The Concise Encyclopedia of Western Philosophy & Philosophers* 272 (3d ed. 2004).

Encyclopedia of Animal Rights and Animal Welfare 34 (Marc Bekoff ed., 2d ed. 2010).

Gerhard Casper, *Constitutionalism, in* 2 *Encyclopedia of the American Constitution* 633 (Leonard W. Levy & Kenneth L. Karst eds., 2d ed. 2000).

22.4(b)FN Full citations to encyclopedias with named authors or editors in academic footnotes

ACADEMIC FORMATTING

Analogize to **Rule 20.1(f)FN**.[44] To cite a specific author's article within an encyclopedia, refer to **Rule 20.3(e)FN**.[45]

Examples

61 J.O. URMSON & JONATHAN RÉE, THE CONCISE ENCYCLOPEDIA OF WESTERN PHILOSOPHY & PHILOSOPHERS 272 (3d ed. 2004).

79 ENCYCLOPEDIA OF ANIMAL RIGHTS AND ANIMAL WELFARE 34 (Marc Bekoff ed., 2d ed. 2010).

135 GERHARD CASPER, *Constitutionalism*, *in* 2 ENCYCLOPEDIA OF THE AMERICAN CONSTITUTION 633 (Leonard W. Levy & Kenneth L. Karst eds., 2d ed. 2000).

22.4(c) Short citations to encyclopedias with named authors or editors

When *id.* is not appropriate (**Rule 11.3(c)**), analogize to **Rules 20.6(a)**[46] and **20.6(b)**.[47] Begin with the author's surname or the title (if the encyclopedia has an editor instead of a named author), followed by a comma and one space, the italicized word *supra*, a comma and one space, and a new pinpoint reference.[48]

Examples

Urmson & Rée, supra, at 273.

Encyclopedia of Animal Rights and Animal Welfare, supra, at 37.

Casper, *supra*, at 634.

22.4(d)FN Short citations to encyclopedias with named authors or editors in academic footnotes

Follow **Rule 22.4(c)**, but after the author name (or title, if the encyclopedia has an editor instead of a named author), insert a *supra* reference to the earlier footnote containing the full citation, followed by a pinpoint reference.[49]

In citing a specific article within an encyclopedia, only use *id.* if you are referring to the same article in the immediately preceding footnote.[50] If you are citing to a new article in the encyclopedia, follow **Rule 20.6(d)**; set out the new author's surname and new article title (or just the title, if the encyclopedia has an editor instead of a named author), followed by a *supra* reference to the earlier footnote containing the full citation, followed by a pinpoint reference.[51]

Examples

61 J.O. URMSON & JONATHAN RÉE, THE CONCISE ENCYCLOPEDIA OF WESTERN PHILOSOPHY & PHILOSOPHERS 272 (3d ed. 2004).

62 *Id.*

. . .

69 URMSON & RÉE, *supra* note 61, at 273.

79 ENCYCLOPEDIA OF ANIMAL RIGHTS AND ANIMAL WELFARE 34 (Marc Bekoff ed., 2d ed. 2010).

80 *Id.* at 36.

. . .

112 ENCYCLOPEDIA OF ANIMAL RIGHTS AND ANIMAL WELFARE, *supra* note 79, at 33.

135 *American Association of University Women*, *in* ENCYCLOPEDIA OF WOMEN IN AMERICAN POLITICS 13 (Jeffrey D. Schultz & Laura van Assendelft eds., 1999).

136 *Id.*

. . .

156 *State Status of Women Commissions*, *in* ENCYCLOPEDIA OF WOMEN IN AMERICAN POLITICS, *supra* note 135, at 217.

157 *American Association of University Women*, *in* ENCYCLOPEDIA OF WOMEN IN AMERICAN POLITICS, *supra* note 135, at 13.

22.5 Full Citations to Annotations in *American Law Reports*

An annotation is a detailed article on a narrow topic of the law, containing extensive references to judicial opinions and other sources dealing with that topic. Annotations are collected and published in volumes of the *American Law Reports* series ("A.L.R.") and online in Westlaw.

A full citation to an annotation contains eight components.[52] (Also use this format to cite the predecessor of A.L.R., *Lawyer's Reports Annotated* (substituting the abbreviation "L.R.A.").[53])

Author, | Annotation, | *Title*, | Volume number | A.L.R. series abbreviation | Article number or initial page, | Pinpoint reference | (Year of publication).

Example (spaces denoted by ▲)

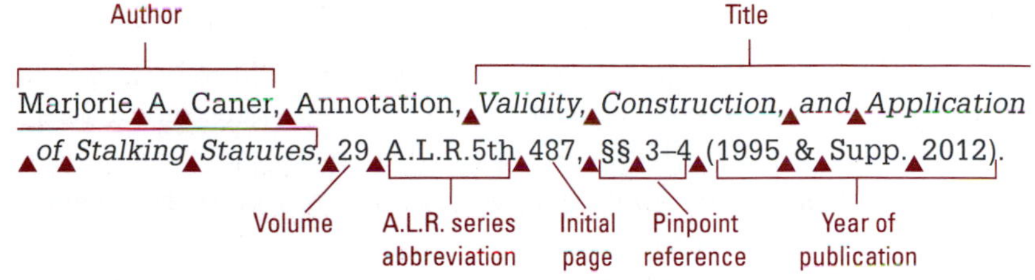

22.5(a) Author and annotation designation

Begin with the author's name, following **Rule 20.1(b)** for books.[54] After the author's name, add a comma, one space, the word "Annotation," in ordinary type, followed by another comma and space.[55] If the annotation shows no author, begin the citation with the designation "Annotation."

Examples

Marjorie A. Shields, Annotation, *Construction and Application of Professional Conduct Rules Concerning False or Misleading Claims About Legal Services*, 5 A.L.R.7th Art. 2, § 1 (2015).

Annotation, *Per Diem Compensation of Public Officer*, 1 A.L.R. 276, 279 (1919).

22.5(b) Annotation title

Present the title exactly as it appears on the first page of the annotation, without omitting any words. Italicize the title and subtitle, if any, but use ordinary type for words italicized in text, such as case names (**Rule 1.3**).[56] Capitalize words according to **Rule 3.2**, **Rule 3.3**, and **Chart 3.1**.[57] Insert a comma and one space after the title.[58]

Examples

Ann K. Wooster, Annotation, *Issues Concerning Bankruptcy Proceedings of Limited Liability Companies*, 37 A.L.R. Fed. 2d 129, § 11 (2009).

Daniel L. Kresh, Annotation, *Stray Remark or Comment Toward Female Plaintiffs Regarding Pregnancy, Child-Rearing, and Related References in Title VII Action for Sex Discrimination*, 6 A.L.R. Fed. 3d Art. 3, § 11 (2015).

22.5(c) Volume number and A.L.R. series

Following the title, set out the volume number of the series in which the annotation appears. Insert one space after the volume number.[59] Immediately following the volume number, indicate the abbreviation for the A.L.R. series in which the work is published, in ordinary type.[60] The A.L.R. series uses the abbreviation "A.L.R." followed by an ordinal number (for the second and later series) or another designation (for the federal or international series), followed by one space.[61] Individual ordinal numbers are treated as single capitals and thus there is no space between them and the abbreviation "A.L.R."[62] Abbreviations for the A.L.R. series are shown in **Chart 22.2**.

Examples

Marilyn E. Phelan, Annotation, *Stolen and Illegally Exported Cultural Property and International Legislation and Treaties Protecting Cultural Property*, 6 A.L.R. Int'l 527, § 1 (2012).

Cara Yates, Annotation, *Application of State Law to Age Discrimination in Employment*, 51 A.L.R.5th 1, § 1(a) n.3 (1997).

Marjorie A. Shields, Annotation, *Admissibility of Evidence Discovered in Search of Defendant's Property or Residence Authorized by Defendant's Spouse*, 154 A.L.R. Fed. 579, § 3(a) (1999).

22.5(d) Article number or initial page

Newer series of A.L.R. are designed for medium-neutral access. For that reason, each annotation is designated as a numbered "Article." Older series of A.L.R. use an initial page number. Following the series abbreviation, set out the annotation's article number (using the abbreviation "Art.") or its initial page number. If the citation has a pinpoint reference, add a comma and one space.[63]

CHART 22.2	Abbreviations for A.L.R. Series (spaces denoted by ▲)
First Series (1919–1947)	A.L.R.
Second Series (1948–1965)	A.L.R.2d
Third Series (1965–1980)	A.L.R.3d
Fourth Series (1980–1991)	A.L.R.4th
Fifth Series (1992–2004)	A.L.R.5th
Sixth Series (2005–2015)	A.L.R.6th
Seventh Series (2015–present)	A.L.R.7th
Federal Series (1969–2005)	A.L.R.▲Fed.
Federal Series, Second (2005–2015)	A.L.R.▲Fed.▲2d
Federal Series, Third (2015–present)	A.L.R.▲Fed.▲3d
International (2010–present)	A.L.R.▲Int'l

Example

George L. Blum, *Zoning Ordinances Addressing Medical Marijuana Businesses*, 30 A.L.R.7th Art. 3, § 7 (2017).

22.5(e) Pinpoint references

When possible, include a pinpoint reference to the cited portion of the annotation, using a section number (preferred), a page number, a footnote number, or a combination of these references.[64] See **Rules 5** through **9** and **Appendix 3(C)** for guidance on pinpoint references and subdivisions.

Example

William H. Danne, Jr., Annotation, *"Palimony" Actions for Support Following Termination of Nonmarital Relationships*, 21 A.L.R.6th 351, § 13 cmt. (2007).

22.5(f) Publication date

End the citation with a publication parenthetical setting out the publication year for the article or the print volume (including any supplement relevant to the citation).[65] See **Rule 8** for more information on citing print supplements.[66]

Annotations published in Westlaw's American Law Reports database are updated weekly. If your source for the annotation is the Westlaw database, construct the publication parenthetical with the name "Westlaw" and the exact date (Month Day, Year) of your access to it.[67]

Examples

Gregory G. Sarno, Annotation, *Legal Malpractice in Handling or Defending Medical Malpractice Claim*, 78 A.L.R.4th 725, § 4(b) (1990 & Supp. 2012).

Kimberly J. Winbush, Annotation, *Construction and Application of Four-Fifths Rule for Finding Evidence of Adverse Impact in Federal Employment Discrimination Cases*, 7 A.L.R. Fed. 3d Art. 1, §§ 17–18 (Westlaw through Nov. 9, 2020).

22.5(g)FN Full citations to annotations in academic footnotes

ACADEMIC FORMATTING

Cite annotations following **Rule 22.5(a)–(f)**; there is no difference in citations to the A.L.R. in academic formatting.[68]

Examples

78 Cara Yates, Annotation, *Application of State Law to Age Discrimination in Employment*, 51 A.L.R.5th 1, § 1(a) n.3 (1997).

82 Marjorie A. Shields, Annotation, *Admissibility of Evidence Discovered in Search of Defendant's Property or Residence Authorized by Defendant's Spouse*, 154 A.L.R. Fed. 579, § 3(a) (1999).

22.6 Short Citations to Annotations

22.6(a) Using *id.* or other short citations to annotations

Analogize to **Rule 21.7(a)** for periodicals.[69]

Examples

Full citation: Deborah F. Buckman, Annotation, *Reverse Confusion Doctrine Under State Trademark Law*, 114 A.L.R.5th 129, § 1(a) (2003).

Daniel L. Kresh, Annotation, *Stray Remark or Comment Toward Female Plaintiffs Regarding Pregnancy, Child-Rearing, and Related References in Title VII Action for Sex Discrimination*, 6 A.L.R. Fed. 3d Art. 3, § 11 (2015).

Short citations: *Id.* § 4.

Buckman, *supra*, § 6.

Kresh, *supra*, § 12.

22.6(b)FN Short citations to annotations in academic footnotes

ACADEMIC FORMATTING

Analogize to **Rule 21.7(b)** for periodicals.[70]

Example

[2] Deborah F. Buckman, Annotation, *Reverse Confusion Doctrine Under State Trademark Law*, 114 A.L.R.5th 129, § 1(a) (2003).

[3] *Id.* § 4.

. . .

[27] Buckman, *supra* note 2, § 6.

23 Restatements, Principles of the Law, Model Codes, Uniform Laws, and Sentencing Guidelines

Fast Formats

Restatement	Restatement (Second) of Agency § 27 (Am. L. Inst. 1958).
Principle	Principles of the L. of Gov't Ethics § 4.01 (Am. L. Inst., Tentative Draft No. 1, 2015).
Model code	Model Penal Code § 2.02(2)(a)(i) (Am. L. Inst. 1985).
ABA model ethics codes	Model Rules of Pro. Conduct r. 2.1 (Am. Bar Ass'n 2004). Model Code of Pro. Resp. DR 5-105(B) (Am. Bar Ass'n 1978).
Uniform law	Unif. Trade Secrets Act § 1(4), 14 U.L.A. 438 (1990).
Sentencing guidelines	U.S. Sent'g Guidelines Manual § 4B1.2(a) (U.S. Sent'g Comm'n 2015).
Citations in academic footnotes	ACADEMIC FORMATTING 33 RESTATEMENT (THIRD) OF PROP.: MORTGS. § 3.1 (AM. L. INST. 1997). 34 MODEL CODE OF PRO. RESP. EC 7-1 (AM. BAR ASS'N 1981). 35 UNIF. ELEC. TRANSACTIONS ACT § 3(b) (1999). 36 U.S. SENT'G GUIDELINES MANUAL § 4A1.1 (U.S. SENT'G COMM'N 2015).
Short citations	Restatement (Second) of Contracts § 90. § 90. 37 UNIF. ELEC. TRANSACTIONS ACT § 3(a). 38 *Id.* § 3(b).

Snapshot

RESTATEMENT OF THE LAW

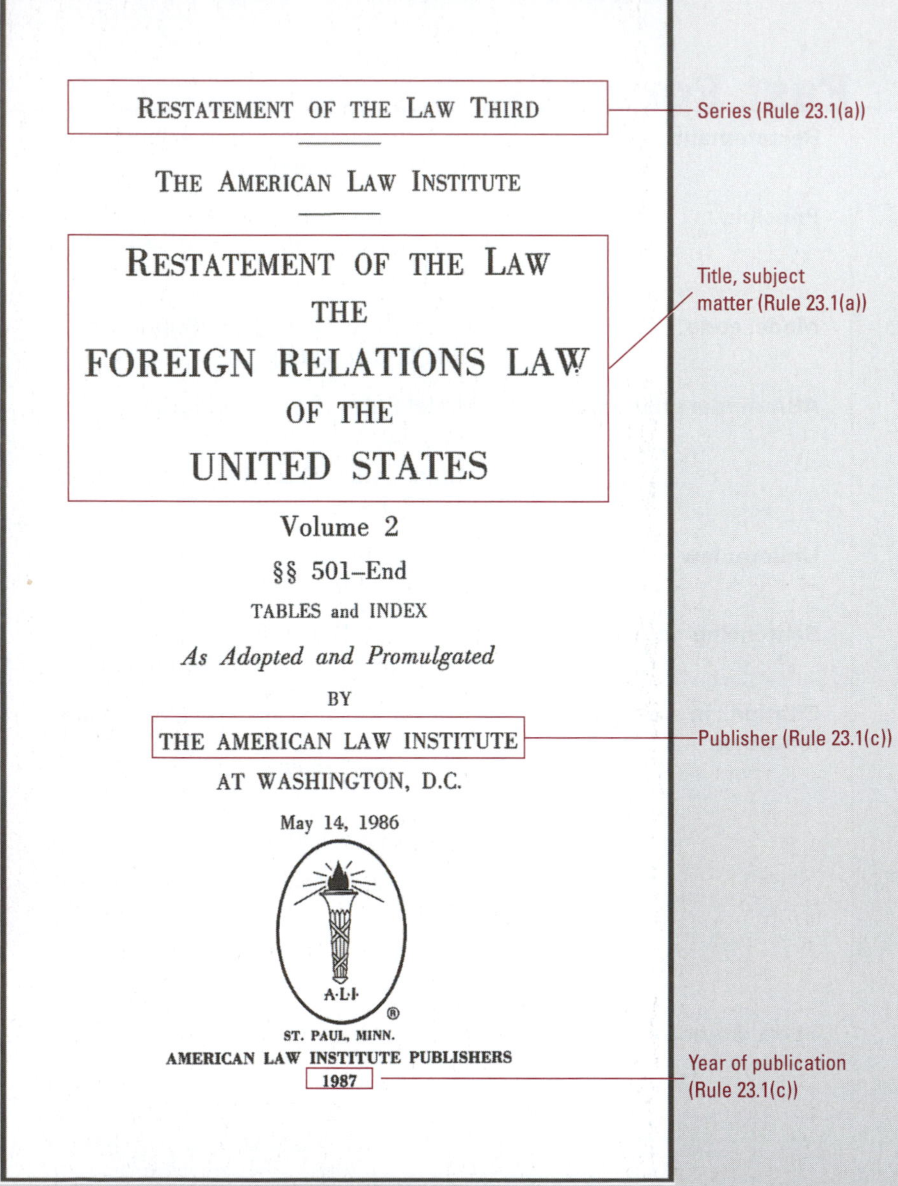
RESTATEMENT OF THE LAW THIRD

THE AMERICAN LAW INSTITUTE

RESTATEMENT OF THE LAW
THE
FOREIGN RELATIONS LAW
OF THE
UNITED STATES

Volume 2
§§ 501–End
TABLES and INDEX

As Adopted and Promulgated
BY
THE AMERICAN LAW INSTITUTE
AT WASHINGTON, D.C.
May 14, 1986

ST. PAUL, MINN.
AMERICAN LAW INSTITUTE PUBLISHERS
1987

Title Page

Snapshot

Chapter Three

HIGH SEAS

§ 521. Freedom of High Seas

Pinpoint reference (Rule 23.1(b))

(1) The high seas are open and free to all states, whether coastal or land-locked.

(2) Freedom of the high seas comprises, *inter alia*:

(a) freedom of navigation;

(b) freedom of overflight;

(c) freedom of fishing;

(d) freedom to lay submarine cables and pipelines;

(e) freedom to construct artificial islands, installations, and structures; and

(f) freedom of scientific research.

(3) These freedoms must be exercised by all states with reasonable regard to the interests of other states in their exercise of the freedom of the high seas.

Source Note:

This section is based on Article 2 of the 1958 Convention on the High Seas, and Articles 87 and 89 of the LOS Convention.

Comment:

a. Area in which high seas freedoms can be exercised. This section applies to all parts of the sea that are not included in the internal waters, the territorial sea, or the exclusive economic zone of any state, or in the archipelagic waters of an archipelagic state. Certain of these freedoms may be exercised also in the exclusive economic zone of other states, as specified in § 514. See LOS Convention, Article 86; compare 1958 Convention on the High Seas, Article 1.

No state may appropriate any part of the high seas or otherwise subject the high seas to its sovereignty. See LOS Convention,

78

Inside Page

Citation: Restatement (Third) of the L. of Foreign Rels. of the U.S. § 521(2)(a)–(f) (Am. L. Inst. 1987).

23.1 Full Citations to Restatements and Principles of the Law

The American Law Institute (ALI) has developed a wide-ranging collection of basic legal concepts, collectively known as "Restatements of the Law." A full citation to a restatement has up to seven components, depending on whether the restatement is in its first, second, or third series, whether it was published in 2015 or later, and whether it is in final or draft form.[1] Beginning in 2015, ALI stopped numbering series, but any restatement belonging to an existing series will remain in that series.

Restatement | [(Series, if not the first)] | of Subject matter | Pinpoint reference | (Am. L. Inst. | [, Draft information] | Year of publication).

Example (spaces denoted by ▲)

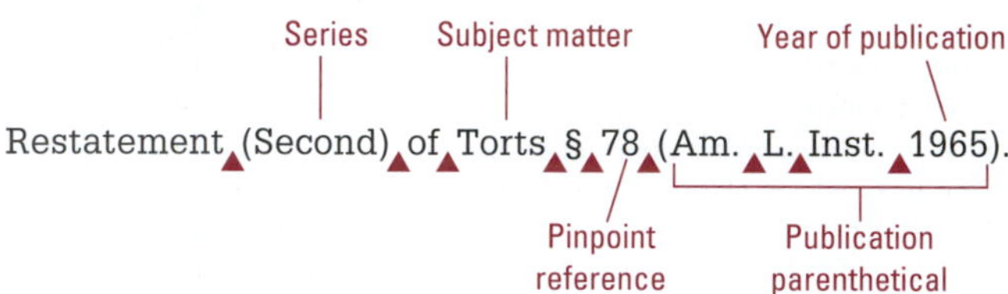

ALI also publishes sets of principles and best practices reflecting emerging areas of law, with the goal of sharing their development. Citations to these "Principles of the Law" have up to six components.[2]

Principles of the L. of | Subject matter | Pinpoint reference | (Am. L. Inst. | [, Draft information] | Year of adoption).

Example (spaces denoted by ▲)

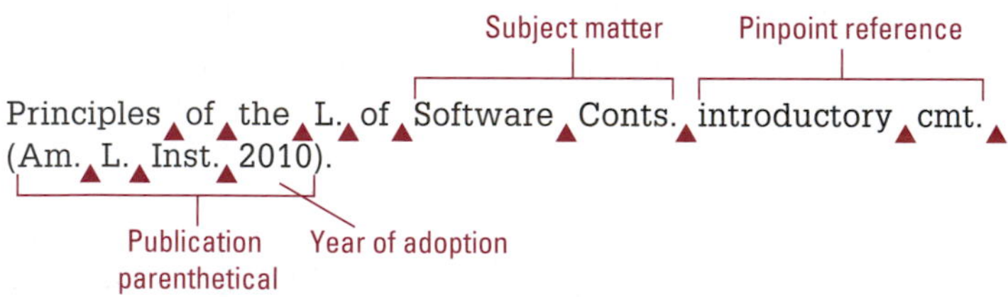

23.1(a) Title, subject matter, and series

Begin with the title "Restatement" or "Principles of the L." followed by the preposition "of" and the subject matter (see **Chart 23.1**), abbreviating any words that appear in **Appendix 3(E)**.[3] Do not omit any words.[4] Retain all subtitles; insert a colon and one space before a subtitle.[5] Except for the first series,

CHART 23.1 Subject Matters of Restatements and Principles of the Law

Current subject matters and drafts of the **Restatements** are as follows:

- Agency
- Charitable Nonprofit Organizations
- Children and the Law
- Conflict of Laws
- Consumer Contracts
- Contracts
- Copyright
- Employment Law
- Foreign Relations Law of the United States
- International Commercial Arbitration
- Judgments
- Law Governing Lawyers
- Law of American Indians
- Liability Insurance
- Property
- Property: Landlord & Tenant
- Property: Mortgages
- Property: Servitudes
- Property: Wills & Other Donative Transfers
- Restitution & Unjust Enrichment
- Security
- Suretyship & Guaranty
- Torts
- Torts: Apportionment of Liability
- Torts: Intentional Torts to Persons
- Torts: Liability for Economic Harm
- Torts: Liability for Physical & Emotional Harm
- Torts: Products Liability
- Trusts
- Unfair Competition
- U.S. Law of International Commercial and Investor-State Arbitration

Current subject matters and drafts of **Principles of the Law** are as follows:

- Aggregate Litigation
- Compliance, Risk Management, and Enforcement
- Corporate Governance
- Data Economy
- Data Privacy
- Election Administration: Non-precinct Voting and Resolution of Ballot-Counting Disputes
- Family Dissolution: Analysis and Recommendations
- Government Ethics
- Intellectual Property: Principles Governing Jurisdiction, Choice of Law, and Judgments in Transnational Disputes
- Policing
- Software Contracts
- Student Sexual Misconduct: Procedural Frameworks of Colleges and Universities
- Transnational Civil Procedure
- Transnational Insolvency

indicate the restatement series, if any, in a parenthetical, spelling out the ordinal number.[6] Capitalize words according to **Rule 3.2**, **Rule 3.3**, and **Chart 3.1**, and use ordinary type for the title, subject matter, and series.[7]

Examples

Restatement (Second) of Conts. § 90 (Am. L. Inst. 1981).

Restatement (Third) of Torts: Prods. Liab. § 2 cmt. d (Am. L. Inst. 1998).

Principles of the L. of Fam. Dissolution: Analysis & Recommendations § 2.05 (Am. L. Inst. 2002).

23.1(b) Pinpoint references

Following the title, provide a pinpoint reference, indicating sections, subsections, or other relevant subdivisions such as comments.[8] Abbreviate subdivisions using **Appendix 3(C)**.[9]

Examples

Restatement (Second) of Conflict of L. § 291 cmt. g (Am. L. Inst. 1971).

Restatement of Prop.: Servitudes § 453 illus. 1 (Am. L. Inst. 1944).

Principles of the L. of Policing § 11.01 cmt. b (Am. L. Inst., Tentative Draft No. 2, 2019), Westlaw Edge ALI-POLICING § 11.01 TD 2.

23.1(c) Publication parenthetical

Begin the publication parenthetical with the abbreviation for the institutional author of both the restatements and principles of law, the American Law Institute ("Am. L. Inst.").[10] Following the author abbreviation, indicate the year of publication for the restatements.[11] But for principles of law, give the year of adoption.[12]

23.1(d) Draft

When citing a draft restatement or principle, add a comma and one space after the author abbreviation, followed by a description of the type of draft, in ordinary type, capitalized, or without abbreviation (e.g., "Draft," "Tentative Draft," "Discussion Draft," or "Proposed Draft").[13] When the draft is numbered, add the abbreviation "No." before its number, and place a comma between the number and the year of publication.[14]

Examples

Numbered tentative draft:	Restatement of L. of Am. Indians § 105 (Am. L. Inst., Tentative Draft No. 3, 2019).
	Restatement of the L. of Charitable Nonprofit Orgs. § 5.02(b)(5) (Am. L. Inst., Tentative Draft No. 3, 2019).
Unnumbered proposed or tentative draft:	Restatement of U.S. L. of Int'l Com. and Inv.-State Arb. § 4.33 (Am. L. Inst., Proposed Final Draft 2004).
	Principles of the L. of Data Priv. § 11 (Am. L. Inst., Tentative Draft 2019).
Unnumbered discussion draft:	Restatement (Third) of Torts §§ 3–4 (Am. L. Inst., Discussion Draft 1999).
	Principles of the L. of Student Sexual Misconduct: Procedural Framework for Colls. and Univs. § 3.5b (Am. L. Inst., Discussion Draft 2018).

23.1(e) Commercial databases and other online sources

When your source is in a commercial database, follow **Rule 23.1(a)–(d)** with these exceptions.[15] In place of the year of publication or adoption, insert a comma and one space after the author abbreviation or draft designation and then give the database name and the date information provided by the database itself, which may be a year, an exact date, a publishing body's meeting session, or some combination thereof.[16] Abbreviate words in **Appendices 3(A)** and **3(E)**.

Examples

Restatement (Second) of Judgments § 75(3)(a) (Am. L. Inst., Lexis+ 1982).

Principles of the L. of Student Sexual Misconduct: Procedural Framework for Colls. and Univs. § 2.2 (Am. L. Inst., Discussion Draft, Westlaw Edge Oct. 2018).

23.1(f)[FN] Full citations to restatements or principles in academic footnotes

ACADEMIC FORMATTING

Follow **Rule 23.1(a)–(e)**, but use large and small capital letters for the title, series, subject matter, and author abbreviation.[17]

Examples

21 RESTATEMENT OF PROP.: SERVITUDES § 453 illus. 1 (AM. L. INST. 1944).

64 PRINCIPLES OF THE L. OF FAM. DISSOLUTION: ANALYSIS & RECOMMENDATIONS § 2.02 (AM. L. INST. 2002).

71 RESTATEMENT OF LIAB. INS. § 50 (AM. L. INST., Westlaw Edge Oct. 2020).

23.2 Short Citations to Restatements or Principles

23.2(a) Using *id.* or other short citations to restatements or principles

When appropriate (**Rule 11.3(c)**), use *id.* as the short citation.[18] When *id.* is not appropriate, keep all components of the full citation except the publication parenthetical.

Examples

Full citation:	Short citation:
Restatement (Second) of Conts. § 90 (Am. L. Inst. 1979).	Restatement (Second) of Conts. § 90.
Restatement (Third) of Restitution § 37(2) (Am. L. Inst., Westlaw Edge Oct. 2020).	Restatement (Third) of Restitution § 37(2).

23.2(b)FN Short citations to restatements or principles in academic footnotes

ACADEMIC FORMATTING

Follow **Rule 23.2(a)**, but use large and small capital letters for the title, series, subject matter, and author abbreviation.[19] Repeat the full citation if the guideline, code, or act has not been cited, in full or in short form (including *id.*) in the same footnote or in one of the previous five footnotes.[20] Do not use *supra* (**Rule 11.4**).[21]

Examples

51 RESTATEMENT OF PROP.: SERVITUDES § 451 (AM. L. INST. 1944).

52 *Id.*

53 PRINCIPLES OF THE L. OF AGGREGATE LITIG. § 2.01 (AM. L. INST., Westlaw Edge Oct. 2020).

. . .

55 RESTATEMENT OF PROP.: SERVITUDES § 450.

56 PRINCIPLES OF THE L. OF AGGREGATE LITIG. § 2.02.

. . .

64 RESTATEMENT OF PROP.: SERVITUDES § 451 (AM. L. INST. 1944).

23.3 Full Citations to Sentencing Guidelines, Model Codes, and Model Acts

For the ABA model code or rules of professional responsibility, see **Rule 23.5**. Use this rule for all other model codes.

23.3(a) Full citation to sentencing guideline, model code, or model act

Begin the citation with the title of the guideline, code, or act, using ordinary type and abbreviating words found in **Appendix 3(E)**.[22] For federal sentencing guidelines, abbreviate "United States" as "U.S."[23] For state sentencing guidelines, use the state's abbreviation from **Appendix 3(B)**.

Following the title, provide a pinpoint reference, indicating sections, subsections, or relevant subdivisions such as comments and illustrations.[24] Abbreviate subdivisions as indicated in **Appendix 3(C)**.[25]

Following the pinpoint reference, add a publication parenthetical.[26] The parenthetical begins with an abbreviation for the promulgator of the guidelines, code, or act (using **Appendices 3(B)** and **3(E)** for abbreviations), followed by the year of adoption, not the year of publication.[27] If the cited version was subsequently amended, use the year of its most recent amendment, even if the portion you are citing was not amended at that time.[28] To cite a tentative or proposed draft, analogize to **Rule 23.1(d)**.[29]

Examples

U.S. Sent'g Guidelines Manual § 2D1.1 (U.S. Sent'g Comm'n 2015).

U.S. Sent'g Guidelines Manual ch. 3, pt. A, introductory cmt. (U.S. Sent'g Comm'n 1990).

U.S. Sent'g Guidelines Manual § 3B1.4 cmt. n.2 (U.S. Sent'g Comm'n 1995).

U.S. Sent'g Guidelines Manual app. A (U.S. Sent'g Comm'n 2014).

Model Penal Code § 2.05 cmt. 1 (Am. L. Inst. 1985).

Model Land Dev. Code § 2-301 (Am. L. Inst. 1976).

Model Relocation Act § 10 (Am. Acad. Matrim. Laws., Tentative Draft 1996).

23.3(b) Commercial databases and other online sources

Cite an online version that is an exact copy (e.g., a PDF) of the sentencing guideline, model code, or model act in the same manner as its print counterpart.[30] You may also append a URL to the full citation if it will substantially improve access to the source.[31] When your source is in a commercial database, follow **Rule 23.3(a)** with these exceptions.[32] In place of the year of adoption, insert a comma and one space after the author abbreviation or draft designation, if any, and then give the database name and the date information provided by the database itself, which may be a year, an exact date, a publishing body's meeting session, or some combination thereof.[33] Abbreviate words in **Appendices 3(A)** and **3(E)**. If you are citing to another online source, check **Rules 30.2** and **30.3** to see if you need to append a URL or cite it as a website.[34]

Examples

Model Penal Code § 401.9(2) (Am. L. Inst., Westlaw Edge through 2019 Ann. Meeting of Am. L. Inst.).

Model Code for Pub. Infrastructure Procurement § 5-202(1)(a) (Am. Bar Ass'n, Westlaw Edge 2007).

U.S. Sent'g Guidelines Manual § 2D1.1 (U.S. Sent'g Comm'n 2015), https://www.ussc.gov/sites/default/files/pdf/guidelines-manual/2018/GLMFull.pdf.

23.3(c)FN Full citations to sentencing guidelines, model codes, or model acts in academic footnotes

ACADEMIC FORMATTING

Follow **Rule 23.3(a)–(b)**, but use large and small capital letters for the title and promulgator abbreviations.[35]

Examples

[35] Model Penal Code § 2.05 cmt. 1 (Am. L. Inst. 1985).

. . .

[57] U.S. Sent'g Guidelines Manual § 1B1.3 cmt. background (U.S. Sent'g Comm'n 2015).

23.4 Short Citations to Sentencing Guidelines, Model Codes, or Model Acts

23.4(a) Using *id.* or other short citations to sentencing guidelines, model codes, or model acts

When appropriate (**Rule 11.3(c)**), use *id.* as the short citation.[36] When *id.* is not appropriate, use one of the short citation options below.[37] In selecting an option, choose one with enough information for the reader to easily recognize the source.[38]

Examples

Full citation:	Model Penal Code § 2.02(2)(a)(i) (Am. L. Inst., Westlaw Edge through 2019 Ann. Meeting of Am. L. Inst.).
Short citation options:	Model Penal Code § 2.02(2)(a)(i). § 2.02(a)(i). *Id.* § 2.02(a)(i).
Full citation:	U.S. Sent'g Guidelines Manual § 4B1.2(a) (U.S. Sent'g Comm'n 2012).
Short citation options:	U.S. Sent'g Guidelines Manual § 4B1.2(a). § 4B1.2(a). *Id.* § 4B1.2(a).

23.4(b)FN Short citations to sentencing guidelines, model codes, or model acts in academic footnotes

ACADEMIC FORMATTING

Follow **Rule 23.4(a)**, but use large and small capital letters for the title and promulgator abbreviations.[39] Repeat the full citation if the guideline, code, or act has not been cited, in full or in short form (including *id.*) in the same footnote or in one of the previous five footnotes.[40] Do not use *supra* (**Rule 11.4**).[41]

Examples

55 MODEL PENAL CODE § 2.02(2)(a)(i) (AM. L. INST. 1985).

56 *Id.* § 2.02(b).

. . .

59 MODEL PENAL CODE § 2.02(a)(ii).

. . .

67 MODEL PENAL CODE § 2.02(a)(i) (AM. L. INST. 1985).

23.5 ABA Model Code or Rules of Professional Responsibility

23.5(a) Full citation to the ABA model code or rules of professional responsibility

A full citation to the American Bar Association's old *Code of Professional Responsibility* and the new *Model Rules of Professional Conduct* contains four or five components, depending on whether a pinpoint reference is available.[42]

Abbreviated name of code or rules | [Pinpoint reference] | (Am. Bar Ass'n | Date).

Example (spaces denoted by ▲)

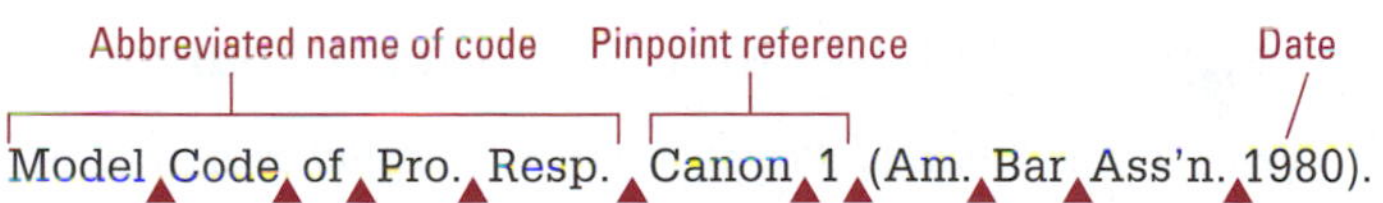

Begin with the title in ordinary type.[43] Abbreviate the *Model Code of Professional Responsibility* as "Model Code of Pro. Resp." Abbreviate the current *Model Rules of Professional Conduct* as "Model Rules of Pro. Conduct."[44]

Following the title, provide a pinpoint reference, indicating sections, subsections, or relevant subdivisions such as comments.[45] Following the pinpoint reference, add a publication parenthetical.[46] Begin the publication parenthetical with the abbreviation for the works' institutional author, the American Bar Association ("Am. Bar Ass'n").[47] Following the author abbreviation, indicate the year of publication.[48]

When citing to a specific part of the *Model Code of Professional Responsibility*:

- Cite an *ethical consideration* using "EC" before the specific ethical consideration number in a pinpoint reference.[49]

Example

Model Code of Pro. Resp. EC 8-2 (Am. Bar Ass'n 1980).

- When citing a specific *disciplinary rule*, use the prefix "DR."[50]

Example

Model Code of Pro. Resp. DR 7-107 (Am. Bar Ass'n 1980).

- If the source is a note to a section, indicate that using "note" and the note number in the pinpoint reference.[51]

Example

Model Code of Pro. Resp. Canon 7 note 2 (Am. Bar Ass'n 1980).

When citing to a specific part of the *Model Rules of Professional Conduct*:

- Use the abbreviation "r." and then a space before the rule number in a pinpoint reference.[52]

Example

Model Rules of Pro. Conduct r. 1.15 (Am. Bar Ass'n 1983).

- If the source is a comment on a rule, indicate that using the abbreviation "cmt." and the comment number, if any, in the pinpoint reference.[53]

Example

Model Rules of Pro. Conduct r. 3.5 cmt. 4 (Am. Bar Ass'n 1983).

23.5(b) Commercial databases and other online sources

If you are citing to the *Code of Professional Responsibility* or the *Model Rules of Professional Conduct* as it appears on the American Bar Association's website, treat it as an official version;[54] follow **Rule 23.5(a)** with no changes. You may append a URL to the full citation if it will substantially improve access to the source.[55] When your source is in a commercial database, follow **Rule 23.5(a)** with these exceptions.[56] In place of the year, insert a comma and one space after "Am. Bar Ass'n," and then give the database name and the date information provided by the database itself.[57] Abbreviate words in **Appendices 3(A)** and **3(E)**. If you are citing to another online source, check **Rules 30.2** and **30.3** to see if you need to append a URL or cite it as a website.[58]

Examples

Model Rules of Pro. Conduct r. 1.4 (Am. Bar Ass'n, Westlaw through 2018).

Model Rules of Pro. Conduct r. 1.18 (Am. Bar Ass'n 1983), https://www.americanbar.org/groups/professional_responsibility/publications/model_rules_of_professional_conduct/rule_1_18_duties_of_prospective_client/.

23.5(c)FN Full citations to the ABA model code or rules of professional responsibility in academic footnotes

ACADEMIC FORMATTING

Follow **Rule 23.5(a)**, but use large and small capital letters for the name of the code or rule and the author abbreviation.[59]

Examples

135 MODEL RULES OF PRO. CONDUCT r. 3.2 (AM. BAR ASS'N 1983).

136 MODEL CODE OF PRO. RESP. EC 3-5 (AM. BAR ASS'N 1980).

23.5(d) Short citation to the ABA model code or rules of professional responsibility

When appropriate (**Rule 11.3(c)**), use *id.* as the short citation to ethics opinions.[60] When *id.* is not appropriate, use all the components of the full citation except the date parenthetical.

Example

Full citation: Model Rules of Pro. Conduct r. 1.8 (Am. Bar Ass'n 1983).

Short citation: Model Rules of Pro. Conduct r. 1.8.

23.5(e)FN Short citations to uniform laws in academic footnotes

ACADEMIC FORMATTING

Follow **Rule 23.5(d)**, but use large and small capital letters as described in **Rule 23.5(c)FN**.[61] Repeat the full citation if the guideline, code, or act has not been cited, in full or in short form (including *id.*) in the same footnote or in one of the previous five footnotes.[62] Do not use *supra* (**Rule 11.4**).[63]

Example

Full citation: MODEL RULES OF PRO. CONDUCT r. 1.8 (AM. BAR ASS'N 1983).

Short citation: MODEL RULES OF PRO. CONDUCT r. 1.8.

23.6 Citations to Uniform Laws

Use this rule when citing to a uniform act itself, and not the act as it has been adopted by a particular state.[64] When citing a uniform law as adopted by a particular state, cite it as a statute, using **Rule 14.4** and the components of the state's statutory code (consult **Appendix 1(B)**).

23.6(a) Full citation to uniform law

In general, cite uniform laws analogously to federal statutes under **Rule 14.2.**[65] Begin with the title of the uniform law.[66] Abbreviate the Uniform Commercial

Code as "U.C.C."; for other uniform laws, abbreviate words in the title, in ordinary type, using **Appendix 3(E)**.[67] You may omit articles and prepositions not needed for clarity. Following the title, provide a pinpoint reference, indicating sections, subsections, or other relevant subdivisions such as comments.[68] Abbreviate subdivisions using **Appendix 3(C)**.[69]

After the pinpoint reference, provide a publication parenthetical with an abbreviation of the name of the uniform act's author according to **Rule 20.1(b)(3)**.[70] Then indicate the year of publication.[71] To cite a tentative or proposed draft, analogize to **Rule 23.1(d)**.[72]

Examples

Unif. Common Int. Ownership Act § 4-113 (Unif. L. Comm'n 2014).

U.C.C. § 2-207(1) (Am. L. Inst. & Unif. L. Comm'n 1977).

23.6(b) Publication in *Uniform Laws Annotated*

When citing a uniform law to its publication in *Uniform Laws Annotated* (abbreviated as "U.L.A."), first provide the title and the section number as described in **Rule 23.6(a)**, and then insert a comma followed by one space.[73] Then provide the volume number or supplement number of the U.L.A. and the page number on which the cited section begins.[74] If the uniform act was withdrawn, superseded, or amended, indicate that status and the year it took place in a parenthetical.[75]

Examples

Unif. Parentage Act § 803(b)(2), 9B U.L.A. 364 (2001).

Unif. Sales Act § 17, 1 U.L.A. 309 (1950) (withdrawn 1962).

23.6(c) Commercial databases and online sources

Cite an online version that is an exact copy (e.g., a PDF) of a uniform act in the same manner as its print counterpart.[76] You may also append a URL to the full citation if it will substantially improve access to the source.[77] When your source is in a commercial database, follow **Rule 23.6(a)–(b)** with these exceptions.[78] In place of the year of adoption, insert a comma and one space after the author abbreviation or draft designation, if any, and then give the database name and the date information provided by the database itself, which may be a year, an exact date, a publishing body's meeting session, or some combination thereof.[79] Abbreviate words in **Appendices 3(A)** and **3(E)**. If you are citing to another online source, check **Rules 30.2** and **30.3** to see if you need to append a URL or cite it as a website.[80]

Examples

U.C.C. § 5-102 (Am. L. Inst. & Unif. L. Comm'n, Westlaw Edge Apr. 2020).

U.C.C. § 4A-301(a) (Am. L. Inst. & Unif. L. Comm'n, Lexis+ 2020).

Unif. Ltd. Liab. Co. Act § 205 (Unif. L. Comm'n, Westlaw Edge through 2019 Ann. Meeting of the Nat'l Conference of Comm'rs on Unif. State L.).

Unif. Elec. Wills Act § 2(3) (Unif. L. Comm'n 2019), https://www.uniformlaws.org/HigherLogic/System/DownloadDocumentFile.ashx?DocumentFileKey=8529b916-8ede-67e4-68eb-e0f7b1cb6528&forceDialog=0.

23.6(d)FN Full citations to uniform laws in academic footnotes

ACADEMIC FORMATTING

Follow **Rule 23.6(a)–(c)**, but use large and small capital letters for the title of the uniform law, the abbreviation U.L.A, and the author abbreviation.[81]

Examples

80 UNIF. COMMON INT. OWNERSHIP ACT § 4-113 (1994).

87 UNIF. SALES ACT § 17, 1 U.L.A. 309 (1950) (withdrawn 1962).

90 UNIF. STATUTORY FORM OF POWER OF ATT'Y ACT prefatory n. (UNIF. L. COMM'N, Lexis+ 2020).

23.6(e) Using *id.* or other short citations to uniform laws

When appropriate (**Rule 11.3(c)**), use *id.* as the short citation.[82] When *id.* is not appropriate, use one of the short citation options below.[83] In selecting an option, choose one with enough information for the reader to easily recognize the source.[84]

Example

Full citation:	Unif. P'ship Act § 202(c) (1997).
Short citation options:	Unif. P'ship Act § 202(c).
	§ 202(c).
	Id. § 202(c).

23.6(f)FN Short citations to uniform laws in academic footnotes

ACADEMIC FORMATTING

Follow **Rule 23.6(e)**, but use large and small capital letters as described in **Rule 23.6(d)FN**.[85] Repeat the full citation if the guideline, code, or act has not been cited, in full or in short form (including *id.*) in the same footnote or in one of the previous five footnotes.[86] Do not use *supra* (**Rule 11.4**).[87]

Example

Full citation:	UNIF. P'SHIP ACT § 202(c) (1997).
Short citation options:	UNIF. P'SHIP ACT § 202(c).
	§ 202(c).
	Id. § 202(c).

24 Looseleaf Services

Fast Formats

Case in looseleaf reporter	*Glasow v. DuPont de Nemours & Co.*, 7 Trade Reg. Rep. (CCH) ¶ 74,791, at 101,998 (N.D. May 17, 2005).
Material in transfer binder	*Copyright.net Music Publ'g v. MP3 .com*, [2002–2003 Transfer Binder] Copyright L. Dec. (CCH) ¶ 28,613, at 35,941 (S.D.N.Y. 2003).
Non-case material in looseleaf service	*Environmental Groups Appeal BLM Decision to Allow Coal Mine to Expand in Colorado*, 44 Env't Rep. 292 (BNA) (Feb. 1, 2013).
Citation in academic footnote	ACADEMIC FORMATTING 25 Glasow v. DuPont de Nemours & Co., 7 Trade Reg. Rep. (CCH) ¶ 74,791, at 101,998 (N.D. May 17, 2005).
Short citations	*Glasow*, 7 Trade Reg. Rep. (CCH) ¶ 74,795, at 102,002. 31 *Glasow*, 7 Trade Reg. Rep. (CCH) ¶ 74,795, at 102,002.

24.1 Full Citations to Case Materials in Looseleaf Services

A full citation to a case or administrative decision printed in a looseleaf service or topical reporter is similar to a full citation to a case under **Rule 12**, and it uses the following components.[1]

Case name, | Looseleaf volume | Looseleaf name or abbreviation | (Publisher abbreviation) | Initial subdivision | Pinpoint reference | (Court abbreviation | Date), | [Subsequent history].

Example (spaces denoted by ▲)

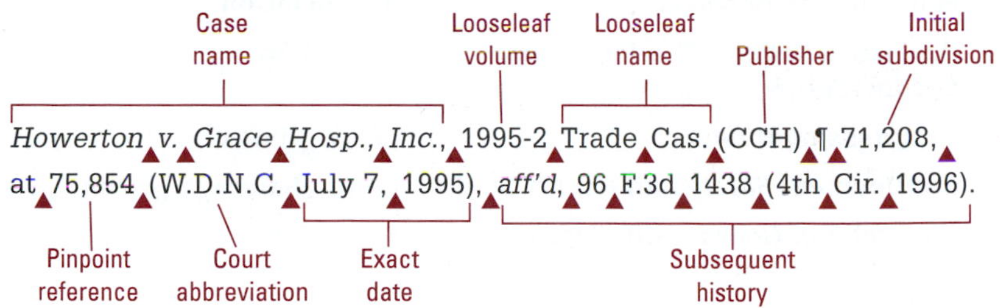

24.1(a) Case name

Present case names in italics, following **Rule 12.2** for components and abbreviating words that appear in **Appendix 3(E)**.[2] After the case name, insert a comma and one space.[3]

24.1(b) Looseleaf volume designation

Designate the volume of the looseleaf service in which the case appears, followed by one space.[4] Volumes may be designated by a number, a year, a descriptive subtitle from the volume's spine, or a combination of these. If the volume designation, or part thereof, might be confused with the looseleaf service's abbreviation, enclose the volume designation in square brackets.[5] If the volume is a transfer binder, indicate the years it covers.[6]

Examples (volume designation in red)

United States v. Med. Mut. of Ohio, 1998-1 Trade Cas. (CCH) ¶ 50,846, at 51,942 (N.D. Ohio Sept. 30, 1998).

Bradley v. United States, 91-2 U.S. Tax Cas. (CCH) ¶ 50,332 (2d Cir. June 24, 1991).

Black & Decker Corp. v. United States, [2004] 2 Stand. Fed. Tax Rep. (CCH) (U.S. Tax Cas. (CCH)) ¶ 50,359 (D. Md. Aug. 3, 2004).

Taft v. Ackermans, [Current Transfer Binder] Fed. Sec. L. Rep. (CCH) ¶ 93,245, at 96,224 (S.D.N.Y. Apr. 13, 2005).

Bishop v. PCS Admin., [2006 Transfer Binder] Fed. Sec. L. Rep. (CCH) ¶ 93,882 (N.D. Ill. May 23, 2006).

24.1(c) Looseleaf service abbreviation

Treat looseleaf service abbreviations analogously to reporter abbreviations in **Rule 12.4**.[7] Present them in ordinary type, and abbreviate any words appearing in **Appendix 5(B)** or **Appendix 3(E)** (but note unique abbreviations for some common reporters below).[8] Insert spaces between adjacent abbreviations if one of them has two or more letters.[9] Use ordinal contractions as shown in **Rule 4.3**.[10] Insert one space after the looseleaf abbreviation.[11]

Examples (spaces denoted by ▲)

Full name of looseleaf:	**Abbreviation:**
American Federal Tax Reporters, Second Series	A.F.T.R.2d
Congressional Index	Cong.▲Index
Employment Safety and Health Guide	Empl.▲Safety▲&▲Health▲Guide
Federal Tax Coordinator Second	Fed.▲Tax▲Coordinator▲2d
Media Law Reporter	Media▲L.▲Rep.
Standard Federal Tax Reporter **(bound as *U.S. Tax Cases*)**	Stand.▲Fed.▲Tax▲Rep. (U.S.▲Tax▲Cas.)
United States Patent Quarterly, Second Series	U.S.P.Q.2d

24.1(d) Publisher

Immediately following the looseleaf service abbreviation, indicate the name of the looseleaf publisher, in parentheses, using the abbreviations in **Chart 24.1**.[12] If the publisher is not listed in **Chart 24.1**, abbreviate any words in its name appearing in **Appendices 3(B)**, **3(E)**, or **5(B)** and according to **Rule 20.1(b)(3)**.[13] Insert one space after the closing parenthesis.[14]

24.1(e) Initial subdivision and pinpoint references

To cite a looseleaf that is updated by interfiling new material, indicate the initial subdivision with a paragraph (¶) or section (§) symbol, followed by one space and the paragraph or section number.[15] To assist the reader in locating specific material, you may add the preposition "at" and a pinpoint reference to a page number.[16]

Newsletter-style looseleafs are typically organized in a binder by report number. For looseleafs organized that way, use the abbreviation "No." followed by the report number.[17] If possible, add a pinpoint reference to a paragraph, section, or page number within the report.[18]

If a looseleaf uses page numbers or another form of subdivision, analogize to the rules above to the extent possible, providing enough information for readers to locate the cited material.[19] See **Rules 5** through **9** for more information on pages and other subdivisions.

Examples

In re Silicon Graphics, Inc. Sec. Litig., [1997 Transfer Binder] Fed. Sec. L. Rep. (CCH) ¶ 99,468 (N.D. Cal. May 23, 1997).

SEC v. Eskind, 29 Sec. Reg. & L. Rep. (BNA) No. 27, at 934 (N.D. Cal. June 26, 1997).

EEOC v. Golden St. Glass Co., EEOC Compl. Man. (CCH) § 615.1, at 3202 (C.D. Cal. Mar. 6, 1980).

CHART 24.1 Abbreviations for Names of Looseleaf Publishers

Publisher name:	Abbreviation (spaces denoted by ▲):
American Bar Association	ABA
Bloomberg Law	BL
Bloomberg BNA or Bureau of National Affairs	BNA
Clark Boardman Callaghan	CBC
Commerce Clearing House, Inc. *or* CCH	CCH
Environmental Law Institute	Env't Law Inst.
LexisNexis	LexisNexis
LRP Publications	LRP
Matthew Bender	MB
National Association of College and University Attorneys	NACUA
Pike & Fischer	P▲&▲F
Practising Law Institute	PLI
Prentice-Hall	P-H
Research Institute of America, Inc.	RIA
Thomson Reuters West	West
University Publications of America	Univ.▲Pub.▲Am.
University Publishing Group	Univ.▲Pub.▲Group
William S. Hein & Co.	Hein
Wolters Kluwer Law & Business *or* Aspen Publishers	Wolters▲Kluwer▲L.▲&▲Bus.

24.1(f) Commercial databases and other parallel citations

There are two instances in which you will need at least a partial parallel citation. First, if the service material is in a commercial database, after the pinpoint reference, insert a comma and one space and then add a parallel citation indicating the name of the database provider and then the unique database identifier, if any.[20] Second, if a publisher will eventually bind the looseleaf material, add the name of the bound work in parentheses immediately after the volume designation.[21]

24.1(g) Court abbreviation

Follow **Rule 12.6** for cases.[22] Abbreviations for court names are in **Appendices 1** and **4**.

SIDEBAR 24.1 Understanding Paragraphs in Looseleaf Services

In looseleaf terminology, a "paragraph" usually does not refer to one block of type. Instead, it can designate any quantity of material and often spans several pages. A case published in a looseleaf service is typically assigned a single paragraph number. The process of determining the paragraph number can be confusing, because some pages within the source may contain both a paragraph number and a page number. When a service contains both paragraph and page numbers, use the paragraph symbol (¶) before the paragraph number, followed by a comma, the preposition "at," and the page number.

24.1(h) Date of decision

Follow **Rule 12.7** for cases, but always provide the exact date (Month Day, Year) of the decision if it is in a looseleaf service (and just the year if it is in a bound service).[23]

24.1(i) Subsequent history

Present subsequent history information in accordance with **Rule 12.8**.

24.1(j) Prior history and other information

Follow **Rules 12.9** (prior history) and **12.10** (parenthetical information).

24.1(k)^FN Full citations to looseleaf service case materials in academic footnotes

ACADEMIC FORMATTING

Follow **Rule 24.1(a)–(j)**, but present case names in ordinary type, as shown in **Rule 12.2(a)(2)^FN**.[24]

24.1(l) Short citations to looseleaf service case materials

Follow **Rule 12.16** for cases.[25]

24.1(m)^FN Short citations to looseleaf service case materials in academic footnotes

ACADEMIC FORMATTING

In academic footnotes, italicize a single party's name in the case's short citation.[26] Analogize to examples in **Rule 12.16(g)^FN**.[27]

24.2 Full Citations to Non-Case Materials in Looseleaf Services

Follow the rule that covers an analogous source (e.g., **Rule 21** for periodicals), and substitute the looseleaf service citation components as shown in

Rule 24.1.[28] Cite the exact date (Month Day, Year) of enactment when citing a statute or regulation.[29] Citations to articles or commentary should also use the exact date (Month Day, Year), if available.[30]

Examples

Internet Service Provider Not Liable for User's Infringement, 2 Copyright L. Rep. (CCH) No. 290, at 4 (May 24, 2002).

Comparison of Rights of Legitimated and Legitimate Children, 2 Immigr. L. Serv. 2d (West) § 7:38 (Aug. 2016).

24.3 Short Citations to Non-Case Materials in Looseleaf Services

Follow the rules for short citations to an analogous source.[31]

25 Court Documents, Transcripts, and Appellate Records

Fast Formats

Affidavit	Corcoran Aff. ¶¶ 1–3.
Brief	Br. Supp. Mot. Reh'g 19:4–9, ECF No. 92.
Court order	Order 3:23–4:5, ECF No. 45.
Discovery document	Pl.'s Interrogs. Nos. 3, 6, & 9.
Pleading	2d Am. Answer ¶¶ 5–12, ECF No. 8.
Hearing transcript	TRO Hr'g Tr. 45:3, Jan. 15, 2014.
Hearing recording	Oral Arg. 0:23:12–0:25:34, Nov. 16, 2020 (audio).
Deposition transcript	Montgomery Dep. 28:12–29:16.
Short citations	Corcoran Aff. ¶ 5. Pl.'s Interrogs. Nos. 6 & 9. TRO Hr'g Tr. 46:15.

25.1 Scope of Rule

Rule 25 applies to documents associated with the same case as the document for which you are drafting the citation. These include, but are not limited to, pleadings, motions and responses, briefs, memoranda of law, discovery and disclosure material, affidavits, declarations, evidence, notices, stipulations, orders, and judgments. See **Rule 12.15** to cite court documents, transcripts, or records in cases other than the one in which you are litigating.

There are two overarching considerations when crafting citations to documents that have to do with a particular case: the narrow audience and the word count. First, the typical audience for these documents will be the parties involved and one or more judges. This is a much narrower audience than a document that may be disseminated through a state bar publication or a law review. Thus, this rule's simplified citation format reflects the shared understanding of the judge and the parties in that case. It also reflects the relative ease of access the judge(s) and parties have to the particular documents being cited. Second, many jurisdictions now have word counts for documents filed in a case. Consequently, practitioners are particularly sensitive to lengthy citations that convey redundant or otherwise unnecessary information to their narrow audience.

Where applicable, the text notes long-standing conventions and contrasts them with modern conventions, which are guided by these two concerns. When applying **Rule 25**, you must occasionally decide whether to follow the traditional format or the modern format based on the jurisdiction and other factors of your particular case.

25.2 Full Citations to Court Documents in the Same Case

A full citation to a court document has the following components, depending on whether you include a date and whether the document has an Electronic Case Filing (ECF) number from PACER.[1] See **Sidebar 25.1** for information on ECF and PACER.

Document name | Pinpoint reference, | [ECF No. | Electronic Case Filing number] | [Month Day, Year].

Examples (spaces denoted by ▲)

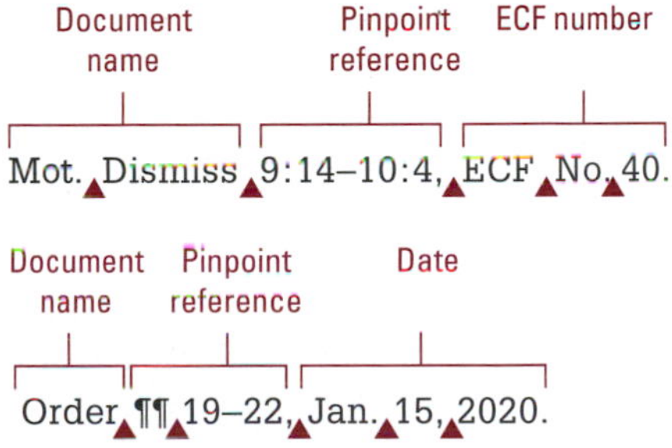

SIDEBAR 25.1 PACER and ECF

All federal courts and many state courts use an online case management system called PACER, which stands for Public Access to Court Electronic Records. Each case filed in any court, including one filed electronically through PACER, is assigned a docket number, also known as a case number. See **Sidebar 12.7** for more about docket numbers. When a jurisdiction uses PACER, each document filed in a particular case is further assigned a unique Electronic Case File (ECF) number. For example, Ronald Albert filed a civil complaint against the Social Security Administration Commissioner in the U.S. District Court of Maine using PACER on June 17, 2020. PACER automatically assigned that case the docket number 2:20-cv-00210-JDL. The first document filed under that particular docket number happens to be the complaint, so the complaint in case 2:20-cv-00210-JDL is ECF number 1. Many documents in a case are not filed with the court, such as transcripts of depositions taken outside of court. Those documents do not have ECF numbers. You can still cite to those, but the citation will not include an ECF number.

25.2(a) Document name

Begin with the name of the document, set out in ordinary type.[2] Unless local court rules provide otherwise (consult **Appendix 2**), you may abbreviate any word that appears in **Appendix 3(G)** or any word of seven letters or more, so long as the result is unambiguous.[3] Eliminate articles and prepositions not needed for clarity.[4] If you must use a party's name, abbreviate it according to **Rule 12.2**.

For documents that include a person's full name in the title, such as an affidavit, declaration, or deposition, use only the person's surname unless there are two people with the same surname in the case, and thus using both a given name and surname in the document name would reduce confusion.[5] Drop any prefixes or suffixes to a person's names such as "Dr.," "Mrs.," "General," or "III."

Affidavits, depositions, and declarations are titled with the person's name and then the document abbreviation, no matter how the title appears on the document.[6] In other words, an affidavit entitled "Affidavit of Soleil Patel" and an affidavit entitled "Soleil Patel's Affidavit" would both be abbreviated as "Patel Aff." See **Sidebar 25.2** for more guidance regarding document names.

Examples

Document name:	**Abbreviation:**
Declaration of Jinfeng Su	Su Decl.
Affidavit of Lieutenant Cynthia Allen	Allen Aff.
Dr. Tyrone Gein's Deposition (when Shelly Gein is also a plaintiff in the case)	Tyrone Gein Dep.

For pleadings, motions, and discovery, you may also eliminate any words on the face of the document not needed for clarity; do not eliminate a word,

SIDEBAR 25.2 **More on Document Names**

Rule 25.2(a) captures the modern trend in court documents to reduce the number of words in a document title so long as the result is unambiguous. Because most court documents are filed electronically, many courts have shifted to imposing word count limits rather than page limits on filings. Some attorneys still use a person's full name the first time the source is cited in a document, sometimes including prefixes and suffixes, and then use only the surname for subsequent citations. Additionally, some attorneys prefer to completely spell out a document name the first time it is cited and then use its abbreviation in subsequent citations. And still others do not omit any words from the title on the face of the document. Unless required by a local court rule (or supervising attorney) to do something different, following **Rule 25.2(a)** in modern times is sufficient. The most important rule is to be consistent within each document.

however, if there would be any confusion as to what document you were referring to. Traditionally, motions for summary judgment would be abbreviated as "Mot. Summ. J." The modern trend, however, is to abbreviate that motion as "MSJ." See **Sidebar 25.2**.

Examples

	Document name:	**Abbreviation:**
When there is only one plaintiff:	Plaintiff's Complaint	Compl.
When there are two or more defendants:	Defendant Gloria Hawking's Answer	Hawking's Answer
When there is only one defendant and motion:	Defendant's Objection to Motion in Limine	Obj. to Mot. Lim.
When there is one plaintiff, but more than one defendant, and the interrogatories have sequential numbering:	Plaintiff GroundZerious Network Company's 2nd Set of Interrogatories to Defendant Martin Armstrong	Pl.'s Interrog. to Def. Armstrong
When there is only one motion for reconsideration in the case:	Petitioners' Motion for Reconsideration Under Rule 71.2	Mot. for Recons.
When there are multiple defendants and motions for summary judgment:	Defendant Sony Corporation's Motion for Partial Summary Judgment No. 3	Sony Corp.'s Partial MSJ No. 3

25.2(b) Pinpoint references

Following the document name, use its subdivisions to provide the most specific pinpoint reference possible.[7] Litigation documents commonly use paragraph numbers, page numbers, or page and line numbers (joined by a colon and no spaces). If the document has volume numbers such as a lengthy deposition or trial transcript, include the volume number.[8] Insert one space after the title, insert "vol." as the abbreviation, one space, the number in either Roman or Arabic numerals depending on how it appears on the front cover of the document, and a comma and one space before the appropriate pinpoint reference.[9]

If there is a possibility of confusion between a number used in the document's name and the pinpoint reference, you may insert the preposition "at" before a pinpoint *page* number.[10] See also **Sidebar 5.2** for guidance on presenting a span of pinpoint references.

Examples

1st Am. Answer ¶¶ 1–5, ECF No. 26.

MSJ No. 2 at 3:19–4:10, ECF No. 78.

Pl.'s Interrogs. to Rawley ¶¶ 21–32, July 8, 2016.

Pl.'s Mot. Lim. 3 at 4:7–11, ECF No. 131.

Reese Dep. vol. 4, 276:01–27.

25.2(c) ECF number

The ECF number is the fastest way to locate a specific filed document. If a document has an ECF number, always use it in the citation by inserting a comma and a space immediately following the pinpoint reference; then insert the abbreviation "ECF No." and the number.[11] There is no need to include both a date and the ECF number in the citation. See **Sidebar 25.1** for more about ECF numbers.

Example

Correct: Pls.' Am. Answer ¶ 67, ECF No. 14.

Incorrect: Pls.' Am. Answer ¶ 67, ECF No. 14, Oct. 10, 2020.

25.2(d) Date of filing, service, or preparation

Generally, a date is not required.[12] If the presiding court's rules require a date, if a date will help identify a particular document that does not have an ECF number (e.g., if two documents have the same title), or if the date is particularly relevant, set out the month, day, and year of the document's filing after the pinpoint reference.[13] Orders issued by the court may have been written a few days before being filed. If the date shown on the face of the order is different than the filing date, use the filing date.

For material served on opposing counsel but not filed with the court, use the date shown in the certificate of service. If the document was neither filed nor served, use its date of preparation (e.g., the date a deposition was taken). In any of these situations, abbreviate the month according to **Appendix 3(A)**.

Examples

Discovery document with no ECF number when the date is important:	Def.'s Req. Admiss. Nos. 12–14, May 26, 2020.
Order from municipal court that does not have an ECF number:	Order of Protection at 2, July 13, 2020.

25.3 Full Citations to Exhibits

Court documents frequently have attachments referred to as exhibits. When citing to an exhibit, it will usually be attached to the document you are drafting, to a different filing in the same case, or to an affidavit or declaration. If the exhibit is going to be attached to the document you are creating, and it is the first time you have cited to the exhibit, begin with "Ex." and the number or letter you have chosen to designate it followed by a comma. Then, as much as possible, give your exhibit a title, following **Rule 25.2(a)** and abbreviating any words in **Appendix 3(E)**, and give the pinpoint reference to the exhibit following **Rule 25.2(b)**. You will not have an ECF number to include.

To cite to an exhibit that was attached to another filing in your case, but is not attached to the document you are currently drafting, begin with the other document's title following **Rule 25.2(a)**, then one space, and the abbreviation "Ex." and its exhibit number.[14] Add a comma and one space after the exhibit number and then insert a pinpoint reference.[15] Pinpoint references should refer to specific locations within the attachment. Most attorneys use an "at" after the comma if the pinpoint reference is a page number.[16] Include the ECF number after the pinpoint reference and, if it would be helpful to the reader, include a parenthetical explaining what the exhibit is.

To cite an exhibit attached to an affidavit or declaration, begin with the title of the document, following **Rule 25.2(a)**, followed by a space, the abbreviation "Ex." and the exhibit number or letter, a comma and one space, and the pinpoint reference.[17]

If the exhibit has a Bates number, you may use that as a pinpoint reference if the exhibit does not have any other subdivision markings or using Bates numbers would prevent confusion. See **Sidebar 25.3** for more about Bates numbering.

Examples

Exhibit to be attached to the document being created:	Ex. 8, Chávez Dep. vol. I, 34:11–17.
	Ex. T, Email from Bakian to Jones at KJ0009482.
Exhibit attached to another filing:	Defs.' MSJ Ex. B, at 4:11–18, ECF No. 76 (deposition of Fred Guong).
	Compl. Ex. 4, ¶ 9.7, ECF No. 2 (contract amendment).
Exhibit attached to an affidavit or declaration:	Ronnow Aff. Ex. H, ¶ 18.
	Doty Decl. Ex. 5, at 2.

SIDEBAR 25.3 Bates Numbering

Bates numbering (also known as Bates stamping, Bates branding, Bates coding, or Bates labeling) refers to the unique identifier that a party assigns to every page of documents it produces during the discovery phase of trial. Bates numbering typically begins with the producing party's name or initials and starts with the number 1, preceded by 4 or more zeros. In each case, there may be as many sets of Bates numbered documents as there are parties. For example, in the fictitious case of *Catalina Foothills School District v. Durham School Bus Services*, the school district may label pages it produces as "CFSD0000001" through "CFSD0004336," meaning there are 4,336 *pages* produced in total, not 4,336 *documents*. The defendant may label pages it produces as "Durham00001" through "Durham00964," which amounts to 964 pages produced. Parties Bates number each page even if the documents produced have their own internal page numbers.

25.4 Full Citations to Transcripts or Recordings

Use this rule unless a local court rule requires otherwise (consult **Appendix 2**) or the transcript will be attached as an exhibit, in which case, cite it according to **Rule 25.3**. A full citation to the transcript or recording of a trial, hearing, or deposition in your own case contains four components.

Title | Pinpoint reference | [, Month Day, Year] | [(Medium designation)].

Examples (spaces denoted by ▲)

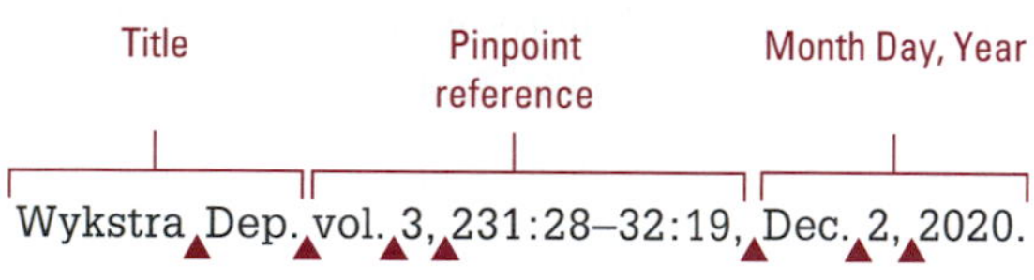

Recording:

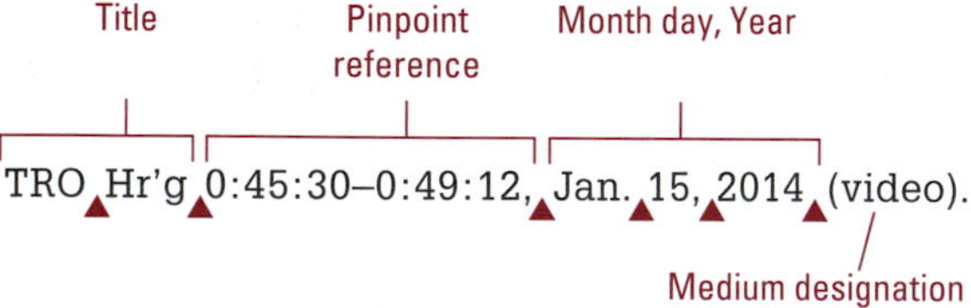

25.4(a) Transcript or recording title

Begin the citation with the name of the transcribed or recorded proceeding, following **Rule 25.2(a)** and abbreviating any word that appears in **Appendix 3(G)**.[18] If in the text you have sufficiently identified a hearing or argument, the title need not be long, but you should always include at least one word. See **Rule 25.2(a)** for more about deposition titles.

Examples

Oral Arg. 0:01:13–0:03:10, Sept. 10, 2020 (audio).

Prelim. Inj. Hr'g Tr. 5:10–29, July 22, 2020.

Zavoli Dep. 114:23–116:3.

25.4(b) Pinpoint references

Follow **Rule 25.2(b)**. To denote a line number within the transcript, use the page number, a colon (with no space on either side), and the line number(s) on which the cited material appears.[19] For example, the number 12:3 represents cited material on line 3 of page 12. If there is a possibility of confusion between a number used in the document's name and the pinpoint reference, you may insert the preposition "at" before a pinpoint page number.[20] See also **Sidebar 5.2** for guidance on presenting a span of references.

If a recording makes use of pinpoint references such as timestamps, provide that information immediately following the title in hours, minutes, and seconds (XX:XX:XX) or the smallest increments possible.

Examples

Document and pinpoint reference:	Citation:
Video of a hearing at 1 hour, 6 minutes, and seconds 4 through 22	Hr'g 1:06:04–22, Aug. 14, 2020 (video).
Trial transcript volume 2, pages 47 through 49	Trial Tr. vol. 2, at 47–49.
Deposition of Marie Ducote at page 120, line 17, through page 122, line 3	Ducote Dep. 120:17–122:3. *or* Ducote Dep. 120:17 to 122:3.

25.4(c) Date of proceeding

Consult **Rule 25.2(c)** to determine whether you need a date.[21] Court proceedings, whether in transcript form or audio or video recorded, are more likely to require a date because they rarely have an ECF number and the title alone may not clearly identify a particular proceeding if there were multiple days or hearings. If needed, following the pinpoint reference, provide the exact date of the transcribed proceeding (Month Day, Year), abbreviating the month according to **Appendix 3(A)**.

Example

Trial Tr. vol. 1, at 6:29–8:06, Feb. 5, 2019.

25.5 Short Citations to Court Documents or Transcripts

Traditional convention prohibits the use of *id.* as a short citation unless the name of the document or transcript is extremely long.[22] Instead, it permits using a shortened form of the document name and a pinpoint reference if the full citation appears in the same general discussion and the reader would be able to locate the full citation quickly.[23] The modern trend, however, is to use *id.* as you would for any other document.[24] If *id.* is inappropriate and the full citation refers to an individual's name, retain the surname only, unless doing so would cause confusion. For more information on surnames, see **Rule 12.2(d)**, **Rule 25.2(a)**, and **Sidebar 25.2**. Do not use "at" before a section or paragraph symbol in a short citation.[25]

Example

Document:	Plaintiff's Amended Answer to Defendant's Counterclaim filed May 22, 2019
Full citation:	Am. Answer to Countercl. ¶ 66, ECF No. 22.
Short citation:	Am. Answer to Countercl. ¶ 66.
	or
	Id. ¶ 66.

25.6 Full Citations to Appellate Records

25.6(a) Full citation options

When a case is on appeal, the court clerks will compile a court record containing all of the relevant documents to the appeal, assigning each page a unique number. Unless a local court rule requires otherwise (see **Appendix 2**), a full citation to an appellate record has two components: an abbreviation for the form of the record and a pinpoint page reference following the preposition "at."[26] Depending on the jurisdiction, the collection of documents from the lower court may be denominated, for example, as a "Record," "Appendix," or "Joint Appendix." See **Appendix 3(G)** for abbreviations. The entire citation may be enclosed in parentheses if desired.[27] Acceptable formats are illustrated below.[28] Once you select a format, use it consistently throughout the document.

Examples

R. at 4:28–5:24.

App. at 37.

(J.A. at 103.)

25.6(b) Pinpoint reference to line numbers

To denote a line number within a specific page of the record, use the page number, a colon (with no space on either side), and the line number.[29] For example, the number 45:16 represents cited material on line 16 of page 45.

Example

The Petitioner, Monique Vasquez, worked as a bank teller for seventeen years. (R. at 6:21.) Her primary job duty was to complete customer transactions. (R. at 7:12–15.)

25.7 Short Citations to Appellate Records

Do not use *id.* as a short citation for record citations unless it will save significant space.[30] Instead, repeat the full citation, as reflected in **Rule 25.6** and its examples.

26 Speeches, Addresses, and Other Oral Presentations

Fast Formats

Unpublished speech	Sonia Sotomayor, Assoc. Justice, U.S. Supreme Court, Commencement Address at New York University School of Law (May 16, 2012).
Transcribed speech	Anna Howard Shaw, The Fundamental Principle of a Republic, at the New York State equal suffrage campaign, City Opera House, Ogdenburg, N.Y. (June 21, 1915) (transcript at http://gos.sbc.edu/s/shaw.html).
Published transcript of a speech	Stephen Breyer, Our Democratic Constitution (Oct. 22, 2001), *in* 77 N.Y.U. L. Rev. 245 (2002).
Citation in academic footnote	ACADEMIC FORMATTING 62 Anna Howard Shaw, The Fundamental Principle of a Republic, at the New York State equal suffrage campaign, City Opera House, Ogdenburg, N.Y. (June 21, 1915) (transcript at http://gos.sbc.edu/s/shaw.html).
Short citations	Shaw, The Fundamental Principle of a Republic. 73 Shaw, *supra* note 62.

26.1 Full Citations to Unpublished Speeches, Addresses, and Other Oral Presentations

A full citation to an unpublished speech, address, or other oral presentation may contain as many as seven components.[1] In this context, "unpublished" means that a transcript of the speech, address, or oral presentation is not available in another publication, such as a newspaper or book; the transcript may nevertheless be available online or may be on file with the author or publisher. See **Sidebar 26.1** for more information on whether to use this rule or **Rule 31.1** for speeches, addresses, or other oral presentations found online.

Speaker's name, | [Speaker's title,] | [Speaker's institutional affiliation,] | Title or subject of presentation | [Pinpoint reference] | (Month Day, Year of presentation) | [(Location of transcript or recording)].

SIDEBAR 26.1 **The Difference Between Using Rule 26 or Using Rule 31.1 for Online Sources**

Citing speeches, addresses, or other oral presentations presents unique challenges in our modern world. Traditional rules of legal citation assume that either you were physically present for the speech or that you have access to a transcript. If this is the case, you can confidently rely on **Rule 26**, including if you watched the oral presentation while it was live streaming, such as on Periscope, or while it was presented live through an online meeting platform such as Zoom or Virbela.

The traditional rules do not account, however, for the pervasive recording of live oral presentations that we encounter today. It is common now for a host to record a presentation given live during an online conference and to post it on a conference website, or for audience members to record a political speech they attend and post it on social media platforms.

If you are referring to an online oral presentation, you have a choice of whether to cite using traditional rules or the more modern rules. If you want to follow the most *traditional* rules, which you should for academic formatting, cite the presentation as an online source using **Rule 31.1** to cite directly to the web page on which you located the video or audio.[2] If the audio or video is embedded in a social media post, refer to **Rule 31.2** as well.[3] For examples of how to cite to online audio or video recordings and broadcasts of speeches, presentations, and other oral presentations according to **Rule 31.1**, see **Rules 28.1(f)** (online videos) and **28.5** (podcasts and other online audio recordings).

Your second choice is to cite using *modern* citation rules. Rather than lumping all online sources into one citation format, the modern rules value retaining the components that identify the source as an online speech, address, or presentation, but include a URL to facilitate access. To cite online speeches, addresses, and other oral presentations using modern citation rules, follow **Rule 26**, paying particular attention to **Rule 26.1(e)**, which requires you to include the URL at which you located the audio or video.

Example (spaces denoted by ▲)

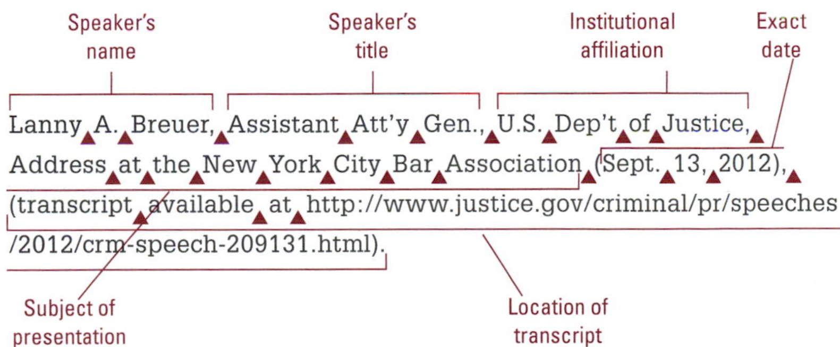

Speaker's name
Speaker's title
Institutional affiliation
Exact date
Lanny▲A.▲Breuer,▲Assistant▲Att'y▲Gen.,▲U.S.▲Dep't▲of▲Justice,▲
Address▲at▲the▲New▲York▲City▲Bar▲Association▲(Sept.▲13,▲2012),▲
(transcript▲available▲at▲http://www.justice.gov/criminal/pr/speeches
/2012/crm-speech-209131.html).
Subject of presentation
Location of transcript

26.1(a) Speaker's name, title, and institutional affiliation

Give the speaker's full name, followed by a comma and one space. Analogize to **Rule 20.1(b)** for book authors. When the speaker is not generally known to the public, or when the information would help the reader appreciate the speaker's significance, you may set out the speaker's title and/or institutional affiliation after his or her name, set off by a comma.[4] You may abbreviate words in the speaker's title or affiliation that appear in **Appendices 3(B)** and **3(E)**.

26.1(b) Subject or title of presentation

When the presentation has a formal title, set it out in full. When it has no formal title, provide a concise description of the subject matter.[5] Present the title or subject in ordinary type, following **Rule 3.2**, **Rule 3.3**, and **Chart 3.1** on capitalization.[6] Insert one space after the subject or title.

Example

Barack Obama, Inaugural Address (Jan. 20, 2009) (video recording at http://www.whitehouse.gov/the_press_office/President_Barack_Obamas_Inaugural_Address).

26.1(c) Pinpoint references

When possible, provide a pinpoint reference to the location of specific material within the presentation, such as a page, paragraph, or section number.[7] See **Rule 5.2** for guidance. If there is no transcript of the speech, but there is a recording, you may use a time marker as the pinpoint reference (XX:XX).

Examples

Deborah Platt Majoras, Chairperson, Fed. Trade Comm'n, Finding the Solutions to Fight Spyware: The FTC's Three Enforcement Principles 7 (Feb. 9, 2006) (transcript at http://www.ftc.gov/speeches/majoras/060209cdtspyware.pdf).

J.K. Rowling, Author, Harvard University Commencement Address 14:37–15:57 (June 5, 2008) (video recording at https://www.youtube.com/watch?v=wHGqp8lz36c).

26.1(d) Date of presentation

Following the title or subject, in parentheses, indicate its exact date (Month Day, Year), if the date is ascertainable.[8] Abbreviate the month according to **Appendix 3(A)**. At a minimum, provide the year. When no date is available, use the abbreviation "n.d." (no date) in place of the year.

Example

Tom Vilsack, Sec'y, U.S. Dep't of Agric., Keynote Address at 2013 USDA Ag Outlook Conference (Feb. 21, 2013).

Russell H. Conwell, Pastor, Grace Baptist Church, Phila., Acres of Diamonds (n.d.) (transcript and audio excerpt available at http://www.americanrhetoric.com/top100speechesall.html).

26.1(e) Information for locating source of transcript or recording

If the speech was transcribed or recorded, add a parenthetical that indicates its location or availability in a private or publicly accessible location.[9]

Example

Barbara Babcock, Judge John Crown Professor of Law, Emerita, Justice Ruth Bader Ginsburg Lecture on Women and the Law at the New York City Bar 2–3 (May 22, 2018) (transcript on file with author).

Steve Jobs, CEO of Apple and Pixar Animation, Commencement Address at Stanford University (n.d.) (video recording available at https://vimeo.com/7976699).

Janelle Monáe, Actress, We Are Not Receptacles . . . We Birthed This Nation (Mar. 6, 2017) (video recording available at https://www.youtube.com/watch?v=lg8jGCab-0I).

26.1(f)FN Full citations to unpublished speeches, addresses, or other oral presentations in academic footnotes

ACADEMIC FORMATTING

There is no difference in the full citation format used in academic footnotes when you are not citing directly to an online source or if you chose to cite to an online source using **Rule 26** (see **Sidebar 26.1**). Follow **Rule 26.1(a)–(e)**. If you chose to cite an online speech, address, or other oral presentation using **Rule 31.1** or **31.2** (see **Sidebar 26.1**), you must use **Rule 31.1(h)** to cite to them in academic footnotes.[10]

26.2 Presentation Transcript Published in Text

When a transcript of the presentation has been published, begin the citation with the first six components of the component diagram in **Rule 26.1**. Do not italicize the title.[11] Omit the "(Location of transcript or recording)" component and instead insert a comma, space, and "*in*" after the date parenthetical. Then insert the citation of the source in which the transcript can be found, analogizing to **Rule 20.3** (collected works), **Rule 21.2** (consecutively paginated periodical), **Rule 21.3** (nonconsecutively paginated periodical), or other relevant rules, depending on the nature of the publication source.[12]

Example

Rev. Martin Luther King, Jr., Christian Minister & Activist, I Have a Dream (Aug. 28, 1963), *in* The Ten Greatest Speeches of the 20th Century 45, 47 (Laura Dysart ed., 2003).

26.3 Short Citations to Speeches, Addresses, and Other Oral Presentations

26.3(a) Using *id.* or other short citations to speeches, addresses, or presentations

When appropriate (**Rule 11.3(c)**), use *id.* as the short citation. When *id.* is not appropriate, use the last name of the speaker, the title of the presentation, and a pinpoint reference (e.g., "at" before a pinpoint page number), if available.[13]

26.3(b)FN Short citations to speeches, addresses, or presentations in academic footnotes

ACADEMIC FORMATTING

When *id.* is not appropriate (**Rule 11.3(c)**), use the *supra* format that follows, cross-referencing the footnote containing the full citation, and providing a pinpoint reference, if available, and using "at" when appropriate.[14] See **Rule 11.4** for additional information on *supra*.

Speaker's last name, | *supra* | note | Note number | [, at Pinpoint reference].

27 Interviews, Letters, and Memoranda

Fast Formats

In-person interview	Interview with Sonia Sotomayor, Assoc. Justice, U.S. Sup. Ct., in Washington, D.C. (Apr. 21, 2011).
Telephone interview	Telephone Interview with Melissa Mikesell, Attorney, All. for Just. (July 18, 2012).
Anonymous or confidential source	Interview with anonymous canine officer (June 19, 2012).
Virtual video interview	Virtual Video Interview with Elizabeth J. McFarland, M.D., Professor of Pediatrics-Infectious Diseases, Univ. of Colo. Anschutz Med. Campus, on Zoom (Feb. 5, 2020).
Interview conducted by another	Telephone Interview by Carrie Gerber with Sofia Dominik, Chief Exec. Officer, Naperville Ltd. (Aug. 24, 2013).
Interview found online (cited per Rule 31.1)	Am. Ass'n of L. Schs., *Becoming a Law Teacher: Interview with a Visiting Associate Professor*, YouTube (Aug. 21, 2019), https://www.youtube.com/watch?v=fd82k89jBkQ.
Unpublished memorandum or letter	Memorandum from Jonathan B. Perlin, Undersec'y for Health, Dep't of Veterans Affs., to Dep't of Veterans Affs. Primary Care Clinicians, Screening and Clinical Management of Traumatic Brain Injury 1 (Jan. 25, 2006) (on file with Fordham Law Review).
Published memorandum or letter	Letter from William Lloyd Garrison to Reverend Samuel J. May (July 17, 1845), *in* 3 *The Letters of William Lloyd Garrison* 303 (Walter M. Merrill ed., 1974).
Citations in academic footnotes	ACADEMIC FORMATTING 52 Interview with Sonia Sotomayor, Assoc. Just., U.S. Sup. Ct., in Washington, D.C. (Apr. 21, 2011). 78 Memorandum from Jonathan B. Perlin, Undersec'y for Health, Dep't of Veterans Affs., to Dep't of Veterans Affs. Primary Care Clinicians, Screening and Clinical Management of Traumatic Brain Injury 1 (Jan. 25, 2006) (on file with Fordham Law Review).

	[135] Letter from William Lloyd Garrison to Reverend Samuel J. May (July 17, 1845), *in* 3 THE LETTERS OF WILLIAM LLOYD GARRISON 303 (Walter M. Merrill ed., 1974).
Short citations	Telephone Interview with Melissa Mikesell. Virtual Video Interview with Elizabeth J. McFarland. Memorandum from Jonathan B. Perlin to Dep't of Veterans Affs. Primary Care Clinicians at 1. [148] Letter from William Lloyd Garrison to Reverend Samuel J. May, *supra* note 135, at 303.

27.1 Full Citations to Interviews Conducted by the Author

A full citation to an interview that you as the writer conducted may contain as many as six components.[1] See **Rule 27.3** for instructions on how to cite to interviews posted online.

Designation with | Interviewee's name, | [Interviewee's title,] | [Institutional affiliation,] | [in Location of interview] | (Month Day, Year).

Example (spaces denoted by ▲)

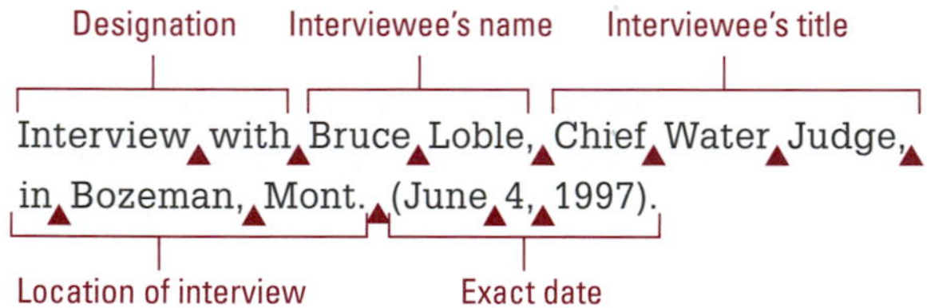

27.1(a) Designation of interview

Depending on the type of interview conducted, the citation begins with a capitalized designation such as "Interview with" (for in-person interview), "Telephone Interview with," "Written Interview with," or "Virtual Video Interview with" (for interviews conducted virtually using a camera through either a video-chat app such as FaceTime or Google Duo or through online video meeting platforms such as Zoom or GoToMeeting).[2]

Examples

Interview with Heather J. Boysel, Managing Member, Gammage & Burnham, PLLC, in Phx., Ariz. (May 18, 2019).

Telephone Interview with Tomiko Brown-Nagin, Daniel P.S. Paul Professor of L., Harvard L. Sch. (Sept. 18, 2020).

Written Interview with Juan Tokatlian, Dir., Dep't Pol. Sci. & Int'l Relations, Univ. San Andrés, Buenos Aires, Arg. (May 16, 2004).

Virtual Video Interview with Amy K. Langenfeld, Clinical Professor L., Ariz. State Univ. Sandra Day O'Connor Coll. L., on Zoom (Sept. 5, 2020).

27.1(b) Interviewee's name, title, and institutional affiliation

Following the designation, set out the interviewee's full name, analogizing to **Rule 20.1(b)** for book authors, using ordinary type.[3] Following the name of the interviewee, add a comma and one space, followed by the interviewee's official title, if any, then a comma, a space, and the interviewee's institutional affiliation, if any.[4] Abbreviate words found in **Appendices 3(B)** and **3(E)**, and capitalize according to **Rule 3.2, Rule 3.3**, and **Chart 3.1**.[5] You may delete articles and prepositions not needed for clarity.

Example

Virtual Video Interview with Laura Sixkiller, Partner, DLA Piper, on JioMeet (Dec. 10, 2020).

27.1(c) Anonymous or confidential interviewee

If it is not possible to identify an interviewee due to privacy or related concerns, indicate that the source is anonymous or confidential, and, to the extent possible, provide a description of the interviewee.

Examples

Interview with anonymous canine officer (June 19, 2012).

Virtual Video Interview with confidential source, on JusTalk (July 27, 2020).

27.1(d) Location of interview

Indicate the location of an on-site, in-person interview with a named interviewee in a prepositional phrase beginning with ", in," abbreviating words found in **Appendix 3(B)**.[6] Indicate the application or online platform that you used for a virtual video interview with a named interviewee in a prepositional phrase beginning with ", on."

Example

Interview with Denise Brogan-Kator, Chief Pol'y Officer, Fam. Equal., in N.Y.C., N.Y. (Oct. 2, 2019).

Virtual Video Interview with Mary Beth Beazley, Professor L., Univ. Nev. Las Vegas, on Google Hangouts (Aug. 23, 2020).

27.1(e) Date parenthetical

In parentheses, set out the exact date (Month Day, Year) of the interview.[7] For a written interview, use the date on which the written answers were provided by the interviewee. Abbreviate the month using **Appendix 3(A)**.

27.2 Full Citations to Interviews Conducted by Another Person

If the author did not personally conduct the interview, follow **Rule 27.1**, but change the designation (**Rule 27.1(a)**) to add a "by" and the interviewer's full name before "with."[8]

Example

Telephone Interview by Razvan Axente with Thomas J. Miner, Assistant Dist. Att'y, 31st Jud. Dist. (June 20, 2012).

27.3 Recorded Interviews Posted Online

Traditional rules of citation assume that interviews will only be conducted in person or over the telephone.[9] **Rules 27.1** and **27.2** cover those instances, in addition to covering those conducted by the author using video cameras for "live" interviews through the use of a video-chat application such as JioMeet or Google Duo or through an online video platform such as Zoom or Skype. In modern times, interviewers frequently record interviews that they conduct using a virtual video application or online platform and then post the interview online. If you are citing to an interview that you either video or audio recorded and posted online for others to access, follow **27.1**; you may choose to append a URL. However, if citing to an interview conducted by someone else that you accessed via an online source, cite to it using **Rule 31.1** or **31.2**, depending on what media the recording is posted to.[10]

27.4FN Full Citations to Interviews in Academic Footnotes

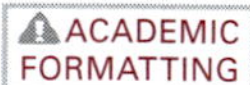

Follow **Rules 27.1–27.2**. There is no difference in the full citation format used in academic footnotes when you are not citing directly to an online source. If you are citing in academic footnotes to a recorded interview found online, use **Rule 31.1(h)**.

27.5 Full Citations to Unpublished Letters and Memoranda

A full citation to an unpublished letter or memorandum has as many as nine components.[11] In this context, "unpublished" means that the letter or memorandum is not available in another publication, such as a newspaper or book; it may nevertheless be available online or may be on file with the author or publisher.

The formatting for a citation to an unpublished letter or memorandum found online depends on whether it appears as an exact copy of the letter or memorandum; whether it retains print characteristics, if not an exact copy; or neither. If the letter or memorandum is an exact copy of the original print source, meaning one that is an unaltered copy of the original, printed source such as a PDF or picture, then use **Rule 27.5**, and a URL is not required.[12] Likewise, if the letter or memorandum online has all the components required to cite it as a letter or memorandum according to **Rule 27.5**, then you use this rule, but in place of the document's location you must append a URL to the end of the citation by placing a comma after the date parenthetical, one space, and then the URL.[13] If neither of these situations apply, you must cite the online letter or memorandum as the website page on which it can be found, using **Rule 31.1** rather than adding the URL as the location at which a reader can find a copy of the letter or memorandum as explained in **Rule 27.5(g)**.[14]

Designation from | Author's name, | [Author's title and affiliation,] | [to] [Recipient's name,] | [Recipient's title and affiliation,] | [Title or subject,] | [Pinpoint reference] | (Month Day, Year) | [(Document's location)] or [, URL].

Example (unpublished memorandum) (spaces denoted by ▲)

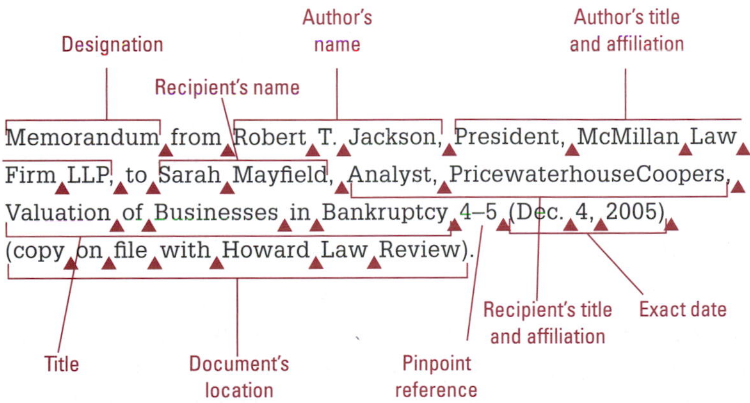

27.5(a) Designation of unpublished letter or memorandum

Begin the citation with the phrase "Letter from," "Memorandum from," or a similar description, in ordinary type, followed by one space.[15]

27.5(b) Author's name, title, and affiliation

Set out the author's full name as shown in the source, analogizing to **Rule 20.1(b)**. Following the surname, add a comma, one space, and the author's title and affiliation, if any, as shown in **Rule 27.1(b)**.[16] Abbreviate any words in the title and institutional affiliation according to **Appendices 3(B)** and **3(E)** and **Chart 12.5**.[17] When there is no title or affiliation, omit the comma between the author's name and "to."[18]

27.5(c) Recipient's name, title, and affiliation

Following the author's name, title, and affiliation, insert a comma, one space, the word "to," another space, and the full name of the recipient or addressee, as shown in the source.[19] Follow **Rule 27.1(b)** to indicate the recipient's title and affiliation, if any. Abbreviate any words in the title and institutional affiliation according to **Appendices 3(B)** and **3(E)** and **Chart 12.5**.[20] Omit the recipient's name and use "to author" in its place when the recipient or addressee of the letter is the author of the work in which the letter is being cited.[21] For "open letters" and other letters without a named recipient, follow the second example.

Examples

Memorandum from Robert E. Fabricant, Gen. Counsel, EPA, to Marianne L. Horinko, Acting Adm'r, EPA, EPA's Authority to Impose Mandatory Controls to Address Global Climate Change Under the Clean Air Act 4–5 (Aug. 28, 2003) (copy on file with Columbia Law Review).

Open Letter from Gregory L. Parham, Adm'r, Animal & Plant Health Inspection Serv., U.S. Dep't of Agric., to Stakeholders, Reducing Backlog of Investigations (Jan. 11, 2012), http://www.aphis.usda.gov/ies/pdf/ies_stakeholders_letter.pdf.

Letter from Bruce P. Smith, Dean, Univ. of Denver Strum Coll. of L., to author (Nov. 11, 2019) (on file with author).

27.5(d) Title or subject of letter or memorandum

Traditionally, legal citation did not require that you include the subject of the letter or memorandum. However, because it is helpful information for the reader, you may provide the title or concisely describe the subject of the letter or memorandum, if you wish. Use **Rule 3.2**, **Rule 3.3**, and **Chart 3.1** for capitalization. Do not abbreviate words unless they are abbreviated in the source.

Example

Letter from Thomas E. Perez, Assistant Att'y Gen., U.S. Dep't of Just., to Kamala D. Harris, Cal. Att'y Gen. & George H. Brown, Gibson, Dunn & Crutcher, 2011 Redistricting Plans for California Congressional Delegation (Jan. 17, 2012), http://redistricting.lls.edu/files/CA%20 preclearance%2020120117.pdf.

27.5(e) Pinpoint references

Indicate, if possible, the page or other subdivision on which the cited material appears, followed by one space.[22] See **Rule 5.2** for more information about pinpoint references.

27.5(f) Date parenthetical

In parentheses, set out the exact date (Month Day, Year) shown on the letter or memorandum.[23] Abbreviate the month using **Appendix 3(A)**. If no date is displayed, use the abbreviation "n.d." (no date) in the parenthetical.

27.5(g) Information for locating copy of letter or memorandum

If possible, indicate a private or publicly accessible location for the letter or memorandum.[24] If it is privately maintained (e.g., in the files of a law review or in the author's own files), describe in a parenthetical where or how readers might obtain a copy (e.g., "copy on file with . . ."). Do not use abbreviations from **Appendix 5(A)**. If an unpublished letter or memorandum is publicly available on the internet, insert a comma followed by the URL.[25] See **Rule 27.5** for when to cite directly to the website on which the letter or memorandum appears, using **Rule 31**.

Examples

Letter from Henry L. Stimson, Sec'y of War, to Earl Warren, Governor of Cal. (Jan. 8, 1943) (on file with Army Corps of Engineers, L.A. District, and copy on file with author).

Letter from Thomas O. Barnett, Assistant Att'y Gen., Dep't of Just., to Robert A. Skitol, Drinker, Biddle & Reath, LLP, Business Review Letter re Proposed Patent Policy 4 (Oct. 30, 2006), http://www.justice.gov/atr/public/busreview/219380.pdf.

27.6 Citations to Published Letters or Memoranda

Cite letters to the editor or other letters published in nonconsecutively paginated periodicals according to **Rule 21.3** (see **Rule 21.3(f)(1)** for an example).[26] Cite letters published in consecutively paginated journals according to **Rule 21.2**.

Cite other published letters and memoranda — such as historical letters collected in other publications — according to **Rule 20.3**, except that you should print the name or the description of the letter or memorandum, if any, in ordinary Roman type, and not in italics.[27] If the letter or memorandum has a date or other identifying information on it, include that information in a parenthetical immediately preceding ", *in* [the source in which the letter or memorandum is published]."[28]

Examples

Letter from T. Broughton to John Wesley, Admonition to Celibacy (Nov. 27, 1735), *in A Collection of Letters on Religious Subjects, from Various Eminent Ministers, and Others* 4–5 (1797).

Letter from Henry David Thoreau to Charles Wyatt Rice (Aug. 5, 1836), *in 1 The Correspondence of Henry D. Thoreau* 19 (Robert N. Hudspeth ed., 2013).

27.7FN Citations to Letters or Memoranda in Academic Footnotes

ACADEMIC FORMATTING

For *unpublished* letters or memoranda cited according to **Rule 27**, there is no difference in the full citation format used in academic footnotes; follow **Rules 27.5–27.6**.

For *published* letters, make sure to check the academic formatting required for the source in which it is published.

If you are citing to a published or unpublished letter found online using **Rule 31**, use **Rule 31.1(h)** to cite to it in academic footnotes.

27.8 Short Citations to Interviews, Letters, or Memoranda

27.8(a) Using *id.* or other short citations to interviews, letters, or memoranda

When appropriate (**Rule 11.3(c)**), use *id.* as the short citation.[29] When *id.* is not appropriate, use the following format for an interview:

Designation | Interviewee's full name.

When *id.* is not appropriate, use the following format for letters or memoranda[30]:

Designation | Author's full name | to Recipient's full name | [at] [Pinpoint reference].

Examples

Full citation: Interview with Heather J. Boysel, Managing Member, Gammage & Burnham, PLLC, in Phx., Ariz. (May 18, 2019).

Telephone Interview by Razvan Axente with Thomas J. Miner, Assistant Dist. Att'y, 31st Jud. Dist. (June 20, 2012).

Letter from Thomas O. Barnett, Assistant Att'y Gen., Dep't of Just., to Robert A. Skitol, Drinker, Biddle & Reath, LLP, Business Review Letter re Proposed Patent Policy 4 (Oct. 30, 2006), http://www.justice.gov/atr/public/busreview/219380.pdf.

Short citation: Interview with Heather J. Boysel.

Telephone Interview with Thomas J. Miner.

Letter from Thomas O. Barnett to Robert A. Skitol at 3.

27.8(b)FN Short citations to interviews, letters, or memoranda in academic footnotes

Use this rule for interviews that are in person, over the telephone, or through virtual video, but that are *not* recorded *and* posted online. For virtual video interviews that are posted online, see **Rule 31.1(h)**. For short forms for letters or memoranda that you must cite using **Rule 31.1** (see **Rule 27.5** and **27.7FN**), use **Rule 31.3**. Otherwise, when *id.* is not appropriate (**Rule 11.3(c)**), use the *supra* format that follows, cross-referencing the earlier footnote containing the full citation of the interview, letter, or memorandum. See **Rule 11.4** for additional information on *supra*.

Designation with | Interviewee's or Author's and Recipient's full names | *supra* | note | Note number, | [at | Pinpoint reference].

Examples

65 Interview with Heather J. Boysel, Managing Member, Gammage & Burnham, PLLC, in Phx., Ariz. (May 18, 2019).

66 *Id.*

...

112 Interview with Heather J. Boysel, *supra* note 65.

...

[178] Letter from Thomas O. Barnett, Assistant Att'y Gen., Dep't of Just., to Robert A. Skitol, Drinker, Biddle & Reath, LLP, Business Review Letter re Proposed Patent Policy 4 (Oct. 30, 2006), http://www.justice.gov/atr/public/busreview/219380.pdf.

[179] *Id.*

...

[191] Letter from Thomas O. Barnett to Robert A. Skitol, *supra* note 178, at 3.

28 Video and Visual Programs, Radio, Audio Recordings, and Microforms

Fast Formats

Movie	*The Adventures of Priscilla, Queen of the Desert* (PolyGram Filmed Entertainment 1994).
Television broadcast	*The Crown: Windsor* (Netflix television broadcast Nov. 4, 2016).
Radio broadcast	*All Things Considered: Critics Question Reporter's Airing of Personal Views* (NPR broadcast Sept. 26, 2006).
Video only available online	Reno May, *California Gun Law Basics*, YouTube (Mar. 23, 2020), https://www.youtube.com/watch?v=T8nkQKm2_TI.
Audio recording	Beyoncé, *4* (Parkwood Entertainment & Columbia Records 2011).
Audio recording in larger collection	P!nk, *Can We Pretend (featuring Cash Cash), on Hurts 2B Human* (RCA Records 2019).
Podcast	Jamie, *Boudica's Rebellion, Part 1*, The British History Podcast (July 8, 2011), https://www.thebritishhistorypodcast.com/boudicas-rebellion-part-one/.
Audiobook	George R.R. Martin, *Game of Thrones: A Song of Ice and Fire* (Aug. 14, 2003) (audiobook downloaded using iTunes and read by Roy Dotrice).
Photograph or illustration with a title	An Emblematical Print on the South Sea Scene (illustration), *in* Ian Crofton, *Kings and Queens of England* 191 (2006).
Photograph or illustration without a title	Photograph of Sandra Day O'Connor, *in Battling Dementia, Sandra Day O'Connor Leaves Public Life with Plea for Bipartisanship*, N.Y. Times (Oct. 23, 2018), https://www.nytimes.com/2018/10/23/us/politics/dementia-sandra-day-supreme-court.html.

Microform	Rex A. Martin, Cardboard Warriors: The Rise and Fall of an American Wargaming Subculture, 1958–1998, at 202 (Aug. 2001) (unpublished Ph.D. dissertation, Pennsylvania State University), *microformed on* UMI Microform 3020503 (Univ. Microforms Int'l).
Citations in academic footnotes	⚠ACADEMIC FORMATTING [23] THE ADVENTURES OF PRISCILLA, QUEEN OF THE DESERT (PolyGram Filmed Entertainment 1994). [37] *The Crown: Windsor* (Netflix television broadcast Nov. 4, 2016). [51] P!NK, *Can We Pretend (featuring Cash Cash), on* HURTS 2B HUMAN (RCA Records 2019). [83] Rex A. Martin, Cardboard Warriors: The Rise and Fall of an American Wargaming Subculture, 1958–1998, at 202 (Aug. 2001) (unpublished Ph.D. dissertation, Pennsylvania State University), *microformed on* UMI Microform 3020503 (Univ. Microforms Int'l).
Short citations	*The Crown: Windsor.* Beyoncé. [64] P!NK, *supra* note 51. [97] Martin, *supra* note 83, at 199.

28.1 Full Citations to Broadcasted Video and Visual Programs

A citation to a video or visual program considers the nature of the program (e.g., a movie or a television broadcast), whether the program is nonepisodic (e.g., a television special) or episodic (e.g., a television series), and whether the program or video was originally broadcast online. If the program is episodic, the citation varies depending on whether it refers to a particular episode or to the series as a whole. For video and visual recordings originally broadcast on the internet, see **Rule 28.1(f)**. For audio or visual recordings of court proceedings, see **Rule 12.15(b)** or **Rule 25.4**.

A full citation to a movie has three components.[1]

Title | [, at Pinpoint reference] | (Producer or broadcaster name | Year).

Example (movie) (spaces denoted by ▲)

Hidden▲*Figures,*▲at▲1:02:30–1:03:37▲(20th▲Century▲Fox▲2016).

Title | Pinpoint reference | Producer name | Year

A full citation to a *nonepisodic* program has four or five components.[2]

Title | [, at Pinpoint reference] | (Producer or broadcaster name | Type of program | Month Day, Year).

Example (nonepisodic program) (spaces denoted by ▲)

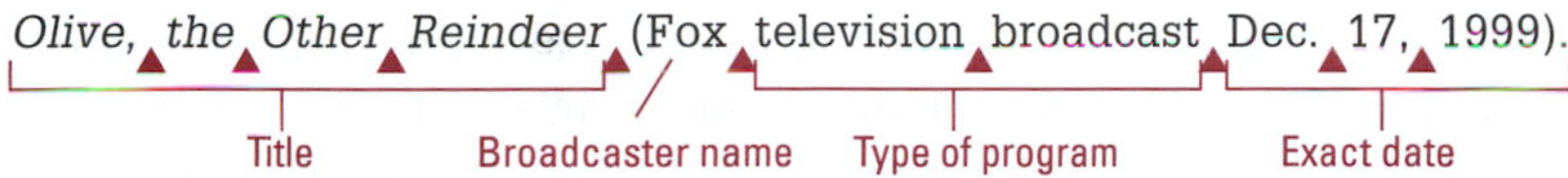

A full citation to an *episodic* program typically has five or six components.[3]

Title: Name of Episode | [, at Pinpoint reference] | (Producer or broadcaster name | Type of program | Month Day, Year).

Example (episodic program — single episode) (spaces denoted by ▲)

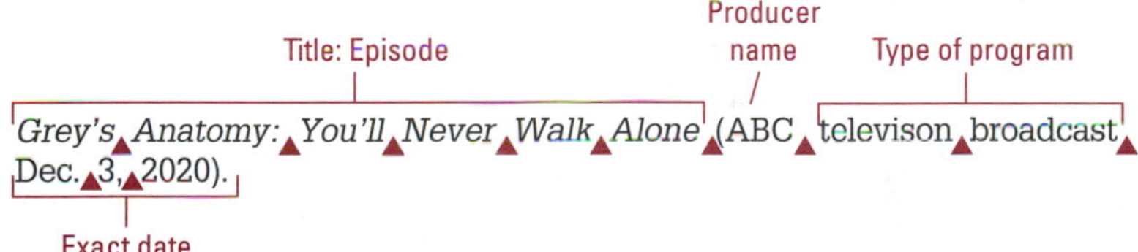

28.1(a) Title of program

Begin the citation with the title of the program, in italics. Follow **Rule 3.2, Rule 3.3,** and **Chart 3.1** for capitalization. If the program is episodic, such as a weekly television series or a daily news broadcast, begin with the name of the program, not the name of the episode, even if you will also cite an episode by its title (see **Rule 28.1(b)**).[4]

28.1(b) Title of episode

When citing a specific episode of a program, following the program title, insert a colon and one space, followed by the episode title, in italics.[5]

Example

Orange Is the New Black: Just Desserts (Netflix television broadcast July 26, 2019).

28.1(c) Pinpoint references

If the cited program makes use of pinpoint references such as scene numbers or timestamps, you may provide that information immediately following the program title or episode title, but it is not necessary.[6]

Examples

Booksmart, at 1:07:52–1:10:36 (United Artists Releasing 2019).

I Am Greta, at 12:10–14:54 (B-Reel Films 2020).

28.1(d) Producer, broadcaster, and program/date parenthetical

After the title and pinpoint reference, add a parenthetical identifying the person or company that produced, broadcast, or recorded the program, followed by one space.[7] If the program was not commercially made, use the name of the individual or organization that made it. Use common acronyms, such as ABC, CBS, CNN, CSPAN, ESPN, and HBO.

Following the name of the producer or broadcaster, set out the date of the program.[8] For a movie, use the year in which it was released. For other programs, indicate their type (e.g., television broadcast), followed by the exact date (Month Day, Year) of the broadcast, if it is available.[9] When the entire season's episodes of an original series are released all at once on a streaming service, use the exact date (Month Day, Year) all the episodes were first available on the service. Treat original television series, specials, and movies on any streaming services (e.g., Disney+, Netflix, HULU, Amazon Prime) the same as you would any other broadcast. Abbreviate months as shown in **Appendix 3(A)**.

To cite an entire series, use the span of years during which the program originally aired. If the series is still running, use the word "present" after the hyphen or en dash that indicates the span.

Examples

The Color Purple (Amblin Entertainment 1985).

Schitt's Creek: Sunrise, Sunset (CBC television broadcast Mar. 10, 2020).

The Great: Parachute (HULU television broadcast May 15, 2020).

Good Morning, America (ABC television series 1975–present).

28.1(e) Transcript

If a transcript of the program is available, following the producer, broadcaster, and program/date parenthetical, you may add a parenthetical reference to the transcript's location.

Example

Face the Nation (CBS television broadcast July 26, 2009) (host Bob Schieffer interviews White House adviser David Axelrod) (transcript available in LEXIS, News library, CBS News Transcripts file).

28.1(f) Videos available online

For commercial movies, television broadcasts, or other video programs that you can cite using **Rule 28.1(a)–(d)** but that can also be found in full on an internet page, there is no difference in the citation format. If appending a URL to the citation will help facilitate finding the source, you may do so.

Examples

Home Again (Open Road Films 2017), https://www.imbd.com/tv/watch/tt5719700?ref_=tt_wbr_fdv.

`*black·ish: Age Against the Machine* (ABC television broadcast Nov. 4, 2020), https://abc.com/shows/blackish/episode-guide/season-07/05-age-against-the-machine.

CBS Evening News (CBS television broadcast Nov. 12, 2020), https://www.cbsnews.com/video/111220-cbs-evening-news/#x.

Cite any other videos available on an internet page, especially those videos that were originally broadcast online or are only available online (i.e., they were never commercially available other than on the internet) according to **Rule 31.1** or **Rule 31.2**.[10] If you have any doubt as to whether the video was ever broadcast anywhere other than online (e.g., a news clip that may or may not have been broadcast on television first), cite it as an online video using **Rule 31.1** or **Rule 31.2**.

When using **Rule 31.1** or **Rule 31.2** for online videos, use the creator of the video as the author or owner, or if the creator is not available, use the person or entity that posted the video as the author,[11] unless it's the same entity that owns the website and the domain ownership is clear from the website's title.[12] Use the title of the video rather than the title of the webpage, especially if there is more than one video on that particular web page. If the video doesn't have a discernible title, create a detailed descriptive title of the subject matter, analogizing to **Rule 26.1(b)** (subject or title of unpublished presentation). Just as with **Rule 31.1(f)**, use the most specific URL for the video, and if needed, use an explanatory parenthetical to describe how to access the specific video you are referencing.[13] When the web page containing the video you are citing indicates that the video contains contents from another source, you should indicate that source in an explanatory parenthetical at the end of the citation.[14] To cite to videos not broadcasted that are also not available publicly on the internet, see **Rule 28.7**.

Examples

Howard University, *Chadwick Boseman's Howard University 2018 Commencement Speech*, YouTube (May 14, 2018), https://www.youtube.com/watch?v=RIHZypMyQ2s&feature=emb_title.

Dave Flanders, *Mikisew Cree Nation Land Use Plan*, Vimeo, at 0:10 (Sept. 7, 2015), https://vimeo.com/138557770.

General Motors, *Keep America Rolling*, Periscope (Sept. 2001), https://www.periscope.com/news/how-will-you-be-remembered-the-importance-of-brand-bravery-during-the-covid-19-pandemic/ (video linked from YouTube).

Health Officials Warn of Potential Spike in COVID-19 Cases After Labor Day Weekend, Fox News (Sept. 7, 2020), https://video.foxnews.com/v/6188323232001#sp=show-clips.

Emory Follies, *Laws Misérables: Emory Law Follies 2013*, YouTube, at 02:56–04:39 (Apr. 12, 2013), http://www.youtube.com/watch?v=IxMxDFbgFzo.

28.1(g)[FN] Full citations to broadcasted video, radio, or visual programs in academic footnotes

Use large and small capital letters for a movie title. Continue using italics for titles of television programs, other video or visual sources, and radio programs.[15]

When a television broadcast is broadcast online as well as on television, you may choose to cite it according to **Rule 31.1** or **Rule 31.2** instead of using **Rule 28.1(a)–(d)**.[16] Traditional citation rules require that you cite all other online videos according to **Rule 31.1** or **Rule 31.2**, depending on the type of website in which the video is embedded.[17] Follow the academic formatting rules in **Rule 31.1(h)[FN]** for online sources by using large and small capital letters for the home page or domain name and italics for the video title.[18]

Examples

[165] THE COLOR PURPLE (Amblin Entertainment 1985).

[177] *Schitt's Creek: Sunrise, Sunset* (CBC television broadcast Mar. 10, 2020).

[180] *CBS Evening News*, CBS NEWS (Nov. 12, 2020), https://www.cbsnews.com/video/111220-cbs-evening-news/#x.

[185] Howard University, *Chadwick Boseman's Howard University 2018 Commencement Speech*, YOUTUBE (May 14, 2018), https://www.youtube.com/watch?v=RIHZypMyQ2s&feature=emb_title.

[189] *Discrimination—What's the Law?*, VICT. LEGAL AID, https://www.legalaid.vic.gov.au/find-legal-answers/videos-about-the-law/discriminationvideo (last visited July 17, 2020) (linked from YouTube).

28.2 Full Citations to Radio Broadcasts and Series

Follow **Rule 28.1** for video and visual programs.[19] You may include the AM or FM channel and location of the radio station, abbreviated according to **Appendix 3(B)**, in a parenthetical after the broadcaster/date parenthetical.

Examples

The Joe Scarborough Show (WABC radio broadcast July 27, 2009) (AM channel 77, N.Y.C., N.Y.).

All Things Considered: Critics Question Reporter's Airing of Personal Views (NPR broadcast Sept. 26, 2006) (transcript and audio at http://www.npr.org/templates/story/story.php?storyId_6146693).

The Hitchhiker's Guide to the Galaxy (BBC radio series 4 1978–2005).

There is no change for academic formatting.[20]

ACADEMIC FORMATTING

Example

[78] *Max, Shannon, & Porkchop* (KiiM radio broadcast Nov. 2, 2020) (FM channel 99.5, Tucson, Ariz.).

28.3 Full Citations to Audio Recordings

Use this rule even if you download or stream the commercial recording from a hosting platform such as iTunes or Spotify. To cite a single audio recording in a collection, follow **Rule 28.4**. For audio or visual recordings of court proceedings, see **Rule 12.15(b)** or **Rule 25.4**. A full citation to an audio recording contains up to five components.[21]

Performer or composer name, | *Title* | [, at Pinpoint reference] | (Recording entity | Year of release).

Example (spaces denoted by ▲)

28.3(a) Performer or composer name

Begin the citation with the performer's or composer's full name in ordinary type, followed by a comma and one space.[22] Analogize to **Rule 20.1(b)** for authors of books.

28.3(b) Title of audio recording

Present the title of the recording, including any subtitle, in italics, analogizing to **Rule 20.1(c)** (book titles).[23] Capitalize according to **Rule 3.2**, **Rule 3.3**, and **Chart 3.1**.

28.3(c) Pinpoint references

If the recording makes use of pinpoint references such as timestamps you may provide that information immediately following the title by adding a comma, then a space, "at" and another space, and finally the timestamp in hours and minutes (XX:XX).[24] If the portion you are providing a pinpoint reference to is within the first ten minutes of the recording, make sure to put a "0" as the first digit.[25]

28.3(d) Recording parenthetical

In parentheses, set out the name of the recording entity (e.g., a record company) in ordinary type, followed by the year of the recording's release.[26] Analogize to **Rule 28.1(d)** for video and visual programs.

Examples

Hayley Kiyoko, *Expectations* (EMPIRE/Atlantic Recording Corp. 2018).

Shea Diamond, *Seen It All* (East West Records 2018).

28.4 Full Citation to Single Audio Recording in a Collection

A full citation to a single audio recording in a collection (e.g., a single track on an album) contains the components that are analogous to those shown in **Rule 20.3** for collected works in print.[27] Follow **Rule 28.3(d)** for the recording parenthetical.

Performer or composer name, | *Title of shorter work*, | *on* | *Title of collection* | (Recording entity | Year of release).

Example

Ray Charles, *Here We Go Again*, *on Genius Loves Company* (Concord Records 2004).

28.5 Podcasts, Audiobooks, and Other Audio Recordings Available Online

Citations to podcasts or other audio recordings online that can be found on an internet page contain components that are analogous to those shown in **Rule 31.1** or **Rule 31.2** for website pages.[28]

Host, author, creator, or owner name, | *Title of recording or episode*, | Website or domain name | [, at Pinpoint reference] | [(Month Day, Year)], | URL | [(last visited Month Day, Year)] | [(Media designation)].

Example (spaces denoted by ▲)

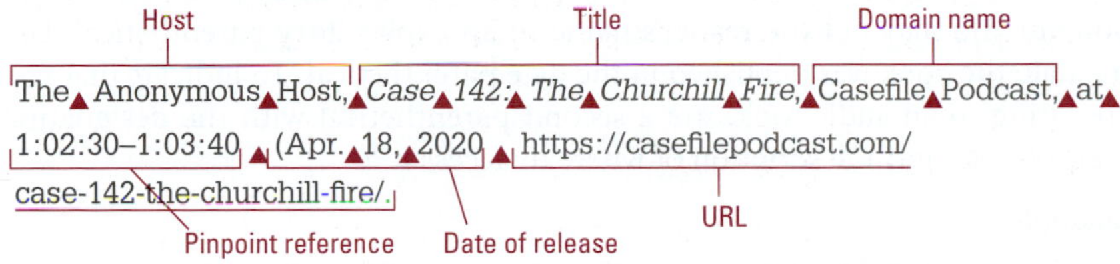

If the date of the recording is available, use that in a date parenthetical before the URL.[29] If there is no date associated with the recording, use a "last visited" parenthetical after the URL.[30] See **Rule 31.1(e)** for more information about dates relating to websites. Use time markers for the pinpoint reference, if any, using the format "XX:XX" for minutes and seconds or "XX:XX:XX" for hours, minutes, and seconds.[31] If the portion you are providing a pinpoint reference to is within the first ten minutes of the recording, make sure to put a "0" as the first digit.[32] If it isn't clear from the title or domain name what the source is, include a parenthetical telling the reader it is a podcast or other audio recording.

Examples

Joy-Ann Reid & Jacque Reid, *It's Official . . . We're Sick and Tired*, Reid This, Reid That, at 06:00–08:50 (June 14, 2020), https://reidthisreidthat.libsyn.com/its-official-were-sick-and-tired (podcast).

Malcolm Gladwell, *The Prime Minister and the Prof*, Revisionist Hist., at 27:00–27:49, http://revisionisthistory.com/episodes/15-the-prime-minister-and-the-prof (last visited Nov. 14, 2020) (podcast).

If there is no access to a podcast or audio recording through a stable URL, such as when the only way to access a recording is to stream or download it from a service like Spotify, omit the website or domain name component, and replace it with the name of the podcast or audio recording, if any.[33] Omit the URL component, and instead, append an explanatory parenthetical describing how you accessed the source and what the source is.[34]

Examples

Law & Order, Sound Effect Network (last visited Aug. 22, 2020) (sound effect downloaded using iTunes).

Jenna Fischer & Angela Kinsey, *Diversity Day*, Office Ladies (Oct. 22, 2019) (podcast streamed using Spotify).

For audiobooks, whenever possible, cite to the print version.[35] You should cite to audiobooks only if they are the sole media through which the book is available or there is something about the audio version that is important and cannot be captured by a print version (such as who the reader is).[36] If you must cite to an audiobook, follow the instructions in this rule for podcasts and other audio recordings found online. Use the book author's name as the first component; you may put the reader's name in an explanatory parenthetical. Use the date the book was published in the date parenthetical. To indicate that you are citing to an audiobook, use a second parenthetical with the designation "audiobook" and a description of where to access it.[37]

Examples

Irin Carmon & Shana Knizhnik, *The Notorious RBG: The Life and Times of Ruth Bader Ginsburg*, at 32:10–43:46 (2019) (audiobook downloaded using Audible and read by Andi Arndt).

Malcolm Gladwell, *Talking to Strangers*, at 1:20:00 (Sept. 10, 2019) (audiobook downloaded using Audible and read by Malcolm Gladwell).

Georgiana Cavendish, *The Sylph* (1778) (audiobook downloaded from LibriVox).

28.6FN Full Citations to Audio Recordings in Academic Footnotes

ACADEMIC FORMATTING

Present both the name of the performer or composer and the title of the recording in large and small capital letters.[38] To cite a collection or a single recording in a collection, italicize the title of the shorter work, but use large and small capital letters for the title of the larger work.[39] For audiobooks, analogize to **Rule 20.4(d)FN**; use large and small capital letters for the author and book title.[40] For other online audio recordings cited using **Rule 28.5**, follow the academic formatting rules in **Rule 31.1(h)FN** for online sources.

Examples

50 BILLIE EILISH, WHEN WE ALL FALL ASLEEP, WHERE DO WE GO? (Darkroom/Interscope Records 2019).

72 CARRIE UNDERWOOD, *Mama's Song*, *on* PLAY ON (Arista Nashville/19 2009).

79 IRIN CARMON & SHANA KNIZHNIK, THE NOTORIOUS RBG: THE LIFE AND TIMES OF RUTH BADER GINSBURG, at 32:10–43:46 (2019) (audiobook downloaded using Audible and read by Andi Arndt).

86 Joy-Ann Reid & Jacque Reid, *It's Official . . . We're Sick and Tired*, REID THIS, REID THAT, at 16:00–18:50 (June 14, 2020), https://reidthisreidthat.libsyn.com/its-official-were-sick-and-tired (podcast).

28.7 Full Citation to Private Audio or Visual Recordings and Pictures

Use this rule for pictures, audio recordings, or visual recordings that you cannot cite according to any other rule, including **Rules 31–33**. This would include audio or visual recordings that are not available on the internet, those that could not be streamed or downloaded from an application, and those that were never commercially available. The picture, audio recording, or visual recording may be available on a personal digital device such as a mobile phone or thumb drive, on old media such as a DVD or VHS tape, or even saved to a private cloud digital repository such as Google Docs, Dropbox, or iCloud. For example, you would use this rule if you are citing to a video that you took yourself and did not upload to a website like YouTube or if you are citing a picture you took that is saved in iCloud, but you never posted on social media.

A citation to a private picture, audio recording, or video recording has up to six components.[41]

Media designation: | Title or descriptive title | [, at Pinpoint reference] | ([Producer or person who recorded the video] | Month Day, Year) | (Location of recording).

Example (spaces denoted by ▲)

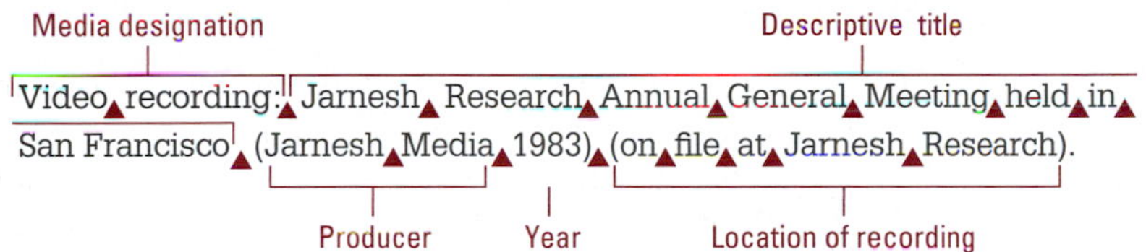

Begin citations to private pictures, audio recordings, or video recordings by designating it as one of those.[42] If the source is untitled, create a detailed descriptive title of the subject matter, analogizing to **Rule 26.1(b)** (subject or title of unpublished presentation).[43] Use time markers for the pinpoint reference, if any, using the format "XX:XX" or "XX:XX:XX."[44] If the portion you are providing a pinpoint reference to is within the first ten minutes of the recording, make sure to put a "0" as the first digit.[45] Always indicate in an explanatory parenthetical where the reader could find a copy of the picture or recording.[46] A private video also has a space for the name of the person or institution that produced the video, if any, and the year it was produced.[47] If it has an exact date it was recorded, substitute that for the year of production.

Examples

Audio recording: The Multi-Generational Teaching of Legal Writing Discussion Group at the 2020 AALS Annual Meeting, at 05:10 (AALS Jan. 3, 2020) (on file with AALS Legal Writing, Reasoning, and Research).

Photograph: Crowd at the Million MAGA March (Nov. 14, 2020) (on file with author).

Video recording: Protesters in Downtown St. Louis, Mo. Marching for Black Lives Matter (Dale Trent June 24, 2020) (on file with author).

For academic formatting, instead of simply saying "Video recording" or "Audio recording" for the media designation, be more specific about what type of media the source is on (e.g., DVD, VHS, thumb drive).[48] Otherwise, there is no difference.

ACADEMIC FORMATTING

28.8 Full Citations to Photographs and Illustrations

A full citation to a titled photograph or illustration has up to six components.[49]

[Artist's name,] | *Title* | ([photograph] or [illustration]), | *in* | Full citation of appropriate work | [, following p. Pinpoint reference to page preceding the image].

A full citation to an *untitled* photograph or illustration has up to six components.[50]

[Artist's name,] | [Photograph] or [Illustration] of | description of the image, | *in* | Full citation of appropriate work | [, following p. Pinpoint reference to page preceding the image].

Example (spaces denoted by ▲)

Description of image | Full Citation to work | Pinpoint reference

Illustration of a brain, *in* Gary Small & Gigi Vorgan, *iBrain* (2008), following p. 85.

Only include the artist's name in either circumstance if it is available and significant or relevant.[51] The pinpoint reference is usually in the citation to the appropriate work itself, whether a page number, URL, or section. However, if the page on which the image appears is not numbered, then omit the pinpoint reference in the work's citation, and insert ", following p." and the page number that precedes the image.[52] If a photograph or illustration is a private one and therefore does not have the components listed above (i.e., does not appear online or in another source), use **Rule 28.7**.

Examples

Illustration of formatting for indented contract sections, *in* Bryan A. Garner, *Garner's Coursebook on Drafting & Editing Contracts* 92 (2020).

Edvard Munch, *The Scream* (photograph), *in* Alastair Sooke, *Edvard Munch's Portrait of Existential Angst Is the Second Most Famous Image in Art History—but Why?*, BBC (Mar. 3, 2016), https://www.bbc.com/culture/article/20160303-what-is-the-meaning-of-the-scream.

28.9FN Full Citations to Photographs and Illustrations in Academic Footnotes

ACADEMIC FORMATTING

Follow **Rule 28.8**, but also consult academic footnote rules for the original source (e.g., **Rule 20.1(f)FN**).[53] For instance, if the original source is online, the website or domain name will be presented in large and small capital letters.

Example

[44] Sean Parker, Photograph of the Big Horn Wildfire, *in Landscapes*, SEAN PARKER PHOTOGRAPHY, https://www.sean-parker.com/Recent-Uploads/i-4RxmJhH/A (last visited Sept. 6, 2020).

28.10 Full Citations to Microforms

28.10(a) When to cite a microform

A microform contains a small image or microreproduction of a document, usually on film. Microfilm is a *roll* of film. Microfiche is a *flat sheet* of film. For purposes of this rule, treat them both the same. The images on microform have been shrunk to about 1/25th of the documents' original size. Because the images are so tiny, readers need a special machine or scanner to be able to read the document. Microforms are not as easily accessible a source as your other options.

If a source is readily available in print, cite its print version, using the appropriate rule for that format; if it is available online but not in print, cite to the online version.[54] Provide a parallel citation to a microform version only if it would be helpful for readers to locate or obtain the original.[55]

Prepare the primary citation by analogizing to the relevant rules for the particular type of source.[56] For example, if citing a letter, follow **Rule 27**; if citing an unpublished manuscript, follow **Rule 29.2**.

28.10(b) Parallel citation to microform

Create a parallel citation to a source's microform version by appending to its full citation a comma, one space, the phrase "*microformed on*" and the name of the collection, in ordinary type.[57] You may abbreviate any words in the collection name that appear in **Appendices 3(B)** and **3(E)**, and you may omit articles and prepositions not needed for clarity.

If the microform bears a unique identifier number or code, indicate that identifier after the name of the collection.[58] If the publisher uses its own system for identifying documents within a collection, follow that system.[59]

Conclude the citation with a parenthetical identifying the publisher of the microform collection.[60] Abbreviate words in the publisher name as shown in **Appendices 3(B)** and **3(E)**.

Examples

H.R. Rep. No. 52-1290, at 3 (1892), *microformed on* CIS No. 3045-H.r.p. 1290 (Cong. Info. Serv.).

Letter from E. Polk Johnson to John Marshall Harlan (Apr. 24, 1911), *microformed on* John Marshall Harlan Papers, Reel 8 (Library of Cong.).

Rex A. Martin, Cardboard Warriors: The Rise and Fall of an American Wargaming Subculture, 1958–1998, at 202 (Aug. 2001) (unpublished Ph.D. dissertation, Pennsylvania State University), *microformed on* UMI Microform 3020503 (Univ. Microforms Int'l).

28.10(c)FN Full citations to microforms in academic footnotes

ACADEMIC FORMATTING

Follow **Rule 28.10(a)–(b)**, but also consult academic footnote rules for the original source (e.g., **Rule 20.1(f)FN**).[61] For example, if the original source is a book, both the author name and the book title will be presented in large and small capital letters.

Examples

112 Francis Bacon, Novum Organum 4 (London, Thomas Lee 1676), *microformed on* Ann Arbor, Mich. Early English Books, 1641–1700, 1115:7 (Univ. Microfilms Int'l).

194 S. Rep. No. 93-690, at 43 (1974), *microformed on* CIS No. 74-S543-3 (Cong. Info. Serv.).

28.11 Short Citations to Video and Visual Programs, Radio, Recordings, Photographs, Illustrations, and Microforms

28.11(a) Using *id.* or other short citations to program, recording, images, or microform

When appropriate (**Rule 11.3(c)**), use *id.* as the short citation.[62] When *id.* is not appropriate, the short citation will vary depending on the source. For video and visual programs, radio, photographs, illustrations, and audio recordings, use the title of the program, image, or recording or the name of the performer, artist, or composer, followed by a pinpoint reference, if available.[63] For microforms, use only the short citation for the original source; omit reference to the microform.[64] For any citation created using **Rules 28.1(f)** (videos found online) and **28.5** (podcasts, audio books, and other audio recordings available online), follow the short forms in **Rule 31.3** for online sources.

Examples

Full citation:	**Short citation:**
Lorena, Light-footed Woman (Netflix 2019).	*Lorena, Light-footed Woman* scene 6.
Katy Perry, *Waking Up in Vegas*, *on Katy Perry* (Capital Music Grp. 2008).	Katy Perry.
Adele, *21* (XL Recordings Ltd. 2010).	Adele.
Letter from E. Polk Johnson to John Marshall Harlan (Apr. 24, 1911), *microformed on* John Marshall Harlan Papers, Reel 8 (Library of Cong.).	Letter from E. Polk Johnson to John Marshall Harlan.

28.11(b)FN Short citations to programs, recordings, images, or microforms in academic footnotes

ACADEMIC FORMATTING

When appropriate (**Rule 11.3(c)**), use *id.* as the short citation.[65] When *id.* is not appropriate, the short citation will vary depending on the source. For video and visual programs, radio, photographs, illustrations, and audio recordings, use the *supra* format that follows, referring to the earlier note containing the full citation.[66] See **Rule 11.4** for more information on *supra*. You may use [hereinafter] to shorten a title. See **Rule 11.5**.

AUTHOR, PERFORMER, composer, or title, | *supra* | note | Note number.

Examples

38 REVERSAL OF FORTUNE (Sovereign Pictures 1990).

39 *Id.*

40 Photograph of overturned train, *in* RANSOM RIGGS, A MAP OF DAYS (2018), following p. 22.

. . .

60 REVERSAL OF FORTUNE, *supra* note 38.

61 *World News with Charles Gibson* (ABC television broadcast Aug. 22, 2009) [hereinafter *World News*].

...

108 *World News*, *supra* note 61.

109 LADY GAGA & BRADLEY COOPER, *Shallow*, *on* A STAR IS BORN SOUNDTRACK (Interscope Records 2018).

...

[120] Lady Gaga & Bradley Cooper, *supra* note 109.

[121] Photograph of overturned train, *supra* note 40.

For a microform, use the appropriate type of short citation for the original source, omitting reference to the microformed version.[67]

Example

[112] Francis Bacon, Novum Organum 4 (London, Thomas Lee 1676), *microformed on* Ann Arbor, Mich. Early English Books, 1641–1700, 1115:7 (Univ. Microfilms Int'l).

[113] *Id.*

...

[141] Bacon, *supra* note 112, at 10.

29 Forthcoming Works, Unpublished Manuscripts, and Working Papers

Fast Formats

Forthcoming work	*Research Handbook on Law and Emotion* (Susan A. Bandes et al. eds., forthcoming Apr. 2021). Diana Simon, *Laughing Your Way to Academic Success: Can Laughter Impact Learning and Well-being in the Law School Classroom and Are There Cross-cultural Differences?*, Conn. L. Rev. Online (forthcoming May 2021) (manuscript at 7-8), https://papers.ssrn.com/sol3/papers.cfm?abstract_id=3664308.
Unpublished manuscript	John Asker et al. Comparing the Investment Behavior of Public and Private Firms 12–13 (July 29, 2011) (unpublished manuscript), http://pages.stern.nyu.edu/~jasker/AFML.pdf. T.B. McCord, Jr., John Page of Rosewell: Reason, Religion, and Republican Government from the Perspective of a Virginia Planter, 1743–1808, at 605 (1990) (Ph.D. dissertation, American University) (on file with American University).
Working paper	Allen N. Berger et al., *Bank Competition and Financial Stability* 14 (World Bank, Working Paper No. 4696, 2008), http://ssrn.com/abstract=1243102.
Citations in academic footnotes	17 Research Handbook on Law and Emotion (Susan A. Bandes et al. eds., forthcoming Apr. 2021). 28 Diana Simon, *Laughing Your Way to Academic Success: Can Laughter Impact Learning and Well-being in the Law School Classroom and Are There Cross-cultural Differences?*, Conn. L. Rev. Online (forthcoming May 2021) (manuscript at 7-8), https://papers.ssrn.com/sol3/paper.cfm?abstract_id=3664308.
Short citations	Asker et al., *supra*, at 15. 38 Simon, *supra* note 28, at 20.

29.1 Full Citations to Forthcoming Works

If a work has not yet been published but is scheduled for publication, cite the work using the rules that will apply to the work when published, with the modifications described below.[1] Do not use **Rule 29** to cite cases that are awaiting their publication in a reporter; for such cases, follow **Rule 12.13**.

29.1(a) Omission of initial page reference

For works whose full citation requires reference to an initial page (e.g., a law review article), omit the initial page reference.[2] Do not insert underlined spaces to indicate the missing page number.

29.1(b) Forthcoming publication date

In the citation's date parenthetical, use the term "forthcoming" by itself if the date of publication is unknown.[3] If the date of publication is known, insert "forthcoming" before the intended year of publication.[4] If the month is known, insert it directly before the year, abbreviating the month as shown in **Appendix 3(A)**.

29.1(c) Parentheticals for pinpoint reference and location of manuscript

Omit the pinpoint reference where it would normally appear for the type of work it will be.[5] If a pinpoint reference to the manuscript is available, indicate it in a second parenthetical, using page numbers or other subdivisions from the unpublished manuscript itself (e.g., "(manuscript at 3)").[6]

In a third parenthetical, describe the location of the forthcoming work (e.g., "on file with [law review name]") if you added a pinpoint reference to the manuscript; it is optional otherwise.[7] If you are citing to a forthcoming work in a commercial database (e.g., SSRN or PQDT), omit the location parenthetical and instead, insert a comma, one space, and then the database identifier or code.[8] If the forthcoming work is available both in hard copy and online, you may append a reference to its URL in place of the location parenthetical; insert a comma, one space, and the URL after the pinpoint reference parenthetical.[9]

Examples

Steven M. Sheffrin, *Tax Fairness and Folk Justice* (forthcoming Oct. 2013).

Rachel S. Arnow-Richman, *Temporary Termination: A Layoff Blueprint for the COVID Era*, Wash. U. J.L. & Pol'y (forthcoming 2021) (manuscript at 10-11), https://papers.ssrn.com/sol3/papers.cfm?abstract_id=3727485.

29.2 Full Citations to Unpublished Manuscripts

Use this rule for manuscripts that are both unpublished and not scheduled for publication. Do not use this rule for unpublished cases (see **Rule 12.13**) or forthcoming works (**Rule 29.1**).

A full citation to an unpublished manuscript, including a thesis or dissertation, contains the following components.[10]

Author's name, | Title | Pinpoint reference | (Date) | (Descriptive parenthetical) | (Location) or [, URL] or [Commercial database identifier].

Example (spaces denoted by ▲)

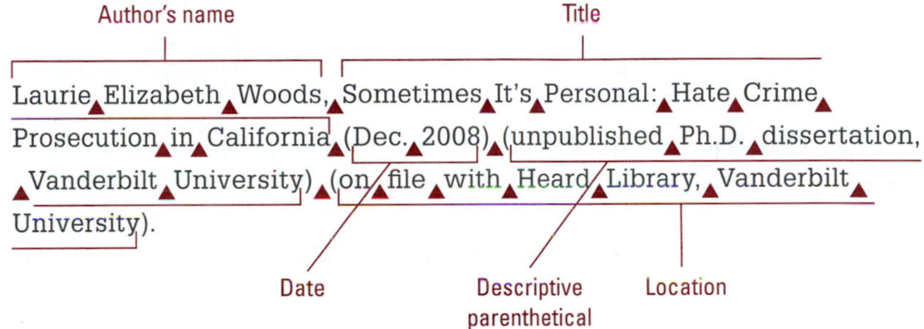

Author's name
Title
Laurie▲Elizabeth▲Woods,▲Sometimes▲It's▲Personal:▲Hate▲Crime▲
Prosecution▲in▲California▲(Dec.▲2008)▲(unpublished▲Ph.D.▲dissertation,
▲Vanderbilt▲University)▲(on▲file▲with▲Heard▲Library,▲Vanderbilt▲
University).
Date
Descriptive parenthetical
Location

29.2(a) Author

Begin with the author's full name, in ordinary type, followed by a comma and one space.[11] Analogize to **Rule 20.1(b)**.

29.2(b) Title

Set out the title as it appears on the cover page of the work, omitting any subtitle unless it is particularly relevant.[12] Present the title in ordinary type.[13] Capitalize words according to **Rule 3.2**, **Rule 3.3**, and **Chart 3.1**.

29.2(c) Pinpoint references

Insert a relevant pinpoint reference, if any, following **Rules 5.2** through **5.4** and **20.1(d)**.[14]

29.2(d) Date parenthetical

Following the title and pinpoint reference, insert a parenthetical with the manuscript's exact date (Month Day, Year), abbreviating months using **Appendix 3(A)**.[15] If the day is not available, use the month and year. If the month is not available, use the year.

29.2(e) Descriptive parenthetical

Following the date parenthetical, insert a second parenthetical describing the cited work (e.g., "unpublished manuscript").[16] For student-written comments and notes that were written under faculty supervision for a law review, describe the work in the parenthetical as an "unpublished comment" or "unpublished note."[17] Describe a student thesis or dissertation beginning with the abbreviation for the degree for which the paper was written (e.g., "M.B.A." or "Ph.D.") and an identification of the type of work (e.g., thesis, dissertation), followed by a comma, one space, and the full name of the school that awarded the degree.[18]

Examples

Andrew Theodore Urban, An Intimate World: Race, Migration, and Chinese and Irish Domestic Servants in the United States, 1850–1920, at 233–84 (June 2009) (Ph.D. dissertation, University of Minnesota) (on file with author).

Christopher W. Bordeaux, Optimizing Nutrient Management and Vegetative Ground Cover on Pastured-Pig Operations 7–10 (Oct. 28, 2010) (M.S. thesis, North Carolina State University), http://repository.lib.ncsu.edu/ir/bitstream/1840.16/6532/1/etd.pdf.

29.2(f) Location of manuscript

In a third parenthetical, describe where or how readers can obtain a copy of the unpublished work.[19] If the work is available in microform, follow **Rule 28.10**. If you are citing to an unpublished work in a commercial database (e.g., SSRN or PQDT), omit the location parenthetical and instead, insert a comma, one space, and then the database identifier or code.[20] If the unpublished work is available both in hard copy and online, you may append a reference to its URL in place of the location parenthetical; insert a comma, one space, and the URL after the pinpoint reference parenthetical.[21] To cite to documents in a shared drive, see **Rule 33.5**.

Examples

Catherine Rehmann, Benevolent Sexism in the Workplace: The Impact on Affect, Behavior, Cognition, and Performance 59 (2019) (M.S. thesis, California State University) (on file with author).

Charlene Y. Taylor, Girls and Boys, Apples and Oranges? A Theoretically Informed Analysis of Gender-Specific Predictors of Delinquency 105–07 (July 21, 2009) (Ph.D. dissertation, University of Cincinnati), http://cech.uc.edu/criminaljustice/dissertations.html.

Sarah Elizabeth Murphy Gray, Deferred but Not Denied: The Impact of Student Debt on Homeownership and the U.S. Racial Wealth Gap 121 (Feb. 2020) (Ph.D. dissertation, Brandeis University), ProQuest 27736680.

29.3 Full Citations to Working Papers

If an unpublished manuscript is identified as a working paper but is not numbered, cite it according to **Rule 29.2.**[22] To cite an unpublished manuscript designated as a working paper that has a number assigned to it, analogize to **Rules 29.1** and **29.2** for other unpublished works, but with the following two modifications. First, place the title of the working paper in italics, followed by a pinpoint reference, if any.[23] Second, begin the date parenthetical with the name of the sponsoring organization, a comma and a space, and then the term "Working Paper," the abbreviation "No." followed by that number.[24] Use a comma to set off the number from the date.[25] Abbreviate words in the sponsoring organization's name (see **Appendices 3(B)** and **3(E)**), and omit prepositions and articles not needed for clarity.[26]

Example

Frederic S. Mishkin & Eugene N. White, *U.S. Stock Market Crashes and Their Aftermath: Implications for Monetary Policy* 50 fig.8 (Nat'l Bureau Econ. Rsch., Working Paper No. 8892, 2002), http://www.nber.org/papers/w8992.pdf.

29.4FN Full Citations to Forthcoming Works, Unpublished Manuscripts, or Working Papers in Academic Footnotes

ACADEMIC FORMATTING

Cite a forthcoming work following **Rule 29.1**, but also consult the academic footnote rules for the analogous source in publication (e.g., **Rule 20.1(f)FN**).[27] For example, if the analogous published source is a book, both the author name and the title will be presented in large and small capital letters.

Cite an unpublished manuscript following **Rule 29.2.**[28] Cite a working paper following **Rule 29.3.**[29] For these, there are no typeface modifications.

29.5 Short Citations to Forthcoming Works, Unpublished Manuscripts, or Working Papers

When appropriate (**Rule 11.3(c)**), use *id.* as the short citation.[30] Otherwise, use the short citation for the analogous published version of the cited authority.[31] For example, use **Rule 20.6** for short citations to works analogous to books, or use **Rule 21.7** for short citations to works analogous to articles in periodicals.

29.6FN Short Citations to Forthcoming Works, Unpublished Manuscripts, or Working Papers in Academic Footnotes

ACADEMIC FORMATTING

When appropriate (**Rule 11.3(c)**), use *id.* as the short citation.[32] If *id.* is inappropriate, use the *supra* format, referring to the earlier note containing the full citation, by analogizing to the short forms for periodicals (**Rule 21.7(b)FN**) or nonperiodicals (**Rule 20.6(d)FN**).[33]

Part 3
Online Sources

30 Online Sources in General

30.1 General Information About Citations to Sources in Print and Online Versions

In general, if a source appears both in print and online versions, cite the print version if it is readily available to most readers.[1] Types of material that are readily available in print include published cases as well as constitutions, statutes, federal administrative materials, and law review articles.

Print has the advantage of permanence, and that is why it is favored in legal citation. No one can deny the convenience of accessing sources on the internet, but at times it can be difficult to find a cited online source, particularly when web pages are constantly being redesigned, moved, or deleted. Moreover, just because information is online does not mean that it is accurate, up to date, or trustworthy. See **Sidebar 30.1** for a list of factors to consider when deciding whether to cite a particular website.

Fortunately, online sources to legal materials increasingly are available as authenticated, official, or exact reproductions of their print counterparts (e.g., the *Code of Federal Regulations* on govinfo.gov or a state judiciary's official opinions maintained on its website). In those instances, you will cite the online version exactly as you would cite the print version.[2] (**Rule 30.2** addresses this topic more fully.)

But when the online version of a source is not a government-sanctioned version, or when it is formatted differently from the print version, its citation will not be identical to the print counterpart. For example, a citation to a statute in a commercial electronic database refers to the date through which the database is current, whereas a citation to the same statute in print refers to its date of publication. A jurisdiction's local rules may require court documents to provide parallel citations to online and print versions of the source in question.

30.2 Citing Online Sources That Are Official, Authenticated, or Exact Reproductions

When an online source is official or authenticated, or when it is an exact reproduction of the print source (e.g., an online PDF displaying the page numbers shown in the print version), cite it the same way you do its print counterpart, without adding the Uniform Resource Locator ("URL") for its home online.[3]

An "official" source is one possessing the same status as its equivalent in print and one that has been approved by the appropriate governmental body, whether or not that body is its publisher (e.g., official versions of state statutes).[4] An "authenticated" source is one whose content has been verified by a governmental entity to be the true representation of the original; it typically bears some indicator of its authenticity, such as a certificate or mark (e.g., the

SIDEBAR 30.1 Types of Websites and Indicia of Reliability

Not all websites are created equal. Before relying on a particular website, assess its "cite-worthiness" using these factors:

- **authority of the author, creator, or host** (e.g., the author's qualifications or expertise, the author's prior publications, the type of organization that created the site);
- **legitimacy** (e.g., whether the site represents an established institution, such as those indicated by domain suffixes .gov, .org, .edu, and whether the information on the site is supported by citations or links to credible sources);
- **currency** (e.g., whether the site is up to date, whether hyperlinks function or redirect to their replacement pages);
- **accuracy** (e.g., whether the site contains obvious errors);
- **objectivity and fairness** (e.g., whether the content of the site reveals its purpose, whether the site is biased);
- **coverage** (e.g., whether the site provides detail, breadth, depth of coverage); and
- **permanence** (e.g., whether the site archives its prior content).

Select sources with high indicia of trustworthiness. Prefer content on a government-sponsored website (e.g., .gov) over the same content on a commercial website (e.g., .com).

eagle logo with the words "Authenticated U.S. Government Information GPO" used for authenticated federal legal materials).[5]

An "exact reproduction" is just what it says — a digital document whose image mirrors its print counterpart, such as a document presented in a Portable Document Format ("PDF").[6] An exact reproduction displays the identical text, font, graphics, and layout of the original. While the same content may be available in HyperText Markup Language ("HTML"), only the PDF document is regarded as an exact reproduction.

Use authenticated, official, or exact reproductions of sources in place of other online versions that may be available.[7]

30.3 Parallel Citing Other Online Sources

There are three instances where you may cite to a source as if it were a print source and merely append a URL to the citation:

- if the source is obscure;
- if the online source can be formatted in full compliance with a rule for print sources; or
- if the rule covering that particular type of source allows.[8]

For the latter category, consult **Chart 30.1** for the rule on online commercial databases or online parallel citation for a particular source.

30.3(a) Parallel citing obscure sources

A parallel URL citation may be used when a traditional print source exists but the source is obscure — one that is rare or essentially unavailable through any means other than online — or citing to the source on the internet would substantially increase a reader's ability to access the source.[9] To cite to the online source, follow the rule for that type of print material; then add a comma, a space, and a URL that links directly to the online source.[10]

Example

Steven Michael Rogers, Accountability in a Federal System 35 (Sept. 2013) (Ph.D. dissertation, Princeton University), https://perma.cc/U9FE-VV3J.

Additional examples may be found in **Rules 27.5** (letters and memoranda) and **29.2(f)** (unpublished manuscripts).

30.3(b) Parallel citing online sources formatted in full compliance with a print source rule

For this rule to apply, an online source must share all characteristics with a print source and not be covered by **Rule 30.2** (as official, authenticated, or an exact reproduction).[11] In this context, the online source must be permanently divided into pages or sections with permanent page numbers or section numbers, which typically would be in the form of a PDF, and not in HTML.[12] Additionally, the online source must have all of the elements present that characterize the printed source being cited, such as a working paper number for a working paper or number of the Congress for a congressional journal.[13] If the online source could be cited in full compliance with the rule for the print source, cite the online source as if citing to the print source and then add a comma, a space, and a URL that links directly to the online source.[14] If the online source can be formatted in full compliance with a rule other than for websites, for purposes of this rule, it does not matter if the online source was ever published in print, as opposed to the sources mentioned in **Rule 30.3(a)** that do have a print counterpart somewhere.[15]

Example

Francine D. Blau & Lawrence M. Kahn, *The Wage Gap: Extent, Trends, and Explanations* 11 (Nat'l Bureau of Econ. Rsch., Working Paper No. 21913, 2016), https://www.nber.org/system/files/working_papers/w21913/w21913.pdf.

This rule would apply when citing a federal legislative agency report or a federal legislative journal online. See **Rule 29.3** (working papers) for another example.

30.3(c) Digital object identifier alternative to URL

A digital object identifier ("DOI") uses a string of numbers and letters to uniquely identify an online source. Before 2011, they always began with "10." After 2011, the preferred format was an active link that begins with http:// or https://. At present, these sources are mostly scholarly articles published in online journals or other archives. Unlike a URL, which may change or even become extinct (the "page not found" error), the DOI is permanent. It will always retrieve the cited source from its online repository. Append a DOI to the source's full citation, preceded by a comma and one space when a rule allows you to parallel cite the source. Represent the capitalization and spacing of the DOI as they appear in the online source.

Examples

Betsy Sparrow et al., *Google Effects on Memory: Cognitive Consequences of Having Information at Our Fingertips*, 333 Science 776, 778 (Aug. 5, 2011), DOI: 10.1126/science.1207745.

Ivica Simonovski & Svetlana Nikoloska, *Profiling of High Risk Profiles of Clients in Order to Prevent Money Laundering and Terrorism*, 1 J. Forensic Anthropology 1, 4 n.13 (2016), DOI: 10.4172/jfa.1000102.

30.4 Other Online Source Rules

The *ALWD Guide* specifically addresses several online sources. **Chart 30.1** cross-references rules for citing specific primary and secondary sources in their online versions. See **Rule 31** for citations to sources on the internet and **Rule 32** for citations to sources in commercial databases.

CHART 30.1	Rules for Online and Parallel Online Citations
Cases not yet available in print reporter	**Rules 12.12, 12.13**
Unpublished cases	**Rule 12.14**
Cases on the internet	**Rules 12.12, 12.14(c)**
Constitutions	**Rule 13.2(d)**
Statutes	**Rules 14.2(h), 14.4(d)**
Session laws	**Rules 14.6(d), 14.8**
Federal legislation	**Rule 15.1(g)**
Congressional reports, documents, debates, journals, and prints	**Rules 15.7(f), 15.9(a), 15.10(a)(6), 15.11(a)**

(*Continued*)

CHART 30.1 Rules for Online and Parallel Online Citations (Continued)

State legislation	**Rules 15.13(f), 15.17(g), 15.18(f), 15.20(a)**
Ordinances	**Rule 17.1(c)**
Federal regulations	**Rules 18.1(e), 18.3(f), Sidebar 18.1**
Federal agency decisions and advisory opinions	**Rules 18.5(b), 18.7(e)**
State administrative codes	**Rule 18.13**
State agency decisions and advisory opinions	**Rules 18.15, 18.16**
Treaties, conventions, and agreements	**Rule 19.1(e)**
Books, treatises, and other nonperiodic materials	**Rule 20.4**
Periodicals	**Rule 21.5**
Dictionaries	**Rule 22.1(b)**
Encyclopedias	**Rule 22.3(f)**
Restatements and principles of law	**Rule 23.1(e)**
ABA model code or rules of professional responsibility	**Rule 23.5(b)**
Uniform laws	**Rule 23.6(c)**
Looseleaf services	**Rule 24.1(f)**
Speeches, addresses, and other oral presentations	**Sidebar 26.1, Rule 26.1(e)**
Interviews	**Rule 27.3**
Letters and memoranda	**Rules 27.5, 27.5(g)**
Broadcasted video and visual programs	**Rule 28.1(f)**
Radio broadcasts	**Rule 28.2**
Podcasts, audio books, and other audio recordings	**Rule 28.5**
Photographs and illustrations	**Rule 28.8**
Forthcoming works	**Rule 29.1(c)**
Unpublished manuscripts	**Rule 29.2(f)**

31 Internet Sites and Blogs

Fast Formats

Owner identified in website title, specific date	*American Memory: A Century of Lawmaking for a New Nation*, Libr. of Cong. (May 1, 2003), http://memory.loc.gov/ammem/amlaw/.
Author, title, website, specific date and time	Holly Thomas, *The UK's Great Scotch Egg Debate Isn't as Funny as It Sounds*, CNN (Dec. 7, 2020, 7:51 PM EDT), https://www.cnn.com/2020/12/07/opinions/uk-vaccine-coronavirus-response-thomas/index.html.
Website requiring a search or that has an unwieldy URL	Driving directions from Las Vegas, Nev. to Cedar City, Utah, Google Maps, https://google.com/maps (follow "Directions" hyperlink; then search starting point field for "Las Vegas, NV" and search destination field for "Cedar City, UT") (last visited Oct. 10, 2020).
Blog	Carolyn Elefant, *The One Law Firm Where There Is NO Partner Pay Gap: The Law Firm of You*, MyShingle.com (Dec. 16, 2020), https://myshingle.com/2020/09/articles/future-trends/the-one-law-firm-where-there-is-no-partner-pay-gap-the-law-firm-of-you/.
Social media posts	Oxford Dictionaries (@OxfordWords), Twitter (Nov. 15, 2016, 11:00 PM), https://twitter.com/OxfordWords/status/798752580872437760. Jacqueline Kaufman (@jaxx2678), Instagram (Jan. 21, 2020), https://www.instagram.com/p/B7mGQ2_FvGm/.
Citation in academic footnote	[103] Abby Budiman et al., *Facts on U.S. Immigrants, 2018*, PEW RSCH. CTR. HISP. TRENDS (Aug. 20, 2020), https://www.pewresearch.org/hispanic/2020/08/20/facts-on-u-s-immigrants/. ⚠ ACADEMIC FORMATTING
Short citations	Budiman et al., *supra*. [115] Budiman et al., *supra* note 103.

31.1 Full Citations to Sources on the Internet

If a source you find online cannot be cited according to **Rule 30.2** as an official, authenticated, or exact copy, and it cannot be cited according to another rule as explained in **Rule 30.3(b)**, you must cite it as a web page according to this rule.[1] If a source is available in both HTML and a PDF (or other format that preserves the pagination, format, and other attributes of printed work), always cite to the PDF version.[2]

A full citation to a source on the internet varies depending on (a) whether the author or owner is specifically identified; (b) whether the writer is citing the entire website or a specific page therein; (c) whether the work has a title; (d) whether the cited source is internally dated or whether the only available date is that of the writer's access to the website; (e) whether there is a time of posting or updating; (f) whether the URL is lengthy or cumbersome; and (g) whether the website is directly accessed from its URL or from a series of links.[3]

[Author or owner], | [*Title*,] | Website or domain name | [Pinpoint reference] | [(Date parenthetical)] | , URL | [(last visited Month Day, Year)].

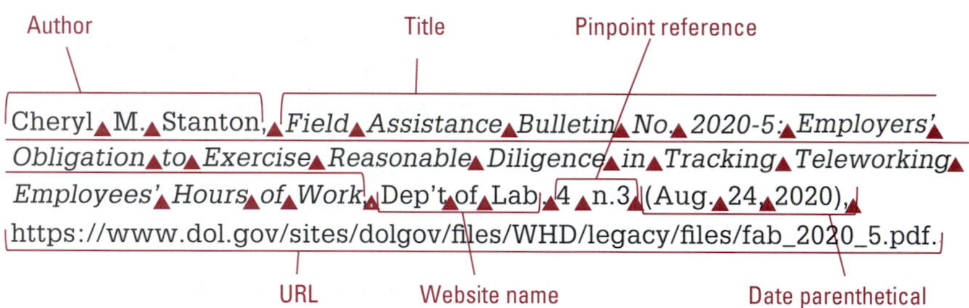

31.1(a) Author or owner

Begin with the full name of the work's author, or if no author is shown, the name of the entity that owns the website, if it is clear from the website name.[4] Before concluding that a website does not have a named author or owner, take time to navigate around the site. You may find the author's name at the end of the cited source or on another page of the site. If you are using the owner's name and that name is evident from the website's title or main page, it does not have to be separately listed.[5]

If you are citing to a comment, cite the username of the commenter as the author; there is no need to use the author's name of the original post.[6] Insert the phrase "Comment to" in ordinary type before the title of the post.[7] See **Rule 31.2** for more information on citing to social media posts.

Follow **Rule 20.1(b)** in presenting an author's or owner's name, and use ordinary type.[8] For institutions or organizations, you may abbreviate any words appearing in **Chart 12.1**, **Appendix 3(B)**, or **Appendix 3(E)**, as long as the name remains clearly identifiable.[9]

Examples

Author's name:	Madison Alder & Allie Reed, *Wear Pants, Sequester Pets: Five Tips from Judges for Zoom Court*, Bloomberg L. (Dec. 8, 2020, 2:46 PM), https://news.bloomberglaw.com/us-law-week/wear-pants-sequester-pets-five-tips-from-judges-for-zoom-court.
Name of website's owner:	Ass'n of Legal Writing Dirs., *ALWD Comments on ABA Standards*, ALWD, https://alwd.org/aba-engagement/alwd-comments-on-aba-standards (last visited Dec. 8, 2020).
Name of owner evident from title of website:	*Native American Tribal Education*, Nat'l Indian L. Libr., https://narf.org/nill/resources/education.html (last visited Dec. 8, 2020).
Name of commenter on an article:	Steve Hubbard (stevioO), Comment to *Lighting the Fuse: It Is Time to Get Rid of Court Reporters in the Federal Courts*, Hercules and the Umpire (Sept. 16, 2013, 12:36 PM), http://herculesandtheumpire.com/2013/07/19/lighting-the-fuse-it-is-time-to-get-rid-of-court-reporters-in-the-federal-courts/.

31.1(b) Title of cited page

Following the author or owner name, provide the title as shown on the cited page, italicized and capitalized according to **Rule 3.2**, **Rule 3.3**, and **Chart 3.1**, even if the website page title uses nonstandard capitalization.[10] To find the title, look for a heading at the top of the page or in the page's title bar.

If you are citing to the main page of the website, omit the title and just list the website or domain name next (see **Rule 31.1(c)**).[11] If you are citing to a comment, begin the title with "Comment to" in regular Roman type followed by the title in italics.[12] As a last resort, if you are citing to a web page whose title or headings are opaque or too obscure, you may use a descriptive title for the page.[13] Do not italicize descriptive titles.[14]

Examples

The CATO Inst., *Introduction to Constitutional Law: 100 Supreme Court Cases Everyone Should Know*, YouTube (Oct. 15, 2019), https://www.youtube.com/watch?v=_f-AqXVjOGU.

Compilation of articles on land use and zoning law, HG.org Legal Res., https://www.hg.org/land-use-and-zoning.html (last visited Sept. 8, 2020).

Interview with Justice Clarence Thomas, Supreme Court of the United States, Part 1, LawProse, http://www.lawprose.org/bryan-garner/garners-interviews/supreme-court-interviews/justice-clarence-thomas-supreme-court-of-the-united-states-part-1/ (last visited Oct. 10, 2020).

U.S. Pat. & Trademark Off., https://www.uspto.gov/ (last visited Dec. 9, 2020).

31.1(c) Website or domain name

Following the title, insert a comma, one space, and the website name, abbreviating words found in **Appendices 3(B)**, **3(E)**, and **5(A)**.[15] The website name will usually be the owner, company, organization, service, product, publication, etc. that appears somewhere on the main web page. For example, website names could be "The New York Times" (abbreviated as "N.Y. Times"), "Bloomberg Law" (abbreviated as "Bloomberg L."), or "YouTube."

If you cannot determine the website's name from the main website page, use its domain name, in ordinary type. The domain name of every website appears in the address bar of the web browser. Domain names may be preceded by prefixes such as "www.," "https://," or "mail." All domain names also have a top level domain, such as ".com" or ".edu," indicating the type of website, or a country code, such as ".ca" (Canada) or ".se" (Sweden). Do not include prefixes or any top level domains in the citation.[16] For example, if the domain name is "https://www.theguardian.com," you would use "The Guardian." Or if the domain name was "en.wikipedia.org," you would use "Wikipedia." Abbreviate any words in the shortened domain name that are found in **Appendices 3(B)**, **3(E)**, and **5(A)**.

If you are citing to a blog within a larger website — that is, a blog that has its own content and space, but is within a larger website — include the website name, a colon, one space, and the name of the subsidiary blog, all in ordinary Roman type.[17]

Examples

Rashida Jones to become President of MSNBC, Nat'l Black Laws. (Dec. 8, 2020), https://nbltop100.org/rashida-jones-to-become-president-of-msnbc/.

Gammage & Burnham, https://www.gblaw.com/ (last visited Dec. 1, 2020).

LawProse Lesson #339: What Is Good Writing?, LawProse: LawProse Lessons (Sept. 22, 2020), https://www.lawprose.org/lawprose-lesson-339-what-is-good-writing/.

31.1(d) Pinpoint references

Indicate a pinpoint reference, such as a page number or a section or paragraph number, if it is a fixed feature of the document.[18] A "fixed feature" is one that does not change when printed on different machines. Do not make up a page number for the screens, because screen sizes vary from computer to computer.[19] Because documents in PDF format replicate the look of the original document, you may use a PDF's page numbers as pinpoint references.[20] Insert the pinpoint reference immediately after the website or domain name.[21] See **Rule 7.1(d)** for rules regarding footnotes or endnotes in online sources.

Examples

Guide to Simplified Proceedings, Occupational Safety & Health Rev. Comm'n § 2 (Mar. 2010), https://www.oshrc.gov/guides/guide-to-simplified-proceedings/#2.

Indian Affairs Manual, Bureau Indian Affs. § 1.4, https://www.bia.gov/sites/bia.gov/files/assets/public/raca/manual/pdf/1_IAM_4_Handbooks_to_the_Indian_Affairs_Manual_508_OIMT.pdf (last updated Feb. 8, 2011).

31.1(e) Date parenthetical

The location and content of the date parenthetical depends on whether the website itself sets out a date or whether the only ascertainable date is that of the writer's visit to the site.[22] Provide as specific a date as possible.[23]

31.1(e)(1) Exact date of the document being cited and specific time of posting

Use the date that is provided on the website for dated reports, articles, blogs, and other information.[24] Make sure that the date clearly refers to the material on the web page that you are citing.[25] In parentheses, set out the exact date (Month Day, Year) immediately after the website or domain name.[26] If the document has only the month and year, or just the year, use those, in that order of preference. Abbreviate months according to **Appendix 3(A)**.

Web pages that indicate a specific time of posting are often seen with news articles and similar items that are updated over a period of time. Whenever it is available, include the timestamp after the date by inserting a comma after the year, one space, the time, and the abbreviations "AM" or "PM" to differentiate morning and evening.[27] If the time of the posting includes a reference to a time zone (e.g., EST (Eastern Standard Time), CDT (Central Daylight Time)), use it as well. Timestamps are especially important when citing to comments to a posting (see **Rule 31.2**).[28] If the website indicates that it was updated or modified after it was posted originally, see **Rule 31.1(e)(2)**.

Examples

Kirsten Williams, *Supreme Court Hears Arguments in Holocaust-era Cases Against Germany and Hungary*, Jurist (Dec. 8, 2020, 10:45 AM), https://www.jurist.org/news/2020/12/supreme-court-hears-arguments-in-holocaust-era-cases-against-germany-and-hungary/.

Elisha Fieldstadt, *"Bombshell" Information from Girlfriend of Chris Watts Helped Investigators*, NBC News (June 3, 2019, 7:53 AM MST), https://www.nbcnews.com/news/us-news/bombshell-information-girlfriend-chris-watts-helped-investigators-n1013121.

Thomas D. Barton & James M. Cooper, *Preventive Law and Creative Problem Solving: Multi-Dimensional Lawyering*, Nat'l Ctr. for Preventive L. 8–9, http://www.preventivelawyer.org/content/pdfs/Multi_Dimensional_Lawyer.pdf [https://web.archive.org/web/08-6-2016/http://www.preventivelawyer.org/content/pdfs/Multi_Dimensional_Lawyer.pdf].

31.1(e)(2) Last visited, updated, or modified dates

When the cited page is not specifically dated, there are two options. First, if the website indicates when it was last updated or modified, use that date with the prefix "last updated" or "last modified."[29] When no date can be ascertained from the cited page or the website itself, indicate the writer's date of access by inserting the phrase "last visited" before the date of access (Month Day, Year).[30] For either of these options, move the date parenthetical from before the URL to a parenthetical following the URL.[31] If you archived a web page in such a way that it indicates when a source was archived, you do not need to include a "last visited" parenthetical and can forgo the date parenthetical either before or after the URL.[32] See **Rule 31.1(f)** for more information about archival tools.

Examples

50 State Surveys of Law, Seattle U. Sch. L. Libr., http://lawlibguides.seattleu.edu/50state (last updated Oct. 23, 2019).

Fed. Bureau of Investigation, *CODIS Combined DNA Index System*, FBI Laboratory Services, https://www2.fbi.gov/hq/lab/html/codisbrochure_text.htm (last visited Dec. 2, 2016).

31.1(f) URL

A Uniform Resource Locator ("URL") is the exact electronic address of the source being cited. A URL typically consists of https:// or the like, followed by the domain name and, sometimes, additional characters that lead to a particular page.

If the URL has a shortlink or shortened URL available that clearly identifies the host site, then you should use the shortened URL.[33] You should not use a shortened URL like bit.ly or ow.ly because they do not clearly identify the host; in other words, any website can use the bit.ly or ow.ly domain name. In contrast, a shortened URL like wapo.st (Washington Post) or imdb.to (for IMDb) do clearly identify the host, and are therefore acceptable.

If there is no appropriate shortened URL, and the URL is relatively short, then set out the entire URL that links directly to the cited material.[34] Because URLs often are case sensitive, cite characters as they are presented without changing capitalization, punctuation, or spacing. The safest way to transcribe a URL correctly is to copy it from the browser window and paste it into the citation.

Do not underline a URL; underlining signifies an active hyperlink. In documents that will be published electronically, however, you may want to keep hyperlinks. Do *not* enclose a URL in angle brackets (< >).

If the online material linked to the URL has been permanently captured by a permalink, append a bracketed URL for the permalink. Likewise, if the web page is archived on an internet archival tool, append the archived URL in brackets after the normal URL.[35] See **Rule 30.3(c)** for information on using a digital object identifier ("DOI") as an alternative to a URL.

Example

> *FAQs*, Facebook, http://investor.fb.com/resources/default.aspx [http://perma.cc/CWD8-N2QF] (last visited Aug. 9, 2016).
>
> Jenny Leonard et al., *U.S. Weighs Sanctions on Chinese Officials, Firms over Hong Kong*, Bloomberg L., https://www .bloombergquint.com/global-economics/u-s-weighs-sanctions -on-chinese-officials-firms-over-hong-kong [https://web.archive .org/web/20200527025106/https://www.bloomberg.com/news/ articles/2020-05-26/u-s-weighs-sanctions-on-chinese-officials -firms-over-hong-kong?srnd=premium] (last updated May 20, 2020, 5:21 AM).

Because URLs can be long, they may not fit onto a single line of text. Break a long URL at a logical point, preferably after a slash (/). You may also break a URL after a colon (:), a double slash (//), or the "at" symbol (@). Break a URL *before* a period; breaking after a period may cause the reader to mistakenly assume the citation has ended. You may need to determine another logical break point, such as before a hyphen or underscore. Never use your own hyphen in breaking a URL, because the hyphen will look like part of the address. If the address is too long, though, you may need to utilize **Rule 31.1(g)** (identifying pathways).[36]

Examples

Preferred breaking point:	http://www.americanbar.org/publications/ law_practice_magazine/2012/january_february/ social-media-networking-for-lawyers.html
Alternative breaking point:	http://www.americanbar.org/publications/law _practice_magazine/2012/january_february/social -media-networking-for-lawyers.html
Incorrect breaking points:	http://www.americanbar.org/publications/law_ practice_magazine/2012/january_february/social- media-networking-for-lawyers.html
	http://www.americanbar.org/publications/ law_practice_magazine/2012/january_febru- ary/social-media-networking-for-lawyers. html

31.1(g) Identifying pathways as an alternative to URL

If the URL is lengthy or unwieldy, or if it will not lead the reader directly to the cited material (such as when you need to search a term to access the article), you should simply explain the path for getting to a particular page.[37] Use the domain name or URL that will get the user closest to the material you are citing; then tell the user in a parenthetical how to get to the particular page being cited, using directions like "click," "select," "follow," "path," "search," or "scroll down."[38] Place search terms in quotation marks.[39]

Examples using pathways

Melissa John, *Law-Suit*, Lawhaha.com, http://lawhaha.com/ (from menu bar, select "Law School Stories," then select "First Year Follies and Foibles" and scroll down to "Law-Suit") (last visited Dec. 8, 2020).

Funding, Bureau of Just. Stat., https://www.bjs.gov/index.cfm?ty=fun#assist (under "On this page," click "BJS funding programs") (last visited Dec. 8, 2020).

Ben Penn & Chris Marr, *Virus Telework Surge Primed for School-Year Reckoning in Court*, Bloomberg L. (Sept. 8, 2020, 2:30 AM), https://news.bloomberglaw.com/ (from advanced search bar, search "unscheduled telework hours," limit date range to "September 8, 2020," and select second article).

31.1(h)^FN Full citations to internet sources in academic footnotes

ACADEMIC FORMATTING

Follow **Rule 31.1(a)–(g)**, but present the website name in large and small capital letters.

Examples

23 *Report on Nuclear Employment Strategy of the United States Specified in Section 491 of 10 U.S.C.*, U.S. DEP'T OF DEF. 3–5 (June 12, 2013), http://www.defense.gov/Portals/1/Documents/pubs/ReporttoCongressonUSNuclearEmploymentStrategy_Section491.pdf.

55 Nat'l Highway Traffic Safety Admin., *Did You Know Archive*, FATALITY ANALYSIS REPORTING SYS. (FARS) ENCYCLOPEDIA, http://www-fars.nhtsa.dot.gov/Main/DidYouKnow.aspx (follow "Trends" hyperlink) (last visited July 8, 2012).

31.2 Blogs, Social Media Platforms, and Wikis

To cite a posting in a blog, a social media platform (e.g., Twitter, Instagram, LinkedIn), or a wiki, follow **Rule 31.1**, with the following additions.[40]

For the author of a social media post, provide the full real name of the person who posted the entry, if you can find and verify it, and include the username or handle of the author on that particular media platform in parentheses after the full name, leaving a space in between the full name and the opening parentheses.[41] If you cannot locate or verify the name of the person who posted the source, use the person's username or handle without parentheses.[42] If the author is a commenter on a post, follow the instructions in **Rule 31.1(a)**.

For social media posts, only include a title if there is one.[43] If a title is not clearly conveyed, omit it; do not attempt to create a descriptive title.[44] After the title (or author's name if no title), include the name of the social media platform.[45]

Examples

Blogs:

Amy Howe, *Justices Seek Government's Views in Antitrust Case*, SCOTUSblog (Dec. 7, 2020, 6:37 PM), https://www.scotusblog.com/2020/12/justices-seek-governments-views-in-antitrust-case/.

Marsi Buckmelter, Comment to *Another Great Statutory Interpretation Case out of Washington State*, Law Professor Blogs Network: Appellate Advocacy Blog (July 7, 2020, 12:33:36 PM), https://lawprofessors.typepad.com/appellate_advocacy/2020/07/another-great-statutory-interpretation-case-out-of-washington-state.html#comments.

Social media posts:

Univ. Ariz. L. (@uarizonalaw), Twitter (July 31, 2020, 1:45 PM), https://twitter.com/uarizonalaw/status/1289301099250253824.

Legal Writing Institute (@LWIonline), *Introducing Your 2020-22 Executive Officers!*, Twitter (July 16, 2020, 11:54 AM), https://twitter.com/LWIonline/status/1283837385697038338.

World Health Org., *COVID-19 Update*, Facebook (Sept. 8, 2020, 2:06 PM), https://www.facebook.com/WHO/videos/2404838886476529.

Wylde Law, Facebook (July 31, 2019, 3:34 PM), https://www.facebook.com/wyldelaw/posts/2133629533596402.

Blair Condoll (@professorbigdawg), Instagram (Sept. 8, 2020), https://www.instagram.com/p/CE48yvqFfQw/.

Sandra Watson, *Nikola and General Motors Form Strategic Partnership*, LinkedIn (Sept. 8, 2020), https://www.linkedin.com/posts/sandra-watson-88249110_nikola-and-general-motors-form-strategic-activity-6709147818818441216-LCLG.

Mike King, *The Small Business Reorganization Act: Blessing or Curse?*, LinkedIn (Dec. 4, 2020), https://www.linkedin.com/pulse/small-business-reorganization-act-blessing-curse-michael-king/?trackingId=moRWbetE6LzrL%2BBSt5%2Bkww%3D%3D.

Wikipedia: *Legal Citation*, Wikipedia, http://en.wikipedia.org/wiki/Legal_citation (last modified July 31, 2016, 9:38 AM).

31.3 Short Citations to Sources on the Internet

31.3(a) Using *id.* or other short citations to internet sources

When appropriate, use *id.* as the short citation (**Rule 11.3(c)**).[46] When *id.* is not appropriate, analogize to **Rule 21.7(a)** for periodicals, setting out the author's last name or the owner's name, or if neither is available, the website or domain name, followed by the italicized word *supra.*[47] If multiple pages of a website with the same website or domain name are cited, or if you are citing to more than one online source from the same author, use the title, too.[48]

Example

Full citation: Elisabeth Frater, *Asian-American Attorneys: Shattering Conventional Notions*, MCCA (May/June 2005), https://www.mcca.com/mcca-article/asian-american-attorneys/.

Short citation: Frater, *supra*.

31.3(b)FN Short citations to internet sources in academic footnotes

ACADEMIC FORMATTING

When *id.* is not appropriate (**Rule 11.3(c)**), use a *supra* reference as described in **Rule 11.4** in addition to presenting the website name in large and small capital letters as described in **Rule 31.1(h)FN**.[49]

Example

263 Laura D. Francis, *Scalia's Absence May Not Affect Immigration Case*, Bloomberg L. Daily Lab. Rep. (Feb. 18, 2016), http://www.bna.com/scalias-absence-may-n57982067466/.

264 132 S. Ct. 2492 (2012).

265 *Id.* at 2501.

266 Francis, *supra* note 263.

32 Commercial Databases

Fast Formats

Database citation using unique identifier	William W. Bassett, *Supreme Court Splits on Same-Sex Marriage—Striking DOMA, Shelving Prop. 8*, 2013 WL 3244866 (June 28, 2013). H.R. 4310, 112th Cong. § 537 (2012), 2011 CONG US HR 4310 (Westlaw).
Database citation without unique identifier	Sheryl Stratton, *Black & Decker to Settle; Bigger Case on Horizon*, Tax Notes Today, Mar. 5, 2007, LEXIS, 2007 TNT 43-1.
Citation in academic footnote	63 Greg Berman & Emily Gold, *Procedural Justice from the Bench*, JUDGES' J., Spring 2012, at *20, Westlaw, JUDGEJ. ⚠ACADEMIC FORMATTING
Short citations	Fla. Att'y Gen. Op. 2013-14, 2013 WL 3388124, at *3. Stratton, *supra*. 81 Berman et al., *supra* note 63, at *22.

32.1 When to Cite Commercial Databases

You may cite a source to a commercial database when the source is not available in print.[1] You may also provide the commercial database information in a parallel citation appended to the source's standard citation when the source will be more readily and easily accessed in the database.[2] (See **Chart 30.1** for rules for citing specific sources to a commercial database or providing parallel citations.)

The best-known commercial databases include Bloomberg Law, Lexis, and Westlaw, but many lawyers also use smaller commercial databases such as Fastcase, and many law libraries provide their users with access to database collections such as HeinOnline.

While the majority of legal sources may be retrieved from these databases by entering their print-version citations into a search box, some sources—particularly those that have no print counterparts—are assigned unique identifiers by the databases, and these identifiers are an integral part of their citations. See **Rule 32.2** for more information about unique database identifiers. For information concerning citations to cases in commercial databases, see **Rules 12.4(b)(5)**, **12.4(c)**, **12.13**, **12.14(b)**, and **12.15(b)**.

32.2 Full Citations When a Unique Identifier Is Available

A unique identifier is a code assigned to a document that will retrieve the document from a specific commercial database directory. The identifier typically consists of a year, the database abbreviation (e.g., BL, WL), and a document number. In Lexis+, you will typically see a subdirectory as part of the main database abbreviation (e.g., U.S. Dist. LEXIS, indicating case law from United States district courts).

Follow the basic citation rule for the print version of the source, but in place of the print publication component of the citation (e.g., volume/periodical abbreviation/initial page), substitute the unique identifier from the commercial database.[3] For legislative, administrative, and executive materials, add a parenthetical reference to the database source if it is not apparent in the database identifier.[4]

Examples

Pending and unreported cases:	*Kagarise v. Savory Sandwiches Enters. 3, LLC*, No. 2014CV034853, 2016 Colo. Dist. LEXIS 489, at *8 (D. Colo. Jan. 6, 2016).
Constitutions:	R.I. Const. art. VI, § 8 (West, Westlaw through ch. 79 of the 2020 2d Reg. Sess.).
Statutes:	Utah Code Ann. § 8-5-1 (Lexis+ 2020).
Article:	William W. Bassett, *Supreme Court Splits on Same-Sex Marriage—Striking DOMA, Shelving Prop. 8*, 2013 WL 3244866 (June 28, 2013).
Court document:	Complaint, *I Am Other Entertainment, LLC v. Adams*, No. 13 CV 4547, 2013 WL 3297482, at *1 (S.D.N.Y. July 1, 2013).
Administrative decision:	*Hisps. United of Buffalo, Inc.*, 359 N.L.R.B. 368 (Dec. 14, 2012), 2012 NLRB LEXIS 852.
Newspaper:	Robert Dodge, *Bush Learning His Economics from Experts*, Dallas Morn. News, June 28, 1999, at 1D, 1999 WL 4131653.
Administrative regulation:	Nev. Admin. Code § 432B.135 (Supp. 2012), NV ADC 432B.135 (Westlaw).

32.3 Full Citations When a Unique Identifier Is Not Available

To cite a source to a commercial database that does not assign it a unique identifier, use the following format.[5]

Regular citation to print source, | Commercial database publisher, | Database name.

Examples

10 Ind. Admin. Code 1.5-4-4 (2009), Westlaw, IN-ADC database.

2 J.I. Clark Hare, *American Constitutional Law* 823 (1889), HeinOnline, Legal Classics Library.

32.4 Short Citations to Commercial Databases

32.4(a) Using *id.* or other short citations to commercial databases

When appropriate (**Rule 11.3(c)**), use *id.* as the short citation.[6] When *id.* is not appropriate, locate the rule for short citations to the analogous print source and adapt it as needed.[7] If the full citation contains a unique identifier, retain it in the short citation, and if needed, change the pinpoint reference.[8]

Example

Full citation: Fla. Att'y Gen. Op. 2013-14, 2013 WL 3388124, at *2 (July 2, 2013).

Short citation: Fla. Att'y Gen. Op. 2013-14, 2013 WL 3388124, at *3.

32.4(b)FN Short citations to commercial databases in academic footnotes

ACADEMIC FORMATTING

When appropriate (**Rule 11.3(c)**), use *id.* as the short citation.[9] When *id.* is not appropriate, use a *supra* reference to the footnote containing the full citation and change only the pinpoint reference, if necessary (**Rule 11.4**).[10]

Example

Full citation: 63 Greg Berman & Emily Gold, *Procedural Justice from the Bench*, JUDGES' J., Spring 2012, at *20, Westlaw, JUDGEJ database.

Short citation: 81 Berman et al., *supra* note 63, at *22.

33 Email, Listservs, Shared Drives, Other Short Electronic Messages, and CD-ROMs

Fast Formats

Email	Email from Jan M. Levine, Professor & Dir. Legal Rsch. & Writing, Duquesne Univ. Sch. of Law, to Richard K. Neumann, Jr., Professor, Hofstra Law Sch., ALWD Conference (June 28, 2009, 3:20 PM EDT) (copy on file with Professor Levine).
Listserv posting	Posting of Carole G. Bremen, cgbremen@gmail.com, to lawclinic@lists.washlaw.edu, *First Arguments in New Term* (Oct. 22, 2013 1:45 PM) (on file with author).
Text	Text from Christina Poletti to Joy Herr-Cardillo, 1L Escape Room Experience (Nov. 17, 2019, 1:51 PM) (on file with Christina Poletti).
Chat	Chat of Brian Larson to LWI members, LWI Scholarship Development Committee Workshop (July 15, 2020) (Zoom) (on file with Legal Writing Institute).
Post on private message board	Post of Xiaoqian Hu to Property-Law-Professors, Property Rights in China (Dec. 12, 2020, 8:12 AM) (Microsoft Teams) (on file with Harvard Law Review).
Generally available shared drive document	Carolyn V. Williams, Assignment Schedule for Intensive Legal Research and Writing 2 (2019) (Dropbox file), https://arizona.box.com/v/color-coded-Intensive-Schedule.
Private shared drive document	Debbie Martin, Rocky Mountain Regional Legal Writing Conference Lodging and Transportation (March 2020) (Microsoft Teams file) (on file with Debbie Martin).
CD-ROM	*Intuitive Estate Planner* (Thomson Reuters CD-ROM, Version 16.2, 2013).

Citations in academic footnotes	[49] Email from Michael Smith to Darby Dickerson, Background on *Jones v. Smith* Case (Dec. 14, 2008, 7:35 AM) (copy on file with Villanova Law Review). ⚠ACADEMIC FORMATTING [68] Mitchell Anderson, COVID-19 Prison/Jail Responses to Survey (last updated June 15, 2020) (Dropbox file) (on file with Practice in Place Podcast).

33.1 Full Citations to Email

A full citation to an email has up to twelve components:

Designation | Author's name | [, Author's title and affiliation] | [, Author's email address] | to | Recipient's name, | [Recipient's title and affiliation,] | [Recipient's email address,] | [Subject line or descriptive title] | [Pinpoint reference] | (Date parenthetical) | (Email's location).

Follow **Rule 27.5** (unpublished letters and memoranda), but with the modifications in **Rule 33.1(a)–(d)** below.

33.1(a) Designation of email

Use "Email from" as the designation.[1] For the title and affiliation of either the author or recipient, abbreviate words found in **Appendix 3(B)** and **Appendix 3(E)**. Including the email addresses of the author or recipient is permissible, but not required.[2] If included, the email address follows the person's title and affiliation, or if there is none, the person's name. If you must break an email address, do so at a logical place, such as after a slash or before a period; do not insert a hyphen, because it may be read as part of the address.

Example

Email from Jodi Wilson, President, Assoc. of Legal Writing Dirs., jlwlson2@memphis.edu, to Anne Mullins, President-elect, Assoc. of Legal Writing Dirs., amullins@law.stetson.edu, New Author Criteria (May 31, 2018, 1:31 PM) (on file with Jodi Wilson).

33.1(b) Subject

As a title, you may use the words in the "Subject" line of the email message, but this component is not required.[3] If the subject line does not describe (or no longer describes, as in the case of an email in a thread) the content, you may use a general description instead. Capitalize according to **Rule 3.2**, **Rule 3.3**, and **Chart 3.1**.

Example

Email from Brooke Bowman, Professor & Dir. Moot Ct. Bd., Stetson U. Coll. of L., to Jessica Barmack, Developmental Ed., The Froebe Grp., Weekly Update (Oct. 20, 2020, 3:20 PM EDT) (copy on file with Professor Bowman).

33.1(c) Date parenthetical

In parentheses, set out the exact date (Month Day, Year) that the email was sent. Whenever it is available, include the exact time of the email (including a reference to the time zone, if available) after the date.[4] See **Rule 31.1(e)(1)** for analogous examples.

33.1(d) Location of copy

Because email messages are generally private, describe where or how readers might obtain a copy of the email in a separate parenthetical.[5]

Example

Email from Jan M. Levine, Professor & Dir. Legal Rsch. & Writing, Duquesne Univ. Sch. of L., to Richard K. Neumann, Jr., Professor, Hofstra L. Sch., ALWD Conference (June 28, 2009, 3:20 PM EDT) (copy on file with Professor Levine).

33.2 Full Citations to Listserv Postings

A posting sent to a listserv is automatically sent to all of the listserv's subscribers. Follow **Rule 33.1** (emails), but with the following modifications. Use "Posting of" as the designation.[6] Following the name, title, and affiliation, if any, of the person who made the posting, add that person's email address, and in place of a recipient's name, provide the email address of the listserv.[7]

Examples

Posting of Coleen Barger, Professor of L., cmbarger@ualr.edu, to LAWFAC-L@ualr.edu, New Scholarly Journal (Sept. 3, 2013, 3:30 PM CDT) (copy on file with author).

Posting of Deborah Borman, Professor of L., Deborah.borman1@gmail.com, to LAWPROF-L@iupui.edu, How to Record a PowerPoint with Voiceover (Mar. 12, 2020, 2:25 PM) (copy on file with Deborah Borman).

33.3 Full Citations to Other Short Electronic Messages

Use this rule to cite to short electronic messages that are not captured by any other rule; these could be texts, chats in video conferences, discussion group postings, internet forum postings, and the like. Short messages can be sent to one person or to a group of people, such as when a participant sends a "chat" to the organizer of a GoToWebinar or "posts" to a channel with all team members on Microsoft Teams. The citation to a short message has seven components:

Designation | Author's name | to | Recipient's name, | [Title or descriptive title] | (Date parenthetical) | (Short message's location).

Follow **Rule 33.1** (emails), but with the modifications in **Rule 33.3(a)–(d)** below.

33.3(a) Designation of short electronic message

Use "Text from," "Chat from," "Post of," or similar phrases for the designation.

Example

Text from Sylvia Lett to Carrie Williams, Background on Open Research Memo (Dec. 11, 2020, 4:56 PM) (on file with author).

33.3(b) Author and recipients

When possible, use the author's or poster's real name; if that is unavailable, use their handle or username for the message's platform. Do not include either the author's or recipient's title or affiliation. These short messages do not display email addresses, so do not include any emails in the citation. Do not include any phone numbers in lieu of an email address.

If the short message is to more than one person (e.g., all participants in a Skype video conference), use the group or team name, if there is one, or description of the group rather than individual names, analogizing to **Rule 20.1(b)(3)**.

Example

Post of Michael Wagenheim to Law-Faculty-Group, How to Use Zoom Whiteboards (Sept. 18, 2020, 1:16 PM) (Microsoft Teams) (on file with University of Arizona Law Library).

33.3(c) Title or descriptive title and descriptive parenthetical

Use the title or description of the presentation or meeting if the message was sent during it. For other short messages, create a descriptive title of the subject matter, analogizing to **Rule 26.1(b)** (subject or title of unpublished presentation). Use **Rule 3.2**, **Rule 3.3**, and **Chart 3.1** for capitalization. Do not abbreviate words in the title or description.

Do not include a pinpoint reference. If the source is not a text, insert a descriptive parenthetical after the date parenthetical that describes the platform on which the message was sent.

Example

Chat from Andrea Gass to Legal Rsch. Working Grp., Native American Court Systems (Nov. 6, 2020) (GoToMeeting) (on file with Arizona State Bar).

33.3(d) Discussion groups and internet forums

If the discussion group message or forum post does not have a URL accessible by anyone with a URL, use **Rule 33.3(a)–(c)**. If it does have a URL associated with it that is accessible by the general public, replace the location parenthetical with a comma, one space, and the URL. For the recipient, list the website or domain name, analogizing to **Rule 31.1(c)**. Italicize the title or descriptive title.

Analogize to **Rule 31.1(a)** if you are citing to a comment on an original post.

Examples

Post of LandlordFrank1975 to The Law.com, *2 Tenants Created Clutter in the Basement* (Dec. 12, 2020, 1:08 PM), https://www.thelaw.com/threads/2-tenants-created-clutter-in-basement.77696/.

Greencedar, Comment to LinuxQuestions, *Linux Predictions for 2020* (Jan. 8, 2020, 10:29 PM), https://www.linuxquestions.org/questions/linux-news-59/linux-predictions-for-2020-a-4175666764/.

33.4FN Citations to Emails, Listserv Posts, and Short Messages in Academic Footnotes

ACADEMIC FORMATTING

There are no differences in the full citation format used in academic notes for emails, listserv posts, or short messages. Follow **Rules 33.1**, **33.2**, and **33.3**.

33.5 Full Citations to Shared Drive Documents

Use this rule when citing to documents on a shared drive such as Dropbox, Microsoft Teams, or Google Docs. A full citation to a shared drive document depends on whether the document is viewable by the general public using a link without having to get permission from the owner for each person accessing the work. If it is viewable, use **Rule 33.5(a)**. If it is not, use **Rule 33.5(b)**.

33.5(a) Full citations to generally available shared drive documents

If the source is published in print (not printed off a personal printer) or on a website other than a shared drive, cite the print or website version, in that order of preference, using the applicable citation rule rather than citing a shared drive version of the source. Citations to works in a shared drive have up to six components:

Author's name, | Title or descriptive title | [Pinpoint reference] | (Date parenthetical) | [(Descriptive parenthetical)] | , URL.

Analogize to **Rule 29.2** (unpublished manuscripts) with the following modifications. If the source is untitled, create a detailed descriptive title of the subject matter, analogizing to **Rule 26.1(b)** (subject or title of unpublished presentation). When the work is not dated, analogize to **Rule 31.1(e)(2)**, including moving the date parenthetical after the URL. If it is not clear from the URL what type of shared drive the document resides in (e.g., "Dropbox file," "Google Doc," "Microsoft Teams file"), create a descriptive parenthetical that describes that information.

Example

Christina Billhartz, Citing to the Record 3 (2020) (Google slides), https://docs.google.com/presentation/d/1u4fW7xnnhywkDyC9fE769LAvGGETNwpdcOBnsMSJ888/edit?usp=sharing.

33.5(b) Full citations to private shared drive documents

Use this rule for shared drive documents that are both not viewable by the general public (see **Rule 33.5(a)**) and not scheduled for publication (see **Rule 29.1**). "Not viewable by the general public" in this context means that either (a) the document's properties are such that anyone with a link cannot view it without the document owner's express permission for each person accessing it, or (b) it could be viewable by anyone with a link, but the owner does not want it to be.

Author's name, | Title or descriptive title | [Pinpoint reference] | (Date parenthetical) | (Descriptive parenthetical) | (Document's location).

Example (spaces denoted by ▲)

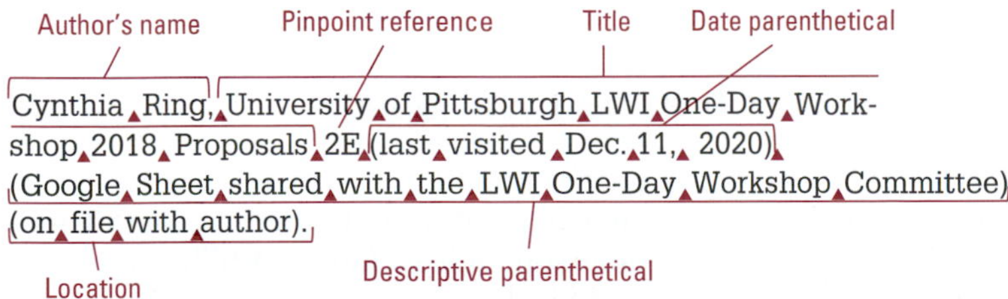

Follow **Rule 33.5(a)** with these three adjustments. When the cited page is not specifically dated, analogize to **Rule 31.1(e)(2)**, but do not move the date parenthetical to the end of the citation. For the descriptive parenthetical, describe the cited work by stating what type of shared drive it resides in (e.g., "Dropbox file," "Google Doc," "Microsoft Teams file"). In lieu of the URL, describe where or how readers might obtain a copy.

Examples

J. App. Prac. & Process, Publication Agreement 4 (last updated July 13, 2020) (Dropbox file) (on file with the Journal of Appellate Practice and Process).

Mitchell Anderson, COVID-19 Prison/Jail Responses to Survey (last updated June 15, 2020) (Dropbox file) (on file with Practice in Place Podcast).

33.5(c)FN Citations to shared drive documents in academic footnotes

ACADEMIC FORMATTING

There are no differences in the full citation format used in academic notes for shared drive documents. Follow **Rule 33.5(a)–(b)**.

33.6 Full Citations to Materials on CD-ROM

A CD-ROM is a compact disc that can be read by a computer. If the work is available in print or on a commercial database, cite the print or commercial database version, in that order of preference, rather than citing a CD-ROM version of the source.[8]

To the extent possible, follow the rule for an analogous source in print, with the following modifications. Add the name of the publisher and the notation "CD-ROM" to the date parenthetical.[9] Indicate the date shown on the actual disc, and, if relevant, the version or release.[10]

Examples

Anderson's Ohio Annotated Bankruptcy Handbook § 107 (LexisNexis CD-ROM current through Sept. 6, 2012).

Intuitive Estate Planner (Thomson Reuters CD-ROM, Version 16.2, 2013).

33.7FN Citations to CD-ROMs in Academic Footnotes

ACADEMIC FORMATTING

Depending on the analogous source in print, you may need to consult academic footnote rules for the analogous source (e.g., **Rule 20.1(f)FN**). For example, if the analogous source is a book, both the author and the name of the book title will be presented in large and small capital letters.

33.8 Short Citations to Emails, Listservs, Short Messages, Shared Drives, and CD-ROMs

When appropriate (**Rule 11.3(c)**), use *id.* as the short citation.[11] When *id.* is not appropriate, use the following format for an email, listserv post, or other short message:

Designation | Author's full name | to | Recipient's full name.

Examples

Full citations:

Email from Brooke Bowman, Professor & Dir. Moot Ct. Bd., Stetson U. Coll. of L., to Jessica Barmack, Developmental Ed., The Froebe Grp., Weekly Update (Oct. 20, 2020, 3:20 PM EDT) (copy on file with Professor Bowman).

Posting of Deborah Borman, Professor of L., Deborah.borman1@gmail.com, to LAWPROF-L@iupui.edu, How to Record a PowerPoint with Voiceover (Mar. 12, 2020, 2:25 PM) (copy on file with Deborah Borman).

Chat from Andrea Gass to Legal Rsch. Working Grp., Native American Court Systems (Nov. 6, 2020) (GoToMeeting) (on file with Arizona State Bar).

Post of LandlordFrank1975 to The Law.com, *2 Tenants Created Clutter in the Basement* (Dec. 12, 2020, 1:08 PM), https://www.thelaw.com/threads/2-tenants-created-clutter-in-basement.77696/.

Short citations:

Email from Brooke Bowman to Jessica Barmack.

Posting of Deborah Borman to LAWPROF-L@iupui.edu.

Chat from Andrea Gass to Legal Rsch. Working Grp.

Post of LandlordFrank1975 to The Law.com.

When *id.* is not appropriate, use the following format for shared drive documents:

Author's surname, | *supra*, | [at] | [Pinpoint reference].

Examples

Full citations:

Christina Billhartz, Citing to the Record 3 (2020), https://docs.google.com/presentation/d/1u4fW7xnnhywkDyC9fE769LAvGGETNwpdcOBnsMSJ888/edit?usp=sharing.

Mitchell Anderson, COVID-19 Prison/Jail Responses to Survey (last updated June 15, 2020) (Dropbox file) (on file with Practice in Place Podcast).

Short citations: Billhartz, *supra*, at 3.

Anderson, *supra*, at 2.

For sources on a CD-ROM, analogize to rules for making short citations to the analogous source.[12] For example, if citing a book on CD-ROM, follow **Rule 20.6**. You do not need to indicate in the short form that the source was a CD-ROM.[13]

Example

Anderson's Ohio Annotated Bankruptcy Handbook, *supra*, § 107.

33.9FN Short Citations to Emails, Listservs, Short Messages, Shared Drives, and CD-ROMs in Academic Footnotes

When *id.* is not appropriate (**Rule 11.3(c)**), use the *supra* format below for an email, listserv post, or other short message, cross-referencing the earlier footnote containing the full citation of the source.[14] See **Rule 11.4** for additional information on *supra*.

Follow **Rule 33.8** for short citations to shared drive documents, with one addition. When *id.* is not appropriate, between *supra* and the comma following it, insert one space, the word "note" in plain type, another space, and the footnote number where the full citation can be found.[15]

The resulting short citations will look like this:

Author's surname, | *supra* | note | Footnote number, | [at] | [Pinpoint reference].

Examples

219 Christina Billhartz, Citing to the Record 3 (2020), https://docs.google.com/presentation/d/1u4fW7xnnhywkDyC9fE769LAvGGETNwpdcOBnsMSJ888/edit?usp=sharing.

220 *Id.*

221 Chat from Andrea Gass to Legal Rsch. Working Grp., Native American Court Systems (Nov. 6, 2020) (GoToMeeting) (on file with Arizona State Bar).

222 Text from Sylvia Lett to Carrie Williams, Background on Open Research Memo (Dec. 11, 2020, 4:56 PM) (on file with author).

. . .

[230] Chat from Andrea Gass to Legal Rsch. Working Grp., *supra* note 221.

[231] Text from Sylvia Lett to Carrie Williams, *supra* note 222.

. . .

[240] Billhartz, *supra* note 219, at 1.

For sources on a CD-ROM, analogize to rules for making short citations for the analogous source in academic formatting.

Example

[117] ANDERSON'S OHIO ANNOTATED BANKRUPTCY HANDBOOK, *supra*, § 107.

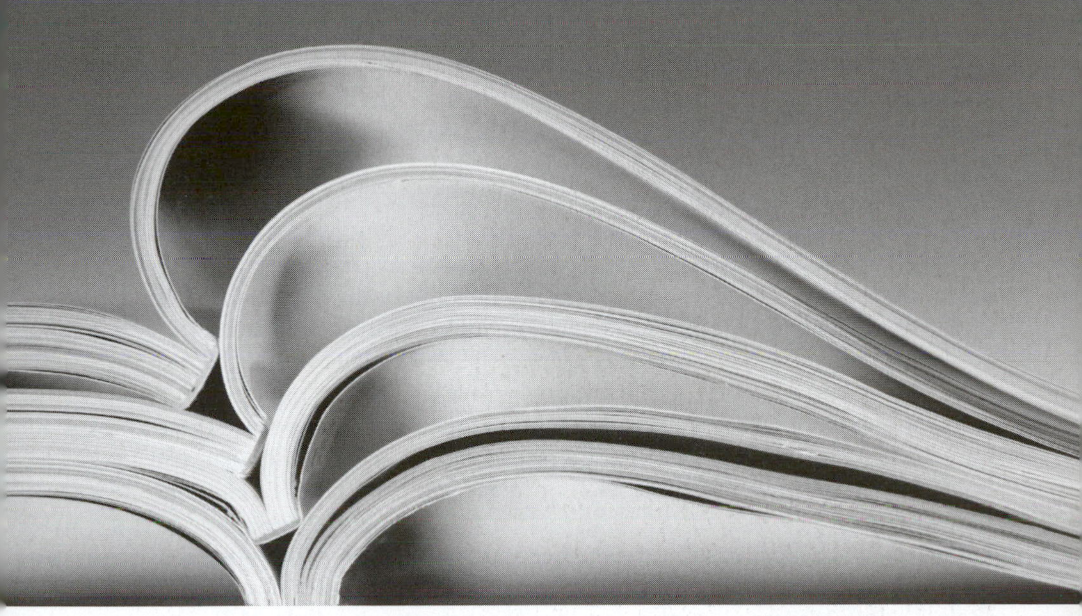

Part 4
Incorporating Citations into Documents

34 Citation Placement and Use

34.1 Placement Options

Legal citations are used in many written situations, including practice-based documents — such as office memoranda, pleadings, motions, and briefs — or academic documents — including books, treatises, and law review articles. In general, practice-based documents place citations within the text, although some courts' rules permit writers to place citations in footnotes. Academic works almost always relegate citations to footnotes or endnotes.[1] Therefore, the first determination for citation placement is whether your document calls for citations in its text (**Rule 34.2**) or in academic footnotes or endnotes (**Rule 34.3**).

Placement also depends on *what* the citation supports — an entire sentence or a block quotation (**Rule 34.1(a)**) or a phrase or portion of a sentence (**Rule 34.1(b)**). Writers must also consider *how often* to cite (**Rule 34.2**). That frequency depends upon the document and the expectations of its readers. Finally, writers must consider the *kind* of support the citation indicates. For guidance on ways to indicate the nature and degree of support a citation provides for a stated proposition, see **Rule 35** (Signals), and for using citations to multiple sources to support a single proposition, see **Rule 36** (Order of Authorities).

34.1(a) Citation sentences

When a citation provides any form of support for the single proposition of an entire textual sentence, it immediately follows the final punctuation ending the textual sentence.[2] When a citation indicates the source of a quotation of fifty words or more, place it on its own line, beneath the block quotation, at the left margin (see **Rule 38.5**).[3] These forms of placement are known as "citation sentences."[4] A citation sentence, like a textual sentence, begins with a capital letter and ends with a period.[5] Both full and short citations (including *id.*) function as citation sentences.

Examples (citation sentences in red)

> In our system, state-operated schools may not be enclaves of totalitarianism. School officials do not possess absolute authority over their students. Students in school as well as out of school are "persons" under our Constitution. They are possessed of fundamental rights which the State must respect, just as they themselves must respect their obligations to the State.

Tinker v. Des Moines Indep. Cmty. Sch. Dist., 393 U.S. 503, 511 (1969).

The federal judicial power is limited, extending only to certain categories of cases or controversies. *See* U.S. Const. art. III, § 2, cl. 1.

34.1(b) Citation clauses

When a cited source relates to only part of a textual sentence, place its citation in a clause within the textual sentence, immediately following the proposition or short quotation it concerns, set off with commas.[6] If the citation clause concludes the textual sentence, use a period as the final punctuation.[7] Both full and short citations (with some exceptions for *id.*) function as citation clauses. Do not use *id.* in a citation clause that refers to a *different* authority than the one immediately preceding it.[8]

Examples (citation clauses in red)

Although the Fourth Amendment prohibits unreasonable searches, *Elkins v. United States*, 364 U.S. 206, 222 (1960), each case must be decided on its own facts and circumstances, *Harris v. United States*, 331 U.S. 145, 150 (1947).

Courts have defined the viewpoint variously as that of "an ordinary reader of a particular race," *e.g.*, *Ragin v. N.Y. Times Co.*, 923 F.2d 995, 1000 (2d Cir. 1991), and that of "a reasonable black person," *e.g.*, *Harris v. Int'l Paper Co.*, 765 F. Supp. 1509, 1516 n.12 (D. Me. 1991).

34.1(c) Embedded citations

A citation may be used as a grammatical element of a textual sentence, such as the object of a preposition or a direct object. Such citations are called "embedded citations"; while they still function as citations, they are necessary to the grammatical sense of the text. For that reason, you should avoid using embedded citations. If you do write a textual sentence using an embedded citation, do not preface it with any signal, and do not repeat the citation following the sentence. Do not use *id.* as an embedded citation.

Examples (embedded citations in red)

In *International Shoe Co. v. Washington*, 326 U.S. 310, 316 (1945), the Court held that if the defendant was not present in the forum, due process required that he have certain minimum contacts with that forum.

The court's opinion quoted 49 U.S.C. § 16(3)(f) (2012) as authority for the one-year statute of limitations.

34.1(d) Textual references

In appropriate circumstances, you may refer to authorities in text without using all of their citation components. A textual reference is appropriate only when the source has previously been cited nearby in a full citation or when all the information typically conveyed in a full citation is present.

Examples (textual references in red)

Federal Rule of Civil Procedure 30(a)(2)(A) presumptively limits each party to ten depositions.

The argument centered on the Privileges or Immunities Clause of the Fourteenth Amendment.

34.1(e)FN Placement of citations in documents with academic footnotes or endnotes

ACADEMIC FORMATTING

All full and short citations belong in the notes.[9] Do not use citation sentences, or citation clauses in the text, and rewrite sentences to avoid using embedded citations.[10]

A "note reference number" is displayed as a superscript numeral, set slightly above the regular text (example: [75]).[11] Note reference numbers correspond to the footnotes or endnotes containing the citations. Notes are numbered consecutively, beginning with the number [1].

When a single source relates to the entire sentence, place its note reference number at the end of that sentence.[12] If it concerns only a portion of the sentence, however, place the note reference number *within* the sentence, immediately following the portion to which it refers (much as you would place a citation clause in practice-based writing).[13] For example, if you make a textual reference to a case (the third example below), insert the note reference number immediately after your first use of the case's name, placing the remaining citation components in the note, and if the textual reference did not do so, setting out the full case name. A note reference number *follows* most marks of punctuation (e.g., periods, commas, semicolons), but it should *precede* a dash or a colon.[14]

SIDEBAR 34.1FN Using Your Word Processor to Format Footnotes

Most word-processing programs have a footnote and endnote function. If you insert note numbers using this function, the program automatically will superscript the note reference numbers, place the notes on the appropriate pages with corresponding text, number and renumber notes if other notes are added or deleted, insert separator lines, and adjust the main text. However, when notes are added or deleted, the program may not automatically renumber textual cross-references (see **Rule 10** (cross-references) and **Rule 11.4** (*supra*)).

Therefore, if a note reference number changes, always check the document's cross-references to that note. As a practical matter, you can use only full citations in the notes — or short citations other than *id.* — and then substitute appropriate short citations and cross-references to them in the final editing stages.

Examples (note reference numbers in red)

Source relates to entire sentence:

The Family and Medical Leave Act grants twelve weeks of leave during a twelve-month period to any eligible employee who, because of a serious health condition, cannot perform the functions of the position she holds.[11]

---

[11] 29 U.S.C. § 2612.

Sources relate to portions of sentence:

Although one court held that an interrogatory with multiple related subparts constituted a single interrogatory,[42] another court ruled that these subparts amounted to multiple interrogatories.[43]

---

[42] *Am. Chiropractic Ass'n v. Trigon Healthcare, Inc.*, 2002 WL 1792062, at *2 (W.D. Va. Aug. 5, 2002).

[43] *Valdez v. Ford Motor Co.*, 143 F.R.D. 296, 298 (D. Nev. 1991).

First textual reference to case:

In *International Shoe Co. v. Washington*,[104] the Court held that if the defendant was not present in the forum, due process required that he have certain minimum contacts with that forum.

---

[104] 326 U.S. 310, 316 (1945).

Although you may use more than one note reference number within a single sentence, do not use two *consecutive* note number references with no intervening text. When two or more citations relate to the same proposition, put them in a string citation (see **Rule 34.3**).

Correct (two authorities support second clause):

In federal cases, all phases of civil deposition are subject to court control;[61] the court has discretion to issue orders designed to prevent abusive tactics during depositions.[62]

***Incorrect* (problem marked in red):**

In federal cases, all phases of civil deposition are subject to court control;[61] the court has discretion to issue orders designed to prevent abusive tactics during depositions.[62] [63]

A note reference number generally should not appear *within* quoted material because it is not part of the quoted text. If you must place a note reference number within a quotation, use brackets around the note reference number (example: [[17]]). **Rule 40.3(d)** addresses the omission of note reference numbers within the original quoted material.

34.2 Frequency of Citation

Legal writing requires appropriate attribution. Place a full or short citation immediately after each sentence—or if applicable, part of a sentence—that contains a statement of legal principle, a reference to or a description of an authority, or an idea, thought, or expression borrowed from another source, including quotations.

When you refer to two or more sentences from the *same* page, section, or other subdivision of the *same* source within a single paragraph and there are no other intervening citations, you may place a single citation to the source at the end of the paragraph. This convention can be confusing for your reader, however, so the best practice is to include a citation after every sentence, even when it is to the same material. Additionally, do not use this convention if the pinpoint reference to the cited material changes. In that situation, use an appropriate short citation with a new pinpoint reference.

Example

An Illinois court has discussed whether a covenant not to compete prohibits a seller from engaging in "any conceivable business activity." *Smith v. Burkitt*, 795 N.E.2d 385, 392 (Ill. App. Ct. 2003). In September 1999, Billy and Brenda Smith entered into a contract with Fred and Dorothy Burkitt to purchase the Burkitts' business. The contract included a noncompetition agreement. In November 2001, the Smiths sued the Burkitts for conducting business in violation of the noncompetition agreement. *Id.* at 387.

Although the agreement provided for the sale of the Burkitts' business assets, including real property and sales inventory, it was silent about the nature of the business. The Burkitts' complaint did not specify the manner in which the Smiths impermissibly violated the agreement, and so the Smiths filed a motion to dismiss on grounds that the vagueness of the agreement made it impossible to enforce. *Id.*

34.3 Number of Sources to Cite

The number of sources you cite for a single proposition depends on several factors: the document you are writing; the audience for whom you are writing; the type and number of sources relevant to the proposition; and the status of those sources in terms of their primacy, acceptance, or influence. A citation sentence or citation clause that contains citations to multiple authorities for a single proposition is called a "string citation." (For guidance on selecting the order of authorities in a string citation, see **Rule 36**.)

34.3(a) Type of document and audience

Academic writing features more string citations than found in practice-based documents such as office memoranda or briefs. Those who use scholarly materials expect abundant citations, showing such things as historical precedent. String citations provide academic readers with the depth of reference necessary to place scholarly topics in context. In contrast, judges and practitioners typically want to see citations only to those authorities providing the best and strongest support for a stated proposition, and therefore, they find string citations to be unhelpful or distracting.

34.3(b) Number of relevant authorities

The more authorities relating to a proposition, the more from which you have to choose, and the greater the likelihood you will cite more than one to support or contradict a proposition. In such a case, the "*e.g.*," introductory signal, which can be used alone or combined with another signal, should prove helpful.[15] See **Rule 35** for more information on signals.

If the proposition is well established, it may be sufficient to cite fewer supporting sources, particularly if they are mandatory primary authorities. If the proposition is novel or contested, you may need to cite more sources to persuade the reader.

34.4 Guidelines for Determining Which Authorities to Cite in a Practice-Based Document

It can be challenging to determine which and how many authorities to cite to show readers you have conducted thorough research, while not overwhelming them with too many citations. Begin by predicting the amount of citation and explanation that interested, but busy, readers would want to see. Put yourself in the reader's position. Ask which authorities — whether favorable to one side or the other — would be most likely to affect a decisionmaker's reasoning. Ask how you would feel if you made a decision without knowing about a particular authority. Cite and discuss (or argue) those authorities. Discard peripheral sources unless you need them to fill gaps in your argument or analysis.

A primary source is always more persuasive than a secondary source. In addition, mandatory authority from the jurisdiction is preferable to persuasive authority from other jurisdictions. Remember that primary authority is more than just case law. Consider whether statutes or regulations, for example, may apply to the issues.

As for case law, particularly if you have limited space, select the case that not only addresses the same legal issue but also is factually the most on point. If two or more cases are equally good, select the case from the highest court. If the cases are from the same court, select either the most recent case or the landmark case — the case to which all later cases refer.

35 Signals

35.1 Function of Signals

A signal prefaces a citation to indicate the type and degree of support or contradiction the cited authority provides for a proposition in text. Use signals not only before full citations but also before short citations.

35.2 Significance of *No Signal*

The *absence of a signal* before a citation is itself a signal (see **Chart 35.1**), signifying one of three things[1]:

- the cited authority provides *direct support for a stated proposition*;
- the cited authority is the *source of a quotation*; or
- the cited authority is the *source of a general reference in text.*

If an authority is cited for a reason other than one of those listed above, the citation must be preceded by one of the *other* signals listed in **Chart 35.1**.

Examples (no signal)

Direct support for proposition:	The Family and Medical Leave Act grants twelve work weeks of leave during any twelve-month period to any eligible employee who, because of a serious health condition, cannot perform the functions of the position she holds. 29 U.S.C. § 2612.
Source of quotation:	Summary judgment is appropriate "if the pleadings, the discovery and disclosure materials on file, and any affidavits show that there is no genuine issue as to any material fact and that the movant is entitled to judgment as a matter of law." Fed. R. Civ. P. 56(c)(2).
Source of general reference in text:	The Supreme Court faced the issue surrounding Title II in *Tennessee v. Lane.*[21] ——— [21] 541 U.S. 509 (2004).

35.3 Categories of Signals

Unless an authority is cited for a reason identified in the "no-signal" group (**Rule 35.2**), use another signal from **Chart 35.1** that is appropriate to the type and degree of support (or contradiction) the authority provides for the text.

CHART 35.1 Categories of Signals: Types and Degrees of Support

A signal is a shortcut indicator of a cited source's relationship to a stated proposition. Signals are categorized by four *types*[2]:

- indicating the source's *support* for the proposition;
- inviting *comparison* between the cited sources' treatment or conclusions about the proposition;
- demonstrating the source's *contradiction* to the proposition; and
- providing *general background* relevant to the proposition.

Most categories contain multiple signals. While multiple signals within a category offer the same *type* of support, the signals' *degree* of support differs. The chart arranges signals from strongest to weakest in terms of their relationship to the proposition and their degree of support.

Signals indicating support[3]:

[no signal]	Use when the cited authority provides direct support for a proposition or is the source of a quotation; use when making a general reference in text to the existence of a particular authority.
E.g.,	Use when the cited authority is representative of, or merely an example of, many authorities that stand for the same proposition but are not cited. Although the periods in this signal are italicized, the *comma* following it is not. The signal may be combined with another signal, preceded by an *italicized* comma (shown in red). Thus: *See, e.g.,* . . . *Compare, e.g.,* . . . *with, e.g.,* . . . *See generally, e.g.,* . . .
Accord	Use when two or more authorities state or support the proposition but the text quotes or refers to only the first; the others are then preceded by "*accord*." Also use to show that the law of one jurisdiction is essentially the same as that of another jurisdiction.
See	Use when the cited authority gives only implicit support for the stated proposition.
See also	Use to cite authority that supports the proposition *in addition to that previously cited* in its support. In addition, *see also* may be used when the cited authority supports a point but is in some respect distinguishable from previously cited authorities. Strongly consider adding an explanatory parenthetical to the citation **(Rule 37)**.
Cf.	Use when the cited authority supports the stated proposition only by analogy. Strongly consider adding an explanatory parenthetical to the citation (**Rule 37**).

(*Continued*)

CHART 35.1 **Categories of Signals: Types and Degrees of Support (*Continued*)**

Signal drawing a comparison[4]:	
Compare . . . [*, and* . . .]*, with* . . . [*, and* . . .]	Use when the stated proposition is only supported by comparing two authorities—i.e., neither states the proposition or implies it, but the comparison shows it. Also use to compare authorities or groups of authorities that reach different results concerning the stated proposition. Separate the references by using a non-italicized comma and one space. Strongly consider adding an explanatory parenthetical to the citation (**Rule 37**).
Signals indicating contradiction[5]:	
Contra	Use when the cited authority directly contradicts the stated proposition. (*Contra* is the opposite of [no signal].)
But see	Use when the cited authority implicitly contradicts the stated proposition. Omit "*but*" when the signal follows another citation using the *contra* signal.
But cf.	Use when the cited authority contradicts the stated proposition by analogy. Omit "*but*" when the signal follows another citation using the *contra* or *but see* signal. Strongly consider adding an explanatory parenthetical to the citation (**Rule 37**).
Signal indicating background material[6]:	
See generally	Use when the cited authority provides helpful background information related to the stated proposition. Consider adding an explanatory parenthetical to the citation (**Rule 37**).

35.4 Formatting Signals

Capitalize the first letter of a signal that begins a citation sentence (**Rule 34.1(a)**).[7] Use lowercase for the first letter of a signal beginning a citation clause (**Rule 34.1(b)**). Insert one space between the signal and the citation(s) it precedes.[8]

Ordinarily, italicize signals (**Rule 1**).[9] Do not, however, italicize a signal word that functions as the verb of a textual sentence.[10]

Examples (signals marked in red)

Capitalizing first letter of signal beginning a citation sentence:	*See* Ellie Margolis, *Authority Without Borders: The World Wide Web and the Delegalization of Law*, 41 Seton Hall L. Rev. 909 (2011); Jeremy Patrick, *Beyond Case Reporters: Using Newspapers to Supplement the Legal-Historical Record (a Case Study of Blasphemous Libel)*, 3 Drexel L. Rev. 539 (2011).

Not capitalizing first letter of signal appearing at beginning of a citation clause:	Where courts have been willing to accord judicial notice to facts in Wikipedia articles, they typically justify their actions by stating that the noticed facts are not subject to dispute, *e.g.*, *First Nat'l Bank in Sioux Falls v. First Nat'l Bank S.D., SPC*, 655 F. Supp. 2d 979, 992 n.6 (D.S.D. 2009) (geography and population statistics); *Io Group, Inc. v. Veoh Networks, Inc.*, 586 F. Supp. 2d 1132, 1145 n.8 (N.D. Cal. 2008) (ability of multiple users to share an IP address), or by stressing Wikipedia's value in addressing topics unlikely to be found in traditional scholarly works, *see AVS Found. v. Eugene Berry Ent., LLC*, No. 11 CV 01084, 2011 WL 6056903, at *6 (W.D. Pa. Dec. 6, 2011) (in trademark action, as source for judicial notice of a trademark's fame, citing Wikipedia's coverage of a sports towel).
Signal used as verb in textual sentence:	For examples of unprofessionalism in documents filed with courts, see Judith D. Fischer, *Bareheaded and Barefaced Counsel: Courts React to Unprofessionalism*, 31 Suffolk U. L. Rev. 1 (1997).

35.5 Signals for Multiple Authorities; Changing Signals

35.5(a) Same type and degree of support

When more than one authority provides the *same type and degree* of support for a single proposition, use the appropriate signal (**Chart 35.1**) at the *beginning* of a group of citations to those authorities (a "string citation"); do not repeat the signal before each citation in the string. Think of the signal as "carrying through" to the end of the string. (For the order of authorities *within* a single signal, see **Rule 36**.)

Example

Proposition supported by string citation providing direct support, indicated by [no signal]:	Each time it has been asked to examine Congress's enforcement of the Fifteenth Amendment's voting rights guarantees, the Supreme Court has approved the use of any rational means to prevent racial discrimination. *Lopez v. Monterey Cnty.*, 525 U.S. 266, 282–85 (1999); *City of Rome v. United States*, 446 U.S. 156, 175–78 (1980); *Georgia v. United States*, 411 U.S. 526, 535 (1973); *South Carolina v. Katzenbach*, 383 U.S. 301, 325–27 (1966).

35.5(b) Different types or degrees of support

When authorities cited for a single proposition provide *different types* or *different degrees* of support, arrange them by signal in the order shown in

Chart 35.1, separated with semicolons.[11] If the signal "*e.g.*," is combined with another signal (for example, "*see, e.g.*," or "*but see, e.g.*,"), use the order of the first signal.[12] When using "*but see*" or "*but cf.*" after citations introduced by another signal indicating contradiction, omit "*but*."[13]

When the citations for a single proposition appear in a *citation clause* (relating to only a portion of a sentence in text, as described in **Rule 34.1(b)**), separate them with semicolons, even if the signal changes to a different *type* of support.[14]

When the cited authorities relate to the entire textual sentence, group those of the *same type* in a single *citation sentence* (**Rule 34.1(a)**), separating the citations with semicolons, even if the *degree* of support changes.[15] When the *type* of support changes, however, begin a new citation sentence.[16]

The citations in the example below show *different types* and *degrees* of support for a single proposition in text. The group in the first citation sentence provides the *same type* of support: direct support, indicated by [no signal]; and implicit support, indicated by *see*. When the type of support *changes* to background material, however, a *second* citation sentence is needed, prefaced by *see generally*.

Example (signals marked in red)

> The crime-fraud exception to the attorney-client privilege "is not without its costs." *United States v. Zolin*, 491 U.S. 554, 563 (1989); *see Clark v. United States*, 289 U.S. 1, 15 (1933) (explaining that "[t]he privilege takes flight if the relation is abused"); *In re Grand Jury Matter 91-01386*, 969 F.2d 995, 997 (11th Cir. 1992) (stating that the attorney-client privilege is, as a matter of law, construed narrowly so as not to exceed the means necessary to support the policy it promotes). *See generally* Edna Selan Epstein, *The Attorney-Client Privilege and the Work-Product Doctrine* 251 (3d ed. 1997) (commenting that "[s]ociety . . . has no interest in facilitating the commission of contemplated but not yet committed crimes, torts, or frauds").

The citations in the next example show different types and degrees of support for the two propositions in text, each supported by its own citation clause. The first clause provides direct support for the first proposition ([no signal]). The second clause supports the second proposition, but the signals show both direct support and contradiction (*but cf.*). Because both citations in the second clause relate to the second proposition, they are joined with a semicolon. If they were not joined, it would not be clear that *Nooner* related only to the second proposition.

Example (signal marked in red)

> A witness's opinion is not objectionable solely because his opinion embraces an issue that the trier of fact will decide, Ark. R. Evid. 704, but in order for such evidence to be admissible, its probative value cannot be substantially outweighed by the likelihood of misleading the jury,

Ark. R. Evid. 403; *but cf.* *Nooner v. State*, 907 S.W.2d 677, 685 (Ark. 1995) (permitting any lay witness testimony that is reasonably based and helpful).

35.5(c)FN Changing signals in academic footnote citations

ACADEMIC FORMATTING

When multiple authorities provide the *same type* and *degree* of support for a proposition, follow **Rule 35.5(a)**, placing all their citations after the appropriate signal in a single string citation in the footnote.[17]

When multiple authorities provide the *same type* of support but *different degrees* of that support, the footnote follows the order of signals shown in **Chart 35.1**, with a semicolon between each group.[18] If the signal *e.g.*, is combined with another signal (for example, *see, e.g.*, or *but see, e.g.*,), the footnote uses the order of the other signal.[19]

When additional citations related to a proposition provide a *different type* of support, the footnote uses the appropriate signal to begin a new citation sentence.[20] In the following example, the proposition is supported by a string citation with four authorities, all providing the *same* direct support, indicated by [no signal].

Example

Each time it has been asked to examine Congress's enforcement of the Fifteenth Amendment's voting rights guarantees, the Supreme Court has approved the use of any rational means to prevent racial discrimination.[23]

---

[23] Lopez v. Monterey Cnty., 525 U.S. 266, 282–85 (1999); City of Rome v. United States, 446 U.S. 156, 175–78 (1980); Georgia v. United States, 411 U.S. 526, 535 (1973); South Carolina v. Katzenbach, 383 U.S. 301, 325–27 (1966).

The citations in the next example show *different types* and *degrees* of support for the single proposition in text. The group in the first citation sentence provides the *same type* of support: direct support, indicated by [no signal]; and implicit support, indicated by *see*. When the *type* of support changes to background material, however, a second citation sentence is needed, prefaced by *see generally*.

Example (signal marked in red)

The crime-fraud exception to the attorney-client privilege "is not without its costs."[35]

---

[35] United States v. Zolin, 491 U.S. 554, 563 (1989); *see* Clark v. United States, 289 U.S. 1, 15 (1933) (explaining that "[t]he privilege takes flight if the relation is abused"); *In re* Grand Jury Matter 91-01386, 969 F.2d 995, 997

(11th Cir. 1992) (narrowly construing attorney-client privilege so as not to exceed the means necessary to support the policy it promotes). *See generally* Edna Selan Epstein, The Attorney-Client Privilege and the Work-Product Doctrine 251 (3d ed. 1997) (commenting that "[s]ociety . . . has no interest in facilitating the commission of contemplated but not yet committed crimes, torts, or frauds").

The citations in the next example show *different types* and *degrees* of support for the two propositions in text. Footnote 57 cites authority giving direct support for the first proposition ([no signal]). Footnote 58 relates to the second proposition, but the signals show both direct support ([no signal]) and contradiction (*but cf.*). Because Nooner is cited in footnote 58, it is clear that the case relates only to the second proposition.

Example (signal marked in red)

A witness's opinion is not objectionable solely because his opinion embraces an issue that the trier of fact will decide,[57] but in order for such evidence to be admissible, its probative value cannot be substantially outweighed by the likelihood of misleading the jury.[58]

---

57 Ark. R. Evid. 704.

58 Ark. R. Evid. 403. *But cf.* Nooner v. State, 907 S.W.2d 677, 685 (Ark. 1995) (permitting any lay witness testimony that is reasonably based and helpful).

36 Order of Cited Authorities

36.1 Ordering Multiple Authorities

Sometimes citation sentences will have multiple authorities following the same signal (a "string citation"). In contrast to the order of the signals themselves, the order of authorities within each signal is flexible. Instead of a rigid rule for ordering the authorities within each signal, authorities should be ordered logically.[1] If a particular authority is more significant than others within the same signal, cite it first, regardless of its type, origin, or age.[2] For example, the authorities that are more authoritative, that is, higher on the hierarchy of authority than others in the string citation, or are more useful to the reader should come first.[3] Authorities that are less helpful or lower on the hierarchy of authority should follow others.[4] Separate the citations following a signal with a semicolon and one space.[5]

For example, the string cite below has two signals: *e.g.*, and *but see*. The order of the signals themselves is determined by the order in which they appear in **Chart 35.1**, so *e.g.*, and all the authorities that need that signal will come first. For more information on the order of signals themselves, see **Rule 35.5(b)** and **Chart 35.1**. Within each signal are multiple cases, one of which must precede the others. The three cases following the *e.g.*, signal are all federal district court cases from different states; the first one listed is a couple years earlier than the second — its recency makes it a bit more weighty than the other case — and the second is many years more recent than the third one listed. There are two unreported federal district court cases following the *but see* signal, but this time they are from the same year; ostensibly they carry the same weight. But assuming that the facts in the case before the court were whether a CFO should be deposed before the opposing side serves interrogatories, you would choose to list *Scotch Whiskey* first because it is more factually similar to the case at hand than *Matarazzi* — i.e., *Scotch Whiskey* is more helpful.

Example (cases that are more helpful or authoritative than the other cases within the signal in red)

> Even if the high-ranking official has personal knowledge, courts will examine whether the party seeking the deposition can obtain the same information through another form of discovery, such as interrogatories. *E.g.*, *Stone City Music v. Thunderbird, Inc.*, 116 F.R.D. 473, 474 (N.D. Miss. 1987); *Mulvey v. Chrysler Corp.*, 106 F.R.D. 364 (D.R.I. 1985); *Buryan v. Max Factor & Co.*, 41 F.R.D. 330, 332 (S.D.N.Y. 1967). *But see* *Scotch Whiskey Ass'n v. Majestic Distilling Co.*, 1988 U.S. Dist. LEXIS 16531, at *15 (D. Md. Nov. 30, 1988) (denying request that interrogatories be served before CFO was deposed); *Matarazzi v. H.J. Williams Co.*, 1988 U.S. Dist. LEXIS 8706, at *2 (E.D. Pa. Nov. 30, 1988) (denying request for protective order that discovering party had to submit interrogatories before deposing the defendant's CEO).

36.2 General Guidelines for Ordering Authorities

Rules 36.2 and **36.3** are merely guidelines to follow if you are struggling with how to order authorities within each signal. They generally order authority by its hierarchy or weight of authority. The mandate of logical ordering laid out in **Rule 36.1** can override any of the provisions in **Rules 36.2** and **36.3**.

36.2(a) Primary authority before secondary authority

Cite primary authority (such as statutes or cases) before secondary authority (such as treatises or legal periodicals).

36.2(b) Federal authority before state authority

Within a specific category of primary law (e.g., statutes, cases), cite a federal authority before a state authority.

36.2(c) Cases from the same jurisdiction

For cases from the *same jurisdiction*, cite those decided by higher courts before those decided by lower courts. For example, cite a case from the United States Supreme Court before a case from the United States Court of Appeals for the Seventh Circuit. Cite a Seventh Circuit case before a case from the United States District Court for the Northern District of Illinois. Cite a case from the Alabama Supreme Court before a case from the Alabama Court of Appeals.

36.2(d) Cases from the same court

For cases from the *same court*, cite in reverse chronological order. For example, cite a 2010 case from the United States Supreme Court before a 2007 case from the United States Supreme Court. Cite a 2009 case from the Kentucky Court of Appeals before a 2003 case from the Kentucky Court of Appeals.

Treat all United States Circuit Courts of Appeal as a *single* court; similarly, treat all United States District Courts as a *single* court. For example, cite a 2013 case from the Ninth Circuit before a 2011 case from the Third Circuit before a 2008 case from the Ninth Circuit. Cite a 1985 case from the United States District Court for the Southern District of New York before a 1962 case from the United States District Court for the Northern District of Alabama.

This principle holds true even when the cases were decided the same year. For example, a case decided by the Third Circuit on October 2, 2009, comes before a case that court decided on October 1, 2009. And if cases from the same court display the same date of decision, put the case with the highest initial page number first.

36.2(e) Position of case unaffected by subsequent or prior history

When ordering cases, ignore subsequent and prior histories. Histories merely "tag along" with a case's full citation.

Example (subsequent history marked in red)

Dravo Corp. v. Liberty Mut. Ins. Co., 164 F.R.D. 70, 75 (D. Neb. 1995); *Frazier v. S.E. Pa. Transp. Auth.*, 161 F.R.D. 309, 316 (E.D. Pa. 1995), *aff'd*, 91 F.3d 123 (3d Cir. 1996).

36.2(f) Position of case unaffected by publication status

When ordering cases, ignore a case's publication status (published, unpublished, slip opinion, not designated for publication).

36.2(g) Authored materials

In general, order authored material alphabetically by the author's last name. Law review pieces written by other authors should precede all student-written pieces. When citing multiple pieces by a single author, put them in reverse chronological order. When a document has more than one author, order by the last name of the first-listed author. When citing material attributed to an organization as author, order alphabetically by the first word of the organization's name. If no author's name is shown, order alphabetically by the first word of the work's title, disregarding any initial article ("A," "An," or "The") in the title.

36.2(h) Forthcoming works

Place forthcoming works in the order they would fall if published.

36.2(i) Material available in online version

If material is available in both print and online versions, follow the ordering rule for the print version of the source (as shown in **Rule 36.3**). If the material is available only in an online version, follow **Rule 36.3(i)(13)**.

36.2(j) Position of short citation

Position a short citation in the same place that the authority's full citation would fall.

36.3 Order of Specific Sources

As explained in **Rule 36.2**, cite specific sources in the order set out in this rule only if you are struggling with how to apply **Rule 36.1**.

36.3(a) Constitutions

Within each category, cite constitutions from the same jurisdiction in reverse chronological order; cite a constitution in force before one that has been repealed or superseded:

(1) Federal Constitution;

(2) State constitutions (alphabetically by state);

(3) Foreign constitutions (alphabetically by country); and

(4) Foundational documents of the United Nations, the League of Nations, and the European Union, in that order.

36.3(b) Statutes; rules of evidence and procedure

Within each category, cite statutes or rules in force before repealed or superseded versions. "Sequential" ordering puts lower numbers before higher numbers:

(1) Codified federal statutes (sequentially by title number, then sequentially by section number);

(2) Uncodified federal statutes (in reverse chronological order of enactment);

(3) Federal rules of evidence and procedure (alphabetically by code name; within a code, sequentially by rule number);

(4) Repealed or superseded federal statutes (in reverse chronological order of enactment);

(5) Codified state statutes (alphabetically by state; within a state, sequentially by title number, then sequentially by section number);

(6) Uncodified state statutes (alphabetically by state; within a state, in reverse chronological order of enactment);

(7) State rules of evidence and procedure (alphabetically by state; within a state, alphabetically by code name; within a code, sequentially by rule number);

(8) Repealed or superseded state statutes (alphabetically by state; within a state, in reverse chronological order of enactment);

(9) Codified foreign statutes (alphabetically by country; within a country, sequentially by title number, then sequentially by section number);

(10) Uncodified foreign statutes (in reverse chronological order of enactment);

(11) Foreign rules (alphabetically by country; within a country, alphabetically by code name; within a code, sequentially by rule number); and

(12) Repealed or superseded foreign statutes (in reverse chronological order of enactment).

36.3(c) Treaties, international rules, and international agreements

Cite United Nations, League of Nations, and European Union, in that order; within each, in reverse chronological order.

36.3(d) Cases

Within each category, cite in reverse chronological order:

(1) Federal cases:

—United States Supreme Court;

—United States Courts of Appeals;

—Emergency Court of Appeals;

—Temporary Emergency Court of Appeals;

—Court of Claims;

—Court of Customs and Patent Appeals;

—Bankruptcy Appellate Panels;

—United States District Courts;

—Judicial Panel on Multidistrict Litigation;

—Court of International Trade (formerly Customs Court);

—District Bankruptcy Courts;

—Railroad Reorganization Court;

—Court of Federal Claims (formerly the trial division for the Court of Claims);

—Court of Appeals for the Armed Forces (formerly the Court of Military Appeals);

—Court of Appeals for Veterans Claims;

—Tax Court (formerly the Board of Tax Appeals); and

—Agencies (alphabetically by agency; within an agency, in reverse chronological order).

(2) State cases:

—Courts (alphabetically by state; within a state, by rank of court); and

—Agencies (alphabetically by state; within a state, alphabetically by agency name).

(3) Foreign cases:

—Courts (alphabetically by country; within a country, by rank of court); and

—Agencies (alphabetically by country; within a country, alphabetically by name of agency).

(4) International cases:

—International Court of Justice;

—Permanent Court of International Justice; and

—Other international tribunals and arbitral panels (alphabetically by name); and

(5) Any other cases, followed by any other agency decisions.

36.3(e) Legislative material

Within each category, cite in reverse chronological order:

(1) Federal legislative material:

—Bills and resolutions;

—Committee hearings (alphabetically by committee or subcommittee name);

—Reports, documents, and committee prints;

—Floor debates; and

—Any other legislative material.

(2) State legislative material (alphabetically by state):

—Bills and resolutions;

—Committee hearings (alphabetically by committee or subcommittee name);

—Reports, documents, and committee prints;

—Floor debates; and

—Any other state legislative material.

36.3(f) Executive and administrative materials

Within each category, cite in reverse chronological order; cite material currently in force before repealed or superseded material. "Sequential" ordering puts lower numbers before higher numbers:

(1) Federal administrative and executive materials:

- Executive orders and presidential proclamations;
- Current Treasury regulations;
- Proposed Treasury regulations;
- Regulations (sequentially by title in C.F.R., then sequentially by chapter, part, or section number);
- Proposed regulations or rules (sequentially by proposed title in C.F.R.; otherwise, in reverse chronological order of proposal);
- *Federal Register*; and
- Other administrative or material (alphabetically by source).

(2) State executive and administrative material (alphabetically by state);

(3) Foreign administrative and executive material (alphabetically by country); and

(4) Other executive and administrative materials.

36.3(g) Materials from intergovernmental organizations

Within each category, cite in reverse chronological order:

(1) Resolutions, decisions, and regulations from the United Nations and League of Nations (General Assembly, then Security Council, then other organs, in alphabetical order); and

(2) Resolutions, decisions, and regulations from other organizations (alphabetically by name of organization).

36.3(h) Case-related material

Cite records, pleadings, briefs, or petitions in that order; within each category, by rank of court (see **Rule 36.3(d)**); within each court, in reverse chronological order. Cite briefs in the same case and same court by party, in this order: plaintiff, appellant, or petitioner; defendant, appellee, or respondent; amicus curiae (if more than one, alphabetically by first word of amicus party's name).

36.3(i) Secondary sources

Unless otherwise noted, cite alphabetically by author's last name:

(1) Uniform laws, model codes, restatements, and principles of law (in that order; within each category, in reverse chronological order);

(2) Books, treatises, and shorter works in a collection of a single author's works;

(3) Works in consecutively paginated law reviews and journals;

(4) Shorter works in a collection of multiple authors' works;

(5) Book reviews (alphabetically by last name of reviewer, excluding those written by students);

(6) Student-written works in consecutively paginated law reviews and journals, including student-written book reviews; if no author shown, by first word of title;

(7) A.L.R. articles and annotations (in reverse chronological order);

(8) Works in nonconsecutively paginated sources, including magazines and newspapers; if no author shown, by first word of title;

(9) Encyclopedias (alphabetically by encyclopedia name; then alphabetically by topic or title name);

(10) Dictionaries;

(11) Working papers;

(12) Unpublished material that is not forthcoming; if no author shown, by first word of title;

(13) Works available solely in electronic sources, including those on the internet; and

(14) Any other secondary source.

36.3(j) Internal cross-references

Order the cross-references in each category sequentially. "Sequential" ordering puts lower numbers before higher numbers:

(1) *Supra* references; and

(2) *Infra* references.

37 Explanatory Parentheticals, Commentary, and Treatment

37.1 Using Explanatory Parentheticals

An explanatory parenthetical is appended to a citation; it typically uses a participial phrase, a quotation, or a short description to help readers understand the cited source's significance.[1] Unlike other parentheticals, an explanatory parenthetical is optional, added to the citation as a service to the reader.[2] An explanatory parenthetical is appropriate for use when the information to be conveyed is relatively short and uncomplicated. Explanatory parentheticals can also be useful in providing a set of brief examples to illustrate a rule's meaning or operation. The more significant or complex the ideas represented by the source, the more the writer should deal with them in the text. Too much information — or too many words — will destroy the parenthetical's effectiveness.

Examples

Using participial phrases for commentary:	Very few cases actually proceed to trial. *See* Harry T. Edwards, *Alternative Dispute Resolution: Panacea or Anathema?*, 99 Harv. L. Rev. 668, 670 (1986) (reporting that about ninety percent of state and federal cases settle or are dismissed before trial); Marc Galanter & Mia Cahill, *"Most Cases Settle": Judicial Promotion and Regulation of Settlements*, 46 Stan. L. Rev. 1339, 1340 (1994) (noting that approximately two-thirds of federal cases settle before trial).
Using brief illustrations:	Courts have held that a qualifying expense under the Illinois Family Expense Act includes both household goods and services. *E.g.*, *Carter v. Romano*, 662 N.E.2d 883, 884 (Ill. 2007) (doctor and hospital bills); *Armani v. Gucci*, 893 N.E.2d 99, 101 (Ill. App. Ct. 2009) (clothing); *Crocker v. Hines*, 645 N.E.2d 583, 587 (Ill. App. Ct. 1998) (food); *Broyhill v. Lane*, 559 N.E.2d 32, 33 (Ill. App. Ct. 1992) (furniture).

37.2 Placement of Explanatory Parentheticals

37.2(a) Placement in general

In general, an explanatory parenthetical immediately follows the citation to the source to which it relates.[3] In full citations to cases, place the explanatory parenthetical immediately after the court/date parenthetical, preceding any subsequent history.[4] In full citations to online sources, place the explanatory parenthetical after the URL.[5]

Examples

See, e.g., 29 C.F.R. § 1910.6 (2012) (identifying various standards incorporated by reference into OSHA regulations).

Bensusan Rest. Corp. v. King, 937 F. Supp. 295, 299 (S.D.N.Y. 1996) (refusing to exercise personal jurisdiction when defendant limited its advertising to local audience), *aff'd*, 126 F.3d 25 (2d Cir. 1997).

American Memory: A Century of Lawmaking for a New Nation, Libr. of Cong. (May 1, 2003), http://memory.loc.gov/ammem/amlaw/ (containing published records from the Continental Congress to the 43rd Congress (1774–1875)).

37.2(b) Placement with other parentheticals

Place an explanatory parenthetical *after* any parenthetical that must be included as part of a citation.[6] For more information, see **Sidebar 37.1**.

SIDEBAR 37.1 Order of Parentheticals

Parentheticals are common elements in legal citations. For example, most source citations contain a date parenthetical; citations to minority opinions parenthetically indicate their authors; and omissions to quotations are often noted parenthetically. Use this guide to order multiple parentheticals within a citation[7]:

- court/date and other date/publication parenthetical;
- [hereinafter *shortened reference*];
- en banc opinion;
- dissenting or concurring opinion;
- plurality opinion;
- per curiam or memorandum opinion;
- alteration, including added emphasis;
- omission of footnote;
- omission of citation;
- quotation or citation of other source;
- URL, if any;
- any other explanatory parenthetical;
- prior or subsequent history.

Example

The court stressed that the Rehabilitation Act "addresses the confidentiality of medical records only in the *limited context* of pre-employment examinations." *Lee v. City of Columbus*, 636 F.3d 245, 252 (6th Cir. 2011) (emphasis added) (agreeing with district court that ADA limitations on disclosure of medical information are incorporated by reference into the Rehabilitation Act).

37.2(c) Parenthetical requiring its own parenthetical

When an explanatory parenthetical itself requires a parenthetical, insert it immediately following the main parenthetical's text, closing both sets of parentheses.[8]

Examples

Byron C. Keeling, *A Prescription for Healing the Crisis in Professionalism: Shifting the Burden of Enforcing Professional Standards of Conduct*, 25 Tex. Tech L. Rev. 31, 38 (1993) (warning that "[u]ntil the profession takes active steps to eliminate [discovery] abuses, the public will continue to hold the legal profession in the same moral contempt that it reserves for used car salesmen" (footnote omitted)).

[362] Inker, *supra* note 350, at 27 (explaining that "[d]omestic relations litigants may be particularly vulnerable because *a spouse or former spouse* can reveal confidential information that will embarrass or otherwise harm the other" (emphasis added)).

37.3 Constructing Explanatory Parentheticals

To add parenthetical commentary about a source, writers may construct a participial phrase, beginning with a verb's present participle ("–ing" form) in lower case and in ordinary type.[9] Because a participial phrase is not a complete sentence, do not place a period inside the parentheses.[10] As long as the meaning is clear, you may omit small, unimportant words such as "the."[11] Use the rules in this paragraph when only quoting a short phrase from the source, as in the last example below.[12]

Examples

In re Kerr, 548 P.2d 297, 302 (Wash. 1976) (en banc) (ruling that attorney who knowingly participates in subornation of perjury should be disbarred).

Turman-Kent v. Merit Sys. Prot. Bd., 657 F.3d 1280, 1290 n.5 (Fed. Cir. 2011) (citing three medical dictionaries for proposition that "brain damage resulting from a stroke is irreversible").

When the explanatory parenthetical contains a quotation that is a grammatically complete sentence, however, the sentence should begin with a capital letter, and final punctuation is required.[13] If you must capitalize a lowercase letter to comply with this rule, follow the instructions and examples in **Rule 39.1**.[14] Use **Rule 39** to indicate any other alterations in the quoted text.[15]

Examples

Clark v. United States, 289 U.S. 1, 15 (1933) ("The privilege takes flight if the relation is abused.").

[92] Quan v. Gonzales, 428 F.3d 883, 891 n.1 (9th Cir. 2005) (O'Scannlain, J., dissenting) (citation omitted) ("The majority's reliance on a website of unknown reliability to establish that 'banks in China are *typically* open on Sundays,' is a novel—and, I would respectfully suggest, misguided—application of the doctrine of judicial notice.").

ACADEMIC FORMATTING

37.4 Commentary About Source or Treatment of Source

A source's citation can refer to *a different* source in two general ways: (1) by providing some sort of commentary or information about the other source, such as citing it, quoting it, or otherwise discussing it; or (2) by providing information about the way the other source treats the subject of the citation, such as indicating its reprint in that other source, its quotation in that other source, its citation in that other source, and so forth. The distinction is important, because the commentary or information is presented in a parenthetical appended to the citation, while the source's treatment is introduced with an italicized descriptive phrase, as explained and illustrated below.[16]

37.4(a) Commentary about external source

When indicating a source's commentary on or additional information *about an external source*, place the reference to the external source in a parenthetical appended to the original source's citation.[17] Such parenthetical commentary commonly uses a participial phrase to indicate the nature of the commentary or information (e.g., "citing," "quoting," "reviewing," "disagreeing with"). The citation to the source inside the parenthetical should follow all the citation rules for that type of source.[18]

Examples

Carter v. Helmsley-Spear, Inc., 71 F.3d 77, 84 (2d Cir. 1995) (citing H.R. Rep. No. 101-54, at 11 (1990)).

Tellabs, Inc. v. Makor Issues & Rts., Ltd., 551 U.S. 308, 314 (2007) (construing 15 U.S.C. § 78u-4(b)(2) (2006)).

Qualley v. Clo-Tex Int'l, Inc., 212 F.3d 1123, 1128 (8th Cir. 2000) (quoting Fed. R. Evid. 201(a) advisory committee's note).

[61] Larry Alexander & Lawrence B. Solum, *Popular? Constitutionalism?*, 118 HARV. L. REV. 1594, 1640 (2005) (reviewing LARRY D. KRAMER, THE PEOPLE THEMSELVES: POPULAR CONSTITUTIONALISM AND JUDICIAL REVIEW (2004)).

ACADEMIC FORMATTING

37.4(b) Treatment by an external source

When a cited source has been treated in some way *by another source*, do not use a parenthetical.[19] Instead, following the citation, add a comma, one space, and an italicized phrase describing the treatment, followed by a citation to the external source.[20] Such phrases commonly use a descriptive verb and a preposition (e.g., "*cited in*," "*quoted in*," "*construed in*," "*reprinted in*," "*repealed by*").[21]

Examples

Kan. Stat. Ann. § 21-3502(1)(d) (1969), *quoted in State v. Chaney*, 5 P.3d 492, 495 (Kan. 2000).

Robert H. Bork, *The Antitrust Paradox* 81–89 (1978), *cited with approval in Aspen Skiing Co. v. Aspen Highlands Skiing Corp.*, 472 U.S. 585, 603 n.29 (1985).

ACADEMIC FORMATTING

[81] Gregory P. Joseph, *Internet and Email Evidence*, 13 PRAC. LITIGATOR, Mar. 2002, at 21, *reprinted in* 5 STEPHEN A. SALTZBURG ET AL., FEDERAL RULES OF EVIDENCE MANUAL, Pt. 4, at 21 (9th ed. 2006).

[97] St. Clair v. Johnny's Oyster & Shrimp, Inc., 76 F. Supp. 2d 773, 774–75 (S.D. Tex. 1999), *cited in* Crochet v. Wal-Mart Stores, Inc., No. 6:11-01404, 2012 WL 489204, at *4 (W.D. La. Feb. 13, 2012).

Part 5
Quotations

38 Quotations

38.1 When to Quote

Use quotations sparingly. Reserve their use for statutory language, for language that must be presented exactly as represented in the original, and for particularly famous, unique, or vivid language. Resist the temptation to quote rather than explain in your own words. When readers encounter a lot of quotations, they may skip sections or read less attentively. They may also conclude that the writer did not understand the material well enough to paraphrase it or to establish its connection to surrounding text.

38.2 Quoting Accurately

Present quotations accurately; reproduce words exactly as they appear in the original source. Never misrepresent a quotation's original meaning. Make no changes to the original without indicating what is altered (**Rule 39**) or omitted (**Rule 40**). To indicate an error in the original quotation, see **Rule 39.6**.

38.3 Quotation Formats

A quotation's format generally depends on its length. "Short quotations" (forty-nine or fewer words) are surrounded by double quotation marks (" ") and typically run into the text.[1] **Rule 38.4** covers short quotations. "Long quotations" (fifty words or more) or quotations of poetry or verse of any length are typically set off as indented blocks.[2] Use **Rule 38.5** for long quotations.

38.4 Short Quotations

38.4(a) Enclosure in double quotation marks

When a quotation of forty-nine or fewer words is not testimony (**Rule 38.6**), an epigraph (**Rule 38.7**), or a quotation of poetry or verse, enclose it in double quotation marks, but do not otherwise set it off from the surrounding text.[3]

Example

> The Eighth Amendment's prohibition of cruel and unusual punishment "guarantees individuals the right not to be subjected to excessive sanctions." *Roper v. Simmons*, 543 U.S. 551, 560 (2005).

38.4(b) Punctuation of short quotations

38.4(b)(1) Quotation of whole sentence

When you quote an entire sentence of forty-nine or fewer words without alteration, enclose it in quotation marks,[4] and keep its original punctuation.

Examples

Explaining why juveniles should not be treated as adults for sentencing purposes, Justice Kagan wrote, "Mandatory life without parole for a juvenile precludes consideration of his chronological age and its hallmark features—among them, immaturity, impetuosity, and failure to appreciate risks and consequences." *Miller v. Alabama*, 567 U.S. 460, 477 (2012).

"The Federal district courts shall have exclusive original jurisdiction of all suits to which a China Trade Act corporation, or a stockholder, director, or officer thereof in his capacity as such, is a party." 15 U.S.C. § 146a.

38.4(b)(2) Commas and periods

When integrating a short quotation into text, set it off with a comma only when the quotation is used in conjunction with a speaker identification tag (e.g., she said, the court stated) or when the sentence would need a comma even if there were no quotation.

Examples

Comma follows speaker identification tag:	The Iowa Supreme Court stated, "Our rule is that words in a criminal statute are to be interpreted strictly."
Comma required by sentence structure:	Under the jurisprudence of the Iowa Supreme Court, "words in a criminal statute are to be interpreted strictly."
No comma needed:	The Iowa Supreme Court has held that "words in a criminal statute are to be interpreted strictly."

When concluding a short quotation in text, place periods and commas *inside* the closing quotation marks, whether or not they are part of the original quotation.[5]

Examples

Original (material to be quoted in red):	Every patent shall contain a short title of the invention and a grant to the patentee, his heirs or assigns, of the right to exclude others from making, using, offering for sale, or selling the invention throughout the United States or importing the invention into the United States, and, if the invention is a process, of the right to exclude others from using, offering for sale or selling throughout the United States, or importing into the United States, products made by that process, referring to the specification for the particulars thereof.

Quotation with period:	The Patent Act grants a patentee "the right to exclude others from making, using, offering for sale, or selling the invention." 35 U.S.C. § 154(a)(1).
Quotation with comma:	Although patentees have "the right to exclude others from making, using, offering for sale, or selling the invention," 35 U.S.C. § 154(a)(1), that right is limited by the doctrine of patent exhaustion.

38.4(b)(3) Colons and semicolons

Place colons or semicolons *outside* the closing quotation marks, even if the language in the original used that punctuation. In selecting the words to quote, stop short of the quotation's *own* colon or semicolon.

Examples

Original (material to be quoted in red):	Except as authorized by this subchapter, it shall be unlawful for any person knowingly or intentionally—(1) to manufacture, distribute, or dispense, or possess with intent to manufacture, distribute, or dispense, a controlled substance; or (2) to create, distribute, or dispense, or possess with intent to distribute or dispense, a counterfeit substance.
Quotation:	The defendants say that it was impossible for them to "possess with intent to manufacture, distribute, or dispense, a controlled substance"; therefore, they argue, they did not violate the statute.

38.4(b)(4) Question marks and exclamation marks

Place question marks and exclamation marks *either inside or outside* the closing quotation marks according to whether you're using the original punctuation of the quoted passage.[6]

Examples

Original (material to be quoted in red):	(4) "Deadly weapon" means: (A) A firearm or anything manifestly designed, made, or adapted for the purpose of inflicting death or serious physical injury.
Quotation:	Why did the State fail to argue that the antique rifle was "manifestly designed, made, or adapted for the purpose of inflicting death"?

Original (material to be quoted in red): Having started with "was there clear error," the court then finds itself in the unpleasant circumstance of later lamenting the pointlessness of sending this case back to be inevitably reversed. Surely Congress wouldn't have wanted to prevent an interlocutory challenge to an incorrect ruling!

Quotation: The article describes the court's reluctance to remand the case: "Surely Congress wouldn't have wanted to prevent an interlocutory challenge to an incorrect ruling!"

38.4(c) Quotation within a short quotation

To punctuate a short quotation that itself contains a quotation, use double quotation marks around the primary quotation and single quotation marks around the internal quotation.[7] Either cite both sources, putting the source of the internal quotation in a parenthetical, or append a parenthetical stating "citation omitted."[8]

ACADEMIC FORMATTING

For academic writing, however, do not append a "citation omitted" parenthetical if you can attribute the source of the nested quote in a parenthetical.[9]

Example (quotation marks in red)

The "enquiry focuses on whether the new work merely supersedes the objects of the original creation, or whether and to what extent it is 'transformative,' altering the original with new expression, meaning, or message." *Campbell*, 510 U.S. at 579 (citation omitted).

or

ACADEMIC FORMATTING

The "enquiry focuses on whether the new work merely supersedes the objects of the original creation, or whether and to what extent it is 'transformative,' altering the original with new expression, meaning, or message."[8]

---

[8] *Campbell*, 510 U.S. at 579 (quoting Pierre N. Leval, *Toward a Fair Use Standard*, 103 HARV. L. REV. 1105, 1111 (1990)).

38.4(d) Placement of citation to source of short quotation

Place the citation to the source of a short quotation immediately after the sentence containing the quoted material.[10] When the sentence contains quotations from two or more sources, however, place each citation in a clause that immediately follows its quotation.[11] For more information about citation clauses, see **Rule 34.1(b)**.

Examples (citations in red)

Under the common-fund doctrine in equity, "a litigant or a lawyer who recovers a common fund for the benefit of persons other than himself or his client is entitled to a reasonable attorney's fee from the fund as a whole." *Boeing Co. v. Van Gemert*, 444 U.S. 472, 478 (1980).

Courts may vacate an arbitrator's decision "only in very unusual circumstances," *First Options of Chi., Inc. v. Kaplan*, 514 U.S. 938, 942 (1995), in a limited judicial review that "maintain[s] arbitration's essential virtue of resolving disputes straightaway," *Hall St. Assocs., L.L.C. v. Mattel, Inc.*, 552 U.S. 576, 588 (2008).

38.4(e)FN Placement of citations to short quotation sources in academic footnotes

ACADEMIC FORMATTING

Place the note reference number for the citation to a short quotation's source immediately after its closing quotation marks.[12] When a sentence contains quotations from different sources, place the note reference number for each cited source immediately after its quotation's closing quotation marks.[13]

Examples

Under the common-fund doctrine in equity, "a litigant or a lawyer who recovers a common fund for the benefit of persons other than himself or his client is entitled to a reasonable attorney's fee from the fund as a whole."[17]

---

[17] Boeing Co. v. Van Gemert, 444 U.S. 472, 478 (1980).

Courts may vacate an arbitrator's decision "only in very unusual circumstances,"[32] in a limited judicial review that "maintain[s] arbitration's essential virtue of resolving disputes straightaway."[33]

---

[32] First Options of Chi., Inc. v. Kaplan, 514 U.S. 938, 942 (1995).

[33] Hall St. Assocs., L.L.C. v. Mattel, Inc., 552 U.S. 576, 588 (2008).

38.4(f) Source of quotation identified in sentence

When all of the components of a citation to a quotation's source can be identified from material within the sentence in which the quotation is placed, no duplicative citation is necessary. Citing a source in full in the text rather than in a citation sentence or citation clause should be avoided whenever possible, though.

Example

Under Federal Rule of Evidence 803(2), an out-of-court statement is admissible as an excited utterance if the statement "relat[es] to a startling event or condition made while the declarant was under the stress of excitement caused by the event or condition."

38.5 Long Quotations

38.5(a) Block quotation format

When a quotation contains fifty words or more, when the quoted material is a transcription of testimony (**Rule 38.6**), or when the quoted material is a verse, poem, or epigraph (**Rule 38.7**), present it in a single-spaced block indented by one tab on both the right and the left.[14] Do not use quotation marks around a block quotation.[15] Separate the block quotation from the text above and below it with a blank line, creating a surrounding frame of white space.[16]

Example

In fact, the Court recognized the value of speech that

> induces a condition of unrest, creates dissatisfaction with conditions as they are, or even stirs people to anger. Speech is often provocative and challenging. It may strike at prejudices and preconceptions and have profound unsettling effects as it presses for acceptance of an idea. That is why freedom of speech, though not absolute, is nevertheless protected against censorship or punishment, unless shown likely to produce a clear and present danger of a serious substantive evil that rises far above public inconvenience, annoyance, or unrest.

Terminiello v. City of Chi., 337 U.S. 1, 4–5 (1949) (internal citations omitted). Some would argue that the Court's view of speech has been expanded much farther than the drafters could have anticipated.

38.5(b) Quotation within a block quotation

When a block quotation contains a quotation from another authority, punctuate the block exactly as it appears in the original, enclosing the internal quotation in double quotation marks.[17] Follow punctuation conventions described in **Rule 38.4(b)**.[18]

Example

Not all agree on the constitutionality of incitement-to-riot statutes:

> The Supreme Court itself said in dicta that "[n]o one would have the hardihood to suggest that the principle of freedom of speech sanctions incitement to riot . . . ." But that comment depends on a limited understanding of incitement, and a limited understanding of riot. If "riot" is defined broadly—which it often is—and "incitement" is not defined at all—which it often is not—then incitement to riot can sweep in innocuous or even socially beneficial activity.

Margot E. Kaminski, *Incitement to Riot in the Age of Flash Mobs*, 81 U. Cin. L. Rev. 1, 8 (2012) (quoting *Cantwell v. Connecticut*, 310 U.S. 296, 308 (1940)). These statutes are likely to be challenged by . . . .

38.5(c) Long quotation in parenthetical

Do not use block formatting to present a long quotation in a parenthetical.[19] If you cannot shorten the quotation by editing, enclose it in double quotation marks.[20] For placement of the parenthetical, see **Rule 37.2**.

Example

> [Text of sentence supported by citation.] *See* 4 U.S.C. § 124(12) (defining "taxing jurisdiction" as "any of the several States, the District of Columbia, or any territory or possession of the United States, any municipality, city, county, township, parish, transportation district, or assessment jurisdiction, or any other political subdivision within the territorial limits of the United States with the authority to impose a tax, charge, or fee").

38.5(d) Paragraphing within block quotation

Retain the original source's paragraphing.[21] When a long quotation comes from the beginning of a paragraph, block indent the whole paragraph, but further indent the first line.[22] If a long quotation spans multiple paragraphs, reflect the original paragraph breaks by indenting the first line of each quoted paragraph.[23]

Example

> There is reason to question that approach:
>
>> The categorical approach to admitting hearsay relies on the use of external generalizations. The categorical exceptions are substantive generalizations not formulated by the trier of fact, but drafted by judges and legislators to represent their collective beliefs about what kinds of hearsay statements are more likely to be reliable. All hearsay that does not conform to these generalizations about reliability is excluded from the trier of fact.
>>
>> However, there is little support for the claim that the categorical approach admits individual items of hearsay that are more reliable than the items it excludes. First, the categorical generalizations about what enhances the reliability of hearsay are unvalidated. We lack systematic empirical research about how the testimonial circumstances of declarants actually affect reliability. The research conducted on a few exceptions flatly contradicts their underlying assumptions about enhanced reliability of perception, memory, and sincerity.
>
> Eleanor Swift, *A Foundation Fact Approach to Hearsay*, 75 Calif. L. Rev. 1339, 1351 (1987).

38.5(e) Placement of citation to quotation source

The citation to the source of a long quotation is not part of the quoted material; therefore, do not place that citation within the block.[24] Following the block, return to regular margins and line spacing, and place the citation at the left margin on the first line of text beneath the block.[25] If you do not want to start a new paragraph after the citation, continue the text on the same line as the citation.[26]

Example (source citation in red)

> Some crimes must be charged with greater specificity. As the Supreme Court has explained,
>
> > [T]he very core of criminality under 2 U.S.C. § 192 is pertinency to the subject under inquiry of the questions which the defendant refused to answer. What the subject actually was, therefore, is central to every prosecution under the statute. Where guilt depends so crucially upon such a specific identification of fact, our cases have uniformly held that an indictment must do more than simply repeat the language of the criminal statute.
>
> *Russell v. United States*, 369 U.S. 749, 764 (1962).

When a block quotation itself contains a quotation, you may place the internal quotation source's citation in a parenthetical following the citation to the main quotation.[27]

Example (parenthetical citation in red)

> These days, "friends" do not necessarily live in the same locale:
>
> > It is not that communities are disappearing; they are simply transforming—traditional neighborhood and small-community groups giving way to social networks that defy location, but include vigorous, nourishing, deeply personal relationships. These networks are thriving as a result of the human need to "preserve the benefits of community in a more splintered world: remaining connected in our relationships, creating and retaining common experience, engaging peer opinion, and building reputation."
>
> Kristin R. Brown, Comment, *Somebody Poisoned the Jury Pool: Social Media's Effect on Jury Impartiality*, 19 Tex. Wesleyan L. Rev. 809, 814–15 (2013) (quoting H. Brian Holland, *Privacy Paradox 2.0*, 19 Widener L.J. 893, 918 (2010)). Social media sites such as Facebook encourage such "friending."

When the source of an internal quotation is cited within the block quotation, retain that citation, and do not repeat it in a parenthetical.

Example (internal citation in red)

> Although the Court rejected the position cited in *Hildwin*, it characterized the nature of capital sentencing by quoting *Poland v. Arizona*, 476 U.S. 147, 156 (1986). In that case, the Court described statutory specifications or aggravating circumstances in capital sentences as "standards to guide the . . . choice between the

> alternative verdicts of death and life imprisonment." *Id.* The Court thus characterized the finding of aggravating facts as a choice between a greater and lesser penalty, not a process of raising the ceiling of the sentencing range available.

Jones v. United States, 526 U.S. 227, 251 (1999).

38.5(f)FN Placement of block-quotation citations in academic footnotes

ACADEMIC FORMATTING

In general, place the note reference number at the end of the block itself, as shown in the first example below.[28]

When a block quotation contains an internal quotation, do not create a footnote for citing the source of the internal quotation.[29] Place the internal source's citation in a parenthetical appended to the block-quotation citation, as shown in the second example below. (To add a note reference number *within* a block quotation, see **Rule 39.5FN**.)

Examples (illustrations in red)

> Some crimes must be charged with greater specificity. As the Supreme Court has explained,
>
> > [T]he very core of criminality under 2 U.S.C. § 192 is pertinency to the subject under inquiry of the questions which the defendant refused to answer. What the subject actually was, therefore, is central to every prosecution under the statute. Where guilt depends so crucially upon such a specific identification of fact, our cases have uniformly held that an indictment must do more than simply repeat the language of the criminal statute.[18]
>
> ---
>
> 18 Russell v. United States, 369 U.S. 749, 764 (1962).

> These days, "friends" do not necessarily live in the same locale:
>
> > It is not that communities are disappearing; they are simply transforming—traditional neighborhood and small-community groups giving way to social networks that defy location, but include vigorous, nourishing, deeply personal relationships. These networks are thriving as a result of the human need to "preserve the benefits of community in a more splintered world: remaining connected in our relationships, creating and retaining common experience, engaging peer opinion, and building reputation."[27]
>
> Social media sites such as Facebook encourage such "friending."
>
> ---
>
> 27 Kristin R. Brown, Comment, *Somebody Poisoned the Jury Pool: Social Media's Effect on Jury Impartiality*, 19 Tex. Wesleyan L. Rev. 809, 814–15 (2013) (quoting H. Brian Holland, *Privacy Paradox 2.0,* 19 Widener L.J. 893, 918 (2010)).

38.6 Testimony

The testimony of a witness, whether rendered at trial or in some other proceeding (e.g., a deposition), is frequently quoted in documents submitted to a court. To provide context, quoted testimony ordinarily reflects the question asked as well as the answer given.

Do not place testimony in quotation marks, regardless of its length. Format testimony as a block quotation under **Rule 38.5(a)**. Although block quotations are ordinarily set out in single space, you may use double spacing throughout or between each Q and A.

Example

> Q: Isn't it true that before you began law school, you knew nothing about legal citation?
>
> A: Well, yes, but that's because I didn't need to know.
>
> Q: Would you agree that accurate citation adds value to your legal writing?
>
> A: Of course.
>
> Q: Then why didn't you indicate the name of the court who decided this case or the date the opinion was issued?
>
> A: I guess I forgot. I'm not very good at editing my own work. Next time, I'll have the *ALWD Guide* beside me as I write.

38.7 Epigraphs

An epigraph is a quotation set at the beginning of a work or chapter. Do not place an epigraph in quotation marks, regardless of its length.

38.7(a) Placement of citation to epigraph

Place the citation to the source of the epigraph underneath the quotation, flush right. Skip one line between the epigraph and the citation. Single-space the citation if it does not fit on a single line. You may place an em dash (—) before the citation.

Example

> This scarecrow of a suit has, in course of time, become so complicated, that no man alive knows what it means.
>
> — Charles Dickens, *Bleak House* 14 (Stephen Gill ed., Oxford Univ. Press 2008) (1853).

38.7(b)FN Placement of citations to epigraphs in academic footnotes

ACADEMIC FORMATTING

Place the note reference number at the end of the epigraph, and set out the source's citation in the corresponding footnote.[30]

Example

> This scarecrow of a suit has, in course of time, become so complicated, that no man alive knows what it means.[1]

---

[1] Charles Dickens, Bleak House 14 (Stephen Gill ed., Oxford Univ. Press 2008) (1853).

39 Altering Quotations

39.1 Altering the Case of a Single Letter in a Word

When you change a letter within a quotation from uppercase to lowercase, or vice versa, enclose the altered letter in square brackets.[1]

Original:	**Alteration:**
"The court held . . . ."	Moreover, "[t]he court held . . . ."
"In the latter event, the court shall permit the parties or their attorneys to supplement the examination by such further inquiry as it deems appropriate . . . ."	"[T]he court shall permit the parties or their attorneys to supplement the examination by such further inquiry as it deems appropriate . . . ."

39.2 Adding, Changing, or Omitting One or More Letters in a Word

Other than indicating a change in capitalization (**Rule 39.1**), when you add or change one or more letters in a quoted word, enclose the added or changed letters in brackets.[2] Alternatively, replace the entire word, as described in **Rule 39.3**. Indicate the omission of one or more letters with empty brackets.[3]

Original:	**Alterations:**
state	state[d], stat[ing], state[s]
held	h[o]ld
the employee	the employee[s]
the employees	the employee[]

39.3 Substituting or Adding Words to a Quotation

When you substitute or add words to a quotation, enclose the substituted or new words in brackets.[4] For example, you may add material to clarify an ambiguity, to supply a missing word, or to provide necessary explanations or translations.

Original:	**Alteration:**
"The court ruled for Mr. Jamison."	"The court ruled for [the defendant]."
"He found the hammer there."	"He found the hammer [by the door]."

39.4 Altering Typeface in a Quotation

Sometimes your only change to a quotation is to alter its typeface, such as italicizing certain words or substituting ordinary type for words that appeared in a different typeface in the original. Do not use brackets around words that have undergone merely a typeface change.[5] Instead, indicate the changes parenthetically, as described below.

39.4(a) Parenthetical description of alteration

When altering the typeface of quoted material, such as creating emphasis by italicizing, describe the alteration in a parenthetical that follows the citation (e.g., "emphasis added").[6] (For placement of the parenthetical, see **Rule 37.2**.) It is not necessary to parenthetically indicate emphasis used in the original (but see **Rule 39.4(b)** for handling original and added emphasis in a single quotation).[7]

Example

Original:

> We think a "permanent physical occupation" has occurred, for purposes of this rule, where individuals are given a permanent and continuous right to pass to and fro, so that the real property may continuously be traversed, even though no particular individual is permitted to station himself permanently upon the premises.

Nollan v. Cal. Coastal Comm'n, 483 U.S. 825, 832 (1987).

Alteration (illustration in red):

> We think a "permanent physical occupation" has occurred, for purposes of this rule, where individuals are given a *permanent and continuous right to pass to and fro*, so that the real property may continuously be traversed, even though no particular individual is permitted to station himself permanently upon the premises.

Nollan v. Cal. Coastal Comm'n, 483 U.S. 825, 832 (1987) (emphasis added).

39.4(b) Distinguishing original and added emphasis

When a quotation contains two or more instances of emphasis, some of which was in the original and some of which was added, parenthetically indicate which emphasis was added, but not which emphasis was in the original.[8]

Example

In *Shaw v. Reno*, 509 U.S. 630 (1993), Justice O'Connor, writing for the majority, described the relationship between race and redistricting:

> [R]edistricting differs from other kinds of state decisionmaking in that the legislature always is aware of race when it draws district lines, just as it is *aware* of age, economic status, religious and political persuasion, and a variety of other demographic factors. That sort of race consciousness does not lead *inevitably* to impermissible race discrimination.

Id. at 646 (second emphasis added).

39.5[FN] Adding a Footnote Within a Block Quotation

ACADEMIC FORMATTING

As explained in **Rule 38.5(f)[FN]**, a note reference number ordinarily is used *at the end* of a block quotation. Should it be necessary or desirable to add a note reference number *within* a block quotation, enclose the superscripted note reference number in brackets.

Example (illustration in red)

> [T]here is something unsettling about a rule of law that regulates humans and gives robots free rein.[[7]] . . . To the extent that the rule depends on the inhuman scale of robotic reading, it also encourages them to scale up their copying. Rebroadcast one radio station for humans and you're an infringer; copy a thousand TV stations for computers and you're a fair use hero.[8]

---

[7] And what about animals? In *Naruto v. Slater*, No. 15-CV-04324-WHO, 2016 WL 362231 (N.D. Cal. Jan. 28, 2016), the court dismissed a copyright suit filed by PETA on behalf of a monkey who used the defendant's camera to take a "selfie."

[8] James Grimmelmann, *Copyright for Literate Robots*, 101 IOWA L. REV. 657, 674–75 (2016).

39.6 Indicating Mistakes in the Original

An original source may contain mistakes, such as spelling, typographical, or grammatical errors. It is your choice whether to correct the mistake or to indicate that the mistake appeared in the original.

To correct the mistake, enclose the correction in brackets as described in **Rules 39.2** and **39.3**. To retain the mistake but indicate that it appeared in the original (and thus is not attributable to you), insert the bracketed term "[sic]" immediately after the word containing the mistake.[9] When quoting obviously archaic or nonstandard writing, you may dispense with inserting [sic] or making other alterations.

Examples

Alternative 1: Correcting the mistake

Original:	**Alteration:**
"The court dismissed there motion."	"The court dismissed [their] motion."
"The court hold that"	"The court h[e]ld that" "The court[s] hold that"

Alternative 2: Using [sic]

Original:	**Alteration:**
"The court dismissed there motion."	"The court dismissed there [sic] motion."
"The court hold that"	"The court hold [sic] that"

SIDEBAR 39.1 "Cleaned up" Quotations

A few scholars have advocated for "cleaning up quotations" by omitting the brackets and ellipses that indicate where a writer has altered quotations and instead indicating those changes by adding the parenthetical "(cleaned up)" at the end of the citation. A writer cleaning up citations could also omit internal quotation marks, internal footnotes, and internal citations from quotations without acknowledging those deletions except with the same parenthetical. It allows a writer to make non-substantive changes to the quotation such as changing the case of a letter without, in the proponents' view, cluttering the text with marks that detract from the message of the quote. For a thorough explanation and proposed legal citation rules for the "(cleaned up)" parenthetical, see Jack Metzler, *Cleaning Up Quotations*, 18 J. App. Prac. & Process 143 (2017).

As attractive as this idea may be for students, professors may disagree. Always check with your professor—and in practice, with your supervising attorney or judge—before "cleaning up" quotations in your writing. Although some judges have embraced it, and the Supreme Court has used it on at least one occasion (see *Brownback v. King*, No. 19-546, slip op. at 6 (U.S. Feb. 25, 2021), https://www.supremecourt.gov/opinions/20pdf/19-546_7mip.pdf), it is far from standard practice. Never use a "(cleaned up)" parenthetical in academic writing. And when merely suspecting it would cause you to use credibility with your audience, always indicate alterations in a quote using **Rule 39**.

40 Indicating Omissions from Quotations

40.1 Indicating Omissions with Ellipsis

An ellipsis alerts readers that one or more words—and perhaps even several sentences or paragraphs—have been omitted from the quotation. To indicate an omitted *letter* within a single word, use empty brackets (**Rule 39.2**).[1]

Type an ellipsis as three spaced points (periods), as shown in the examples below.[2] Insert spaces between the ellipsis points;[3] to do so, you may need to override your word processor's default settings. Do not allow ellipsis points to break across a line; think of the spaces between them as the glue that holds them together. You can prevent this separation by using your word processor to insert a nonbreaking space (also known as a "hard space") between the points. A space always precedes and follows an ellipsis.[4] When the ellipses are at the end of a sentence, still insert a space after the last ellipsis point, and then insert the ending punctuation followed immediately by the closing quotation mark (e.g., ▲.▲.▲.▲." or ▲.▲.▲.▲?").[5]

Examples (spaces denoted by ▲)

Correct uses of ellipsis:

"Where▲.▲.▲.▲the Government uses a device that is not in general public use, to explore details of the home that would previously have been unknowable without physical intrusion, the surveillance is a 'search' and is presumptively unreasonable without a warrant." *Kyllo v. United States*, 533 U.S. 27, 40 (2001).

"When Congress does legislate nationally, imposing burdens▲.▲.▲.▲on the states, it often does so by granting federal money to states or localities▲.▲.▲.▲." Stephen Breyer, *Making Our Democracy Work: A Judge's View* 127 (2011).

Incorrect uses of ellipsis:

"Where▲ . . . ▲the Government uses a device that is not in general public use, to explore details of the home that would previously have been unknowable without physical intrusion, the surveillance is a 'search' and is presumptively unreasonable without a warrant." *Kyllo v. United States*, 533 U.S. 27, 40 (2001).

"When Congress does legislate nationally, imposing burdens.▲.▲.on the states, it often does so by granting federal money to states or localities.▲.▲.▲." Stephen Breyer, *Making Our Democracy Work: A Judge's View* 127 (2011).

40.2 When to Use Ellipsis

40.2(a) Omission of words within quoted sentence or phrase

When you omit one word or a group of words from *within* the text of a quoted passage, insert an ellipsis to indicate the omission.[6] Never begin a quotation with an ellipsis.[7] For omissions of internal citations or footnotes from a quoted passage, see **Rule 40.3(d)**.

Example (spaces denoted by ▲)

Original passage:	This implicit license typically permits the visitor to approach the home by the front path, knock promptly, wait briefly to be received, and then (absent invitation to linger longer) leave. *Florida v. Jardines*, 569 U.S. 1, 8 (2013).
Correct use of ellipsis:	While custom and tradition invite "the visitor to approach the home by the front path, knock promptly, wait briefly to be received, and then▲.▲.▲.▲leave," *Florida v. Jardines*, 569 U.S. 1, 8 (2013), they do not permit greater intrusion without a warrant.

40.2(b) Omission of words from end of quoted sentence

When you quote a grammatically correct sentence without adding words of your own before or after the quote, and you omit one or more words from the end of the quoted sentence, insert an ellipsis, followed by the sentence's final punctuation.[8] Do not end the sentence with only the ellipsis; an ellipsis does not substitute for a period.[9] Do not insert an ellipsis at the end of a quoted phrase or clause (**Rule 40.3(a)**).[10]

Examples (spaces denoted by ▲)

Original:	We hold today that the Sixth Amendment's right of an accused to confront the witnesses against him is likewise a fundamental right and is made obligatory on the States by the Fourteenth Amendment.
Correct use of ellipsis:	"[T]he Sixth Amendment's right of an accused to confront the witnesses against him is . . . a fundamental right▲.▲.▲.▲."
Incorrect uses of ellipsis:	"[T]he Sixth Amendment's right of an accused to confront the witnesses against him is . . . a fundamental right▲.▲.▲."
	The Court held "that the Sixth Amendment's right of an accused to confront the witnesses against him is . . . a fundamental right▲.▲.▲.▲."

40.2(c) Omissions of words or full sentences when the quoted passage has multiple sentences

When you quote a passage originally composed of three or more sentences, indicate the omission of a full sentence within that passage with an ellipsis.[11] Retain the ending punctuation of the sentence prior to the omitted one if you are not omitting any of the words from that prior sentence.[12]

Example (spaces denoted by ▲)

> "Certainly the presence of reporters inside the home was not related to the objectives of the authorized intrusion.▲.▲.▲.▲The reporters therefore were not present for any reason related to the justification for police entry into the home—the apprehension of Dominic Wilson." *Wilson v. Layne*, 526 U.S. 603, 611 (1999).

If you are omitting the end of a prior sentence and also omitting the next sentence or beginning of the next sentence, use only one ellipsis to indicate both omissions.[13] Omit the ending of the prior sentence, then insert the ellipsis, the ending punctuation of the prior sentence, one space, and the remaining quoted material.[14] If deleting the beginning part of a sentence, indicate the change in case using brackets according to **Rule 39.1**.[15] Follow **Rule 40.2(a)** when omitting only phrases from the middle of one sentence.[16]

Examples (spaces denoted by ▲)

> "Once again, the question is asked: what more were the fishermen supposed to do▲.▲.▲.▲? [T]he Park Service suggested that the fishermen could have violated the law and then sued." *S.F. Herring Ass'n v. Dep't of the Interior*, 946 F.3d 564, 582 (9th Cir. 2019).

> "Mr. Chafin seeks▲.▲.▲.▲an order that E.C. be returned to the United States▲.▲.▲.▲. Mr. Chafin is asking for typical appellate relief: that the Court of Appeals reverse the District Court and that the District Court undo what it has done." *Chafin v. Chafin*, 568 U.S. 165, 173 (2013).

40.2(d) Omission of one or more paragraphs from quoted passage

When you omit one or more paragraphs from a quoted passage, indicate that omission by placing the ellipsis on its own line, centered, with five to seven spaces between each ellipsis point.

Example (spaces denoted by ▲)

> The Congress shall have Power To lay and collect Taxes, Duties, Imposts and Excises, to pay the Debts and provide for the common Defence and general Welfare of the United States; but all Duties, Imposts and Excises shall be uniform throughout the United States;
>
> To borrow Money on the credit of the United States;

> To regulate Commerce with foreign Nations, and among the several States, and with the Indian Tribes;
>
> . . . .
>
> To make all Laws which shall be necessary and proper for carrying into Execution the foregoing Powers, and all other Powers vested by this Constitution in the Government of the United States, or in any Department or Officer thereof.

U.S. Const. art. I, § 8.

40.3 When *Not* to Use Ellipsis

40.3(a) Before or after words and phrases incorporated into writer's sentence

Do not use an ellipsis to denote an omission before or after a single word, phrase, or fragment of a sentence that is incorporated into your own sentence structure.[17]

Examples

Original (material to be quoted in red):	But introducing a trained police dog to explore the area around the home in hopes of discovering incriminating evidence is something else. There is no customary invitation to do *that*. An invitation to engage in canine forensic investigation assuredly does not inhere in the very act of hanging a knocker.
Quotation correctly incorporated into writer's sentence:	While the presence of a door knocker is an implied invitation to enter a home, it does not invite "a trained police dog to explore the area around the home in hopes of discovering incriminating evidence." *Florida v. Jardines*, 569 U.S. 1, 8 (2013).
Incorrect use of ellipsis:	While the presence of a door knocker is an implied invitation to enter a home, it does not invite ". . . a trained police dog to explore the area around the home in hopes of discovering incriminating evidence . . . ." *Florida v. Jardines*, 569 U.S. 1, 8 (2013).

40.3(b) At beginning of quotation

Do not use an ellipsis to denote an omission at the beginning of a quotation, whether the quotation is the entire sentence or just a phrase incorporated into your own sentence structure.[18] If the quotation is not incorporated into your own sentence structure, but is instead a grammatically correct sentence on its own, after omitting the beginning of the sentence, capitalize the first letter of the word beginning the sentence, using square brackets as shown in **Rule 39.2**.[19]

Examples

Original (material to be quoted in red):	"But, in our system, undifferentiated fear or apprehension of disturbance is not enough to overcome the right to freedom of expression." *Tinker v. Des Moines Indep. Cmty. Sch. Dist.*, 393 U.S. 503, 508 (1969).
Correct omissions:	"[I]n our system, undifferentiated fear or apprehension of disturbance is not enough to overcome the right to freedom of expression." *Tinker v. Des Moines Indep. Cmty. Sch. Dist.*, 393 U.S. 503, 508 (1969).
	The Court held that "undifferentiated fear or apprehension of disturbance is not enough to overcome the right to freedom of expression." *Tinker v. Des Moines Indep. Cmty. Sch. Dist.*, 393 U.S. 503, 508 (1969).
Incorrect omissions:	". . . [I]n our system, undifferentiated fear or apprehension of disturbance is not enough to overcome the right to freedom of expression." *Tinker v. Des Moines Indep. Cmty. Sch. Dist.*, 393 U.S. 503, 508 (1969).
	The Court held that ". . . undifferentiated fear or apprehension of disturbance is not enough to overcome the right to freedom of expression." *Tinker v. Des Moines Indep. Cmty. Sch. Dist.*, 393 U.S. 503, 508 (1969).

40.3(c) To indicate omission of material following complete sentence

Do not use an ellipsis to indicate an omission following the ending punctuation of a complete sentence (when not continuing to quote further from the source) or at the end of a block quotation that concludes with a complete sentence.[20]

Example

Original (material to be quoted in red): "Joint proceedings are not only permissible but are often preferable when the joined defendants' criminal conduct arises out of a single chain of events. Joint trial may enable a jury 'to arrive more reliably at its conclusions regarding the guilt or innocence of a particular defendant and to assign fairly the respective responsibilities of each defendant in the sentencing.' " *Kansas v. Carr*, 577 U.S. 108, 125 (2016) (citing *Buchanon v. Kentucky*, 483 U.S. 402, 418 (1987)).

Correct omission of ellipsis: "Joint proceedings are not only permissible but are often preferable when the joined defendants' criminal conduct arises out of a single chain of events." *Kansas v. Carr*, 577 U.S. 108, 125 (2016).

Incorrect use of ellipsis: "Joint proceedings are not only permissible but are often preferable when the joined defendants' criminal conduct arises out of a single chain of events. . . ." *Kansas v. Carr*, 577 U.S. 108, 125 (2016).

40.3(d) To indicate omission of footnotes or citations

Do not use an ellipsis to indicate the omission of a footnote or a citation from a quoted passage.[21] Indicate the omission in a parenthetical after the citation.[22] For placement of the parenthetical, see **Rule 37.2**.

Examples

Original (footnote to be omitted in red): "Even electronic surveillance substantially contemporaneous with an individual's arrest could hardly be deemed an 'incident' of that arrest.[20]" *Katz v. United States*, 389 U.S. 347, 357 (1967).

Correct omission: "Even electronic surveillance substantially contemporaneous with an individual's arrest could hardly be deemed an 'incident' of that arrest." *Katz v. United States*, 389 U.S. 347, 357 (1967) (footnote omitted).

Incorrect omission: "Even electronic surveillance substantially contemporaneous with an individual's arrest could hardly be deemed an 'incident' of that arrest. . . ." *Katz v. United States*, 389 U.S. 347, 357 (1967) (footnote omitted).

Original (citations to be omitted in red):

The Supreme Court has articulated four factors to determine whether an area is within the curtilage: (1) the proximity of the area to the house; (2) whether the area is included within an enclosure surrounding the home; (3) the nature of the use to which the area is put; and (4) the steps taken by the resident to protect the area from observation. *United States v. Dunn*, 480 U.S. 294, 301, 107 S. Ct. 1134, 94 L. Ed. 2d 326 (1987). The central inquiry is "whether the area in question is so intimately tied to the home itself that it should be placed under the home's 'umbrella' of Fourth Amendment protection." *Id.*

United States v. McDowell, 713 F.3d 571, 574 (10th Cir. 2013).

Correct omissions:

The Supreme Court has articulated four factors to determine whether an area is within the curtilage: (1) the proximity of the area to the house; (2) whether the area is included within an enclosure surrounding the home; (3) the nature of the use to which the area is put; and (4) the steps taken by the resident to protect the area from observation. The central inquiry is "whether the area in question is so intimately tied to the home itself that it should be placed under the home's 'umbrella' of Fourth Amendment protection."

United States v. McDowell, 713 F.3d 571, 574 (10th Cir. 2013) (citations omitted).

Incorrect omissions:

The Supreme Court has articulated four factors to determine whether an area is within the curtilage: (1) the proximity of the area to the house; (2) whether the area is included within an enclosure surrounding the home; (3) the nature of the use to which the area is put; and (4) the steps taken by the resident to protect the area from observation. . . . The central inquiry is "whether the area in question is so intimately tied to the home itself that it should be placed under the home's 'umbrella' of Fourth Amendment protection." . . .

United States v. McDowell, 713 F.3d 571, 574 (10th Cir. 2013).

Part 6
Appendices

Appendix 1 Primary Sources by Jurisdiction

Appendix 1 lists the reporters, statutory compilations, session laws, administrative compilations, and administrative registers most commonly used in federal, state, and territorial jurisdictions, current through December 2020. It excludes federal and state constitutions, all of which use the same citation format (**Rule 13**). For federal tax materials, see **Appendix 6**. For federal agencies and their reporters and publications, see **Appendix 7**.

Sources are listed in order of preference, if any. Official sources are denoted with a red star (★). The red star *does not* necessarily mean that the official source is preferred. The preferred sources for a national audience, if any, are indicated with a red asterisk (*). The abbreviations and formats in this appendix are standardized, i.e., designed to be generally recognizable. They *do not* reflect unique citation formats that readers outside the jurisdiction may not recognize (e.g., statutory abbreviations ACA, G.L., ILCS, and T.C.A.). See **Appendix 2** for local rules of citation.

Use the abbreviations in **Appendix 1** to cite these primary sources even if they differ from abbreviations used in another appendix or publication (e.g., the abbreviations used by a commercial database publisher). Deviate from them only when you are following local rules. Component diagrams are furnished for states using public domain citations.

The diagrams indicate required spaces with red triangles (▲). Omit this symbol when you type the citation or abbreviation. A citation component printed in red indicates a variable (e.g., numbers and dates). The brackets enclosing a citation component indicate that the component is optional or only applicable in certain situations. For example, a component that appears as "[(year)]" means that including the year parenthetical is optional. Do not include the brackets in the citation if you include the optional component.

This appendix uses typefaces appropriate to everyday legal writing. Academic writing changes the typeface of some components to LARGE AND SMALL CAPITAL LETTERS; check rules with the FN suffix.

Each jurisdiction's entry lists its courts in hierarchical order. Beside each court's name, in parentheses, is its abbreviation. See **Appendix 4** for additional court abbreviations. Beneath each court's name is a table listing the reporters in which the court's opinions are most commonly published, the abbreviations for those reporters, and their coverage dates. If a state uses a public citation format, that is indicated before the reporters are listed. For more information on public citation formats, see that state's entry in **Appendix 2**.

Statutory compilation tables list current codes. Because publishers can change, confirm the publisher rather than relying solely on the current publisher listed here. Follow the numbering system used by the code (e.g., numbers connected by hyphens or periods, subsection letters in parentheses). Where a jurisdiction's session laws, administrative compilations, or administrative registers are published, the appendix provides tables with the names of those sources and format diagrams.

1(A) Federal Primary Sources

Court system and reporters (official reporters denoted with ★ and preferred sources denoted with *):		
United States Supreme Court (U.S.)		
★*United States Reports	U.S.	1790–present
Supreme Court Reporter	S. Ct.	1882–present
United States Supreme Court Reports, Lawyers' Edition	L. Ed.	1790–1956
Second Series	L. Ed. 2d	1956–present
United States Law Week	U.S.L.W.	1933–2018
United States Circuit Courts of Appeals (e.g., 1st Cir., 2d Cir., D.C. Cir.)		
*Federal Reporter	F.	1880–1924
*Second Series	F.2d	1924–1993
*Third Series	F.3d	1993–present
Federal Appendix	F. App'x	2001–present
United States Circuit Courts (abolished in 1912) (e.g., C.C.D. Mass., designated by name of district court)		
Federal Cases	F. Cas.	1789–1880
Federal Reporter	F.	1880–1912
Temporary Emergency Court of Appeals (Temp. Emer. Ct. App.) **Emergency Court of Appeals (Emer. Ct. App.)** **Commerce Court (Comm. Ct.)**		
Federal Reporter	F.	1880–1924
Second Series	F.2d	1924–1993
United States Court of Appeals for the Federal Circuit (Fed. Cir.) **United States Court of Customs and Patent Appeals (C.C.P.A.)** **Court of Customs Appeals (Ct. Cust. App.)** **Court of Claims (Ct. Cl.)** (appellate jurisdiction)		
*Federal Reporter	F.	1880–1924
*Second Series	F.2d	1924–1993
*Third Series	F.3d	1993–present
★Court of Customs Appeals Reports	Ct. Cust.	1910–1929

Reporter	Abbreviation	Years
★Court of Customs and Patent Appeals Reports	C.C.P.A.	1929–1982
★Court of Claims Reports	Ct. Cl.	1956–1982
United States Court of Federal Claims (Fed. Cl.) **United States Claims Court (Cl. Ct.)** **Court of Claims (Ct. Cl.)** (original jurisdiction)		
Federal Claims Reporter	Fed. Cl.	1992–present
United States Claims Court Reporter	Cl. Ct.	1983–1992
Federal Reporter, Second Series	F.2d	1930–1932, 1960–1982
Federal Supplement	F. Supp.	1932–1960
★Court of Claims Reports	Ct. Cl.	1863–1982
United States Court of International Trade (Ct. Int'l Trade) **United States Customs Court (Cust. Ct.)**		
★*Customs Bulletin and Decisions	Cust. B. & Dec.	1967–present
★*Court of International Trade Reports	Ct. Int'l Trade	1980–present
★*Customs Court Reports	Cust. Ct.	1938–1980
Federal Supplement	F. Supp.	1980–1998
Second Series	F. Supp. 2d	1998–2014
Third Series	F. Supp. 3d	2014–present
International Trade Reporter Decisions	I.T.R.D. (BL)	1980–present
United States District Courts (e.g., S.D. Cal., W.D.N.Y., D. Colo.)		
*Federal Supplement	F. Supp.	1932–1998
*Second Series	F. Supp. 2d	1998–2014
*Third Series	F. Supp. 3d	2014–present
*Federal Rules Decisions	F.R.D.	1938–present
*Bankruptcy Reporter	B.R.	1979–present
Federal Rules Service	Fed. R. Serv.	1938–present
Federal Cases (citations should give the case number in a parenthetical)	F. Cas.	1789–1880
Federal Reporter	F.	1880–1924
Second Series	F.2d	1924–1932
United States Bankruptcy Courts (e.g., Bankr. S.D.N.Y.) **Bankruptcy Appellate Panels** (e.g., B.A.P. 1st Cir.)		
*Bankruptcy Reporter	B.R.	1979–present

Judicial Panel on Multidistrict Litigation (J.P.M.L.) **Special Court, Regional Rail Reorganization Act (Reg'l Rail Reorg. Ct.)**		
*Federal Supplement	F. Supp.	1968–1998
*Second Series	F. Supp. 2d	1998–2014
*Third Series	F. Supp. 3d	2014–present
Tax Court (T.C.); Board of Tax Appeals (B.T.A.)		
*United States Tax Court Reports	T.C.	1942–present
*Reports of the United States Board of Tax Appeals	B.T.A.	1924–1942
Tax Court Memorandum Decisions (CCH)	T.C.M. (CCH)	1942–present
Tax Court Memorandum Decisions (P-H)	T.C.M. (P-H)	1942–1991
Tax Court Memorandum Decisions (RIA)	T.C.M. (RIA)	1991–present
Board of Tax Appeals Memorandum Decisions	B.T.A.M. (P-H)	1928–1942
United States Court of Appeals for Veterans Claims (Vet. App.) **United States Court of Veteran Appeals (Vet. App.)**		
*West's Veterans Appeals Reporter	Vet. App.	1900–present
United States Court of Appeals for the Armed Forces (C.A.A.F.) **United States Court of Military Appeals (C.M.A.)**		
*Decisions of the United States Court of Military Appeals	C.M.A.	1951–1975
West's Military Justice Reporter	M.J.	1978–present
Court Martial Reports	C.M.R.	1951–1975
Military Service Courts of Criminal Appeals (A. Ct. Crim. App.; A.F. Ct. Crim. App.; C.G. Ct. Crim. App.; N-M Ct. Crim. App.) **Courts of Military Review (e.g., A.C.M.R.)** **Boards of Review (e.g., A.B.R.)**		
*West's Military Justice Reporter	M.J.	1978–present
*Court Martial Reports	C.M.R.	1951–1975
Statutory compilations:		
★*United States Code	Title number U.S.C. § section number [(year)].	
United States Code Annotated	Title number U.S.C.A. § section number (West [year]).	
United States Code Service	Title number U.S.C.S. § section number (LexisNexis [year]).	
Gould's United States Code Unannotated	Title number U.S.C.U. § section number (Gould [year]).	
Revised Statutes of the United States	Title number Rev. Stat. § section number [(edition] [year)].	

Session laws:	
★United States Statutes at Large	Pub. L. No. public law number, volume number Stat. page number (enactment or effective date). Priv. L. No. private law number, volume number Stat. page number (enactment or effective date).
Administrative compilation:	
★Code of Federal Regulations	Title number C.F.R. § section number (year).
Administrative register:	
★Federal Register	Volume number Fed. Reg. page number (month day, year).

1(B) States' and District of Columbia's Primary Sources

Alabama

Court system and reporters:		
Alabama Supreme Court (Ala.)		
*Southern Reporter	So.	1886–1941
★*Second Series (official since 1976)	So. 2d	1941–2008
★*Third Series	So. 3d	2008–present
★Alabama Reports	Ala.	1840–1976
Alabama Court of Civil Appeals (Ala. Civ. App.) **Alabama Court of Criminal Appeals (Ala. Crim. App.)** previously Alabama Court of Appeals (Ala. Ct. App.)		
*Southern Reporter	So.	1911–1941
★*Second Series (official since 1976)	So. 2d	1941–2008
★*Third Series	So. 3d	2008–present
★Alabama Appellate Court Reports	Ala. App.	1911–1976
Statutory compilations:		
★*Code of Alabama, 1975	Ala. Code § section number (year).	
Michie's Alabama Code, 1975	Ala. Code § section number (LexisNexis year).	
Session laws:		
★*Alabama Laws	Year Ala. Laws page number.	
West's Alabama Legislative Service	Year Ala. Legis. Serv. page number (West).	
Michie's Alabama Code Year Advance Legislative Service	Year–pamphlet number Ala. Adv. Legis. Serv. page number (LexisNexis).	

Administrative compilation:	
Alabama Administrative Code	Ala.▲Admin.▲Code▲r.▲rule number▲(year).
Administrative register:	
Alabama Administrative Monthly	Volume number▲Ala.▲Admin.▲Monthly▲page number▲(month▲day,▲year).

Alaska

Court system and reporters:		
Alaska Supreme Court (Alaska)		
★*Pacific Reporter, Second Series	P.2d	1959–2000
★*Third Series	P.3d	2000–present
★Alaska Reports	Alaska	1887–1958
Alaska Court of Appeals (Alaska▲Ct.▲App.)		
★*Pacific Reporter, Second Series	P.2d	1980–2000
★*Third Series	P.3d	2000–present

Statutory compilations:	
★*Alaska Statutes	Alaska▲Stat.▲§▲section number▲(year).
West's Alaska Statutes Annotated	Alaska▲Stat.▲Ann.▲§▲section number▲(West▲year).
Session laws:	
★*Session Laws of Alaska	Year▲Alaska▲Sess.▲Laws▲ch.▲chapter number,▲§▲section number.
Alaska Statutes Year Advance Legislative Service	Year–pamphlet number▲Alaska▲Adv.▲Legis.▲Serv.▲page number▲(LexisNexis).
West's Alaska Legislative Service	Year▲Alaska▲Legis.▲Serv.▲page number▲(West).
Administrative compilation:	
Alaska Administrative Code	Alaska▲Admin.▲Code▲tit.▲title number,▲§▲section number▲(year).
Administrative register:	
Alaska Administrative Journal (discontinued May 2000)	Issue number▲Alaska▲Admin.▲J.▲page number▲(month▲day,▲year).

Arizona

Court system and reporters:		
Arizona Supreme Court (Ariz.)		
*Pacific Reporter	P.	1883–1931
*Second Series	P.2d	1931–2000
*Third Series	P.3d	2000–present
★Arizona Reports	Ariz.	1866–present
Arizona Court of Appeals (Ariz. Ct. App.)		
*Pacific Reporter, Second Series	P.2d	1965–2000
*Third Series	P.3d	2000–present
★Arizona Appeals Reports	Ariz. App.	1965–1976
★Arizona Reports	Ariz.	1976–present
Arizona Tax Court (Ariz. Tax Ct.)		
*Pacific Reporter, Second Series	P.2d	1989–2000
*Third Series	P.3d	2000–present

Statutory compilations:	
★Arizona Revised Statutes Annotated	Ariz. Rev. Stat. Ann. § section number (year).
Arizona Revised Statutes	Ariz. Rev. Stat. § section number (LexisNexis year).
Session laws:	
★*Session Laws of Arizona	Year Ariz. Sess. Laws page number.
West's Arizona Legislative Service	Year Ariz. Legis. Serv. page number (West).
Arizona Advance Legislative Service (last published in 2017)	Year-pamphlet number Ariz. Adv. Legis. Serv. page number (LexisNexis).
Administrative compilation:	
Arizona Administrative Code	Ariz. Admin. Code § section number (year).
Administrative register:	
Arizona Administrative Register	Volume number Ariz. Admin. Reg. page number (month day, year).

Arkansas

Court system and reporters:	
Public domain format (for opinions issued since February 14, 2009):	
★Arkansas Supreme Court (official since 2009)	Year Ark. opinion number, at page number.
★Arkansas Court of Appeals (official since 2009)	Year Ark. App. opinion number, at page number.

Arkansas Supreme Court (Ark.)		
*South Western Reporter	S.W.	1886–1928
*Second Series	S.W.2d	1928–1999
*Third Series	S.W.3d	1999–present
★Arkansas Reports	Ark.	1837–2009
Arkansas Court of Appeals (Ark.▲Ct.▲App.)		
South Western Reporter	S.W.	1886–1928
*Second Series	S.W.2d	1928–1999
*Third Series	S.W.3d	1999–present
★Arkansas Appellate Reports (bound with Ark.)	Ark.▲App.	1981–2009
★Arkansas Reports	Ark.	1979–1981
Statutory compilations:		
★*Arkansas Code of 1987 Annotated	Ark.▲Code▲Ann.▲§▲section number▲(year).	
West's Arkansas Code Annotated	Ark.▲Code▲Ann.▲§▲section number▲(West▲year).	
Session laws:		
★*Acts of Arkansas	Year▲Ark.▲Acts▲page number.	
West's Arkansas Legislative Service	Year▲Ark.▲Legis.▲Serv.▲page number▲(West).	
Arkansas Code of 1987 Annotated Advance Legislative Service	Year–pamphlet number▲Ark.▲Adv.▲Legis.▲Serv.▲page number▲(LexisNexis).	
Administrative compilation:		
Code of Arkansas Rules	Agency number–sub-agency number–chapter number▲Ark.▲Code▲R.▲§▲section number▲(LexisNexis▲year).	
Administrative registers:		
*Arkansas Register	Volume number▲Ark.▲Reg.▲page number▲(month▲year).	
Arkansas Government Register	Issue number▲Ark.▲Gov't▲Reg.▲page number▲(LexisNexis▲month▲year).	

California

Court system and reporters:		
California Supreme Court (Cal.)		
*Pacific Reporter	P.	1883–1931
*Second Series	P.2d	1931–2000
*Third Series	P.3d	2000–present
★California Reports	Cal.	1850–1934
★Second Series	Cal.▲2d	1934–1969
★Third Series	Cal.▲3d	1969–1991
★Fourth Series	Cal.▲4th	1991–present
West's California Reporter	Cal.▲Rptr.	1959–1991
Second Series	Cal.▲Rptr.▲2d	1991–2003
Third Series	Cal.▲Rptr.▲3d	2003–present
California Unreported Cases	Cal.▲Unrep.	1855–1910
California Court of Appeal (Cal.▲Ct.▲App.) previously California District Court of Appeal (Cal.▲Dist.▲Ct.▲App.)		
*Pacific Reporter	P.	1905–1931
*Second Series	P.2d	1931–1959
*West's California Reporter	Cal.▲Rptr.	1959–1991
*Second Series	Cal.▲Rptr.▲2d	1991–2003
*Third Series	Cal.▲Rptr.▲3d	2003–present
★California Appellate Reports	Cal.▲App.	1905–1934
★Second Series	Cal.▲App.▲2d	1934–1969
★Third Series	Cal.▲App.▲3d	1969–1991
★Fourth Series	Cal.▲App.▲4th	1991–present
Appellate Division of California Superior Court (Cal.▲App.▲Dep't▲Super.▲Ct.)		
*Pacific Reporter	P.	1929–1931
*Second Series	P.2d	1931–1959
*West's California Reporter	Cal.▲Rptr.	1959–1991
*Second Series	Cal.▲Rptr.▲2d	1991–2003
*Third Series	Cal.▲Rptr.▲3d	2003–present
★California Appellate Reports Supplement	Cal.▲App.▲Supp.	1929–1934
★Second Series	Cal.▲App.▲2d▲Supp.	1934–1969

★Third Series (bound with Cal. App. 3d)	Cal. App. 3d Supp.	1969–1991
★Fourth Series (bound with Cal. App. 4th)	Cal. App. 4th Supp.	1991–present

Statutory compilations:

*West's Annotated California Codes	Cal. Subject abbreviation Code § section number (West year).
*Deering's California Codes Annotated	Cal. Subject abbreviation Code § section number (Deering year).

Subject abbreviations for statutory compilations:

Subject	Abbreviation	Subject	Abbreviation
Agricultural	Agric.	Elections	Elec.
Business and Professions	Bus. & Prof.	Evidence	Evid.
Civil	Civ.	Family	Fam.
Civil Procedure	Civ. Proc.	Financial	Fin.
Commercial	Com.	Fish and Game	Fish & Game
Corporations	Corp.	Food and Agricultural	Food & Agric.
Education	Educ.	Government	Gov't
Harbors and Navigation	Harb. & Nav.	Public Resources	Pub. Res.
Health and Safety	Health & Safety	Public Utilities	Pub. Util.
Insurance	Ins.	Revenue and Taxation	Rev. & Tax.
Labor	Lab.	Streets and Highways	Sts. & High.
Military and Veterans	Mil. & Vet.	Unemployment Insurance	Unemp. Ins.
Penal	Penal	Vehicle	Veh.
Probate	Prob.	Water	Water
Public Contract	Pub. Cont.	Welfare and Institutions	Welf. & Inst.

Session laws:

★*Statutes of California	Year Cal. Stat. page number.
West's California Legislative Service	Year Cal. Legis. Serv. page number (West).
Deering's California Advance Legislative Service	Year–pamphlet number Cal. Adv. Legis. Serv. page number (LexisNexis).

Administrative compilation:	
★California Code of Regulations	Cal. Code Regs. tit. title number, § section number (year).
Administrative register:	
California Regulatory Notice Register	Issue number Cal. Regulatory Notice Reg. page number (month day, year).

Colorado

Court system and reporters:		
Public domain format (for opinions issued since January 1, 2012):		
Colorado Supreme Court	*Case name*, year CO opinion number, ¶ paragraph number.	
Colorado Court of Appeals	*Case name*, year COA opinion number, ¶ paragraph number.	
Colorado Supreme Court (Colo.)		
*Pacific Reporter	P.	1883–1931
★*Second Series (official since 1980)	P.2d	1931–2000
★*Third Series	P.3d	2000–present
★Colorado Reports	Colo.	1864–1980
★Colorado Lawyer	Colo. Law.	1972–present
★Brief Times Reporter	Brief Times Rep.	1977–1996
★Colorado Journal	Colo. J.	1996–2002
★Law Week Colorado	L. Week Colo.	2002–present
Colorado Court of Appeals (Colo. App.)		
★Colorado Court of Appeals Reports	Colo. App.	1891–1980
*Pacific Reporter	P.	1891–1931
★*Second Series (official since 1980)	P.2d	1970–2000
★*Third Series	P.3d	2000–present
★Colorado Lawyer	Colo. Law.	1972–present
★Brief Times Reporter	Brief Times Rep.	1977–1996
★Colorado Journal	Colo. J.	1996–2002
★Law Week Colorado	L. Week Colo.	2002–present

Statutory compilations:	
★*Colorado Revised Statutes	Colo. Rev. Stat. § section number (year).
West's Colorado Revised Statutes Annotated	Colo. Rev. Stat. Ann. § section number (West year).

Session laws:	
★*Session Laws of Colorado	Year▲Colo.▲Sess.▲Laws▲page number.
West's Colorado Legislative Service	Year▲Colo.▲Legis.▲Serv.▲page number▲(West).
Colorado Advance Legislative Service	Year-pamphlet number▲Colo.▲Adv.▲Legis.▲Serv.▲page number▲(LexisNexis).
Administrative compilations:	
★*Colorado Code of Regulations (online)	Colo.▲Code▲Regs.▲§▲section number▲(year).
Code of Colorado Regulations	Volume number▲Colo.▲Code▲Regs.▲§▲section number▲(LexisNexis▲year).
Administrative register:	
Colorado Register (official since 2007)	Issue number▲Colo.▲Reg.▲page number▲(month▲year).

Connecticut

Court system and reporters:		
Connecticut Supreme Court (Conn.) previously Connecticut Supreme Court of Errors (Conn.)		
*Atlantic Reporter	A.	1885–1938
*Second Series	A.2d	1939–2010
*Third Series	A.3d	2010–present
★Connecticut Reports	Conn.	1814–present
Day	Day	1802–1813
Root	Root	1789–1798
Kirby	Kirby	1785–1789
Connecticut Appellate Court (Conn.▲App.▲Ct.)		
*Atlantic Reporter, Second Series	A.2d	1983–2010
*Third Series	A.3d	2010–present
★Connecticut Appellate Reports	Conn.▲App.	1983–present
Connecticut Superior Court (Conn.▲Super.▲Ct.) **Connecticut Court of Common Pleas (Conn.▲C.P.)**		
*Atlantic Reporter, Second Series	A.2d	1954–2010
*Third Series	A.3d	2010–present
★Connecticut Supplement	Conn.▲Supp.	1935–present
Connecticut Law Reporter	Conn.▲L.▲Rptr.	1990–present
Connecticut Superior Court Reports	Conn.▲Super.▲Ct.	1986–1994

Connecticut Circuit Court (Conn. Cir. Ct.)		
*Atlantic Reporter, Second Series	A.2d	1961–1974
*Third Series	A.3d	2010–present
★Connecticut Circuit Court Reports	Conn. Cir. Ct.	1961–1974
Statutory compilations:		
★*General Statutes of Connecticut	Conn. Gen. Stat. § section number (year).	
West's Connecticut General Statutes Annotated	Conn. Gen. Stat. Ann. § section number (West year).	
Session laws:		
★*Connecticut Public and Special Acts	Year Conn. Acts page number ([Reg. or Spec.] Sess.).	
★*Connecticut Public Acts	Year Conn. Pub. Acts page number.	
★*Connecticut Special Acts	Year Conn. Spec. Acts page number.	
Connecticut Advance Legislative Service (last published in 2019)	Year–pamphlet number Conn. Adv. Legis. Serv. page number (LexisNexis).	
West's Connecticut Legislative Service	Year Conn. Legis. Serv. page number (West).	
Administrative compilation:		
Regulations of Connecticut State Agencies	Conn. Agencies Regs. § section number (year).	
Administrative register:		
★*Connecticut Law Journal	Volume number Conn. L.J. page number (month day, year).	
Connecticut Government Register	Issue number Conn. Gov't Reg. page number (LexisNexis month year).	

Delaware

Court system and reporters:		
Delaware Supreme Court (Del.) previously Delaware High Court of Errors and Appeals (Del.)		
*Atlantic Reporter	A.	1885–1938
★*Second Series (official since 1966)	A.2d	1939–2010
★*Third Series	A.3d	2010–present
★Delaware Reports	Del.	1832–1966
Delaware Cases	Del. Cas.	1792–1830

Delaware Court of Chancery (Del. Ch.)		
*Atlantic Reporter	A.	1885–1938
★*Second Series (official since 1966)	A.2d	1939–2010
★*Third Series	A.3d	2010–present
★Delaware Chancery Reports	Del. Ch.	1814–1968
★Delaware Cases	Del. Cas.	1792–1830
Delaware Superior Court (Del. Super. Ct.) previously Delaware Superior Court and Orphans' Court (Del. Super. Ct. & Orphans' Ct.)		
*Atlantic Reporter	A.	1885–1938
★*Second Series (official since 1966)	A.2d	1938–2010
★*Third Series	A.3d	2010–present
★Delaware Reports	Del.	1832–1965
Delaware Family Court (Del. Fam. Ct.)		
★*Atlantic Reporter, Second Series	A.2d	1977–2010
★*Third Series	A.3d	2010–present

Statutory compilations:	
★*Delaware Code Annotated	Del. Code Ann. tit. title number, § section number (year).
West's Delaware Code Annotated	Del. Code Ann. tit. title number, § section number (West year).
Session laws:	
★*Laws of Delaware	Volume number Del. Laws page number (year).
Delaware Code Annotated Advance Legislative Service	Year–pamphlet number Del. Code Ann. Adv. Legis. Serv. page number (LexisNexis).
West's Delaware Legislative Service	Year Del. Legis. Serv. page number (West).
Administrative compilation:	
★*Delaware Administrative Code	Title number Del. Admin. Code § regulation number–section number (year).
Code of Delaware Regulations (LexisNexis)	Title number Del. Code Regs. § regulation number–section number (LexisNexis year).
Administrative register:	
★*Delaware Register of Regulations	Volume number Del. Reg. Regs. page number (month day, year).
Delaware Government Register	Issue number Del. Gov't Reg. page number (LexisNexis month year).

District of Columbia

Court system and reporters:		
District of Columbia Court of Appeals (D.C.) previously Municipal Court of Appeals (D.C.)		
★*Atlantic Reporter, Second Series	A.2d	1943–2010
★*Third Series	A.3d	2010–present
District of Columbia Superior Court (D.C. Super. Ct.)		
Daily Washington Law Reporter	Daily Wash. L. Rptr.	1971–present

Statutory compilations:	
★*District of Columbia Official Code	D.C. Code § section number (year).
West's District of Columbia Code Annotated	D.C. Code Ann. § section number (West year).
Session laws:	
★*United States Statutes at Large	Volume number Stat. page number (Year).
*District of Columbia Register	Volume number D.C. Reg. page number (month day, year).
*District of Columbia Official Code Lexis Advance Legislative Service	Year–pamphlet number D.C. Code Adv. Leg. Serv. page number.
District of Columbia Session Law Service (West)	Year D.C. Sess. L. Serv. page number (West).
Municipal regulations:	
★*District of Columbia Municipal Regulations	D.C. Mun. Regs. tit. title number, § section number (year).
Code of District of Columbia Municipal Regulations (LexisNexis)	D.C. Code Mun. Regs. tit. title number § section number (LexisNexis year).
Administrative register:	
★District of Columbia Register	Volume number D.C. Reg. page number (month day, year).

Florida

Court system and reporters:		
Florida Supreme Court (Fla.)		
*Southern Reporter	So.	1887–1941
★*Second Series (official since 1948)	So. 2d	1941–2008
★*Third Series	So. 3d	2008–present
★Florida Reports	Fla.	1846–1948
Florida Law Weekly	Fla. L. Weekly	1978–present

Florida District Court of Appeal (Fla. Dist. Ct. App.)		
★*Southern Reporter, Second Series	So. 2d	1957–2008
★*Third Series	So. 3d	2008–present
Florida Law Weekly	Fla. L. Weekly	1978–present
Florida Circuit Court (Fla. Cir. Ct.) **Florida County Court (Fla. County Name County Ct.)** **Florida Public Service Commission (Fla. P.S.C.)** and other Florida lower courts		
★Florida Supplement	Fla. Supp.	1952–1980
★Second Series	Fla. Supp. 2d	1980–1992
Florida Law Weekly Supplement	Fla. L. Weekly Supp.	1992–present
Statutory compilations:		
★*Florida Statutes	Fla. Stat. § section number (year).	
West's Florida Statutes Annotated	Fla. Stat. Ann. § section number (West year).	
LexisNexis Florida Statutes Annotated	Fla. Stat. Ann. § section number (LexisNexis year).	
Session laws:		
★*Laws of Florida	Year Fla. Laws page number.	
West's Florida Session Law Service	Year Fla. Sess. Law Serv. page number (West).	
Administrative compilation:		
Florida Administrative Code Annotated	Fla. Admin. Code Ann. r. rule number (year).	
Administrative register:		
*Florida Administrative Register	Volume number Fla. Admin. Reg. page number (month day, year).	
Florida Administrative Weekly	Volume number Fla. Admin. Weekly page number (month day, year).	

Georgia

Court system and reporters:		
Georgia Supreme Court (Ga.)		
*South Eastern Reporter	S.E.	1886–1939
*Second Series	S.E.2d	1939–present
★Georgia Reports	Ga.	1846–present

Georgia Court of Appeals (Ga. Ct. App.)		
*South Eastern Reporter	S.E.	1906–1939
*Second Series	S.E.2d	1939–present
★Georgia Appeals Reports	Ga. App.	1906–present
Statutory compilations:		
★*Official Code of Georgia Annotated	Ga. Code Ann. § section number (year).	
West's Code of Georgia Annotated	Ga. Code Ann. § section number (West year).	
Session laws:		
★*Georgia Laws	Year Ga. Laws page number.	
Georgia Advance Legislative Service	Year-pamphlet number Ga. Code Ann. Adv. Legis. Serv. page number (LexisNexis).	
West's Georgia Legislative Service	Year Ga. Code Ann. Adv. Legis. Serv. page number (West).	
Administrative compilation:		
★Official Compilation of Rules and Regulations of the State of Georgia	Ga. Comp. R. & Regs. § title number-chapter number-section number (year).	
Administrative register:		
Georgia Government Register	Issue number Ga. Gov't Reg. page number (LexisNexis month year).	

Hawai'i

Court system and reporters:		
Hawai'i Supreme Court (Haw.)		
★*Pacific Reporter, Second Series	P.2d	1959–2000
★*Third Series	P.3d	2000–present
★West's Hawaii Reports	Haw.	1847–1994
★Hawai'i Reports	Haw.	1994–present
Hawai'i Intermediate Court of Appeals (Haw. Ct. App.)		
★*Pacific Reporter, Second Series	P.2d	1980–present
★*Third Series	P.3d	2000–present
★West's Hawaii Reports	Haw.	1994–present
★Hawai'i Appellate Reports	Haw. App.	1980–1994
Statutory compilations:		
★*Hawai'i Revised Statutes	Haw. Rev. Stat. § section number (year).	

Michie's Hawaii Revised Statutes Annotated	Haw. Rev. Stat. Ann. § section number (LexisNexis year).
West's Hawaii Revised Statutes Annotated	Haw. Rev. Stat. Ann. § section number (West year).
Session laws:	
★*Session Laws of Hawai'i	Year Haw. Sess. Laws page number.
Michie's Hawaii Revised Statutes Annotated Advance Legislative Service	Year-pamphlet number Haw. Rev. Stat. Ann. Adv. Legis. Serv. page number (LexisNexis).
West's Hawaii Legislative Service	Year Haw. Legis. Serv. page number (West).
Administrative compilation:	
Weil's Code of Hawai'i Rules	Haw. Code R. § section number (LexisNexis year).
Administrative register:	
Hawaii Government Register	Issue number Haw. Gov't Reg. page number (LexisNexis month year).

Idaho

Court system and reporters:		
Idaho Supreme Court (Idaho)		
*Pacific Reporter	P.	1883–1931
*Second Series	P.2d	1931–2000
*Third Series	P.3d	2000–present
★Idaho Reports	Idaho	1866–present
Idaho Court of Appeals (Idaho Ct. App.)		
*Pacific Reporter, Second Series	P.2d	1982–2000
*Third Series	P.3d	2000–present
★Idaho Reports	Idaho	1982–present
Statutory compilations:		
★*Idaho Code	Idaho Code § section number (year).	
West's Idaho Code Annotated	Idaho Code Ann. § section number (West year).	
Session laws:		
★*Idaho Session Laws	Year Idaho Sess. Laws page number.	
Idaho Code Annotated Advance Legislative Service	Year-pamphlet number Idaho Code Ann. Adv. Legis. Serv. page number (LexisNexis).	
West's Idaho Legislative Service	Year Idaho Legis. Serv. page number (West).	

Administrative compilations:	
★Idaho Administrative Code (online)	Idaho ▲Admin. ▲Code ▲r. ▲title number. chapter number.section number ▲(year).
Administrative register:	
Idaho Administrative Bulletin	Volume number ▲Idaho ▲Admin. ▲Bull. ▲ page number ▲(month ▲day, ▲year).

Illinois

Court system and reporters:		
Public domain format (for opinions issued since July 1, 2011):		
★Illinois Supreme Court	*Case name*, ▲year ▲IL ▲opinion number, ▲¶ ▲paragraph number.	
★Illinois Court of Appeals	*Case name*, ▲year ▲IL ▲App ▲(District abbreviation) ▲opinion number, ▲¶ ▲paragraph number.	
Illinois Supreme Court (Ill.)		
*North Eastern Reporter	N.E.	1885–1936
*Second Series	N.E.2d	1936–2013
*Third Series	N.E.3d	2014–present
★Illinois Reports	Ill.	1819–1954
★Second Series	Ill. ▲2d	1954–2011
West's Illinois Decisions	Ill. ▲Dec.	1976–present
Illinois Appellate Court (Ill. ▲App. ▲Ct.)		
*North Eastern Reporter, Second Series	N.E.2d	1936–2013
*Third Series	N.E.3d	2014–present
★Illinois Official Reports	Year ▲IL ▲docket no.	2011– present
★Illinois Appellate Court Reports	Ill. ▲App.	1877–1954
★Second Series	Ill. ▲App. ▲2d	1954–1972
★Third Series	Ill. ▲App. ▲3d	1972–2011
West's Illinois Decisions	Ill. ▲Dec.	1976–present
Illinois Circuit Court (Ill. ▲Cir. ▲Ct.) **Illinois Court of Claims (Ill. ▲Ct. ▲Cl.)**		
★*Illinois Court of Claims Reports	Ill. ▲Ct. ▲Cl.	1889–present
Statutory compilations:		
★*Illinois Compiled Statutes	Chapter number ▲Ill. ▲Comp. ▲Stat. ▲Act number/section number ▲(year).	
West's Smith-Hurd Illinois Compiled Statutes Annotated	Chapter number ▲Ill. ▲Comp. ▲Stat. ▲Ann. ▲Act number/section number ▲(West ▲year).	

Illinois Compiled Statutes Annotated	Chapter number▲Ill.▲Comp.▲Stat.▲Ann.▲Act number/section number▲(LexisNexis▲year).
Session laws:	
★*Laws of Illinois	Year▲Ill.▲Laws▲page number.
Illinois Legislative Service	Year▲Ill.▲Legis.▲Serv.▲page number▲(West).
Illinois Compiled Statutes Annotated Advance Legislative Service	Year–pamphlet number▲Ill.▲Comp.▲Stat.▲Ann.▲Adv.▲Legis.▲Serv.▲page number▲(LexisNexis).
Administrative compilations:	
★*Illinois Administrative Code	Ill.▲Admin.▲Code▲tit.▲title number,▲§▲section number▲(year).
Code of Illinois Rules	Volume number▲Ill.▲Code▲R.▲rule number▲(LexisNexis▲year).
Administrative register:	
Illinois Register	Volume number▲Ill.▲Reg.▲page number▲(month▲day,▲year).

Indiana

Court system and reporters:		
Indiana Supreme Court (Ind.)		
*North Eastern Reporter	N.E.	1885–1936
★*Second Series (official since 1981)	N.E.2d	1936–2013
★*Third Series	N.E.3d	2014–present
★Indiana Reports	Ind.	1848–1981
Blackford	Blackf.	1817–1847
Indiana Court of Appeals (Ind.▲Ct.▲App.) previously Indiana Appellate Court (Ind.▲App.)		
*North Eastern Reporter	N.E.	1891–1936
★*Second Series (official since 1979)	N.E.2d	1936–2013
★*Third Series	N.E.3d	2014–present
★Indiana Court of Appeals Reports	Ind.▲App.	1891–1979
Indiana Tax Court (Ind.▲T.C.)		
North Eastern Reporter	N.E.	1885–1936
★*Second Series (official since 1979)	N.E.2d	1936–2013
★*Third Series	N.E.3d	2014–present

Statutory compilations:	
★*Indiana Code	Ind. Code § section number (year).
West's Annotated Indiana Code	Ind. Code Ann. § section number (West year).
Burns Indiana Statutes Annotated	Ind. Code Ann. § section number (LexisNexis year).
Session laws:	
★*Acts of Indiana	Year Ind. Acts page number.
West's Indiana Legislative Service	Year Ind. Legis. Serv. page number (West).
Burns Indiana Statutes Annotated Advance Legislative Service	Year–pamphlet number Ind. Stat. Ann. Adv. Legis. Serv. page number (LexisNexis).
Administrative compilations:	
★*Indiana Administrative Code	Title number Ind. Admin. Code rule number (year).
West's Indiana Administrative Code	Title number Ind. Admin. Code rule number (West year).
Administrative register:	
Indiana Register	Volume number Ind. Reg. page number (month day, year).

Iowa

Court system and reporters:		
	Iowa Supreme Court (Iowa)	
*North Western Reporter	N.W.	1879–1941
★*Second Series (official since 1968)	N.W.2d	1941–present
★Iowa Reports	Iowa	1855–1968
	Iowa Court of Appeals (Iowa Ct. App.)	
★*North Western Reporter, Second Series	N.W.2d	1977–present

Statutory compilations:	
★*Code of Iowa	Iowa Code § section number (year).
West's Iowa Code Annotated	Iowa Code Ann. § section number (West year).
Session laws:	
★*Iowa Acts	Year Iowa Acts page number.
West's Iowa Legislative Service	Year Iowa Legis. Serv. page number (West).

Administrative compilation:	
Iowa Administrative Code	Iowa Admin. Code r. rule number (year).
Administrative register:	
Iowa Administrative Bulletin	Volume number Iowa Admin. Bull. page number (month day, year).

Kansas

Court system and reporters:		
Kansas Supreme Court (Kan.)		
*Pacific Reporter	P.	1883–1931
*Second Series	P.2d	1931–2000
*Third Series	P.3d	2000–present
★Kansas Reports	Kan.	1862–present
McCahon	McCahon	1858–1868
Kansas Court of Appeals (Kan. Ct. App.)		
*Pacific Reporter	P.	1895–1931
*Second Series	P.2d	1977–2000
*Third Series	P.3d	2000–present
★Kansas Court of Appeals Reports	Kan. App.	1895–1901
★Second Series	Kan. App. 2d	1977–present

Statutory compilations:	
★*Kansas Statutes Annotated	Kan. Stat. Ann. § section number (year).
West's Kansas Statutes Annotated	Kan. Stat. Ann. § section number (West year).
Session laws:	
★*Session Laws of Kansas	Year Kan. Sess. Laws page number.
West's Kansas Legislative Service	Year Kan. Legis. Serv. page number (West).
Administrative compilation:	
Kansas Administrative Regulations	Kan. Admin. Regs. § section number (year).
Administrative register:	
Kansas Register	Volume number Kan. Reg. page number (month day, year).

Kentucky

Court system and reporters:		
Kentucky Supreme Court (Ky.) previously Kentucky Court of Appeals (Ky.)		
*South Western Reporter	S.W.	1886–1928
★*Second Series (official since 1973)	S.W.2d	1928–1999
★*Third Series	S.W.3d	1999–present
★Kentucky Reports	Ky.	1785–1951
Kentucky Opinions	Ky. Op.	1864–1886
Kentucky Law Reporter	Ky. L. Rptr.	1880–1908
Kentucky Appellate Reporter	Ky. App.	1994–2000
Kentucky Attorney's Memo	Ky. Att'y Memo	2001–2007
Kentucky Law Summary	Ky. L. Summ.	1966–present
Kentucky Court of Appeals (Ky. Ct. App.)		
★*South Western Reporter, Second Series	S.W.2d	1976–1999
★*Third Series	S.W.3d	1999–present
Kentucky Attorney's Memo	Ky. Att'y Memo	2001–2007
Kentucky Law Summary	Ky. L. Summ.	1966–present

Statutory compilations:	
Baldwin's Kentucky Revised Statutes Annotated (certified)	Ky. Rev. Stat. Ann. § section number (West year).
Michie's Kentucky Revised Statutes Annotated (certified)	Ky. Rev. Stat. Ann. § section number (LexisNexis year).

Session laws:	
★*Kentucky Acts	Year Ky. Acts page number.
Kentucky Revised Statutes and Rules Service	Year Ky. Rev. Stat. & R. Serv. page number (West).
Kentucky Revised Statutes Advance Legislative Service	Year–pamphlet number Ky. Rev. Stat. Adv. Legis. Serv. page number (LexisNexis).

Administrative compilation:	
Kentucky Administrative Regulations Service	Title number Ky. Admin. Regs. rule number (year).

Administrative register:	
Administrative Register of Kentucky	Volume number Ky. Admin. Reg. page number (month year).

Louisiana

Court system and reporters:		
Public domain format (for opinions issued since December 31, 1993):		
Louisiana Supreme Court	*Case name*, opinion number, p. page number (La. month number/day number/last two digits of year); parallel citation to Southern Reporter.	
Louisiana Court of Appeal	*Case name*, opinion number, p. page number (La. App. Circuit number Cir. month number/day number/last two digits of year); parallel citation to Southern Reporter.	
Louisiana Supreme Court (La.) previously Superior Court of Louisiana (La.), Superior Court of the Territory of Orleans (Orleans)		
*Southern Reporter	So.	1887–1941
*Second Series	So. 2d	1941–2008
*Third Series	So. 3d	2008–present
★Louisiana Reports	La.	1901–1972
Louisiana Annual Reports	La. Ann.	1846–1900
Robinson	Rob.	1841–1846
Martin (Louisiana Term Reports)	Mart.	1809–1830
Louisiana Court of Appeal (La. Ct. App.)		
*Southern Reporter	So.	1928–1941
*Second Series	So. 2d	1941–2008
*Third Series	So. 3d	2008–present
★Louisiana Court of Appeals Reports	La. App.	1924–1932
Peltier's Decisions, Parish at Orleans	Pelt.	1917–1924
Teissier, Orleans Court of Appeals	Teiss.	1903–1917
Gunby's Reports	Gunby	1885
McGloin	McGl.	1881–1884

Statutory compilations:	
West's Louisiana Statutes Annotated	La. Stat. Ann. § section number (year).
West's Louisiana Children's Code Annotated	La. Child. Code Ann. art. article number (year).
West's Louisiana Civil Code Annotated	La. Civ. Code Ann. art. article number (year).

West's Louisiana Code of Civil Procedure Annotated	La. Code Civ. Proc. Ann. art. article number (year).
West's Louisiana Code of Criminal Procedure Annotated	La. Code Crim. Proc. Ann. art. article number (year).
West's Louisiana Code of Evidence Annotated	La. Code Evid. Ann. art. article number (year).
Session laws:	
★*State of Louisiana: Acts of the Legislature	Year La. Acts page number.
West's Louisiana Session Law Service	Year La. Sess. L. Serv. page number (West).
Louisiana Advance Legislative Service	Year-pamphlet number La. Ann. Stat. Adv. Legis. Serv. page number (LexisNexis).
Administrative compilation:	
★Louisiana Administrative Code	La. Admin. Code tit. title number, § section number (year).
Administrative register:	
Louisiana Register	Volume number La. Reg. page number (month day, year).

Maine

Court system and reporters:		
Public domain format (for opinions issued since December 31, 1996):		
Maine Supreme Judicial Court	*Case name*, year ME opinion number, volume number A.2d initial page number.	
Maine Supreme Judicial Court (Me.)		
*Atlantic Reporter	A.	1885–1938
★*Second Series (official since 1966)	A.2d	1939–2010
★*Third Series	A.3d	2010–present
★Maine Reports	Me.	1820–1965
Statutory compilations:		
*West's Maine Statutes	Me. Stat. tit. title number, § section number (year).	
Maine Revised Statutes Annotated (West) (certified)	Me. Rev. Stat. Ann. tit. title number, § section number (West year).	
Session laws:		
★*Laws of the State of Maine	Year Me. Laws page number.	
Maine Legislative Service	Year Me. Legis. Serv. page number (West).	

Administrative compilation:	
Code of Maine Rules	Agency number–sub-agency number–chapter number▲Me.▲Code▲R.▲§▲section number▲(LexisNexis▲year).
Administrative register:	
Maine Government Register	Issue number▲Me.▲Gov't▲Reg.▲page number▲(LexisNexis▲month▲year).

Maryland

Court system and reporters:		
Maryland Court of Appeals (Md.)		
*Atlantic Reporter	A.	1885–1938
*Second Series	A.2d	1939–2010
*Third Series	A.3d	2010–present
★Maryland Reports	Md.	1851–present
Gill	Gill	1843–1851
Gill and Johnson	G.▲J.	1829–1842
Harris and Gill	H.▲G.	1826–1829
Harris and Johnson	H.▲J.	1800–1826
Harris and McHenry	H.▲M.	1770–1799
Maryland Court of Special Appeals (Md.▲Ct.▲Spec.▲App.)		
*Atlantic Reporter, Second Series	A.2d	1967–2010
*Third Series	A.3d	2010–present
★Maryland Appellate Reports	Md.▲App.	1967–present

Statutory compilations:	
Michie's Annotated Code of Maryland	Md.▲Code▲Ann.,▲Subject abbreviation▲§▲section number▲(LexisNexis▲year).
West's Annotated Code of Maryland	Md.▲Code▲Ann.,▲Subject abbreviation▲§▲section number▲(West▲year).

Subject abbreviations for statutory compilations:			
Agriculture	Agric.	Election Law	Elec.▲Law
Alcoholic Beverages	Alco.▲Bev.	Environment	Env't
Business Occupations and Professions	Bus.▲Occ.▲&▲Prof.	Estates and Trusts	Est.▲&▲Trusts
Business Regulation	Bus.▲Reg.	Family Law	Fam.▲Law

Commercial Law	Com.▲Law	Financial Institutions	Fin.▲Inst.
Constitutions	Const.	General Provisions	Gen.▲Provis.
Corporations and Associations	Corps.▲&▲Ass'ns	Health–General	Health–Gen.
Correctional Services	Corr.▲Servs.	Health Occupations	Health▲Occ.
Courts and Judicial Proceedings	Cts.▲&▲Jud.▲Proc.	Housing and Community Development	Hous.▲&▲Cmty.▲Dev.
Criminal Law	Crim.▲Law	Human Services	Hum.▲Servs.
Criminal Procedure	Crim.▲Proc.	Insurance	Ins.
Economic Development	Econ.▲Dev.	Labor and Employment	Lab.▲&▲Empl.
Education	Educ.	Land Use	Land▲Use
Local Government	Local▲Gov't	State Government	State▲Gov't
Natural Resources	Nat.▲Res.	State Personnel and Pensions	State▲Pers.▲&▲Pens.
Public Safety	Pub.▲Safety	Tax–General	Tax–Gen.
Public Utilities	Pub.▲Util.	Tax–Property	Tax–Prop.
Real Property	Real▲Prop.	Transportation	Transp.
State Finance and Procurement	State▲Fin.▲&▲Proc.		

Session laws:	
★*Laws of Maryland	Year▲Md.▲Laws▲page number.
Michie's Annotated Code of Maryland Advance Legislative Service	Year–pamphlet number▲Md.▲Code▲Ann.▲Adv.▲Legis.▲Serv.▲page number▲(LexisNexis).
West's Maryland Legislative Service	Year▲Md.▲Legis.▲Serv.▲page number▲(West).
Administrative compilation:	
Code of Maryland Regulations	Md.▲Code▲Regs.▲regulation number▲(year).
Administrative register:	
Maryland Register	Volume number▲Md.▲Reg.▲page number▲(month▲day,▲year).

Massachusetts

Court system and reporters:		
Massachusetts Supreme Judicial Court (Mass.)		
*North Eastern Reporter	N.E.	1885–1936
*Second Series	N.E.2d	1936–2013
*Third Series	N.E.3d	2014–present
★Massachusetts Reports	Mass.	1804–present
Massachusetts Appeals Court (Mass. App. Ct.)		
*North Eastern Reporter, Second Series	N.E.2d	1972–2013
*Third Series	N.E.3d	2014–present
★Massachusetts Appeals Court Reports	Mass. App. Ct.	1972–present
Massachusetts District Court, Appellate Division (Mass. Dist. Ct.) Boston Municipal Court, Appellate Division (Bos. Mun. Ct.)		
★*Massachusetts Appellate Division Reports (official since 1980)	Mass. App. Div.	1936–present
*Massachusetts Supplement	Mass. Supp.	1980–1983
*Massachusetts Appellate Decisions	Mass. App. Dec.	1941–1977
Appellate Division Advance Sheets	Year Mass. App. Div. Adv. Sh. page number.	1975–1979
Massachusetts Superior Court (Mass. Super. Ct.)		
Massachusetts Law Reporter	Mass. L. Rptr.	1993–present
Statutory compilations:		
★*General Laws of Massachusetts	Mass. Gen. Laws ch. chapter number, § section number (year).	
Massachusetts General Laws Annotated	Mass. Gen. Laws Ann. ch. chapter number, § section number (West year).	
Annotated Laws of Massachusetts	Mass. Ann. Laws ch. chapter number, § section number (LexisNexis year).	
Session laws:		
★*Acts and Resolves of Massachusetts	Year Mass. Acts page number.	
Massachusetts Legislative Service	Year Mass. Legis. Serv. page number (West).	
Massachusetts Advance Legislative Service	Year-pamphlet number Mass. Adv. Legis. Serv. page number (LexisNexis).	

Administrative compilation:	
*Code of Massachusetts Regulations	Title number Mass. Code Regs. section number (year).
Code of Massachusetts Regulations (LexisNexis)	Title number Mass. Code Regs. section number (LexisNexis year).
Administrative register:	
Massachusetts Register	Issue number Mass. Reg. page number (month day, year).

Michigan

Court system and reporters:		
	Michigan Supreme Court (Mich.)	
*North Western Reporter	N.W.	1879–1941
*Second Series	N.W.2d	1941–present
★Michigan Reports	Mich.	1847–present
Douglass	Doug.	1843–1847
Blume, Unreported Opinions	Blume Unrep. Op.	1836–1843
Blume, Supreme Court Transactions	Blume Sup. Ct. Trans.	1805–1836
	Michigan Court of Appeals (Mich. Ct. App.)	
*North Western Reporter, Second Series	N.W.2d	1965–present
★Michigan Appeals Reports	Mich. App.	1965–present
	Michigan Court of Claims (Mich. Ct. Cl.)	
Michigan Court of Claims Reports	Mich. Ct. Cl.	1939–1942
Statutory compilations:		
★*Michigan Compiled Laws	Mich. Comp. Laws § section number (year).	
Michigan Compiled Laws Annotated	Mich. Comp. Laws Ann. § section number (West year).	
Michigan Compiled Laws Service	Mich. Comp. Laws Serv. § section number (LexisNexis year).	
Session laws:		
★*Michigan Public Acts (online)	Year Mich. Pub. Acts act number.	
Michigan Legislative Service	Year Mich. Legis. Serv. page number (West).	
Michigan Advance Legislative Service	Year-pamphlet number Mich. Adv. Legis. Serv. page number (LexisNexis).	

Administrative compilation:	
Michigan Administrative Code (online)	Mich. Admin. Code r. rule number (year).
Administrative register:	
Michigan Register	Issue number Mich. Reg. page number (month day, year).

Minnesota

Court system and reporters:		
Minnesota Supreme Court (Minn.)		
*North Western Reporter	N.W.	1879–1941
★*Second Series (official since 1978)	N.W.2d	1941–present
★Minnesota Reports	Minn.	1851–1977
Minnesota Court of Appeals (Minn. Ct. App.)		
★North Western Reporter, Second Series	N.W.2d	1983–present

Statutory compilations:	
★*Minnesota Statutes	Minn. Stat. § section number (year).
Minnesota Statutes Annotated	Minn. Stat. Ann. § section number (West year).
Session laws:	
★*Laws of Minnesota	Year Minn. Laws page number.
Minnesota Session Law Service	Year Minn. Sess. Law Serv. page number (West).
Administrative compilation:	
Minnesota Rules	Minn. R. rule number (year).
Administrative register:	
Minnesota State Register	Volume number Minn. Reg. page number (month day, year).

Mississippi

Court system and reporters:	
Public domain format (for opinions issued since July 1, 1997):	
Mississippi Supreme Court	*Case name*, case identification number (¶ paragraph number) (Miss. year).
Mississippi Court of Appeals	*Case name*, case identification number (¶ paragraph number) (Miss. Ct. App. year).

Mississippi Supreme Court (Miss.) previously High Court of Errors and Appeals (Miss.)		
*Southern Reporter	So.	1887–1941
★*Second Series (official since 1966)	So. 2d	1941–2008
★*Third Series	So. 3d	2008–present
★Mississippi Reports	Miss.	1818–1966
Mississippi Decisions	Miss. Dec.	1820–1885
Mississippi Court of Appeals (Miss. Ct. App.)		
★Southern Reporter, Second Series	So. 2d	1995–2008
★Third Series	So. 3d	2008–present
Statutory compilations:		
★*Mississippi Code of 1972 Annotated	Miss. Code Ann. § section number (year).	
West's Annotated Mississippi Code	Miss. Code Ann. § section number (West year).	
Session laws:		
★*General Laws of Mississippi	Year Miss. Laws page number.	
Mississippi General Laws Advance Sheets	Year–pamphlet number Miss. Laws Adv. Sh. page number (LexisNexis).	
West's Mississippi Legislative Service	Year Miss. Legis. Serv. page number (West).	
Administrative compilation:		
Code of Mississippi Rules	Title number–chapter number Miss. Code R. § section number (LexisNexis year).	
Administrative register:		
Mississippi Government Register	Issue number Miss. Gov't Reg. page number LexisNexis month year).	

Missouri

Court system and reporters:		
Missouri Supreme Court (Mo.)		
*South Western Reporter	S.W.	1887–1928
★*Second Series (official since 1956)	S.W.2d	1928–1999
★*Third Series	S.W.3d	1999–present
★Missouri Reports	Mo.	1821–1956
Missouri Court of Appeals (Mo. Ct. App.)		
*South Western Reporter	S.W.	1902–1928
★*Second Series (official since 1954)	S.W.2d	1928–1999

★*Third Series	S.W.3d	1999–present
★Missouri Appeal Reports	Mo.▲App.	1876–1954
Statutory compilations:		
★*Missouri Revised Statutes	Mo.▲Rev.▲Stat.▲§▲section number▲(year).	
Vernon's Annotated Missouri Statutes	Mo.▲Ann.▲Stat.▲§▲section number▲(West▲year).	
Session laws:		
★*Laws of Missouri	Year▲Mo.▲Laws▲page number.	
Missouri Legislative Service	Year▲Mo.▲Legis.▲Serv.▲page number▲(West).	
Administrative compilation:		
Missouri Code of State Regulations Annotated	Mo.▲Code▲Regs.▲Ann.▲tit.▲title number,▲§▲section number▲(year).	
Administrative register:		
Missouri Register	Volume number▲Mo.▲Reg.▲page number▲(month▲day,▲year).	

Montana

Court system and reporters:		
Public domain format (for opinions issued since December 31, 1997):		
Montana Supreme Court	*Case name*,▲year▲MT▲opinion number,▲¶▲paragraph number,▲parallel citations to Montana Reports and Pacific Reporter.	
Montana Supreme Court (Mont.)		
*Pacific Reporter	P.	1883–1931
*Second Series	P.2d	1931–2000
*Third Series	P.3d	2000–present
★Montana Reports	Mont.	1868–present
State Reporter	State▲Rptr.	1945–present
Statutory compilations:		
★*Montana Code Annotated	Mont.▲Code▲Ann.▲§▲section number▲(year).	
West's Montana Code Annotated	Mont.▲Code▲Ann.▲§▲section number▲(West▲year).	
Session laws:		
Laws of Montana	Year▲Mont.▲Laws▲page number.	

Administrative compilation:	
Administrative Rules of Montana	Mont. Admin. R. rule number (year).
Administrative register:	
Montana Administrative Register	Issue number Mont. Admin. Reg. page number (month day, year).

Nebraska

Court system and reporters:		
Nebraska Supreme Court (Neb.)		
*North Western Reporter	N.W.	1879–1941
*Second Series	N.W.2d	1941–present
★Nebraska Reports (online only, effective Jan. 1, 2016)	Neb.	1860–present
Nebraska Court of Appeals (Neb. Ct. App.)		
*North Western Reporter, Second Series	N.W.2d	1992–present
★Nebraska Appellate Reports (online only, effective Jan. 1, 2016)	Neb. App.	1992–present

Statutory compilations:	
★*Revised Statutes of Nebraska	Neb. Rev. Stat. § section number (year).
Revised Statutes of Nebraska Annotated	Neb. Rev. Stat. Ann. § section number (LexisNexis year).
West's Revised Statutes of Nebraska Annotated	Neb. Rev. Stat. Ann. § section number (West year).
Session laws:	
★*Laws of Nebraska	Year Neb. Laws page number.
West's Nebraska Legislative Service	Year Neb. Legis. Serv. page number (West).
Administrative compilation:	
Nebraska Administrative Code	Title number Neb. Admin. Code § section number (year).

Nevada

Court system and reporters:		
Nevada Supreme Court (Nev.)		
*Pacific Reporter	P.	1883–1931
*Second Series	P.2d	1931–2000
*Third Series	P.3d	2000–present
★Nevada Reports	Nev.	1865–present

Nevada Court of Appeals (Nev. Ct. App.)		
*Pacific Reporter, Third Series	P.3d	2015–present
Statutory compilations:		
★*Nevada Revised Statutes	Nev. Rev. Stat. § section number (year).	
Michie's Nevada Revised Statutes Annotated	Nev. Rev. Stat. Ann. § section number (LexisNexis year).	
West's Nevada Revised Statutes Annotated	Nev. Rev. Stat. Ann. § section number (West year).	
Session laws:		
★*Statutes of Nevada	Year Nev. Stat. page number.	
West's Nevada Legislative Service	Year Nev. Legis. Serv. page number (West).	
Administrative compilation:		
Nevada Administrative Code	Nev. Admin. Code § section number (year).	
Administrative register:		
Nevada Register of Administrative Regulations	Volume number Nev. Reg. Admin. Regs. regulation number (month day, year).	

New Hampshire

Court system and reporters:		
New Hampshire Supreme Court (N.H.)		
*Atlantic Reporter	A.	1885–1938
*Second Series	A.2d	1939–2010
*Third Series	A.3d	2010–present
★New Hampshire Reports	N.H.	1816–present
Statutory compilations:		
★*New Hampshire Revised Statutes Annotated (West)	N.H. Rev. Stat. Ann. § section number (year).	
LexisNexis New Hampshire Revised Statutes Annotated	N.H. Rev. Stat. Ann. § section number (LexisNexis year).	
Session laws:		
★*Laws of the State of New Hampshire	Year N.H. Laws page number.	
*New Hampshire Legislative Service	Year N.H. Legis. Serv. page number.	
LexisNexis New Hampshire Revised Statutes Annotated Advance Legislative Service	Year–pamphlet number N.H. Rev. Stat. Ann. Adv. Legis. Serv. page number (LexisNexis).	

Administrative compilations:	
*New Hampshire Code of Administrative Rules Annotated	N.H.▲Code▲Admin.▲R.▲Ann.▲Abbreviated department name▲rule number▲(year).
Code of New Hampshire Rules	N.H.▲Code▲R.▲Abbreviated department name▲rule number▲(LexisNexis▲year).
Administrative register:	
*New Hampshire Rulemaking Register	Volume number▲N.H.▲Rulemaking▲Reg.▲page number▲(month▲day,▲year).
New Hampshire Government Register	Issue number▲N.H.▲Gov't▲Reg.▲page number▲(LexisNexis▲month▲year).

New Jersey

Court system and reporters:		
New Jersey Supreme Court (N.J.) previously New Jersey Court of Errors and Appeals (N.J.)		
*Atlantic Reporter	A.	1885–1938
*Second Series	A.2d	1939–2010
*Third Series	A.3d	2010–present
★New Jersey Reports	N.J.	1948–present
★New Jersey Law Reports	N.J.L.	1790–1948
★New Jersey Equity Reports	N.J.▲Eq.	1830–1948
New Jersey Miscellaneous Reports	N.J.▲Misc.	1923–1948
New Jersey Superior Court Appellate Division (N.J.▲Super.▲Ct.▲App.▲Div.) **New Jersey Superior Court Chancery Division (N.J.▲Super.▲Ct.▲Ch.▲Div.)** **New Jersey Superior Court Law Division (N.J.▲Super.▲Ct.▲Law▲Div.)** previously New Jersey Supreme Court (N.J.▲Sup.▲Ct.), New Jersey Court of Chancery (N.J.▲Ch.), and New Jersey Prerogative Court (N.J.▲Prerog.▲Ct.) **New Jersey County Courts (**Name of County▲**County▲Ct.)** and other New Jersey lower courts		
*Atlantic Reporter	A.	1885–1938
*Second Series	A.2d	1939–2010
*Third Series	A.3d	2010–present
★New Jersey Superior Court Reports	N.J.▲Super.	1948–present
★New Jersey Law Reports	N.J.L.	1790–1948
★New Jersey Equity Reports	N.J.▲Eq.	1830–1948
New Jersey Miscellaneous Reports	N.J.▲Misc.	1923–1948
New Jersey Tax Court (N.J. Tax C.)		
New Jersey Tax Court Reports	N.J.▲Tax	1979–present

Statutory compilations:	
★*New Jersey Statutes Annotated	N.J. Stat. Ann. § section number (West year).
New Jersey Revised Statutes	N.J. Rev. Stat. § section number (year).
Session laws:	
★Laws of New Jersey	Year N.J. Laws page number.
New Jersey Session Law Service	Year N.J. Sess. Law Serv. page number (West).
Administrative compilation:	
New Jersey Administrative Code	N.J. Admin. Code § title:chapter–subchapter-section number (year).
Administrative register:	
New Jersey Register	Volume number N.J. Reg. page number (month day, year).

New Mexico

Court system and reporters:		
Public domain format (effective July 1, 2013, for papers to be filed on or after Aug. 1, 2013):		
★New Mexico Supreme Court	*Case name*, year-NM-opinion number, parallel citation to New Mexico Appellate Reports[, optional citation to Pacific Reporter].	
★New Mexico Court of Appeals	*Case name*, year-NMCA-opinion number, parallel citation to New Mexico Appellate Reports[, optional citation to Pacific Reporter].	
New Mexico Supreme Court (N.M.)		
*Pacific Reporter	P.	1883–1931
*Second Series	P.2d	1931–2000
*Third Series	P.3d	2000–present
★New Mexico Reports	N.M.	1852–2012
New Mexico Court of Appeals (N.M. Ct. App.)		
*Pacific Reporter, Second Series	P.2d	1966–2000
*Third Series	P.3d	2000–present
★New Mexico Reports	N.M.	1966–2012

Statutory compilations:	
★*New Mexico Statutes Annotated 1978 (Conway Greene) (print and online)	N.M. Stat. Ann. § section number (year).
West's New Mexico Statutes Annotated	N.M. Stat. Ann. § section number (West year).
Michie's Annotated Statutes of New Mexico	N.M. Stat. Ann. § section number (LexisNexis year).
Session laws:	
★*Laws of the State of New Mexico	Year N.M. Laws page number.
New Mexico Advance Legislative Service	Year N.M. Adv. Legis. Serv. page number.
West's New Mexico Legislative Service	Year N.M. Legis. Serv. page number (West).
Administrative compilation:	
★New Mexico Administrative Code (online)	N.M. Admin. Code R. title number.chapter number.part number.section number.
Code of New Mexico Rules (LexisNexis)	N.M. Code R. § title number.chapter number.part number.section number (LexisNexis year).
Administrative register:	
New Mexico Register	Volume number N.M. Reg. page number (month day, year).

New York

Court system and reporters:

New York Court of Appeals (N.Y.)
previously New York Court for the Correction of Errors (N.Y. Errors),
New York Supreme Court of Judicature (N.Y.),
and New York Court of Chancery (N.Y. Ch.)

*North Eastern Reporter	N.E.	1885–1936
*Second Series	N.E.2d	1936–2013
*Third Series	N.E.3d	2014–present
★New York Reports	N.Y.	1847–1956
★Second Series	N.Y.2d	1956–2013
★Third Series	N.Y.3d	2014–present
West's New York Supplement	N.Y.S.	1888–1937
Second Series	N.Y.S.2d	1938–2014
Third Series	N.Y.S.3d	2015–present

New York Supreme Court, Appellate Division (N.Y. App. Div.) previously Supreme Court, General Term (N.Y. Gen. Term)		
*West's New York Supplement	N.Y.S.	1888–1937
*Second Series	N.Y.S.2d	1938–present
★New York Appellate Division Reports	A.D.	1896–1955
★Second Series	A.D.2d	1956–2003
★Third Series	A.D.3d	2004–present
Supreme Court Reports	N.Y. Sup. Ct.	1874–1896
Lansing's Reports	Lans.	1869–1873
Barbour's Supreme Court Reports	Barb.	1847–1877
Other New York lower courts (e.g., N.Y. App. Term., N.Y. Sup. Ct., N.Y. Ct. Cl., N.Y. Civ. Ct., N.Y. Crim. Ct., N.Y. Fam. Ct.)		
*West's New York Supplement	N.Y.S.	1888–1937
*Second Series	N.Y.S.2d	1938–2014
*Third Series	N.Y.S.3d	2015–present
★New York Miscellaneous Reports	Misc.	1893–1955
★Second Series	Misc. 2d	1956–2003
★Third Series	Misc. 3d	2003–present

Statutory compilations:	
McKinney's Consolidated Laws of New York Annotated (West)	N.Y. *Subject abbreviation* Law § *section number* (McKinney *year*).
New York Consolidated Laws Service (LexisNexis)	N.Y. *Subject abbreviation* Law § *section number* (Consol. *year*).
New York Consolidated Laws Unannotated (LexisNexis)	N.Y. *Subject abbreviation* Law § *section number* (LexisNexis *year*).

Subject abbreviations for statutory compilations:			
Abandoned Property	Aband. Prop.	Banking	Banking
Agricultural Conservation	Agric. Conserv.	Benevolent Orders	Ben. Ord.
Agriculture and Markets	Agric. & Mkts.	Business Corporation	Bus. Corp.
Alcoholic Beverage Control	Alco. Bev. Cont.	Canal	Canal
Alternative County Government	Alt. County Gov't	Civil Practice Law and Rules	N.Y. C.P.L.R. *rule number* (McKinney *year*). **or** N.Y. C.P.L.R. *rule number* (Consol. *year*).
Arts and Cultural Affairs	Arts & Cult. Aff.		

Civil Rights	Civ. Rights	Highway	High.
Civil Service	Civ. Serv.	Indian	Indian
Commerce	Com.	Insurance	Ins.
Cooperative Corporations	Coop. Corp.	Judiciary	Jud.
Correction	Correct.	Judiciary Court Acts	Jud. Ct. Acts
County	County	Labor	Lab.
Criminal Procedure	Crim. Proc.	Legislative	Legis.
Debtor and Creditor	Debt. & Cred.	Lien	Lien
Domestic Relations	Dom. Rel.	Limited Liability Company	Ltd. Liab. Co.
Economic Development	Econ. Dev.	Local Finance	Local Fin.
Education	Educ.	Mental Hygiene	Mental Hyg.
Elder	Elder	Military	Mil.
Election	Elec.	Multiple Dwelling	Mult. Dwell.
Eminent Domain Procedure	Em. Dom. Proc.	Multiple Residence	Mult. Resid.
Employers' Liability	Empl'rs Liab.	Municipal Home Rule	Mun. Home Rule
Energy	Energy	Navigation	Nav.
Environmental Conservation	Env't Conserv.	Not-for-Profit Corporation	Not-for-Profit Corp.
Estates, Powers and Trusts	Est. Powers & Trusts	Optional County Government	Opt. Cnty. Gov't
Executive	Exec.	Parks, Recreation and Historic Preservation	Parks Rec. & Hist. Preserv.
Financial Services	Fin. Serv.	Partnership	P'ship
General Associations	Gen. Ass'ns	Penal	Penal
General Business	Gen. Bus.	Personal Property	Pers. Prop.
General City	Gen. City	Private Housing Finance	Priv. Hous. Fin.
General Construction	Gen. Constr.	Public Authorities	Pub. Auth.
General Municipal	Gen. Mun.	Public Buildings	Pub. Bldgs.
General Obligations	Gen. Oblig.	Public Health	Pub. Health
		Public Housing	Pub. Hous.
		Public Lands	Pub. Lands
		Public Officers	Pub. Off.

Public Service	Pub. Serv.	State Finance	State Fin.
Racing, Pari–Mutuel Wagering and Breeding	Rac. Pari–Mut. Wag. & Breed.	State Printing and Public Documents	State Print. & Pub. Docs.
Railroad	R.R.	State Technology	State Tech.
Rapid Transit	Rapid Trans.	Statute of Local Governments	Stat. Local Gov'ts
Real Property	Real Prop.	Surrogate's Court Procedure Act	Surr. Ct. Proc. Act
Real Property Actions and Proceedings	Real Prop. Acts	Tax	Tax
Real Property Tax	Real Prop. Tax	Town	Town
Religious Corporations	Relig. Corp.	Transportation	Transp.
Retirement and Social Security	Retire. & Soc. Sec.	Transportation Corporations	Transp. Corp.
Rural Electric Cooperative	Rural Elec. Coop.	Unconsolidated	Unconsol.
Second Class Cities	Second Class Cities	Uniform Commercial Code	U.C.C.
Social Services	Soc. Serv.	Vehicle and Traffic	Veh. & Traf.
Soil and Water Conservation Districts	Soil & Water Conserv. Dist.	Village	Village
State	State	Volunteer Ambulance Workers' Benefit	Vol. Ambul. Workers' Ben.
State Administrative Procedure Act	A.P.A.	Volunteer Firefighters' Benefit	Vol. Fire. Ben.
		Workers' Compensation	Workers' Comp.

Session laws:

★*Laws of New York	Year N.Y. Laws page number.
McKinney's Session Laws of New York	Year N.Y. Sess. Laws page number (McKinney).
New York Consolidated Laws Service Advance Legislative Service	Year–pamphlet number N.Y. Consol. Laws Adv. Legis. Serv. page number (LexisNexis).

Administrative compilation:

Official Compilation of Codes, Rules, and Regulations of the State of New York	N.Y. Comp. Codes R. & Regs. tit. title number, § section number (year).

Administrative register:

New York State Register	Volume number N.Y. Reg. page number (month day, year).

North Carolina

Court system and reporters:		
North Carolina Supreme Court (N.C.)		
*South Eastern Reporter	S.E.	1886–1939
*Second Series	S.E.2d	1939–present
★North Carolina Reports	N.C.	1778–present
North Carolina Court of Appeals (N.C.▲Ct.▲App.)		
*South Eastern Reporter, Second Series	S.E.2d	1968–present
★North Carolina Court of Appeals Reports	N.C.▲App.	1968–present

Statutory compilations:	
★*General Statutes of North Carolina	N.C.▲Gen.▲Stat.▲§▲section number▲(year).
West's North Carolina General Statutes Annotated	N.C.▲Gen.▲Stat.▲Ann.▲§▲section number▲(West▲year).

Session laws:	
*Session Laws of North Carolina	Year▲N.C.▲Sess.▲Laws▲page number.
North Carolina Advance Legislative Service	Year–pamphlet number▲N.C.▲Adv.▲Legis.▲Serv.▲page number▲(LexisNexis).
North Carolina Legislative Service	Year▲N.C.▲Legis.▲Serv.▲page number▲(West).

Administrative compilation:	
North Carolina Administrative Code	Title number▲N.C.▲Admin.▲Code▲rule number▲(year).

Administrative register:	
North Carolina Register	Volume number▲N.C.▲Reg.▲page number▲(month▲day,▲year).

North Dakota

Court system and reporters:	
Public domain format (for opinions issued since December 31, 1996):	
North Dakota Supreme Court	*Case name*,▲year▲ND▲opinion number,▲¶▲paragraph number,▲parallel citation to North Western Reporter.
North Dakota Court of Appeals	*Case name*,▲year▲ND▲App▲opinion number,▲¶▲paragraph number,▲parallel citation to North Western Reporter.

North Dakota Supreme Court (N.D.)		
*North Western Reporter	N.W.	1890–1941
★*Second Series (official since 1953)	N.W.2d	1941–present
★North Dakota Reports	N.D.	1890–1953
North Dakota Court of Appeals (N.D. Ct. App.)		
★North Western Reporter, Second Series	N.W.2d	1987–present
Statutory compilations:		
★*North Dakota Century Code	N.D. Cent. Code § section number (year).	
West's North Dakota Century Code Annotated	N.D. Cent. Code Ann. § section number (West year).	
Session laws:		
★*Laws of North Dakota	Year N.D. Laws page number.	
North Dakota Century Code Advance Legislative Service	Year–pamphlet number N.D. Cent. Code Adv. Legis. Serv. page number (LexisNexis).	
West's North Dakota Legislative Service	Year N.D. Legis. Serv. page number (West).	
Administrative compilation:		
North Dakota Administrative Code (online)	N.D. Admin. Code rule number (year).	

Ohio

Court system and reporters:		
Public domain format (for opinions issued since April 30, 2002):		
★Ohio Supreme Court	*Case name*, parallel citation to Ohio State Reports, year-Ohio-opinion number, parallel citation to North Eastern Reporter, ¶ paragraph number from public domain version.	
★Ohio Court of Appeals	*Case name*, parallel citation to Ohio Appellate Reports, year-Ohio-opinion number, parallel citation to North Eastern Reporter, ¶ paragraph number from public domain version.	
Ohio Supreme Court (Ohio)		
*North Eastern Reporter	N.E.	1885–1936
*Second Series	N.E.2d	1936–2013
*Third Series	N.E.3d	2014–present
★Ohio Reports	Ohio	1821–1851

★Ohio State Reports	Ohio St.	1852–1964
★Second Series	Ohio St. 2d	1964–1982
★Third Series	Ohio St. 3d	1982–present
Wilcox's Condensed Reports	Wilc. Cond. Rep.	1821–1831
Wright	Wright	1831–1834
Ohio Unreported Cases	Ohio Unrep. Cas.	1809–1899
Ohio Court of Appeals (Ohio Ct. App.)		
*North Eastern Reporter	N.E.	1923–1936
*Second Series	N.E.2d	1936–2013
*Third Series	N.E.3d	2014–present
★Ohio Appellate Reports	Ohio App.	1913–1965
★Second Series	Ohio App. 2d	1965–1982
★Third Series	Ohio App. 3d	1982–present
Ohio Circuit Court Reports	Ohio C.C.	1914–1917
Ohio Court of Appeals Reports	Ohio Ct. App.	1916–1922
Other Ohio lower courts (e.g., Ohio Court of Common Pleas (Ct. Com. Pl.)		
*North Eastern Reporter	N.E.	1885–1936
*Second Series	N.E.2d	1936–2013
*Third Series	N.E.3d	2014–present
★Ohio Miscellaneous Reports	Ohio Misc.	1962–1982
★Second Series	Ohio Misc. 2d	1982–2012
★Ohio Opinions	Ohio Op.	1934–1957
★Second Series	Ohio Op. 2d	1957–1976
★Third Series	Ohio Op. 3d	1976–1982
Statutory compilations:		
Page's Ohio Revised Code Annotated	Ohio Rev. Code Ann. § section number (LexisNexis year).	
Baldwin's Ohio Revised Code Annotated	Ohio Rev. Code Ann. § section number (West year).	
Session laws:		
★*State of Ohio: Legislative Acts Passed and Joint Resolutions Adopted	Year Ohio Laws page number.	
Page's Ohio Legislative Bulletin	Year Ohio Legis. Bull. page number (LexisNexis).	

Baldwin's Ohio Legislative Service Annotated	Year▲Ohio▲Legis.▲Serv.▲Ann.▲page number▲(West).
Administrative compilation:	
Baldwin's Ohio Administrative Code	Ohio▲Admin.▲Code▲rule number▲(year).
Administrative and executive registers:	
Baldwin's Ohio Monthly Record	Ohio▲Monthly▲Rec.▲page number▲(month▲year).
Ohio Government Reports	Ohio▲Gov't▲page number▲(month▲day,▲year).
Ohio Department Reports	Ohio▲Dep't▲page number▲(month▲day,▲year).

Oklahoma

Court system and reporters:		
★Public domain format (for opinions decided after May 1, 1997)		
★Oklahoma Supreme Court	*Case name*,▲year▲OK▲opinion number[,▲optional parallel citation to Pacific Reporter].	
★Oklahoma Court of Criminal Appeals	*Case name*,▲year▲OKCR▲opinion number[,▲optional parallel citation to Pacific Reporter].	
Oklahoma Supreme Court (Okla.)		
*Pacific Reporter	P.	1890–1931
★*Second Series (official 1953–2013)	P.2d	1931–2000
★*Third Series (official through Dec. 31, 2013)	P.3d	2000–present
★Oklahoma Reports	Okla.	1890–1953
Oklahoma Court of Criminal Appeals (Okla.▲Crim.▲App.) previously Oklahoma Criminal Court of Appeals (Okla.▲Crim.▲App.)		
*Pacific Reporter	P.	1908–1931
★*Second Series (official since 1953)	P.2d	1931–2000
★*Third Series (official through Dec. 31, 2013)	P.3d	2000–present
★Oklahoma Criminal Reports	Okla.▲Crim.	1908–1953
Oklahoma Court of Civil Appeals (Okla.▲Civ.▲App.)		
★*Pacific Reporter, Second Series	P.2d	1967–2000
★*Third Series (official through Dec. 31, 2013)	P.3d	2000–present

Oklahoma Court of Appeals for the Indian Territory (Indian Terr.)		
*South Western Reporter	S.W.	1896–1907
★Indian Territory Reports	Indian Terr.	1896–1907
Statutory compilations:		
★*Oklahoma Statutes (West)	Okla. Stat. tit. title number, § section number (year).	
Oklahoma Statutes Annotated	Okla. Stat. Ann. tit. title number, § section number (West year).	
Session laws:		
*Oklahoma Session Laws	Year Okla. Sess. Laws page number.	
Oklahoma Session Law Service	Year Okla. Sess. Law Serv. page number (West).	
Administrative compilation:		
Oklahoma Administrative Code	Okla. Admin. Code § section number (year).	
Administrative register:		
Oklahoma Register	Volume number Okla. Reg. page number (month day, year).	
Oklahoma Gazette	Volume number Okla. Gaz. page number (month day, year).	

Oregon

Court system and reporters:		
Oregon Supreme Court (Or.)		
*Pacific Reporter	P.	1883–1931
*Second Series	P.2d	1931–2000
*Third Series	P.3d	2000–present
★Oregon Reports	Or.	1853–present
Oregon Court of Appeals (Or. Ct. App.)		
*Pacific Reporter, Second Series	P.2d	1969–2000
*Third Series	P.3d	2000–present
★Oregon Reports, Court of Appeals	Or. App.	1969–present
Oregon Tax Court (Or. T.C.)		
★Oregon Tax Reports	Or. Tax	1962–present
Statutory compilations:		
★*Oregon Revised Statutes	Or. Rev. Stat. § section number (year).	
West's Oregon Revised Statutes Annotated	Or. Rev. Stat. Ann. § section number (West year).	

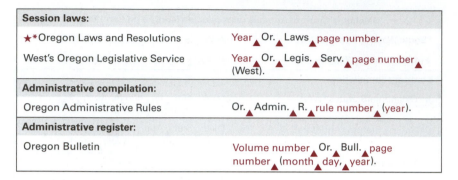

Session laws:	
★*Oregon Laws and Resolutions	Year Or. Laws page number.
West's Oregon Legislative Service	Year Or. Legis. Serv. page number (West).
Administrative compilation:	
Oregon Administrative Rules	Or. Admin. R. rule number (year).
Administrative register:	
Oregon Bulletin	Volume number Or. Bull. page number (month day, year).

Pennsylvania

Court system and reporters:		
Pennsylvania Supreme Court (Pa.) previously High Court of Errors and Appeals (Pa.)		
*Atlantic Reporter	A.	1885–1938
*Second Series	A.2d	1939–2010
*Third Series	A.3d	2010–present
★Pennsylvania State Reports	Pa.	1845–present
Pennsylvania Superior Court (Pa. Super. Ct.)		
★Public domain format:		
Pennsylvania Superior Court slip opinions prior to publication in Atlantic Reporter, effective Jan. 1, 1998	*Case name*, Year PA Super opinion number, paragraph number.	
*Atlantic Reporter	A.	1930–1938
★*Second Series (official since 1997)	A.2d	1939–2010
★*Third Series	A.3d	2010–present
★Pennsylvania Superior Court Reports	Pa. Super.	1895–1997
Pennsylvania Commonwealth Court (Pa. Commw. Ct.)		
★*Atlantic Reporter, Second Series (official since 1995)	A.2d	1970–2010
★*Third Series	A.3d	2010–present
★Pennsylvania Commonwealth Court Reports	Pa. Commw.	1970–1994
Pennsylvania District and County Courts (Pa. Name of County or District Ct.)		
★*Pennsylvania District and County Reports	Pa. D. & C.	1922–1954

★*Second Series	Pa. D. & C.2d	1955–1977
★*Third Series	Pa. D. & C.3d	1977–1989
★*Fourth Series	Pa. D. & C.4th	1989–2007
★*Fifth Series	Pa. D. & C.5th	2007–present
Pennsylvania District Reports	Pa. D.	1892–1921
Pennsylvania County Court Reports	Pa. C.	1870–1921
Statutory compilations:		
★*Pennsylvania Consolidated Statutes	Title number Pa. Cons. Stat. § section number (year).	
Purdon's Pennsylvania Statutes and Consolidated Statutes Annotated	Title number Pa. Stat. and Cons. Stat. Ann. § section number (West year).	
Purdon's Pennsylvania Statutes and Consolidated Statutes	Title number Pa. Stat. and Cons. Stat. § section number (West year).	
Session laws:		
*Laws of Pennsylvania	Year Pa. Laws page number.	
Purdon's Pennsylvania Legislative Service	Year Pa. Legis. Serv. page number (West).	
Administrative compilation:		
Pennsylvania Code	Title number Pa. Code § section number (year).	
Administrative register:		
Pennsylvania Bulletin	Volume number Pa. Bull. page number (month day, year).	

Rhode Island

Court system and reporters:		
Rhode Island Supreme Court (R.I.)		
*Atlantic Reporter	A.	1885–1938
★*Second Series (official since 1980)	A.2d	1939–2010
★*Third Series	A.3d	2010–present
★Rhode Island Reports	R.I.	1828–1980
Statutory compilations:		
★*General Laws of Rhode Island	R.I. Gen. Laws § section number (year).	
West's General Laws of Rhode Island Annotated	Title number R.I. Gen. Laws Ann. § section number (West year).	

Session laws:	
★Public Laws of Rhode Island and Providence Plantations	Year R.I. Pub. Laws page number.
Acts and Resolves of Rhode Island and Providence Plantations	Year R.I. Acts & Resolves page number.
West's Rhode Island Advance Legislative Service	Year R.I. Adv. Legis. Serv. page number (West).
Rhode Island Advance Legislative Service	Year–pamphlet number R.I. Adv. Legis. Serv. page number (LexisNexis).
Administrative compilation:	
Code of Rhode Island Rules	Title number–chapter number R.I. Code R. § section number (LexisNexis year).
Administrative register:	
Rhode Island Government Register	Issue number R.I. Gov't Reg. page number (LexisNexis month year).

South Carolina

Court system and reporters:		
South Carolina Supreme Court (S.C.)		
*South Eastern Reporter	S.E.	1887–1939
*Second Series	S.E.2d	1939–present
★South Carolina Reports	S.C.	1868–present
South Carolina Court of Appeals (S.C. Ct. App.)		
*South Eastern Reporter, Second Series	S.E.2d	1983–present
★South Carolina Reports	S.C.	1983–present
Statutory compilation:		
★Code of Laws of South Carolina 1976 Annotated	S.C. Code Ann. § section number (year).	
Session laws:		
Acts and Joint Resolutions of South Carolina	Year S.C. Acts page number.	
Administrative compilation:		
Code of Laws of South Carolina 1976 Annotated: Code of Regulations	S.C. Code Ann. Regs. regulation number (year).	
Administrative register:		
South Carolina State Register	Volume number S.C. Reg. page number (month day, year).	

South Dakota

Court system and reporters:		
Public domain format (for opinions issued since December 31, 1996):		
South Dakota Supreme Court	*Case name*, year SD opinion number, ¶ paragraph number, parallel citation to North Western Reporter.	
South Dakota Supreme Court (S.D.)		
*North Western Reporter	N.W.	1890–1941
★*Second Series (official since 1976)	N.W.2d	1941–present
★South Dakota Reports	S.D.	1890–1976
Statutory compilation:		
★South Dakota Codified Laws	S.D. Codified Laws § section number (year).	
Session laws:		
★Session Laws of South Dakota (online)	Year S.D. Sess. Laws ch. chapter number, § section number.	
Administrative compilation:		
Administrative Rules of South Dakota	S.D. Admin. R. rule number (year).	
Administrative register:		
South Dakota Register	Volume number S.D. Reg. page number (month day, year).	

Tennessee

Court system and reporters:		
Tennessee Supreme Court (Tenn.) previously Tennessee Supreme Court of Errors and Appeals (Tenn.)		
*South Western Reporter	S.W.	1886–1928
★*Second Series (official since 1972)	S.W.2d	1928–1999
★*Third Series	S.W.3d	1999–present
★Tennessee Reports	Tenn.	1791–1971
Tennessee Court of Appeals (Tenn. Ct. App.) (created 1925) preceded by Tennessee Court of Civil Appeals (Tenn. Civ. Ct. App.)		
★*South Western Reporter, Second Series (official since 1972)	S.W.2d	1932–1999
★*Third Series	S.W.3d	1999–present
★Tennessee Appeals Reports	Tenn. App.	1925–1971
Court of Civil Appeals: Tennessee	Tenn. Civ. App.	1910–1918

Tennessee Court of Criminal Appeals (Tenn. Crim. App.)		
★*South Western Reporter, Second Series (official since 1972)	S.W.2d	1967–1999
★*Third Series	S.W.3d	1999–present
★Tennessee Criminal Appeals Reports	Tenn. Crim. App.	1967–1971
Statutory compilations:		
★*Tennessee Code Annotated	Tenn. Code Ann. § section number (year).	
West's Tennessee Code Annotated	Tenn. Code Ann. § section number (West year).	
Session laws:		
*Public Acts of the State of Tennessee	Year Tenn. Pub. Acts ch. chapter number.	
*Private Acts of the State of Tennessee	Year Tenn. Priv. Acts ch. chapter number.	
Tennessee Code Annotated Advance Legislative Service	Year-pamphlet number Tenn. Code Ann. Adv. Legis. Serv. page number (LexisNexis).	
West's Tennessee Legislative Service	Year Tenn. Legis. Serv. page number (West).	
Administrative compilation:		
Official Compilation — Rules and Regulations of the State of Tennessee	Tenn. Comp. R. & Regs. rule number (year).	
Administrative register:		
Tennessee Administrative Register	Volume number Tenn. Admin. Reg. page number (month year).	

Texas

Court system and reporters:		
Texas Supreme Court (Tex.)		
*South Western Reporter	S.W.	1886–1928
★*Second Series (official since 1962)	S.W.2d	1928–1999
★*Third Series	S.W.3d	1999–present
★Texas Reports	Tex.	1846–1962
Texas Court of Criminal Appeals (Tex. Crim. App.) previously Texas Court of Appeals (Tex. Ct. App.)		
*South Western Reporter	S.W.	1892–1928
★*Second Series (official since 1962)	S.W.2d	1928–1999
★*Third Series	S.W.3d	1999–present
★Texas Criminal Reports	Tex. Crim.	1892–1962
Texas Court of Appeals Reports	Tex. Ct. App.	1876–1883

Texas Court of Appeals (Tex. App.) previously Texas Court of Civil Appeals (Tex. Civ. App.)		
★*South Western Reporter (official since 1911)	S.W.	1892–1928
★*Second Series	S.W.2d	1928–1999
★*Third Series	S.W.3d	1999–present
★Texas Civil Appeals Reports	Tex. Civ. App.	1892–1911
Statutory compilations:		
*Vernon's Texas Codes Annotated	Tex. Subject abbreviation Code Ann. § section number (West year).	
Vernon's Texas Revised Civil Statutes Annotated	Tex. Rev. Civ. Stat. Ann. art. article number, § section number (West year).	
Vernon's Texas Business Corporation Act Annotated	Tex. Bus. Corp. Act Ann. art. article number (West year).	
Vernon's Texas Code of Criminal Procedure Annotated†	Tex. Code Crim. Proc. Ann. art. article number (West year).	
Vernon's Texas Insurance Code Annotated	Tex. Ins. Code Ann. art. article number (West year).	
Vernon's Texas Probate Code Annotated	Tex. Prob. Code Proc. Ann. § section number (West year).	

Subject abbreviations for Texas Codes Annotated:

Agriculture	Agric.	Insurance	Ins.
Alcoholic Beverage	Alco. Bev.	Labor	Lab.
Business and Commerce	Bus. & Com.	Local Government	Loc. Gov't
Business Organizations	Bus. Orgs.	Natural Resources	Nat. Res.
Civil Practice and Remedies	Civ. Prac. & Rem.	Occupations	Occ.
Criminal Procedure†	Crim. Proc.	Parks and Wildlife	Parks & Wild.
Education	Educ.	Penal	Penal
Election	Elec.	Property	Prop.
Estates	Est.	Special District Local Laws	Spec. Dists.
Family	Fam.	Tax	Tax
Finance	Fin.	Transportation	Transp.
Government	Gov't	Utilities	Util.
Health and Safety	Health & Safety	Water	Water
Human Resources	Hum. Res.		

†When it enacts the Code of Criminal Procedure, Texas will complete a codification project begun in 1963, superseding the Revised Texas Statutes of 1925 with twenty-seven subject-matter codes. Note that it still may be necessary to refer to both the newer subject-matter codes and the older codes. *See* Legis. Ref. Lib. of Tex., *Statutory Revision*, http://www.lrl.state.tx.us/legis/revisorsNotes.cfm (last visited Dec. 27, 2020).

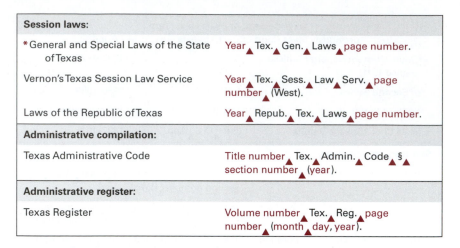

Session laws:	
*General and Special Laws of the State of Texas	Year Tex. Gen. Laws page number.
Vernon's Texas Session Law Service	Year Tex. Sess. Law Serv. page number (West).
Laws of the Republic of Texas	Year Repub. Tex. Laws page number.
Administrative compilation:	
Texas Administrative Code	Title number Tex. Admin. Code § section number (year).
Administrative register:	
Texas Register	Volume number Tex. Reg. page number (month day, year).

Utah

Court system and reporters:		
Public domain format (for opinions issued since December 31, 1998):		
Utah Supreme Court	*Case name*, year UT opinion number, ¶ paragraph number, parallel citation to Pacific Reporter.	
Utah Court of Appeals	*Case name*, year UT App opinion number, ¶ paragraph number, parallel citation to Pacific Reporter.	
Utah Supreme Court (Utah)		
*Pacific Reporter	P.	1881–1931
★*Second Series (official since 1974)	P.2d	1931–2000
★*Third Series	P.3d	2000–present
★Utah Reports	Utah	1855–1952
★Second Series	Utah 2d	1953–1974
Utah Court of Appeals (Utah Ct. App.)		
★*Pacific Reporter, Second Series	P.2d	1974–2000
★*Third Series	P.3d	2000–present
Statutory compilations:		
★Utah Code (online)	Utah Code § section number.	
Utah Code Annotated	Utah Code Ann. § section number (LexisNexis year).	
West's Utah Code Annotated	Utah Code Ann. § section number (West year).	

Session laws:	
*Laws of Utah	Year▲Utah▲Laws▲page number.
Utah Legislative Service	Year▲Utah▲Legis.▲Serv.▲page number▲(West).
Utah Code Advance Legislative Service	Year–pamphlet number▲Utah▲Adv.▲Legis.▲Serv.▲page number▲(LexisNexis).
Administrative compilation:	
Utah Administrative Code	Utah▲Admin.▲Code▲r.▲rule number▲(LexisNexis▲year).
Administrative register:	
Utah State Bulletin	Issue number▲Utah▲Bull.▲page number▲(month▲day,▲year).

Vermont

Court system and reporters:		
Public domain format (for opinions issued since December 31, 2002):		
Vermont Supreme Court	*Case name*,▲year▲VT▲opinion number,▲¶▲paragraph number,▲parallel citations to Vermont Reports and Atlantic Reporter.	
Vermont Supreme Court (Vt.)		
*Atlantic Reporter	A.	1885–1938
*Second Series	A.2d	1939–2010
*Third Series	A.3d	2010–present
★Vermont Reports	Vt.	1826–present
Statutory compilations:		
★*Vermont Statutes Annotated	Vt.▲Stat.▲Ann.▲tit.▲title number,▲§▲section number▲(year).	
West's Vermont Statutes Annotated	Vt.▲Stat.▲Ann.▲tit.▲title number,▲§▲section number▲(West▲year).	
Session laws:		
*Acts and Resolves of Vermont	Year▲Vt.▲Acts▲&▲Resolves▲page number.	
West's Vermont Legislative Service	Year▲Vt.▲Legis.▲Serv.▲page number▲(West).	
Vermont Advance Legislative Service	Year–pamphlet number▲Vt.▲Adv.▲Legis.▲Serv.▲page number▲(LexisNexis).	
Administrative compilation:		
Code of Vermont Rules	Title number–chapter number▲Vt.▲Code▲R.▲§▲section number▲(year).	
Administrative register:		
Vermont Government Register	Issue number▲Vt.▲Gov't▲Reg.▲page number▲(LexisNexis▲month▲year).	

Virginia

Court system and reporters:		
Virginia Supreme Court (Va.) previously Virginia Supreme Court of Appeals (Va.)		
*South Eastern Reporter	S.E.	1887–1939
*Second Series	S.E.2d	1939–present
★Virginia Reports	Va.	1790–present
Virginia Court of Appeals (Va. Ct. App.)		
*South Eastern Reporter, Second Series	S.E.2d	1985–present
★Virginia Court of Appeals Reports	Va. App.	1985–present
Virginia Circuit Court (Va. Cir. Ct.)		
★Virginia Circuit Court Opinions	Va. Cir.	1957–present
Statutory compilations:		
★*Code of Virginia 1950 Annotated	Va. Code Ann. § section number (year).	
West's Annotated Code of Virginia	Va. Code Ann. § section number (West year).	
Session laws:		
*Acts of the General Assembly of the Commonwealth of Virginia	Year Va. Acts page number.	
West's Virginia Legislative Service	Year Va. Legis. Serv. page number (West).	
Virginia Advance Legislative Service	Year–pamphlet number Va. Adv. Legis. Serv. page number (LexisNexis).	
Administrative compilation:		
Virginia Administrative Code	Title number Va. Admin. Code § section number (year).	
Administrative register:		
Virginia Register of Regulations	Volume number Va. Reg. Regs. page number (month day, year).	

Washington

Court system and reporters:		
Washington Supreme Court (Wash.)		
*Pacific Reporter	P.	1880–1931
*Second Series	P.2d	1931–2000
*Third Series	P.3d	2000–present
★Washington Reports	Wash.	1889–1939
★Second Series	Wash. 2d	1939–present

Washington Territory Reports	Wash. Terr.	1854–1888
Washington Court of Appeals (Wash. Ct. App.)		
*Pacific Reporter, Second Series	P.2d	1969–2000
*Third Series	P.3d	2000–present
★Washington Appellate Reports	Wash. App.	1969–present
Statutory compilations:		
★*Revised Code of Washington	Wash. Rev. Code § section number (year).	
West's Revised Code of Washington Annotated	Wash. Rev. Code Ann. § section number (West year).	
Annotated Revised Code of Washington	Wash. Rev. Code Ann. § section number (LexisNexis year).	
Session laws:		
*Session Laws of the State of Washington	Year Wash. Sess. Laws page number.	
West's Washington Legislative Service	Year Wash. Legis. Serv. page number (West).	
Administrative compilation:		
Washington Administrative Code	Wash. Admin. Code § section number (year).	
Administrative register:		
Washington State Register	Issue number Wash. Reg. page number (month day, year).	

West Virginia

Court system and reporters:		
West Virginia Supreme Court of Appeals (W. Va.)		
*South Eastern Reporter	S.E.	1886–1939
*Second Series	S.E.2d	1939–present
★West Virginia Reports	W. Va.	1864–present
Statutory compilations:		
*West Virginia Code	W. Va. Code § section number (year).	
Michie's West Virginia Code Annotated	W. Va. Code Ann. § section number (LexisNexis year).	
West's Annotated Code of West Virginia	W. Va. Code Ann. § section number (West year).	

Session laws:	
*Acts of the Legislature of West Virginia	Year W. Va. Acts page number.
West's West Virginia Legislative Service	Year W. Va. Legis. Serv. page number.
West Virginia Advance Legislative Service	Year–pamphlet number W. Va. Adv. Legis. Serv. page number (LexisNexis).
Administrative compilation:	
West Virginia Code of State Rules (online)	W. Va. Code R. § title number-series (year).
Administrative register:	
West Virginia State Register	Volume number W. Va. Reg. page number (month day, year).

Wisconsin

Court system and reporters:		
Public domain format (for opinions issued since December 31, 1999):		
Wisconsin Supreme Court	*Case name*, year WI opinion number, ¶ paragraph number, parallel citations to Wisconsin Reports and North Western Reporter.	
Wisconsin Court of Appeals	*Case name*, year WI App opinion number, ¶ paragraph number, parallel citations to Wisconsin Reports and North Western Reporter.	
Wisconsin Supreme Court (Wis.)		
*North Western Reporter	N.W.	1879–1941
*Second Series	N.W.2d	1941–present
★Wisconsin Reports	Wis.	1853–1957
★Second Series	Wis. 2d	1957–present
Wisconsin Court of Appeals (Wis. Ct. App.)		
*North Western Reporter, Second Series	N.W.2d	1978–present
★Wisconsin Reports, Second Series	Wis. 2d	1978–present
Statutory compilations:		
★*Wisconsin Statutes	Wis. Stat. § section number (year).	
West's Wisconsin Statutes Annotated	Wis. Stat. Ann. § section number (West year).	
Session laws:		
*Wisconsin Session Laws	Year Wis. Sess. Laws page number.	
West's Wisconsin Legislative Service	Year Wis. Legis. Serv. page number (West).	

Administrative compilation:		
	Wis. Admin. Code agency abbreviation § section number (year).	
Note: Use agency abbreviation shown in code.		
Administrative register:		
Wisconsin Administrative Register (online)	Issue number Wis. Admin. Reg. page number (month day, year).	

Wyoming

Court system and reporters:		
Public domain format (for opinions issued since December 31, 2003):		
Wyoming Supreme Court	*Case name*, year WY opinion number, ¶ paragraph number, parallel citation to Pacific Reporter.	
	Wyoming Supreme Court (Wyo.)	
*Pacific Reporter	P.	1883–1931
★*Second Series (official since 1959)	P.2d	1931–2000
★*Third Series	P.3d	2000–present
★Wyoming Reports	Wyo.	1870–1959
Statutory compilations:		
★*Wyoming Statutes Annotated	Wyo. Stat. Ann. § section number (year).	
West's Wyoming Statutes Annotated	Wyo. Stat. Ann. § section number (West year).	
Session laws:		
*Session Laws of Wyoming	Year Wyo. Sess. Laws page number.	
West's Wyoming Legislative Service	Year Wyo. Legis. Serv. page number (West).	
Administrative compilation:		
Code of Wyoming Rules	Title number–chapter number Wyo. Code R. § section number (LexisNexis year).	
Administrative register:		
Wyoming Government Register	Issue number Wyo. Gov't Reg. page number (LexisNexis month year).	

1(C) Territories' and Tribal Courts' Primary Sources

American Samoa

Court system and reporters:		
High Court of American Samoa (Am. Samoa)		
★American Samoa Reports	Am. Samoa	1900–1975
★Second Series	Am. Samoa 2d	1983–1997
★Third Series	Am. Samoa 3d	1997–present
Statutory compilation:		
★American Samoa Code Annotated	Am. Samoa Code Ann. § section number (year).	
Administrative compilation:		
American Samoa Administrative Code	Am. Samoa Admin. Code § section number (year).	

Guam

Court system and reporters:		
Public domain format:		
Supreme Court of Guam	*Case name*, year Guam opinion number ¶ paragraph number.	
Supreme Court of Guam (Guam) and District Court of Guam (D. Guam)		
*Federal Supplement	F. Supp.	1951–1998
*Second Series	F. Supp. 2d	1998–2014
*Third Series	F. Supp. 3d	2014–present
★Guam Reports	Guam	1955–1987
Statutory compilation:		
★Guam Code Annotated	Title number Guam Code Ann. § section number (year).	
Session laws:		
Guam Session Laws	Guam Pub. L. law number (year).	
Administrative compilation:		
Administrative Rules and Regulations of the Government of Guam	Title number Guam Admin. R. & Regs. § section number (year).	

Navajo Nation

Court system and reporters:		
Supreme Court of the Navajo Nation (Navajo) previously Navajo Court of Appeals (Navajo)		
★*Navajo Reporter	Navajo Rptr.	1969–present
Navajo District Court (Navajo D. Ct.)		
★*Navajo Reporter	Navajo Rptr.	1969–present
Statutory compilations:		
Navajo Nation Code Annotated	Navajo Nation Code Ann. tit. title number, § section number (year).	

Northern Mariana Islands

Court system and reporters:		
Public domain format (for opinions issued since June 12, 1996):		
★Supreme Court of the Commonwealth of the Northern Mariana Islands	*Case name*, year MP opinion number ¶ paragraph number.	
★Northern Mariana Islands Superior Court	*Case name*, year CR opinion number ¶ paragraph number.	
Supreme Court of the Commonwealth of the Northern Mariana Islands (N. Mar.)		
★Northern Mariana Islands Reporter	N. Mar. I.	1989–present
Commonwealth Superior Court of the Northern Mariana Islands (N. Mar. I. Commw. Super. Ct.) previously Commonwealth Trial Court of the Northern Mariana Islands (N. Mar. Commw. Trial Ct.)		
*Federal Supplement	F. Supp.	1979–1998
*Second Series	F. Supp. 2d	1998–2014
*Third Series	F. Supp. 3d	2014–present
★Northern Mariana Islands Commonwealth Reporter	N. Mar. I. Commw.	1979–present
Statutory compilation:		
★Northern Mariana Islands Commonwealth Code	Title number N. Mar. I. Code § section number (year).	
Session laws:		
Northern Mariana Islands Session Laws	Year N. Mar. I. Pub. L. number.	
Administrative compilation:		
★Northern Mariana Islands Administrative Code	Title number N. Mar. I. Admin. Code § section number (year).	
Administrative register:		
Northern Mariana Islands Commonwealth Register	Volume number N. Mar. I. Reg. page number (month day, year).	

Oklahoma Native Americans

Court system and reporters:		
Tribal courts (e.g., Supreme Court of the Cheyenne and Arapaho Tribes, Supreme Court of the Muscogee (Creek) Nation, Supreme Court of the Pawnee Nation)		
Courts of Indian Appeals; Courts of Indian Offenses		
Oklahoma Tribal Court Reports	Okla. Trib.	1979–present

Puerto Rico

Court system and reporters:		
Public domain format (for opinions issued since January 1, 1998):		
Tribunal Supreme de Puerto Rico (Spanish)	*Case name*, year TSPR page number (year).	
Puerto Rico Supreme Court (English)	*Case name*, year PRSC page number (year).	
Puerto Rico Supreme Court (P.R.) (Tribunal Supremo de Puerto Rico)		
★*Puerto Rico Reports	P.R.	1899–1978
★*Official Translations of the Supreme Court of Puerto Rico	P.R. Offic. Trans.	1978–present
★Decisiones de Puerto Rico	P.R. Dec.	1899–present
Sentencias del Tribunal Supremo de Puerto Rico	P.R. Sent.	1899–1902
Jurisprudencia del Tribunal Supremo de Puerto Rico	J.T.S.	1973–present
Puerto Rico Circuit Court of Appeals (P.R. Cir.) (Tribunal de Circuito de Apelaciones)		
Decisiones del Tribunal de Circuito de Apelaciones de Puerto Rico	T.C.A.	1995–present
Statutory compilation:		
Laws of Puerto Rico Annotated (Leyes de Puerto Rico Anotadas)	P.R. Laws Ann. tit. title number, § section number (year).	
Session laws:		
Laws of Puerto Rico (Leyes de Puerto Rico)	Year P.R. Laws page number.	
Administrative register:		
Puerto Rico Register of Regulations	Volume number P.R. Reg. Issue number (month day, year).	

United States Virgin Islands

Court system and reporters:		
Supreme Court of the United States Virgin Islands (V.I.)		
★Virgin Islands Reports	V.I.	1917–present
Superior Court of the Virgin Islands (Super. Ct. V.I.) previously Territorial Court of the Virgin Islands		
★Virgin Islands Reports	V.I.	1917–present
Statutory compilation:		
★Virgin Islands Code Annotated	V.I. Code Ann. tit. title number, § section number (year).	
Session laws:		
*Session Laws of the Virgin Islands	Year V.I. Sess. Laws page number.	
Virgin Islands Code Annotated Advance Legislative Service	Year–pamphlet number V.I. Code Ann. Adv. Legis. Serv. page number (LexisNexis).	
Administrative compilation:		
Code of U.S. Virgin Islands Rules	Title number–chapter number V.I. Code R. § section number (LexisNexis year).	
Administrative register:		
Virgin Islands Government Register	Issue number V.I. Gov't Reg. page number (LexisNexis month year).	

Appendix 2 Local Court Citation Rules

Appendix 2 addresses citation rules promulgated by all levels of federal, state, and other United States territorial courts. It indicates whether a jurisdiction has rules governing public domain citation, and it provides URLs and citations to information relevant to legal citation in federal, state, and territorial jurisdictions.

In order to facilitate easily updating these local rules, **Appendix 2** is fully online. You can find it on the CasebookConnect platform for the ALWD Guide to Legal Citation, Seventh Edition, or on the book's product page under Student Resources or Professor Resources at https://www.wklegaledu.com/Williams-ALWDGuideLegalCitation7. If you discover that a local rule has changed from the last update or you believe a local rule of practice that is missing from this list would help others, you may email the author at cvwilliams@email.arizona.edu so that the change can be incorporated in the next update. The most recent date of each **Appendix 2** update is noted online.

Appendix 3 General Abbreviations

Appendix 3 contains abbreviations for the following citation components:

(A) Calendar divisions (months);
(B) United States and world geography (e.g., cities, states, territories, countries, regions);
(C) Subdivisions (e.g., appendix, section, paragraph, volume);
(D) Publishing terms (e.g., copyright, draft, edition, printing, serial);
(E) Case names, statutes, and institutional authors;
(F) Legislative terms; and
(G) Court documents.

With the exception of **Appendix 3(A)**, entries are in alphabetical order. Required spaces are indicated by red triangles (▲). Some **Appendix 3** abbreviations differ from those in appendices relating to other types of citation components; for example, in **Appendix 3(G)**, "J." stands for "Judge," while in **Appendix 5(A)**, "J." stands for "Journal." In academic footnote citations, some abbreviations should be presented in LARGE AND SMALL CAPITAL LETTERS or in *italics*; check the FN rules corresponding to the specific source to be cited.

3(A) Calendar Divisions

Month	Abbreviation	Month	Abbreviation
January	Jan.	July	July
February	Feb.	August	Aug.
March	Mar.	September	Sept.
April	Apr.	October	Oct.
May	May	November	Nov.
June	June	December	Dec.

3(B) United States and World Geography

Use these abbreviations for geographic terms in names of non-governmental parties (**Rule 12.2(e)(2),(f)**); courts (**Rule 12.6**); institutional authors (**Rule 20.1(b)(3)**); and treaties (**Rule 19.1**). When a government entity is a party to a case, consult **Rule 12.2 (h)–(k)** to determine whether to use an abbreviation. Note that some geographical names are listed because they should *not* be abbreviated.

3(B)(1) States and Territories of the United States

State or Territory	Abbreviation	State or Territory	Abbreviation
Alabama	Ala.	Montana	Mont.
Alaska	Alaska	Nebraska	Neb.
American Samoa	Am. Sam.	Nevada	Nev.
Arizona	Ariz.	New Hampshire	N.H.
Arkansas	Ark.	New Jersey	N.J.
California	Cal.	New Mexico	N.M.
Colorado	Colo.	New York	N.Y.
Connecticut	Conn.	North Carolina	N.C.
Delaware	Del.	North Dakota	N.D.
District of Columbia	D.C.	Northern Mariana Islands	N. Mar. I.
Florida	Fla.	Ohio	Ohio
Georgia	Ga.	Oklahoma	Okla.
Guam	Guam	Oregon	Or.
Hawaii	Haw.	Pennsylvania	Pa.
Idaho	Idaho	Puerto Rico	P.R.
Illinois	Ill.	Rhode Island	R.I.
Indiana	Ind.	South Carolina	S.C.
Iowa	Iowa	South Dakota	S.D.
Kansas	Kan.	Tennessee	Tenn.
Kentucky	Ky.	Texas	Tex.
Louisiana	La.	Utah	Utah
Maine	Me.	Vermont	Vt.
Maryland	Md.	Virgin Islands	V.I.
Massachusetts	Mass.	Virginia	Va.
Michigan	Mich.	Washington	Wash.
Minnesota	Minn.	West Virginia	W. Va.
Mississippi	Miss.	Wisconsin	Wis.
Missouri	Mo.	Wyoming	Wyo.

3(B)(2) Major Cities of the United States

City	Abbreviation	City	Abbreviation
Baltimore	Balt.	Los Angeles	L.A.
Boston	Bos.	Miami	Mia.
Chicago	Chi.	New York City	N.Y.C.
Dallas	Dall.	Oklahoma City	Okla. City
District of Columbia	D.C.	Philadelphia	Phila.
Houston	Hous.	Phoenix	Phx.
Kansas City	Kan. City	San Francisco	S.F.

3(B)(3) Countries, Provinces, and Regions

Country, Province, or Region	Abbreviation	Country, Province, or Region	Abbreviation
Afghanistan	Afg.	Andorra	Andorra
Africa	Afr.	Angola	Angl.
Albania	Alb.	Anguilla	Anguilla
Alberta	Alta.	Antarctica	Antarctica
Algeria	Alg.	Antigua and Barbuda	Ant. & Barb.
America	Am.	Argentina	Arg.

Country, Province, or Region	Abbreviation
Armenia	Arm.
Asia	Asia
Australia	Austl.
Australian Capital Territory	Austl. Cap. Terr.
Austria	Austria
Azerbaijan	Azer.
Bahamas	Bah.
Bahrain	Bahr.
Bangladesh	Bangl.
Barbados	Barb.
Belarus	Belr.
Belgium	Belg.
Belize	Belize
Benin	Benin
Bermuda	Berm.
Bhutan	Bhutan
Bolivia	Bol.
Bosnia and Herzegovina	Bosn. & Herz.
Botswana	Bots.
Brazil	Braz.
British Columbia	B.C.
Brunei	Brunei
Bulgaria	Bulg.
Burkina Faso	Burk. Faso
Burundi	Burundi
Cambodia	Cambodia
Cameroon	Cameroon
Canada	Can.
Cape Verde	Cape Verde
Cayman Islands	Cayman Is.
Central African Republic	Cent. Afr. Rep.
Chad	Chad
Channel Islands	Channel Is.
Chile	Chile
China, People's Republic of	China
Colombia	Colom.
Comoros	Comoros
Congo, Democratic Republic of the	Dem. Rep. Congo
Congo, Republic of the	Congo
Costa Rica	Costa Rica
Côte d'Ivoire	Côte d'Ivoire
Croatia	Croat.
Cuba	Cuba
Cyprus	Cyprus
Czech Republic	Czech
Denmark	Den.
Djibouti	Djib.
Dominica	Dominica
Dominican Republic	Dom. Rep.
Ecuador	Ecuador

Country, Province, or Region	Abbreviation
Egypt	Egypt
El Salvador	El Sal.
England	Eng.
Equatorial Guinea	Eq. Guinea
Eritrea	Eri.
Estonia	Est.
Ethiopia	Eth.
Europe	Eur.
Falkland Islands	Falkland Is.
Fiji	Fiji
Finland	Fin.
France	Fr.
Gabon	Gabon
Gambia	Gam.
Georgia [for U.S. state, see **Appendix 3(B)(1)**]	Geor.
Germany	Ger.
Ghana	Ghana
Gibraltar	Gib.
Great Britain	Gr. Brit.
Greece	Greece
Greenland	Green.
Grenada	Gren.
Guadeloupe	Guad.
Guatemala	Guat.
Guinea	Guinea
Guinea–Bissau	Guinea–Bissau
Guyana	Guy.
Haiti	Haiti
Honduras	Hond.
Hong Kong	H.K.
Hungary	Hung.
Iceland	Ice.
India	India
Indonesia	Indon.
Iran	Iran
Iraq	Iraq
Ireland	Ir.
Israel	Isr.
Italy	It.
Jamaica	Jam.
Japan	Jap.
Jordan	Jordan
Kazakhstan	Kaz.
Kenya	Kenya
Kiribati	Kiribati
Korea, North	N. Kor.
Korea, South	S. Kor.
Kosovo	Kos.
Kuwait	Kuwait
Kyrgyzstan	Kyrg.
Laos	Laos

Country, Province, or Region	Abbreviation
Latin America	Lat. Am.
Latvia	Lat.
Lebanon	Leb.
Lesotho	Lesotho
Liberia	Liber.
Libya	Libya
Liechtenstein	Liech.
Lithuania	Lith.
Luxembourg	Lux.
Macau	Mac.
Macedonia	Maced.
Madagascar	Madag.
Malawi	Malawi
Malaysia	Malay.
Maldives	Maldives
Mali	Mali
Malta	Malta
Manitoba	Man.
Marshall Islands	Marsh. Is.
Martinique	Mart.
Mauritania	Mauritania
Mauritius	Mauritius
Mexico	Mex.
Micronesia	Micr.
Moldova	Mold.
Monaco	Monaco
Mongolia	Mong.
Montenegro	Montenegro
Montserrat	Montserrat
Morocco	Morocco
Mozambique	Mozam.
Myanmar	Myan.
Namibia	Namib.
Nauru	Nauru
Nepal	Nepal
Netherlands	Neth.
New Brunswick	N.B.
New South Wales	N.S.W.
New Zealand	N.Z.
Newfoundland & Labrador	Nfld.
Nicaragua	Nicar.
Niger	Niger
Nigeria	Nigeria
North America	N. Am.
Northern Ireland	N. Ir.
Northern Territory (Australia)	N. Terr.
Northwest Territories (Canada)	N.W.T.
Norway	Nor.
Nova Scotia	N.S.

Country, Province, or Region	Abbreviation
Nunavut	Nun.
Oman	Oman
Ontario	Ont.
Pakistan	Pak.
Palau	Palau
Panama	Pan.
Papua New Guinea	Papua N.G.
Paraguay	Para.
Peru	Peru
Philippines	Phil.
Pitcairn Island	Pitcairn Is.
Poland	Pol.
Portugal	Port.
Prince Edward Island	P.E.I.
Qatar	Qatar
Québec	Que.
Queensland	Queensl.
Réunion	Réunion
Romania	Rom.
Russia	Russ.
Rwanda	Rwanda
Saint Helena	St. Helena
Saint Kitts and Nevis	St. Kitts & Nevis
Saint Lucia	St. Lucia
Saint Vincent and the Grenadines	St. Vincent
Samoa	Samoa
San Marino	San Marino
São Tomé and Príncipe	São Tomé & Príncipe
Saskatchewan	Sask.
Saudi Arabia	Saudi Arabia
Scotland	Scot.
Senegal	Sen.
Serbia	Serb.
Seychelles	Sey.
Sierra Leone	Sierra Leone
Singapore	Sing.
Slovakia	Slovk.
Slovenia	Slovn.
Solomon Islands	Solom. Is.
Somalia	Som.
South Africa	S. Afr.
South America	S. Am.
South Australia	S. Austl.
Spain	Spain
Sri Lanka	Sri Lanka
Sudan	Sudan
Suriname	Surin.
Swaziland	Swaz.
Sweden	Swed.
Switzerland	Switz.

Country, Province, or Region	Abbreviation
Syria	Syria
Taiwan	Taiwan
Tajikistan	Taj.
Tanzania	Tanz.
Tasmania	Tas.
Thailand	Thai.
Timor–Leste	Timor–Leste
Togo	Togo
Tonga	Tonga
Trinidad and Tobago	Trin. & Tobago
Tunisia	Tunis.
Turkey	Turk.
Turkmenistan	Turkm.
Turks and Caicos Islands	Turks & Caicos Is.
Tuvalu	Tuvalu
Uganda	Uganda
Ukraine	Ukr.
United Arab Emirates	U.A.E.
United Kingdom	U.K.
United States of America	U.S.
Uruguay	Uru.
Uzbekistan	Uzb.
Vanuatu	Vanuatu
Vatican City	Vatican
Venezuela	Venez.
Victoria	Vict.
Vietnam	Viet.
Virgin Islands, British	Virgin Is.
Wales	Wales
Western Australia	W. Austl.
Yemen	Yemen
Yukon Territory	Yukon
Zambia	Zam.
Zimbabwe	Zim.

3(C) Subdivisions

Use these abbreviations to indicate a subdivision or pinpoint reference of a cited work. For specific information about the role of these subdivisions in citations, including whether to insert a space between an abbreviation and the number(s) that follow it, see **Rules 6–10**. Words in red text indicate that there is no space between the abbreviation and the pinpoint reference. When the cited source uses paragraph (¶) or section (§) symbols, use those symbols instead of the indicated abbreviation. To form a plural, append "s" to the abbreviation unless the word listed below indicates otherwise or the abbreviation would end awkwardly with "ss."

Word/Term	Abbreviation
addendum	add.
amendment	amend.
annotation	annot.
appendices	apps.
appendix	app.
article	art.
attachment	attach.
bibliography	bibliog.
book	bk.
chapter	ch.
clause	cl.
column	col.
comment(ary)	cmt.
decision	dec.
department	dept.
division	div.
endnote	n.
endnotes	nn.
example	ex.
figure	fig.
folio	fol.
footnote (in internal cross-reference)	note
footnote	n.
footnotes (in internal cross-reference)	notes
footnotes	nn.
historical note	hist. n.
historical notes	hist. nn.
hypothetical	hypo.
illustration(s)	illus.
introduction	intro.

Word/Term	Abbreviation
line	l.
lines	ll.
note (in internal cross-reference)	note
note	n.
notes (in internal cross-reference)	notes
notes	nn.
number	no.
page (in internal cross-reference)	p.
pages (in internal cross-reference)	pp.
paragraph	¶ *or* para.
paragraphs	¶¶ *or* paras.
part	pt.
preamble	pmbl.
principle	princ.
publication	pub.
record	rec.
reference	ref.
rule	r.
schedule	sched.
section	§ *or* sec.
sections	§§ *or* secs.
seri(al, es)	ser.
subdivision	subdiv.
subsection	subsec.
subpart	subpt.
supplement	supp.
table	tbl.
title	tit.
volume	vol.

3(D) Publishing Terms

Word/Term	Abbreviation
abridge(d, ment)	abr.
annotated	ann.
anonymous	anon.
circa	c.
compil(ation, ed)	comp.
copyright	copy.
draft	drft.
edit(ion, or)	ed.
editors	eds.
manuscript	ms.
mimeograph	mimeo.
new series	n.s.
no date	n.d.
no place	n.p.
no publisher	n. ▲ pub.
offprint	offprt.
old series	o.s.
permanent	perm.
photoduplicated reprint	photo. ▲ repr.
printing	prtg.
replacement	repl.
reprint	reprt.
revis(ed, ion)	rev.
seri(al, es)	ser.
special	spec.
temporary	temp.
tentative	tent.
translat(ion, or)	trans.
unabridged	unabr.
volume	vol.

3(E) Names of Cases, Institutional Authors, and Periodical Titles

Use the abbreviations in **Appendix 3(E)** for words in the names of cases, institutional authors, and periodical titles not listed in **Appendix 5** or where specifically directed by an ALWD rule. While most end in a period, others are contractions formed with apostrophes, and those do not end with a period. For abbreviations of names of case reporters, see **Chart 12.2** or a jurisdiction's entry in **Appendix 1**. For abbreviations of statutory compilations, see a jurisdiction's entry in **Appendix 1**.

To form a plural, add "s" to the end of the abbreviation unless the word listed indicates otherwise or the abbreviation would end awkwardly with "ss." For example, the "(s)" in "Resource(s)" means to use "Res." for "Resource" (singular) or "Resources" (plural).

When an abbreviation differs depending its reference, you will see a bracketed note. For example, the abbreviation "Fed." stands for "Federal," but this abbreviation is not used to refer to the *Federal Reporter*. Some abbreviations refer to more than one word or to related forms of a word (indicated in parentheses). For example, "Corp." stands for either "Corporate" or "Corporation."

You may abbreviate a word of eight or more letters that is not listed here if doing so not only shortens the word but also produces a recognizable abbreviation. To prevent reader confusion, you may need to spell out a word instead of abbreviating it.

Word/Term	Abbreviation
Academ(ic, y)	Acad.
Account(ant, ing, ancy)	Acct.
Administrat(ion, ive)	Admin.
Administrator	Adm'r
Administratrix	Adm'x
Advertising	Advert.
Advoca(cy, te)	Advoc.
Affair	Aff.
Africa(n)	Afr.
Agricultur(al, e)	Agric.
Alliance	All.
Alternative	Alt.
Amendment	Amend.
America(n)	Am.
Ancestry	Anc.
and	&
Annual	Ann.
Appellate	App.
Arbitrat(ion, or)	Arb.
Artificial Intelligence	A.I.
Associate	Assoc.
Association	Ass'n
Atlantic [*Note: not* for reporter; see **Chart 12.2**]	Atl.
Attorney	Att'y
Authority	Auth.
Automo(bile, tive)	Auto.
Avenue	Ave.
Bankruptcy [*Note: not* for reporter; see **Chart 12.2**]	Bankr.
Behavior(al)	Behav.
Board	Bd.
British	Brit.
Broadcast(er, ing)	Broad.
Building	Bldg.
Bulletin	Bull.
Business(es)	Bus.
Capital	Cap.
Casualt(ies, y)	Cas.
Catholic	Cath.
Cent(er, re)	Ctr.
Central	Cent.
Chemical	Chem.
Children	Child.
Chronicle	Chron.
Circuit	Cir.
Civil	Civ.
Civil Libert(ies, y)	C.L.
Civil Rights	C.R.
Coalition	Coal.
College	Coll.
Commentary	Comment.
Commerc(e, ial)	Com.
Commission	Comm'n
Commissioner	Comm'r
Committee	Comm.
Communication	Commc'n
Community	Cmty.
Company	Co.
Comparative	Compar.
Compensation	Comp.
Computer	Comput.
Condominium	Condo.
Conference	Conf.
Congress(ional)	Cong.
Consolidated	Consol.
Constitution(al)	Const.
Construction	Constr.
Contemporary	Contemp.
Continental	Cont'l
Contract	Cont.
Conveyance(r)	Conv.

Word/Term	Abbreviation	Word/Term	Abbreviation
Cooperat(ion, ive)	Coop.	Fidelity	Fid.
Corporat(e, ion)	Corp.	Financ(e, ial, ing)	Fin.
Correction(al, s)	Corr.	Fortnightly	Fort.
Cosmetic	Cosm.	Forum	F.
Counsel(or, ors, or's)	Couns.	Foundation	Found.
County [*Note:* See **Rule 12.2(j)**]	Cnty.	General	Gen.
		Global	Glob.
Court	Ct.	Government	Gov't
Criminal	Crim.	Group	Grp.
Defen(d, der, se)	Def.	Guarant(or, y)	Guar.
Delinquen(cy, t)	Delinq.	Hispanic	Hisp.
Department	Dep't	Histor(ical, y)	Hist.
Detention	Det.	Hospital(ity)	Hosp.
Develop(er, ment)	Dev.	Housing	Hous.
Digest	Dig.	Human	Hum.
Digital	Digit.	Humanity	Human.
Diplomacy	Dipl.	Immigration	Immigr.
Director	Dir.	Import(ation, er)	Imp.
Discount	Disc.	Incorporated	Inc.
Dispute	Disp.	Indemnity	Indem.
Distribut(ing, ion, or)	Distrib.	Independen(ce, t)	Indep.
District	Dist.	Industr(ial, ies, y)	Indus.
Division	Div.	Inequality	Ineq.
Doctor	Dr.	Information	Info.
East(ern)	E.	Injury	Inj.
Econom(ic, ical, ics, y)	Econ.	Institut(e, ion)	Inst.
Editor(ial)	Ed.	Insurance	Ins.
Education(al)	Educ.	Intellectual	Intell.
Electr(ic, ical, icity, onic)	Elec.	Intelligence	Intel.
Employ(ee, er, ment)	Emp.	Interdisciplinary	Interdisc.
Enforcement	Enf't	Interest	Int.
Engineer	Eng'r	International	Int'l
Engineering	Eng'g	Invest(ment, or)	Inv.
English	Eng.	Journal(s)	J.
Enterprise	Enter.	Judicial	Jud.
Entertainment	Ent.	Juridical	Jurid.
Environment(al)	Env't	Jurisprudence	Juris.
Equality	Equal.	Justice	Just.
Equipment	Equip.	Juvenile	Juv.
Estate	Est.	Labor	Lab.
Europe(an)	Eur.	Laboratory	Lab'y
Examiner	Exam'r	Law(s) (*Note:* Law is *not* abbreviated if it is the first word)	L.
Exchange	Exch.		
Executive	Exec.		
Executor	Ex'r	Lawyer	Law.
Executrix	Ex'x	Legislat(ion, ive)	Legis.
Explorat(ion, ory)	Expl.	Liability	Liab.
Export(ation, er)	Exp.	Librar(ian, y)	Libr.
Faculty	Fac.	Limited	Ltd.
Family	Fam.	Limited Liability Company	LLC *or* L.L.C.
Federal [*Note: not* for reporter; see **Chart 12.2**]	Fed.	Limited Liability Limited Partnership	LLLP *or* L.L.L.P.
Federation	Fed'n	Limited Liability Partnership	LLP *or* L.L.P.

Word/Term	Abbreviation
Limited Partnership	LP *or* L.P.
Litigation	Litig.
Local	Loc.
Machine(ry)	Mach.
Magazine	Mag.
Maintenance	Maint.
Management	Mgmt.
Manufacturer	Mfr.
Manufacturing	Mfg.
Maritime	Mar.
Market	Mkt.
Marketing	Mktg.
Matrimonial	Matrim.
Mechanic(al)	Mech.
Medic(al, inal, ine)	Med.
Memorial	Mem'l
Merchan(dise, dising, t)	Merch.
Metropolitan	Metro.
Military	Mil.
Mineral	Min.
Modern	Mod.
Mortgage	Mortg.
Municipal(ity)	Mun.
Mutual	Mut.
National	Nat'l
Nationality	Nat'y
National Association	N.A.
National Trust and Savings Association	NT & SA *or* N.T. & S.A.
Natural	Nat.
Negligence	Negl.
Negotiat(ion, or)	Negot.
Newsletter	Newsl.
North(ern)	N.
Northeast(ern) [*Note: not* for reporter; see **Chart 12.2**]	Ne.
Northwest(ern) [*Note: not* for reporter; see **Chart 12.2**]	Nw.
Number	No.
Offic(e, ial)	Off.
Opinion	Op.
Order	Ord.
Organiz(ation, ing)	Org.
Pacific [*Note: not* for reporter; see **Chart 12.2**]	Pac.
Parish	Par.
Partnership	P'ship
Patent	Pat.
Person(al, nel)	Pers.
Perspective	Persp.
Pharmaceutic(al)	Pharm.
Philosoph(ical, y)	Phil.
Planning	Plan.

Word/Term	Abbreviation
Policy	Pol'y
Politic(al, s)	Pol.
Practi(cal, ce, tioner)	Prac.
Preserv(ation, e)	Pres.
Priva(cy, te)	Priv.
Probat(e, ion)	Prob.
Problems	Probs.
Proce(edings, dure)	Proc.
Product(ion)	Prod.
Profession(al)	Pro.
Professional Association	PA *or* P.A.
Professional Corporation	PC *or* P.C.
Professional Limited Liability Company	PLLC *or* P.L.L.C.
Property	Prop.
Protection	Prot.
Psycholog(ical, ist, y)	Psych.
Public	Pub.
Publication	Publ'n
Publishing	Publ'g
Quarterly	Q.
Railroad	R.R.
Railway	Ry.
Record	Rec.
Referee	Ref.
Refin(ement, ing)	Refin.
Regional	Reg'l
Register	Reg.
Registered Limited Liability Partnership	RLLP *or* R.L.L.P.
Regulat(ion, or, ory)	Regul.
Rehabilitat(ion, ive)	Rehab.
Relation	Rel.
Report(er)	Rep.
Reproduct(ion, ive)	Reprod.
Research	Rsch.
Reserv(ation, e)	Rsrv.
Resolution	Resol.
Resource(s)	Res.
Responsibility	Resp.
Restaurant	Rest.
Retirement	Ret.
Review, Revista	Rev.
Rights	Rts.
Road	Rd.
Savings	Sav.
School(s)	Sch.
Scien(ce, tific)	Sci.
Scottish	Scot.
Secretary	Sec'y
Securit(ies, y)	Sec.
Sentencing	Sent'g
Service	Serv.
Shareholder or Stockholder	S'holder

Word/Term	Abbreviation
Social	Soc.
Sociedad Anónima, Société Anonyme	SA *or* S.A.
Societa per Azioni, Sociedad por acciones	S.p.A.
Society	Soc'y
Sociolog(ical, y)	Socio.
Solicitor	Solic.
Solution	Sol.
South(ern) [*Note: not* for reporter; see **Chart 12.2**]	S.
Southeast(ern) [*Note: not* for reporter; see **Chart 12.2**]	Se.
Southwest(ern) [*Note: not* for reporter; see **Chart 12.2**]	Sw.
Statistic(al, s)	Stat.
Steamship(s)	S.S.
Street	St.
Studies	Stud.
Subcommittee	Subcomm.
Supreme Court [*Note: not* for reporter; see **Chart 12.2**]	Sup. Ct.
Surety	Sur.
Survey	Surv.
Symposium	Symp.
System(s)	Sys.
Taxation	Tax'n
Teacher	Tchr.
Techn(ical, ique, ological, ology)	Tech.
Telecommunication	Telecomm.
Tele(graph, phone)	Tel.
Temporary	Temp.
Township [*Note:* See **Rule 12.2(j)**]	Twp.
Transcontinental	Transcon.
Transnational	Transnat'l
Transport(ation)	Transp.
Tribune	Trib.
Trust(ee)	Tr.
Turnpike	Tpk.
Uniform	Unif.
United States	U.S.
University [*Note: not* for periodical; see **Appendix 5(A)**]	Univ.
Urban	Urb.
Utility	Util.
Village	Vill.
Week	Wk.
Weekly	Wkly.
West(ern)	W.
Yearbook or Year Book	Y.B.

3(F) Legislative Terms

Use these abbreviations in citations to legislative measures and related documents. To form the plural, add "s" to the end of the abbreviation unless the word listed indicates otherwise or the abbreviation would awkwardly end with "ss." Note that some words in this appendix are *not* abbreviated. You may, however, abbreviate other words of more than six letters not appearing in this appendix if the resulting abbreviation is unambiguous. Omit articles and prepositions from titles of documents if not needed for clarity.

Word/Term	Abbreviation
Annals	Annals
Annual	Ann.
Assembly(man, woman, member)	Assemb.
Bill	B.
Attorney General	Att'y Gen.
Commissioner	Comm'r
Committee	Comm.
Concurrent	Con.
Conference	Conf.
Congress(ional)	Cong.
Debate	Deb.
Delegate	Del.
Document(s)	Doc.
Executive	Exec.
Federal	Fed.
General	Gen.
House	H.
House of Delegates	H.D.
House of Representatives	H.R.

Word/Term	Abbreviation
Joint	J.
Law	L.
Legislat(ion, ive)	Legis.
Legislature	Leg.
Miscellaneous	Misc.
Number	No.
Order	Order
Public	Pub.
Record	Rec.
Register	Reg.

Word/Term	Abbreviation
Regular	Reg.
Report	Rep.
Representative	Rep.
Resolution(s)	Res.
Senate	S.
Senator	Sen.
Service	Serv.
Session(s)	Sess.
Special	Spec.
Subcommittee	Subcomm.

3(G) Court Documents

Use these abbreviations in citations to legal documents connected to a case formerly or presently litigated (**Rule 12.15** or **Rule 25**), and use them when specific *ALWD Guide* rules refer you here. Combine abbreviations as needed to reflect a document's name, adding appropriate spaces between abbreviations two or more letters in length. Note that some words in **Appendix 3(G)** are *not* abbreviated. You may, however, abbreviate other words of seven or more letters not appearing in this appendix if the resulting abbreviation is unambiguous. Omit articles and prepositions from titles of documents if not needed for clarity.

Word/Term	Abbreviation
Administrative	Admin.
Administrative Law Judge	A.L.J.
Admiralty	Adm.
Admission	Admis.
Affidavit	Aff.
Affirm	Affirm
Aldermen's	Alder.
Amended	Am.
And	&
Answer	Answer
Appeal	Appeal
Appeals Court	App. Ct.
Appellant	Appellant
Appellate	App.
Appellee	Appellee
Appendix [*Note: not* when citing Joint Appendix]	App.
Application	Appl.
Arbitrat(ion, or)	Arb.
Argument	Arg.
Armed Services Board of Contract Appeals	ASBCA
Assembly(man, member, woman)	Assemb.

Word/Term	Abbreviation
Attachment	Attach.
Attorney	Att'y
Attorney General	Att'y Gen.
Bankruptcy	Bankr.
Bankruptcy Appellate Panel	B.A.P.
Baron	B.
Board of Contract Appeals	B.C.A.
Board of Immigration Appeals	B.I.A.
Board of Patent Appeals and Interferences	B.P.A.I.
Board of Tax Appeals	B.T.A.
Borough	Bor.
Brief	Br.
Central District	C.D.
Certiorari	Cert.
Chancellor	C.
Chancery	Ch.
Chief Baron	C.B.
Chief Justice, Chief Judge	C.J.
Circuit	Cir.
City	City
Civil	Civ.
Compel	Compel
Complaint	Compl.

Word/Term	Abbreviation
Counterclaim	Countercl.
County	Cnty.
Court	Ct.
Criminal	Crim.
Cross-claim	Cross-cl.
Decision	Dec.
Declaration	Decl.
Defendant	Def.
Defendant's	Def.'s
Defendants	Defs.
Defendants'	Defs.'
Defense	Def.
Demurrer	Dem.
Deny[ing]	Den.
Department	Dep't
Deposition	Dep.
Discovery	Disc.
Dismiss	Dismiss
District [federal]	D.
District [state]	Dist.
District Attorney	D.A.
Division	Div.
Document	Doc.
Eastern District	E.D.
Evidence	Evid.
Examination	Exam.
Exhibit	Ex.
General	Gen.
Grant	Grant
Hearing	Hr'g
Independent	Indep.
Information	Info.
Injunction	Inj.
Instruction	Instr.
Interrogatory	Interrog.
Joint Appendix	J.A.
Judge	J.
Judges	JJ.
Judgment	J.
Justice	J.
Justices	JJ.
Juvenile	Juv.
Letter	Ltr.
Limine	Lim.
Litigation	Litig.
Magistrate	Mag.
Mediat(ion, or)	Med.
Memorandum	Mem.
Middle District	M.D.
Minute	Min.
Motion	Mot.
Number	No.
Numbers	Nos.
Objection	Obj.
Opinion	Op.
Opposition	Opp'n
Order	Order
Permanent	Perm.
Petition	Pet.
Petitioner	Pet'r
Petitioner's	Pet'r's
Petitioners	Pet'rs
Petitioners'	Pet'rs'
Plaintiff	Pl.
Plaintiff's	Pl.'s
Plaintiffs	Pls.
Plaintiffs'	Pls.'
Points and Authorities	P. & A.
Preliminary	Prelim.
Probat(e, ion)	Prob.
Produc(e, tion)	Prod.
Quash	Quash
Report & Recommendation	R. & R.
Reconsideration	Recons.
Record	R.
Referee	Ref.
Rehearing	Reh'g
Reply	Reply
Reporter	Rep.
Request	Req.
Respondent	Resp't
Respondent's	Resp't's
Respondents	Resp'ts
Respondents'	Resp'ts'
Response	Resp.
Review	Rev.
Rule(s)	R.
Session(s)	Sess.
Solicitor	Sol.
Special	Spec.
State	St.
Stay	Stay
Subpoena	Subpoena
Summary	Summ.
Supplement(al)	Supp.
Support	Supp.
Suppress	Suppress
Surrogate's Court	Sur. Ct.
Temporary	Temp.
Temporary Restraining Order	TRO
Testimony	Test.
Transcript	Tr.
Trial	Trial
Verified Statement	V.S.
Versus	v.

Appendix 4 Court Abbreviations

Appendix 4 contains abbreviations for names of courts at both the appellate and trial levels. Required spaces are indicated by red triangles (▲). A citation component printed in red indicates a variable (e.g., a city's name). If you cannot find an entry for the court you wish to cite, consult **Appendix 1** before constructing an abbreviation using **Appendix 4(C)**. Many court names incorporate numbers; see **Rule 4.3** for information about ordinal numbers. This appendix has three subdivisions: **Appendix 4(A)**, Federal Court Abbreviations; **Appendix 4(B)**, State Court Abbreviations; and **Appendix 4(C)**, Other Abbreviations in Court Names.

4(A) Federal Court Abbreviations

Court	Abbreviation
United States Supreme Court	U.S.
United States Courts of Appeals	
First Circuit	1st▲Cir.
Second Circuit	2d▲Cir.
Third Circuit	3d▲Cir.
Fourth Circuit	4th▲Cir.
Fifth Circuit	5th▲Cir.
Sixth Circuit	6th▲Cir.
Seventh Circuit	7th▲Cir.
Eighth Circuit	8th▲Cir.
Ninth Circuit	9th▲Cir.
Tenth Circuit	10th▲Cir.
Eleventh Circuit	11th▲Cir.
District of Columbia Circuit	D.C.▲Cir.
Federal Circuit	Fed.▲Cir.
United States District Courts	
Middle District of Alabama	M.D.▲Ala.
Northern District of Alabama	N.D.▲Ala.
Southern District of Alabama	S.D.▲Ala.
District of Alaska	D.▲Alaska
District of Arizona	D.▲Ariz.
Eastern District of Arkansas	E.D.▲Ark.
Western District of Arkansas	W.D.▲Ark.
Central District of California	C.D.▲Cal.
Eastern District of California	E.D.▲Cal.
Northern District of California	N.D.▲Cal.
Southern District of California	S.D.▲Cal.
District of the Canal Zone	D.C.Z.
District of Colorado	D.▲Colo.
District of Connecticut	D.▲Conn.
District of Delaware	D.▲Del.
District of the District of Columbia	D.D.C.

Court	Abbreviation
Middle District of Florida	M.D. Fla.
Northern District of Florida	N.D. Fla.
Southern District of Florida	S.D. Fla.
Middle District of Georgia	M.D. Ga.
Northern District of Georgia	N.D. Ga.
Southern District of Georgia	S.D. Ga.
District of Guam	D. Guam
District of Hawaii	D. Haw.
District of Idaho	D. Idaho
Central District of Illinois	C.D. Ill.
Northern District of Illinois	N.D. Ill.
Southern District of Illinois	S.D. Ill.
Northern District of Indiana	N.D. Ind.
Southern District of Indiana	S.D. Ind.
Northern District of Iowa	N.D. Iowa
Southern District of Iowa	S.D. Iowa
District of Kansas	D. Kan.
Eastern District of Kentucky	E.D. Ky.
Western District of Kentucky	W.D. Ky.
Eastern District of Louisiana	E.D. La.
Middle District of Louisiana	M.D. La.
Western District of Louisiana	W.D. La.
District of Maine	D. Me.
District of Maryland	D. Md.
District of Massachusetts	D. Mass.
Eastern District of Michigan	E.D. Mich.
Western District of Michigan	W.D. Mich.
District of Minnesota	D. Minn.
Northern District of Mississippi	N.D. Miss.
Southern District of Mississippi	S.D. Miss.
Eastern District of Missouri	E.D. Mo.
Western District of Missouri	W.D. Mo.
District of Montana	D. Mont.
District of Nebraska	D. Neb.
District of Nevada	D. Nev.
District of New Hampshire	D.N.H.
District of New Jersey	D.N.J.
District of New Mexico	D.N.M.
Eastern District of New York	E.D.N.Y.
Northern District of New York	N.D.N.Y.
Southern District of New York	S.D.N.Y.
Western District of New York	W.D.N.Y.

Court	Abbreviation
Eastern District of North Carolina	E.D.N.C.
Middle District of North Carolina	M.D.N.C.
Western District of North Carolina	W.D.N.C.
District of North Dakota	D.N.D.
District of the Northern Mariana Islands	D. N. Mar. I.
Northern District of Ohio	N.D. Ohio
Southern District of Ohio	S.D. Ohio
Eastern District of Oklahoma	E.D. Okla.
Northern District of Oklahoma	N.D. Okla.
Western District of Oklahoma	W.D. Okla.
District of Oregon	D. Or.
Eastern District of Pennsylvania	E.D. Pa.
Middle District of Pennsylvania	M.D. Pa.
Western District of Pennsylvania	W.D. Pa.
District of Puerto Rico	D.P.R.
District of Rhode Island	D.R.I.
District of South Carolina	D.S.C.
District of South Dakota	D.S.D.
Eastern District of Tennessee	E.D. Tenn.
Middle District of Tennessee	M.D. Tenn.
Western District of Tennessee	W.D. Tenn.
Eastern District of Texas	E.D. Tex.
Northern District of Texas	N.D. Tex.
Southern District of Texas	S.D. Tex.
Western District of Texas	W.D. Tex.
District of Utah	D. Utah
District of Vermont	D. Vt.
Eastern District of Virginia	E.D. Va.
Western District of Virginia	W.D. Va.
District of the Virgin Islands	D.V.I.
Eastern District of Washington	E.D. Wash.
Western District of Washington	W.D. Wash.
Northern District of West Virginia	N.D. W. Va.
Southern District of West Virginia	S.D. W. Va.
Eastern District of Wisconsin	E.D. Wis.
Western District of Wisconsin	W.D. Wis.
District of Wyoming	D. Wyo.
Military Courts	
Air Force Court of Criminal Appeals	A.F. Ct. Crim. App.
Armed Services Board of Contract Appeals	ASBCA
Army Court of Criminal Appeals	A. Ct. Crim. App.
Coast Guard Court of Criminal Appeals	C.G. Ct. Crim. App.
Court of Appeals for Veterans Claims	Vet. App.
• Was: Court of Veterans Appeals	Vet. App.

Court	Abbreviation
Navy–Marine Court of Criminal Appeals	N.–M. Ct. Crim. App.
United States Court of Appeals for the Armed Forces	C.A.A.F.
• Was: United States Court of Military Appeals	C.M.A.
Bankruptcy Courts	
Bankruptcy Appellate Panels	Examples
• Each United States Circuit Court of Appeals has a corresponding bankruptcy appellate panel. Insert "B.A.P." before the circuit court abbreviation.	B.A.P. 5th Cir. B.A.P. 8th Cir.
Bankruptcy Courts	
• Each United States District Court has a corresponding bankruptcy court. Insert "Bankr." before the district court abbreviation.	Bankr. N.D. Ala. Bankr. D. Mass.
Other Select Federal Courts and Boards of Special Jurisdiction	
Board of Contract Appeals	B.C.A.
Board of Immigration Appeals	B.I.A.
Board of Patent Appeals and Interferences	B.P.A.I.
Board of Tax Appeals	B.T.A.
Commerce Court	Comm. Ct.
Court of Claims	Ct. Cl.
Emergency Court of Appeals	Emer. Ct. App.
Foreign Intelligence Surveillance Court	FISA Ct.
Foreign Intelligence Surveillance Court of Review	FISA Ct. Rev.
Judicial Panel on Multidistrict Litigation	J.P.M.L.
Special Court, Regional Rail Reorganization Act	Reg'l Rail Reorg. Ct.
Temporary Emergency Court of Appeals	Temp. Emer. Ct. App.
Trademark Trial and Appeal Board	T.T.A.B.
United States Circuit Court [for specific district]	C.C. district court abbreviation
United States Claims Court	Cl. Ct.
United States Court of Customs and Patent Appeals	C.C.P.A.
United States Court of Customs Appeals (1910–1982)	Ct. Cust. App.
United States Court of Federal Claims	Fed. Cl.
United States Court of International Trade	Ct. Int'l Trade
United States Customs Court (1890–1980)	Cust. Ct.
United States Tax Court	T.C.

4(B) State Court Abbreviations

Appendix 4(B) lists abbreviations for each state's court of last resort, intermediate appellate courts, and trial courts of general jurisdiction. Required spaces are indicated by red triangles (▲). For courts not listed here, analogize to the entries here and consult **Appendix 4(C)** for additional abbreviations that may be applicable.

Court	Abbreviation
Alabama Supreme Court	Ala.
Alabama Court of Civil Appeals	Ala. Civ. App.
Alabama Court of Criminal Appeals	Ala. Crim. App.
Alabama Court of Appeals (through 1969)	Ala. Ct. App.
Alabama Circuit Court	Ala. Cir. Ct.

Court	Abbreviation
Alaska Supreme Court	Alaska
Alaska Court of Appeals	Alaska Ct. App.
Alaska Superior Court	Alaska Super. Ct.
Arizona Supreme Court	Ariz.
Arizona Court of Appeals	Ariz. Ct. App.
Arizona Tax Court	Ariz. Tax C.
Arizona Superior Court	Ariz. Super. Ct.
Arkansas Supreme Court	Ark.
Arkansas Court of Appeals	Ark. Ct. App.
Arkansas Circuit Court	Ark. Cir. Ct.
Arkansas Chancery Court (through 2001)	Ark. Ch. Ct.
California Supreme Court	Cal.
California Court of Appeal	Cal. Ct. App.
California District Court of Appeal	Cal. Dist. Ct. App.
California Superior Court Appellate Department	Cal. App. Dep't Super. Ct.
California Superior Court	Cal. Super. Ct.
Colorado Supreme Court	Colo.
Colorado Court of Appeals	Colo. App.
Colorado District Court	Colo. Dist. Ct.
Connecticut Supreme Court	Conn.
Connecticut Appellate Court	Conn. App. Ct.
Connecticut Superior Court	Conn. Super. Ct.
Connecticut District Court	Conn. Dist. Ct.
Connecticut Court of Common Pleas	Conn. C.P.
Connecticut Circuit Court	Conn. Cir. Ct.
Delaware Supreme Court	Del.
Delaware Court of Chancery	Del. Ch.
Delaware Superior Court	Del. Super. Ct.
Delaware Superior Court and Orphans' Court	Del. Super. Ct. & Orphans' Ct.
Delaware Family Court	Del. Fam. Ct.
District of Columbia Court of Appeals	D.C.
District of Columbia Superior Court	D.C. Super. Ct.
Florida Supreme Court	Fla.
Florida District Court of Appeal	Fla. Dist. Ct. App.
Florida Circuit Court	Fla. Cir. Ct.
Georgia Supreme Court	Ga.
Georgia Court of Appeals	Ga. Ct. App.
Georgia Superior Court	Ga. Super. Ct.
Hawaii Supreme Court	Haw.
Hawaii Intermediate Court of Appeals	Haw. Ct. App.
Hawaii Circuit Court	Haw. Cir. Ct.
Idaho Supreme Court	Idaho
Idaho Court of Appeals	Idaho Ct. App.
Idaho District Court	Idaho Dist. Ct.
Illinois Supreme Court	Ill.
Illinois Appellate Court	Ill. App. Ct.
Illinois Court of Claims	Ill. Ct. Cl.
Illinois Circuit Court	Ill. Cir. Ct.

Court	Abbreviation
Indiana Supreme Court	Ind.
Indiana Court of Appeals	Ind. Ct. App.
Indiana Tax Court	Ind. T.C.
Indiana Superior Court	Ind. Super. Ct.
Iowa Supreme Court	Iowa
Iowa Court of Appeals	Iowa Ct. App.
Iowa District Court	Iowa Dist. Ct.
Kansas Supreme Court	Kan.
Kansas Court of Appeals	Kan. Ct. App.
Kansas District Court	Kan. Dist. Ct.
Kentucky Supreme Court	Ky.
Kentucky Court of Appeals	Ky. Ct. App.
Kentucky Circuit Court	Ky. Cir. Ct.
Louisiana Supreme Court	La.
Louisiana Court of Appeal	La. Ct. App.
Louisiana District Court	La. Dist. Ct.
Maine Supreme Judicial Court	Me.
Maine Superior Court	Me. Super. Ct.
Maryland Court of Appeals	Md.
Maryland Court of Special Appeals	Md. Ct. Spec. App.
Maryland Circuit Court	Md. Cir. Ct.
Massachusetts Supreme Judicial Court	Mass.
Massachusetts Appeals Court	Mass. App. Ct.
Trial Court of the Commonwealth	Mass. Commw. Ct.
Massachusetts District Court	Mass. Dist. Ct.
Michigan Supreme Court	Mich.
Michigan Court of Appeals	Mich. Ct. App.
Michigan Court of Claims	Mich. Ct. Cl.
Michigan Circuit Court	Mich. Cir. Ct.
Minnesota Supreme Court	Minn.
Minnesota Court of Appeals	Minn. Ct. App.
Minnesota District Court	Minn. Dist. Ct.
Mississippi Supreme Court	Miss.
Mississippi Court of Appeals	Miss. Ct. App.
Mississippi Circuit Court	Miss. Cir. Ct.
Mississippi Chancery Court	Miss. Ch. Ct.
Missouri Supreme Court	Mo.
Missouri Court of Appeals	Mo. Ct. App.
Missouri Circuit Court	Mo. Cir. Ct.
Montana Supreme Court	Mont.
Montana District Court	Mont. Dist. Ct.
Nebraska Supreme Court	Neb.
Nebraska Court of Appeals	Neb. Ct. App.
Nebraska District Court	Neb. Dist. Ct.
Nevada Supreme Court	Nev.
Nevada District Court	Nev. Dist. Ct.
New Hampshire Supreme Court	N.H.
New Hampshire Superior Court	N.H. Super. Ct.

Court	Abbreviation
New Jersey Supreme Court	N.J.
New Jersey Superior Court, Appellate Division	N.J. Super. Ct. App. Div.
New Jersey Superior Court, Chancery Division	N.J. Super. Ct. Ch. Div.
New Jersey Superior Court, Law Division	N.J. Super. Ct. Law Div.
New Jersey Tax Court	N.J. Tax C.
New Jersey Court of Chancery	N.J. Ch.
New Jersey Prerogative Court	N.J. Prerog. Ct.
New Mexico Supreme Court	N.M.
New Mexico Court of Appeals	N.M. Ct. App.
New Mexico District Court	N.M. Dist. Ct.
New York Court of Appeals	N.Y.
New York Supreme Court, Appellate Division	N.Y. App. Div.
New York Supreme Court	N.Y. Sup. Ct.
New York Court of Claims	N.Y. Ct. Cl.
New York Civil Court	N.Y. Civ. Ct.
New York Criminal Court	N.Y. Crim. Ct.
New York Family Court	N.Y. Fam. Ct.
North Carolina Supreme Court	N.C.
North Carolina Court of Appeals	N.C. Ct. App.
North Carolina Superior Court	N.C. Super. Ct.
North Dakota Supreme Court	N.D.
North Dakota Court of Appeals	N.D. Ct. App.
North Dakota District Court	N.D. Dist. Ct.
Ohio Supreme Court	Ohio
Ohio Court of Appeals	Ohio Ct. App.
Ohio Court of Common Pleas	Ohio Ct. C.P.
Oklahoma Supreme Court	Okla.
Oklahoma Court of Criminal Appeals	Okla. Crim. App.
Oklahoma Court of Civil Appeals	Okla. Civ. App.
Oklahoma District Court	Okla. Dist. Ct.
Oregon Supreme Court	Or.
Oregon Court of Appeals	Or. Ct. App.
Oregon Tax Court	Or. T.C.
Oregon Circuit Court	Or. Cir. Ct.
Pennsylvania Supreme Court	Pa.
Pennsylvania Superior Court	Pa. Super. Ct.
Pennsylvania Commonwealth Court	Pa. Commw. Ct.
Pennsylvania District and County Court	Pa. Dist. & County Ct.
Rhode Island Supreme Court	R.I.
Rhode Island Superior Court	R.I. Super. Ct.
South Carolina Supreme Court	S.C.
South Carolina Court of Appeals	S.C. Ct. App.
South Carolina Circuit Court	S.C. Cir. Ct.
South Dakota Supreme Court	S.D.
South Dakota Circuit Court	S.D. Cir. Ct.
Tennessee Supreme Court	Tenn.
Tennessee Court of Appeals	Tenn. Ct. App.
Tennessee Court of Criminal Appeals	Tenn. Crim. App.
Tennessee Circuit Court	Tenn. Cir. Ct.
Tennessee Criminal Court	Tenn. Crim. Ct.
Tennessee Chancery Court	Tenn. Ch. Ct.

Court	Abbreviation
Texas Supreme Court	Tex.
Texas Court of Criminal Appeals	Tex. Crim. App.
Texas Court of Appeals	Tex. Ct. App.
Texas Commission of Appeals	Tex. Comm'n App.
Texas Courts of Appeals	Tex. App.
Texas Courts of Civil Appeals	Tex. Civ. App.
Texas District Court	Tex. Dist. Ct.
Texas Criminal District Court	Tex. Crim. Dist. Ct.
Utah Supreme Court	Utah
Utah Court of Appeals	Utah Ct. App.
Utah District Court	Utah Dist. Ct.
Vermont Supreme Court	Vt.
Vermont Superior Court	Vt. Super. Ct.
Vermont District Court	Vt. Dist. Ct.
Virginia Supreme Court	Va.
Virginia Court of Appeals	Va. Ct. App.
Virginia Circuit Court	Va. Cir. Ct.
Washington Supreme Court	Wash.
Washington Court of Appeals	Wash. Ct. App.
Washington Superior Court	Wash. Super. Ct.
West Virginia Supreme Court of Appeals	W. Va.
West Virginia Circuit Court	W. Va. Cir. Ct.
Wisconsin Supreme Court	Wis.
Wisconsin Court of Appeals	Wis. Ct. App.
Wisconsin Circuit Court	Wis. Cir. Ct.
Wyoming Supreme Court	Wyo.
Wyoming District Court	Wyo. Dist. Ct.

4(C) Other Abbreviations in Court Names

If the court deciding a case is not listed in **Appendix 1(A)**, **1(B)**, **4(A)**, or **4(B)**, you may use the following abbreviations to construct its name for the parenthetical described in **Rule 12.6**.

Word/Term	Abbreviation	Word/Term	Abbreviation
Administrative Court	Admin. Ct.	Children's Court	Child. Ct.
Admiralty	Adm.	Circuit Court (old federal)	C.C.
Aldermen's Court	Alder. Ct.	City Court	City Ct.
Appeal(s, late)	App.	Civil	Civ.
Bankruptcy [Court, Judge]	Bankr.	Civil Appeals	Civ. App.
Borough Court	Bor. Ct.	Civil Court of Record	Civ. Ct. Rec.
Central District	C.D.	Civil District Court	Civ. Dist. Ct.
Chancery	Ch.	Commerce Court	Comm. Ct.

Word/Term	Abbreviation
Commission	Comm'n
Common Pleas	C.P.
Commonwealth Court	Commw. Ct.
Conciliation Court	Concil. Ct.
County Court	Cnty. Ct.
County Judge's Court	Cnty. J. Ct.
Court	Ct.
Court of Appeal[s]	Ct. App.
Court of Civil Appeals	Civ. App.
Court of Common Pleas	Ct. Com. Pl.
Court of Errors and Appeals	Ct. Err. & App.
Court of [General, Special] Sessions	Ct. [Gen. or Spec.] Sess.
Court of Special Appeals	Ct. Spec. App.
Criminal Appeals	Crim. App.
Criminal District Court	Crim. Dist. Ct.
Department	Dep't
District Court (federal)	D.
District Court (state)	Dist. Ct.
District Court of Appeal[s]	Dist. Ct. App.
Division	Div.
Domestic Relations Court	Dom. Rel. Ct.
Eastern District	E.D.
Equity	Eq.
Errors	Err.
Estate	Est.
Family Court	Fam. Ct.
General	Gen.
High Court	High Ct.
Judicial District	Jud. Dist.
Judicial Division	Jud. Div.
Justice('s)	J.
Justice of the Peace's Court	J.P. Ct.
Juvenile Court	Juv. Ct.
Land Court	Land Ct.
Law Court	Law Ct.
Law Division	Law Div.
Magistrate	Magis.
Middle District	M.D.
Municipal	Mun.
Northern District	N.D.
Orphans' Court	Orphans' Ct.
Parish Court	Parish Ct.
Police Justice's Court	Police J. Ct.
Prerogative Court	Prerog. Ct.
Probate Court	Prob. Ct.
Public Utilities Commission	P.U.C.
Real Estate Commission	Real Est. Comm'n
Recorder's Court	Rec's Ct.
Regular	Reg.
Session(s)	Sess.
Southern District	S.D.
Special	Spec.
Superior Court	Super. Ct.
Supreme Court (other than U.S. Supreme Court)	Sup. Ct.
Supreme Court, Appellate Division	App. Div.
Supreme Court, Appellate Term	App. Term
Supreme Court of Errors	Sup. Ct. Err.
Supreme Judicial Court	Sup. Jud. Ct.
Surrogate's	Sur.
Tax Appeal Court	Tax App. Ct.
Tax Court	T.C.
Teen Court	Teen Ct.
Territor(ial, y)	Terr.
Traffic Court	Traffic Ct.
Tribal Court	Tribunal Ct.
Tribunal	Trib.
Water Court	Water Ct.
Western District	W.D.
Workers' Compensation	Workers' Comp.
Workmen's Compensation Division	Workmen's Comp. Div.
Youth Court	Youth Ct.

Appendix 5 Periodicals and Looseleaf Services

Appendix 5 contains two sets of abbreviations, one for titles of periodicals and one for words commonly used in titles of looseleaf services. To help you determine spacing in each abbreviation, each appendix uses the symbol ▲ to designate a required space. Omit this symbol when you type the abbreviation. Follow **Rule 2** to properly space abbreviations.

Appendix 5 is fully online so all law review students can more easily access full periodical abbreviations and to facilitate more timely revisions to periodical names. You can find it on the CasebookConnect platform for the ALWD Guide to Legal Citation, Seventh Edition, or on the book's product page under Student Resources or Professor Resources at https://www.wklegaledu.com/Williams-ALWDGuideLegalCitation7. If you discover that a periodical name has changed from the last update or there is a periodical that you think should be added, you may email the author at cvwilliams@email.arizona.edu. The most recent date of each **Appendix 5** update is noted online.

Appendix 6 Federal Taxation Materials

Appendix 6 addresses statutory, judicial, and administrative sources of federal taxation materials. Cite U.S. tax treaties and secondary sources relating to taxation — such as treatises, books, legal periodicals, and looseleaf services — using the rules for those sources set out elsewhere in the *ALWD Guide*.

This appendix is divided into the following sections and subsections:

6(A) Statutory Compilations

Title 26 of the *United States Code* contains the Internal Revenue Code ("I.R.C."). Tax courts and practitioners typically cite the Internal Revenue Code directly instead of using "26 U.S.C."[1] (Note: The Internal Revenue Code does not contain every federal tax statute. For example, Titles 11 and 28 contain some tax-related statutes; to cite these statutes, follow **Rule 14.2.**)

To cite a statute in Title 26, begin with the abbreviation I.R.C. followed by a section symbol, one space, and the section number.[2] When citing to an official or unofficial version of the I.R.C., including a date in a parenthetical at the end is optional.[3] See **Rule 14.2(f)** for more information about constructing a date parenthetical if you choose to include it. When citing an unofficial version of I.R.C., such as in the *United States Code Annotated* or the *United States Code Service*, add the publisher's name in a parenthetical at the end of the citation, followed by the volume's publication date, if choosing to include it.[4]

To cite a provision of the I.R.C. that is no longer in effect, enclose in an initial parenthetical the year of the I.R.C. version under which the section was promulgated. In a second parenthetical, indicate the year of repeal.[5] See **Sidebar A6.1** for additional information on versions of the Internal Revenue Code.

Examples

Official version:	I.R.C. § 165(g).
Unofficial version:	I.R.C. § 212 (West).
Repealed section:	I.R.C. § 275(c) (1939) (repealed 1954).

SIDEBAR A6.1 **Versions of the Internal Revenue Code**

The current Internal Revenue Code (I.R.C.) was enacted in 1986 and applies to transactions made after October 22, 1986. Other versions since 1900 were the I.R.C. of 1939 (applying to most transactions between January 1, 1939, and August 16, 1954) and the I.R.C. of 1954 (until the 1986 I.R.C. was enacted, applying to income tax transactions that occurred on or after January 1, 1954; to estate tax matters that occurred after August 16, 1954; and to gift tax transactions that occurred on or after January 1, 1955).

6(B) Tax Courts and Reporters

When the Commissioner of Internal Revenue is a party to a case, use the abbreviation "*Comm'r*" (omitting "of Internal Revenue") (**Rule 12.2(l)**).[6] (*Note:* In their writing, tax practitioners commonly prefer and use the spelled-out term "*Commissioner*.") Cite tax cases to official reporters where available, following **Rule 12.4**. Where one of these cases has subsequent history, follow **Rule 12.8**.[7] Consult **Rule 12.16** for short citation formats.[8] Cases cited to looseleaf services should add a parenthetical with the publisher's abbreviation (see **Chart 24.1**), as illustrated in several of the examples below.[9] Pinpoint references should reflect the subdivisions (pages, paragraph numbers) used by the reporter or service.[10]

Do not italicize case names in full citations used in academic writing; see **Rule 12.2(a)(2)**[FN].[11]

ACADEMIC FORMATTING

6(B)(1) Trial Courts Hearing Federal Tax Cases

▪ **United States District Courts**

Certain categories of tax cases fall under the jurisdiction of the United States District Courts. These cases were published in the *Federal Reporter* through 1931 and now are found in the *Federal Supplement*; cite cases to one of these reporters if therein. Unreported cases and cases of particular interest are often published by looseleaf services, such as *United States Tax Cases* (abbreviated "U.S.T.C." or "U.S. Tax Cas."), published by Commerce Clearing House ("CCH"), and *American Federal Tax Reports* ("A.F.T.R." and "A.F.T.R.2d"), published by Research Institute of America ("RIA"). Practitioners typically provide parallel citations to these services.

Example

LPCiminelli Interests, Inc. v. United States, 2012-2 U.S. Tax Cas. (CCH) ¶ 50,671, 110 A.F.T.R.2d (RIA) 2012-6631, 6633 (W.D.N.Y. 2012).

▪ **United States Tax Court (1942 to present)**

The United States Tax Court is a federal trial court specializing in tax disputes. It issues three types of decisions: Regular Decisions, Memorandum Decisions, and Summary Decisions. Prior to 1942, the court was known as the United States Board of Tax Appeals.

The Tax Court publishes its Regular Decisions in its official reporter, *Reports of the United States Tax Court* ("T.C."). Because no other court publishes its opinions in this reporter, omit the court abbreviation from the date parenthetical (see **Rule 12.6(a)**). The United States Tax Court website, https://ustaxcourt.gov, contains Regular Decisions beginning with those issued September 25, 1995; it contains opinions in published format beginning January 11, 2010. Cite opinions from this official website just as you would cite them in print.

Example

Weber v. Commissioner, 138 T.C. 348, 356 (2012).

Regular Decisions are also available in looseleaf reporters, such as *Tax Court Reports* ("Tax▲Ct.▲Rep."), published by Commerce Clearing House (CCH) and *Tax Court Reported Decisions* ("Tax▲Ct.▲Rep.▲Dec."), published by Research Institute of America (RIA). Include a parenthetical with the publisher abbreviation following the reporter abbreviation.[12]

Example

Estate of Saunders, Tax Ct. Rep. (CCH) 58,610 (2011).

Tax Court Memorandum Decisions ("T.C.M.")[13] typically involve the application of well-settled law to factual disputes. Memorandum Decisions are not officially reported, but they may be obtained from the United States Tax Court website, http://ustaxcourt.gov (beginning with cases decided September 25, 1995). Cite opinions from the website just as you would cite them in print, using the opinion abbreviation, the case number, and a date parenthetical. Unofficial versions are published by CCH, Prentice-Hall (P-H) (before April 15, 1991), and RIA (after April 15, 1991).[14]

Examples

Leyshon v. Commissioner, T.C.M. (RIA) 2012-248 (2012).

Leyshon v. Comm'r, 104 T.C.M. (CCH) 243 (2012).

Tax Court Summary Opinions ("T.C.▲Summ.▲Op.") are non-precedential opinions from the small case division; the taxpayer can elect this division for controversies valued at $50,000 or less. Summary Opinions (beginning January 10, 2001) are also available on the Tax Court's website, http://www.ustaxcourt.gov. When citing a Tax Court Summary Opinion, provide a parallel citation to a looseleaf service, website, or commercial database. Cite it the same as its print counterpart, using the opinion abbreviation and the case number; depending on the source, the parallel citation should follow the format set out in **Rules 12.14(b)**, **24**, **31**, or **32**.

Example

Sjoberg v. Comm'r, T.C. Summ. Op. 2008-162, 2008 Tax Ct. Summary LEXIS 160 (Dec. 23, 2008).

▪ **United States Board of Tax Appeals (1924–1942)**

The United States Board of Tax Appeals was the predecessor of the United States Tax Court. Its official reporter is *United States Board of Tax Appeals Reports* ("B.T.A.").[15] Widely used unofficial reporters are *Board of Tax Appeals Service* ("B.T.A. Serv. (CCH)") and *Board of Tax Appeals Memorandum Decisions* ("B.T.A. Mem. Dec. (P-H)").

Examples

Am. Cigar Co. v. Comm'r, 21 B.T.A. 464 (1930).

Standard Oil Co. v. Comm'r, 43 B.T.A. 973, 998 (1941), *aff'd*, 129 F.2d 363 (7th Cir. 1942).

Martin Wunderlich Co. v. Comm'r, 1952 B.T.A. Mem. Dec. (P-H) ¶ 52,029, at 52-96 (1952).

▪ **United States Court of Federal Claims (Oct. 29, 1992 to present)**

The official reporter is the *Federal Claims Reporter* ("Fed. Cl.").[16] Unofficial reporters for the court are *American Federal Tax Reports* ("A.F.T.R.," "A.F.T.R.2d") and *United States Tax Cases* ("U.S.T.C." or "U.S. Tax Cas."). Omit the court abbreviation when citing the official reporter. If citing an unofficial reporter, enclose the publisher's abbreviation in parentheses after the reporter abbreviation.

Examples

Pereira v. United States, 84 Fed. Cl. 597, 600 (2008).

BP Expl. & Oil, Inc. v. United States, 2000-1 U.S.T.C. (CCH) ¶ 50,460, at 84,493 (Fed. Cl. 2000).

▪ **United States Claims Court (1982–Oct. 28, 1992)**

The United States Claims Court preceded the United States Court of Federal Claims. The official reporter is the *United States Claims Court Reporter* ("Cl. Ct.").[17] Unofficial reporters include *American Federal Tax Reports* ("A.F.T.R.," "A.F.T.R.2d") and *United States Tax Cases* ("U.S.T.C." or "U.S. Tax Cas."). Omit the court abbreviation when citing the official reporter. If citing an unofficial reporter, enclose the publisher's abbreviation in parentheses after the reporter abbreviation.

SIDEBAR A6.2 Case Names in Older Tax Authorities

Some sources use the administrative style of the case — the plaintiff's full name in place of the adversarial case name. In these situations, it is preferable to convert the case name to an adversarial style, such as the hypothetical *Plaintiff v. Comm'r.*

Examples

Shook v. United States, 26 Cl. Ct. 1477, 1478 (1992).

Kircher v. United States, 61 A.F.T.R.2d (RIA) 88-1182, 88-1183 (Cl. Ct. 1988).

▪ **Court of Claims (1855–1982)**

This court of original jurisdiction preceded the United States Claims Court. Its official reporter is *Court of Claims Reports* ("Ct. ▲ Cl.").[18] Some of its cases were also published in the *Federal Reporter* and the *Federal Supplement*.[19] The unofficial reporter is *United States Tax Cases* ("U.S.T.C." or "U.S. ▲ Tax ▲ Cas."). Omit the court abbreviation when citing the official reporter.

Example

Henry v. United States, 139 Ct. Cl. 362 (1957).

6(B)(2) Appellate Courts for Federal Tax Cases

Decisions of United States District Courts and the United States Tax Court are appealed to the appropriate United States Court of Appeals — whose cases are reported in the *Federal Reporter* and may ultimately receive review by the United States Supreme Court. Cases from the circuit courts of appeal and Supreme Court cases are unofficially reported in *American Federal Tax Reports* ("A.F.T.R.," "A.F.T.R.2d")[20] and *United States Tax Cases* ("U.S.T.C." or "U.S. ▲ Tax ▲ Cas."). When citing a United States Supreme Court case to one of these unofficial reporters, add the court abbreviation ("U.S.") to the date parenthetical.

Examples

Comm'r v. Simmons, 646 F.3d 6 (D.C. Cir. 2011).

Grogan v. Garner, 70 A.F.T.R.2d 92-5639, 92-5640 (U.S. 1991).

Crisp v. United States, 2002-2 U.S.T.C. ¶ 50,765, at 85,791 (9th Cir. 2000).

6(B)(3) Unreported Opinions

To cite unreported opinions available only in a separately paginated slip opinion, refer to **Rule 12.12**.[21] Use **Rule 12.14(b)** to cite a case that is unreported but available on an electronic database such as Bloomberg Law, Lexis+, or Westlaw Edge.[22]

6(C) Administrative Materials

6(C)(1) Administrative Announcements

Treasury Regulations ("Treas. Reg.") are published in the *Federal Register* and codified in Title 26 of the *Code of Federal Regulations*.[23] These regulations have their own form of citation; do not refer to C.F.R. Begin with the abbreviation "Treas. Reg." followed by a section symbol, the section number, and in parentheses, the year of the regulation's promulgation.[24] If the regulation was amended, give the year of the last amendment instead.[25] For temporary regulations, add the abbreviation "Temp." before "Treas. Reg."[26] For proposed treasury regulations, add the abbreviation "Prop." and use the exact date of the regulation's proposal;[27] if possible, add a parallel citation to their publication in the *Federal Register* (**Rule 18.3**).[28]

Examples

Treas. Reg. § 1.409A-1(b)(4) (2007).

Temp. Treas. Reg. § 1.482 (2006).

Prop. Treas. Reg. § 301.7701-2(a), 4 Fed. Reg. 75,709 (Apr. 4, 2008).

6(C)(2) I.R.S. Compilations

The *Internal Revenue Bulletin* ("I.R.B.") is a weekly publication containing I.R.S. pronouncements such as Revenue Rulings, Revenue Procedures, Treasury Decisions, Notices, and Announcements. Until 2008, it served as the advance sheet for the *Cumulative Bulletin* (for more on the *Cumulative Bulletin*, see below). Although the I.R.S. ceased publishing the *Internal Revenue Bulletin* in print in March 2013, issues are available online at https://apps.irs.gov/app/picklist/list/internalRevenueBulletins.html. Each issue is numbered sequentially by year and week of issue, separated by a hyphen. Provide an initial page number, and if appropriate, a pinpoint page number.[29]

Examples

I.R.S. Notice 2012-31, 2012-20 I.R.B. 906, 908–09.

I.R.S. Ann. 2009-53, 2009-25 I.R.B. 1107.

Until 2008, contents of the weekly I.R.B. were consolidated semiannually into a permanent and indexed *Cumulative Bulletin*. A citation to the *Cumulative Bulletin* ("C.B.") begins with its volume number (composed of the year, a hyphen, and the compilation number (usually 1 or 2)), followed by its abbreviation, the initial page, and if relevant, a pinpoint page number.[30]

Examples

Rev. Proc. 92-59, 1992-2 C.B. 411.

Rev. Rul. 74-330, 1974-2 C.B. 278.

6(C)(3) Officially Published I.R.S. Pronouncements

Cite an I.R.S. Announcement ("I.R.S. Ann.") by year and number of issue, separated by a hyphen. If the announcement was published prior to 2000, use only the last two digits of the year. Provide a parallel citation to C.B. or I.R.B. You may use an announcement's title as the first component of the citation.

Examples

I.R.S. Ann. 2013-12, 2013-11 I.R.B. 651.

Mutual Agreement on U.K. Pension Arrangements, I.R.S. Ann. 2005-30, 2005-18 I.R.B. 988.

The I.R.S. reviews tax decisions made by the courts and issues its own opinion about whether it agrees with the decision. The opinion is published as either an acquiescence (*acq.*,), meaning that the I.R.S. will not contest the point in later cases; an acquiescence in result (*acq. in result*,), in which the I.R.S. agrees with the result of the decision, but disagrees with one or more stated reasons; or a nonacquiescence (*nonacq.*,), meaning that the I.R.S. will not appeal but will not follow the decision with other taxpayers.[31] Nonacquiescence and either form of acquiescence may be indicated.[32] Append the acquiescence information to the case citation, using the relevant abbreviation, followed by a comma and a citation to the opinion in C.B. or I.R.B.[33]

Examples

Dean v. Comm'r, 35 T.C. 1083 (1961), *nonacq.*, 1973-2 C.B. 4.

Lemmen v. Comm'r, 77 T.C. 1326, 1348 (1981), *acq.*, 1983-1 C.B. 1.

Cite a Delegation Order ("I.R.S. Deleg. Order") by order number and, when available, revision number ("Rev.").[34] Provide a parallel citation to C.B., I.R.B., the *Internal Revenue Manual* ("I.R.M."), or the *Federal Register*.[35]

Examples

I.R.S. Deleg. Order 42 (Rev. 12), 1979-2 C.B. 482.

I.R.S. Deleg. Order 5 (Rev. 18), 2000-51 I.R.B. 587.

Cite an I.R.S. Notice ("I.R.S. Notice"), Revenue Procedure ("Rev. Proc."), or Revenue Ruling ("Rev. Rul.") by year and sequential number of issue, separated by a hyphen.[36] If published prior to 2000, use only the last two digits of the year. Provide a parallel citation to C.B. or I.R.B.[37] It is appropriate to include the title of an I.R.S. Notice in its citation.[38]

Examples

I.R.S. Notice 2009-21, 2009-13 I.R.B. 724.

Weighted Average Interest Rate Update, I.R.S. Notice 99-7, 1999-1 C.B. 351.

Rev. Proc. 99-25, 1999-1 C.B. 1117.

Rev. Rul. 2004-52, 2004-1 C.B. 973.

Treasury Decisions ("T.D.") are proposed and final treasury regulations pertaining to tax matters, issued by the Secretary of the Treasury. Proposed regulations are identified by the prefix "REG," followed by a project number. Provide a parallel citation to I.R.B., C.B., *Treasury Decisions Under Internal Revenue Laws* (Treas. Dec. Int. Rev.), or the *Federal Register*.[39]

Examples

REG-112815-12, 2013-35 I.R.B. 162.

T.D. 4723, 34 Treas. Dec. Int. Rev. 4 (1937).

Cite a Treasury Directive ("Treas. Dir.") or Treasury Order ("Treas. Order") by number and provide a parallel citation to C.B. or I.R.B.[40]

Examples

Treas. Dir. 15-42, 1995-41 I.R.B. 32.

Treas. Order 150-02, 1994-1 C.B. 721.

6(C)(4) Taxpayer Forms and Publications

Cite Taxpayer Forms ("I.R.S. Form") by number. For forms that are issued or revised annually, enclose the year in parentheses. For forms that are not issued or revised annually, enclose the date of last revision in parentheses, preceded by the term "last rev." Current and prior forms are available on the I.R.S. website at https://www.irs.gov/forms-pubs.

Examples

I.R.S. Form 1040 (2008).

I.R.S. Form 1040 sched. R (2009).

I.R.S. Form 1000 (last rev. Dec. 2005).

Cite a Taxpayer Publication ("I.R.S. Pub.") by italicized title, I.R.S. publication number, pinpoint page if available, and year of publication.

Examples

Farmer's Tax Guide, I.R.S. Pub. No. 225, at 19 (2012).

6(C)(5) Other I.R.S. and Treasury Materials

General Counsel Memoranda ("I.R.S. Gen. Couns. Mem.") are numbered sequentially but without reference to the year of issue; enclose the exact date of issue in parentheses.[41]

Example

I.R.S. Gen. Couns. Mem. 39,892 (Nov. 26, 2002), 2002 IRS GCM LEXIS 1.

The *Internal Revenue Manual* ("I.R.M.") is cited in decimal format. The first digit is the part number, the second number is the chapter number, the third number is the section number, and the fourth number is the subsection number. Sub-subsections are set off by an additional decimal. If citing the official version published by the I.R.S., enclose the year of issue in parentheses. If citing an unofficial version, add the publisher and the year of publication.

Examples

I.R.M. 5.7.5 (1996).

I.R.M. 5.7.5.4 (RIA 2001).

Cite a News Release ("I.R.S.▲News▲Release") by year and sequential release number, separated by a hyphen; enclose the exact date in parentheses.[42] It is appropriate to include the title of the release in italics and to provide a parallel citation to an electronic database, website, or looseleaf service.

Example

I.R.S. News Release 2009-77 (Aug. 25, 2009).

Cite a Private Letter Ruling ("I.R.S.▲Priv.▲Ltr.▲Rul.") by year (two- or four-digit, depending on whether it was issued before 2000) followed by a hyphen, the week of release followed by a hyphen, and the three-digit sequential item number for the week; enclose the exact date of issue in parentheses.[43] It is appropriate to provide a parallel citation to an electronic database, website, or looseleaf service.

Examples

I.R.S. Priv. Ltr. Rul. 90-31-022 (May 7, 1990).

I.R.S. Priv. Ltr. Rul. 2005-29-001 (July 22, 2005), 2005 WL 1707488.

Cite a Technical Advice Memorandum ("I.R.S.▲Tech.▲Adv.▲Mem.") by year (two- or four-digit, depending on whether it was issued before 2000) followed by a hyphen, the week of release followed by a hyphen, and the three-digit sequential item number for the week; enclose the exact date of issue in parentheses.[44]

Example

I.R.S. Tech. Adv. Mem. 87-14-008 (Dec. 17, 1986).

Appendix 7 Federal Administrative Agencies and Publications

Appendix 7 lists major official federal administrative publications and their abbreviations. For tax sources, use **Appendix 6**. Required spaces are indicated by red triangles (▲).

7(A) Selected Official Federal Administrative and Executive Reporters and Publications

Reporter/Publication	Abbreviation
Administrative Decisions Under Immigration and Nationality Laws	I. & N. Dec.
Agriculture Decisions	Agric. Dec.
Atomic Energy Commission Reports	A.E.C.
Board of Contract Appeals Decisions	B.C.A.
Civil Aeronautics Board Reports	C.A.B.
Copyright Decisions	Copy. Dec.
Cumulative Bulletin	C.B.
Customs Bulletin and Decisions	Cust. B. & Dec.
Daily Compilation of Presidential Documents	Daily Comp. Pres. Doc.
Decisions and Orders of the National Labor Relations Board	N.L.R.B.
Decisions of the Commissioner of Patents	Dec. Comm'r Pat.
Decisions of the Comptroller General of the United States	Comp. Gen.
Decisions of the Department of the Interior	Interior Dec.
Decisions of the Department of the Interior and General Land Office in Cases Relating to Public Lands	Pub. Lands Dec.
Decisions of the Federal Labor Relations Authority	F.L.R.A.
Decisions of the National Mediation Board	N.M.B.
Decisions of the United States Merit Systems Protection Board	M.S.P.B.
Environmental Administrative Decisions	E.A.D.
Equal Opportunity Employment Commission Decisions	E.E.O.C. Dec.
Federal Communications Commission Reports	F.C.C., F.C.C.2d
Federal Energy Guidelines: FERC Reports	FERC
Federal Maritime Commission Reports	F.M.C.
Federal Mine Safety and Health Review Commission Decisions	FMSHRC
Federal Power Commission Reports	F.P.C.
Federal Service Impasses Panel Releases	Fed. Serv. Imp. Pan. Rels.
Federal Trade Commission Decisions	F.T.C.
Interior and General Land Office Cases Relating to Public Lands	Pub. Lands Dec.
Interior Decisions	Interior Dec.
Interstate Commerce Commission, Motor Carrier Cases	M.C.C.
Interstate Commerce Commission Reporter	I.C.C., I.C.C.2d
Manual of Patent Examining Procedure	MPEP
National Transportation Safety Board Decisions	N.T.S.B.
Nuclear Regulatory Commission Issuances	N.R.C.
Ocean Resources and Wildlife Reporter	O.R.W.
Official Gazette of the United States Patent Office	Off. Gaz. Pat. Office
Official Gazette of the United States Patent and Trademark Office	Off. Gaz. Pat. & Trademark Office
Opinions of the Attorneys General	Op. Att'y Gen.
Opinions of the Office of Legal Counsel of the Department of Justice	Op. O.L.C.
Public Papers of the Presidents	Pub. Papers

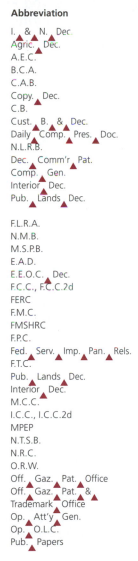

Reporter/Publication	Abbreviation
Securities and Exchange Commission Decisions and Reports	S.E.C.
Social Security Rulings, Cumulative Edition	S.S.R. Cum. Ed.
Surface Transportation Board Reporter	S.T.B.
Trademark Manual of Examining Procedure	TMEP
Trademark Trial and Appeal Board Manual of Procedure	TBMP
Weekly Compilation of Presidential Documents	Weekly Comp. Pres. Doc.

7(B) Selected Federal Agency Abbreviations and Acronyms

Agency	Abbreviation
Armed Services Board of Contract Appeals	ASBCA
Benefits Review Board	Ben. Rev. Bd.
Board of Patent Appeals and Interferences	B.P.A.I.
Civilian Board of Contract Appeals	CBCA
Commodity Futures Trading Commission	CFTC
Consumer Financial Protection Bureau	CFPB
Department of Agriculture	USDA
Department of Commerce, National Oceanic and Atmospheric Administration	NOAA
Department of Commerce, Patent and Trademark Office	USPTO
Department of Defense	DOD
Department of Education	ED
Department of Energy	DOE
Department of the Interior	DOI
Department of Justice	DOJ
Department of Labor	Dep't of Labor *or* DOL
Department of State	Dep't of State
Environmental Appeals Board	EAB
Environmental Protection Agency	EPA
Equal Employment Opportunity Commission	EEOC
Federal Aviation Administration	FAA
Federal Bureau of Investigation	FBI
Federal Communications Commission	FCC
Federal Energy Regulatory Commission	FERC
Federal Labor Relations Authority	FLRA
Federal Mine Safety and Health Review Commission	FMSHRC
Federal Trade Commission	FTC
Government Accountability Office	GAO
Interior Board of Contract Appeals	IBCA
Interior Board of Indian Appeals	IBIA
Interior Board of Land Appeals	IBLA
International Trade Commission	USITC
Interstate Commerce Commission	ICC
Merit Systems Protection Board	MSPB
National Labor Relations Board	NLRB
National Mediation Board	NMB
National Transportation Safety Board	NTSB
Nuclear Regulatory Commission	NRC

Agency	Abbreviation
Occupational Safety and Health Review Commission	OSHRC
Office of Dispute Resolution for Acquisition	ODRA
Securities and Exchange Commission	SEC
Small Business Administration	SBA
Social Security Administration	SSA
Surface Transportation Board	STB

Appendix 8 Cross-References for Law Reviews

Some law reviews and journals require their staff writers and editors to include a *Bluebook* rule when suggesting changes to an article. Now, with **Appendix 8**, they can rely exclusively on the *ALWD Guide* for this purpose. Using reference numbers in **Parts 1–5** and **Appendix 6**, **Appendix 8** accurately correlates information in the text of the *ALWD Guide* with the corresponding rules from *The Bluebook: A Uniform System of Citation* (Columbia Law Review Ass'n et al. eds., 21st ed. 2020). For example, in **Part 1**, **Rule 1** of the *ALWD Guide*, reference number seven ([7]) is at the end of the first sentence under **Rule 1.3(d)**; it refers to the number seven in the list under **Part 1**, **Rule 1** (the first section) of this appendix, where you'll find the corresponding *Bluebook* rule cite: [7] 2.1(a). Thus, the information in the first sentence under **Rule 1.3(d)** of the *ALWD Guide* correlates to the information in *The Bluebook* under **Rule 2.1(a)**.

Because the references in **Appendix 8** are all to one source, they are not set up like typical citations. **Appendix 8** does not use *id.* Note that only the pinpoint reference is listed next to the reference number, not the entire *Bluebook* citation. And the callouts begin again at "[1]" when starting a new rule in the *ALWD Guide*. When a signal precedes a pinpoint reference, however, it means the same as the signals in **Chart 35.1** of the *ALWD Guide*. For instance, when "*see*" precedes the pinpoint reference, the twenty-first edition of *The Bluebook* gives only implicit support for the stated proposition — usually in the form of an example at that pinpoint reference — rather than explaining the citation rule clearly or plainly. Also, if there are nonconsecutive pinpoint references for a reference number, they are separated by a comma if there is no intervening signal.

You will find that many rules, sidebars, charts, and other parts of the *ALWD Guide* do not have a callout. Occasionally, a callout isn't necessary because the information would not cause a law review staff writer to make a change. Much more commonly, though, no callout indicates that the twenty-first edition of *The Bluebook* does not contain that information — it is silent on how to treat a particular source or does not explain the background of a legal source. In those instances, the *ALWD Guide* fills the gaps that would likely frustrate or confuse legal writers.

Part 1

Rule 1

[1] 2.

[2] *See* B2, 2.2.

[3] *See* B2.

[4] *See* B2.

[5] 2.1(f).

[6] 2.2(c).

[7] 2.1(a).

[8] *See* 2.1(a).

[9] 5.2(d)(i).

[10] 5.2(d)(iii).

[11] 7(b).

[12] *See* 2, 2.1(c)–(d); *see also* 2.2(a).

[13] *See* B2.

[14] *See* 2.2(a).

[15] *See* 1.1.

Rule 2

[1] 6.1(b)
[2] *See* 6.2(b).
[3] 6.1(a).
[4] 6.1(a).
[5] 6.1(a).
[6] 6.1(a).
[7] 6.2(c).
[8] *See* 3.3(b)–(c).
[9] B6.
[10] 10.2.
[11] 10.2.1(c).
[12] 10.2.1(c).
[13] *See* 8(c)(ii).

Rule 3

[1] *See* 5.2(c).
[2] *See* 8(a).
[3] *See* 8(c)(i).
[4] *See* 8(c)(i).
[5] *See also* 8(c)(ii).

Rule 4

[1] 6.2(a)(vii).
[2] 6.2(a)(vii).
[3] *See, e.g.*, 10.1, 10.5(c), 15.1(b), 16.4, 16.7.1(b)–(c).
[4] 6.2(a).
[5] 6.2(a)(iv).
[6] 6.2(a)(iii).
[7] 6.2(a)(i).
[8] 6.2(c).
[9] *See* B3, 3.1(a).
[10] 6.2(b)(i).
[11] 6.2(b)(ii).
[12] 6.2(b)(ii).

Rule 5

[1] *See* 10, 16.
[2] *See* 15.
[3] 3.2(a).
[4] 3.2(a).
[5] 3.2(a).
[6] 3.2(a).
[7] 3.2(a), 3.3(b).
[8] 3.2(a).
[9] 3.2(a).
[10] *See* 3.2(a).
[11] 3.2(a).
[12] 15.8(b).
[13] *See* 10.8.1(a).
[14] *See* 10.8.1.
[15] *See* 15.8(b).
[16] B10.1.2; *see also* 3.2(a).

Rule 6

[1] *See* 3.3, 6.2(c).
[2] 3.3(b)–(c).
[3] *See* 3.3.
[4] 3.3(d).
[5] 6.2(c).
[6] *See* 3.3.
[7] *See* 3.3(b)–(c).
[8] *See* 3.3(b).
[9] 3.3(a).
[10] 3.3.
[11] 3.3(b)–(c).
[12] 3.3(b)–(c).
[13] 3.3(b).
[14] 3.3(b).
[15] 3.3(b)–(c).
[16] 3.3(b)–(c).
[17] 3.3(b)–(c).
[18] 3.3.
[19] 3.3.
[20] 3.3.
[21] 3.3.
[22] 6.2(c).
[23] 6.2(c).
[24] 6.2(c).

Rule 7

[1] 3.2(b).
[2] 3.2(c).
[3] 3.2(b)–(c).
[4] 3.2(b).
[5] 3.2(b).
[6] 3.2(b).
[7] *See* 3.2(b).
[8] 3.2(b).
[9] *See* 3.2(b).
[10] 3.2(b).

Rule 8

[1] 3.1(c).
[2] 3.1(c).

Rule 9

[1] 3.2(d).
[2] 3.2(d).
[3] 3.2(d).
[4] 3.4.
[5] *See* 3.4.

Rule 10

[1] 3.5.
[2] 3.5.
[3] 3.5.

Rule 11

[1] 10.9, 12.10(b), 13.8(c), 14.5(c).
[2] *See* 4.2, 15.10, 16.9, 17.6, 18.9.
[3] *See* 4.1.
[4] *See* 4.1.
[5] 4.1.
[6] *See* 4.1.
[7] 4.1.
[8] 4.1.
[9] *See* 4.1.
[10] 4.1.
[11] *See* 4.1.
[12] *See* 4.1.
[13] 4.1; 15.10.1.
[14] 4.1.
[15] *See* 4.2(a).
[16] 4.2 and B4.
[17] 4.2(a).
[18] *See* 4.2(a).
[19] 4.2.
[20] *See* 4.2(a).
[21] 4.2(b).
[22] 4.2(b).
[23] 4.2(b).
[24] 4.2(b).

Part 2

Rule 12

[1] B10.1, 10.
[2] 10.2.1.
[3] *See* B10.
[4] B10, 2.2(a)(i), 2.2(b)(i).
[5] B10.1.1(v).
[6] 2.1(a).
[7] 2.1(a).
[8] B10.1.1(v).
[9] 10.2.1(a).

[10] 10.2.1(a).
[11] *See* 10.2.
[12] 10.2.1(a).
[13] *See* B10.1.1(i).
[14] 10.2.1(a).
[15] 10.2.1(a).
[16] 10.2.1.
[17] 10.2.1(a).
[18] 10.2.1(e).
[19] 10.2.1(g).
[20] 10.2.1(g).
[21] *See* 10.2.1(g).
[22] *See* 10.2.1(a).
[23] 10.2.1(a).
[24] *See* 10.2.1(a).
[25] 10.2.1(b).
[26] 10.2.1(g).
[27] 10.2.1(g).
[28] *See* 10.2.1(g).
[29] B10.1.1(ii), 10.2.1(g).
[30] 10.2.1.
[31] 10.2.1(g).
[32] 10.2.1(h).
[33] 10.2.1(d).
[34] *See* 10.2.1(a).
[35] 10.2.2.
[36] T6.
[37] 10.2.2, T6.
[38] 6.1(b).
[39] 6.1(b); 10.2.1(c).
[40] 6.1(b); *see* 10.2.1(c).
[41] *See* 6.1(b), 10.2.1(c), T6.
[42] 10.2.2.
[43] 6.1(b).
[44] 10.2.1(f).
[45] 10.2.1(f).
[46] 10.2.1(f).
[47] 10.2.1(f).
[48] 10.2.1(f).
[49] 10.2.1(i).
[50] 10.2.1(i)(i).
[51] 10.2.1(i)(iv).
[52] 10.2.1(i)(ii).
[53] 10.2.2; *see* 6.1(b).
[54] 10.2.1(f).
[55] *See* 10.2.2; 6.1(b).
[56] 10.2.1(f).
[57] 10.2.1(f).
[58] 10.2.1(d).
[59] 10.2.1(f).
[60] 10.2.1(f).
[61] *See generally* 10.2.1.
[62] 10.2.2.
[63] 10.2.1(f).
[64] 6.1(b).
[65] 10.2.1(j).
[66] 10.2.1(a).
[67] 10.2.1(a).
[68] *See* 10.2.1(a).
[69] 10.2.2.
[70] 10.2.1(b).
[71] *See* 10.2.1(b).
[72] 10.2.1(b).
[73] 10.2.1(b).
[74] 10.2.1(b).
[75] 10.2.1(a).
[76] 10.2.1(a).
[77] 10.2.1(a).
[78] *See* 10.2.1(k).
[79] 10.2.1(k).
[80] 10.2.1(k).
[81] 10.2.1(k).
[82] 10.2.1(d).
[83] 10.2.1(d).
[84] *See* 10.2.1(k).
[85] 10.2.1(k), 4.2(b).
[86] 10.2.1(k).
[87] B10.1.2, 10.3.2.
[88] 10.3.2.
[89] *See* T1.
[90] 6.1(a).
[91] 6.1(a).
[92] 10.3.1(a).
[93] *See* T1.1, T1.3.
[94] *See* T1.1, T1.3.
[95] 10.3.1(a).
[96] 10.3.1(a).
[97] *See* 10.3.1(b).
[98] T1.1.
[99] T1.1.
[100] 10.3.2.
[101] 10.3.2.
[102] 10.3.2.
[103] 10.3.2.
[104] T1.1.
[105] *See* 10.3.1, 10.3.1(b), T1.3.
[106] *See* 10.3.1(a).
[107] 10.3.1(b).
[108] 10.3.1(a).
[109] 10.3.1(a).
[110] 10.3.1(b).
[111] 10.3.1(a)–(b).
[112] B10.1.2.
[113] 10.
[114] B10.1.3.
[115] B10.1.2.

[116] B10.1.2., 3.2(a).

[117] 6.2(a); *see, e.g.*, 10.1, 10.5(c).

[118] 10.3.3.

[119] *See* 10.3.1(b).

[120] *See* 10.3.1(b).

[121] 10.4.

[122] 10.4; *see* T1.1, T1.3.

[123] *See* 10.4.

[124] 10.4(b).

[125] 10.4(a).

[126] 10.4(a).

[127] *See* 10.4(a).

[128] *See* 10.4(a).

[129] 10.4(a).

[130] 10.8.2.

[131] 10.8.2.

[132] 10.8.2.

[133] 10.4(a).

[134] 10.4(a).

[135] 10.4(b).

[136] 10.4(b).

[137] 10.4(b).

[138] *See* 10.4(b).

[139] 10.4(b).

[140] 10.5(a); *see* 10.

[141] 10.5(a), (b).

[142] 10.5(b).

[143] 10.7.

[144] *See* T8.

[145] T8.

[146] T8.

[147] 10.7.1(b).

[148] 10.7.

[149] 10.7.

[150] 10.7.

[151] 10.7.

[152] *See* 10.7.

[153] *See* 10.7.

[154] *See* 10.7, T8.

[155] 10.7.1(a).

[156] 10.7.2.

[157] 10.7.1(a)

[158] 10.7.1(d).

[159] *See* 10.7.

[160] *See* 10.7.

[161] 10.7.

[162] 10.7.

[163] 10.5(d).

[164] 10.5(d).

[165] 10.7.2(a).

[166] 10.7.2(a).

[167] 10.7.2(a).

[168] 10.7.2(c).

[169] 10.7.2(c).

[170] 10.7.2(c).

[171] 10.7.1(c).

[172] 10.7.1(c)(i).

[173] 10.7.1(c)(ii).

[174] 10.7.1(c)(iii).

[175] 10.7.1(c)(iii).

[176] 10.7.1(c)(iii).

[177] 1.5(a).

[178] 1.5(b).

[179] 1.5(b).

[180] 10.7.

[181] 10.7.1(a).

[182] 10.7.1(a).

[183] 10.7.1(a).

[184] 10.6.1(a).

[185] 10.6.1(a).

[186] 10.6.1(a).

[187] *See* 10.6.1(a).

[188] 10.6.1(b).

[189] 10.6.1(b).

[190] 10.6.1(a); 10.9(b)(i).

[191] 9; *see* 10.6.1(a).

[192] 9(a).

[193] 10.6.1(a).

[194] 10.6.2.

[195] 10.6.2.

[196] 10.6.2.

[197] 10.6.2.

[198] 10.6.2.

[199] *See* 10.6.1(a), 10.6.2.

[200] 10.9(b)(i).

[201] 10.9(b)(i).

[202] 10.9(b)(i).

[203] 10.3.3.

[204] 10.3.3.

[205] *See* 10.3.3.

[206] 10.3.3.

[207] 10.3.3.

[208] 10.3.3.

[209] 10.3.3.

[210] *See* 10.3.3.

[211] 10.8.1(b).

[212] *See* 10.8.1(b).

[213] *See* 10.8.1(b).

[214] *See* 10.8.1(b).

[215] *See* 10.8.1(b).

[216] *See* 10.8.1(b).

[217] 10.8.1(b).

[218] B10.1.4(iii).

[219] *See* 10.5(b).

[220] 10.8.1(a).
[221] 10.8.1(a).
[222] 10.8.1(a).
[223] *See* 10.8.1(a).
[224] *See* 10.8.1(a).
[225] 10.8.1(c).
[226] 10.8.1(c), 18.2.2.
[227] 3.3.
[228] 10.8.3.
[229] 10.8.3.
[230] 10.8.3.
[231] 10.8.3.
[232] 10.8.3.
[233] 10.8.1(a).
[234] 10.8.3.
[235] 10.8.3.
[236] 10.8.3.
[237] 10.8.3.
[238] 10.8.3.
[239] 10.8.3.
[240] B4, 4.1.
[241] 10.8.3.
[242] 4.1; *see* 10.9(b).
[243] 4.1.
[244] 4.1.
[245] *See* 10.9(a)(i).
[246] *See* 10.9(a)(i).
[247] 10.9(a)(i).
[248] 10.9(a)(i).
[249] *See* 10.9(a)(i).
[250] 10.9(c).
[251] 10.9(b).
[252] 4.1, 10.3.1.
[253] 10.9(b)(ii).
[254] *See* 10.9(a)(ii).
[255] *See* 10.9(a)(ii).
[256] *See* 10.9(a)(iii).
[257] *See* 10.9(a)(iii).
[258] 10.9(a)(iii).
[259] 10.9(a).
[260] 2.1(a), 10.9(a)(i).
[261] 2.1(a).
[262] 10.9(a).
[263] 10.9(a).
[264] 4.2.

Rule 13

[1] 11.
[2] 11.
[3] B11.
[4] T16.
[5] *See* 11.
[6] *See* 11.
[7] 11.
[8] 11.
[9] 11.
[10] 11.
[11] 11.
[12] 11.
[13] 11.
[14] 11.
[15] 11.
[16] 11.
[17] 11.
[18] 11.
[19] 11.
[20] 11.
[21] 11.
[22] 11.
[23] 11.

Rule 14

[1] 12.1, 12.3.
[2] 12.2.1(a), 18.2.1(a).
[3] 12.3.
[4] 12.2.1(a).
[5] 12.3.1(a).
[6] 12.3.1(a).
[7] 12.3.1(a).
[8] *See* 12.3.1(a).
[9] 12.3.1(b).
[10] 12.3.1(b).
[11] 12.9.1.
[12] *See* 12.
[13] 12.2.1(a), 12.3.
[14] 12.2.1(a), 12.3.
[15] *See* 3.3(b), 12.
[16] *See* 12.
[17] *See* 12.
[18] 3.3(b).
[19] *See* 12.
[20] *See* 3.3(b).
[21] 12.2.2(a).
[22] 12.3.1(g).
[23] 12.3.1(h).
[24] 12.3.1(h).
[25] *See* 12.
[26] 12.3.2.
[27] 12.3.1(d).

[28] 12.3.1(d).
[29] 12.3.2.
[30] 12.3.2.
[31] 12.3.2.
[32] 12.3.2.
[33] 12.5(a).
[34] 12.8.
[35] *See, e.g.*, 1.5(b), 12.8.
[36] 12.5(b); *see* 12.2.1(a).
[37] 12.5(b).
[38] 12.3.1(d); 12.5(a).
[39] 12.3.
[40] 12.2.1(b).
[41] 12.7.2, 12.7.3.
[42] 12.7.2, 12.7.3.
[43] 12.7.3.
[44] 12.7.3.
[45] 12.7.1.
[46] *See generally* 12.
[47] 12.3.1(c).
[48] 12.3.2.
[49] 12.3.2.
[50] 12.5(b).
[51] 12.5(b).
[52] 12.3.
[53] *See* 4.1.
[54] *See* 12.10.
[55] 12.10(d).
[56] 12.10(d).
[57] 12.10(c).
[58] 12.10(c).
[59] 12.10(b).
[60] 12.10(b).
[61] 12.10(b).
[62] *See generally* 12.4.
[63] 12.4(a).
[64] 12.4(a).
[65] 12.4(a).
[66] 12.4(a).
[67] *See* 12.4(a).
[68] 12.2.1(b).
[69] *See* 12.2.1(c), 12.4.
[70] *See* 12.4(a).
[71] *See* 12.4(a).
[72] 12.4(b).
[73] 12.4(b).
[74] 12.6.
[75] 12.4(c).
[76] 12.4(c).
[77] 12.4(e).
[78] 12.4(e).
[79] 12.4(f).
[80] 12.2.2(b).
[81] 12.2.2(b).
[82] 12.7.1–.3.
[83] 12.7.2–.3.
[84] 12.4(a).
[85] *See* 12.4.
[86] *See* 12.10(b), 4.1.
[87] *See* 12.10(b).
[88] *See* 12.10(b).
[89] 12.10(b).
[90] 12.10(b).
[91] 4.2.

Rule 15

[1] 13, 13.2(a).
[2] 13.2(a).
[3] *See* 13.1.
[4] 13.2(a).
[5] *See* 13.2(a).
[6] *See* 13.2(a).
[7] *See* 13.2(a).
[8] *See* 13.2(a).
[9] *See* 13.2(a).
[10] *See* 13.2(a).
[11] 13.2(a).
[12] 13.
[13] 13.
[14] *See* 13.1.
[15] 13.
[16] 13.
[17] 13.2(a).
[18] *See* 13.2(a), T6, T9, T10.
[19] 13.7(b).
[20] 13.7(b), 18.2.1(a).
[21] *See* 13.7(b), 18.2.1(a).
[22] 13.7(b).
[23] 13.2(a).
[24] 13.7(a).
[25] 13.7(b).
[26] *See* 13.2(a).
[27] 13.8(c).
[28] 4.1.
[29] 13.8(c).
[30] 13.8(d).
[31] 13.8(d).
[32] 13.8(c).

[33] 13.8(c).
[34] 4.2.
[35] 13.2(b).
[36] 13.2(b).
[37] 13.8(c)–(d).
[38] *See* 13.2(b).
[39] 13.8(c).
[40] *See* 13.8(c).
[41] 4.2; *see* 13.8(c).
[42] 13.2(b).
[43] 13.2(b).
[44] *See* 13.2(b).
[45] *See* 13.2(b).
[46] 13.2(b).
[47] 13.8(c)–(d).
[48] *See* 13.2(b).
[49] 13.8(c).
[50] 13.8(c).
[51] 4.2; *see* 13.8(c).
[52] *See* 13.3(a).
[53] 13.3(a).
[54] 13.3(a).
[55] 13.3(a).
[56] 13.3(a).
[57] 13.3(a).
[58] *See* 13.3(a).
[59] *See* 13.2(a).
[60] 13.3(a).
[61] *See* 13.2(a), 13.3(a).
[62] *See* 13.3(a).
[63] 13.3(a).
[64] 13.7.
[65] *See* 13.3(a).
[66] 13.8(c).
[67] 4.1.
[68] 13.8(d).
[69] 13.8(d).
[70] 4.2.
[71] 4.2(a).
[72] 13.4(a).
[73] 13.4(b).
[74] 13.4(b).
[75] *See* 13.4(b), 15.1(c).
[76] B13.
[77] 13.4(a).
[78] 13.4(a).
[79] *See* 13.4(a).
[80] 13.4(a).
[81] *See* 13.4(a).
[82] *See* 13.4(a).
[83] 13.4(a).
[84] 13.
[85] 6.2(b).
[86] 13.
[87] 13.4(a).
[88] 18.2.1(a).
[89] 13.7(a).
[90] 13.8(d).
[91] 13.6.
[92] 13.6.
[93] 13.4(a).
[94] *See* 13.4(b).
[95] 13.6.
[96] 4.1.
[97] 4.1.
[98] *See* 13.8(c).
[99] 13.8(c).
[100] 13.8(d).
[101] 13.8(d).
[102] 13.8(c).
[103] *See* 13.8(c).
[104] 4.2(a).
[105] 13.4(c).
[106] 13.4(c), 15.1(c).
[107] 13.4(c).
[108] 13, B2.
[109] *See* 13.4(c).
[110] 13.7(a).
[111] 13.7(b), 18.2.1(b).
[112] 13.4(c).
[113] 4.1, 13.8(c).
[114] 4.1.
[115] *See* 13.8(c).
[116] 13.8(d).
[117] 13.8(d).
[118] 13.8(c).
[119] *See* 13.8(c).
[120] 4.2(a).
[121] 13.5.
[122] 13.5.
[123] 13.5.
[124] *See* 13.5.
[125] 13, 13.5.
[126] *See* 13.5.
[127] 13.5.
[128] 13.5.
[129] *See* 13.5.
[130] 13.5.
[131] 13.
[132] 18.2.1(a).
[133] 13.7(a).
[134] 13.8(d).
[135] *See* 13.5.
[136] *See* 13.8(c), 4.1.
[137] 4.1.

138 *See* 13.8(c).
139 13.8(d).
140 13.8(d).
141 13.5.
142 13.8(c).
143 *See* 13.8(c).
144 4.2(a).
145 13.5.
146 *See* B2, 13.
147 13.7(b).
148 *See* 13.5.
149 13.5.
150 13.5.
151 *See* 13.8(c).
152 4.1.
153 *See* 13.8(c).
154 13.8(d).
155 13.5.
156 13.8(c).
157 *See* 13.8(c).
158 4.2(a).
159 13.4(e).
160 *See* 13, 13.4(e).
161 13.7(a).
162 13.4(e).
163 *See* 13.8(c).
164 4.1.
165 *See* 13.8(c).
166 13.8(d).
167 13.8(d).
168 13.4(e).
169 13.8(c).
170 *See* 13.8(c).
171 4.2(a).
172 *See* B2, 3.3.
173 3.3.
174 3.3.
175 13.2(c).
176 13.2(c).
177 13.2(c).
178 13.2(c).
179 13.2(c).
180 *See* 13.2(c).
181 13.2(c).
182 *See* 6.2(b).
183 *See* 13.2(c).
184 13.2(c).
185 *See* 13.2(c).
186 *See* 13.2(c).
187 13.2(c).
188 13.2(c).
189 18.2.1(a).
190 13.7(a).
191 13.7(b), 18.2.1(b)(2).
192 *See* 13.2(c).
193 *See* 13.8(c).
194 4.1.
195 13.8(c).
196 13.8(c).
197 3.2(a).
198 13.8(d).
199 13.8(d).
200 13.8(c).
201 *See* 13.8(c).
202 4.2.
203 *See* 13.2(b).
204 *See* 13.2(b).
205 *See* 13.8(c).
206 *See* 13.2(b)–(c).
207 *See* 13.8(c).
208 13.3(a)–(b).
209 *See* 13.3(b).
210 *See* 13.8(c).
211 *See* 13.2(b)–(c).
212 13.4(f).
213 13.4(f).
214 13.4(f).
215 13.4(f), 15.1(c).
216 B2, 13.4(f).
217 *See* 13.4(a), (f).
218 *See* 13.4(a).
219 13.4(f).
220 *See* 13.2(c), 13.4(f).
221 13.4(f).
222 13.4(f).
223 13.4(f).
224 13.4(f).
225 13.4(f).
226 13.8(c).
227 *See* 13.8(c).
228 4.2(a).
229 *See* 13.7(b).
230 *See* 13.5.
231 4.1.
232 4.1.
233 13.8(d).
234 3.2.
235 4.1.
236 *See* 13.5.
237 3.2.
238 4.2.
239 *See* 13.4(e)–(f).
240 13.7(a).
241 13.7(b).
242 *See* 13.4(e)–(f).

[243] 4.1.
[244] 4.1.
[245] 3.2.
[246] 13.8(d).
[247] 13.8(d).
[248] *See* 13.4(e)–(f).
[249] 4.1.
[250] *See* 13.4(e)–(f).
[251] 4.2.

Rule 16

[1] 12.9.3.
[2] *See* 12.9.3.
[3] *See* 12.9.3.
[4] *See* 12.9.3.
[5] *See* B12.1.3.
[6] *See* 12.9.3.
[7] *See* 12.9.3.
[8] 12.9.3.
[9] 10.8.4.
[10] *See* 10.8.4.
[11] *See* 10.8.4, 12.9.3.
[12] 4.1.
[13] *See* 10.8.4, 12.9.3.
[14] *See* 12.9.5.
[15] 12.9.5.
[16] *See* 12.9.5.
[17] *See* 12.9.5.
[18] *See* B2, 12.9.5.
[19] 3.2.
[20] 12.9.5.
[21] 4.1.
[22] 4.1.
[23] 4.2.

Rule 17

[1] *See* 12.9.2.
[2] 12.9.2
[3] 12.9.2.
[4] 12.9.2.
[5] *See* 12.9.2.
[6] *See* B2.
[7] *See* 12.9.2.
[8] *See* 12.9.2.
[9] 12.5(b), 18.2.1.
[10] *See* 12.5(b).
[11] 12.9.2.
[12] 12.9.2.
[13] *See* 12.9.2.
[14] *See* 12.9.2.
[15] 12.9.2.
[16] T12.
[17] 12.9.2.
[18] 12.9.2.
[19] 4.1.
[20] 4.1.
[21] 4.1.
[22] 4.2.

Rule 18

[1] 14.2(a).
[2] *See* 14.2.
[3] 14.2(a).
[4] *See* 14.2(a).
[5] 14.2(a).
[6] 14.2(a).
[7] *See* 14.2.
[8] *See* 14.2.
[9] 14.2(a).
[10] *See* 18.2.1(a).
[11] *See* 18.2.1(a).
[12] *See* 18.2.1(b)(ii).
[13] 14.4.
[14] *See* 14.2(a), T1.2 (under Department of the Treasury, Regulations).
[15] 14.2(a), T1.2 (under Department of the Treasury, Regulations).
[16] 4.1.
[17] *See* 14.5(c).
[18] *See* 14.5(c).
[19] *See* 14.5(c).
[20] 14.5(c).
[21] 4.2.
[22] 14.2(a).
[23] 14.2(a).
[24] 14.2(a).
[25] 14.2(b).
[26] *See* 14.2(a).

[27] *See* 14.2(a).

[28] 14.2(a).

[29] *See* 14.2(a).

[30] *See* 14.2(a).

[31] 14.2(a).

[32] 14.2(b).

[33] 14.2(a).

[34] *See* 18.2.1(a).

[35] 14.4.

[36] 14.4.

[37] 4.1.

[38] *See* 14.5(c).

[39] *See* 14.5(c).

[40] *See* 14.5(c).

[41] 14.5(c).

[42] 4.2.

[43] 14.3.

[44] *See* 14.3.1.

[45] 14.3.1(b).

[46] 14.3.1(a).

[47] 10.2; *see* T6.

[48] *See* 14.3; B2.

[49] 14.3.2(a).

[50] *See* T1.2.

[51] 14.3.2(c).

[52] 14.3.2(c).

[53] 14.3.2(b).

[54] 14.3.2(c).

[55] *See* 14.4.

[56] *See* 14.3, 14.4, 10.8.1(a).

[57] 18.2.1(a)–(b).

[58] *See* 14.3.1(a).

[59] *See* 14.3.1–.2.

[60] *See* 14.3.1(a).

[61] 14.3.3, 15.1(d).

[62] *See* 14.3.3.

[63] 14.3.1(b).

[64] *See* 14.3, 10.2.

[65] *See* 14.3.

[66] *See* T1.2 (under Department of Justice, Advisory Opinions).

[67] *See* 14.3.1, T1.2, T6.

[68] *See* T1.2 (under Department of Justice, Advisory Opinions).

[69] *See* T1.2 (under Department of Justice, Advisory Opinions).

[70] *See* T1.2 (under Department of Justice, Advisory Opinions).

[71] *See* T1.2 (under Department of Justice, Advisory Opinions).

[72] *See* T1.2 (under Department of Justice, Advisory Opinions).

[73] *See* T1.2 (under Department of Justice, Advisory Opinions).

[74] *See* T1.2 (under Department of Justice, Advisory Opinions).

[75] *See* T1.2 (under Department of Justice, Advisory Opinions).

[76] 14.4.

[77] 14.4.

[78] 18.2.1(a)–(b).

[79] 4.1, 14.5(c).

[80] 14.5(d), 18.9(b).

[81] 14.5(d), 18.9(b).

[82] 4.1; *see* 14.5(c).

[83] 4.2.

[84] *See* 14.2(a), T1.2 (under Executive Office of President, Executive Orders, Presidential Proclamations, and Reorganization Plans).

[85] *See* T1.2 (under Executive Office of President, Executive Orders, Presidential Proclamations, and Reorganization Plans).

[86] *See* T1.2 (under Executive Office of President, Executive Orders, Presidential Proclamations, and Reorganization Plans).

[87] *See* T1.2 (under Executive Office of President, Executive Orders, Presidential Proclamations, and Reorganization Plans).

[88] *See* T1.2 (under Executive Office of President, Executive Orders, Presidential Proclamations, and Reorganization Plans).

[89] T1.2 (under Executive Office of President, Executive Orders, Presidential Proclamations, and Reorganization Plans).

[90] T1.2 (under Executive Office of President, Executive Orders, Presidential Proclamations, and Reorganization Plans).

[91] *See* T1.2 (under Executive Office of President, Other Presidential Papers).

[92] *See* T1.2 (under Executive Office of President, Other Presidential Papers).

[93] *See* T1.2 (under Executive Office of President, Executive Orders, Presidential Proclamations, and Reorganization Plans); 14.2(a).

[94] *See* T1.2 (under Executive Office of President, Executive Orders, Presidential Proclamations, and Reorganization Plans); 14.2(a).

[95] T1.2 (under Executive Office of President, Executive Orders, Presidential Proclamations, and Reorganization Plans).

[96] *See* T1.2 (under Executive Office of President, Executive Orders, Presidential Proclamations, and Reorganization Plans); 14.2(a).

[97] *See* T1.2 (under Executive Office of President, Executive Orders, Presidential Proclamations, and Reorganization Plans); 14.2(a).

[98] T1.2 (under Executive Office of President, Executive Orders, Presidential Proclamations, and Reorganization Plans).

[99] *See* T1.2 (under Executive Office of President, Executive Orders, Presidential Proclamations, and Reorganization Plans).

[100] *See* T1.2 (under Executive Office of President, Executive Orders, Presidential Proclamations, and Reorganization Plans).

[101] 4.1, 14.5.

[102] *See* 14.5(c).

[103] *See* 14.2(c).

[104] *See* 14.5(c).

[105] 14.5(c).

[106] 4.2.

[107] *See* T1.2 (under Department of Commerce, Patent and Trademark Office).

[108] T1.2 (under Department of Commerce, Patent and Trademark Office).

[109] T1.2 (under Department of Commerce, Patent and Trademark Office).

[110] *See* T1.2 (under Department of Commerce, Patent and Trademark Office).

[111] T1.2 (under Department of Commerce, Patent and Trademark Office).

[112] T1.2 (under Department of Commerce, Patent and Trademark Office).

[113] T1.2 (under Department of Commerce, Patent and Trademark Office).

[114] 14.

[115] 14.

[116] 14.

[117] 14.

[118] 14.4.

[119] 14.4.

[120] 18.2.1(a)–(b).

[121] 14.4.

[122] 14.4.

[123] 18.2.1(a)–(b).

Rule 19

[1] *See* 21.4.
[2] *See* 21.1(a), 21.4.
[3] *See* 21.1(a), 21.4.
[4] 21.4.1.
[5] 21.4.1(a)(i)–(ii).
[6] 21.4.1(a)(i).
[7] *See* 21.4.
[8] 21.4(b).
[9] 21.4.3.
[10] *See* 21.4.3.
[11] *See* 21.4, 21.4.3.
[12] *See* 21.4.3.
[13] *See* 21.4.3.
[14] *See* 21.4.2.
[15] *See* 21.4.2.
[16] *See* 21.4, 21.4.2.
[17] 21.4.4.
[18] 21.4.4.
[19] 21.4.4.
[20] 21.4.4.
[21] 21.4.4.
[22] 21.4.4.
[23] 21.4.5.
[24] 21.4.5(a)(i).
[25] 21.4.5(a)(ii).
[26] 21.4.5(b).
[27] 21.4.5(b).
[28] 21.3, 21.4.5(b).
[29] 21.4.5(c).
[30] 21.4.5(c).
[31] *See* 21.4.5.
[32] 18.2.1(a)–(b).
[33] *See* 21.4.5(a)(i), T4.1.
[34] *See* 21.4.5(a)(ii), T4.2.
[35] *See* 21.4.5(c), T4.3.
[36] *See* T4.1.
[37] 21.17(a); *see* 4.1.
[38] 21.17(a).
[39] 21.17(a); *see* 4.2.
[40] 21.17(a).

Rule 20

[1] *See* 15.
[2] 15.1.
[3] *See* B2, B15.1.
[4] 15.1.
[5] 15.1.
[6] 15.1(a).
[7] 15.1(b).
[8] *See* 15.1(b).
[9] *See* 15.1(b).
[10] 15.1(b).
[11] 15.1(b).
[12] *See* 15.1(b).
[13] 15.1.
[14] 15.1(c)–(d).
[15] 15.1(d).
[16] *See* 15.1(d).
[17] 15.1(c).
[18] 15.1(c).
[19] *See* 15.6.
[20] 15.6.
[21] 15.3; *see* B15.1.
[22] 15.3; *see* B15.1.
[23] 15.3.
[24] 15.3.
[25] 15.3.
[26] *See* B15.1.
[27] 15.3.
[28] 20.2.2(a).
[29] 20.2.2(b).
[30] 20.2.2(a).
[31] *See* 3.2(a).
[32] *See* 3.2(a).
[33] *See* 3.2(a).
[34] *See* 3.1(a).
[35] 3.2(a), 15.3.
[36] *See* 3.2–.3.
[37] *See, e.g.*, 15.1(b).
[38] 15.4.
[39] *See* 15.4.
[40] 15.2(a).
[41] 15.2(a).
[42] 15.2(b).
[43] 15.2(a).
[44] 15.2(a).
[45] 15.2(a).
[46] 15.2(a).
[47] 15.2(a).
[48] 15.4(a)(iii).
[49] 15.2(c).
[50] 15.4(a)(iii).
[51] 15.4(a).
[52] 15.4(a)(iii).
[53] 15.4(a)(iii).
[54] 15.4(a)(i).

[55] 15.7(a).

[56] *See* 15.7.

[57] 15.7(b).

[58] *See* 15.7(b).

[59] 15.4(a)(i).

[60] 15.4(a)(i).

[61] *See* 15.4(a)(ii).

[62] 15.4(d).

[63] 15.4(c).

[64] 15.4(c).

[65] *See* 15.4(c).

[66] 15.4(c).

[67] 15.1, 15.3.

[68] 15.8(b).

[69] 15.8(b).

[70] 15.8(b).

[71] 15.5.1(b).

[72] *See* B2, 15.5.1(b).

[73] 15.5.1(a).

[74] *See* B2, 15.5.1(a).

[75] *See* 15.5.1(a).

[76] 15.5.1(a).

[77] *See* 15.5.1(a).

[78] *See* 15.6.

[79] 15.5.2(a).

[80] 15.5.2(a).

[81] 15.5.2(b).

[82] 15.5.2(b).

[83] 15.5.1(b).

[84] 15.5.1(a).

[85] *See* 15.9(b)–(c).

[86] 15.9(a).

[87] 18.2.1(a)(iii).

[88] *See* 18.2.1(b)(ii).

[89] 15.9(b).

[90] 15.9(b).

[91] 15.9(c).

[92] *See* 15.9(c).

[93] 15.9(c).

[94] 15.9(c).

[95] *See* 15.9(a), (c).

[96] *See* 15.9(b), 18.2.2.

[97] *See* 15.8(c)(iv).

[98] 15.8(c)(iv).

[99] *See* 15.8(c)(iv).

[100] *See* 15.8(c)(iii).

[101] *See* 15.8(c)(iii).

[102] 15.8(c)(iii).

[103] *See* T2.22.

[104] *See* T2.22.

[105] T2.22.

[106] *See* B2, 15.8(c)(i).

[107] 15.8(c)(i).

[108] *See* 15.8(c)(i).

[109] 15.8(c)(i).

[110] 15.8(c)(i).

[111] *See* 15.8(c)(ii).

[112] *See* 15.8(c)(ii).

[113] 15.4(a)(i).

[114] 15.8(c)(ii).

[115] *See* 15.10.

[116] 15.10, B15.2.

[117] 4.1.

[118] 15.10.

[119] *See* 15.10, B15.2.

[120] *See* 4.2(a).

[121] *See* B15.2, 4.2(b).

[122] 4.2(a).

[123] 4.2(a).

[124] 4.2(b).

[125] *See* B15.2, 3.2(a), 3.3, 4.2(a).

[126] 3.3.

[127] 3.2(b).

[128] 3.1(c).

[129] 3.2(d).

[130] 15.10.1.

[131] 15.10.1.

[132] 15.10.1.

[133] *See* B15.2, 3.2(a), 3.3, 4.2(a).

[134] 4.1, 15.10.1.

[135] *See* 4.2(a), 15.10.1.

[136] *See* 15.10.1.

[137] 15.10.1.

[138] 15.10.

[139] 15.1, 15.3.

[140] 15.5.

[141] 15.9.

[142] 15.8(c)(iv).

[143] 15.8(c)(i).

[144] 15.8(c)(ii).

[145] *See* 15.10, 15.10.1.

[146] 15.10, 4.2.

[147] 15.10.1.

[148] 15.10.1.

Rule 21

[1] B16.1.1, 16.4, 16.7.1.
[2] 16.2.
[3] 16.2.
[4] 16.2.
[5] *See* 15.1(c); 16.2.
[6] *See* 15.6; 16.2.
[7] *See* 15.1(c); 16.2.
[8] 16.7.1(a).
[9] B16.1.3, 16.7.1(a).
[10] 16.7.1(b); *see* B16.1.3.
[11] 16.7.1(b).
[12] 16.7.1(c).
[13] 16.7.1(c).
[14] 16.7.1(c).
[15] 16.3.
[16] 16.3.
[17] B16.1.1; 16.3.
[18] 16.3; *see* 8.
[19] 16.3; *see* 20.2.2(b).
[20] *See* 16.7.1(a).
[21] *See* 16.2, 16.6.
[22] *See* 16.4.
[23] 8.
[24] *See* 16.4.
[25] 16.4.
[26] 16.1, T6, T13.
[27] *See* 16.1, T6, T13.
[28] 16.1, T10.
[29] T13.
[30] T13.
[31] *See* 16.1, T6, T10, T13.
[32] B16.1.1.
[33] 6.1(a).
[34] 6.1(a).
[35] T6, T13.
[36] T6, T13.
[37] T13.
[38] *See* 16.4.
[39] 16.4.
[40] 16.4.
[41] *See, e.g.*, 16.4, 16.7.1(b), 16.7.1(c).
[42] 16.4.
[43] 16.4.
[44] *See* 16.4.
[45] 16.4.
[46] 16.7.3.
[47] *See* 16.7.3.
[48] 16.4.
[49] 16.4.
[50] 16.7.4.
[51] 16.7.4.
[52] 16.7.5.
[53] 16.7.5.
[54] 16.7.5.
[55] 16.7.2.
[56] 16.7.2.
[57] 16.7.2.
[58] 16.7.2.
[59] 16.7.2.
[60] 16.5; *see* B16.1.2.
[61] *See* 16.5.
[62] *See* B16.1.2, 16.5.
[63] *See* B16.1.2, 16.5.
[64] *See* 16.5.
[65] 16.5.
[66] 16.5.
[67] T12; *see* 16.5.
[68] *See* 16.5.
[69] 16.5.
[70] 16.5.
[71] 16.5.
[72] *See* 16.5.
[73] 16.6(a); *see* B16.1.4.
[74] 16.6(c).
[75] 16.6(a).
[76] 16.6(a).
[77] 16.6(a); *see* B16.1.4.
[78] 16.6(a).
[79] 16.6(a).
[80] 16.6(a); *see* B16.1.4.
[81] 16.6(b).
[82] *See* 16.6(b).
[83] T10.
[84] *See* 16.6(b).
[85] 16.6(a).
[86] 16.6(a).
[87] 16.6(a).
[88] 16.6(f).
[89] 16.6(f).
[90] 16.7.8; *see* 16.5.
[91] 16.7.8; *see* 16.5.
[92] 16.7.8; *see* 16.5.
[93] 16.7.8; *see* T6, T13.
[94] 16.7.8.
[95] 16.7.8.
[96] 16.8(b).
[97] 16.8(a).
[98] 16.6(f).
[99] 18.2.1(a)(iii).

[100] *See* 18.2.1(b)(ii).
[101] 16.8.
[102] 16.8(b).
[103] *See* 15.9(c).
[104] 16.
[105] 16.9(a).
[106] 4.1.
[107] 4.1, 16.9(a).
[108] B16.2, 16.9(b).
[109] B16.2, 16.9(b).
[110] 16.9(b).
[111] *See* B16.2, 4.2(b).
[112] 16.9(b).
[113] *See* 4.2(a).
[114] 3.3.
[115] 3.2(b).
[116] 3.1(c).
[117] 3.2(d).
[118] 16.9(b).
[119] *See* 16.9(b).
[120] 16.9(b).
[121] *See* 16.9(b).
[122] *See* 16.9(b).

Rule 22

[1] *See* 15.8(a).
[2] *See* 15.5.
[3] *See* B15.1, 15.8(a).
[4] *See* 15.9(b).
[5] *See* 15.9(b).
[6] *See* 15.9(b).
[7] *See* 15.9(b).
[8] *See* 15.9(b).
[9] *See* B15.1, 15.8(a).
[10] *See* B15.1, 15.8(a).
[11] *See* B15.1, 15.8(a).
[12] *See* B15.1, 15.8(a).
[13] *See* 15.1, 15.3, 15.8(a).
[14] 4.1, 15.10.
[15] 4.2(a), 15.10.
[16] 4.1, 15.10.
[17] 4.1.
[18] *See* 4.2(a), 15.10.
[19] *See* 4.2(a), 15.1, 15.10.
[20] *See* 4.2(a), 15.3, 15.10.
[21] *See* 4.2(a), 15.10.
[22] *See* 15.1, 15.3, 15.8(a).
[23] *See* 15.8(a).
[24] *See* 15.8(a).
[25] *See* 15.8(a).
[26] *See* 15.8(a), 15.4(a)(ii).
[27] *See* 15.8(a).
[28] 8(a).
[29] *See* 15.3.
[30] *See* 15.3.
[31] *See* 3.3, 15.8(a).
[32] *See* 15.8(a).
[33] *See* 15.9(a).
[34] 15.9(a).
[35] *See* 15.9(a).
[36] *See* 15.8(a).
[37] 4.1, 15.10.
[38] *See* 15.8(a).
[39] 3.3.
[40] 3.3.
[41] *See* 4.2(a), 15.10.
[42] *See* 15.1.
[43] *See* 15.5.1(a).
[44] *See* 15.1–.4.
[45] *See* 15.5.1(a).
[46] B15.2, 15.10.
[47] 15.10.1.
[48] *See* 4.2(a), 15.10.1.
[49] *See* 4.2(b), 15.10.1.
[50] *See* 15.10.1.
[51] *See* 15.10.1.
[52] *See* 16.7.6.
[53] 16.7.6.
[54] 16.7.6.
[55] 16.7.6.
[56] 16.7.6.
[57] 8(a).
[58] 16.7.6.
[59] *See* 16.7.6.
[60] *See* 16.7.6.
[61] *See* 16.7.6.
[62] 6.1(a).
[63] *See* 16.7.6.
[64] *See* 3.1(b), 16.7.6.
[65] *See* 16.7.6.
[66] *See* 3.1(c).
[67] *See* 16.8(a).
[68] *See* 16.7.6.
[69] 16.9.
[70] 16.9.

Rule 23

[1] *See* 12.9.4.
[2] *See* 12.9.4.
[3] 12.9.4.
[4] *See* 12.9.4.
[5] *See* 12.9.4.
[6] *See* 12.9.4.
[7] *See* B12.1.3, 12.9.4.
[8] *See* 12.9.4.
[9] *See* 12.9.4.
[10] 12.9.4.
[11] 12.9.4.
[12] 12.9.4.
[13] *See* 12.9.4.
[14] *See* 12.9.4.
[15] *See* 12.5(a).
[16] 12.5(a).
[17] 12.9.4.
[18] 4.1, 12.10(b).
[19] 12.9.4.
[20] 12.10(b).
[21] 4.2.
[22] *See* B12.1.3, 12.9.4.
[23] *See* 12.9.4.
[24] *See* 12.9.4.
[25] 12.9.4; *see* 3.4.
[26] *See* 12.9.4.
[27] 12.9.4.
[28] 12.9.4.
[29] 12.9.4.
[30] 18.2.1(a).
[31] 18.2.1(b)(i).
[32] *See* 12.5(a).
[33] 12.5(a).
[34] 18.2.1.
[35] 12.9.4.
[36] 4.1.
[37] 12.10(b).
[38] *See* 12.10(b).
[39] 12.9.4.
[40] 12.10(b).
[41] 4.2.
[42] *See* 12.9.5.
[43] *See* B12.1.3; 12.9.5.
[44] *See* 12.9.5.
[45] *See* 12.9.5.
[46] *See* 12.9.5.
[47] 12.9.5.
[48] 12.9.5.
[49] *See* 12.9.5.
[50] *See* 12.9.5.
[51] *See* 12.9.5.
[52] *See* 12.9.5.
[53] *See* 12.9.5.
[54] *See* 12.5(b), 18.2.1(a)(ii).
[55] 18.2.1(b)(i).
[56] *See* 12.5(a).
[57] 12.5(a).
[58] 18.2.1.
[59] *See* 10.8.4, 12.9.5.
[60] 4.1.
[61] *See* 12.9.5.
[62] 12.10(b).
[63] 4.2.
[64] 12.9.4.
[65] *See* 12.9.4.
[66] *See* 12.9.4.
[67] 12.9.4; *see* B12.1.3.
[68] *See* 12.9.4.
[69] *See* 12.9.4.
[70] 12.9.4.
[71] 12.9.4.
[72] 12.9.4.
[73] 12.9.4; *see* T6.
[74] 12.9.4.
[75] 12.9.4.
[76] 18.2.1(a).
[77] 18.2.1(b)(i).
[78] *See* 12.5(a).
[79] 12.5(a).
[80] 18.2.1.
[81] 12.9.4.
[82] 4.1.
[83] 12.10(b).
[84] *See* 12.10(b).
[85] *See* 12.9.4, 12.10(b).
[86] 12.10(b).
[87] 4.2.

Rule 24

[1] 19.1.
[2] *See* B19.1, 19.1.
[3] *See* B19.1, 19.1.
[4] *See* 19.1(a).
[5] 19.1(a).
[6] 19.1(a).
[7] *See* 19.1, T15.
[8] 19.1.
[9] 6.1(a); *see* T15.

[10] 6.1(a); *see* 19.1, T15.
[11] *See* 19.1.
[12] 19.1(b).
[13] 19.1(b).
[14] *See* 19.1.
[15] 19.1(c).
[16] *See* 19.1(c).
[17] 19.1(c).
[18] 19.1(c).
[19] *See* 19.1(c).
[20] 19.1.
[21] 19.1.
[22] 19.1.
[23] 19.1(d).
[24] 19.1.
[25] 19.2(a).
[26] 19.2(a).
[27] 19.2(a).
[28] *See* 19.1.
[29] 19.1(d).
[30] 19.1(d).
[31] 19.2(b).

Rule 25

[1] *See* B17.1.
[2] B17.1.1.
[3] *See* B17.1.1; BT1.
[4] *See* B17.1.4.
[5] *See* B17.1.2.
[6] *See* B17.1.
[7] B17.1.2.
[8] *See* B17.1.2.
[9] *See* B17.1.2.
[10] *See* B17.1.2.
[11] B17.1.4.
[12] B17.1.3.
[13] B17.1.3.
[14] *See* B17.1.2.
[15] *See* B17.1.2.
[16] *See* B17.1.1–.3.
[17] *See* B17.1.2.
[18] *See* B17.1.1.
[19] *See* B17.1.2.
[20] B17.1.2.
[21] B17.1.3.
[22] B17.2.
[23] B17.2.
[24] *See* 4.1.
[25] *See* 3.3.
[26] *See* B17.1.2.
[27] B17.1.1.
[28] *See* B17.1.1.
[29] *See* B17.1.2.
[30] *See* B17.2.

Rule 26

[1] *See* 17.2.6, 18.2.2.
[2] 17.5(b).
[3] 18.2.2.
[4] *See* 17.2.6.
[5] 17.2.6.
[6] *See* 17.2.6.
[7] 17.2.6.
[8] 17.2.6.
[9] *See* 17.2.6.
[10] *See* 18.2.2, 18.6.
[11] 15.5.2(b); 17.2.6.
[12] 17.2.6.
[13] *See* 17.6.
[14] 17.6.

Rule 27

[1] *See* 17.2.5.
[2] *See* 17.2.5.
[3] *See* 17.2.5.
[4] *See* 17.2.5.
[5] *See* 17.2.5.
[6] *See* 17.2.5.
[7] 17.2.5.
[8] *See* 17.2.5.
[9] *See* 17.2.5.
[10] *See* 18.6.
[11] *See* 17.2.3.
[12] *See* 18.2.1(a)(iii), 18.2.2.
[13] *See* 18.2.1(b)(ii).
[14] *See* 18.2.2, 17.5(b); *see also* 18.2.1.
[15] *See* 17.2.3.
[16] *See* 17.2.3.
[17] *See* 17.2.3.
[18] *See* 15.5.2(b), 17.2.3.
[19] *See* 17.2.3.

[20] *See* 17.2.3.

[21] 17.2.3.

[22] *See* 17.2.3.

[23] *See* 17.2.3.

[24] *See* 17.2.3.

[25] *See* B18.1.2, 18.2.1(b)(ii).

[26] *See* 16.6(b).

[27] 15.5.2(b).

[28] 15.5.2(b).

[29] 17.6.

[30] *See* 17.6.

Rule 28

[1] *See* 18.6.

[2] *See* 18.6.

[3] *See* 18.6.

[4] *See* 18.6.

[5] *See* 18.6.

[6] 18.6.

[7] 18.6.

[8] 18.6.

[9] *See* 18.6.

[10] 18.6.

[11] 18.6.

[12] 18.2.2(a).

[13] *See* 18.2.2(d), 18.6.

[14] 18.6.

[15] 18.6.

[16] 18.6

[17] 18.6.

[18] 18.6.

[19] *See* 18.6.

[20] *See* 18.6.

[21] 18.7.1.

[22] *See* 18.7.1.

[23] *See* B15.1, 18.7.1.

[24] 18.7.1.

[25] *See* 18.7.3.

[26] 18.7.1.

[27] *See* 18.7.1.

[28] *See* 18.7.3.

[29] *See* 18.7.3.

[30] 18.2.2(c).

[31] 18.7.3.

[32] *See* 18.7.3.

[33] *See* 18.7.3.

[34] *See* 18.7.3.

[35] 15.9(c).

[36] *See* 15.9(c).

[37] *See* 15.9(c).

[38] 18.7.1.

[39] 18.7.1.

[40] *See* 15.9(c).

[41] *See* 18.6, 18.7.2.

[42] *See* 18.6, 18.7.2.

[43] *See* 18.6, 18.7.2.

[44] 18.6, 18.7.2.

[45] *See* 18.7.3.

[46] *See* 18.6, 18.7.2.

[47] *See* 18.6.

[48] 18.6.

[49] *See* 18.8.

[50] *See* 18.8.

[51] 18.8.

[52] 18.8.

[53] *See* 18.8.

[54] *See* 18.5.

[55] 18.5.

[56] 18.5.

[57] 18.5.

[58] 18.5.

[59] 18.5.

[60] 18.5.

[61] 18.5.

[62] 18.9.

[63] 18.9(d).

[64] 18.9(c).

[65] 18.9.

[66] 18.9(d).

[67] 18.9(c).

Rule 29

[1] *See* 17.3.

[2] 17.3.

[3] 17.3.

[4] 17.3.

[5] 17.3.

[6] 17.3.

[7] 17.3.

[8] 17.5(a).

[9] 17.5(a).

[10] *See* 17.2.1.

[11] 17.2.1.

[12] 17.2.1.

[13] 17.2.1.
[14] 17.2.1.
[15] 17.2.1.
[16] 17.2.1.
[17] 17.2.1.
[18] 17.2.1.
[19] 17.2.1.
[20] 17.5(a).
[21] 17.5(a).
[22] *See* 17.4.
[23] 17.4.
[24] 17.4.
[25] *See* 17.4.
[26] *See* 17.4, 15.1(d).
[27] *See* 17.3.
[28] *See* 17.2.1.
[29] *See* 17.4.
[30] *See* 17.6.
[31] *See* 17.6.
[32] *See* 17.6.
[33] *See* 17.6.

Part 3

Rule 30

[1] *See* 18.2.1(a).
[2] *See* 18.2.1(a)(i)–(iii).
[3] 18.2.1(a)(i)–(iii).
[4] 18.2.1(a)(ii).
[5] 18.2.1(a)(i).
[6] 18.2.1(a)(iii).
[7] 18.2.1(a).
[8] 18.2.1(b).
[9] 18.2.1(b)(i).
[10] 18.2.1(b)(i).
[11] 18.2.1(b)(ii).
[12] 18.2.1(b)(ii).
[13] 18.2.1(b)(ii).
[14] 18.2.1(b)(ii).
[15] 18.2.1(b)(ii).

Rule 31

[1] 18.2.2.
[2] 18.2.2(f).
[3] *See* 18.2.2.
[4] 18.2.2(a).
[5] 18.2.2(a).
[6] 18.2.2(a).
[7] 18.2.2(a).
[8] *See* 18.2.2(a).
[9] *See* 18.2.2(a).
[10] 18.2.2(b), (b)(ii).
[11] 18.2.2(b)(i).
[12] *See* 18.2.2(a), 18.2.2(b)(ii).
[13] 18.2.2(b)(iv).
[14] 18.2.2(b)(iv).
[15] *See* 18.2.2(b)(i).
[16] *See* 18.2.2(b)(i)–(iii).
[17] 18.2.2(b)(iii).
[18] 18.2.2(g).
[19] 18.2.2(g).
[20] 18.2.2(g).
[21] 18.2.2(g).
[22] 18.2.2(c).
[23] *See* 18.2.2(c).
[24] 18.2.2(c).
[25] 18.2.2(c).
[26] 18.2.2(c).
[27] *See* 18.2.2(c).
[28] 18.2.2(c).
[29] 18.2.2(c).
[30] 18.2.2(c).
[31] 18.2.2(c).
[32] 18.2.2(c).
[33] 18.2.2(d).
[34] 18.2.2(d).
[35] 18.2.1(d).
[36] *See* 18.2.2(d).
[37] 18.2.2(d).
[38] *See* 18.2.2(d).
[39] *See* 18.2.2(d).
[40] *See generally* 18.2.2.
[41] 18.2.2(a).
[42] 18.2.2(a).
[43] 18.2.2(a), (b)(v).
[44] 18.2.2(b)(v).
[45] 18.2.2(a).
[46] 18.9(a).
[47] 18.9(a).
[48] 18.9(a).
[49] 18.9(a).

Rule 32

[1] *See* 10.8.1, 12.5(a), 13.7(a), 14.4, 15.9(a), 16.8, 17.5(a).

[2] *See* 10.8.1, 12.5(a), 13.7(a), 14.4, 15.9(a), 16.8, 17.5(a).

[3] *See* 10.8.1, 12.5(a), 13.7(a), 14.4, 15.9(a), 16.8, 17.5(a).

[4] *See* 13.7(a), 14.4.

[5] *See* 10.8.1(a), 12.5(a), 13.7(a), 14.4, 15.9(a), 16.8, 17.5(a).

[6] 4.1.

[7] *See* 10.9(a)(ii), 12.10(d), 13.8(d), 14.5(d), 15.10.

[8] *See* 10.9(a)(ii), 12.10(d), 13.8(d), 14.5(d), 15.10.

[9] 4.1.

[10] 4.2.

Rule 33

[1] *See* 17.2.4.

[2] 17.2.4.

[3] *See* 17.2.4.

[4] 17.2.4.

[5] *See* 17.2.4.

[6] *See* 17.2.4.

[7] *See* 17.2.4.

[8] *See* 18.4(a).

[9] *See* 18.4(b).

[10] *See* 18.4(b).

[11] 4.1.

[12] 18.9(c).

[13] 18.9(c).

[14] 4.2.

[15] 4.2.

Part 4

Rule 34

[1] 1.1.

[2] B1.1.

[3] 5.1(a)(i).

[4] B1.1.

[5] B1.1.

[6] B1.1.

[7] B1.1.

[8] B4.

[9] 1.1.

[10] *See* 1.1(a).

[11] 1.1(a).

[12] 1.1(a).

[13] 1.1(a).

[14] 1.1(a).

[15] *See* 1.2(a).

Rule 35

[1] 1.2(a).

[2] 1.2.

[3] 1.2(a).

[4] 1.2(b).

[5] 1.2(c).

[6] 1.2(d).

[7] B1.2.

[8] *See* 1.3.

[9] *See* 1.2.

[10] 1.2(e).

[11] B1.2, 1.3.

[12] 1.3.

[13] 1.2(c).

[14] 1.3.

[15] *See* 1.3.

[16] 1.3.

[17] 1.3.

[18] 1.3.

[19] 1.3.

[20] 1.3.

Rule 36

[1] 1.4.
[2] 1.4.
[3] 1.4.
[4] 1.4.
[5] 1.4.

Rule 37

[1] *See* B1.3, 1.5(a).
[2] *See* B1.3, 1.5(a).
[3] B1.3.
[4] *See* B1.3.
[5] 1.5(b).
[6] *See* 1.5(b).
[7] 1.5(b).
[8] 10.6.4.
[9] B1.3, 1.5(a)(i).
[10] B1.3.
[11] 1.5(a)(ii).
[12] B1.3, 1.5(a)(i) .
[13] B1.3, 1.5(a)(ii).
[14] *See* 1.5(a)(ii).
[15] 1.5(a)(ii).
[16] 1.6(c).
[17] *See* 10.6.3.
[18] 10.6.3.
[19] *See* 1.6.
[20] *See* 1.6(a)–(c).
[21] *See* 1.6(a)–(c).

Part 5

Rule 38

[1] 5.1(b)(i).
[2] 5.1(a)(i), (b)(iii).
[3] 5.1(b)(i).
[4] B5.1, 5.1(b)(i).
[5] B5.1, 5.1(b)(iv).
[6] B5.1, 5.1(b)(iv).
[7] 5.1(b)(i); *see* B5.1.
[8] B5.1.
[9] 5.2(e).
[10] *See* B5.1.
[11] 5.1(b)(ii).
[12] 5.1(b)(ii).
[13] *See* 5.1(b)(ii).
[14] B5.2, 5.1(a)(i), 5.1(b)(iii).
[15] B5.2, 5.1(a)(i).
[16] *See* B5.2, 5.1(a)(i).
[17] B5.2, 5.1(a)(i).
[18] *See* B5.2, 5.1(a)(i).
[19] 5.1(a)(ii).
[20] 5.1(a)(ii).
[21] 5.1(a)(iii).
[22] 5.1(a)(iii).
[23] 5.1(a)(iii).
[24] 5.1(a)(ii).
[25] 5.1(a)(ii).
[26] *See* 5.1(a)(i).
[27] *See* B5.2, 5.1.
[28] 5.1(a)(ii).
[29] *See* 5.2(e).
[30] *See* 5.1(a)(ii).

Rule 39

[1] 5.2(a).
[2] 5.2(a).
[3] 5.2(b).
[4] 5.2(a).
[5] 5.2(d)(i).
[6] 5.2(d)(i).
[7] 5.2(d)(iii).
[8] *See* 5.2(d)(i), (iii).
[9] 5.2(c).

Rule 40

[1] 5.2(b), 5.3.
[2] 5.3.
[3] 5.3.
[4] 5.3.
[5] 5.3(b)(iii).
[6] 5.3(a), (b)(ii).
[7] 5.3.
[8] 5.3(b)(iii).
[9] *See* 5.3(b)(iii).
[10] 5.3(a).
[11] 5.3(b)(v).
[12] 5.3(b)(v).
[13] 5.3(b)(vi).
[14] 5.3(b)(vi).
[15] *See* 5.3(b)(vi).
[16] 5.3(b)(ii).
[17] 5.3(a).
[18] 5.3, 5.3(b)(i).
[19] 5.3(b)(i).
[20] 5.3(b)(iv).
[21] 5.3(c).
[22] 5.3(c).

Part 6

Appendix 6

[1] 12.9.1.
[2] *See* 12.9.1.
[3] 12.3.2; *see* 12.9.1.
[4] 12.9.1.
[5] 12.7.2.
[6] 10.2.1(j).
[7] *See* 10.7.1(a).
[8] *See* 10.9.
[9] *See* 19.1(b).
[10] 3.2(a); *see* 10; 19.1(c).
[11] 2.1(a).
[12] *See* 19.1(b), T15.
[13] T1.1 (under Tax Court).
[14] *See* T1.1 (under Tax Court).
[15] *See* T1.1 (under Tax Court).
[16] *See* T1.1 (under United States Court of Federal Claims).
[17] *See* T1.1 (under United States Court of Federal Claims).
[18] *See* T1.1 (under United States Court of Federal Claims).
[19] *See* T1.1 (under United States Court of Federal Claims).
[20] *See* 19.1.
[21] *See* 10.8.1(b).
[22] *See* 10.8.1(a).
[23] T1.2 (under Department of the Treasury, Regulations).
[24] *See* T1.2 (under Department of the Treasury, Regulations).
[25] T1.2 (under Department of the Treasury, Regulations).
[26] *See* T1.2 (under Department of the Treasury, Regulations).
[27] *See* T1.2 (under Department of the Treasury, Regulations).
[28] *See* T1.2 (under Department of the Treasury, Regulations).
[29] *See* T1.2 (under Department of the Treasury, Other Treasury Determinations).
[30] *See* T1.2 (under Department of the Treasury, Treasury Determinations).
[31] *See* T1.2 (under Department of the Treasury, Cases).
[32] T1.2 (under Department of the Treasury, Cases).
[33] *See* T1.2 (under Department of the Treasury, Cases).

[34] *See* T1.2 (under Department of the Treasury, Other Treasury Determinations).

[35] *See* T1.2 (under Department of the Treasury, Other Treasury Determinations).

[36] *See* T1.2 (under Department of the Treasury, Treasury Determinations and Other Treasury Determinations).

[37] *See* T1.2 (under Department of the Treasury, Treasury Determinations).

[38] *See* T1.2 (under Department of the Treasury, Other Treasury Determinations).

[39] *See* T1.2 (under Department of the Treasury, Treasury Determinations).

[40] *See* T1.2 (under Department of the Treasury, Other Treasury Determinations).

[41] *See* T1.2 (under General Counsel Memoranda).

[42] *See* T1.2 (under Department of the Treasury, Other Treasury Determinations).

[43] *See* T1.2 (under Private Letter Rulings).

[44] *See* T1.2 (under Technical Advice Memoranda)

Index

References are to page numbers.